D1616781

We Are an African People

We Are an African People

Independent Education, Black Power,
and the Radical Imagination

RUSSELL RICKFORD

OXFORD
UNIVERSITY PRESS

OXFORD
UNIVERSITY PRESS

Oxford University Press is a department of the University of
Oxford. It furthers the University's objective of excellence in research,
scholarship, and education by publishing worldwide.

Oxford   New York

Auckland   Cape Town   Dar es Salaam   Hong Kong   Karachi
Kuala Lumpur   Madrid   Melbourne   Mexico City   Nairobi
New Delhi   Shanghai   Taipei   Toronto

With offices in

Argentina   Austria   Brazil   Chile   Czech Republic   France   Greece
Guatemala   Hungary   Italy   Japan   Poland   Portugal   Singapore
South Korea   Switzerland   Thailand   Turkey   Ukraine   Vietnam

Published in the United States of America by
Oxford University Press
198 Madison Avenue, New York, NY 10016

Library of Congress Cataloging-in-Publication Data
Rickford, Russell John.
We are an African people : independent education, black power, and the radical
imagination / Russell Rickford.
pages cm
Includes bibliographical references and index.
ISBN 978–0–19–986147–7 (hardcover : acid-free paper)   1. African Americans—Education—History—
20th century.   2. African American schools—History—20th century.   3. Black power—United States—
History—20th century.   4. Black nationalism—United States—History—20th century.   5. Racism in
education—United States—History—20th century.   6. Discrimination in education—United States—
History—20th century.   I. Title.
LC2741.R54 2016
371.829'96073—dc23
2015018301

1 3 5 7 9 8 6 4 2
Printed by Sheridan, USA

For Manning Marable,
with gratitude.

And for Adrienne,
eternally.

One of the most important things we must now begin to do is to call ourselves "African."

—Stokely Carmichael (Kwame Ture), 1969

CONTENTS

ACKNOWLEDGMENTS

I came to the topic of Black Power and independent education while grappling with my own contradictions. In fall 1995, as a Howard University junior, I attended the Million Man March (MMM). The idea of hundreds of thousands of black men converging on the National Mall in Washington, DC, ignited my political imagination. In high school, I had aspired to open an Afrocentric academy as a symbol of my commitment to black nationalist development. In college, I continued to see black unity, Afrocentric cultural expression, and charismatic, male leadership as paths to African-American liberation. Though the MMM featured all these elements, its theme of black patriarchal solidarity and atonement struck me as curiously anemic. Keynoted by the Nation of Islam's Min. Louis Farrakhan, the rally lacked the searing indictment of the state, white supremacy, and the accommodationist black establishment that Malcolm X had once embodied.

In subsequent years, I developed a materialist analysis of structural racism. As my critique of narrow or "bourgeois" black nationalism deepened, I recognized that the MMM and similar rituals of black cohesiveness largely ignored or denied class and gender inequities, overlooked or discounted systemic origins of racial exploitation in the capitalist system, and envisioned no wholesale transfer of wealth and capital to workers and the poor. I concluded that most contemporary expressions of black nationalism posed little or no threat to the ruling class and primarily served the interests of people like me—comfortable members of the African-American middle class.

As I entered graduate school in my late 20s, I wanted to understand why the strains of black nationalist ideology that I had absorbed as an adolescent lacked overtly anticapitalist themes. My theory was that radical impulses within the eclectic black nationalist revival of the 1960s had reinvigorated popular critiques of capitalist society, but that those tendencies had waned (or had been suppressed) as revolutionary nationalism was eclipsed by more benign varieties that stressed identity politics. Probing the genealogy of my own bourgeois national-ist origins led to an analysis of the fate of Black Power ideologies in the age of neoliberalism. *We Are an African People* is the product of that inquiry.

Along the way, I learned that the transmutation of black nationalism and Pan Africanism in the aftermath of the mass movements of the 1960s was far more complicated than I had imagined. I discovered that the "Pan African nationalist" renaissance of the 1970s had generated an incredibly fertile insti-tutional life, part of a larger outpouring of theory and cultural production that changed African-American politics, and that raised critical questions of class, gender, and citizenship. This flourishing of activity included powerful inter-nationalist elements and inspired a crusade to remake black America through a conversion from "Negro" to "African." Attempts to construct what I call the African-American "postcolony," a projected condition of cultural and political sovereignty, were central to that quest. Yet the dominant motif of contemporary Pan African nationalism was not "identity," but rather, "liberation." Using the medium of education to explore the complex relationship between these two themes is the primary objective of this book.

The task has been challenging. Thankfully, I have had plenty of support. This study benefited from grants from the National Academy of Education Spencer Postdoctoral Fellowship; the Faculty Research Grant, Rockefeller Center, Dartmouth College; the Walter and Constance Burke Research Award, Dartmouth College; and the Bancroft Awards Committee, Columbia University. It also was enriched by a John Sloan Dickey Center manuscript review at Dartmouth.

For providing an intellectual and spiritual "home" and an extended family, I wish to thank the faculty and staff of the history departments of Columbia University, Dartmouth College, and Cornell University, as well as the faculty and staff of the Institute for Research in African American Studies at Columbia, the Program in African and African American Studies at Dartmouth, and the Africana Studies and Research Center at Cornell.

I would like to thank the staff of the institutions identified in this book's table of archives, especially the good and patient stewards of the Schomburg Center. I am indebted to the staff of the libraries at Columbia, Dartmouth, and Cornell, particularly to those who administer the Borrow Direct and Interlibrary loan services.

I am deeply grateful to the following for providing encouragement, sup-port for this project, and camaraderie, fellowship, and inspiration: Eric Acree, Hannibal Afrik, Vanessa Agard-Jones, Zaheer Ali, Aimee Bahng, Ed Baptist, Martha Biondi, Liz Blum, Stefan Bradley, Scot Brown, Judi Byfield, Colin Calloway, James E. Campbell, Azikiwe Chandler, Osei Chandler, Derek Chang, Soyica Colbert, Matthew Countryman, Jeff Cowie, Ray Craib, Joe Cullon, Josh

Davis, Andre Elizee, Ansley Erickson, Johanna Fernandez, Natalege Fields, Zinga Fraser, Lonnetta Gaines, Maria Cristina Garcia, Durba Ghosh, Larry Glickman, Reena Goldthree, Sandra Greene, Chrissie Greer, Vincent Harding, Alexis Jetter, Rashauna Johnson, Peniel Joseph, Juba Kalamka, Robin D. G. Kelley, Baba Kemit, Ibram Kendi, Deborah King, Julilly Kohler-Hausmann, Kwasi Konadu, Oneka LaBennett, Carol D. Lee, Kofi Lomotey, Seth Markle, Samir Meghelli, Derek Musgrove, Celia Naylor, Jeff O. G. Ogbar, Tanalís Padilla, Charles M. Payne, Dan Perlstein, Brian Purnell, Julie Rabig, Barbara Ransby, Sam K. Roberts, Noliwe Rooks, Naaborko Sackeyfio-Lenoch, Nick Salvatorre, Robert Self, Victor Seow, Jeff Sharlet, Mwalimu Shujaa, Nikhil Pal Singh, Robyn Spencer, Quito Swan, Jeanne Theoharis, Antonio Tillis, Elizabeth Todd-Breland, Keith Walker, Margaret Washington, Jitu Weusi, Derrick E. White, Preston Wilcox, Craig Wilder, Fanon Che Wilkins, Gertrude Wilks, Danielle Terrazas Williams, Yohuru Williams, Joy Williamson-Lot, Chris Wohlforth, and Komozi Woodard.

I am especially indebted to Anthony Bogues, Eric Foner, V. P. Franklin, Kevin K. Gaines, Cedric Johnson, Ira Katznelson, Annelise Orleck, and Penny Von Eschen for extensive and generous feedback and mentorship. Your kindness and generosity are testaments to what the profession can be at its elegant best.

Thank you to the anonymous reviewers; to my editor, Susan Ferber; and to Maya Bringe and the staff of Oxford University Press.

My adviser and mentor, the late Manning Marable, had an immense impact on my life and work. I need him now, more than ever, and I miss him every day. Thank you, Professor.

I also wish to thank the Black Historians Matter crew, all guerilla historians, and the progressive and radical students, workers, and staff of Dartmouth College and Cornell University. *A Luta Continua.*

My siblings, Shiyama Clunie, Anakela Washington, and Luke Rickford, provided steadfast support and encouragement.

My parents, John and Angela Rickford, read every word of what has been, for long stretches, a meandering and torturous tome. Their pride has been a continuous ovation that has immeasurably enriched this work and this writer. I have nothing with which to repay their evangelical belief. They have only my profound respect and love.

My daughter, Anaya Truth Rickford, has been patient and loving. Her patience has worn thin. Yes, Sweet Girl, we can finally go outside and play.

My partner, Adrienne Clay, remains a revelation in my life. Despite the rigors imposed by this book, our friendship is unbroken. Undying. She above all is responsible for the completion of this study, and for the grace that envelops me every day. For that, and for past and future journeys, my love, thank you.

No one, not even the rain . . .

ABBREVIATIONS

ATA	Afro-American Teachers Association
AFS	African Free School
ALD	African Liberation Day
ALSC	African Liberation Support Committee
CAP	Congress of African People
CBE	Center for Black Education
CFUN	Committee for a Unified Newark
CIBI	Council of Independent Black Institutions
CORE	Congress of Racial Equality
FST	Free Southern Theater
HBCUs	Historically Black Colleges and Universities
HPC	Harlem Parents Committee
IS 201	Intermediate School 201
LEI	Lynn Eusan Institute
MPLA	People's Movement for the Liberation of Angola
MXLU	Malcolm X Liberation University
NAAAE	National Association of Afro-American Educators
NOI	Nation of Islam
NSM	Northern Student Movement
PASP	Pan African Services Project
Six-PAC	Sixth Pan African Congress
SNCC	Student Nonviolent Coordinating Committee
SOBU	Student Organization for Black Unity
TABU	Toward a Black University
UFT	United Federation of Teachers
UNIA	Universal Negro Improvement Association
UNITA	National Union for the Total Independence of Angola

PARTIAL LIST AND LOCATIONS OF INDEPENDENT BLACK NATIONALIST SCHOOLS

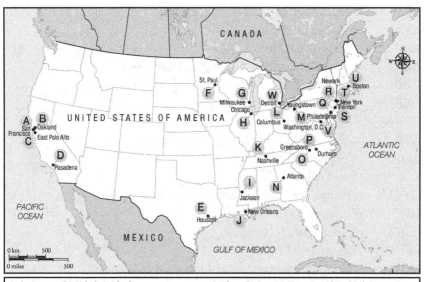

A. San Francisco, CA: **Malcolm X School**
B. Oakland, CA: **Oakland Community School**
C. East Palo Alto, CA: **Nairobi Day School and High School; Nairobi College**
D. Pasadena, CA: **Omowale Ujamaa Community School**
E. Houston, TX: **Kazi Shule; Lynn Eusan Institute**
F. St. Paul, MN: **Institute of African Learning**
G. Milwaukee, WI: **Clifford McKissick Community School**
H. Chicago, IL: **Arusha-Konakri Institute; New Concept Development Center; Shule Ya Watoto; Black People's Topographical Research Center**
I. Jackson, MS: **Black and Proud Liberation School**
J. New Orleans, LA: **Ahidiana Work/Study Center**
K. Nashville, TN: **Nashville Liberation School; People's College**
L. Columbus, OH: **Umoja Sasa Shule**
M. Youngstown, OH: **Marcus Garvey School**

N. Atlanta, GA: **Learning House; Pan African Work Center; Martin Luther King, Jr. Community School**
O. Greensboro, NC: **Malcolm X Liberation University**
P. Durham, NC: **Pan African Early Education Center**
Q. Philadelphia, PA: **ARD Self-Help Center; Freedom Library Day School; Nidhamu Sasa School**
R. Newark, NJ: **African Free School; Chad School**
S. Trenton, NJ: **African People's Action School**
T. New York, NY: **Our School; Uhuru Sasa Shule; School of Common Sense**
U. Boston, MA: **Highland Park Free School; St. Joseph's Community School**
V. Washington, D.C.: **Center for Black Education; Nationhouse Watoto School; New School of Afro-American Thought; New Thing Art & Architecture Center**
W. Detroit, MI: **Aisha Shule**

We Are an African People

Introduction

Education, Black Power, and the Radical Imagination

> Our education must therefore inculcate a sense of commitment to the
> whole community and help the pupils to accept the values appropriate
> to our kind of future, not those appropriate to our colonial past.
> —Julius Nyerere, *"Education for Self-Reliance"*

On a July evening in 1968, a television audience witnessed a demonstration of
the new black militancy and its exacting pedagogy. Some 22 million viewers of
a CBS special on the African-American experience watched John Churchville,
a former Student Nonviolent Coordinating Committee member and one of
the pioneering institution builders of the Black Power era, preside over North
Philadelphia's Freedom Library Day School. They saw him train preschoolers to echo phrases like "My nationality is Afro-American!" designed to crush
the "Negro" cowering within the black child. During the program, Churchville
posed a series of ritualized questions meant to test the resolve of his three- to
five-year-old students, all residents of the surrounding riot-scarred neighborhood. In one sequence, Jenell, a four-year-old girl, answered her teacher:

CHURCHVILLE: What do you want, Jenell?
JENELL: I want freedom.
CHURCHVILLE: When do you want it?
JENELL: I want my freedom now.
CHURCHVILLE: No, you have to wait until next week, Jenell, you can't have it now.
    Can you wait until next week?[1]

Scenes of the exchange played during *Black History: Lost, Stolen or Strayed*,
the first installment in a series about the cultural representation of African
Americans. Churchville's methods, a narrator explained, reflected a struggle for
psychological fortification. Freedom Library was a reaction—an overreaction,

the program suggested—to white racial hostility. Following the broadcast, a few commentators praised Churchville's attempt to prepare African-American children for future encounters with public schools modeled on the cultural values of the white middle class. Black writer Toni Cade argued that Freedom Library's "lesson in selfhood" would ensure that its students never became sycophants of white America. "I know of no blacks who did not rejoice in that [televised] sequence," a *Negro Digest* contributor declared. But many viewers saw the Churchville segment as a case of indoctrination. Several people telephoned CBS or their local station to complain. "I don't believe that a major network should contribute to white backlash and resentment," one caller said.[2]

If *Black History* sparked controversy, it also offered an inside look at a new breed of private school. Churchville's goal of resocializing the oppressed was no more unique than his brand of black nationalist and Pan Africanist education—an approach combining concepts of black American nationality with commitment to linking black struggles worldwide. By 1970, more than 60 "Pan African nationalist" institutions, from preschools to postsecondary ventures, had appeared in cities across the country.[3] The small, independent enterprises were often accused of teaching hate and were routinely harassed by authorities. Yet these institutions served as vital mechanisms of "black consciousness"—a sense of pride and awareness defined against the self-abnegation of "Negro" mentality.[4]

Founded by young activist-intellectuals, Pan African nationalist schools strove not simply to bolster the academic skills and self-image of inner-city African-American youth but also to "decolonize" minds, to nurture the next generation of activists, and to embody the principles of self-determination and African identity. As grassroots "counterinstitutions" built on a thoroughgoing critique of white cultural hegemony, Pan African nationalist schools, or "independent black institutions" as they were known by the 1970s, served as successors to the civil rights movement's "freedom schools"—temporary organs linked to mass struggles of the early to mid-1960s—and as forerunners to modern Afrocentric academies, alternative models that sparked debates about race, ideology, and pedagogy beginning in the 1980s and '90s.[5] Independent black institutions were more than sites of indoctrination. They constituted a vibrant Black Power submovement, a crusade rooted in the renascent idea that African Americans were a subjugated nation, an "internal colony" that needed to claim intellectual and cultural autonomy before achieving true liberation through formal statehood or community self-rule.[6]

In the late 1960s and '70s, an array of African-American activists and educators embraced black independent schools as symbols of a new phase of struggle: the quest to concretize the ideals of "blackness" and "Africanness" that had been rekindled by the mass movements of the 1960s. Scores of organizers—from artists and cultural figures to college students, parents, antipoverty workers, and insurgent public school teachers—helped start "liberation schools," "community schools," and other avowedly ideological academies in basements and storefronts, while many more black-consciousness advocates actively supported such ventures. The growth of these institutions signaled a strategic and philosophical shift from the pursuit of reform within a liberal democracy to the attempt to build the prospective infrastructure for an independent black nation, an entity that many activists imagined as a political and spiritual extension of the Third World.

This reconceptualization occurred during and after the mid-1960s amid the upsurge of theory that characterized the Black Power renaissance. Independent black institutions exemplified the contemporary politics of personal and collective conversion. They were the instruments of a stratum of radicalized, largely middle-class activist-intellectuals. Some of these figures were known nationwide, such as Owusu Sadaukai (Howard Fuller) of Greensboro, North Carolina's Malcolm X Liberation University, and Black Arts Movement leaders Amiri Baraka and Haki Madhubuti, respective cofounders (along with their spouses, educators Amina Baraka and Safisha Madhubuti) of Newark's African Free School and Chicago's New Concept Development Center. Others, such as Nairobi Day School founder Gertrude Wilks of East Palo Alto, California, were recognized only in their local communities. All were veterans of social battles in the Jim Crow South and northern metropolises who wished to initiate a rebirth of blackness, a revolution in culture and political theory that could connect poor and working-class African Americans to Africa, the Caribbean, and the masses of the nonwhite world.

Creators of the schools—cultural and revolutionary nationalists, Pan Africanists, and a few budding Marxists—strove to codify a major insight of civil rights campaigns and earlier liberation struggles, namely, that black people could develop alternatives to the oppressive social institutions that dominated their lives. The schools reflected a search for indigenous structures that could "house our aspirations" while forming "liberated zones" of self-determination within deteriorating urban centers. Subsisting on donations, private grants, modest tuition fees, and, to a lesser extent, federal antipoverty funds, the academies served only a tiny fraction of urban schoolchildren and young adults.[7] The significance of the ventures lies less in the size of their enrollments (generally from 25 to 250 students) than in their role as organs of radical imagination and products of the effort to fashion a new peoplehood—styled as "Afro-American" or simply "African"—through a transformation of consciousness.

Organizers of Pan African nationalist schools understood citizenship as a cultural construct. Though postwar struggles had expanded the scope of legal equality and civil rights, these theorists believed white supremacy remained the central reality of black existence throughout the world. For them, cultivating

an alternative citizenship—a sense of transnationalism that defied the cultural
norms and political dictates of the American empire—was a vital means of subverting Western hegemony and combatting the psychology of the oppressed, a
syndrome described by thinkers from Frantz Fanon to Malcolm X.[8] *We Are an
African People* describes a moment in which cadres of activist-intellectuals saw
rethinking schools in poor and working-class African-American communities
both as a way to redeem the process of formal learning and as a way to pursue,
indeed *prefigure*, black cultural and political sovereignty.

Pan African nationalists viewed the classroom as the placenta of a nation.
They believed formal education could sever sociopolitical, material, and psychological dependencies and aid in the creation of what I call the African-American
"postcolony"—an independent polity ready to take its place among the rising powers of the non-Western world. They believed that black America must
prepare its youth not merely to navigate a racist society or an increasingly specialized job market but also to contribute technical expertise to the cause of
"national development" wherever in the African world they were called to serve.
Over the course of the 1970s, this stunningly romantic premise foundered in
the face of complex political, economic, and social circumstances in the United
States, Africa, and the Caribbean, revealing the perils of an ahistorical mystique
of global blackness and invented Africanness.

The goal of black cultural redefinition through independent education nevertheless generated a tremendous surge of theory and practice. A "struggle in
the arenas of ideas" over the definition of the black experience, this cause rever-
berates today in everything from African-American home schooling to black
enthusiasm for charter schools.[9] Pan African nationalist schools did not spawn
organizations that oversaw the day-to-day instruction of tens of thousands of
children (though a handful of the campuses, including Chicago's New Concept
Development Center, survive to this day). Their legacy lies instead in the tena-
cious belief that African Americans must be educated to recognize and develop
the subordinate nation to which they belong by right of birth.

The quest for independent black institutions was not solely or primarily
defined by classroom experiences. Pan African nationalist schools were far more
than vessels of formal education. They were cooperatives, collectives, cultural
centers, organs of community action and agitprop, and laboratories for a spectrum of ideas—from anti-imperialism and Third Worldism on the left to patriarchy and racial fundamentalism on the right. This book examines the broad
ideals that animated these institutions and galvanized their founders. It explores
the political imagination of a collection of organizers who, having witnessed the
limitations of desegregation battles, struggles on college campuses, antipoverty
work, and grassroots campaigns for decent public education, concluded that
autonomous social and cultural structures were essential tools of black liberation

and regeneration in an age that combined the discourse of "colorblind" equality with a racialized matrix of mass incarceration, chronic unemployment, and dwindling social welfare.

Seeing themselves as a people's intelligentsia fostering resistance through African reidentification, operators of independent black institutions consciously blended pedagogy, organizing, and propaganda. *We Are an African People* illuminates their philosophies of education, their attempts to foster global solidarities, and their crusade to reimagine blackness. It offers an intellectual history of subaltern education, a critical analysis of the fate of Black Power ideologies in the postsegregation era, and a portrait of African-American self-activity at the neighborhood level.

In a sense, this is a study of Black Power's afterlife. *We Are an African People* depicts an aspect of the movement that flourished in the early to mid-1970s, a time not often associated with vigorous black nationalist and Pan Africanist efforts in multiple communities. For many African-American urbanites, local organizations and establishments—not spectacular events or charismatic leaders—gave the contemporary struggle its thrust and meaning.[10] Yet the political and cultural practices of independent black institutions are enshrined in neither the iconography nor the popular memory of Black Power. Notwithstanding the televised scenes of Freedom Library Day School described earlier, relatively few reporters or TV cameras entered the schools. My narrative of Black Power begins after the media spotlight faded.

We Are an African People offers a glimpse at a lost 1970s, a moment of political flux and cultural ferment whose creative social possibilities remain unfulfilled. The story contained in these pages will be unfamiliar to most readers. To some, the ideological and conceptual underpinnings of Pan African nationalist schools will seem esoteric. We are used to imagining the 1970s as a moment of malaise, retrenchment, and decline. What are we to make of a small yet formidable movement that arose substantively during that decade, that proved remarkably resilient, and that posited education as the final battlefield of "the colonized," with no less at stake than the very meaning and future of the oppressed in relation to "the mother country"?[11]

Many of the theories and discursive strategies associated with independent black institutions were highly abstract. The political rhetoric of the schools was steeped in idealism. Though Pan African nationalists touted institution building as a viable frontier for mass action, the vast majority of African-American schoolchildren remained in public institutions. Indeed, the turn to private education reflected some of the elements of fragmentation and retreat from radical agitation that afflicted the larger liberation struggle. Many operators of Black Power counterinstitutions were justifiably criticized for preoccupation with "internal purification," a trait that reinforced strains of dogmatism and social isolation.[12]

Yet the quest for independent black institutions cannot be dismissed as empty symbolism or narrow identity politics. The schools served as key programmatic expressions of Black Power. They represented conscious attempts to transcend rhetoric and create enduring mechanisms of consciousness and resistance. Many of the establishments were centers of radical commitment. Their organizers expressed solidarity with liberation fronts in Africa and throughout the Third World while engaging social justice campaigns within African-American neighborhoods. They strove to provide decent, socially relevant education in places where such amenities were severely limited. At their best, Pan African nationalist schools honored the activist tradition of addressing pragmatic, everyday needs while "preparing the field" of struggle for tomorrow.[13]

We Are an African People conveys a panorama of possibilities even as it offers sober critiques. To understand the rise of independent black institutions in the 1970s, we must be willing to examine social movements—especially complex, highly symbolic movements—on their own terms. We must heed historian Nikhil Pal Singh's assertion that "Aspirations for black freedom and equality have long been deemed exorbitant in the normative and normalizing frames . . . used to contain them." This study accepts radical exorbitance and elaborate symbolism as genuine modes of opposition and as necessary spiritual and intellectual components of self-liberation. As Robin D. G. Kelley has noted, neither utopian outlooks nor imagined communities are apolitical.[14]

In the pages that follow, I attempt both to grapple with nationalist myths and to comprehend the social functions that they perform for the oppressed. Despite its shortcomings, the political imaginary of Pan African nationalism—the philosophical and ideological architecture of its beliefs—offered powerful, alternative visions of African-American cultural citizenship, by which I mean the discourses of identity and belonging within the social production of subordinate groups.[15] This book demonstrates how those visions were invigorated by the mystique of postcoloniality and instantiated by activist-intellectuals who saw revolution as the primary imperative of their lives.

The rise of Pan African nationalist schools highlights important dimensions of modern African-American thought. Much of the original impetus for the movement sprang from dissatisfaction with the politics and strategies of integration. The 1970s marked the high tide of official desegregation efforts in many municipalities. African-American resistance to separate schools remained strong and continued to offer a crucial means of seeking access to resources and opportunities overwhelmingly concentrated in white institutions.[16]

However, the profound flaws of the integrationist strategy and agenda deepened black ambivalence toward the approach. Those misgivings intensified amid feeble and inequitable desegregation plans, virulent white opposition to racial intermingling, black concerns about isolation in white-controlled establishments, and the demographic realities of white flight from city centers and public education. As New York City school boycott leader Milton Galamison acknowledged in 1968, "Black people who had not previously thought the matter through decided that it might not be an advantage to have their children educated beside the children whose parents sanctioned bigotry and hatred."[17]

Some African Americans rejected integration on strategic, philosophical, and ideological grounds. Traditionally a site of African-American struggle for social inclusion, education was also a historic arena of black self-determination. African-American schools have served as instruments for instilling "race pride" and nurturing "race leaders" since the late eighteenth and nineteenth centuries. Following the Civil War, freed people bolstered traditions of black educational autonomy by establishing and running their own schools. African Americans continued to pursue self-help in education during the twentieth century, even as they endured the stifling repression of Jim Crow. Black nationalist sentiment and encounters with systemic discrimination in the urban North and West, as well as the South, led some African-American migrants to create separate educational models, including the private schools of the Universal Negro Improvement Association and the Nation of Islam.[18]

The vast majority of black inner-city children, however, remained in public schools, many of which were severely neglected as white ethnic populations abandoned the city core in the postwar era. By the 1960s, some African-American urbanites viewed local systems of public education as colonial apparatuses designed to stultify children of color. They accused neighborhood schools of preparing youngsters for lives of marginality and servitude on the fringes of an opulent society. Nor did "multiethnic" studies and "integrated" textbooks end the chronic alienation of African-American students. Organizers of Milwaukee's Clifford McKissick Community School, an independent black institution, noted in 1970 that inclusion of African-American history and culture in public school curricula had created little more than "a black patchwork on a snow-white blanket of white nationalist education."[19]

The contemporary black drive for educational justice included ongoing campaigns for desegregation and parity, creation of professional associations and advocacy groups, and demands for curricular changes, more black personnel, and parent participation in school governance. The range of strategies suggested the diversity of African-American visions of dignified schooling. Though some of these efforts yielded substantial concessions, the thrust for reform never fulfilled overarching goals of social mobility, collective advancement, and open opportunity, and thus failed to produce the democratic revolution in school and society envisioned by many African-American parents. In the late 1960s, pragmatism and political growth revitalized black nationalist themes in educational struggles, a development that fueled the drive for local control over public schools in the Ocean Hill–Brownsville section of Brooklyn. As urban "community control" initiatives foundered, however, the search for alternatives continued.[20]

As "ghetto schools" spawned functional illiterates and white resistance to busing and other methods of achieving "racial balance" intensified, a small but growing segment of African-American urbanites sought educational salvation beyond public education. They were not alone. The era witnessed a flourishing of alternative school movements. "Free schools" were created by counterculture activists who argued that the compulsory nature and authoritarian methods of public schools bred conformity and smothered the creative genius of children. While innovative, free schools were overwhelmingly white and middle-class. Their organizers shared black radicals' disdain for the materialism and individualism of bourgeois culture. Yet free schoolers hoped to humanize a decadent and "overdeveloped" society, while black radicals wished to cultivate communities that a racist power structure had willfully "underdeveloped."[21]

The constellation of alternative establishments included urban "street academies" geared toward dropouts and the underprivileged, as well as politically moderate black private schools serving middle-class populations and offering black studies along with traditional college preparation. Few of those models appear in this study. Rather than attempt a taxonomy of black private schools, *We Are an African People* examines a cluster of secular institutions expressly devoted to fostering black national and transnational consciousness as a primary pedagogical and social mission. In the heyday of Black Power, the phrase "independent black institution" was closely associated with grassroots, militant enterprises in major cities.[22] It was these outfits—not traditional African-American boarding schools or historically "Negro" colleges and universities—that embodied the contemporary meaning of "independent" (both private and free from the influence and control of the white power structure) and "black" (racially assertive, proud, and uncompromising).

Pan African nationalist schools engaged in academic uplift, but their primary purpose was sociopolitical and counterhegemonic. In this respect, they resembled contemporary American Indian "survival schools," Chicano heritage academies, and the liberation schools of the Young Lords, a radical Puerto Rican group. Forged by nationalist movements, these institutions encouraged their students to speak indigenous tongues and regard native territories as proud homelands rather than degraded reservations. In their strenuous efforts to socialize children, their wariness toward mainstream culture, and their close ties to neighborhoods, independent black institutions mirrored older ethnic and parochial models as well, including Catholic schools, Chinese private schools, and Jewish day schools.[23] Unlike these more traditional establishments, however, Pan African nationalist schools paired separatist impulses with strains of radical internationalism and anti-imperialism.

The breakthrough year for independent black institutions was 1970. Operators of the schools and other black-consciousness devotees gathered at conferences and Afro-American teacher conventions to share visions of nationalist development and educational autonomy. They concluded that independent institutions must nurture communitarian values, encourage "rediscovery of self as an African," and attempt to train and export "teachers and technicians, scientists, engineers, whatever is needed by any African nation anywhere in the world."[24]

In June 1972, almost 30 teachers and organizers from throughout the country assembled in the Frogmore section of the historic South Carolina Sea Island of St. Helena—a former refuge for escaped slaves and now a retreat for civil rights workers seeking recuperation and Neo-Pan Africanists seeking African "restoration"—to formalize the Council of Independent Black Institutions (CIBI), a national federation. Attendees hailed from 14 schools, including campuses in Atlanta, Chicago, New York, and Columbus, Ohio. They chose as their mantra the Pan-African slogan "We Are an African People." They agreed that independent institutions must offer programs for welfare recipients and prisoners, maintain strict regimens of self-defense training, and avoid insidious, "Western" distinction between physical and intellectual labor. Finally, the new alliance crafted an ambitious statement of purpose. CIBI would be "the political vehicle through which a qualitatively different people is produced . . . a people who can be trusted to struggle uncompromisingly for the liberation of all African people everywhere."[25]

To fully comprehend this mission, we must trace the genealogy of post-1960s struggle. The history of independent black institutions illuminates larger transformations of African-American political culture. As young civil rights veterans outgrew obsolete protest strategies, powerful currents thrust them toward new analyses and approaches, re-energizing them and giving them a sense of control over their lives. The themes "from freedom to liberation" and "from colony to capital" illustrate the paths that these figures traveled to Pan African nationalist education. Though the phrases were not used by contemporaries, they offer a useful framing for the transitions that propelled activists from a first wave of mass insurgency in the early 1960s to a second wave of grassroots organizing in the late '60s and '70s.

The genesis of many independent black institutions began with the dissolution of the Student Nonviolent Coordinating Committee (SNCC). After emerging from the southern desegregation movement and scattering to various cities, former SNCC workers John Churchville, Jimmy Garrett, Cleveland Sellers, Judy

Richardson, Willie Ricks, Ralph Featherstone, Jean Wiley, Stanley Wise, Karen Edmonds, Courtland Cox, Bernice Reagon, Charlie Cobb, Fred Brooks, George Ware, and Syrtiller Kabat helped create, staff, or sustain an array of institutions, including Philadelphia's Freedom Library Day School, Atlanta's Pan African Work Center, Greensboro's Malcolm X Liberation University, Washington, DC's Center for Black Education, and the Nairobi Day School of East Palo Alto, California.

They and other organizers hoped to hasten the conversion from civil rights to human rights, a reorientation heralded by Malcolm X. They shed the vestiges of Cold War parochialism, trading the mantra of "freedom"—an ideal associated with the quest for legal equality—for that of "national liberation," a concept that connoted black self-determination and identification with the revolutionary world. Some of these figures again joined cadres of activists, believing that such "organizations of organizers" could help prepare black America for coming struggles.[26]

In their hunt for forms of political and cultural sovereignty that the mainstream civil rights movement had failed to deliver and neglected to pursue, young black progressives and militants (like many of their white, New Left counterparts) looked to the Third World as a source of social models. For them, the critical divide was not the American South versus the North, but rather, the colonizer versus the colonized. This theoretical turn reflected growing contempt for liberalism, recognition of dwindling possibilities for social reform via traditional channels, and, not infrequently, a dose of romanticism. But black "Third Worldism" also signaled genuine optimism about the radical potential of transnational solidarity. Contemporary black nationalism was inextricable from Pan Africanism, because black nation-states were viewed as key indexes of the freedom and power of African-descended people across the globe.[27]

Many African-American internationalists thus evinced a bold form of nationalism, a core element of black consciousness whose cultural and political influence markedly increased. African Americans, these thinkers insisted, were not merely another ethnic group. To realize their destiny, black Americans needed "to die a tribe and be born a nation," as the people of Mozambique and other revolutionary lands were attempting to do.[28] Nationhood was the true condition of African America and the ultimate mechanism of self-determination.

However, formal statehood remained a distant ideal, and there was no consensus about what form it should take or whether it was even necessary. What most young radicals could agree on was the need to foster national consciousness and rehabilitate African-American identity. Escaping colonial mentality meant spurring the cultural and psychological reorientation that Malcolm X had advocated. Collective redefinition would bring redemption. As the Nation of

Islam had long demonstrated, the construction of a new and meaningful peoplehood could begin with the rigorous restructuring of individual lives.[29]

Looking to stimulate a transformation of consciousness, a host of battle-tested activists returned to the arena of education, refining theories of liberatory pedagogy drawn from their experiences in freedom schools, black studies campaigns, and student protests. Not all these figures were associated with SNCC. Former or current members of the Republic of New Africa and the Nation of Islam created Omowale Ujamaa Northwest Community School in Pasadena, California. Abdullah Abdur-Razzaq, who as "James Shabazz" had been a top Malcolm X aide, helped his spouse, Ohra, establish the Al-Karim School in the Crown Heights section of Brooklyn. The borough was also home to the 150-student School of Common Sense, a venture founded by Sonny Carson, militant director of Brooklyn's breakaway Congress of Racial Equality chapter. The local community control struggle, a Carson ally later recalled, had convinced the leader that the education of African-American children could not remain in the hands of "white working class teachers aspiring to become members of the petit-bourgeoisie."[30]

The new institution builders were seasoned organizers who had remolded themselves. Like the Black Panthers, who launched similar "liberation schools" in the late 1960s (though with more explicit emphasis on Marxist-Leninist themes), Pan African nationalists continued to see education as a route to black empowerment. Now, however, they envisioned permanent ventures that could replace, rather than merely critique or destabilize, the institutions of the dominant culture. They also broadened their theoretical base. Some read Brazilian theorist Paulo Freire, whose 1970 treatise, *Pedagogy of the Oppressed*, argued that the reconstruction of subject peoples required the cultivation of critical consciousness. Even more influential was "Education for Self-Reliance," a 1968 essay by Tanzanian president Julius Nyerere that discussed the need to eliminate the psychological and political residue of colonialism by reshaping education.[31]

This message resonated with black liberationists, many of whom believed a quasi-colonial education had "depersonalized" African Americans, preparing them for subservience in much the same way that European empires had denatured their nonwhite subjects. Such theorists looked to postcolonial and revolutionary societies for solutions, impressed by accounts of how Cubans, North Vietnamese, and others had reduced illiteracy and used education as a tool for nation building. Especially inspiring were reports of how Southern African liberation movements had constructed temporary schools for the benefit of their cadres and indigenous populations, a practice depicted in *A Luta Continua*, an African-American-made documentary about the anticolonial struggle.[32]

The idea of converted military camps deep in the liberated zones of Mozambique (a Portuguese colony until 1974) where "bush schools"—often little more than a blackboard on a tree—transformed guerillas and villagers into "new men and women" captivated African-American radicals and deep-ened their vision of education as the reclamation of a subject people's human-ity. They concluded that a revolution *by* education required a revolution *in* education. Schools would have to be dramatically reimagined if they were to be engines of the new society rather than bulwarks of the status quo. They would need to become "liberated zones" that could function as self-contained commu-nities and embryos of the coming nation.[33]

If education was a crucial realm of struggle, the African-American metropo-lis was the new land. Young militants regarded the black city core as a sup-pressed political territory and as a key site for reimagining community. In the mid-1960s, SNCC cadres had expanded efforts to establish pilot programs in urban areas, especially in the North, recognizing that "the axis of the struggle appeared to be shifting away from the rural South." As SNCC leader Stokely Carmichael maintained, the time had come "to return to the ghetto to organize these communities to control themselves."[34] After SNCC's demise in the late 1960s, civil rights veterans continued to regard the inner city as a test site for linking revolutionary theory and everyday attempts to serve the oppressed.

The call for experienced organizers to "return" to urban enclaves meant a recommitment to territories that exemplified both the oppressive nature of racial capitalism and the "national" character of black America. The reconcep-tualization of "second ghettoes"—repositories for waves of African-American migration since World War II—as the future province of black sovereignty reinforced the concept of inner cities as potential powerbases. The challenge lay in transforming these colonial domains into capitals of black dignity, and in doing so largely (or entirely) without the aid of the War on Poverty.

From their inception, many Pan African nationalist institutions had ben-efited from antipoverty funds. The community action arm of the Great Society sustained many of the self-help projects that later evolved into independent schools. However, the belief that the poverty programs were designed to mol-lify and coopt militants bred growing disillusionment with the federal initia-tives. By the late 1960s and early '70s, amid dwindling social spending and intensifying critiques of antipoverty measures as sophisticated pacification schemes, many African-American organizers concluded that independent, grassroots initiatives—not federal programs—were the critical instruments of community self-sufficiency and revival.[35]

The explosion of urban uprisings after 1964, and especially the insurrec-tions of 1967–1968, underscored the "proto-revolutionary" potential of ghetto territories. Authorities depicted "riots" as responses to concentrated poverty and inequality, and as outbursts of frustration, criminality, and vio-lence. Yet elements of empowerment accompanied the turmoil. While some observers saw evidence of pathology, many organizers sensed that a reservoir of political energy had been exposed.

Radical theorists understood the uprisings not simply as responses to the failure of racial reform to alleviate the suffering of the slums but also as local expressions of global revolt and as opportunities for sustained organizing. The police slaying of an unarmed 18-year-old during Milwaukee's 1967 insurrection, for example, led to the conversion of a local youth center into the Clifford McKissick Community School, an independent senior high offering instruction in algebra, chemistry, karate, African affairs, and the West African language of Yoruba. Throughout the "long hot summers" of the 1960s, community activists strove to harness the wave of militancy and to develop the restive, inchoate nation that postwar migration had engendered.[36]

Autonomous institutions offered a means of doing so. The concept of urban enclaves as incipient sovereignties deepened the appeal of parallel black structures. Black Power advocates hailed the construction of such entities as a step toward formal self-determination and as a practical survival strategy at a time of economic stagnation and retrenchment. The "mounting proclivity of black people to create their own independent organs of struggle," as one journalist put it, accompanied ongoing attempts to improve existing schools, hospitals, and public accommodations within African-American neighborhoods.[37] However, the deficiencies of community control campaigns strengthened the conviction that the redevelopment of black urban centers required the creation of grassroots enterprises able to remain separate from the state and existing power apparatuses.

The construction of parallel institutions, a cornerstone of black nationalist practice, offered a means of pursuing self-reliance, meeting social needs, and conveying moral and political principles. New African-American cultural centers, publishing houses, theaters, and health clinics emerged. Intellectuals, activists, and artists created influential Pan African nationalist organs such as Atlanta's Institute of the Black World, a think tank, and the Drum & Spear Bookstore, a radical political salon that opened in a riot-torn section of Washington, DC. At a time when reshaping consciousness was considered indispensable, schools were among the most cherished forms of autonomy. They included establishments like Uhuru Sasa Shule (Kiswahili for "Freedom Now School") of Brooklyn, West Side Chicago's Shule Ya Watoto ("School for Children"), and the Black and Proud Liberation School of Jackson, Mississippi.[38]

The appeal of parallel institutions had grown as the freedom struggle evolved. Emphasis on independent structures and power blocs had re-emerged in the early to mid-1960s, producing northern and southern freedom schools, the Freedom Now Party in Michigan, and the Lowndes County Freedom Organization in

Alabama. "A conscious bid for political power is being made, and in the course of that effort a tactical shift is being effected," civil rights strategist Bayard Rustin noted in 1964. "Direct-action techniques are being subordinated to a strategy calling for the building of community institutions or power bases. Clearly, the implications of this shift reach far beyond Mississippi." Offering a more nationalistic framing, SNCC in 1966 called upon African Americans "to begin building independent political, economic and cultural institutions that they will control and use as instruments of social change in this country."[39]

The construction of parallel institutions assumed richer symbolic meaning in the late 1960s as autonomous black trade unions (including Detroit's League of Revolutionary Black Workers) proliferated, the Black Panthers unveiled a series of "survival programs" designed to deliver social services directly to poor communities, and Pan African nationalism enjoyed a moment of ideological hegemony in black political culture. "The most crucial work for this particular era of African existence is the building of revolutionary nationalist institutions," editors of the newly launched *Rhythm Magazine* asserted in 1970. "By 'institutions' we mean schools, political parties, cultural centers, military units, presses—all those programmatic structures that enable a people to see beyond survival; in short, the elemental ingredients of a viable nation."[40]

Such establishments promised to supplement the social services that were vanishing from the urban core, a site of massive disinvestment and neglect. Parallel institutions seemed capable of offering an alternative structure of authority, a provisional power that could replace hostile and inadequate local agencies. By presenting credible alternatives that fulfilled human needs, such ventures could win the loyalty of the people, exposing the failings of the existing social apparatus and serving as tools for mass politicization. The metaphor of black nationhood could become material reality, crystallizing in an emerging network of independent enterprises.[41]

Though it was rarely invoked explicitly, the concept of "dual power," or the formation of alternative institutions as a means of supplanting corrupt state authority, captures the aims and exuberance of Black Power's autonomous establishments. A mainstay of leftist practice since the formation of workers' "soviets" during the Russian Revolution of 1917, the approach appealed to African-American organizers who wished to formalize elements of intellectual independence from a majority culture they viewed as rapidly decaying. The principle of dual power provided a rationale for constructing within black neighborhoods institutional models of a free and just society. It offered a method of discrediting the structures of white elite power while gradually subverting their control over black life.[42]

The dual power model had many African-American antecedents. Some of the mutual aid societies and other indigenous establishments devoted to strengthening the viability of southern black communities during and after Reconstruction performed quasi-governmental functions, including maintaining internal order and discipline, delivering social services, and providing for collective defense. In the interwar years, Marcus Garvey's Universal Negro Improvement Association organized schools, a nurse and paramilitary corps, and other parallel institutions. As theorists James and Grace Boggs observed, the growth of the Nation of Islam in black urban neighborhoods between the 1930s and the 1960s rested in part on the strength of an organizational framework that "approximates the structure of government, including leaders, followers, taxation, discipline, and enforcement agencies." *Freedomways* editor Jack O'Dell later argued that the most profound characteristic of the civil rights movement of the 1950s and '60s was its role as an independent center of authority that "represented the people's alternative to the power of institutionalized racism and colonialist war." By 1970, the creation of "alternative forms or institutions" was closely associated with Pan African nationalist development and the "We Are an African People" slogan.[43]

Despite its contemporary relevance, the principle of dual power contained a number of contradictions. The construction of autonomous social prototypes reflected awareness that revolution required more than spontaneous eruption. Yet institutional preservation often meant supplementing rather than confronting the dominant political apparatus, a strategy seemingly inconsistent with broad social transformation. Dual power reflected both practical and utopian ideas. It strove to address material conditions at the grassroots, but it could also reinforce the fantasy that the state would simply wither away or foster the belief that official authority might be usurped by a few isolated counterinstitutions. Finally, the drive to create separate structures encompassed both egalitarian and authoritarian impulses, embodying the ideal of widespread, democratic participation while replicating the hierarchy of a vanguard formation.

The rediscovery of dual power enriched the black renaissance of the 1960s and '70s, conflicting tendencies notwithstanding. At a time when anticolonial theory shaped the discourse of liberation, efforts to craft alternative structures shifted the radical gaze toward future horizons. The practice of dual power suggested that black people could design viable prototypes of the societies they wished to inhabit. The postcolonial process of establishing a political culture based on the aims of the revolution could thus begin immediately, even amid the throes of struggle.[44]

To the young organizers who remade African-American politics in the 1960s, the conversion from "freedom" to "liberation" seemed necessary and promising. The ferment of street uprisings, the rejuvenation of nationalism, the rise of black consciousness, the rendezvous with the Third World, the colonial analogy, the

Pan African resurgence—all were essential to the transformation of the movement. Black Power, or that phase of insurgency known to participants as "the black liberation struggle," was a social awakening, a period of intense political maturation that helped shape African-American modernity. The movement, or conglomeration of submovements, was led by grassroots organizers and charismatic mobilizers. It was local as well as national and transnational, strategic and sustained as well as abortive, and democratic as well as authoritarian.

Examining Black Power through the lens of independent schools opens new vistas of struggle. Schools are rich sites of knowledge production. They generate a fertile set of political ideas and offer a valuable means of assessing contemporary efforts to model a postrevolutionary future. Black nationalism and Pan Africanism did not simply disrupt or derail educational struggles in the 1960s, as some scholars suggest. *We Are an African People* presents nationalism as an organic outgrowth of the range of impulses within black educational thought and practice.[45]

The narratives of disillusionment with which historians once explained transitions to black nationalism and to speculative varieties of radicalism seem curiously one-dimensional. A rich corpus of scholarship has demonstrated that Black Power's multiple political and cultural expressions were neither merely phenomena of the urban North nor purely manifestations of frustration or bravado. They were not simply episodes of rhetoric or catharsis.[46]

As scholars have argued, the radicalism of the late 1960s and 1970s reformulated rather than ruptured the "organizing tradition," the painstaking, egalitarian approach that helped define earlier stages of struggle.[47] This was the case in the realm of education. Organizers who adopted revolutionary outlooks increasingly scorned progressive Western pedagogy, believing that its ideals of self-actualization and individual expression masked an underlying commitment to capitalist accumulation and racial hierarchy. But many Black Power institutions maintained democratic philosophies and instructional techniques. Overemphasis on decline—in the methods and objectives of alternative education or in the transformation of black political culture more broadly—obscures the progressive ethics that marked all phases of the movement.[48]

Independent black institutions exemplified another critical dimension of Black Power organizing—its pragmatism. Pan African nationalist schools were more than sources of theory. They were also direct responses to material and other deficiencies in urban infrastructure and schooling. Organizers and supporters of the institutions recognized that "people do not just fight for ideas."[49] They yearned to politicize black residents of core cities, but they also wanted the children of such territories to become fully literate and conscious of the world as it was and as it might be. Anything less would compromise the political and cultural transfiguration they envisioned.

Focusing on the activities of Pan African nationalist educators helps highlight the everyday practices of Black Power while challenging the notion that advocates of the movement abandoned community work for proselytizing and "skillful manipulation of media." Black Powerites were pedagogues and propagandists. They engaged bread-and-butter issues of education, housing, and employment even as they forged new political paths and created centralized organizations. "There will be no instant revolution this year," a SNCC officer acknowledged in 1968. "We have to prepare our people for a very long haul. We have to propose programs."[50]

Depictions of the late 1960s and '70s as an incomprehensible welter of events and ideas, or as a mere splintering of groups and coalitions, require reconsideration.[51] The dynamics of chaos and fracture strongly marked contemporary politics. Yet the period also offered elements of intellectual and tactical coherence. Despite the intricate organizational and ideological realignments that accompanied their rebirth, Pan Africanism and African reidentification supplied an intellectual matrix upon which an array of activists and cultural workers coalesced.

Tales of post-1960s political failure have eclipsed not just Black Power's pragmatism and coherence but also its radical optimism.[52] During the pregnant moment between the mid-1960s civil rights legislation and the political alienation of the late 1970s, bitter disenchantment and exhilarating possibilities commingled. The turn to Pan African nationalism was an expression of hope more than a symptom of despair. Radical internationalism reinvigorated the freedom struggle and enlarged its political visions.

A holistic view of the Black Power era must depict its fusion of alienation and expectation while conveying the depth and scope of its intellectual production. *We Are an African People* stresses the ideological diversity and complexity of Pan Africanism (or "Neo-Pan Africanism"), a major tendency of the movement. Like other scholars of transnational African-American consciousness, I do not regard African cultural identity and solidarity efforts as illusory.[53] In such crusades, the politics of engagement and escape often coincide. The freedom dreams of black internationalists were audacious, but rarely were they flimsy or ephemeral.

Nor were such visions markers of larger, inexorable processes of decline. A detailed mapping of discursive practices and countersymbolic strategies can highlight the political fertility of the 1970s. Upon careful analysis, many of the decade's seemingly evanescent struggles appear rigorous, theoretically expansive, and influential. Such campaigns belie accounts of the abrupt collapse of grassroots activity.

New scholarship has reframed the decade. "Far from belonging to the post-civil rights era," historian Stephen Tuck writes, the 1970s represented "the high-water mark of the black liberation movement." A number of grassroots struggles, from the revolts of rank-and-file workers to welfare rights campaigns, unfolded during a period that is often viewed as the "tragic denouement" of 1960s protests.[54] The rise of a generation of black independent schools under-scores the need to rethink the decade. Dismissing even seemingly quixotic Black Power institutions as symbols of hubris and fantasy conceals the liminal moment in which they flourished and leads to truncated and reductionist accounts of the liberation struggle.

Historicizing Pan African nationalism's quest to remake African-American identity in the post–Jim Crow era means reconstructing a range of visions and activities. It also means transcending the impulse to vindicate Black Power. Serious movements demand rigorous scrutiny. I accept Ann McClintock's asser-tion that "All nationalisms are gendered, all are invented, and all are dangerous," as well as E. Frances White's premise that black nationalism contains both liber-ating and repressive discourses.[55] *We Are an African People* offers a sympathetic yet critical analysis of Pan African nationalism's ideological groundings. In so doing, it expands an ongoing discussion of the internal contradictions of Black Power and black nationalism.[56]

As this study demonstrates, a host of theoretical and practical weaknesses plagued the quest for independent black institutions. Patriarchy was an espe-cially severe deficiency. Many Pan African nationalist schools were founded and operated by women, including Atlanta's Learning House (Lonnetta Gaines and Victoria Skaggs); St. Paul, Minnesota's Institute of African Learning (Sylvia Hill); Philadelphia's ARD Self-Help Center (Alice Walker); and Durham, North Carolina's Pan African Early Education Center (Mary McDonald). Overall, however, independent black institutions reproduced the pronounced male supremacy inherent in the majority culture. Their masculinist framing of libera-tion marginalized black women, including those who played central roles in their organization. As Christina Greene has noted, such male-centered approaches "obscured the critical contributions of women to Black Power projects, particu-larly those undertaken at the local level."[57]

An exaggerated view of the significance of identity was another serious shortcoming. Leaders of the schools attempted to preserve "blackness" and "Africanness" as a set of specific cultural behaviors and political values, even as those motifs were commoditized, appropriated by liberal and conservative forces, and stripped of oppositional meaning as symbols of mass resistance to racial capitalism.[58]

Preoccupation with internal conversion and the inculcation of values sug-gested that resocialization could replace other forms of struggle, or that resocial-ization *was* the struggle. The effort to forge a new peoplehood, an ideal closely associated with cultural nationalism, was embraced by practically every Black Power tendency. Yet the authoritarian implications of campaigns to govern consciousness and "win the mind" were often ignored. At times, emphasis on re-education and psychological liberation eclipsed more substantive challenges to structural racism. The fixation of activist-intellectuals on reconditioning students, staff—indeed, all black Americans—threatened to reduce emancipation to an act of culture or a psychic quest.[59]

The equation of Pan Africanism with the activities of true believers, and the notion that the enculturation of the masses was the duty of an advance guard of ideologues, further separated some varieties of black radicalism from the everyday realities and aspirations of the African-American working classes. The real value of "liberated territories" lay in their capacity to return decision-making power to the people, not in the creation of a new layer of intellectual or political elites.

Finally, organizers of independent schools misjudged the capacity of black self-help and communitarianism to prefigure more robust forms of political autonomy and to mitigate the effects of capitalist restructuring. Wedded to notions of urban centers as sites of racial solidarity, they were ill equipped to confront the social devastation spawned by the growing isolation and poverty of postindustrial cities.

Despite these and other flaws, independent black institutions were more than rearguard formations or distractions from confrontation politics. The schools embodied the rich institutional life of the Black Power and Black Arts movements; they were products of a cultural efflorescence that remains remarkably underappreciated. They disseminated ideas through their own small libraries, radio programs, night courses, newsletters, publishing houses, pamphlets, bookstores, cooperatives, study groups, lecture series, rallies, prison programs, plays, festivals, cultural centers, concerts, and films.[60] Pan African nationalist institutions were emblems of ingenuity and organs of a vibrant black radical counterpublic.

They were also dynamic social and intellectual experiments. *We Are an African People* chronicles the transformation of ideas in the context of daily practice. It avoids analytical compartmentalism, the tendency to treat activists and organizations as if they were politically static. Physical travel almost always accompanied intellectual growth and transition. The political realm of Pan African nationalist thinkers encompassed Cuba, Algeria, Guyana, Tanzania, Trinidad, Angola, and China. International fellowship and exchange with revolutionaries—from Mozambique's Samora Machel to Guinea-Bissau's Amilcar Cabral—spurred the ideological development of individual activists and that of the institutions they represented. This study traces those complex circuits and metamorphoses. It strengthens the burgeoning scholarship on Black Power's global trajectories.[61] It charts an extraordinary struggle to build the new society, within and beyond the classroom, at home and abroad.

We Are an African People begins with the 1960s community control, "relevance," and black studies battles that inspired many independent black institutions and that helped popularize the theories of "black education" they attempted to refine. Chapters 1 and 2 address the practical inadequacies of school desegregation campaigns and describe alternative approaches to which black urban parents, activists, and students turned. Demands for curricular changes and "home rule" in school governance were part of larger, grassroots efforts to reimagine the classroom as a site of social democracy and cultural dignity. As these ambitions strained the limits of reform, some organizers looked for solutions beyond public education. Separatist impulses and persistent conflict with public school bureaucrats led to the founding in 1970 of Brooklyn's Uhuru Sasa Shule, one of the most influential Pan African nationalist establishments of the era.

Uhuru Sasa and other contemporary institutions extended a long-standing tradition of constructing autonomous schools within black mass movements. Chapter 3 chronicles the evolution of such "movement schools," from the "universities" of the Universal Negro Improvement Association in the early twentieth century to the freedom schools and liberation schools of the 1960s. Changing philosophies of citizenship helped determine whether movement schools attempted to supplement, challenge, or replace the dominant institutions of the larger society. Chapter 4 describes the emergence of the Nairobi School System of East Palo Alto, a Northern California town whose struggles for self-government and educational opportunity fueled a transition from militant integrationism to pragmatic black nationalism. The quest of young East Palo Altans to change the town's name to "Nairobi" frames the chapter's discussion of the "African restoration movement," the limitations of culturalist politics, and the competing impulses within the "We Are an African People" concept.

While the first four chapters of this study emphasize experimentation and redefinition, Chapters 5 and 6 examine more fully the construction and ideological evolution of Pan African nationalist schools. Chapter 5 chronicles the rise of Neo-Pan Africanism in the late 1960s as a major tendency of Black Power and identifies the Congress of African People, a national formation, as a central organizational framework for contemporary institution building. The chapter concludes with an analysis of the shortcomings of "Racial Pan Africanism," an approach whose essentialism severely constrained African-American internationalist politics. The revival of "Left Pan Africanism," an alternative tendency that offered a more critical, anti-imperialist perspective, is discussed.

Chapter 6 explores the paradigm of the "Black University" and the innovative prototypes of adult education that it inspired. Rebellions on college campuses produced Malcolm X Liberation University in Durham and then Greensboro, North Carolina; the Center for Black Education in Washington, DC; and Nairobi College of East Palo Alto, California. Similar impulses triggered a revolt at Howard University (also in Washington), whose students rejected the school's status as a "Negro" institution largely disconnected from surrounding, poor and working-class African-American neighborhoods. Ideological growth led to the creation of African Liberation Day in North America, an expression of the popular internationalism that undergirded the Black University theme. The appearance of "left" models of the Black University, including the Lynn Eusan Institute of Houston, Texas, raised hopes for a progressive, radical turn in the politics of institution building.

Chapter 7 and the Epilogue depart from the theme of radicalization and demonstrate instead how the ascent of "Afrocentrism" after the late 1970s signaled the consolidation of a more conservative brand of nationalism and provided another case of the domestication of 1960s insurgencies. Chapter 7 outlines the forces of demobilization and demoralization that activists confronted in the first half of the 1970s. As the liberation struggle endured escalating violence and state repression, new crises of factionalism and sectarianism arose. Disputes between Left Pan Africanists and Racial Pan Africanists plunged independent black institutions into bitter ideological combat. The political intricacies of the Sixth Pan African Congress further disoriented African-American radicalism and internationalism.

By the end of the decade, many surviving Pan African nationalist schools were politically divided, destitute, and crisis ridden. New black alternative models appeared in the last two decades of the century, but most lacked the explicit anticapitalism, anti-imperialism, and Third Worldism that had characterized radical institutions of the early 1970s. The new generation of black nationalist schools generally accepted, or were unable to substantially challenge, the brittle tenets of corporate multiculturalism. Some Afrocentric educators aligned politically with conservatives who wished to recast educational reform as a drive for privatization, vouchers, and charter schools. As the discourses and rituals of Pan African nationalism separated from the politics of mass opposition, few alternative institutions were able to reinvigorate the radical and progressive traditions of Black Power organizing.

Though the most expansive, global impulses of independent black institutions were ultimately blunted, *We Are an African People* is not primarily a narrative of decline. My purpose is not simply to disentangle radical and conservative tendencies. Rather, I hope to illustrate complexities and possibilities, casting alternative social visions in the full span of their development, always mindful of the enduring potential for positive adaptation and growth.

Long after the tides of 1960s radicalism had receded, many marginalized Americans continued to imagine the schoolhouse as a locus of self-determination. Education remains an arena of struggle. We still need counterinstitutions, radical democratic spaces in which people of all colors can craft and enact creative theories of social reconstruction. Today, as many parents, students, and activists strive to reimagine and redesign schools that have long stood as sites of civic abandonment and criminalization, a re-examination of recent traditions of educational dissent may prove invaluable. The following pages, then, seek to capture the spirit of the liberation struggle and to acknowledge its triumphs and errors in the hopes of crafting more resilient movements in the future.

1

Community Control
and the Struggle for
Black Education in the 1960s

The most damaging thing a people in a colonial situation can do is to
allow their children to attend any educational facility organized by the
dominant enemy culture.
                                        —George Jackson, *Soledad Brother*, 1970[1]

On January 6, 1965, an elementary school student at Harlem's Public School
(PS) 80 wrote the following composition for class, a piece cryptically titled "Sen
Feel Sad":

> 1. Why a baby Rabbit's eyes are clos
>   It was a letter baby and her
>   eyes Hurt him
> 2. what baby Rabbit's like to eat
>   baby Rabbit's eat caBBage
> 3. a mother Rabbit's and six new
>   babies, is all children
> 4. Bunny and Her Babies
>   are a little children
> 5. why the Rabbit make a nest
>   they makes they nest with
>   grass

In a way, the essay was poignant. Almost poetic. It was also depressingly
typical—another testament, it seemed, to the effects of the community's public schools. Circulating copies of the prose as further vindication of their cause,
members of a local campaign for educational justice acknowledged what many

Harlemites already knew: that such inaptitude in the language arts placed a disgraceful share of local children among the legions of "the doomed." What lay ahead for the essay's author if not the indignity of menial employment, and perhaps even the frontlines of the Vietnam War or the narcotics trade?

Harlem children performed two to four years behind national and citywide academic norms. The longer they remained in school, the further behind they fell. A 1964 study reported that "less than half of Central Harlem's youth seem destined to complete high school, and of those that do, most will join the ranks of those with no vocational skills, no developed talents, and, consequently, little or no future." Chronic miseducation had already relegated countless local youngsters to lives of drudgery in a land of abundance. Over the course of the 1960s, as they mounted a minor revolution to reclaim the neighborhood's schools, Harlem's black and Puerto Rican parents rediscovered an appropriately unsettling term for such degradation: "educational genocide."[2]

In the mid- to late 1960s, the militant cry for "quality integrated education" in Harlem and other mobilized African-American communities gave way to demands for African-American control of schools in black neighborhoods. The patent shortcomings of desegregation campaigns helped spur the transition. Working-class African-American urbanites had long seen desegregation as a pragmatic way to gain access for their children to the educational resources overwhelmingly reserved—in the North and the South—for white students. Most members of the black rank and file had no particular affinity for white middle-class institutions or norms. They willingly embraced a quest for African-American educational autonomy when changing demographic and political realities suggested that such a tactical adjustment was necessary.

However, the community control movement and the theories of "black education" that it helped spawn transcended purely academic concerns. Grassroots opposition to the underdevelopment of African-American schools and communities signaled a broader crusade to liberate both the black urban "colony" and African-American consciousness itself. Black parents, children, and activists sought educational dignity and the right to define themselves within and beyond the classroom. In time, these rudimentary desires would produce a new generation of independent schools.

"The Road Upward": Intermediate School 201 and the Transition from Integrationism

Local schools had long been cruel symbols of the oppression of Harlem, a place described by one of its resident journalists as "a six square mile festering black scar on the alabaster underbelly of the white man's indifference." Though Harlem remained the cultural capital of black America, its schools epitomized the official neglect so evident in the community's streets and tenements. If a local junior high proved notoriously unsanitary, with overflowing latrines and roach-infested cafeteria food, its deterioration reflected broader afflictions, including "rent gouging landlords, graft grabbing cops, and usurious loan sharks."[3] It was the intersection of such indignities—compounded by the violence of a malignant police presence—that ignited the Harlem uprising of 1964, an omen of coming summers of unrest.

While bitter resentment propelled some Harlemites toward street action, others found more sustained paths of resistance. By the early 1960s, the community's schools had become decisive theaters in the black quest for freedom. The local fight escalated in the late 1950s as the outcry over inferior public schools spawned acts of civil disobedience. Emboldened by *Brown v. Board of Education*, the 1954 Supreme Court ruling against public school segregation, an incipient parent movement pressed New York City's Board of Education to fulfill its promises to eradicate the district's "racial imbalance," a counterpart to the southern system of formal apartheid recently struck down by the Court. Nine Harlem mothers resolved to boycott their children's schools, incensed by the duplicity by which distant bureaucrats preserved a racially stratified system. The striking mothers declared that they would "go to jail and rot" before permitting neighborhood schools to further debase their children.[4]

The intransigence of district officials and other municipal authorities deepened in the 1960s as white residents continued to flee both the inner city and public education, and the concentration of African Americans and Puerto Ricans in substandard "ghetto schools" increased. An era of militancy emerged as the southern freedom struggle invigorated a northern battle for rights that also had flourished in the postwar years. In 1964, alliances of New York parents, anti-poverty workers, civic leaders, and other activists mounted boycotts against the inferior schools that served the majority of the district's black and Latino pupils. "The Harlems of the north and west are joining the new democratic revolution which was born of the southern Negroes' desegregation battles," *Freedomways* magazine proclaimed.[5]

Like the southern-based movement, the New York campaign portrayed segregation as the chief obstacle to educational equity, condemning *any* scheme of racial separation, whether forged by law and custom or by ostensibly "natural" residential patterns, as undemocratic and immoral. New York parents and activists rejected spurious distinctions between de facto and de jure segregation, seeing "dual systems" of both northern and southern provenance as evils rooted in systemic practices of exclusion and subordination. Despite the opposition's resolve ("How would it look to have the children of the madams attending the same school as the children of the maids?" one Brooklyn principal asked), the desegregation crusade displayed great faith that agitation would sweep aside the anachronistic structures of white supremacy and initiate a new age of opportunity.

That optimism soon vanished. New York's Board of Education continued to make "miserly concessions to parental despair," commissioning studies and offering the palliatives of open enrollment and voluntary transfers while resisting meaningful desegregation of declining inner-city schools. Authorities relied on the growing exodus of white pupils from the district to explain the persistence of what activists dubbed the "status crow" (a play on "Jim Crow," the southern edifice of white supremacy). When feeble gestures toward integration *were* made, like one that involved shuttling black Brooklynites to white schools in Queens, the efforts siphoned off handfuls of children without restructuring the system. As the mid-1960s unfolded, segregation in the city's black and Puerto Rican schools intensified and a new mood of confrontation engulfed the movement.[6]

The hunger for decent education, the accumulated bitterness over years of bureaucratic obstruction, and the rising spirit of defiance among local desegregation forces converged in the struggle over Harlem's Intermediate School 201 (IS 201). Pressure on the Board of Education to relieve overcrowding in two local junior highs yielded plans for the new school, which authorities vowed would be built in a "fringe" area to attract both white and minority students. Evidence soon materialized that the facility, touted as a modern showcase, would constitute yet another insult. Residents initially objected to the proposed name—Arthur A. Schomburg—believing that it honored a white man. (Schomburg, a past luminary of the neighborhood, was actually a distinguished Afro-Puerto Rican bibliophile.) Parents also complained that by locating the planned school near elevated railroad tracks in a gritty section of East Harlem, the city had precluded white enrollment, which many black residents regarded as the only reliable guarantor of adequate funding, innovative curricula, and experienced teachers.

Harlemites grew more irate when they discovered that the penal-style building under construction would lack windows, a feature designed to mute the rumble of passing trains. In truth, quipped a political cartoonist for the local *Amsterdam News*, the windowless design "was to keep parents from looking in and seeing it wasn't integrated and the kids from looking out to see it was in Harlem." The edifice itself—a "cheesebox on stilts" according to one critic—was not the ultimate affront. That blow came in early 1966 when the Board of Education revealed the sort of "integration" that would prevail at the new school—50-50 black and Puerto Rican. Outraged parents from both groups condemned the maneuver and prepared to boycott, determined to resist the opening of IS 201 as a "segregated ghetto school."[7]

The ensuing clashes between local desegregation forces and the Board of Education came to symbolize the powerlessness of inner-city residents to wrest concessions from remote bureaucracies. The campaign also demonstrated the limitations of the desegregation crusade. In the New York movement, as in other urban school struggles, militant integrationists had provided the most uncompromising impetus for social change, a reality that reflected the dominant character of the mass movement that had emerged in the 1950s. Though some black Harlemites embraced the creed of interracialism, many more local parents viewed desegregation in strictly pragmatic terms, believing that the presence of white bodies ensured the sort of educational provisions that their children had been denied in aging schools abandoned by European immigrants. "The public schools of our nation have been the road upward for all groups who have come to our shores and prospered," the integrationist Harlem Parents Committee (HPC) asserted in 1965. "The Negro, the Puerto Rican and all other minorities must now have the opportunity to travel that road."[8]

Hardly content to lobby for integration alone, local parents kept pushing for assurances that IS 201 would feature "a curriculum commensurate with the demands of the space age." However, the viability and relevance of the integrationist agenda began to unravel amid the realities of urban life and the changing priorities of black protest. The vanguard of the New York struggle had long affirmed interracial living as a vital part of a child's education, seeing reforms that failed to intermingle white, black, and Puerto Rican students as accommodations to the status quo and betrayals of the cause of full equality. This approach had produced little substantive change over the past dozen years, as black parents had grown desperate for an academic program that could prepare their children for college and specialized jobs in a technocratic age that threatened to cast aside the unskilled.

The token desegregation envisioned by many white moderates and the overt hostility others displayed toward integration experiments suggested that insistence upon fair and equitable school integration would continue to meet with failure. Growing emphasis on black pride diminished acceptance of many of the theories of social psychology upon which *Brown* rested, especially the dubious premise that "racial concentration" in black schools damaged the culture and psyches of African-American children. HPC continued to hail desegregation as inevitable; New York's white bigots could escape public school integration only in "a Gemini space capsule to the moon," the organization proclaimed in the spring of 1966. This was mostly bluster. All parties involved recognized the obsolescence of "quality integrated education" as the mantra of the campaign.

The Harlem movement was changing rapidly by summer 1966. While its cultural touchstone had been the southern struggle, with allusions to that battlefront scattered throughout its literature, the campaign now adopted the rhetoric of the internal colony, an idiom that seemed more relevant to circumstances in the urban North. (In a typical expression of the colonial metaphor, one imperious, white principal was described in an HPC circular as ruling "with pith helmet and riding crop"). Demands increased for "heritage classes" featuring black history. Critiques of the classroom hegemony of "dominant group culture" began to replace concerns about the link between segregation and black "cultural deprivation." The movement's churchly tone of moral indignation gave way to naked scorn for the white establishment. Parents spoke of "breaking the back" of the Board of Education, and white angst over the new slogan of black radicalism provoked bitter condemnation. "If white power reads a connotation of violence in the manifesto of Black Power," one local activist asserted, "it is because white power intends to use violence to maintain the status quo."[9]

The struggle was growing increasingly militant and complex. IS 201 demonstrations now drew the visible participation of the Student Nonviolent Coordinating Committee (SNCC), the Congress of Racial Equality (CORE), and Harlem's fledgling Black Panther formation, groups that conveyed unapologetic visions of black autonomy. These forces allied with the local parent and civic organizations at the movement's core, some of which continued to espouse elements of the integrationist worldview. All parties agreed, however, on the call for an African-American principal for IS 201—a figure that might present to Harlem children "the right kind of image." (Given the contemporary equation of group progress with the reclamation of masculine prerogatives, the presence of a black *man* was seen as especially capable of bolstering self-esteem.)[10]

Hope for desegregation, if not precisely dead, was mostly moribund. "We must no longer pursue the myth that integrated education is equated with quality education," one local antipoverty worker declared in 1966. Parents continued to weigh other strategies, striving to meet the critical need for black self-determination and educational excellence. By that fall, they had shifted their hopes to one particular approach: local self-government. "If you won't integrate I.S. 201," Harlem residents told the Board of Education, "give us control of the school. We know you can't run a segregated school that teaches our children. We never ran a school before, but we couldn't do worse."[11]

With this bit of pragmatism, a new phase of struggle was born. It was now clear that IS 201's student body would remain as solidly black and Latino as any other Harlem school, and that "quality education, segregated style" had become the seemingly novel rallying cry of a growing portion of the community. It was not long before a more affirming formulation emerged, one that heralded the positive cultural and political characteristics of "black education."

"Worse Than Segregation": The Underdevelopment of Black Communities

The IS 201 affair, a prelude to the well-known educational rebellion of Brooklyn's Ocean Hill–Brownsville section, and a campaign that helped force the 1969 decentralization of New York's school district, immediately struck observers as significant. One longtime activist called it Harlem's Bastille. Another asserted that Black Power "took its first steps at the doorstep of Harlem's Arthur A. Schomburg Intermediate School." During that autumn of 1966, the embattled middle school became a symbol of the forces then transforming black educational struggles—and African-American politics—across the country. The metamorphosis of the IS 201 campaign heralded the shift from desegregation to "community control," another signal of the rebirth of black nationalism in African-American thought. The era of striving for entry into the white American mainstream on the dominant culture's terms had ended. Now the drive was toward self-determination and the refashioning of slums as more viable communities.

Harlem's demand for a decisive voice in school governance marked a major transition. Since its inception in 1963, the HPC had embraced Frederick Douglass's old command to "educate your colored and your white children together in your day and night school and they will learn to know each other better and be able to cooperate for the mutual benefit." By late 1966, however, the post-*Brown* view of segregation as a fading relic that could be ushered into oblivion by grassroots pressure seemed naïve; racial apartheid in its northern and southern iterations stood exposed as a pillar of the social order. Still, parents and activists within and beyond New York bristled at the charges of "separatism" and "reverse racism" that the turn to community control produced. Many proponents of black control of African-American schools were longtime desegregation advocates who saw themselves as making a tactical adjustment rather than undergoing a wholesale change of course. "The goal of our community has always been one of quality education," a New Boston Urban League officer explained in 1968. "But three to five years ago it seemed that the strategy which would achieve the goal had to be integration."[12]

Rising optimism about community control as the defining thrust in the quest for educational equity was tempered by anxieties about appearing to have abandoned desegregation, a cause still widely seen as an essential route to black freedom. And though the question of neighborhood control of black schools produced broad African-American accord, elements of dissent remained. Within communities like Harlem, however, there was no denying the force with which the principle of black self-rule redefined indigenous struggles for racial justice through the schools.

Such campaigns had evolved during the early to mid-1960s as African Americans throughout the country re-evaluated the nature of racism in American life. Pragmatism and ideological growth engendered new strategies and outlooks. Most movement workers recognized political adaptation as essential to a diverse and dynamic struggle. However, many critics then and since have

depicted the pursuit of alternatives to desegregation in contemporary black educational battles as detours from a defining cause. In their accounts, the demand
for community control of schools belongs to the larger "tragedy" of the late '60s,
a moment of crisis in which Black Power upset the moral balance of the civil
rights movement. Separatism, "a sour goal of the disappointed, the disillusioned
and the betrayed," thus becomes the emblematic source of disorder, the gremlin
intent on imperiling hard-fought reforms and squandering liberal goodwill.[13]

Versions of this narrative aggravated Harlem parents in 1966. They might
have been astonished to read in the *New York Times* that their neighborhood's
departure from the ideal of quality integrated education had been orchestrated
by "Negro nationalist and Black Muslim elements who are segregationist." Local
activists objected to their bid for educational control being reduced to a squabble
over the color of a principal. Whatever their individual views of the black nationalist renaissance, they found dismaying the tendency of pundits to cast Black
Power—whose practical manifestation was community control—as "the black
analogue of white racism." As Harlem leader Babette Edwards observed, "We are
branded racist by the same people who have always called us apathetic."[14]

Community control of education within and beyond New York City represented not a crude expression of extremism, but rather, a mass-based, grassroots
campaign, one that helped stimulate the less visible but more enduring black
independent school movement of the late 1960s and '70s. To understand the
quest for educational self-determination and the role of black nationalism in
African-American philosophies of education, one must transcend the tropes of
alienation and decline that continue to enshroud the memory of Black Power.
The mid-1960s nationalist revival was a natural and vital development in the
context of a postwar freedom movement that, as historian Robert Self notes,
"nurtured multiple strategies and ideologies of resistance, accommodation, and
liberation."[15] The heroic black push for integration never existed as uncontested
orthodoxy. Throughout their efforts to reform public education in the urban
North, African Americans waged complex struggles guided both by the troubled
crusade for full citizenship and by the need to develop black communities from
within.

Those quests for decent schooling form a record of black America's systematic
underdevelopment and consonant will to resist. Their contemporary beginnings
lie in the Great Migration that swelled during and after World War I, when waves
of African Americans began departing the rural South for urban destinations in
the North and West. Minute black populations in cities outside the South had
shared the mediocre school conditions experienced by the largely immigrant
urban poor and working classes. With the influx of southern migrants, however,
the familiar pattern of separate and inferior black education began to materialize
in the North. Conditions remained better than those that prevailed throughout

the Jim Crow South. Yet a parallel caste system took shape as northern officials shunted black pupils into congested and underfunded schools.[16]

By the 1930s Harlem's African-American children faced double or triple sessions (the splitting of large school populations into morning and afternoon shifts) in overcrowded schools staffed by inexperienced teachers and stocked with racist materials. African Americans resisted total marginalization, devising self-help campaigns designed to transmit cultural knowledge and traditions. Scholar-activist W. E. B. DuBois acknowledged the need to preserve the benefits of black educational autonomy, even as he decried growing racial segregation in northern school districts. "Negro children must not be allowed to grow up in ignorance," he declared. "This is worse than segregation, worse than anything we could contemplate."[17]

With the emergence in the 1940s of the Great Migration's second, more expansive phase, the black population of the urban North soared and its social and geographic isolation intensified. The emancipatory themes surrounding World War II raised expectations about the possibilities of equal citizenship, as northern racial segregation came to be seen by more African Americans as methodically enforced and patently degrading. Then in 1954 the Supreme Court issued its *Brown* decision, vindicating the protracted crusade against Jim Crow and galvanizing a postwar black insurgency. "Jubilation, optimism, and hope filled my home," black sociologist Sara Lawrence Lightfoot, a 10-year-old northerner at the time, later remembered. "Through a child's eyes, I could see the veil of oppression lift from my parents' shoulders."[18]

For all the grandeur of the Supreme Court edict, its immediate aftermath suggested that generations of struggle lay ahead. In 1955, the Court delivered its "all deliberate speed" order, underscoring the cautiousness and constraints of a Cold War–era decision that lacked the power or will to erase profound historical inequities. A southern mass movement nevertheless mobilized, armed with a mandate and rationale for desegregation and a willingness to face ferocious white opposition. As the confrontation at Little Rock's Central High vividly demonstrated in 1957, the question of education and democracy had flown to the center of black revolt.

Brown provided a catalyst for grassroots action in the North as well. Activists there also stretched the boundaries of the decision, reinvigorating existing battles for high-quality education or launching new struggles centered on eliminating racially separate schools. The landmark ruling spurred a "vibrant and multifaceted campaign" for integrated education in New York City, as African-American protesters strove to expose the deceptiveness of municipal authorities who depicted racial concentration in the district's schools as "natural" and unplanned. Long regarded by African Americans as one of many barriers to social equality, enforced separation now appeared to be the very embodiment of racial injustice—"the great evil" that had to be eliminated before an open society conducive to black advancement could be constructed. Yet ambivalence persisted. Many African Americans were convinced that white power structures would furnish black children with decent schooling "only if there were white children as hostages in their classroom." This position required neither a spiritual embrace of white society nor a willingness to adopt its cultural norms.[19]

Historian Richard Kluger argues that "Separate schools for Negroes carried with them a legacy of social untouchability and psychological inferiority, and so their very presence in a community held the promise of yet another generation of second-class citizenship." On the other hand, "segregated" and underfunded black schools often played essential social roles and cultivated rich cultural traditions within black communities, and thus "could be simultaneously a source of pride and a symbol of inadequacy." Some African Americans simply preferred all-black schools on practical and ideological grounds.[20] In short, integration, a cause imbued with exhilarating promise during the 1950s and early '60s, at no time represented an end in itself.

Even tactical support for integration began to seem inauspicious over the course of the 1960s. It was not until the early 1970s that the Supreme Court appeared to sanction immediate and utter dissolution of both de jure and de facto school segregation. By then, judicial decrees, federal policy, and grassroots pressure had desegregated public education in parts of the South, despite virulent white opposition. However, desegregation forces also met bitter resistance in the North. "White backlash" conjures images of peaceable citizens pushed to the wall by black rioters and busing ordinances and pressed into action to preserve "neighborhood schools" and ethnic enclaves. The phrase hardly captures the fury with which many white northerners combated desegregation in the 1960s and '70s. Boston became a paradigmatic site of antibusing hysteria, but scores of other communities also rallied against the "invasion" of black children, who were viewed as such a grave threat that in Pontiac, Michigan, empty buses were dynamited.[21] White racism reinforced the matrix of postwar changes that transformed urban centers, devastating black schools and constricting the futures of the children they served. One such shift was the exodus of white residents from the city core. "White flight" was a highly subsidized process, not simply the result of independent household decisions. The state served as mass suburbanization's most aggressive sponsor, though discriminatory banks, realtors, and other private interests bolstered the outmigration.[22] Federal funds enriched booming residential frontiers from which African Americans were excluded, and deindustrialization spurred the loss of urban manufacturing, further eviscerating the job market and tax bases of cities with rapidly expanding black populations. By the 1960s, it was clear that the primary victims of postwar capitalist restructuring were African Americans, who had been systematically denied the housing, social services, political patronage, and employment that buttressed white social mobility.

The structural shifts that depleted central cities ensured that impoverished urban schools became increasingly black domains. "By 1965," legal scholar Davidson M. Douglas reports, "the percentage of black elementary school students attending majority black schools in Chicago, Detroit, and Philadelphia ranged from 87 to 97 percent, a sharp increase from the 1940s." Racial segregation also intensified in New York. Historian Martha Biondi writes that in that city between 1954 and 1960, "the number of schools with a black and Puerto Rican student population of 90 percent or more rose from zero to thirty-eight, and by 1963 to sixty-one, or 22 percent of borough schools." Inner-city public education sequestered and stigmatized whole populations of children. As African Americans entered the 1960s, increasingly clustered in ghettos amid American's golden age of prosperity, they were often forced to rely on substandard public schools to propel their children into a credentials society that in coming years would all but bar the undereducated from dignified employment.[23]

"Their Own Turf": The New Black Militancy

In the early 1960s, a blend of frustration and rising expectations converted northern desegregation struggles into militant vehicles for mass action. The movement for quality, integrated education had reached its peak. Radical momentum radiated from the South following the student sit-in crusades of 1960. Grassroots coalitions of parents, workers, and other activists escalated local battles against school bureaucracies, whose representatives had greeted their demands for equal education with indifference or condescension. ("You have a nice little demonstration," New York's school superintendent told Harlem parents during one protest.)[24] By 1963, negotiation and incrementalism had given way to confrontation and direct action. Massive demonstrations unfolded in northern and midwestern cities, with tens of thousands of children boycotting classes and attending "freedom schools" during city-wide campaigns.[25]

The upsurge of militancy yielded concessions from national and local authorities. By the mid-1960s, dozens of northern school districts took decisive steps toward desegregation, transcending parsimonious "voluntary transfer" programs and turning instead to busing, school mergers, and the redrawing of attendance boundaries to intermingle white and black students. The federal government supplied a stream of funding to local school districts to support equal educational opportunity and attempted to boost the school readiness of poor children by enhancing basic skills. Though these reforms had some positive effects, they failed to redeem public schooling for the masses of African Americans, whose educational fates reflected their larger socioeconomic subordination. The pedagogic failure of ghetto schools, one critic acknowledged, "must be blamed on the whole complex of social arrangements whose cumulative viciousness creates a Harlem or a Watts."[26]

African Americans began to suspect that both well-meaning white people and the mechanism of liberal reform itself might be powerless to dismantle—might indeed be implicated in perpetuating—the very edifice of oppression. Street insurgents demonstrated this awareness by mounting spontaneous attacks on the property and symbols of white supremacy (extortionist stores, repressive police) in black central cities beginning in the summer of 1964.[27] African Americans asked searching questions of American democracy as the economic containment of black inner cities intensified and the failures of integrationist reform were exposed. How could black people move from brokering concessions to seizing genuine power?

This question had haunted the freedom movement long before Stokely Carmichael and Willie Ricks of SNCC raised the call for Black Power in the summer of 1966. Growing insistence on its resolution reflected the struggle's maturation, as did the regeneration of black nationalism within African-American political culture. Black nationalism had always been a factor in the movement. Renewed emphasis on racial pride and commitment to political autonomy now drove more black people to define liberation as the pursuit of group empowerment, and to shun assimilationist models of integration as tantamount to submersion in a hostile and alien culture. The rebirth of black nationalism highlighted political questions inherent in African-American urbanization and the emergence of postwar "second ghettos." Were black inner cities simply reservations for the poor? Were black people primarily oriented toward "opening the opportunity structure within the existing system" or toward transforming "their own turf" into a more powerful and independent community?[28]

If black people never eschewed the former path, during the 1960s they made remarkable strides in the latter direction. Black Power drew momentum from grassroots traditions of radicalism, from the long-standing cultural value of self-determination, from recent political victories, from the tactical and theoretical inadequacies of "civil rights," from shifts in the postwar economy, from Third World independence movements, from the eruption and suppression of riots, from renewed awareness of African heritage, from the searing insights of Malcolm X, and from widespread revulsion against U.S. imperialism in Vietnam and other lands. Its main impetus, however, lay in the rising determination of black people to define and defend themselves.

The new politics generated sweeping changes in the realm of education, an area uniquely equipped—because so many African Americans saw it as the critical mechanism of social transformation—to illustrate the influence of the black nationalist renaissance. The struggle to reform deteriorating institutions in black communities, to reimagine the provision of social services, and to develop black cultural identity and consciousness all held profound implications for the conceptualization and delivery of education. Most educational justice movements since the 1950s had sought the training and resources necessary for black children to join mainstream society *as fashioned by the white majority*. After the mid-1960s, the orientation of black activism shifted decisively toward preparing those children to enter society on terms that they might dictate, and to enter in a manner that honored rather than degraded or denied their innermost selves.

Arming black children with a sense of cultural integrity and racial pride had been a long-standing priority for black Americans. What made the late 1960s extraordinary was the intense confluence of these ideas and the fact that they inspired so many black people to seek meaningful autonomy, whether this meant forming black caucuses within largely white educational organizations, agitating for black studies and community control of public schools, or establishing independent black institutions. African-American parents rejected the myth that education was apolitical. They recognized schooling as a matter of power, and they resolved to control the socialization of their children and the definition of their own social reality. They understood that for the oppressed, the transmission between generations of knowledge and cultural wisdom constitutes "a struggle in the arena of ideas," and they realized that other crusades for freedom and justice might come to nothing if victory in this area were denied.[29]

Harlemites and other African Americans across the country strove to cultivate a redemptive vision of "black education." Though no neat consensus emerged, many African Americans saw blackness as a convergence of historical circumstances and cultural values that necessitated distinct pedagogies. "Black," the new symbol, offered a critical modifier for "education," the old hope, and a whole generation of theorists sought to interpret their combined meaning. The definitions produced by these educators, parents, workers, intellectuals, and activists demanded a rethinking of the concepts of community, relevance, and autonomy—themes that provided fertile soil for the next generation of black independent schools. To appreciate the appeal of these concepts and to understand their practical application, one must trace from Manhattan to Brooklyn the evolution of community control.

"A Deluge of Action": The Rise of Ocean Hill–Brownsville

Though the fight over IS 201 continued, by 1967, Brooklyn's troubled neighborhood of Ocean Hill–Brownsville had overtaken Harlem as the vanguard of black educational struggle. If East Harlem provided community control's beachhead, Central Brooklyn supplied its definitive battleground. Therein lay Brownsville, a black and Puerto Rican enclave so blighted that even New York City Mayor John V. Lindsay called it "Bombsville." The conglomerate territory of Ocean Hill–Brownsville, whose rates of poverty and unemployment surpassed those of Harlem, was an especially stark nexus of social decay.

Ocean Hill–Brownsville and its surroundings, including Bedford-Stuyvesant, harbored more than their share of anguish. Yet a spirit of resistance flourished within Central Brooklyn's black populace. The city-wide school boycotts of the early to mid-1960s had drawn some of their most implacable leaders from the area, which featured a full complement of block organizations, antipoverty workers, and parent groups. Black and Puerto Rican residents continued to mobilize, launching rent strikes and pressing slumlords to repair crumbling tenements. As school strike organizer Milton Galamison wrote of a larger portion of black Brooklyn, "Any evidence of injustice can precipitate a deluge of social action."[30]

Some inhabitants resolved to resist the crippling of their children in the area's schools. The local agitators included charismatic Robert "Sonny" Carson of Brooklyn CORE, who in 1967 demanded from Bedford-Stuyvesant principals a detailed plan to bring the community's black children up to grade level, pledging to ensure the removal of the administrators in question should they fail to comply. (Carson later organized the black nationalist School of Common Sense in the borough.) More modest measures were taken by mothers like Lillian Wagner, a Brownsville Parent Teacher Association president. She approached the microphone at a public hearing of the Board of Education in December 1966, hoping to discuss conditions in her neighborhood schools. The body, however, refused to hear the grievances of the single mother, who had not received advance permission to speak at the meeting.

This rebuff prompted a crescendo of objections from assembled antipoverty workers and activists, including participants in the ongoing IS 201 conflict and other aggrieved parents from the city's poorer neighborhoods. Amid audience chants of "Let her speak!" members of the board summarily adjourned and left the meeting hall. Upon the departure of the officials, several protesters filled the dais chairs, proclaiming themselves the "People's Board of Education." The renegade body remained in the public hearing hall through the night, conducting a free-flowing discussion of the divide between the record of the schools and the parents' dreams for their children. As 68-year-old Harlem organizer Mother Audley Moore later remarked, "It was a people's parliament if ever there was one, and each vowed to remain until the rising sun."[31]

The Ocean Hill–Brownsville struggle gained momentum in the wake of the three-day occupation of the central school board headquarters. In the summer of 1967, the Ford Foundation, an outfit that promoted social management as the authoritative response to urban crises, sponsored three "demonstration districts" designed to offer residents of Harlem, Ocean Hill–Brownsville, and a section of Manhattan's Lower East Side a genuine voice in the running of their schools. Appearing to acquiesce to growing pressure, the city's embattled Board of Education agreed to cede a degree of authority to the neighborhood districts. New York's experiment in community control had begun.[32]

A locally elected board of Ocean Hill–Brownsville parents and community leaders began staffing the eight-school district. The board hired a black district administrator who in turn oversaw a team that included four black principals and New York's first Chinese and Puerto Rican principals. (Prior to these appointments, only four African Americans served as principal in a city of more than 850 schools and a largely nonwhite student population.) The board embraced the sensibilities of its neighborhood when choosing personnel, pursuing both minority and white candidates and weighing factors like commitment to the educability of black and Latino children. It ignored civil service and seniority rankings that ensured job security and determined promotion of the city's largely Jewish teachers and school supervisors while keeping such positions almost uniformly white. ("The people in the street considered these laws written to protect the moneyed white power structure of this city," a representative of the Ocean Hill–Brownsville board later argued.) This flouting of conventional merit standards ended the United Federation of Teachers' (UFT) support for community control and brought the local union and black parents in the demonstration districts into open conflict.

The Ocean Hill–Brownsville governing board felt that its mandate to protect black and Puerto Rican children from racist or substandard teachers trumped narrow trade unionism or "professional rights," a concept, it charged, that further entrenched white privilege at the expense of students of color. Nor would the board be satisfied to languish in impotence. Attempting to consolidate its contested power, it abruptly dismissed (or "forcibly transferred") 19 intransigent district teachers and supervisors, most of them white, whom it accused of sabotaging the experiment in self-government. Thereafter, a full-scale conflict flared. Claiming that due process had been violated, the overwhelmingly white UFT launched a series of bitter, district-wide strikes that all but paralyzed the school system and stoked deep-seated racial animosities.[33]

The Ocean Hill–Brownsville confrontation stands as a "watershed moment" in the contemporary efforts of African Americans and other minorities to resist banishment to the social and economic margins of disintegrating urban centers.[34] The affair was both a practical bid for accountability and a sign of blossoming political consciousness. Mobilized parents in Brooklyn and elsewhere hoped to compel school bureaucrats to respond to their desires for their children, whom they wished to see included in the technological revolution engulfing American society. By 1969, battles for greater parent and neighborhood involvement in the decision-making process of local schools had gripped urban centers across the country. Within two years of IS 201's opening skirmishes, grassroots pressure had made community control the most explosive issue in education.[35]

"The Back Way": Black Survival and the Conundrum of Integration

The community control movement garnered much of its mass support from a universal impulse: the will to survive. African-American parents recognized that without adequate preparation for college and dignified employment, their children would remain stranded on the fringes of a technocratic society. Black educational revolts reflected conventional aspirations for social mobility. However, even the seemingly straightforward matter of survival contained multiple meanings, an indication of the complex motives that propelled African-American struggles. "Black survival" entailed not only economic advancement but also the literal preservation of life, as well as the strengthening of black consciousness and social institutions.

When African-American demonstrators decried "educational genocide," a phrase maligned by school officials, they deployed a discourse of survival that acknowledged many assaults, from cultural denigration to political and economic subordination.[36] The social empowerment implications of "survival" deepened in the late 1960s and early '70s. "We do feel that we can develop the kinds of black kids in the ghetto who can withstand the negative influence of white education . . . without undergoing too much psychological damage," African-American social work professor and IS 201 activist Preston Wilcox asserted in 1968.[37] Speaking in 1972 before a gathering of black teachers at a Bedford-Stuyvesant junior high, another community control veteran declared:

> In the Yeshiva schools the teachers teach the Jewish kids what they need to know to survive in this world. This is a black school. It's made up of black and Puerto Rican kids. If you see any white kids here you show them to me because there ain't any. This is a black school for black kids and you've got to teach them what they need to know to survive.[38]

"Survival" encompassed a host of aspirations. The concept could signal a need for greater black representation in mainstream society, affirm the value of black separation as a regrouping strategy, or entail some creative combination of these approaches. By the late 1960s, the broad discourse of survival seemed poised to eclipse narrow visions of integration. Many African Americans welcomed educational models that transcended or rejected integrationist ideals.[39]

Conventional modes of desegregation proved capable of fulfilling neither evolving black aims nor the original objective of high-quality education. Prospects for substantial racial intermingling dwindled further amid the "bitter demographic and political facts" of the day. Nationwide, more children attended racially homogenous schools in 1970 than had done so in 1954. In 1971, the Supreme Court sanctioned busing as a remedy for segregation, yet the specter of "forced busing" continued to generate fierce white resistance. The rhetoric of "neighborhood schools" (versus campuses in outlying communities) masked a deep commitment to segregation. As one observer noted in 1967, "Protecting the neighborhood school has been the Northern equivalent of preserving the Southern way of life."[40]

Integration offered a means of thrusting handfuls of black children toward the centers of social privilege in specific locales. These were often the sons and daughters of more assertive, informed, or better-off families who were positioned to seize limited opportunities to attend more prosperous white schools. But desegregation failed as a mass solution. "If a parent wants to bus a child and can do so, all right," Brooklyn Congresswoman Shirley Chisholm declared in 1970. "But I am talking about the welfare mother. I am talking about the masses whose children will still be left behind."[41] The black schoolchildren who served as desegregation's shock troops in the 1960s and 1970s often discovered that simply enrolling in white schools guaranteed neither equality nor educational opportunity. In 1972, legal scholar Derrick A. Bell recounted the abuse and humiliation that many such youngsters endured:

> Black children are harassed unmercifully by white students, are suspended or expelled for little or no cause (when they are not simply ignored) by white teachers, are taunted and insulted, segregated within classes, excluded from extracurricular activities, shunted off into useless courses, and daily faced with a veritable battleground of racial hostility, much of which is beyond the ability or willingness of courts to rectify.[42]

Meanwhile, beginning in the 1950s, school mergers, closures, and other desegregation-related changes led to the massive dismissal and demotion of black teachers and administrators, particularly in the South. The shuttering of beloved black schools or the stripping of their cultural significance and identity through the loss of cherished traditions, emblems, colors, mascots, and names deepened the ordeal. Many black parents struggled to weigh the trauma black children often suffered during forays onto white campuses against the benefits of what they believed to be an objectively superior academic experience. Despair enveloped one black mother after a Pontiac, Michigan, school bus delivered its African-American passengers to the rear entrance of an elementary school as a way to evade screaming antibusing pickets. "If there's anything that grates on black folks' nerves," she said, "it's going in the back way."[43]

The demeaning implications of integrationist practice intensified black alienation. The power to design and implement desegregation campaigns resided far beyond black communities, reinforcing the white paternalism that many African Americans yearned to escape. The premise that black children should bear the burden of migration angered black parents who envisioned integration as a proportionate exchange in which all involved parties shared burdens and benefits. "Most black folks feel, too, it's always been one-way, it's been black kids being brutalized, psychologically manipulated—it's never been white kids," Brooklyn teacher Leslie Campbell later maintained. "We say, 'O.K., you want integration, why don't you bus white kids into Bedford Stuyvesant?' "[44]

Then there was the question of the basic nature of black schools. The IS 201 affair had evolved from the premise of the inseparability of integrated schools and excellent education. Now the notion of the inherent inferiority of all-black schools seemed grossly insulting—"mix Negroes with Negroes and you get stupidity," as CORE's Floyd McKissick put it in 1966. The Ocean Hill–Brownsville struggle demonstrated the growing reluctance of some residents of the community to disparage black schools by defining them simply as "segregated." Questions of power and control began to rival the old view of racial concentration as the hallmark of oppression.[45]

Other factors eroded black investment in desegregation. Bonds of solidarity and heritage connected many African Americans to black institutions and environments. The prospect of cultural attrition in white schools remained a source of quiet anxiety. A 1968 cartoon in an Ocean Hill–Brownsville community newspaper depicted a black man seated at a table in an upscale restaurant. "No bean 'n' rice, no turnip greens 'n' hog jowl, no kinda soul food!" the diner quipped. "You call this inter-gration? I calls it starvation!"[46]

By the eve of the 1970s, the discrediting of unjust or assimilationist modes of integration appeared all but complete. "Now it is clear to blacks that our initial acceptance of one-way 'integration,' based on a definition of integration developed by whites, put the burden on us and perpetuated the very thing we most desired to end—the one-sided view of who's valuable in this society," Boston activist Mel King maintained. But how absolute was the shift in emphasis toward improving existing black schools or creating new, autonomous ones? Was desegregation "as a broad social goal and a major political objective" truly dead?[47]

Most African Americans remained deeply committed to dismantling the lingering structures of racial segregation. Pragmatic desegregation as a pathway to social and economic advancement remained as critical to black liberation as did strategic separation.[48] Integrationist and nationalist impulses were never mutually exclusive. Many militant integrationists affirmed black institutions while insisting that African-American freedom and dignity required access to the apparatuses of white power. Indeed, desegregation campaigns actually *stimulated* the racial consciousness of young activists, who rejected the idea that cultural dissolution constituted an acceptable cost of full citizenship.[49]

"A Common Mood": The Ideologies of Community Control

To understand the depth of support for community control of black schools in neighborhoods like Ocean Hill–Brownsville, one must consider widespread alienation from narrowly conceived integration, on one hand, and rising optimism about the internal development of black communities, on the other. Black central cities appeared degrading to their occupants not because of the racial composition of these territories, but because of the relative powerlessness of their inhabitants. In such neighborhoods flourished a politicized minority with a conscious, strategic orientation toward either integration or nationalism, and a substantial majority whose politics can best be described as pragmatic. Individuals traversed these categories—or combined their essential perspectives—based on the changing realities of struggle.

By the late 1960s, however, the cultural value of black self-determination had won the allegiance of virtually all political currents. Though vigorous internal debate continued, the idea of a unified, politically and culturally autonomous "black community" captured the imagination of many African Americans. One scholar has argued that "In the late 1960s, the black community stood as a conglomeration of often contradictory interests and directions, dubiously tied together by a common mood which combined centuries of anger with new hope, increasing desperation with new confidence."[50] Reconciling such complexity with the broad mandate for community control requires an examination of the common impulses that connected traditionally competing political outlooks.

Pragmatists, for their part, employed a compelling logic. While African-American advancement required immediate access to decent education, substantial residential and school desegregation appeared unlikely in the foreseeable future. The shift to educational self-rule constituted a rational strategic adjustment given prevailing realities. Underlying this perspective was the proposition that geographic racial concentration might provide a basis for empowering—rather than merely containing—black communities. Preston Wilcox, IS 201 tactician and social work professor, expressed the pragmatist view in 1966 when he urged a gathering of Harlem parents to reassess the premises of integration. "If one believes that a segregated white school can be a good school, then one must believe that a segregated Negro and Puerto Rican school, like I.S. 201, can also be a good school," he argued. "We must be concerned with those who are left behind and who will be left behind even if the best conceivable school desegregation program should be implemented."[51]

Then there were those with an ideological commitment to integration. Many of these figures adopted a compromise position that acknowledged the practical shortcomings of integrationism while offering forthright support for community control. "I don't want segregation," IS 201 parent leader David Spencer declared in 1966, "but if I have it, I want it on my terms." Babbette Edwards of Harlem's community board continued to view black neighborhood involvement in school governance as a reform that might ultimately facilitate integration. Yet she rejected the prospect of further desegregation plans engineered by white officials. "Our priority is black community control," she acknowledged.[52]

The community control movement also contained an avowedly nationalist element. Its ranks included members of New York's Afro-American Teachers Association (ATA), the organization that had split from the UFT to become the union's most intractable adversary. Many who identified with black nationalism saw community control of education as the initial campaign of a struggle for greater authority over police forces, businesses, and other institutions within African-American neighborhoods. Nationalists wished to use public schools to foster a robust racial consciousness and to acculturate black children according to concepts of African identity. "We understand now that the schools have been preparing us to live in a white society as white people," declared Ocean Hill–Brownsville middle school administrator Albert Vann, an ATA official. "They have been preparing us for something we can never be."[53]

On some questions, nationalists, pragmatists, and integrationists remained too closely aligned to constitute separate camps. A broad cross-section of the black working class could understand the concept of community control—could grasp the need for African-American parents to root out racist administrators and materials and ensure that their children's teachers actually believed that they could learn. Yet the mainstream news media and UFT leadership, ignorant or scornful of the political realities of black inner cities, depicted militant impulses within community control campaigns as the bitter fruit of a black nationalist fringe. They saw the organic black impetus toward self-determination as the result of manipulation by foreign ideological agents.[54]

The militancy of the Ocean Hill–Brownsville citizenry deepened throughout 1968 and 1969 as the struggle to resist the subversion of community control wore on. Major news outlets displayed a stark bias, citing as evidence of black extremism any nationalistic or chauvinistic tendency within the politically complex affair. Meanwhile, UFT representatives leveled accusations of "mob rule" and magnified troubling incidents of anti-Semitism to restore public faith in the supremacy of white bureaucratic professionalism over the insurgencies of the urban black poor and working class.[55] The prejudices of the news media and the political establishment incensed Ocean Hill–Brownsville inhabitants. "They must kill Ocean Hill-Brownsville in order to give credibility to their belief that we are not capable of self-determination," declared Rhody McCoy, administrator of the neighborhood district. Black Brooklyn at the height of the struggle was hardly "a unanimously aroused and totally mobilized community." Yet its schools were far from strongholds of "revolutionaries without a following," as a major news magazine opined.[56]

Some African Americans interpreted community control as an explicitly black nationalist demand. Others saw a bid for traditional reform. ("We're like Boston Tea Party Indians," one Harlemite exclaimed.) Sponsors of New York's Black Solidarity Day hailed "all complexions of militancy." Still, few Ocean Hill–Brownsville parents questioned what Marxist theorist Grace Lee Boggs called "the individualist, opportunist orientation of American education."[57] Acceptance of the ethic of schooling as a matter of individual preparation for job competition overshadowed overtly anticapitalist critiques. As a cause that brought into conflict exploited black and Puerto Rican workers and an ascendant class of relatively privileged, overwhelmingly white craft unionists (i.e., New York City public school teachers), the period's defining community control battle further imperiled the links between black militancy and the mainstream labor movement.

Of course, it was organized labor in its conservative, postwar incarnation that had repudiated those ties in the first place. In its struggles to defend newfound class privileges, the UFT appeared to black New Yorkers not as a social democratic ally, but as another lilywhite craft union, like those in the construction trades, that was prepared to close ranks with employers and industry to exclude people of color from the halls of power. By contrast, the community control movement displayed growing awareness of the structural nature of urban poverty and the dual character of racial and class oppression, and thus provided ample groundwork for future challenges to white supremacy.[58]

"Ocean Hill–Brownsville Is Like Kenya": Community Control and the Colonial Analogy

All manner of ideas, reformist and radical alike, circulated within Ocean Hill–Brownsville. While the efforts of the black separatist Republic of New

Africa to promote a plebiscite on the matter of Ocean Hill–Brownsville's formal sovereignty generated only polite interest, a major premise of this drive—the view of black urbanites as a subject people residing in conquered "national" territory—proved ubiquitous. The internal colony theory of black ghettos, an idea derived from Third World struggles and refined by African-American intellectuals like Harold Cruse and Jack O'Dell, permeated popular discourse during the mid-1960s. A Harlem antipoverty official lectured on the concept in 1967, and an IS 201 administrator later interpreted its essential meaning. "Ocean Hill-Brownsville is like Kenya," he said. "We are like another part of West Africa. We have all been excluded from the seats of power."[59]

The idea that African-American communities constituted colonial possessions of white America provided a compelling explanation for the subordination of central cities, whose economies and political will were subject to "foreign" rule. For Brooklyn's Black Caucus, whose members called for United Nations recognition of "30 million Afro Americans within a racist nation of white oppressors," the idea represented a kind of orthodoxy. A less literal conception of colonial status led Brooklyn clergy, activists, and black citizens of all political creeds to describe their schools and neighborhoods as afflicted by absentee domination. The parent council of an Ocean Hill–Brownsville junior high referred to the strike-related police occupation of the community as "an invasion by a foreign military force."[60]

While such declarations revealed the influence of political theory, community control drew much of its momentum from quotidian impulses. Many Ocean Hill–Brownsville parents supported the movement simply because they remained desperate to see their children properly educated. They tended to follow a middle course, declining to demand total autonomy or to deploy inflammatory rhetoric. But the wisdom, even inevitability of their bid to control the schools seemed irrefutable. "This is our community . . . this is our community . . . and we don't own anything in it!" one parent exclaimed. "Not even our own children."[61]

The quest to control the socialization of black and Puerto Rican children fueled larger desires for dignity and power. As parents and workers were drawn into the movement, their capacity for political self-organization was revealed. Alienation from public schools and from other failing civic institutions in black neighborhoods continued to fester. The rising consciousness of Harlem, Ocean Hill–Brownsville, and similarly aroused black communities suggested that a powerful political transformation was underway. In the throes of struggle, very few participants recognized the inherent constraints of home rule.

By the mid-1960s, Harlem's Intermediate School 201 had become a symbol of the militant rejection of superficial and unjust desegregation schemes.

Community control, a pragmatic alternative, reached its apogee in Central Brooklyn. Ocean Hill–Brownsville's bid for authority over local schools encountered staunch opposition from bureaucratic unionists. However, the imperatives of African-American "survival" and educational salvation generated multiple forms of resistance. Far from a symptom of disillusionment, campaigns for black autonomy reflected growing optimism about the prospects for internal development of African-American neighborhoods. Cries of "educational genocide" indicted not only shoddy "ghetto schools" but also the larger structural domination of the black urban core. Redemptive models of education needed to fulfill broad visions of dignity while preparing youngsters to help "decolonize" their communities. These militant ambitions would converge in the principle of "social relevance."

Black Studies and the Politics of "Relevance"

Education means an assimilation of white American culture.
—Gunnar Myrdal, 1944[1]

Pedagogy became an arena of intense political contestation during the 1960s. The flowering of black consciousness expanded popular visions of the purpose and possibilities of schooling. Many progressive theorists believed black children required a distinctive education designed to meaningfully address their social realities and cultural heritage. African-American parents, students, and intellectuals demanded "relevance," a theme that proved as central to notions of black educational salvation as did the ideal of "community."

Concepts of relevance offered alternatives to the paternalistic or racist "cultural deprivation" theories that continued to guide the education of many children of color. Some African-American thinkers strove to identify and affirm distinctly "black" values and styles of learning. The emergence of an array of African-American educational organizations and professional associations bolstered the quest for self-definition. By the late 1960s, however, grassroots activists had discovered the limitations of public education as an instrument of black consciousness and social transformation. A search for new directions led radical organizers from the barricades of Ocean Hill–Brownsville to the struggle for "independent black institutions."

"When the Truth Is Presented": Black Studies and Public Education

The cry for relevance fueled the cultural renaissance known as "black studies." Protest and pressure led to greater acknowledgment of previously denigrated or ignored aspects of the African-American experience. Substantial changes occurred not only at the college level but also in primary and secondary education, further challenging the "melting pot" concept of the public school mission and initiating the second "textbook revolution" of the postwar era.[2] New expressions of cultural pluralism rarely challenged the structural dimensions of white supremacy. Nor could curricular changes alone fulfill desires to foster a deeper sense of African-American peoplehood.

Nevertheless, most black people recognized the need for more accurate and significant representation of African-American life and culture in public school curricula. Despite the flourishing of black mass movements, few school districts had revamped the Eurocentric content of classes in social studies, literature, and other subjects. African-American civic groups, institutions, and intellectuals traditionally had employed a host of strategies to expose children and adults to black history. Yet as the scholar St. Clair Drake observed, such extracurricular activities were unable to overcome "the lethargy, timidity, and often hostile attitudes of school administrators, teachers and textbook publishers who resisted pleas for the curricular and textbook revision needed to 'set the record straight' on the role of black men and women in the history of mankind."[3]

This changed dramatically during the 1960s and '70s. Civil rights activists of the 1950s and early '60s had sought "integrated textbooks" and the removal of racist classroom materials like the children's classic *Little Black Sambo*, reforms that were promoted as paths to "intergroup" harmony. The coming of Black Power eclipsed such approaches. The demand for black studies was presented as an imperative of African-American identity and pride rather than as an obligation of interracial accord.

Though upheavals on college campuses seized headlines, high school students were among the original shock troops of the black studies revolt. Major student demonstrations flared in cities like Philadelphia, Boston, and Chicago, where youngsters launched boycotts and rallied for inclusion of black history in public schools. New York was a key staging ground for militancy in middle schools and senior highs. Black and Puerto Rican student grievances against racist disciplinary procedures, the dearth of teachers of color, and the absence of black studies blended with outrage over police presence in schools and the return to Ocean Hill–Brownsville of unwanted, striking teachers. A series of student protests roiled the district in 1968–1969. Nationwide, tens of thousands of African-American secondary school students claimed the right to wear Afros and dashikis, to fly black liberation flags, or to otherwise fulfill the mandates of black consciousness.[4]

African-American parents, educators, and community control advocates joined the fight for social and curricular relevance. "Do you want your child taught this?" asked one Ocean Hill–Brownsville flyer that suggested that history classes controlled by New York City's central Board of Education deprecated enslaved Africans, dismissed militant abolitionist John Brown as "crazy," and defamed Puerto Ricans as "dirty" intruders who "should go back to Puerto Rico." The parent-community council of Brooklyn's Junior High School (JHS) 271 condemned "John Birch type social studies" (a reference to the right-wing group) and called for African arts and crafts in the classroom.[5] The curricula of community-controlled schools occasionally embraced the contemporary Black Arts movement. Ocean Hill–Brownsville parents who volunteered to serve as substitute elementary school instructors during a United Federation of Teachers strike participated in a workshop whose sample lesson revolved around a LeRoi Jones (Amiri Baraka) poem:

> We are beautiful people
> with African imaginations
> full of masks and dances and swelling chants
> with African eyes, and noses, and arms
> though we sprawl in grey chains in a place
> full of winters, when what we want is sun.[6]

Such pedagogical approaches enhanced earlier reforms enacted by the city. During the mid-1960s, New York emerged as a forerunner among the handful of urban school boards that required "multiethnic" textbooks and classroom coverage of minority-related topics. By 1968, few school districts with substantial nonwhite populations could afford to ignore demands for curricular change. Boards of education across the country responded to mounting pressure by incorporating black studies. After black Philadelphia teenagers marched on their school district's headquarters, authorities mandated that every student in the city complete a program of African and African-American history "as an integral part of his total school experience."[7]

Black studies courses in some public schools proved substantive. Classes in Cleveland engaged meaningful questions like "The Ghetto: Black Prison or Black Community?" and "The Black Artist: Chiefly Black or Chiefly Artist?" Other offerings were less auspicious. "The natives of Africa are not all wild savages," a history unit in Alexandria, Virginia, conceded. Some critics viewed black studies curricula and materials as cynical attempts at appeasement. They noted that textbook publishers, in their haste to exploit a growing market, had exchanged white characters for black ones without genuinely revamping content. Even *Publisher's Weekly* acknowledged the superficiality of such "change-the-color-plate" tactics. Black studies activist Jimmy Garrett condemned cosmetically "integrated" picture books that "[put] ties on black men or [painted] white men a darker shade with the same thin bridged nose, the same thin lips, the same pallid expression, a darker shade of pale."[8]

Critics of token reforms also resented "contributionism," an approach to African-American history that presented the achievements of innocuous black strivers—from Phillis Wheatley to George Washington Carver—as the product of industriousness and self-discipline in an increasingly meritocratic society. One purveyor of educational products claimed that "the best way to study black history" was to ingest trivia that demonstrated that black people accompanied Cortez to Mexico in 1519 and otherwise participated in the conquest of the "New World." When New York's United Federation of Teachers devised a curriculum with a similar theme—African Americans as foot soldiers in the triumphant march of Western civilization—one of Harlem's black nationalist intellectuals denounced the course of study as a case of "cultural genocide."[9]

The community control struggle itself contained elements of contributionism. Groups like the East Harlem Coalition for Community Control resolved that "Spanish and black history and culture are to be offered to the students on a meaningful scale and given [their] rightful place as part of the history of the United States." The premise that the social value of black history lay in demonstrating its indivisibility from the experiences of the white majority had shaped earlier reforms. New York City education officials cited as rationales for a 1966 after-school program in black and Puerto Rican history enhancement of "ethnic group pride" and enrichment of white students' "knowledge of the contribution of minority groups to history and culture."[10]

Contributionism's appeal rested on the premise that a portion of white America, faced with an accurate and balanced record of the nation's past, would recognize the need for racial cooperation. "When the truth is presented," black children's book author Margaret Burroughs suggested in 1966, "these people will find that all people—white, yellow, red, and yes, black—have made worthwhile contributions to society, civilization, and American life and history." Employing the same logic, the NAACP released a 1970 U.S. history syllabus for secondary schools that highlighted "the inventors of every race and nationality [who] helped make America an industrial giant."[11]

Many black nationalists took a different approach. They saw the study of black life and history as a way to forge an African-American personality fully committed to political and cultural autonomy. "It's time for you to realize that your forefathers were the most civilized persons on earth," Brooklyn activist Sonny Carson told an audience at one Ocean Hill–Brownsville rally. "They did not act every time the pig [police and white authorities] said act. But instead they made the pig act." Black studies for its militant proponents constituted an instrument of liberation from "psychological captivity"—not merely a supplement to the master narrative of American exceptionalism.[12]

Most nationalists rejected narrow contributionism as a strategy incapable of reconstructing white America. They recognized that simply "calling the honor roll of great blacks of the past" could not humanize a racist society.[13] A wide spectrum of African Americans resolved to see public schools incorporate programs of study that would truly enhance black consciousness. As community organizer and Harlem parent Maude White Katz observed in 1968:

> A revolutionary change has taken place in the minds of black parents. There will be no more resignation and accommodation to the status quo as a way of life for them. Things must change for them and their children. They may not know all the facts about their history, but since Lumumba, Nkrumah and others, they know they have a history. They have roots.[14]

The pursuit of black awareness in Ocean Hill–Brownsville's community control district remained an accordingly expansive and cosmopolitan project. Some classrooms featured discussions of the ideas of Black Power spokesman H. Rap Brown and Chinese leader Mao Tse-Tung. A poster plastered to the walls of JHS 271 declared "Uncle Sam Wants You, Nigger!"—an indictment of the U.S. imperialist adventure in Vietnam. The middle school staged a production of "A Season in the Congo," Caribbean poet Aimé Césaire's play about martyred African nationalist Patrice Lumumba. Observation of "black liberation week" (a reinterpretation of Negro History Week) in Harlem and Ocean Hill–Brownsville schools included "political prisoner's day" and lessons about the slave insurrections of Nat Turner and Denmark Vesey.[15]

"The Exchange of Respect": Community Control and Progressive Pedagogy

Philosophies of relevance guided community control's most creative pedagogical techniques. Most Ocean Hill–Brownsville teachers and administrators rejected the regimentation that characterized many inner-city classrooms. Local parents learned to question the austere methods that some African Americans, recalling the severe schooling of their own childhoods, accepted as a necessary burden of learning for the oppressed. Elements of innovation and humanity returned to public schools that parents and activists helped occupy and staff during United Federation of Teachers (UFT) strikes. Schools in Harlem's community control district screened animated geometry films and employed a creative phonics method that assigned a distinct color to each sound. At Public School (PS) 64 on the Lower East Side, one observer reported, "Puerto Rican flags hung from the windows, soul music was broadcast on the PA system, and rigid authoritarian control based on mutual fear and hostility between students and teachers disappeared."[16]

Emphasis on humanistic approaches led to more evenhanded disciplinary procedures. The vast majority of suspended New York City schoolchildren were black or Puerto Rican, and the UFT's pursuit of a "disruptive child" rule enabling teachers to unilaterally oust pupils had embittered African-American parents who saw the policy as a license for racist practices. (The Afro-American Teachers Association condemned efforts to grant teachers "the power to act as policeman, judge and jury over our children.") By contrast, the demonstration districts treated excessive suspensions and expulsions as symptoms of abuse and dramatically reduced reliance on such measures. "To the black community, the so-called disruptive child was a result of the murderous system," a dissident UFT member maintained. "He was a politically oppressed child."[17]

Some African-American parents remained convinced that strict discipline alone could prepare their children to face a hostile society. One father received a round of applause during an Ocean Hill–Brownsville meeting when he described the schoolyard whippings of his youth. Black nationalism's emphasis on socialization occasionally inspired authoritarian approaches. Controversial New York City assistant principal Herman Ferguson proposed a "survival curriculum" within a paramilitary-style school outfitted with loudspeakers to continuously bathe students in the words of Malcolm X, filling them with "constant pride in blackness." Yet respect for democratic classroom principles also proliferated. A workshop at the 1968 Black Power Conference in Philadelphia advocated the nurturing of student creativity and acknowledged that "the transmission of knowledge is inseparable from the exchange of respect and mutuality."[18]

Similar ideals led some teachers in New York's demonstration districts to reject standardized tests as culturally biased. Progressive theorists strove to adapt educational content to the circumstances of poor children of color. Harlem theorist Preston Wilcox suggested that such youngsters might relate to social studies lessons that encouraged them to examine Muhammad Ali's motives for resisting the military draft, or to analyze the media's insistence on continuing to address the boxer as "Cassius Clay." James E. Campbell, a New York City assistant principal and former Malcolm X aide, argued that relevant curricula must equip black children to confront the injustice of dilapidated housing, the crisis of poor health services, and the devastation of the heroin trade.[19]

Wilcox imagined guest lecturers who had "earned their PhDs on the street" teaching primary or secondary school students about the ravages of dope and crime while demonstrating the possibility of rehabilitation. Jimmy Garrett, a leader of the pioneering black studies struggle at San Francisco State, envisioned history teachers drawing on the rhythm of the Temptations and the indignity of neighborhood drunks to stimulate the political consciousness of black sixth graders in San Francisco's Fillmore section. These strategies shared a powerful premise: that poor children must confront community realities and needs as part of the public school curriculum, learning to engage rather than disparage or escape their surroundings. Sociologist Joyce Ladner, a Student Nonviolent Coordinating Committee veteran like Garrett, maintained that Head Start and other compensatory programs taught poor black children more about how white "Dick and Jane" characters function in suburbia than about how youngsters in Bedford-Stuyvesant, Watts, or Sunflower County, Mississippi, could "develop skills to transform their environments into more wholesome, habitable areas."[20]

For these intellectuals, education's essential aims were social justice and cultural edification. In "decolonized" schools, black youngsters might learn to shun the bourgeois prerogatives of social climbing and private accumulation, avoiding psychological dissolution into a materialistic, white mainstream. Progressive, self-governing black schools would invert dominant power relations. Welfare recipients would find in such institutions a forum for their expertise in managing cold bureaucracies and meager budgets. Even the police would see their roles reversed. The community-controlled school would house and regulate law enforcement agencies that had functioned as occupying forces of black urban centers. Like the activists of Harlem's Intermediate School (IS) 201, who responded to the area's high rates of tuberculosis and sickle cell anemia by arranging screenings through nearby hospitals, theorists of black relevance regarded the neighborhood school as the core of community life. They imagined institutions that could restore the promise of social democracy, delivering free day care and public assistance along with a superb primary and secondary education.[21]

Community control proponents envisioned schools as instruments for reconstructing the lives of the disinherited, as had earlier generations of reformers. They dreamed of mutual aid committees and credit unions. A 20-point agenda "for real school community control" created by IS 201 administrators included complete medical services and free breakfast and lunch programs for all children featuring rice, beans, and Chinese food ("No more soup and bread and butter sandwiches"), as well as adult education classes, drug rehabilitation programs, and full employment for Harlem residents. The school complex published a 245-page manual designed to help Harlemites fight employment discrimination, earn a high school diploma, and otherwise resist poverty and degradation. In the minds of progressive activists, the neighborhood school became a weapon against police brutality, a mediator of quarrels with the welfare system, and an arena for confronting "those larger issues which impinge so critically on the lives of school children in the ghetto."[22]

"Corn Flakes Instead of Eggs": The Cult of Deprivation

Some of community control's empowerment strategies reflected the familiar historical patterns of urban ethnic groups. Traditionally, as new immigrants and other members of the urban poor gained a measure of stability and clout, they sought greater influence over schools and other municipal agencies as sources of jobs and contracts. African Americans hoped the apparatus of public education—a growth industry in declining cities—could perform the social functions that ward politics and ethnic networks had fulfilled for other marginalized populations. But attempts to convert schools into cultural and economic bases for black communities represented more than a pragmatic response to local needs. The pursuit of educational relevance signaled a larger struggle for self-definition, a crusade that had witnessed the transition from "Negro" to "Afro-American," and that now demanded the severing of other "semantic shackles."[23] Black culture, real and perceived, had long been subject to the interpretations of distant elites. African-American workers and professionals now strove to redefine the reigning social theories of black life.

One source of their indignation was the doctrine of cultural deprivation. Reformers and policymakers of the late 1950s and '60s had constructed remedial and compensatory education programs upon the principle of African-American deficiency. Theories of social disadvantage supplanted crudely racist explanations for black children's academic distress. Experts suggested that many African Americans did poorly in school not because of innate shortcomings, but as a result of cultural defects in their homes and neighborhoods. A vast literature on the socially deprived child arose. Poverty programs sought to correct the presumably crippling influence (on language skills, learning ability, and educational attitudes) of "broken" homes and environments that lacked books.[24]

Many black parents initially embraced compensatory education as an overdue reform, demanding the expansion of programs like Head Start. Increasingly, however, critics of "deficit model" remedies attacked their underlying assumptions as offensive if not racist. Prominent black psychologist Kenneth B. Clark lambasted the deprivation "cult" and proposed "socially denied" as a phrase that more precisely conveyed the systemic racism plaguing poor children of color. African-American parents rejected narratives of crumbling families and deviant communities as explanations for their children's academic struggles. They resisted the smearing of black culture, unable to recognize their lives in official accounts of pathology.[25]

Black parents who boycotted a slum school in the Haight-Ashbury section of San Francisco in early 1966 openly mocked the trope of cultural deficiency.

Confronting the school's principal during a meeting, the striking residents demanded to know why their children had been labeled "culturally disadvantaged." "Well doesn't that mean that their parents earn less than $4,000 a year," the principal replied. "What has culturally disadvantaged got to do with money?" one mother asked. "You've got it," another woman interjected. "Culture is money." A Harlem mother struck a similar note of dissent during the IS 201 struggle. "I don't want to be told that my daughter can't learn because she comes from a fatherless home or because she had corn flakes for breakfast instead of eggs," she declared.[26]

Contemporary studies deepened the insult, linking academic performance to class while overlooking the racist machinations perceived by black parents. Some African Americans resolved to shield their children from further defamation. The Inner City Parents Council of Detroit condemned the "Nazi-like theories of racial inferiority" that guided compensatory education. "I would like to declare a moratorium on white investigators coming into the black community and into black schools and saying we're going to lay the word on you," education professor Chester Davis, a staff member at Atlanta's Institute of the Black World, proclaimed in 1970. "They ain't got the word!"[27]

"How to Spell R-E-S-P-E-C-T": Black Styles, Black Values

A generation of black intellectuals shunned the themes of deviance popularized by "culture of poverty" experts. They proclaimed the positive distinctiveness of black life, spurning Nathan Glazer and Daniel Moynihan's 1965 assertion that "the Negro is only an American and nothing else."[28] African-American children, they argued, required educational methods tailored to their special aptitudes. As Ruther Turner Perot of the Washington-based Black Child Development Institute noted in 1971, "Deficiency is defined by the man who determines the standard."[29]

Some African-American theorists defended the legitimacy of "black learning styles" while accusing public education of reproducing the cultural norms of the white bourgeoisie. Black studies advocate Jimmy Garrett argued that while white children could absorb "high flown rhetoric" all day, black children were equally capable of listening to "soul" records for hours. "Why is it black children [who] cannot spell their own names know how to spell 'r-e-s-p-e-c-t'?" a la Aretha Franklin, he asked. One African-American Brooklyn principal described middle-class white students as docile "captives" of classroom monotony. By contrast, he suggested, black children instinctively rebelled against bland instruction.[30]

Black nationalists feared that a culturally foreign education would "whitewash" African-American children, producing self-abnegating "black Anglo-Saxons." "Are they, in the process of preparing to achieve high scores on 'standardized tests,' being induced to try to emulate the culture of another ethnic or racial group?" political scientist and *Black Power* coauthor Charles V. Hamilton asked. "Are they being given a sense of their own heritage?"[31] Many nationalists believed only black teachers could truly cultivate African-American children. "Our children need teachers with soul," the Afro-American Teachers Association (ATA) proclaimed in ads designed to recruit black New York City instructors. Some theorists suggested that residents of black central cities were inherently better qualified to teach African-American youngsters than were most white professionals. "Expertise is a myth to mystify the community," declared the head of a radical faction of the UFT.[32]

The ATA proposed that white instructors who wished to remain in black, inner-city schools receive a formal orientation to such neighborhoods so that they might comprehend "the home environment" and "style of living" of their inhabitants. Yet critics like black studies professor Nathan Hare doubted that white, middle-class teachers could shed their inclination "to regard as saucy and slovenly mannerisms which slum boys exhibit as symbols of ghetto sophistication and thwarted manliness." Of course, bourgeois black teachers in ghetto schools also risked assuming the role of cultural missionaries. Only those instructors who "identify the community's struggle as their own" could claim relevance. African-American teachers could furnish inner cities with skills and leadership, the ATA's Leslie Campbell conceded, but they must never enter black neighborhoods as "strangers bearing gifts."[33]

For some black educators, remaining "relevant" meant internalizing a new code of ethics. "We can no longer serve our constituents platitudes about the 'American dream,'" an IS 201 administrator proclaimed. Attendees of Detroit's 1968 Black Ministers-Teachers Conference vowed, "We shall not covet that status in society which will serve to isolate us from our goals and those of the black community." Even the head of the Black Caucus of the American Federation of Teachers criticized African-American public school instructors who "accepted uncritically the assumptions of American education and society."[34] Such pronouncements suggested that "relevance" posed a far greater challenge than any textbook could answer. The task of creating an education pertinent to the social realities of African Americans meant confronting the debate over "black values."

The idea of an admirable, distinctly African-American repertoire of social values incensed those who believed that black children required traditional preparation for "the real world of tough interracial competition." These critics suggested that scorning middle-class ideals of self-denial, delayed gratification, and respect for discipline and property would only exacerbate the "self-perpetuating cycle of disadvantages" within black communities. "If Negroes are to make their way in American society," one *New York Times* essayist maintained, "their progress, like that of other ethnic or racial groups, will be judged by their acquisition of the majority culture in all its ramifications."[35] Some working-class black parents were themselves ambivalent about professions of "black values," which seemed to verge on reifying theories of innate racial difference. While they wished public education to assist in developing positive black consciousness, experience had deepened their suspicion of educational methods that appeared to deny their children the tools of mainstream success.

Nevertheless, many black educators and intellectuals remained convinced that the classroom hegemony of "white," bureaucratic values smothered the humanistic instincts of children of color. Preston Wilcox argued that public schools fostered materialism and imparted an overformal and artificial cultural style. Participants in an education workshop at the summer 1969 regional Black Power conference in Bermuda accused the United States and other "colonial powers" of using schools to reinforce a culture of profiteering and individualism. "Even those schools which have 100 percent black student bodies are, in fact, European colonial schools," a contributor to Chicago's *Black Liberator* declared. "They are founded on a European value system, not a black one."[36]

The desire to socialize African-American children according to "a black code of values" spanned a relatively wide ideological spectrum. The proposition that black educational redemption meant considering positive cultural differences whose significance had been disguised or denied generated an exciting sense of possibility. The school experience now seemed replete with opportunities to rehabilitate black identity and prepare children for citizenship not just in a pluralistic American democracy, but also in a nation waiting to be born. "The man is not going to give these values to us," ATA leader and Ocean Hill–Brownsville intermediate school administrator Albert Vann insisted, using the masculine construction to identify both the oppressor and the oppressed. "They have to be earned by a new kind of black man that we don't have yet."[37]

"In the Hands of Black Men": Black Education and the Politics of Separation

The pursuit of black autonomy generated not only crusades for educational relevance but also a remarkable upsurge of organizations. The late 1960s and '70s witnessed the rise of a highly politicized black professional class and a virtually unparalleled proliferation of African-American associations. Scores of professional and occupational groups appeared, including roughly 25 national black educational organizations.[38]

Countless education-related outfits emerged on the local level. Moderate to conservative groups like the Chicago African American Teachers Association (CATA) emphasized "responsible" political agitation and traditional methods of professional advancement. The organization's slogan—"We Are Drum Majors for Quality Education"—evoked the integrationist rhetoric of Martin Luther King, Jr. By contrast, New York's staunchly nationalistic ATA, originally a black teacher caucus within the city's United Federation of Teachers, stressed militant political confrontation. "It is the mis-education and ineffectiveness of education for black youth coupled with the frustrations of being black in white America that has driven youth to the brink of social revolution," ATA leader Albert Vann insisted. Yet both CATA and ATA endorsed community control and black studies—including Swahili courses—in public schools.[39]

By the late 1960s, a sense of growing consensus around black nationalist themes bolstered the idea that racial solidarity could bridge ideological and class divides. As more black occupational pressure groups arose, the ideals of self-determination and "unity without uniformity" began to seem eminently achievable. The 1966 Conference on Racism in Education demonstrated the growing power and indignation of the black thrust toward cultural autonomy. Sponsored by the liberal American Federation of Teachers (AFT), the event saw more than 1,300 teachers, many of them black, descend on Washington, DC, that December to "correct America's image of the past." Organizers had imagined a collegial, integrated gathering dedicated to ridding history textbooks and public school curricula of racist content. Instead, the forum unleashed currents of dissent and amplified calls for black educational independence.

Some professionals saw the Racism in Education conferences of 1966 and 1967 as opportunities to collect imaginative lesson plans, including an outline for a course on "Afro-American in the arts" that recommended shadowboxes of African scenes and *Clever Hands of the African Negro* as text. Radicals like New York City assistant principal James E. Campbell pursued a more trenchant agenda. Campbell, who had directed the Harlem "liberation school" associated with Malcolm X's Organization of Afro-American Unity, questioned the motives behind Racism in Education, describing the meeting as a probe of black minds by the white fathers of "intellectual neocolonialism." He accused conference organizers of ignoring the underlying values of American education, including the sacredness of private property and the nobility of the profit motive. "Are we to assume," he asked, "that the ideological base of racism can be separated from the operation of the American system—capitalism?"[40]

The assaults on liberalism continued. One panel of black educators questioned whether white instructors, no matter how well meaning, possessed the moral and political qualifications to teach African-American children under *any* circumstances. Meanwhile, black nationalists at the parley, including veteran activist Queen Mother Moore and historian John Henrik Clarke, issued searing critiques of white supremacy. The exasperation of black attendees and the force of their rejection of white paternalism lingered long after the conference, inspiring the birth of the AFT Black Caucus, a subgroup of the powerful teacher's union.[41]

Proponents of black self-determination attacked other symbols of liberal reform. In early 1968, a revolt of black educators disrupted an antipoverty summit in New Orleans. The confrontation occurred during the winter conference of Upward Bound, the federal initiative designed to propel poor high school students into college. One source of black frustration was the composition of the national program's leadership; while half of all Upward Bound pupils were black, African Americans constituted only 45 of its 253 directors. The Upward Bound revolt also reflected broader disaffection with the poverty programs. Black social workers and teachers recognized the growing hostility of the African-American lower classes toward the War on Poverty, which eased black destitution while failing to address its origins in the structures of racial capitalism. Many poor African Americans saw antipoverty efforts as pacification schemes, and few black Upward Bound workers wished to be viewed as agents of placation. Harlem activist Preston Wilcox, who attended the New Orleans assembly, suggested that the forum reflected the desire of the white establishment to "engage Hertz Rent-A-Negroes in anaesthetizing the functional anger existent in black ghettos."[42]

A group of African Americans formed a caucus at the conference and produced a position paper that some Upward Bound officials viewed as absolutist. The caucus recommended that black directors alone supervise Upward Bound projects with a plurality of black students, a measure designed to ensure that African-American youngsters might find themselves "in the hands of black men with whom they can identify." (Again a link was drawn between African-American masculinity and the rehabilitation of black self-image.) Many onlookers recoiled. As one delegate remembered, "It was painful to see white directors who perceived themselves as liberals and thought they had great rapport with their Negro students being told: 'Baby, you've been had. You're not getting through to them at all.' "[43]

The pursuit of broad-based, independent black formations reached its practical limits with the establishment of the National Association of Afro-American Educators (NAAAE). None of the familiar slogans, from "relevance" to "black values," could stem the ideological crises that wracked the organization. The endeavor began when some 1,000 representatives from several states gathered in Chicago for the National Conference of Afro-American Educators in June 1968. Organizers defined "educator" loosely, seeing race as the essential characteristic and unity as the overarching goal. "Cultural commonality," they presumed, would trump political difference.[44]

Attendees included teachers, administrators, academics, professionals, parents, students, and activists. Preston Wilcox of Harlem, who emerged as NAAAE chair, boasted that participants ranged from those "wearing natural hair and affecting African dress to those with straightened hair and Westernized attire." Yet philosophical conflicts immediately arose. "Are we educating our children to live in a black society only," someone asked, "or are we educating for a multi-racial group society?" The question resurfaced: "Are we working toward inclusion into the majority culture or are we trying to establish a separate society for blacks?" Wilcox attempted to shroud ideological and class divisions. "We think that we have pulled together the first black-initiated, black-controlled, culturally radical organization," he said. But the cry that emanated from the Chicago proceedings—"Give us a clear ideological base!"—went unanswered.[45]

Clarity again proved elusive during an "excruciating" planning meeting in St. Louis that August and throughout a follow-up conference in Atlanta. Conflict re-emerged when a dissident faction, decrying the dominance of an "educated elite" and insisting that black education must arise from the masses, charged that bourgeois leaders had betrayed the NAAAE's grassroots mission. "Having begun to throw off the mantle of white liberal leadership," they asked, "are we to substitute hard won victory for the same kind of leadership–only this time with black faces?" Factionalism also marred the 1969 NAAAE summit, during which a group of midwestern delegates deplored the concentration of power in the organization's executive committee. "They viewed Black Chicago and Black New York as being two different nations rather than [being] different parts of the same black nation," Wilcox later complained.[46]

Neither the ideal of nationhood nor the "united front" principle could save the NAAAE, which dwindled after the 1969 conference and eventually died. (Successor organizations like the National Alliance of Black Educators, which emerged in 1973, lacked the NAAAE's nationalist character and broad social goals.) The group had projected mostly abstract ideals. "Those who have knowledge primarily from books must be linked with those who have knowledge from the streets," one attendee of the Chicago meeting declared. Another expressed the desire "to translate white materialism into black humanism." Members of the organization designed an elaborate rubric of psycho-political blackness by which the metamorphosis from "Negro" ("a person of color who desires to be like his white master") to "Afro-American educator" (someone who wishes to positively "shape the destiny of black people") was to be measured.[47]

In truth, the aims of the NAAAE were no more concrete than those of other black nationalist assemblages. Attendees of the education workshop at Philadelphia's 1968 Black Power Conference also traded platitudes, proclaiming that African-American children must learn "to be black in thought, in action, in affect, in substance, in spirit, in behavior, in attitudes, in gut reactions." The flimsiness of such statements hardly diminished the zeal with which contemporary theorists pursued concepts of autonomous black education. Consideration of "alternative educational structures" increasingly framed discussions of schooling at black conferences. More African Americans embraced independent institutions as a means of fulfilling mandates for community control and relevance. As Jimmy Garrett observed in 1968, many black parents and educators had simply "given up hope of reaping educational benefits from a system that has refused to recognize the needs of black children."[48]

"A More Potent Force": The Demise of Community Control and the Search for Alternatives

In the end, that system also declined to substantially redistribute decision-making power over inner-city public schools. Community control, a crucial component of contemporary black educational visions, never fulfilled demands for academic redemption and self-rule. Several cities restructured their boards of education and created semiautonomous school districts; more supervisors and teachers of color were hired or promoted. These measures neither furnished black families with decisive authority nor meaningfully involved poor parents in the fashioning and delivery of education. New York City's demonstration districts were finally dissolved by a 1969 "decentralization" law that nominally dispersed the powers of the Board of Education, carving the school system into "community districts" without genuinely reallocating fiscal, personnel, or curricular functions.[49]

Community control proponents recognized the decimation of their cause. Decentralization, once seen as a euphemism for power sharing, lay exposed as an instrument of the status quo, a clerical change that further entrenched rigid bureaucracies. Critics lamented the return of the "plantation system" of ghetto education. The dream of converting inner-city public schools into paragons of dignity and participatory democracy seemed all but dead. The headline of one African-American newspaper captured the bitterness that prevailed in the streets: "Cowardly Racists Dissolve Black Schools."[50]

The crippling of educational justice movements accompanied the conservative turn of the late 1960s, when federal policies of "benign neglect" replaced mandates for "maximum feasible participation" of the poor. The failure of community control experiments to generate substantial reform deepened the conviction that such concessions were little more than "neocolonial" schemes to manage black confrontation politics and deflect radical impulses. Proponents of the internal colony theory concluded that financial and political elites had responded to the growing black presence in major cities not by abandoning these "central mechanisms of industrial capitalism," but by offering token minority participation while ensuring that the capital and political resources remained in the hands of the "mother country." As the parent union of the IS 201 complex declared in 1971, "Injustice is now managed uptown instead of downtown."[51]

Vestiges of the struggle remained. Some New York public schools served soul food or "Latin flavor" lunches in the early 1970s, and the charismatic, young principal of Brooklyn's JHS 57 sported an Afro and a Black Power fist medallion. The city's pilot "minischool," an innovative model aimed at salvaging ghetto dropouts, borrowed its name, Harambee Prep, from a popular Swahili word meaning "let's pull together." These were meager victories for those who had demanded a new social contract for schoolchildren in the urban core. As community control forces disbanded and black class tensions intensified, charges multiplied that self-seeking "Negro professionals" had helped neutralize the movement in return for antipoverty funds or positions within the municipal bureaucracy. "The cripplers in the past (largely white) have now been joined by destructive, opportunistic education pimps (largely black), who prey on the Harlem community," longtime activist Babette Edwards proclaimed in 1971.[52]

Other critics chastised local activists for letting "the myth of government-sponsored revolution" convince them that community control had constituted anything other than riot deterrence—summer "'cool off' money," as one Ocean Hill–Brownsville governing board member put it. Even sympathetic observers derided as "romantic fantasy" the expectation that a humanitarian revolution in education would accompany "a shift in power from the bureaucracy to the people." A columnist for *The Nation* scorned the idea of community control as a viable solution for the slums. "Dashikis, natural hairdos, soul music in the cafeteria, and introductory Swahili all have some symbolic significance," he maintained, "but the children will still leave these schools unable to read and write."[53]

Dismal reading scores seemed to confirm community control's failure to lift black achievement (though to be fair, the experiment had not been granted sufficient time to demonstrate real progress). The academic crisis endured well after the passage of New York's 1969 decentralization law. "I don't care how much the new structure has given people a sense of control over their own destiny," psychologist Kenneth B. Clark declared in 1980. "The schools are no better and no worse than they were a decade ago."[54]

Ultimately, community control struggles in New York and elsewhere underscored the deficiencies of public education as an instrument of social transformation. Noting a re-emergence in "the faith that failed," a host of contemporary critics echoed the familiar argument that American public schools preserve the lowly status of the poor far more efficiently than they aid upward mobility. Sociologist C. Eric Lincoln described black schoolchildren as "programmed for social and economic oblivion" by a power structure that profits from such an arrangement. Leftist theorist Doxey Wilkerson insisted, "It is not the education of black men and women that will achieve their liberation; it is the liberation of black Americans that will assure their effective education." Yet the overwhelming majority of African Americans polled by *Ebony* in 1970 cited improved education as a response to the question, "How will blacks make real progress?"[55]

Some activists wondered whether the entire community control movement had been a farce. "Is all that suffering, all that expense, all that experience going to go for naught?" a former IS 201 administrator asked. The reforms pursued by New York's demonstration districts had failed to satisfy the primary objective of African-American parents—the academic salvation of their children.[56] Observers insisted that more time was needed to nurture modest gains, yet short-term triumphs could hardly replace the dignity of literacy or the promise of social mobility. Still, the burgeoning political consciousness of certain mobilized neighborhoods suggested that community control had achieved at least *some* substantial victories.

Black and Puerto Rican residents of Harlem and Brooklyn remained acutely aware of the dynamics of social oppression that the struggle had underscored. The winter 1970 newsletter of the defunded IS 201 complex carried black history bulletins and infant mortality statistics along with news of prison uprisings and accounts of the repression of political dissidents, from Black Panthers to Young Lords (a Puerto Rican group). Evidence of expanding racial consciousness contrasted with the resistance to black nationalist outlooks that ATA founders had encountered earlier in the 1960s. Living amid picketing, rallies, and strikes radicalized youngsters. In a 1969 issue of *Black Fury*, an IS 201 newspaper, local eighth graders described Latinos and black Americans as "brothers" who must unite to "carry on the struggle." Editors of the school yearbook dedicated that year's edition to neighborhood fifth graders "in the confidence that the struggle will mature in the hands of our younger brothers."[57]

Mounting interest in alternative and independent schools offered another sign of the survival of community control ideals. Some Ocean Hill–Brownsville educators openly admired the Nation of Islam's black nationalist private schools. If African Americans could not gain control of local education, the ATA's Herman Ferguson argued in 1968, they should abandon the public school system and place the instruction of their progeny "in the hands of black people who have demonstrated that they ... have the interests of black children at heart." ATA officials hailed the Nation's academies as "our parochial schools" and assured residents that the institutions—which enrolled both Muslim pupils and the children of nonbelievers—offered a viable, community-based education. Community control advocate Preston Wilcox also favored private models. By 1969, he had developed and circulated a provocative prospectus— "An Independent Black School or a Dependent Nigger School"—that described an enterprise funded by white patrons but governed by "black values."[58]

Meanwhile, there emerged two proposals for an independent Harlem school system lying beyond the jurisdiction of New York's Board of Education. The first, a Congress of Racial Equality (CORE) plan endorsed by an array of civil rights leaders and designed to surpass community control as a mechanism for home rule, imagined a public district of 50,000 students chartered by the state legislature and dedicated to correcting "the impotence of ghetto life." The new district would operate like a sovereign city-state within the existing territory of the city school system. Roy Innis and Victor Solomon, the plan's coauthors, argued that the reorganization would help address "the black man's image of himself and his lack of control over the institutions which control his life." Written by a former IS 201 activist, the second proposal for a Harlem educational system eschewed public funding altogether, envisioning a network of culturally affirming private schools.[59]

Both proposals echoed elements of a plan advanced by Malcolm X's Organization of Afro-American Unity as early as 1964 that called for the group to take control of failing public schools in Harlem and Bedford-Stuyvesant as a means of offering black communities "a more potent force for educational self-improvement." In the late 1960s and early '70s, however, debate erupted among black nationalists over whether public or private institutions provided the more auspicious arena of struggle. Activists like Amiri Baraka saw no conflict between crusades for control of public schools and efforts to establish independent black academies. Yet Roy Innis of CORE emphasized the limitations of private education as a mass solution and reaffirmed the drive for community control of school districts with large black populations.[60]

While the ATA endorsed both approaches, the organization strongly favored independent black institutions. This rapidly became the orthodox position of black nationalists. Members of the New School for Afro-American Thought, a Washington, DC, establishment, acknowledged in 1968 that the push for black educational reform had stalled and argued that constructing models outside the public system represented a dire necessity. Two years later the Congress of African People, a national organization, established as a long-term goal the replacing of public schools in black communities with "Pan African educational alternatives."[61]

Community control veterans entered the 1970s searching for new ways to end the "crucifixion" of black children in urban schools. Harlem theorist Preston Wilcox worked with antipoverty programs to empower the parents of African-American schoolchildren. Activist Babette Edwards became a staunch proponent of "vouchers," or government subsidies designed to enable low-income parents to enroll their children in the public or private schools of their choice. Discharged from his teaching job, Albert Vann of the ATA entered Brooklyn politics, viewing his service as an assemblyman as an extension of the community control thrust, and sensing the limitations of further agitation "outside the system."[62] Leslie Campbell saw no such constraints. Dismissed from the public school system in 1969 along with Vann, the middle-school teacher withdrew into black Brooklyn and started a school.

"The Devil Can Never Educate Us": The Road to Uhuru Sasa

Campbell, a true son of Brooklyn, was born, raised, and educated in the borough. His father, Robert Campbell, an organizer for the Communist Party's Harlem and Bedford-Stuyvesant branches, served as secretary to left-wing New York City councilman Benjamin Davis, taught Campbell about the Mau Mau liberation struggle in Kenya, and once introduced his son to legendary human rights activist Paul Robeson. Campbell's mother, Mardesta Mealing, played a far greater role in his upbringing. A leftist who reared seven children while on public assistance, she nurtured her son's activist inclinations through her own work mobilizing black, Bedford-Stuyvesant parents around demands for decent public education.

Poor but bright, and a voracious reader, Campbell entered prestigious Brooklyn Tech High School in 1952, though isolation among privileged, white classmates led to his withdrawal from the institution. The school to which he transferred offered no refuge; its students, mostly recent European immigrants, regarded acts of antiblack violence as rites of cultural assimilation. Campbell majored in history and minored in education at Long Island University's Brooklyn campus, where his most inspiring professor was a white civil rights veteran. A law career seemed remote and expensive, so after graduating in 1962, Campbell took a teaching job at Bedford-Stuyvesant's overwhelmingly black and Puerto Rican Junior High School 35.[63]

The large cohort of activist, black teachers at JHS 35 included Albert Vann, future ATA leader and one of Campbell's close allies. If JHS 35 was a stronghold of black activist-intellectuals, Central Brooklyn, with its growing population of southern transplants and Caribbean immigrants, was itself a cultural mecca. Its dignitaries included Milton Galamison, civil rights leader and pastor of a Bedford-Stuyvesant church. The failure of Galamison's city-wide school desegregation crusade to transform the educational experiences of the system's black children served as a profound political lesson for Campbell, who participated in the leader's massive 1964 boycotts.

Now a social studies teacher in his mid-20s, Campbell grew increasingly troubled by the racial inequities of urban public education. He began to see the miseducation of black children less as a result of negligence than as the product of an immense system—a colonial structure designed to stultify its inner-city subjects. The ascent of the United Federation of Teachers furnished no solutions. The local union seemed to exemplify white liberal hypocrisy, supporting the southern desegregation movement while narrowly pursuing its own professional interests at home, to the considerable detriment, Campbell believed, of black youths. Seeking alternatives, Campbell, Vann, and other black educators formed the ATA in 1964. The self-help organization challenged New York City's African-American instructors to strengthen bonds of racial solidarity in black schools and communities.

At JHS 35, Campbell helped create a sweeping, diasporic curriculum that included classes on African history and the transatlantic slave trade. His lectures on "the current situation of the black man" and his efforts to politicize youngsters antagonized a vocal group of parents who viewed him as an extremist. Campbell's black nationalist outlook only deepened. For him, the first major Black Power conference at Newark, New Jersey, in 1967 marked the end of the "nightmare" of integrationism and vindicated the dream of black nationhood. He returned from the gathering filled with new resolve to convert black public schools into "tools for molding our communities and our students."[64]

The ATA embraced the demand for community control, a cause bolstered in 1967 by the formation of the experimental Ocean Hill–Brownsville district. This development came amid a national surge of black militancy that Campbell hailed as evidence of a "great awakening." His own "shining moment" of struggle arrived in February 1968 when he violated a Board of Education edict by escorting 40 eighth graders during school hours to a Malcolm X memorial at Harlem's IS 201. The rally echoed with calls for revolutionary violence and was swiftly condemned by the press as "antiwhite." Its sponsors, however, saw a historic occasion, a fiery coronation for black nationalism that attracted a host of luminaries, from Malcolm's widow Betty Shabazz to artist-activist LeRoi Jones (later Amiri Baraka).[65]

During the tribute, ATA member Herman Ferguson (then under indictment—in a time of growing repression of black radicals—for allegedly conspiring to murder moderate civil rights leaders) urged members of the audience to arm themselves for what he described as an imminent race war. Dan Watts of the left-leaning *Liberator* later dismissed the event as the work of "verbal revolutionaries" who substituted "down with whitey" hyperbole for viable political programs. Yet Campbell viewed the memorial as an expression of the nationalist principles that defined his teaching. When school administrators charged him with insubordination and temporarily revoked his license, the ATA denounced the "educational lynching" and 300 teenagers and other admirers rallied in his defense. Acknowledging Campbell's merits as a teacher, authorities agreed to transfer the outspoken instructor to Ocean Hill–Brownsville. "It is unfortunate that my departure from JHS 35 could not have been held in the usual 'punch and cookies' manner," he declared in a parting statement. "But revolutions are never fought that way."[66]

Determined to shape the political meaning of community control, Campbell helped transform JHS 271 into a bastion of black consciousness. He covered a bulletin board with news clippings about the Black Panthers, decorated his eighth-grade classroom with posters of the black Christ, displayed slides of great African civilizations, assigned *Malcolm X on Afro-American History* as his textbook, and oversaw adult evening courses that offered instruction in staging community demonstrations and fomenting peoples' revolutions. He also discussed the merits of formal black sovereignty ("Now, Timmy," he asked one student, "would you like an Afro-American state?") and, according to a disputed report, extolled the tactical value of Molotov cocktails.[67]

A rival social studies instructor at JHS 271 taught that "extremists" on the right and left flanks of the "American Highway" of political beliefs rely on violence and aggression to achieve rapid social change or to preserve the status quo, while those in the great "Center Lane" of politics maintain peace by bringing about change gradually. By contrast, Campbell strove to convince black youths that liberal democratic traditions camouflage the realities of white supremacy. Again parents remonstrated. But many students grew to appreciate the giant iconoclast who patiently explained the cultural significance of dashikis and the principles of Black Power. Campbell's most devoted pupils included youngsters who, largely as a result of his tutelage, adopted African names and "Third World" outlooks. "We became international," one former student recalled.[68]

Campbell solidified his reputation as a firebrand in April 1968 when the murder of Martin Luther King, Jr. prompted a JHS 271 assembly at which the instructor delivered a characteristically intemperate address. Students had rampaged through the school the day after the assassination, scattering chairs and calling for vengeance. During the ensuing assembly, Campbell advised the youngsters to direct their fury at the white power structure. Acts of petty crime, he argued, should be performed with revolutionary intent and in preparation for sustained street combat. "When the enemy taps you on the shoulder," he proclaimed, "send him to the cemetery." This message was cathartic, Campbell later insisted, and actually *cooled* tempers. But the remarks fueled his notoriety, as did an incident that afternoon in which a handful of students assaulted a white teacher who had removed a bulletin board bearing signs that read "Martin Luther King was killed by a vicious white man—Prepare yourselves."[69]

Campbell again faced disciplinary action that fall for harassing teachers who had returned to the classroom after going out on strike. Neither suspension nor arraignment on criminal charges of coercion could bridle the defiant instructor. Writing in the ATA newsletter that fall, Campbell charged the United Federation of Teachers with wringing profits from inner cities while breeding functional illiterates as cheap labor for the service industries and cannon fodder for the battlefields of Vietnam. "The devil can never educate us," he declared.[70]

Some white sympathizers admired Campbell's militancy. "His suspicion of the 'white liberal' arises out of a history of double cross and meaningless rhetoric, and seems to be shared by his true constituency, the black community," one Jewish colleague observed. The journalist I. F. Stone praised Campbell's pedagogy, noting that his lectures on "Our Homeland" mirrored Zionist Sabbath school lessons. A provocation that December, however, alienated would-be allies and seemed to confirm Campbell's incendiary purpose. By then the community control struggle had produced reciprocal charges of racism from the largely Jewish teachers union and from black representatives. Ugly epithets from both camps had poisoned the affair. Thus it seemed especially reckless when Campbell, appearing on a late-night WBAI radio show hosted by Student Nonviolent Coordinating Committee veteran Julius Lester, read over the air a JHS 271 student's poem that began, "Hey, Jew boy, with that yarmulke on your head. You pale-faced Jew boy—I wish you were dead. . . ."[71]

Titled *Anti-Semitism*, the poem attempted crude irony. Its eighth-grade creator had learned from freewheeling discussions at the middle school that the "original Semites" were black, a premise embraced by many black nationalist groups. ("How can they ask a Semite if he's anti-Semitic?" Brooklyn activist Sonny Carson later quipped at an Ocean Hill–Brownsville rally.) Bristling at accusations of anti-Semitism directed at black communities by Jewish teachers she regarded as racist, the adolescent had hurled the indictment back at its authors. Campbell later acknowledged the toxic nature of the poem. Yet he continued to maintain that he had read the passages simply to convey the pain and feelings of betrayal that prevailed in the district. He defended what he saw as the emotional response of a politically unrefined child. "It was not a statement, it was a reaction," he insisted. "Somebody hits you, you react."[72]

Seen as an expression of raw bigotry, the recitation of the poem reinforced Ocean Hill–Brownsville's image as a haven for extremists. The outcry against apparent manifestations of anti-Semitism, one observer noted, "created the political conditions for the defeat and humiliation" of the district. Campbell's infamy increased. "If they could have electrocuted me I would have gone to the chair," he later acknowledged. The radio broadcast proved especially damaging in the context of growing alarm over the deterioration of black–Jewish relations. A *Time* magazine report published shortly after the WBAI incident lamented the rise of "an ominous current of anti-Semitism" among "a small fraction of Negroes."[73]

In truth, the widening gulf between some Jews and African Americans reflected complex contemporary and historical circumstances. Progressive Jews had long been among the most committed allies of black struggle. As the push for black autonomy drove many white participants from the movement, however, deep-seated resentment of Jews as conspicuous symbols of the exploitation and absentee ownership of black ghettoes surfaced. Mounting pro-Palestine sentiment among African Americans, especially in the aftermath of the Arab-Israeli War of 1967—an event that highlighted Israel's status as a settler colony and an imperialist power—intensified anti-Zionist critiques and reinforced black perceptions of the Jewish minority as little more than a new oppressor class. At times, forthright anti-Zionism and vulgar anti-Semitism commingled.

This ideological fusion may have inspired the poem that Campbell read over the air, as well as some of the more chauvinistic pronouncements that he made in subsequent years. Like other African Americans who succumbed to narrow nationalism while pursuing principled Third Worldism, he rarely differentiated between progressive Jews who embodied antiracist traditions and opportunistic members of the group who, having departed the urban reservations now occupied by black people, joined other white "ethnics" in clothing themselves in the social privileges of whiteness. Campbell never acknowledged any current of truth in the ongoing allegations of anti-Semitism. He continued to maintain that leaders of the United Federation of Teachers and their political cronies had exploited the issue to deflect criticism of their opposition to community control. Undeniably, however, the venting of anti-Semitic sentiments alienated principled antiracists who had long supported black educational justice.

Reports of the indoctrination of schoolchildren by black fanatics proliferated, and Campbell became a visible symbol of the purported conspiracy to fan the flames of bigotry. New York progressives tried to ensure that outrage over "intergroup vilification" did not eclipse critical questions of democracy raised by inner-city battles for dignified education. For Campbell, however, this phase of struggle had come to an end. Seen by authorities as the culmination of a series of misdeeds, the poem fiasco (and an additional incident in which a Malcolm X oration was piped through the loudspeakers of JHS 271) brought to a conclusion the educator's eight years with the public schools. In a move that the ATA denounced as the beginning of a purge of militants, Campbell was dismissed from his teaching post in the fall of 1969.[74]

Campbell viewed the termination as an act of retaliation for his unapologetic advocacy of black nationalism. A statement he later issued about deposed Ghanaian leader Kwame Nkrumah seemed to encapsulate his feelings toward his own removal: "He was charged with being a demagogue, an outlaw, a socialist and a dictator," Campbell declared. "Whenever someone attempts to be a positive force for black people he is cut down." The battle-worn instructor struggled to regroup throughout that autumn. He had experienced moments of jubilation in Ocean Hill–Brownsville. "We had shown that this downtrodden community faced with a crisis, using its own resources, could overcome," he later said.[75] Yet he recognized that the movement had won only token concessions, and he resolved to pursue more promising methods of self-determination. Amid the search for new directions, he abandoned the moniker Leslie Campbell and assumed the Kiswahili name Jitu Weusi ("Big Black").

"Revolutionary Appetite": The Role of High School Radicals

Despite his lingering bitterness, Weusi's relationship to a group of 60 militant high school students allowed him to maintain a sense of purpose. In 1967, he had helped organize the African-American Student Association (ASA), a counterpart to the ATA. The organization claimed membership throughout the city, defining itself as a disciplined, black nationalist formation within the waves of social protest that engulfed New York high schools in the late 1960s. Many ASA members lived in Bedford-Stuyvesant and attended Brooklyn's Boys High or Franklin K. Lane High School, institutions that exhibited many of the familiar symptoms of repression and neglect as growing black and Latino enrollment transformed their student bodies. Even those Lane students who evaded the narcotics trade that thrived within the school struggled to escape an academic tracking system that shunted some youngsters toward industrial jobs while preparing others for college.

African-American pupils encountered overt racial hostility in and around Lane, which lay near Queens in a conservative, predominantly white neighborhood. These and other black adolescents also faced broader social crises, including soaring levels of unemployment. Politicized by urban rebellions, the Vietnam War, the slaying of King, and the global student revolts of 1968, many such youths developed an acute social consciousness. The ASA embodied their rebellious spirit and played a critical role in transmitting Black Power ideas throughout New York schools. By 1969, the group was collaborating with other student organizations to mount rallies and school walkouts. Its members achieved fleeting victories, hoisting a red, black, and green liberation flag over Lane High, and defacing a mural at George Washington High that depicted black slaves kneeling before the nation's first president. However, struggles on behalf of more significant objectives—including control over faculty appointments and curricula, official recognition of Malcolm X's birthday, and creation of drug rehabilitation centers—met staunch resistance and spawned disturbances and arrests.[76]

Weusi had mentored ASA members during summer and after-school sessions and remained a volunteer adviser to the organization following his departure from public education. He saw the youngsters as natural allies—gifted activists deeply committed to social change. He delivered speeches at some of the city's most turbulent student demonstrations and was frequently accused of master-minding the disruptions. Yet he continued to see promise in adolescents who others viewed as menaces. The admiration appeared mutual; after Weusi's dismissal from his teaching position, ASA members helped stage a mock funeral for him in which they served as honorary pallbearers.[77]

Weusi regretted that many of the brightest student activists had become casualties of struggle, receiving suspensions or expulsions for their roles in school disorders. He felt a sense of duty to help steer these youngsters toward college by helping them obtain high school diplomas or equivalencies. At the same time, his search for a revolutionary methodology had led him to the concept of "independent black institutions." He hoped to satisfy his own practical need for employment as well, and his experience organizing Ocean Hill–Brownsville evening classes suggested that opening a private institution might fulfill all these impulses. On the other hand, like many young, African-American radicals, he also considered quitting the United States altogether and "repatriating" to Tanzania, where he could contribute to an authentic nation-building campaign while living and working under the command of the philosopher-statesman Julius Nyerere.

In the end, the native son bypassed East Africa and returned to Central Brooklyn. With cash from a bail fund that he and several ASA members had established, Weusi and his young charges in 1969 acquired a battered but sturdy, industrial-era building at 10 Claver Place near the junction of Bedford-Stuyvesant and Fort Greene. The events of the past year had convinced him that public schools no longer offered viable channels for black liberation. Revisiting JHS 271 that September, he discovered that administrators had instituted "law and order" procedures for suppressing student dissent, and that standard textbooks containing "the lies of this reactionary, exploitive, racist society" had returned to the shelves. He now turned to a new arena of struggle, believing that the abandoned, three-story edifice on Claver could house an institution capable of fulfilling the "revolutionary appetite" of black youth.[78]

"Fertile Soil": Building Uhuru Sasa

Weusi and a dozen hardcore ASA members spent weeks rehabilitating the old warehouse. They restored the interior, their efforts supplemented by the volunteer labor of blue-collar men from the area. The crew of students and workers hauled away debris, repaired plumbing and walls, and installed wiring. Efforts to raise $10,000 in contributions and loans continued as the young activists built a kitchen and converted a second-floor loft. Finally they constructed a stage and sound room; live music would be a key component of the cultural center they envisioned, providing crucial revenue to help support its centerpiece: a private school.

By 1970, the institution that became "the East" (a name that suggested a cultural counterpoint to western traditions) hosted the early installments of "Black Experience in Sound," a series of performances by avant-garde jazz artists. In a display of transnational solidarity, Geddes Granger, a leader of the burgeoning Black Power revolt in Trinidad and Tobago, attended one of the first concerts. Granger's presence was meaningful because the movement he represented embodied many of the elements that would define the East: Pan-African consciousness, the fusion of popular culture and radical politics, mobilization of students and youth, and the erection of parallel institutions designed to expose the illegitimacy of existing apparatuses of authority and governance.[79]

The East flourished. A platform for local artists, its concert series also featured many of the celebrated musicians of the day, especially politically oriented figures like Pharoah Sanders, Max Roach, Sun Ra, and Archie Shepp. As a community center, the East attracted a growing coterie of black nationalists and generated an array of cultural and political initiatives, including cooperative businesses, an African street fair, and a polemical, alternative publication named *Black News*. Yet the educational fate of the ousted ASA students remained uncertain. Weusi and other ATA members hastily created an evening school for the pupils, but the effort lacked a coherent political framework or a guiding philosophy. Forced to reorganize, the circle of educators established an affirmative ideology of self-reliance and crafted an instructional program that they deemed appropriate for the edification of the ASA faithful.

Uhuru Sasa Shule ("Freedom Now School") opened in February 1970 as the educational arm of the East. Originally a part-time junior and senior high for ASA members, the school rapidly expanded into a full-time, coed venture serving elementary grades and preschoolers—mostly youngsters from East New York, Bedford-Stuyvesant, Brownsville, and Flatbush whose working-class parents welcomed alternatives to local public schools. Weusi, Albert Vann, Herman Ferguson, and other ATA members made up the volunteer faculty while a corps of modestly paid instructors (current or former black public school teachers) took shape. Tuition stood at $5 a week. By that fall, dozens of children ages 3 to 17 attended the fledgling school, which grouped youngsters according to ability rather than age. Weusi now presided over an institution designed to train children in both traditional academic subjects and black nationalist principles.

"The minds of these kids is fertile soil," Weusi declared, "but it just lays there in the [public] schools."[80]

Weusi had discovered in Julius Nyerere's "Education for Self-Reliance" a compelling theoretical and pedagogical rationale. The 1967 essay outlined the humanist, cooperative principles that the Tanzanian leader deemed necessary to defeat the lingering cultural grip of the colonial period. Nyerere insisted that without educational systems capable of instilling collectivist values and nationalist ideals, African independence would remain incomplete. Weusi embraced the principle, believing that black America needed to escape a colonial mentality of its own. "Our people have been educated to be dependent upon the institutions of our oppression," he argued. No longer simply a matter of "cultural relevance," a worthwhile black education would prepare black children for political self-determination while inspiring them to pursue "physical nationhood for African people in the western hemisphere."[81]

Yet the challenges of sustaining an upstart establishment in a relatively poor neighborhood while striving to craft the cultural and ethical basis for a new society immediately arose. What did the principle of self-reliance mean in practice? Could Uhuru Sasa maintain financial autonomy while plagued by drafty classrooms, teacher shortages, inadequate instructional materials, and spiraling costs? Could the institution compete with public schools? Could it elude extensive state oversight? What were the practical and academic implications of operating a school that remained, for the moment, unaccredited? What were the social and academic aims of a curriculum built upon the concept of "blackness"? Finally, did private education represent a new frontier for mass action, or was the turn to independent institutions another sign of the black freedom struggle's fragmentation and retreat from radical engagement?

These and other questions loomed throughout 1970 as Uhuru Sasa continued to evolve. It was exhilarating to see similar enterprises emerge throughout the country. "With the increase of correct African institutions our day of liberation, and spiritual salvation, is surely on the set," Weusi proclaimed. As an Uhuru Sasa pamphlet asserted, "We are a Pan-African Nationalist school, meaning that we support and participate in the struggles of Africans worldwide, and, secondly, we are in preparation for Nationhood—ultimate control of our lives."[82]

In the mid- to late 1960s, militant black nationalism intensified and transformed crusades for African-American educational justice. Many students and activists rejected white liberal paternalism and attempted to convert public schools into bailiwicks of radical organizing and progressive theory. The demise of community control marked a major setback. For some activists, however, temporary defeat only confirmed the deficiencies of public education as an agent of meaningful social change. Searching for alternatives, Brooklyn's Jitu Weusi and other dissidents turned to private models, an approach that exemplified the contemporary spirit of social experimentation. Institution building promised to fulfill thwarted ambitions for nationalist development and "self-reliance." Of course, parallel educational structures linked to freedom struggles were hardly unprecedented. Prototypes like Uhuru Sasa built on a long tradition of movement schools.

3

The Evolution of Movement Schools

> At one end of the spectrum is the concept of using parallel institutions
> to transform their Establishment counterparts. . . . At the spectrum's
> other end is the conviction that . . . parallel institutions must survive and
> grow into an anti-Establishment network, a new society.
> —Staughton Lynd, 1965[1]

Though the church is the paramount social institution in African-American life, schools have long played a critical role in the black freedom quest. Educational institutions that arose in the context of mass struggle—identified here as "movement schools"—provided significant models of black autonomy. While all such establishments attempted to develop leaders and offer alternative structures of authority, they varied widely in purpose, ideology, and political meaning. African Americans have historically produced two major streams of emancipatory education: one arising from integrationist politics and another embodying black nationalist and Pan Africanist outlooks. These currents often commingle.[2]

The private schools of Marcus Garvey's Universal Negro Improvement Association and Elijah Muhammad's Nation of Islam served as early precursors to the institutions of the Black Power era. Produced by working-class movements during the period between the world wars, these establishments sought to create a separate, orderly black world as a shield against systemic white racism. By the 1950s and early '60s, Citizenship Schools and freedom schools had emerged as vibrant symbols of the postwar thrust for desegregation and full citizenship.

As the freedom struggle evolved, however, questions resurfaced about whether parallel structures should supplement or supplant the dominant institutions of the larger society. Some "liberation schools" of the late 1960s reflected the search for more permanent alternatives. The discursive shift from "freedom" to "liberation" signaled a transition from efforts to redeem American democracy to attempts to furnish the oppressed with the provisional tools of self-government. This strategic adaptation revived the black nationalist and Pan Africanist tradition of movement schools and helped convert the Student

Nonviolent Coordinating Committee, a key civil rights organization, into a seedbed of Black Power.

"Marcus Garvey Personified": Early Black Nationalist Schools and Uplift Politics

The academies of the Universal Negro Improvement Association (UNIA) and the Nation of Islam provide classic models of the black nationalist schools that arose in the first half of the twentieth century. Both served as ideological progenitors of the independent black institutions of the late 1960s and '70s. Like those later movement schools, UNIA and Nation of Islam models were responses to the structural racism that African Americans encountered amid the search for a "Promised Land" in northern metropolises. Unlike the more politically engaged establishments of the Black Power era, however, UNIA and Nation of Islam schools were cloistered affairs dedicated to racial uplift and to promoting within their ranks the teachings of their charismatic patriarchs.[3] They exemplified visions of a disciplined, inward-looking black nation designed to coexist with a hostile and powerful white society.

Education was central to the aims, ideals, and origins of the UNIA, the massive movement that proliferated among the working classes of the African Diaspora after the First World War. Prior to his arrival in the United States in 1916, UNIA founder Marcus Garvey had planned to establish a trade school and cultural center in Jamaica modeled after Booker T. Washington's Tuskegee Institute. In 1914, he founded the UNIA, whose original goals included the creation of colleges and secondary schools for "boys and girls of the race." Many of the UNIA branches that later emerged in North America and the Caribbean operated elementary schools as part of their programs of cultural enrichment. The organization's 1920 "Declaration of the Rights of the Negro Peoples of the World" condemned racist materials in public schools and demanded the introduction of black history curricula.[4]

UNIA officials briefly operated a Booker T. Washington University in Harlem as part of their efforts to produce a leadership class devoted to racial advancement and cultural regeneration. In the late 1930s, Garvey personally presided over a School of African Philosophy in Toronto, a rigorous training course for future UNIA organizers. Yet it was the short-lived Liberty University that embodied Garveyite dreams of redemptive education. The coed institution, actually a "practical" high school, emerged in 1926 when the UNIA acquired Smallwood-Corey Normal and Industrial Institute, a stately but aging enterprise located in Claremont, Virginia, along the banks of the St. James River. Beset with financial woes, Liberty closed in 1929, having offered a handful of Garveyites a

vocational education combined with elements of the liberal arts, including reci-
tations of Paul Laurence Dunbar poems and accounts of the scientific genius of
ancient Egyptians.[5]

Liberty University generated immense enthusiasm among the UNIA faithful. Inaugural exercises on the sprawling campus featured hymns, prayers, a procession of UNIA dignitaries, and uniformed regiments of the Universal African
League and the Black Cross Nurses. W. A. Wallace, the organization's secretary
general, delivered remarks on the theme of "the New Education for the Negro."
As he lamented, "Not five out of 100 of [black] high school boys or girls of
today can tell you of the achievements of three of their race outside of Douglass,
Washington and Dunbar." Liberty, Wallace maintained, would help furnish the
Negro with "the same kind of stimulant that has kept the Japanese proud of a
Japanese, the white proud of a white, and the Chinaman proud of a Chinaman."[6]

Garvey scholar Barbara Bair has observed that, "The true frame of reference
for Liberty University was not the current Jim Crow realities of the United States
but the future possibilities of an independent Africa." Indeed, *all* UNIA educational endeavors were undertaken in the name of racial edification and Pan
African redemption. The Negro, Garvey insisted, "is never thoroughly educated
until he has imbibed racial education." Such instruction would occur in private
arenas far removed from the white world. In Garvey's view, the Negro could no
more expect to receive a worthwhile education from the white majority than
one could expect a stranger "to give you the clothing that you need to cover
your own body." Instead, black people were to acquire a dual education like the
Jew, who receives "the education of the state" and of his people, and therefore
"knows all about the Gentile while the Gentile knows nothing of him."[7]

The UNIA's pedagogical efforts were eminently practical. Individual branches
offered adult classes in basic literacy, nursing, and nutrition. Seen as natural
teachers, women bore primary responsibility for instruction, and thus strongly
influenced the cultural arts of "nation building." Despite the grassroots appeal of
UNIA politics, Garveyite educational philosophies contained deep elements of
conservatism. The movement sought to enable "educated Negroes" to "assume
proper leadership of the race"—an objective that reflected Progressive Era sensibilities and ingrained class biases. "The majority of the Negroes," Garvey believed,
were ignorant and needed educational enrichment to escape a condition akin to
what would later be described as "cultural deprivation." UNIA officials saw social
rehabilitation as central to African redemption, and embraced enculturation as
a political and pedagogical goal. As the organization's supreme leader acknowledged, "I am trying to make everyone a Marcus Garvey personified."[8]

Emphasis on re-education also shaped the instructional endeavors of the
Nation of Islam (NOI), whose independent schools built upon the UNIA model
while proving more enduring. The full time primary and secondary schools

of the "University of Islam" emerged in the early 1930s as the religious body was forming in black Detroit. The earliest version of what became a network of parochial schools took shape in the home of Elijah Muhammad, the Nation's "Messenger." Muhammad's wife, Clara, served as the school's first teacher, faithfully training the children of the expanding congregation.

NOI schools attempted to prepare black children from the age of three to "know self," "love self," and "do for self," a precursor to the Black Power trinity of self-respect, self-determination, and self-defense. Public schools, Muhammad taught, had been "designed by the slave masters" to keep African Americans docile and dependent. The black man "cannot build a future with white people in his mind," the Messenger insisted. African Americans required an education shielded from white control. This devotion to independent, black nationalist instruction aroused the suspicion of authorities. Intelligence and law enforcement agents began monitoring the NOI and its academies—which initially lacked state authorization—almost from their inception. Detroit police raided the city's University of Islam and seized its records in 1934 after scores of black parents began withdrawing their children from local public schools and enrolling them in the Muslim institution. Muhammad and other NOI members were arrested and charged with contributing to the delinquency of minors, and officials attempted to close the parochial school before riotous parishioners forced the establishment of an uneasy modus vivendi between the temple and the city.[9]

White officialdom accused the University of Islam of sheltering a dark and secretive curriculum. In 1962, an Illinois state legislator launched an unsuccessful campaign to shutter the Chicago campus, charging that it taught "race hatred" and arguing that its very existence encouraged "other 'nut' groups to open their own schools." In truth, the Nation's academies were no more exotic than were the parochial schools of other insular, religious orders; even the 1934 police raid revealed nothing more sensational than the devotion of the "Mohammedans" to teaching "general knowledge of spook civilization," a reference to Christian society.[10] Apart from Arabic and a set of idiosyncratic catechisms that combined numerology and religious doctrine, the University of Islam curriculum—arithmetic, science, English, and French—was prosaic. Even the stern, math–science focus reflected the unexceptional belief that raising a nation required the expertise of a generation of technicians. The Muslims supplemented standard grade-school textbooks with homespun materials and publications like *Negro Makers of History* by Carter G. Woodson and *Africa's Gift to America* by J. A. Rogers.[11]

The University of Islam exemplified the NOI's obsession with order and discipline. Students were urged to "gather fruit from the tree of knowledge." Some Muslim teachers emphasized academic drills and rote learning. Their pupils chanted multiplication tables in sync, performing military-style pivots (Left Face! Right Face!), as instructors issued Arabic commands. A somber motto adorned a wall at the Chicago campus: "There is no substitute for intelligence; the nearest thing to it is silence." Classes spanned all but two weeks of the year. Recess, art class, and other "frills" were proscribed. Single-sex classes discouraged "sweethearting," and a rigid dress code (jacket and tie for boys, headscarves and long dresses for girls) was enforced. Dietary regulations and hair and fingernail inspections reinforced the martial aura.[12]

The preoccupation with discipline stemmed in part from the notion that racism had severely damaged the African-American psyche, a familiar theme in American intellectual history.[13] The image of "the so-called Negro" as a creature in need of moral and psychological reconstruction continued to define the NOI worldview. As one University of Islam administrator asserted, only the Messenger could transform "a smiling and shuffling" people into a productive nation. This ethic of rehabilitation did not hinder the growth of the University of Islam. By 1965, the system, which operated on tuition fees and tithes, served 2,000 students in eight schools, including campuses in Los Angeles, Atlanta, Philadelphia, and Boston. Ten years later, 40 more schools had appeared. A Harlem campus opened in 1969 with an enrollment of 500 and soon developed a waiting list of 200 children, most of them non-Muslims. A benefit for the academies held that year at New York's posh Waldorf-Astoria Hotel drew an array of black personages, from local politicians to cultural figures.[14]

Black urbanites whose children were consigned to deteriorating public schools generally viewed the Muslim academies as welcome alternatives. Parents liked the brass-tacks curriculum, the record of boosting academic achievement, and the reputation for eliminating drugs, truancy, and disorder. "There is no juvenile delinquency in Islam," an NOI couple declared in a 1957 letter to the *Pittsburgh Courier*, another reason, the two suggested, that African Americans should "stop fighting and trying to go to those integrated schools." The University of Islam represented only one component of an NOI empire that by the 1960s included bakeries, restaurants, supermarkets, and farms. Operators of the schools sponsored regular field trips to NOI businesses, excursions designed to celebrate independent black enterprise.[15] However, regimenting the black working class and cultivating petit-bourgeois ambitions hardly constituted a viable strategy for mass liberation. It would fall to a new generation of organizers to determine whether emancipatory education could transcend the pieties of moral uplift and black capitalism.

"What Do We Want to Keep?": Freedom Schools and the Promise of Citizenship

Like their black nationalist predecessors, movement schools of the post–World War II era illustrated the political possibilities of education and the enduring faith in its transformative capacity. Yet they represented a different set of priorities than those of the UNIA and NOI academies. A burgeoning African-American insurgency and the crumbling edifice of formal segregation provided a new context for the creation of parallel institutions. The autonomous establishments of the 1950s and early '60s reflected the contemporary struggle's demand for full access to the privileges and prosperity of American citizenship.

The freedom schools of the first half of the 1960s embodied the optimism of the period, a moment when black mass mobilization seemed capable of redeeming America. The institutions honored the conviction that the leadership of everyday people was essential to the process of democratic change. The most influential freedom schools operated under the banner of the 1964 Mississippi Freedom Summer, a set of programs sponsored by the Council of Federated Organizations but largely administered by the youthful Student Nonviolent Coordinating Committee (SNCC), the radical wing of the southern movement for racial equality.

The Mississippi Freedom Schools drew upon a tradition of antiracist education that emphasized participatory democracy, grassroots struggle, and human rights. For years, Tennessee's Highlander Folk School had conveyed these principles while training groups of adults to do political work among laborers and the rural poor. NAACP Youth Councils and the "Nonviolent High" of McComb, Mississippi—a project created by SNCC in 1961—offered additional models of emancipatory education, as did the Prince Edward County, Virginia, freedom schools that emerged in 1963. Northern freedom schools, another antecedent, arose in the early 1960s amid the huge desegregation boycotts that unfolded in Chicago, New York, Boston, and other cities.[16]

Citizenship Schools, a Highlander Folk School initiative adopted by the Southern Christian Leadership Conference in 1961, also served as precursors to the Mississippi Freedom Schools. Organized by South Carolina activist Septima Clark, the adult education project revived traditions of civic activism and prepared African-American southerners to pass literacy tests required for voter registration. Citizenship Schools imparted practical skills while helping adults comprehend and resist systemic oppression. They also reflected a sense of confidence in the nation's essentially democratic character, an article of faith that would come to seem glaringly naïve. During a 1964 discussion of the value of Citizenship Schools, for example, Clark echoed a major premise of Cold War liberalism, asserting that "changes in the structure of the government and all phases of life [are] required *if our democratic government is to survive and be the model for the new nations recently born.*"[17]

The 1964 Mississippi Freedom Schools exhibited similar philosophical complexity. The schools, which operated in borrowed or makeshift facilities, relied heavily on the scores of northern, mostly white and middle-class college students that Freedom Summer brought to the Deep South. These recruits joined black activists who were engaged in organizing poor, African-American communities in a climate of violence and repression. The overall goal of the summer campaign was to erect temporary institutions that could challenge Mississippi's racial caste system, invigorating the local struggle and helping democratize a closed society.

As SNCC organizer and Freedom School originator Charlie Cobb noted, most public schools serving black Mississippians were "wastelands" that destroyed intellectual curiosity. Education was a central component of "the apparatus of oppression" that relegated many of the state's residents to conditions of servitude. Cobb envisioned a program for black teenagers that could fill an intellectual vacuum, encouraging youngsters to "articulate their own desires, demands and questions" and "challenge the myths of our society." Beyond reinforcing academic skills, Freedom Schools would help usher young people into the movement by creating a statewide leadership cadre "committed to critical thinking and social action." To accomplish this, Freedom School instructors practiced an egalitarian pedagogy that affirmed SNCC's commitment to internal democracy and grass-roots leadership. Freewheeling workshops promoted independent thought, and didactic or authoritarian teaching methods were shunned.[18]

This approach helped ensure the project's success. Over the course of the summer, more than 2,000 students—mostly older children, adolescents, and young adults—attended Freedom Schools throughout the state. The classes contrasted with the "standard bleached product" dispensed by Mississippi public schools. "The only thing our kids knew about Negro history was about Booker T. Washington and George Washington Carver and his peanuts," Freedom School coordinator Ralph Featherstone later recalled. Now Freedom School pupils studied everything from the birth of Haiti to Joseph Cinque's 1839 slave revolt aboard the *Amistad*. They also engaged in critical theory. One Freedom School exercise posed a series of questions that encouraged students to analyze mainstream values and those of the movement: "What does the majority culture have that we want? What does the majority culture have that we don't want? What do we have that we want to keep?"[19]

Freedom Schools helped African Americans overcome the paralyzing fear of dissent that pervaded Mississippi culture. They encouraged young people to question white supremacy, a heretical act in the Deep South. "We hadn't even heard that word, 'political power,' because it wasn't taught in the black schools," civil rights worker and native Mississippian Unita Blackwell later remembered. As one scholar noted, "The road from study to action was short." Those who attended the schools began to appear at mass rallies, participate in boycotts, or volunteer to canvass during voter registration drives. "The Freedom School is inspiring the people to lend a hand in the fight," Ralph Featherstone remarked that summer. "The older people are looking to the young people, and their courage is rubbing off."[20]

But questions about the nature of racism and inequality were already puncturing the optimism of Freedom Summer. Even before the movement's failed challenge to the segregationist Mississippi delegation at the 1964 Democratic National Convention—a development that spurred the radicalization of a generation of activists—serious doubts arose within the integrationist struggle about the merits of liberal democracy and nonviolent action. Even as the passage of the 1964 Civil Rights Act ended the formal reign of segregation, the actual apparatus of oppression began to seem vaster and more intractable than the one expiring with the doomed Jim Crow regime.

Historian Daniel Perlstein argues that Freedom Summer represented a moment in which the civil rights movement "simultaneously expressed itself with the rhetoric of American democracy and sought to restructure radically American society." The notion that critical citizenship and mass action could help democratize the country was a major Freedom School premise. Yet instructors also attempted to enable youngsters to recognize "the link between a rotting shack and a rotting America." Some Freedom Schools reflected the ideal of interracialism. (One SNCC organizer defined them as "any place where young people, whether black or white, rich or poor, come to deal with questions as they relate to their lives"). But the irony of white teachers urging African-American youths to exercise independent intellectual and political agency proved unsettling. Signs of waning faith in liberal reform appeared. "What does it mean to be in a mainstream of a cesspool?" SNCC worker Jimmy Garrett asked. "What does it mean to be called a 'normal' American in a decayed society?"[21]

The question of black autonomy deepened the crisis. Freedom Schools, George W. Chilcoat and Jerry A. Ligon have observed, were designed to "parallel but contrast with the repressive, discriminatory Mississippi schools." Freedom Summer organizers had originally proposed "crash programs" that could operate *alongside* existing institutions. "We must think of our programs ultimately as supplementing, not replacing, the regular social institutions," they declared, expressing the widespread desire to both improve and integrate mainstream establishments. However, Charlie Cobb's emphasis on "building our own institutions to replace the old, unjust decadent ones" suggested that competing impulses were present from the start.[22]

The creation of Freedom Schools raised the possibility of forming more permanent structures—separate if not entirely *separatist*—to engage in ideological competition with the dominant society. The very existence of the schools suggested the flourishing of what observers described as black "para-governments," or grassroots mechanisms of governance able to perform some traditional functions of the state while remaining independent of white authority. For some members of the southern movement, the emergence of autonomous structures like Freedom Schools occasioned "the first break in our desire to integrate." As early as fall 1964, SNCC leader Bob Moses began identifying the nationalist principles inherent in parallel institutions. "Why can't we set up our own schools?" he asked during one civil rights conference. "Because when you come right down to it, why integrate their schools? What is it that you will learn in their schools?" It was not long before SNCC staffers began discussing the need for black people to erect their own governments and simply declare the existing one null and void.[23]

"After Atlantic City": SNCC, Black Consciousness, and the Demise of Civil Rights Mentality

The political evolution that reshaped the integrationist, southern movement is familiar to students of the freedom struggle. Over the course of the 1960s, civil rights and antipoverty activists tested the limits of formal equality, critiquing integrationist reform, moral suasion, and nonviolent insurgency, and adopting more radical methods of social change. Shifts in the thought and practice of young organizers influenced black politics throughout the United States and beyond. SNCC's metamorphosis was particularly significant. The group provides an ideal case study in political transformation, in part because it encompassed many of the tendencies that defined radical politics in the late 1960s and '70s. SNCC workers and their northern allies helped forge the political paths that later converged in the form of alternative, Pan Africanist institutions.

An outgrowth of the sit-in crusades of 1960, SNCC embodied the impatience of black college students and other young people who demanded *Freedom Now*. Some portion of its staff embraced the spiritual tenets of nonviolent social change. Other organizers regarded nonviolence more as a pragmatic strategy for achieving desired reforms. In the early days, many SNCC workers equated black liberation with full inclusion in the American social order. As belief in the nation's legitimacy unraveled, broader processes of radicalization took shape.

Fissures in the civil rights coalition and in SNCC's liberal reformism widened in 1963 and 1964. In those years the Cambridge, Maryland, movement transcended nonviolent, integrationist protest; the March on Washington demonstrated how co-optation could deflate black militancy; an audience in Atlanta with Kenyan freedom fighter Oginga Odinga revealed the promise of transnational black solidarity; the outbreak of urban rebellions provided a new touchstone of radicalism; and the defeat of the Mississippi Freedom Democratic Party's quest to unseat the white supremacist Mississippi delegation at the Democratic National Convention in Atlantic City exposed the liberal establishment's hypocrisy and commitment to the status quo. "After Atlantic City," SNCC's Cleveland Sellers later recalled, "our struggle was not for civil rights, but for liberation."[24]

Between 1965 and 1966, alienation and indictment replaced skepticism and doubt. Revolutionary impulses within SNCC deepened amid the bloody debacle of the Selma campaign; the patent constraints of the Voting Rights Act; the explosive power of the Watts, Los Angeles, uprising; and the naked imperialism of the Vietnam War. What historian Clayborne Carson calls "the search for radical political alternatives" crystallized in the rise of independent black political parties like Alabama's Lowndes County Freedom Organization and "black consciousness" splinter movements like the Atlanta Project. In time, the rhetoric of human rights and armed self-defense (long an integral reality of southern, black life) eclipsed the discourse of civil rights and nonviolence. Fanon (a theorist of armed, anticolonial revolution) displaced Camus (an existentialist associated with the ethic of nonviolence) in SNCC's literary repertoire, and the organization expanded its vision of the insurgent Third World and urban landscapes, North and South, as critical realms of struggle. In the context of these changes, the Stokely Carmichael and Willie Ricks cry for "Black Power" in summer 1966—a development that the news media greeted with "warnings of an imminent racial cataclysm"—conferred a populist slogan on a political transfiguration that was already underway.[25]

SNCC imploded in subsequent years, disintegrating amid repression, factionalism, and internal discord. Its dwindling cadre ejected the few remaining white staff members and developed ill-fated alliances with groups like the Black Panthers. Yet SNCC's demise illuminated future trajectories. The organization's black nationalist awakening, a reflection of the belief that the movement "must be black controlled, dominated and led," anticipated more vigorous efforts to establish parallel institutions. Its internationalism, forged in opposition to Western imperialist exploits in Vietnam, the Dominican Republic, Palestine, Southern Africa, and elsewhere, heralded more sophisticated expressions of anticolonialism and Third Worldism. Its captivation with Africa, an identification strengthened in 1964 by a SNCC delegation visit to Guinea, stimulated lifelong engagement with diasporic politics and Pan Africanism. Its nascent anticapitalism, bred by encounters with the underside of the "American way of life," generated Leninist, Maoist, and radical feminist currents that contributed to a brief but powerful resurgence of independent Marxism in the West.[26]

Malcolm X helped foster each of these radical tendencies. The future patron saint of Black Power exerted growing influence on SNCC's young corps after 1962.[27] By the time of his assassination in 1965, he had inspired the revolutionary visions that helped deliver many activists from elements of parochialism that had hampered earlier phases of the movement. In the years after the leader's death, cadres of SNCC personnel, along with other civil rights workers, shed the vestiges of domestic reformism and initiated a host of projects that reflected the political insights of Brother Malcolm.

"Shake These Kids": The Rebirth of Black Nationalist Schools

The transformation of the freedom struggle changed the nature of movement schools. Young organizers continued to embrace the proposition that "an entire school system can be created in any community outside the official order and critical of its suppositions," as scholar-activist Howard Zinn had observed.[28] But no longer preoccupied with the moral redemption of American society, many activists adopted organizing strategies designed to revolutionize black culture and consciousness. During the mid- to late 1960s, autonomous black education reflected the ideological shifts that redefined mass revolt.

SNCC's 1965 black history primer, a booklet designed for use in movement schools across the country, signaled coming changes. On one hand, the primer conveyed much of the spirit of the northern and southern freedom schools of 1963–1964, which had cast black Americans as inheritors of a national heritage of liberty. The 1965 publication placed the black movement within the liberal tradition of the American Revolution. However, the booklet also presented a series of pointed critiques, asking, "Why does the United States support dictators and racists in other countries?" and "As machines put more and more people out of work, what will these people do?" The very origins of the primer suggested growing militancy. Created by a SNCC field secretary and graphic artist as a way to celebrate traditions of political agitation, the publication had stemmed from dissatisfaction with *Color Me Brown*, a children's book dismissed by young activists as "a rotten, bourgeois sort of thing that played up Booker T. [Washington] and didn't even mention Nat Turner or Du Bois."[29]

Other SNCC ventures that summer also presaged future efforts. The organization's first and only residential freedom school allowed a handful of organizers and young adults to confront the complexities of contemporary politics. The project enabled two sets of teenagers—one from Cordele, Georgia, and another from South Side Chicago—to spend almost two months living together in each location while exploring shared social realities. The effort was designed to demonstrate that "the same man was on the back of all Negroes, North and South," thereby forging a sense of unity and underscoring the national character of the freedom struggle. The school bolstered awareness. Students discussed police brutality and African identity, debated protest strategies, met West African dignitaries, visited a Nation of Islam mosque, and analyzed the internal contradictions of black nationalism.

But the program collided with the realities of inner-city life. Debates over nonviolent theory and practice occurred amid one of Chicago's ongoing turf battles. "The kids had to negotiate daily the reality of urban violence," SNCC member Fannie Theresa Rushing later explained. The teenagers pushed organizers to acknowledge the philosophical and practical inconsistencies of nonviolence. One SNCC staffer conceded that the tactic was useful only in the presence of television cameras. As discussions of the potential for armed revolt in the United States unfolded, instructors recognized the challenge they faced transplanting the Mississippi Freedom School model to urban centers. "We went into the South Side talking about 'freedom,' which to the southern kids meant the vote, education, eating where you wanted to, etc.," SNCC's Judy Richardson later recalled. "But 'freedom' to the South Side kids meant getting out of the ghetto . . . and you don't get out of the ghetto with nonviolence."[30]

The experience of the Child Development Group of Mississippi (CDGM) further highlighted the limitations of existing movement schools. Freedom Summer participant Tom Levin, originator of the CDGM concept, had envisioned a system of preschools that shared the Freedom School spirit. An antipoverty initiative under the auspices of Head Start, CDGM would enable Mississippi's poor, black residents to exert greater control over the destinies of their children while addressing their desire to direct their own lives. SNCC workers were skeptical. "Now totally alienated from the federal government," historian John Dittmer explains, "SNCC saw the War on Poverty as a blatant move to co-opt the movement. And while CDGM was a natural extension of the freedom schools and based on egalitarian principles, it was a program conceived and developed by white northerners."[31]

Yet CDGM produced some remarkable victories. A pioneering model of early childhood education, the program employed scores of poor, black women—many of them former maids or farm workers—and armed them with the tools of self-determination. Head Start in Mississippi, SNCC staffers conceded in 1965, had proven to be "radically conceived" and effective. CDGM "offered both parents and teachers a direction away from a state education system unworthy of the name," one writer acknowledged. "It encouraged the exciting notion of community participation in education rather than turning education over to the professionals. It provided social services and medical programs, which demonstrated the corruption and inadequacies of state and federal offerings." Running preschool centers, another observer noted, helped convince many African-American mothers that rather than subject their children to "foreign customs, language and values" or train them to "scorn and escape their origins," education could help them seize their fate. Some activists came to view CDGM as a crucial vehicle for fostering "the next generation of movement children."[32]

But the stratagems of Mississippi segregationists embroiled the program in controversy. Seeing a threat to their hegemony, reactionary politicians accused CDGM workers of funneling money to black militants. Swirling charges of communism and corruption finally toppled CDGM; in 1966, federal officials shifted control of Head Start in Mississippi to a board of industrialists and other figures agreeable to the state's power structure. In the end, CDGM served as another cautionary tale for young radicals. The program's defeat, activist Jean Smith later recalled, "required me to abandon my last hope that American society would willingly make room for us."[33]

Resentment of the machinations of white power made 1966 a decisive year for SNCC and its theories of emancipatory education. That spring, when members of the organization's Atlanta Project assembled to imagine a new program of urban freedom schools, their plans reflected the critiques that would engender Black Power. "Our experience has taught us something about this country—it lies," activist Bill Ware proclaimed during the meeting. "In Freedom Schools we intend to tell it like it is; to get down to the nitty-gritty; to tell our history and the country's history." Participants at the gathering now saw Charlie Cobb's original 1964 Freedom Schools prospectus as largely irrelevant. Whereas Cobb had regarded Mississippi schools as anomalous, organizers now believed that black Americans across the country faced equally contemptible systems of education. The Atlanta staff further rejected the premise, ostensibly present in earlier freedom schools, that outsiders were needed "to bring light to Mississippi Negroes."

The Atlanta activists affirmed SNCC's traditions of grassroots empowerment. They continued to see freedom schools as a means of supplementing academic skills, rebuilding pride, and cultivating poor, African-American communities. They discussed the need to offer instruction not only in African history and international affairs but also in practical legal principles. Rather than grapple with abstract concepts, students could design housing programs or attend meetings of police review boards. The Atlanta Project began soliciting donated books about black American and African history, recognizing that "Very few people in this country know the real story about the 'dark' continent or its 'dark' peoples." Staffers rejected escapism. "Don't sit around talking about going back to Africa," one member cautioned. However, the activists also displayed growing interest in radicalizing African Americans by "creating little insurgencies"—indigenous cadres not overtly linked to SNCC but devoted to disseminating its political philosophies within poor, black communities. Atlanta organizers believed that only a disciplined and militant freedom school faculty—a body immersed in the tenets of black consciousness—could fulfill this mission. "We want to shake these kids," SNCC worker Gwen Robinson explained. "We want to get over to these kids that they live in a depraved society."[34]

In 1967, another vehicle for doing so emerged. That year a Nashville "liberation school" named for slave rebel Nat Turner supplied a new model of autonomous black education and provided further evidence of the scale of the repression that SNCC faced. Operators of the school included Fred Brooks, chair of SNCC's Nashville chapter, and George Ware, the organization's campus coordinator. Both were visible Black Power advocates; Ware had been among those arrested that spring when a Stokely Carmichael visit to Nashville prompted a police crackdown that in turn ignited a riot among black college students. Brooks and Ware helped organize the part-time liberation school amid a national upsurge of black student activism. The school operated three times a week during the summer and served as many as 100 youngsters ages six and up. Its staff included Tennessee State and Fisk University undergraduates who shared SNCC's commitment to exposing local children to black history and culture.

Modeled after the freedom schools, the venture also embodied Black Power sensibilities. Its classroom featured maps of Africa and its instructors stressed that nonviolence "only works because there is a threat of violence." Math, basic reading, crafts, and swimming supplemented the political aspects of the curriculum, another reason many African-American parents welcomed the project. Yet officials within and beyond Nashville mounted a concerted effort to portray the school as virulently antiwhite. Nashville's police captain testified before the U.S. Senate Judiciary Committee that the institution, which received support from one of the city's antipoverty agencies, taught "hatred of the white man." Brooks defended the school and its personnel, declaring, "If [black children] become angry when they learn the truth about the white man, that is not my responsibility."[35]

Conservative congressmen looking to discredit poverty programs and depict black militants as instigators of urban insurrections continued to vilify the school. Federal agents targeted the establishment as part of a government campaign to monitor and disrupt black political activities. Persecution within Nashville intensified. Administrators of the local community action agency made no fewer than 18 visits to the school in a vain search for signs of impropriety. Facing growing pressure, the Episcopal chapel that had hosted the school finally evicted the operation, and Ware was arrested and charged with sedition in connection with statements he had made about the need for black people to acquire power by any means. Eventually the displaced school was forced to convene in a public park, a facility from which authorities promptly removed all benches, picnic tables, and waste cans. The liberation school survived, for the moment. That fall, in a display of defiance, its faculty staged a skit based on Nat Turner's 1831 revolt, a production that required students to pretend to hack white slaveholders to death.[36]

As the brief life of the Nashville institution suggests, the shift from "freedom schools" to "liberation schools" marked a critical transition. While "freedom" evoked the civil rights ideal of equality before the law, "liberation" implied an uncompromising embrace of self-rule. Malcolm X's Organization of Afro-American Unity (OAAU) designated the Harlem weekend school that it established in 1964 a "liberation" school. The operation reflected the political priorities of the OAAU, including opposition to U.S. imperialism and solidarity with progressive African nations. James E. Campbell, the radical educator responsible for the school, saw the venture as an extension of contemporary movement schools. According to historian William Sales, Campbell envisioned "a synthesis between the freedom school orientation toward citizenship and the OAAU orientation toward Pan-African internationalism." The Revolutionary Action Movement, a radical formation closely linked to Malcolm X and to elements within SNCC, also advocated liberation schools as a means of teaching urban black children survival skills that would enable them to avoid "mass extermination."[37]

Temporary enterprises identified as "freedom schools" and linked to mass struggles continued to appear during the late 1960s, but it was the idiom of "liberation" that captured the zeitgeist. Several more SNCC liberation schools materialized. The one linked to the organization's Los Angeles chapter was organized by radical intellectual Angela Davis. In 1968, Davis instituted a curriculum that featured courses on Third World freedom struggles, community organizing, and Marxist theory. She saw the school as "a place where political understanding was forged and sharpened, where consciousness became explicit and was urged in a revolutionary direction." As SNCC's dissolution entered its final stages in 1969, leaders of another ephemeral outgrowth of the group, the Black Revolutionary Action Party, made plans to construct liberation schools that might "create new men and women committed to justice and the liberation of all colonized people."[38]

"A Heavy Rap": Black Panther Liberation Schools and the Ethics of Pedagogy

The most influential liberation schools belonged to the Panthers. The Black Panther Party, a formation that emerged in late 1966 as a means of defending urban black neighborhoods against police brutality, began establishing summertime liberation schools in 1969 to supplement its popular free breakfast programs. The party had started implementing "socialistic and educational programs" that focused on meeting the everyday needs of African-American inner-city residents. Designed to address concrete problems of hunger, health, and education, the initiatives represented what Chicago Panther Fred Hampton called "socialism in action," or the direct provision of social services as a demonstration of communitarian ideals.

By summer 1969, Panthers were serving hot, daily meals to as many as 15,000 children in New York, Chicago, Detroit, Boston, Los Angeles, Kansas City, and the San Francisco Bay Area. "We know that they are hungry because when we were kids we were hungry," one Panther explained. Black Panther Minister of Information Eldridge Cleaver summarized the program's political intent: "If we can understand Breakfast for Children," he said, "can we not also understand Lunch for Children, and Dinner for Children, and Clothing for Children, and Education for Children, and Medical Care for Children?[39]

Liberation schools reflected a key element of the party's platform: "We want education for our people that exposes the true nature of this decadent American society. We want education that teaches us our true history and our role in the present-day society." Panther schools convened in church basements, housing projects, and cultural centers. Conceived as temporary measures, many of the part-time institutions continued to meet intermittently during the school year, supplementing the public education of grade schoolers and adolescents in hard-scrabble neighborhoods. By 1970, scores of Panther chapters across the country operated liberation schools, most of which featured young Panthers as instructors. Some of the establishments opened with as many as 90 registered children, though enrollment was typically more modest. Like other radical enterprises, the schools were designed to infuse youngsters with revolutionary fervor and enable them to "survive this corrupt system and build a new one that serves the people."[40]

Panther schools conveyed the organization's basic political principles. Classes for older children provided a simplified version of the training in "Marxist-Leninist, Mao Tse-Tung Thought" that the Panther rank and file received. Party guidelines stipulated that individual schools were to undergo a strict approval process to ensure that "not one incorrect idea" reached the youth. Panther propaganda needed to be powerful so that when students returned to public schools, "all they will have on their minds is revolution." Liberation schools taught youngsters to identify the entire cast of Panther antagonists, including capitalists and landlords ("the avaricious business pig" or "the big, fat businessman"), law enforcement agents ("the police pig and the National Guard pig"), and crooked politicians ("the President pig"). Students gained a sense of personal connection to Panther leaders. "Dear Bobby Seale, We are fine in Liberation School," one pupil wrote in fall 1969, addressing the organization's chairman. "I am sorry you are in jail." Liberation school students were taught a triumphant refrain about Cleaver, who had fled the country to escape legal prosecution: "Where's Eldridge? He's free, eating watermelon and the pigs can't touch him."[41]

The Panther curriculum displayed elements of creativity. Liberation school instructors arranged field trips to allow children "to check out the genocide" inherent in dilapidated tenements lined with poisonous, exposed lead pipes. Classes covered "the history of the oppression of poor people," providing academic reinforcement while featuring revolutionary songs, discussion of current events, and analysis of cartoons from the Panther newspaper. Principles of class struggle were translated into simple and accessible concepts. The value of inter-racial, proletarian solidarity was a prominent curricular theme. Children learned to identify themselves as "little changers" who belonged to a "BIG FAMILY" or global community of oppressed people. Members of the big family, they were taught, "do not hit or swear at the brothers and sisters. We are all brothers and sisters because we are all not free."[42]

Panther schools honored progressive traditions of emancipatory education by emphasizing pragmatic content (including training in basic legal aid) and affirming the political potential of poor and working-class African Americans. As one liberation school teacher stated, "We recognize that education is only relevant when it teaches the art of survival." Panthers assured themselves that "The message that the kids were getting wasn't a straight, heavy rap." As prominent party member Assata Shakur later observed, "We were all dead set against cramming things in [the children's] heads or teaching them meaningless rote phrases." There were signs that students grasped ideas like "All Power to the People," a slogan that some youngsters accurately interpreted as "taking power away from the few and giving it to the many."[43]

However, evidence of heavy-handed pedagogy also emerged, and the Panthers were frequently accused of using liberation schools and free break-fasts to indoctrinate youngsters. As historian Joy Ann Williamson has observed, "Panther educational ideals did not always translate into practice." Liberation school teachers combined didactic approaches with more open-ended techniques. Some instructors believed it was necessary to "conquer" the minds of their students. Panther Defense Minister Huey P. Newton argued that "The sleeping masses must be bombarded with the correct approach to the struggle." At times, liberation school attendees seemed to spout slogans mechanically. "I am a revolutionary!" the children in one Oakland, California, school chorused during a 1969 session. "I love Huey P. Newton! I love Eldridge Cleaver! I love Bobby Seale! I love being revolutionary! I feel good! Off the pigs! Power to the people!"[44]

Some liberation schools were geared toward rhetoric and memorization. One sample lesson based on the party's political platform encouraged "reverse method" recitation, a pedagogical style reminiscent of Nation of Islam cat-echisms. An instructor would provide the platform's first demand: "We want the power to determine the destiny of our black community." Why, he or she would then ask, do we want this power? Students would deliver the prescribed response: "We believe that black people will not be free until we are able to determine our destiny." The Panthers insisted that pupils absorbed the politi-cal concepts. The children's comprehension "manifests itself in their definitions, i.e. Revolution means Change; Revolutionaries are Changers; Liberation means Freedom," party officials declared.[45] The organization, of course, had painstak-ingly inculcated these catchphrases.

Many rank-and-file Panthers no doubt viewed any form of indoctrination as inimical to the organization's values. The most pressing concerns of liberation school operators, however, were fluctuating enrollments, budget and staffing shortages, and frequent closings. Many black churches refused to open their facilities to the Panthers, and efforts by law enforcement and federal agents to undermine, neutralize, and destroy the organization—a crusade described by one scholar as "far-reaching, comprehensive, and vile"—frequently targeted lib-eration schools. (Police forced the closure of one Panther school in Richmond, California, just hours into its opening day.)[46]

Still, the party's schools successfully exposed black youths and their families to eclectic visions of socialism, revolutionary nationalism, and internationalism. Future black radical institutions would struggle to reconcile the ideals of Third World Marxism and black nationhood that Panther pedagogy inventively fused. In time, the strain of ideological and other contradictions—and the violence of state repression—would exact a massive toll on the party. Yet by develop-ing a provocative model of radical pedagogy, the Panthers demonstrated that movement schools could successfully overcome their traditional linkages to bourgeois nationalism and liberal reform. The great contribution of the libera-tion schools, Seale asserted in 1969, was their capacity to teach black children to identify "pigs" of all colors. As the leader explained, "We're going to be talking about downing the class system, cultural nationalists and capitalists, both black and white, who are the same: exploitative."[47]

"A Revolution Inside": Freedom Library Day School and Black Self-Concept

The new black nationalist institutions embodied the conviction that liberation requires an internal conversion. If Black Power produced a defining principle, it was that revolution in the streets could not succeed without a correspond-ing revolution "in the winding corridors of the mind." Radical theorist Julius

Lester echoed a host of Third World thinkers when he asserted that, "The colonized must kill themselves and awaken the unborn within before they can address themselves directly to the colonizer." Acts of self-mastery, along with collective will to metamorphose from an oppressed minority to a sovereign people, were necessary if black Americans were to seize what Stokely Carmichael called the "dictatorship of definition"—the power to interpret and control their own realities.[48] Freedom Library Day School, a shoestring operation housed in a North Philadelphia storefront, represented an early attempt to institutionalize this consciousness.

Freedom Library's reputation as a stronghold of militancy reflected the vision and labors of John E. Churchville. Churchville was born to a single mother, a devout woman from whom he acquired his love for music. As a youngster growing up in 1950s North Philadelphia, he had "a brush with ruin" when, armed with a zip gun, he confronted a neighborhood tough who had mercilessly tormented him. A serious and intense adolescent, Churchville became an Ahmadiyya Muslim, joining a sect whose universalist themes were popular among African-American jazz artists. Though he gravitated toward philosophy and read Plato and Sartre, jazz piano was his true passion. He attended Temple University on a music scholarship in 1959, only to drop out and move to New York City, where he worked as a musician and janitor while exploring the Lower East Side's radical political circles. After a stint as a member of a communist study group, he followed his black nationalist impulses uptown, visiting the Nation of Islam's Harlem mosque to imbibe the sermons of Minister Malcolm X. The Muslim leader struck him as articulate and fearless—a man, he later recalled, "who didn't look over his shoulder to make sure white folks were pleased with what he had to say."[49]

It was the struggle against Jim Crow, however, that represented the front lines of militancy. The 19-year-old Churchville joined SNCC, serving from 1961 to 1963 as a field secretary in southwest Georgia and the Mississippi Delta. Though he relished his time in the movement, he resented the policy of pairing black and white canvassers during door-to-door voter registration drives. Poor African Americans who responded favorably to such visits, he argued, were merely accepting a new model of paternalism and authority. Their deference suggested a syndrome as deep-seated as the air of superiority (black activists dubbed it the "Tarzan complex") displayed by some white SNCC workers. Churchville persuaded a project director to let him partner with a black colleague on a trial basis, determined to demonstrate that African Americans could motivate one another without the presence of a white person to validate the exchange. He began using what he later termed "black talk" while in the field. Refusing to discuss integration or race relations, he stressed that black residents could advance as a people only by asserting group power and racial pride. The approach caused some unease among SNCC staffers, especially those whose integrationist convictions remained firm.[50]

After leaving SNCC, Churchville briefly served as an administrator for the Nation of Islam in Atlanta before returning to Philadelphia in 1964 and accepting an organizing job with the Northern Student Movement (NSM), an arm of SNCC formed in 1962 to support southern efforts and to initiate parallel campaigns in northern urban slums. NSM was an unlikely institutional base for Churchville. Founded by privileged, white college students as a fundraising vehicle, the organization had grown rapidly in the Northeast while remaining predominantly white. Its original approach to racial injustice involved providing academic tutoring for black teenagers in slum areas. Yet the organization evolved. Its critique of structural racism deepened as it committed itself to the political empowerment of the oppressed.

Between 1963 and 1964, the group strove to transcend the paternalistic view that the exposure of white, middle-class students to ghetto conditions would bring about racial understanding and progress. NSM activities expanded to include rent strikes and boycotts. Critical questions of race and power came to the fore as Bill Strickland, a Harvard graduate and an avowed black nationalist, rose to the group's top office. NSM embarked on an array of programs designed to "instill in the ghetto resident a sense of his own worth." The organization adopted the view that education must relate to concrete community needs. It now sought "to bend education to the 'other America'" and catalyze the ghetto into acting on its own behalf, rather than merely "remake the deprived into some middle class mold."[51]

Churchville's work with NSM helped mark the organization's transition to a more grassroots, nationalistic posture. Integrationist sentiment, however, remained strong within the group's local leadership. So when the SNCC veteran proposed an all-black project in the heart of North Philadelphia, he again framed the venture as experimental. Churchville wished to open a "Freedom Library" in the African-American neighborhood as a model of an indigenous establishment expressly devoted to black self-determination. Designed to nurture racial consciousness, the library would feature books by and about black people. The concept was not new; organizers had operated "freedom libraries" during the Freedom Summer of 1964, providing many black Mississippians with their first exposure to African-American literature. Churchville viewed the NSM Freedom Library as a way to tackle "self-hate and identity ambivalence," problems he saw as pervasive in northern ghettoes. The library would help foster awareness of the community's innate potential and enable residents to "build something that is their own." Black inner cities, Churchville believed, needed stable social structures that could respond to local needs and provide bases for "concerted national action in the future."[52]

Churchville's vision began to materialize in the summer of 1964. With the support of NSM and the aid of a $1,500 grant, the activist acquired a narrow, dilapidated storefront on Ridge Avenue. The setting—a gritty section of North Philadelphia noted for its street gangs and squalid buildings—seemed inauspicious. That August, the area surrounding Freedom Library became the epicenter of the Philadelphia riot, an event that left many adjacent stores encased in plywood. But Churchville, a resident of the area and the project's first staff member, would not be deterred. He collected donated books from public and university libraries, joining Strickland in soliciting further contributions from ministers and literary figures. The makeshift library, no more than a stark, sparsely furnished shop, gradually amassed a few hundred volumes.

Books, however, played only a minor role in Freedom Library's development. Though Churchville had envisioned the project as a platform for launching rent strikes and block cleanups, he increasingly saw the storefront itself as the locus of activity. He organized a neighborhood tutoring program and a weekly, black history lecture series as outgrowths of the library. The initiatives targeted both the community's rougher elements and the upwardly mobile, though Churchville clearly prioritized the former population. To him, Freedom Library, which lay just paces from a bar, was "beautifully" located. "If you want intellectual discussion at its best, go to a bar," he later said. "I'm not kidding. You will find many cats out there high who have a whole lot. I am in there teaching a black history class and the nigger comes in there high as he can be, blowing me away with facts."[53]

Churchville recruited college students, then local high school pupils (including gang members) to tutor younger children at the Ridge Avenue site, which soon became a hub of neighborhood activity. Freedom Library, whose all-black staff grew to include a few other North Philadelphia residents, helped connect area inhabitants with antipoverty programs and served as neutral territory for peace negotiations between warring gangs. In 1965, Churchville opened a part-time preschool to augment his thriving tutorial program, recruiting neighborhood youths and charging $10 a week for day- and after-school sessions designed to bolster poor children's academic skills and racial identity. "We felt that if we instilled a sense of worth in them before the public school system got ahold of them, they might be able to deal with the inconsistencies and falsehoods they would be expected to learn," he later said. Contributions from local black businesses, churches, and fraternal lodges helped sustain the operation. By that summer, more than 130 youngsters, from toddlers to adolescents, participated in the "identity orientation" courses. Churchville regularly gathered students from street corners and homes, returning to the storefront with a column of children in tow.

The driving force behind Freedom Library's programs was the desire to restore black self-image and foment "a revolution inside." Churchville reasoned that knowledge of black history and cultural heritage could stimulate a rich and meaningful identity and combat the psychological consequences of oppression. Poor African Americans, he and Strickland argued, were forced to make "a thousand daily capitulations" that undermined their sense of self-worth. Freedom Library literature was steeped in the contemporary language and assumptions of social science. It decried "the damaging psychological effect on people who had nothing good to believe about themselves except that they helped to build America as slaves."[54]

The Ridge Avenue site also reflected a larger attempt to reshape the freedom struggle. Churchville and Strickland dismissed as feeble and ineffective the moderate reformism of the mainstream movement. Such demands, they insisted, represented little more than cries "from the torture chamber." Endless demonstrations had only exhausted and bewildered black America. What African Americans needed was identity restoration and "knowledge of themselves." The civil rights establishment, Churchville believed, rooted its appeals in a pathetic quest for white acceptance. Freedom Library offered an opportunity to create an alternative "movement from below" that could marshal the power of collective resentment.[55]

Despite the potency of this critique, Churchville's rhetoric contained a web of contradictions. On one hand, residents of black ghettoes symbolized the power of the masses, embodying the aspirations of "the total black community." On the other hand, they exemplified the dehumanizing effects of racism and thus required moral and cultural rehabilitation. By arguing that white domination "bludgeoned" African Americans and crippled their spirit, Freedom Library organizers reified contemporary theories of black "personality damage" and reproduced therapeutic responses to problems of structural racism. Their prescriptions shifted from presumptions of psychological injury and cultural deficiency to uplift solutions, a reflection of the bourgeois premise that the leadership of educated and enlightened African Americans is needed to reform the dispossessed. "If we can create in the Negro community a feeling of identity, based on a knowledge of history and on self-improvement," Churchville argued, "it will help to end antisocial behavior."[56]

It was often unclear whether Freedom Library stood for systemic change or self-help, social reform or revolution, a form of black nationhood or a larger share of American prosperity. At times the school's operators employed the language of personal responsibility and criticized the poverty programs as paternalistic. On these occasions, they seemed to imply that cultural factors—that is, "lack of identity and self-esteem"—were among the main causes of poverty and degradation. "We are the enemy," Churchville later declared, stressing the need for the lower classes to suppress "decadent tendencies." In other instances, the Freedom Library director invoked Marxian themes, emphasized structural forces, depicted poverty as a political crisis rather than a moral or sociological dilemma, and deployed the language of rebellion. Many of Churchville's more conservative outlooks revolved around gender. His contention that matriarchal tendencies had undermined the black movement, and his complaints about the damage to children's psyches done by North Philadelphia mothers who failed to maintain tidy homes, reflected an acutely patriarchal worldview.[57]

In the end, neither patriarchy nor ideological inconsistency prevented Churchville and Freedom Library from becoming major political forces in black Philadelphia. Churchville emerged as a vocal opponent of the 1965 campaign to desegregate North Philadelphia's Girard College, an elite private school for boys. He denounced integrationism as an insidious distraction, even as demonstrators picketed the imposing campus. He also joined increasingly forceful protests against the substandard public schools that served many of the city's children of color. During one fall 1965 rally at which he appeared, several neighborhood groups decried the "fire traps, more than 65 years old, to which we are required to send our children every day." Decaying public schools, Churchville told the gathering, reflected a national conspiracy to strangle black communities.[58]

Churchville and other Freedom Library activists formalized their black nationalist agenda in February 1966—prior to the national explosion of the "Black Power" slogan—when they helped organize Philadelphia's Black People's Unity Movement (BPUM). At the time, many African Americans winced at the mere mention of the word "black." As historian Matthew J. Countryman notes, however, BPUM crafted a compelling message that synthesized "Malcolm X's call for black cultural pride and community control over the social, economic, and political institutions in the black community with SNCC's commitment to community organizing and indigenous leadership development." Churchville supplied the "emotional flashpoint" of BPUM's founding rally. The event drew a crowd of 300, including 45 white onlookers, to a North Philadelphia church. As the proceedings began, Churchville stood and ordered white spectators to surrender their seats so that the African Americans for whom the rally was intended could sit. Murmurs of surprise rippled through the audience. A black newspaper later condemned the incident as a case of "reverse discrimination." But as one witness recalled, Churchville's dramatic act sent an unequivocal signal that "we were embarking on a journey of self-discovery and self-determination."[59]

BPUM became one of the city's leading Black Power formations. Yet Freedom Library remained Churchville's defining crusade—the primary expression of his ambition to transform the black urban core into "a bastion of power." This mission was not universally embraced. Freedom Library came under heavy FBI surveillance. In the summer of 1966, a massive police raid on several of the city's black militant cadres targeted Churchville and the Freedom Library, as well as the local SNCC office. Churchville, who had faced persecution and arrests during his SNCC days, and whose black nationalist activities had precipitated earlier conflicts with Philadelphia police, refused to succumb to the latest wave of repression.[60] Even as he confronted mounting opposition, however, additional battles loomed.

While NSM's African-American membership had sharply increased, Churchville had continued to clash with some of the organization's integrationist, white leaders. Between 1964 and 1966, Freedom Library found itself enmeshed in many of the group's internal conflicts. In 1967, Churchville and NSM parted ways. With a wife to support and a child on the way, the organizer purchased the Ridge Avenue storefront and launched the Freedom Library Day School, a wholly independent, full-time operation. The Black Power phase of the liberation struggle had produced one of its first permanent institutions, a venture designed to replace—rather than merely supplement or reform—failing inner-city schools, thus finally answering the question Bob Moses had posed in 1964: "Freedom School *after* public school, or *instead* of public school?"[61]

"My Homeland Is Africa": Teaching a New World

Like many of the private schools that it helped inspire, Freedom Library fulfilled practical needs. Initially the institution's sole instructor, Churchville encountered fifth graders who were functionally illiterate along with scores of other children who had been deeply neglected and alienated by public education. Freedom Library gradually developed a permanent corps of full-time pupils. By 1969, as many as 30 youngsters attended the school five days a week. By 1971, Churchville presided over a small staff of teachers, 40 children ages two to seven, and several older pupils.[62] There in the austere storefront, neighborhood preschoolers and elementary school students transcribed phrases like "Nat Is Fat," practicing reading, math, and penmanship while following an academic regimen that stressed phonics and repetition.

Of course, Freedom Library did not simply impart academic skills. Like earlier movement schools, Churchville's operation attempted to equip youngsters with the tools of self-liberation. The Ridge Avenue site exemplified Freedom School founder Charlie Cobb's insight that "education is not the development of intellectual skills, but a preparation for participation in living." Black education, Churchville insisted, must cultivate "a new generation of correct thinkers" and prepare youngsters for "total immersion in revolutionary struggle." The molding of uncompromising agents of black liberation, he believed, could begin at the age of two or three. At Freedom Library, preschoolers painstakingly copied affirmations into handwritten workbooks: "I am black and beautiful . . . I am the greatest . . . I deserve the best . . . I want black power."[63]

Emphasis on socialization produced an air of severity. Churchville demanded strict discipline and developed a reputation for using (or threatening to use) corporal punishment. Freedom Library relied heavily on regimentation and memorization—hallmarks of an educational philosophy that favors results over process and compliance over creativity. But Churchville believed harsh approaches were necessary. Black children, he insisted, could ill-afford the luxuries of leisure or free play. They needed rigor to survive in a hostile society. They needed the moral reinforcement and political guidance that would enable them to make sacrifices on behalf of black nationhood. "Don't nobody want to walk up the mountain," Churchville later declared, explaining the need to instill revolutionary discipline.[64]

The headmaster's approach never softened. "You are going to be brilliant!" he commanded his students. Churchville's austere bearing stemmed from his somber religiosity. A born-again Christian, he had converted in 1966 after an intermittent courtship with Islam.[65] A fundamentalist worldview reinforced his tendency toward political and pedagogical absolutism. His notion of the Savior as a stern taskmaster and his vision of damnation as a perpetual and imminent threat reinforced the asceticism and order of his classroom.

Yet Freedom Library also incorporated aspects of progressive instruction. Churchville had read *Pedagogy of the Oppressed* by Paulo Freire and embraced some of the principles that guided the Brazilian philosopher's concept of education as the practice of freedom. In the Ridge Avenue storefront, students sang freedom songs, retold or concocted stories, drew pictures of themselves and their surroundings, and dramatized historical events—activities designed to foster critical awareness and enable children to develop as distinct personalities. The youngsters also confronted open-ended questions—"What is a community? What is a ghetto? What is segregation?"—that encouraged them to apply concepts of justice and equality to their own lives, a technique that mirrored Freedom School pedagogy.[66]

Such methods helped establish Freedom Library as a significant new prototype for black education. Jitu Weusi, the former Ocean Hill–Brownsville teacher, traveled to Philadelphia to observe the Ridge Avenue operation in 1969, prior to founding Brooklyn's Uhuru Sasa Shule. He later described Freedom Library as "the scene of my great enlightenment." The pioneering school also impressed Vincent and Rosemarie Harding of the Institute of the Black World, an Atlanta think tank. Though the activist couple had helped develop progressive, black educational projects in that southern city, including the Martin Luther King, Jr. Community School, in fall 1974 they collected their two children and the 12-year-old son of an old comrade and set off for Philadelphia to enroll the youngsters in Freedom Library. Deliberation over the "demands of the next stages" of black liberation inspired the move. The Hardings, who knew Churchville from his SNCC and NSM days, hoped the school would help nurture the spirit of sacrifice that a protracted struggle demands, producing "men and women who fight on for the new day, no matter how long it takes, no matter what obstacles we must overcome."[67]

Like many black Americans, Churchville saw the cultivation of African identity as central to this mission. Restoration of self-knowledge and self-esteem meant rediscovery of ancestral languages, religions, and cultures. Long before "black" had become a popular designation, Freedom Library preschoolers learned to shun the word "Negro." "I am an Afro-American," their homemade primers reminded them. "My homeland is Africa. Africa is a Continent. I live in America now. I am proud of Africans. Africans are black people. Black people are beautiful. I am beautiful."[68]

By the late 1960s, such themes shaped the curricula of scores of black community schools. Pan Africanism, a commitment to linking struggles for freedom and dignity throughout the African continent and diaspora, seemed to represent a positive and necessary refinement of the Black Power concept. Philadelphia's BPUM embodied the resurgent internationalism. A Tanzanian diplomat appeared at the group's second "unity rally" in March 1966. The visitor hailed the awakening of black consciousness in Africa, the Caribbean, and the United States and described the "establishment of a black government out of a colonial past." Churchville and other revolutionary nationalists believed that achieving this goal in North America meant nurturing "a people totally different from any who have ever existed."[69] Whether the reclamation of African identity could inspire such a genesis or bring about the "postcolonial" black America of contemporary visions remained to be seen.

SNCC's death was remarkably generative. The demise of "civil rights" mentality and the dispersal of young organizers in the late 1960s initiated a period of transition and radical experimentation that gave rise to a host of parallel institutions and movement schools, especially in urban centers. Faith in the transformative power of education endured, as did the conviction that structures created "outside the official order" could serve as vessels of critical thought and consciousness. Models like Freedom Library Day School demonstrated that movement schools could operate on a permanent, full-time basis, housing a broader range of political and cultural activities than had their predecessors. Renewed emphasis on fomenting an internal revolution and practicing a vigorous cultural politics led Black Power formations to seek the "restoration" of African identity. This crusade found an unlikely locale in the tiny, Northern California town of East Palo Alto, and an atypical champion in one Gertrude Wilks.

4

African Restoration and the Promise
and Pitfalls of Cultural Politics

National liberation is necessarily an act of culture.

—Amilcar Cabral[1]

In 1968, the younger residents of East Palo Alto, California, an unincorporated black town of 20,000 on the San Francisco Peninsula, attempted to change the hamlet's name to "Nairobi." The effort, which produced a ballot proposal that fall, seemed improbable. East Palo Alto was a patchwork of flower farms before the 1950s and '60s, when it became a haven for African-American refugees from southern repression and northern slums. It was little more than a "sophisticated colony"—a settlement poised between ghetto blight and suburban tranquility. Yet the rechristening bolstered its reputation as a locus of black consciousness and bestowed an evocative title upon its network of private schools.

The campaign to name a minute, African-American community after the capital of Kenya, an East African nation 10,000 miles away, demonstrated the power of black America's rediscovered African identity. By the late 1960s, the refrain "We Are an African People" encompassed multiple debates about the future course of black life and politics. As culture came to be seen as a critical terrain of struggle, independent schools served as key instruments for rewriting Africa's meaning to black America.

East Palo Alto's cultural and educational renaissance began with a series of desegregation campaigns. Local activist Gertrude Wilks led demonstrations, organized tutoring programs, and devised a plan to "sneak" East Palo Alto youngsters into the affluent, white schools of a nearby district. However, white backlash and the patent flaws of integrationism led Wilks to found Nairobi Day School, an effort to safeguard the minds, lives, and futures of black children within their own community. The recasting of black identity through the recovery of Africa profoundly enriched this cause. The rise of Maulana Karenga and contemporary cultural nationalism appeared to complement grassroots struggles for dignity and freedom. Yet overemphasis on identity proved deeply limiting, theoretically and strategically. In time, fanciful notions of African reclamation clashed with more radical interpretations of culture.

"Yes on Nairobi!": The Africanization of East Palo Alto

The prospective renaming of East Palo Alto electrified many inhabitants of the working-class municipality, a sliver of the peninsula located 35 miles south of San Francisco. The idea surfaced during a spring 1968 public hearing to discuss a federal Model Cities grant. Donald Reid, a black technical writer in his 30s and the originator of the concept, argued that the town's adoption of the name "Nairobi" would make a powerful statement, honoring the African heritage of many local residents the way "New York" or "New Orleans" acknowledged the European derivation of other Americans. Supporters of the measure believed the name would convey black pride while affirming the community's independence from affluent, predominantly white Palo Alto, a neighbor with which it had long had an uneasy relationship.

Older residents, including members of the town's dwindling white population, were unconvinced. To them, the politics of African reclamation seemed arcane if not subversive. For some East Palo Altans, as for many Americans, Africa remained a symbol of backwardness. Residents who were anxious to achieve conventional, middle-class status viewed the renaming scheme as a threat to their attempts to associate themselves with the posh respectability of Palo Alto, home of Stanford University. By contrast, proponents of the Nairobi effort felt that the town's traditional name relegated them to the periphery of the elite white suburb across the creek. "East Palo Alto" suggested a colony subordinate to the metropole. "Nairobi" signaled a center of black autonomy.[2]

As the November 1968 vote approached, debate over the name change intensified and "Yes on Nairobi" buttons and bumper stickers blossomed throughout the community. However, multiple interpretations of the African theme existed even among supporters of the ballot initiative. Some proponents of the renaming cast the proposal as a celebration of pluralism. "If people of all races can live in Rome, New York," one East Palo Altan maintained, "then the same should be true of Nairobi, California." Others stressed the campaign's radical implications, seeing the endeavor as an expression of burgeoning militancy. "No longer will the beautiful black people of [East Palo Alto] allow the community to be considered a mere suburb of honkeyville," the *Black Panther* proclaimed.[3]

The Nairobi proposal was a manifestation of a broader phenomenon. African cities and states had shed European names amid postcolonial "Africanization" campaigns. In 1966, for example, Leopoldville, a place named after Belgium's King Leopold II (a paragon of imperialist brutality and greed), had become Kinshasa, capital of the Congo. Some Westerners found the litany of new names mystifying. "No sooner will we learn where Gaberones, Bechuanaland, is than it will be Gaberones, Botswana," one journalist complained. Yet many African Americans recognized the ritual of renaming as an essential act of self-determination. Black nationalists in the United States launched analogous efforts, reimagining Newark, New Jersey, as a "New Ark" of black salvation.[4]

The "Yes on Nairobi" drive also reflected specific East African influences. The Mau Mau uprising that engulfed Kenya during the 1950s had fascinated and inspired many African Americans. Most white Westerners saw the Kenyan "emergency" as an atavistic expression of savagery. For radical black Americans engaged in their own mass insurgencies, however, the armed rebellion, a prelude to Kenya's 1963 independence, represented an uncompromising quest for land and freedom. "Right here in Harlem . . . we need a Mau Mau," Malcolm X had declared in 1964.[5] East Palo Alto's renaming crusade suggested the admiration African Americans felt for African nationalists like Kenya's Jomo Kenyatta. Unaware of Kenyatta's role as a client of British neocolonialism, many black Americans continued to associate the leader with Africa's heroic struggle for self-rule.[6]

If the Nairobi proposal revealed global visions of black liberation, the effort offered little assurance that East Palo Alto could escape its own colonial status. Since its gold rush origins in the 1840s, the village had been a site of lofty dreams and chronic misfortune. It had hosted a series of failed ventures between the late nineteenth and early twentieth centuries, including a commercial port, a brickyard, and a utopian farming colony. In subsequent years, "East Palo Alto" served as the common-usage name for a hinterland known for saloons, flower nurseries, and ranches. An influx of World War II veterans led to the creation of new housing subdivisions during the 1940s and early '50s. But East Palo Alto remained unincorporated, and thus lacked the political clout to resist the uprooting of its commercial sector in 1955 by the construction of the Bayshore Freeway, another example of the highway and "urban renewal" projects that dislocated many contemporary African-American communities. Surrounding cities further depleted the town's tax base, swallowing its most valuable tracts, shrinking its territory, and delaying its achievement of formal self-government.[7]

Amid these indignities, a black population took root. African Americans gained a foothold in town by the early to mid-1950s. East Palo Alto was one of the few places in the area where black migrants were permitted to buy homes. The allure of suburban living and the appeal of affordable housing and decent jobs widened the stream of newcomers. "Blockbusting" realtors panicked white homeowners with tales of black invasion and collapsing property values, then capitalized on white flight by selling to black settlers. African-American transplants from the South and from nearby San Francisco, Richmond, and Oakland arrived in East Palo Alto. By the early 1970s, more than two-thirds of the town's population was black.

East Palo Alto had become a case study in the modest trend toward black suburbanization. Whether the community could avoid what social scientists called "ghettoization," however, remained uncertain. For the moment, the hamlet resisted the blight of the big city core. Its African-American occupants, most of whom owned their tract homes, held clerical, domestic, or industrial jobs in surrounding areas and saw themselves as having reached the lower rung of the middle class. East Palo Alto's oak trees offered ample shade, and its ranch-style houses boasted wisps of well-kept lawns.[8]

Still, the town remained an island of black aspiration within a sea of white wealth. Lower incomes, economic isolation, declining infrastructure, and a growing plague of drug crimes tied East Palo Alto to other "instant ghettoes" that had sprung up in the West, and further distinguished the community from the nearby habitats of professors and electronics industry executives. Thwarted ambitions linked the municipality to an older generation of unincorporated black settlements. Rural African-American enclaves like Mound Bayou, Mississippi, and Boley, Oklahoma, had provided a degree of sanctuary from white domination since the late nineteenth and early twentieth century. Conceived as models of self-sufficiency, such "all-Negro" colonies had deteriorated in later decades as their populations dwindled and their economies failed.[9]

Even as the dreams of earlier black pioneers faded, East Palo Altans launched their own bids for independence. The town became a seedbed of black self-activity. Agitation led in 1967 to the formation of a shadow "municipal council." Locally elected and equipped only with the authority to advise county administrators, the body, a "halfway house" between genuine autonomy and the dependency of the past, enabled residents to address long-festering crises, including abuse by police from surrounding districts. Other self-help initiatives included youth patrols, a neighborhood health center, and a special civilian court endowed with the power to sentence offenders to perform chores in homes they had burglarized.[10]

Yet it was the "Nairobi" proposal—a marriage of the contemporary themes of localism and African identity—that cemented East Palo Alto's reputation as a bastion of black awareness. Though the ballot question ultimately went down to defeat, the alias survived. The post office began receiving mail marked "Nairobi, CA," and more than a dozen businesses adopted the name. Operators of Nairobi Village (formerly University Village) Shopping Center hung a wooden sign at the mall's entrance proclaiming "Uhuru Na Umoja" ("Freedom and Unity").

Even a local troupe of singing black cowboys now wished to be known as the "Nairobi Wranglers."[11]

Some East Palo Altans embraced the town's renaming campaign as an opportunity to share in the spirit of postcolonialism. But achieving true self-sufficiency required more than symbolism. Meaningful liberation meant controlling one's destiny and fortifying one's community. Local leaders hoped to cultivate an East Palo Alto that would merit its proud pseudonym. They saw in the town's unincorporated status an opportunity to create a model community, a modern frontier city combining the advantages of western living with the southern black ethos of mutual aid.

During the 1960s, a small corps of activists coalesced. Its members, mostly southern migrants propelled to East Palo Alto by chance or fortune and incensed by local black powerlessness, formed a dynamic leadership base within an increasingly galvanized community. The loose coterie of workers, professionals, housewives, and clergy embraced the philosophies of black self-help, grassroots organizing, and community control. Even as East Palo Alto's political and economic plight deepened, its activists strove to create institutions that could help African Americans seize their collective fate.[12]

The determination of these leaders to reverse the drift toward ghetto conditions and the complexity of their transformation from militant integrationism to pragmatic nationalism converged in the person of Gertrude Wilks. A sturdy woman known for her pin-curled hairdo and homemade dresses, Wilks was an anomaly among leaders of contemporary Pan African nationalist private schools. While most such figures were young, male, and intensely ideological, Wilks was an earthy, working-class, slightly older mother who had been driven to institution building more by desperation than by doctrine. Yet her militancy and resolve helped produce Nairobi Day School, one of Black Power's earliest and longest-lived independent establishments. As Pan African nationalist institutions across the country pursued formulaic notions of African culture and identity, Wilks and Nairobi Day School developed practical, humanistic models of Africa-conscious education.

"Escalating the Struggle": Gertrude Wilks and Militant Integrationism

Wilks's struggle for redemptive education began in her youth. Born into a sharecropping family in rural Louisiana on the eve of the Depression, she discovered at an early age the connection between illiteracy, indigence, and racial caste. As a child she toiled alongside her siblings and parents for one plantation owner after another in a brutal system of tenancy and debt. The prerogatives of white planters and the seasonal rhythms of agriculture often determined the extent and nature of schooling for rural African Americans. Yet by outmaneuvering landlords and slipping away from cotton fields, Wilks managed to acquire a 12th-grade education.

Wilks married in the late 1940s and absconded to Northern California, where she and her husband found factory work. By 1952, they had joined the flow of African-American war veterans and other migrants into East Palo Alto. While her husband labored at a nearby assembly plant, Wilks settled into domestic life and launched a brisk dressmaking business from home. She volunteered at church, helped establish a local antipoverty group, and began working with the area NAACP. Ensconced in the modest suburb, she looked to the future, confident that she and her husband could offer their three children all the opportunities that she had been denied.[13]

It soon grew evident, however, that her eldest son was falling by the wayside. Otis was not bringing home homework or showing academic progress. When Wilks shared her concerns with the largely white staff of local schools, she was complimented on her son's pleasant disposition and cautioned against tutoring him at home; doing so, she was told, would only undermine the efforts of professionals. Conscious of her own rudimentary schooling and "crude" speech and loath to be seen as a meddling, overbearing mother (especially given contemporary concerns about domineering African-American "matriarchs"), Wilks relented. "You didn't feel you was *qualified*," she later said, explaining her reluctance to challenge white teachers. Then one day during his junior or senior year, Otis made an alarming confession: though he was on track to graduate, he was totally unprepared for college. Semiliterate at best, he struggled even to complete applications for entry-level jobs. "I am lost," he told his mother. "I don't know nothing."[14]

Wilks felt betrayed. She had played the role of dutiful mother, seeing her domesticity as another advantage that would help propel her children into college and professional life. Now the whole plot seemed to have unraveled.[15] While deeply embittering, Wilks's experience was far from unique. East Palo Alto schools had deteriorated significantly during the 1950s and '60s. As white residents fled, unimpeded by racial discrimination in housing and labor markets, they eased the pressure on educators—most of whom lived outside the community—to uphold academic standards. East Palo Alto's Ravenswood High, a predominantly black school by the late 1960s, shifted to a vocational emphasis as its course offerings and overall rigor declined. The Ravenswood district itself became a symbol of failure. While its first graders scored in the 50th percentile compared to national reading norms, its second and third graders scored in the

35th and 25th percentiles, respectively. By 1966, almost half of East Palo Alto eighth graders ranked in the 25th percentile on standardized reading tests.[16]

Outraged by what she saw as the sabotage of her son, Wilks began to organize. She joined a local civil rights drive that since the early 1960s had focused on de facto segregation in East Palo Alto schools. Embracing the emphasis on religion and education prevalent among many black southerners, she and a handful of community leaders formed a pressure group—the Mothers for Equal Education (or simply, "the Mothers")—at a local church in 1965. "I needed some women because women stick with things," she later recalled. Wilks and her comrades recruited a few other outspoken women who refused to surrender "college plans for our young people." The Mothers met in living rooms and church pews, always convening with a simple prayer: "Oh Lord, here we stand, joined together heart and hand, to help provide better education throughout the land."[17]

Wilks became a warrior for integration. Like other local activists, she accepted prevailing theories about the intellectually uplifting presence of white, middle-class children. Abandoning polite entreaties and the air of respectability associated with black churchwomen, she and the Mothers launched a militant, grassroots desegregation campaign. They joined other leaders in demanding the phasing out of Ravenswood High and the dispersal of its pupils among the area's better-performing, largely white schools. After district administrators rejected the plan, they organized boycotts, wearing black to "mourn the death of our youth" and standing firm as school officials dismissed them as rabble-rousers. They continued to mobilize, staging walkouts and demonstrations in concert with the NAACP and Congress of Racial Equality, and patrolling picket lines with their children at their sides.[18]

Now approaching her 40s, Wilks earned a reputation as an unabashed radical. She harangued at school board meetings and rallies, receiving anonymous threats of "Birmingham-style retaliation" for her attempts to enroll black children (including her own) in lily-white, neighboring schools. She had begun to detect flaws in the integrationist strategy. Many white teachers feared black students or assumed that their parents were unconcerned about education. Wilks recognized, however, that outstanding faculty, curricula, and materials remained concentrated in white, middle-class schools, and she began developing a plan to connect East Palo Alto children with these resources.[19]

The "Sneak-out" was the fruit of her deliberation. As an adolescent she had stolen away from plantations to attend a distant high school. Now she orchestrated an analogous escape. Telephoning a white ally in Palo Alto in 1966, she won a pledge that her second child, Danny, a sophomore, could live in the friend's home while attending one of the town's excellent high schools. Soon dozens of East Palo Alto teenagers were volunteering to live with white families in Palo Alto and neighboring Los Altos four days a week so that they could attend elite junior and senior high schools in the districts. "We have to go out to your schools so we can keep up with you later in life," one teenage Sneak-out participant explained to white peers during a 1967 integration conference.[20]

Over the course of two years, as many as 200 students participated in the informal transfer system, which relied on host households identified by the Mothers. Opponents argued that the transfer scheme further weakened East Palo Alto schools by siphoning off ambitious students. For Wilks, however, immediate enhancement of black educational opportunity was paramount. The Sneak-out, she believed, would enable working-class African Americans to enter college thoroughly prepared. The program immediately garnered widespread recognition. The NAACP's national organ, *The Crisis*, noted in 1966 that a means of "circumventing de facto school segregation" had been devised in East Palo Alto. The publication hastened to add, however, that the solution was only temporary; the Mothers and the local NAACP were pressing forward with other methods of freeing East Palo Alto from "the bonds of de facto segregation."[21]

"We Got Power": East Palo Alto and the Dual Strategy

The Mothers were also hatching a separate plan. That fall, shortly after the birth of the Sneak-out, they organized a Saturday school in East Palo Alto. The aim was to supplement the community's floundering schools with a free program emphasizing literacy. One October day, Wilks and the Mothers held an initial session for 22 students at St. John the Baptist Church, embracing the modest goal of teaching local children "to read and stand tall." Makeshift classes expanded into weekly tutorials serving mainly elementary grades and occupying every corner of the church, where parent volunteers, clergy, and black and white teachers from area districts presided over clusters of children engaged in basic tasks—practicing phonics, studying word formation, and analyzing poetry or coverage of black people in the news. If one pedagogical philosophy prevailed, it was the belief that poor and working-class black children could learn to read and write through repetition of basic skills in a nurturing, disciplined environment familiar to most of them—the black church.[22]

The Saturday school outgrew St. John's. By 1967, as many as 300 students from throughout the San Francisco Peninsula traveled to East Palo Alto to attend classes. The Mothers borrowed larger facilities from a local public school, adding Wednesday evening sessions, a math course, African dance, and a "black awareness" curriculum. As the program evolved, relations with the school district deteriorated. Ravenswood officials began attacking the supplementary school as a drain on the morale of public education. Others questioned the qualifications of the Mothers. "Gertrude, you know you don't have no degree," friends and enemies chided. The constraints of part-time instruction proved daunting. "It's hard to undo the damage of five days [in public schools] in two hours on Saturday," Wilks acknowledged.[23]

Meanwhile, the Sneak-out faltered. East Palo Alto students progressed academically in Palo Alto, where many teachers held Phi Beta Kappa keys and emphasized critical thinking. But the youngsters were deeply alienated. "I couldn't express myself at that school," one student said of his time at a predominantly white junior high. "I was locked up inside. If I stood up to be a man, I was considered rowdy." Some found the experience degrading. "Once in a while one black student would try to fit in with the upper-class whites," another Sneak-out volunteer remembered, "and as soon as they start treating his ass like an animal . . . he would crawl right back through the back entrance to his own black society." Wilks worried that by uprooting and isolating East Palo Alto children, the integration program was damaging its intended beneficiaries. "We had been told that if you could just sit beside the white students, all of the good things was in the hills," she recalled.[24] Now a vexing question emerged: did the price of admission to the "hills" of Palo Alto exceed the practical rewards of decent education?

Local developments compounded the dilemma. The San Francisco–Oakland region was the site of the nation's first voluntary, comprehensive program of school desegregation, a feat achieved by Berkeley in 1968. Palo Alto, the home of an active Friends of the Student Nonviolent Coordinating Committee (SNCC) chapter and other antiracist groups, prided itself on its enlightened sensibilities and its traditions of social justice. Many expressions of Palo Alto liberalism were self-serving and anemic, a reality richly demonstrated by the 1968 attempt of several white residents to "promote racial understanding" by securing "a Negro family as neighbor." However, some Palo Altans were principled foes of white supremacy who vigorously opposed the "subeducation" of black children.[25]

The formalizing of the Sneak-out program in 1968 thus seemed to represent an act of racial goodwill. An interdistrict transfer agreement enabled 75 East Palo Alto youths to enter the Palo Alto district under more dignified terms than those implied by the act of "sneaking." Pledging to enhance "multicultural understanding," local officials that year launched a national campaign to recruit African-American teachers. They also hired a black "multicultural coordinator," selecting a college instructor known for his enthusiastic support for the Black Panthers.

These measures were designed to cleanse the district of "conscious or unconscious" racial bias. Yet the white backlash so visible throughout the land also thrived in Palo Alto. The multicultural coordinator was harried into resigning, and an energized opposition strove to expose the diversity initiatives as reckless experiments that brought "disruptive influences" into the schools. Even the handling of the transfer program revealed underlying prejudices. The willingness of some Palo Alto residents to subject so-called "Sneak-ins" to humiliating scrutiny and to blame them for any and all outbreaks of campus discord compounded the youngsters' stigmatization.[26]

In the months following Martin Luther King, Jr.'s April 1968 assassination, the pall of suspicion gave way to outright hostility. The murder stoked African-American bitterness and white fears of race war. Radicalized Sneak-out students escalated demands for black history, Swahili courses, and more black instructors. Amid the turmoil, some Palo Alto teenagers and adults made earnest attempts to confront institutional racism. (One local group used the outpouring of white guilt to bolster its program of providing seed money for black entrepreneurs.) Other Palo Altans recoiled from the specter of black militancy. A few host families even ejected their resident Sneak-outs. Forthright black advancement, Wilks concluded, was now seen as an imminent threat.[27]

Racial tensions continued to mount. "Nigger stay out!" graffiti and "This bathroom for blacks only" signs (the latter posted by African-American students) materialized in Palo Alto high schools, as did a flood of leaflets anonymously distributed by a group calling itself SPONGE—Society for the Prevention of Niggers Getting Everything. Wilks feared that East Palo Alto transfer students had become targets for the latent hostilities of white liberalism. A host of crises had engulfed the interdistrict program by the 1968–1969 academic year. A final clash underscored the strife. After a period of heightened friction, Wilks's third child, Pat, was involved in a confrontation between administrators and a cluster of defiant black students at a Palo Alto senior high. Gathered in a corridor, the teenagers repeatedly ignored orders to disperse and return to class. Instead, accompanied by a tambourine, they took up a low, insistent chant: "We got power—Black Power. We got that Black Power."[28]

The backdrop of Black Power had indeed catalyzed the growing militancy—and changing political strategies—of East Palo Alto youths and adults. The town hosted several Black Power summits beginning in 1967, and its political reputation attracted a series of prominent black nationalist visitors. The most popular caller was Stokely Carmichael of SNCC. The celebrated militant, then at the peak of his influence, visited East Palo Alto on several occasions during 1967 and 1968. Wilks was among those captivated by the young leader, whose magnetism and common touch belied his firebrand image. "The people just lined up to talk with him," she later remembered.[29]

While in town, Carmichael participated in private strategy sessions with local activists. His influence on one tactical meeting of East Palo Alto's desegregation forces in spring 1967 proved especially significant. The discussion that day revolved around ongoing efforts to integrate local schools and absorbed more than two hours before someone asked the opinion of the special guest. Carmichael, who had remained silent, seemed bewildered. "I don't understand why you are working so hard to turn the minds of your children over to the people who have oppressed you for 400 years," he said. "It seems to me that what we ought to be doing is taking control of the education of our children."[30]

Carmichael's challenge helped mark the genesis of East Palo Alto's two-pronged struggle: a quest for control of public schools and for the formation of independent black institutions. Wilks came to embody this dual strategy. She had long attempted to desegregate and supplement East Palo Alto schools, even as her Sneak-out program enabled some youngsters to circumvent the town's dismal educational offerings. Now she joined the thrust for community control, supporting "militant" school board candidates, agitating for the appointment of more black faculty and staff in East Palo Alto schools, and pressing for greater community and parent participation in selecting administrators and shaping policy.[31]

In the late 1960s and early '70s, Wilks helped lead the growing resistance to desegregation schemes that called for the dispersal of black students among the white majorities of schools in surrounding communities, a strategy that many East Palo Altans now saw as ineffective and unjust. She reversed her long-standing support for the integration of Ravenswood High, even as the school's governing authority, the Sequoia Union High School District, responded to pressure from federal authorities by developing plans to desegregate the now overwhelmingly black campus. Wilks rejected the notion that the presence of white students could redeem Ravenswood. The Sneak-out, she believed, had demonstrated the danger of overreliance on integration. What East Palo Alto youths needed was "a place to get in out of the rain"—an educational base within their community that could nurture leaders and reinforce skills without scattering children "from pillar to post." East Palo Alto organizers embraced community control as a practical alternative to desegregation's "destruction of black self-esteem." They hoped to steer public education away from Western ideals while creating new pedagogical models based on values seen as African inspired.[32]

Emboldened by Carmichael's intervention, local activists also explored the possibilities of independent education. As the Sneak-out continued to deteriorate and debate over the fate of Ravenswood matched the intensity of the desegregation battles polarizing nearby San Francisco, Richmond, and other communities, Wilks began making plans to offer a viable educational alternative within East Palo Alto. "I decided right there that I had to do something about giving a black child some security, by proving that we as black people could build an institution that was as good as anybody's right here in our community," she later said.[33] The shift to independent education signaled the fruition of a spirit of black pride and assertiveness that had burgeoned in the aftermath of the Watts,

Los Angeles, rebellion of 1965. Other factors also prompted the transition. In April 1969, having been involved in a series of racial skirmishes, 18-year-old Pat Wilks was finally expelled from a Palo Alto senior high. The following day, determined to enroll her daughter in a more edifying institution, the elder Wilks fulfilled her long-standing desire to start a full-time school.[34]

"Niggerology": Pragmatic Nationalism and the Nairobi Method

What began as a prayer for fortitude in a circle of mothers evolved into Nairobi Day School, an institution serving preschool through grade 12. Originally housed in a private East Palo residence, the school served 10 initial pupils, including several former Sneak-outs. Enrollment climbed to 40, then 60, then 80. By the early 1970s, 10 teachers oversaw 50 elementary and 30 high school students in several converted houses purchased with funds donated by white sympathizers. A banner near the school entrance bore a simple credo: "Our Children Can Learn."

Wilks assembled a faculty of college students and certified teachers (both black and white) with the assistance of Bob Hoover, a local organizer and the principal of Nairobi's high school program. Hoover's wife, Mary, a reading specialist who later taught at Howard University, designed the school's literacy-oriented curriculum, while Barbara Mouton, an activist who became East Palo Alto's first official mayor upon its incorporation in 1983, served as an administrator. Nairobi's trustee board included area clergy, NAACP officials, and a woman identified in the school's literature as the "first Negro woman to register to vote in Louisville, Kentucky." Hopeful that the institution met state requirements, the officers began the long process of seeking accreditation.[35]

Financial woes immediately engulfed the school, which received regular support from neither government agencies nor major foundations (though San Francisco–area electronics companies and other firms made donations). Administrators embraced the principle of self-sufficiency. "We're not a front for nobody," Wilks declared. But the absence of large, renewable grants meant permanent desperation. While Nairobi's annual operating costs exceeded $65,000, few of its 35 families could pay the full $1,000 tuition. Most families received hefty financial aid from the school; some paid no tuition whatsoever.[36]

The school's facilities were humble, even makeshift. Staff members begged equipment from shuttered public schools in the area. A library took shape in a converted garage. Mortgage payments consumed funds earmarked for teacher salaries. A permanent fundraising blitz helped cover the shortfall. The Mothers sold chicken dinners, sweet potato pies, and quilts; taught dressmaking and arts and crafts; and opened a bookstore linked to the school. Teachers and students organized banquets, fashion shows, carnivals, conferences, and bazaars as benefits for the institution. Local clergy coaxed donations from their congregants. Other contributions came from welfare checks.[37]

Despite the perennial budget crisis, Nairobi fulfilled its mandate to provide an alternative to "the absolute destruction of our black minds" in public schools. Courses included African history, U.S. history, physics, mathematics, communications, music, and sewing.[38] Nairobi staff insisted that their aim was not to subvert public instruction or engender a "hate whitey" mindset, but to impart academic skills while instilling black pride and a sense of civic responsibility. As one East Palo Alto educator observed, "It doesn't mean a damn thing to teach black culture if [African-American children] can't read or write." College preparation was an explicit and unequivocal goal; the objective was to "even the odds" by enabling African Americans to hold their own in a competitive society. ("We cannot be black and proud, or brown and proud, or yellow and proud and also dumb," a Nairobi pledge asserted.)[39] Yet the critical measure of success was the political and socioeconomic empowerment of the entire community. Nairobi officials rejected visions of black progress that emphasized personal advancement. Individual escape from black slums, they believed, too often meant relegation to the "ghettos" of avarice and indifference. Nairobi fostered a critique of the white middle class as a population that was materially rich yet spiritually impoverished. Rather than encourage students to emulate the sterile values of individualism and materialism, the institution sought to nurture a future cohort of selfless, dedicated East Palo Alto leaders. Professional striving was never to alienate the Nairobi alumna from her old neighborhood or diminish her commitment to its deliverance.[40]

Students were taught that they owed the community that had produced them. (As Mary Hoover later declared, "You in debt for life.") But social commitment without scholastic excellence was meaningless. "The people don't need dummies," one pupil observed. Student essays abounded with promises to "get my people together" or to "help my people get ready for the revolution." The practical and political utility of formal knowledge was a familiar theme. "If I get my degree in chemistry," one student wrote, "then I want to teach chemistry to black students in black schools or help make bombs for the revolution, whatever is more necessary at the time."[41]

"Niggerology," the irreverent black-consciousness course that Wilks taught at the secondary-school level, encapsulated Nairobi's pragmatic brand of nationalism. The class conveyed an incisive yet unpretentious social awareness. Its title served as a reminder that neither platitudes nor slogans could transform the material realities of the oppressed. "Niggerology" entailed an ethic of commitment and an understanding that people needed concrete results. The appropriation of "nigger"—a term generally shunned in black middle-class circles—also reflected Nairobi's working-class orientation and unpretentious character.

The course encouraged adolescents to confront their conditions. It sent them trekking through East Palo Alto to identify overgrown lots or malfunctioning traffic lights, problems that they then reported to the Municipal Council. Visits to a local grocery store allowed youngsters to explore the political implications of wilted produce, aging meat, and inflated prices. Students discovered that achieving "black nationhood"—understood as a sense of solidarity and autonomy—meant resolving daily problems through the application of technical knowledge and homegrown wisdom. Political adaptation was essential; one had to deploy a range of tactics while collaborating with everyone from NAACP officers to Black Panthers.[42]

If Nairobi sought to avoid revolutionary dogma, Wilks and the school remained deeply enmeshed with the politics and personalities of Black Power. Former Black Panther Minister of Education George Mason Murray, the controversial San Francisco State instructor whose 1968 dismissal from the college helped spark a rancorous student strike, joined the Nairobi faculty in the fall of 1969. The school's staff and trustee board included figures like former SNCC worker Syrtiller Kabat and Sidney F. Walton—the radical educator and former multicultural coordinator for Palo Alto schools—who embraced the task of fomenting "a revolution of black minds."[43]

Wilks viewed these younger militants as spiritual comrades, though she did not share all their ideological commitments. For her, Black Power simply meant "white power colored black"—a just and necessary reallocation of wealth and resources. She displayed few of the personal accouterments of radicalism. "If you're looking for my natural," she explained to those who mentioned her pressed hair, "it's inside." Yet she venerated Stokely Carmichael, alternately comparing him to her own father and to Jesus Christ. "Every door that he scares the hell out of someone to open, I can enter," she proclaimed.[44]

Wilks hardly concealed her distaste for integrationism. She and other Nairobi leaders continued to spurn models of desegregation that required black children to venture into remote and hostile neighborhoods "to get what was rightfully theirs." Narrow integration threatened to erode black leadership and self-respect—the very qualities that Nairobi strove to cultivate. Wilks no longer believed that desegregation could bring about meaningful social change for the black poor and working class. "It has been 18 years since the landmark decision *Brown versus Board of Education*," she wrote in 1972. "Eighteen long years and most of the poor children born that same year will be graduating from school this June unable to decipher the symbols on this very page."[45]

For Wilks, integration was feasible only when white communities surrendered unjustly accrued privilege. In the absence of such redistribution, white liberal benevolence was a sham. "You ought to have a policy like we have in the South saying, 'No Blacks allowed,'" she once declared. "That's right—I think we ought to be big enough to do that in California. I don't think you ought to take a kid on campus and crucify him alive and then say you want to integrate."[46]

If superficial integration was objectionable, formal separatism was impractical. Many of Nairobi's solidly middle-class allies—those endowed with the surplus time and money upon which the enterprise depended—were white. White teachers initially made up more than half the school's faculty. Nairobi policy required at least one black teacher per classroom. Administrators designed workshops to rid white volunteers of paternalism and notions of black cultural deficiency. Yet they also adopted the principled position that "teaching black" was a matter of ideology rather than skin pigment.[47]

Nairobi organizers rejected narrow racialism. They welcomed any student "irrespective of race, creed or color." They believed that white antiracists could serve as partners—though never managers—in efforts to reinforce black identity. According to black studies scholar St. Clair Drake, Nairobi practiced a "protective racial solidarity" that eschewed chauvinism and affirmed black self-determination while welcoming alliances with white people who operated "on the new wave length.'" Some students embraced this outlook. "Mrs. Rabell is white to other people," one sixth-grader said of a Nairobi instructor, "but to us she is black and beautiful."[48]

Despite such perspectives, Nairobi was widely seen as a stronghold of black separatism. Public school officials continued to portray the institution as a dangerous obstacle to desegregation. Some local families kept their distance, fearing that the school "taught Black Power." Nairobi's politics rankled East Palo Alto residents like Kemp Miller, head of a local group that stressed black professional success and interracialism as paths to gradual social reform. "Separatists want a culture of their own and I think that's good," Miller said in a 1970 interview. "They want their own to educate them, and I don't think that's bad. I can understand their impatience; I can't accept it." Many area foundations also withheld support, viewing the school as aggressively antiwhite. When the county board of supervisors cut funding for a popular Nairobi summer project, staff members blamed the pervasive notion that the school peddled racial hatred. The institution's officers were eventually brought before the Equal Opportunity Commission to answer similar charges.[49]

In truth, Nairobi's politics were milder and more flexible than those of many contemporary independent black institutions. The school's practicality stemmed in part from the convergence of gender and class. From the start, Wilks and the Mothers had pursued basic objectives: dignity, educational equality, and academic achievement. While these aims had broadened over time, they had never fundamentally changed. Like many women who bear primary responsibility for their children's welfare, the Mothers had employed multiple tactics to achieve educational redemption. Pragmatism had been their watchword. In time, more militant ideologies influenced Nairobi's mission. Younger activists attempted to frame the institution as a means of enabling students "to make the radical, complete break away from this system of white control, manipulation and destruction."[50] But Nairobi continued to affirm the possibilities of social mobility through academic success.

Though the perspectives of women and mothers strongly shaped Nairobi's character, neither Wilks nor her supporters imagined the school as a maternalistic enterprise. The defining goals were academic rigor and black awareness; fostering a "nurturing" environment was simply a means to an end. Gender, however, had always played a role in East Palo Alto's struggle for dignified education. Wilks had hesitated to project herself as a militant leader during early encounters with school board officials. Doing so, she feared, meant becoming the emasculating matriarch indicted by the 1965 Moynihan Report and condemned by many black organizers. "I risked being accused of castrating our men," she later said. "I knew that. But I had to stand up, however rough it might be."[51]

Wilks and the Mothers had embraced their image as "raucous" women, sweeping aside bourgeois norms of feminine comportment and respectability. "I'm not gonna promise nobody for money or nothing else that I'm gonna be nice," Wilks proclaimed. The Nairobi founder ignored those who counseled her to "take the militant jacket off." She understood the political value of disruption, believing firmly that "black people received more in the civil rights movement when we was more aggressive."[52] Besides, she insisted, nothing was "moderate" about the educational assault on African-American children.

Still, Wilks never relinquished pragmatism. The Nairobi founder ran her school in the style of a church, shunning political dogma while employing cultural practices familiar to most East Palo Altans. Part of Nairobi's appeal was its legitimation of black vernacular styles within an arena—formal education—that so often had meant degradation and alienation for the African-American lower classes. "I'm bringing you a message straight from the people," Wilks declared. "This is the way it is. This is what we want to say. Now if you want to hear it in a polished way, that's just too bad."[53]

Wilks's vision of social redemption entailed a revaluation of "little blacks" (her phrase) who lacked professional status but possessed a host of skills that could be harnessed on behalf of the larger community. Marshaling that expertise required humility. "We always had enough courage to go to the streets and work with the folks who wasn't doing well," Wilks later said.[54] A common touch was necessary when trying to convince parents to entrust their children to an academic program fashioned by an unlettered woman and her radical allies.

Grassroots sensibilities shaped Wilks's "Recipe for Building a School." The 1971 pamphlet relied on a cooking analogy to address workaday women and men who might have been intimidated by the prospect of institution building. The "Recipe" counseled would-be organizers of independent schools to "never forget the vitality of prayer in the black community" and urged them to seek the influence of ministers able to secure donations even from "conservative black folks."[55] Such strategies helped Nairobi operators construct a remarkable educational complex that grew to include a small college, a preschool, and other facilities. By the early 1970s, East Palo Alto's black institutional renaissance stood as a model for nationalists throughout the country.

The school system's broader significance as a symbol of educational reform, however, remained ambiguous. Nairobi organizers strove to instill communitarian ethics as an alternative to the competitive ethos of mainstream education. They embraced the ideal of the community-based school, applying the principles of *Pedagogy of the Oppressed* author Paulo Freire and other theorists who argued that students learn more effectively and become "more fully human" when motivated by philosophies and rituals rooted in their own cultures. Black ditties, poems, and spirituals suffused the Nairobi curriculum. Pupils sang freedom songs in daily assemblies, often accompanied by piano, guitar, and handclapping.[56]

Nairobi staffers rejected the interventionism of compensatory education and the practice of declaring black students "disadvantaged." They avoided overemphasis on discipline, drilling, or testing and shunned grouping, tracking, and other measures traditionally used by public schools to sort and rank children. "Your job is to teach," Nairobi instructors were told, "not to diagnose." Leaders of the institution stressed creative learning and personal growth while striving to nurture values like deference and sharing that they believed thrived in black homes.[57]

Respect for black vernacular speech represented another Nairobi reform. Guided by Mary Hoover, a language education expert, the school became one of the first black institutions to formally recognize its pupils as "bidialectical" and to affirm Black English as a defining cultural element of many African-American students. Drawing on recent research, Nairobi educators concluded that the linguistic features of black speech were systematic, legitimate, and based, in part, on West African patterns of pronunciation and grammar. A distinct history and cultural background—rather than laziness or ineptitude—led children to employ the alternative structures of black vernacular. Nairobi celebrated dexterous use of proverbs like "The Lord don't like ugly" as a form of cultural proficiency. Students were encouraged to wield the expressive genius of dialect, even as they learned Standard English as a kind of second language.[58]

Yet Nairobi also embraced more conservative ideas, especially as a competitor with public education—the system that continued to serve the vast majority of African-American children. East Palo Alto's struggle with decaying schools reinforced the desire of the private institution to break public education's "monopolistic grasp" on the community's children. The view of public instruction as a stranglehold that smothered innovation led Nairobi leaders to support school vouchers and other measures that promised to empower poorer families, enabling them to divert public funds toward private education. Like other veterans of conflicts with public schools, many East Palo Alto organizers came to regard teachers unions and government regulation as obstacles to community control, which rested on the ability to sever bureaucracy, circumvent conventional curricula, and remove objectionable instructors and administrators.[59] In coming years, some grassroots activists would escalate demands for liberation from the "monopoly" of public education, thus echoing the rhetoric of free market proponents who promoted privatization as the salvation of black education.

"I Am African!": The Rehabilitation of Identity

The most remarkable "reform" pursued by Nairobi staffers was the effort to rehabilitate African identity. Leaders of the institution embraced the crusade to transform black America's prevailing conceptions of Africa. Even as East Palo Alto residents debated the "Yes on Nairobi" question, children in the community continued to disparage the continent and its peoples. When Bob Hoover asked local grade schoolers what they knew about Africans, the youngsters responded with the standard repertoire of slurs: ugly, savage, primitive, dirty. When asked why they believed Africans were ugly, children as young as six described themselves: nappy hair, thick lips, black. "And that's why we started the Nairobi Day School," Hoover later recalled. "We said, 'We have to get our kids out of this damn system before it destroys every one of them.'"[60]

African themes abounded at Nairobi. The ceremony marking the school's first full academic year featured community leaders sporting *bubas* and brandishing spears—still a spectacle for East Palo Altans in 1969. Nairobi grammar books imparted knowledge of African geography (A is for Angola; B is for Botswana; C is for Congo) while instructional rhymes familiarized pupils with East African icons:

> Nyerere believes in work
> Kazi Kazi Kazi
> Nyerere believes in work

> busy busy busy
> Nyerere believes in black people
> share share share
> Nyerere believes in black people
> care care care. . . .[61]

Some expressions of African awareness at Nairobi were unabashedly romantic. The notion that traditional African societies were unfailingly egalitarian proved pervasive. In an imaginative composition, one of the school's 13-year-old pupils contrasted the "fresh smell of pine trees in Africa" with the noxious ecology of the Western world, a result, she asserted, of the manufacture of bombs by white men.[62] Yet African consciousness also generated more concrete references. The Kikuyu initiation oath, a symbol of resistance to British rule in Kenya, was recited at some Nairobi assemblies:

> I resolve on this day:
> That all my strength,
> That all my wit,
> Will be an instrument against oppression;
> That what I have gained
> In the first two stages of life
> Will be applied to making my community,
> My village,
> And my nation free . . .
> That in the name of Ngai
> I will be an instrument
> That will help tear down
> The walls of this Babylon.[63]

Nairobi reminded black studies scholar St. Clair Drake, one of the institution's advisers, of the decrepit but proud "Jim Crow" schools that he had attended as a boy, institutions that had nurtured his lifelong fascination with the African heritage of black Americans. Restoring African pride, however, was never a simple task. Casual denigration of Africa and Africans (a familiar theme in the vernacular rituals of many black Americans) persisted in the corridors of Nairobi. In response, Bob Hoover arranged for a local teenager to perform African dances at the school as a demonstration of the beauty of the continent's cultures. On another occasion, a handsome and somber undergraduate visited the campus to read African myths to the children, a presentation enhanced by the John Coltrane record that played in the background.[64]

Stokely Carmichael himself performed acts of African reaffirmation at Nairobi. The leader conveyed a powerful vision of Pan African identity during a February 1968 lecture at the institution attended by East Palo Alto children and other area youths and adults. Speaking to the youngest members of the audience, Carmichael argued that public schools routinely lied about Africa and that black schoolchildren needed to repudiate those lies by developing a positive sense of heritage. "Where are you from, brother? Where are you from, sister?" Carmichael asked, gesturing to individual children. "Africa!" the youngsters replied, echoing the familiar theme. The activist completed the address with a command: "Don't ever let them make you ashamed of Africa. And the only way they can't make you ashamed of Africa is if you say, 'I'm an African! I'm an African! I am African first and foremost!'"[65]

"To Acquaint Us with Our Past": The Symbols of African Identity

Africa had long formed a mosaic of meaning in black American consciousness. For generations, African Americans had attempted to preserve independent notions of Africa amid Western narratives of a barbaric land. By the early twentieth century, they had imagined the continent as a mysterious and bewitching realm, as a candidate for "civilizing" missions, as a source of ambivalence and alienation, as a potential Zion, as the site of an illustrious past, as a storehouse of cultural essence, as a symbol of deliverance from Western domination, and as a redemptive force for the entire diaspora.

Black internationalist awareness initially expanded in the wake of World War II, a conflict that crippled European colonialism and hastened the reawakening of nonwhite populations. African and Asian peoples returned to the stage of history as African Americans escalated their own quests for freedom. The postwar black American freedom struggle emerged as mass rebellions flared on the African continent. Black Americans glimpsed possibilities of their own redemption in the revolts of colonial subjects, even as news of African-American advances and indignities reverberated throughout Africa.[66]

Yet black America's lingering ambivalence toward its ancestral homeland impeded feelings of Pan African solidarity. Few African Americans possessed the awareness with which to combat routine defamations of Africa. African-American children who misbehaved in church were told to "Stop acting like an African!" A popular black maxim held that "I haven't lost anything in Africa and I'm not going there to find it." Cold War pressures further suppressed diasporic consciousness, stifling the cosmopolitan outlooks that had shaped black culture during the interwar years. By the 1950s, many African Americans viewed their drive for freedom and democracy as an essentially domestic affair.[67]

Then Ghana arose. In 1957, the West African nation became the first Sub-Saharan state to win independence. African-American interest in the "new Africa" surged. The knowledge that Africans were extricating themselves from colonial bondage helped transform black America's sense of its own destiny. In 1960 a host of African nations gained independence. By the mid-1960s, internationalist currents had reshaped African-American politics. Young radicals exemplified the cultural values that critic Harold Cruse dubbed "Afro-Americanism." They recast African-American relations with the non-Western world, applauding the escalation of armed struggle in Africa's settler colonies and viewing the continent as an arsenal of political and social models for black America. Their bible was *The Wretched of the Earth*. Their political muse was Malcolm.[68]

Malcolm X had redefined the black revolt as a human rights struggle, converting a search for African linkages into a modern philosophy of transnational blackness. In the year before his February 1965 death, he had communed with African revolutionaries and nationalist leaders during extended tours of the continent, embodying the possibilities of radical, Pan African solidarity and internationalizing the African-American struggle. "You can't understand what is going on in Mississippi if you don't understand what is going on in the Congo," he proclaimed.[69]

The Black Power generation heeded Malcolm's message. Unlike many of their elders, younger African Americans no longer viewed the continent as a source of revulsion or embarrassment, or worried that acknowledgment of their African heritage would jeopardize the pursuit of full citizenship in America. "Black Americans have returned spiritually to Africa," Amy Ashwood Garvey, Marcus Garvey's first wife, noted in 1968.[70] Yet far from simply reclaiming Africa, African Americans engaged in a process of reinvention driven by a fierce desire for self-definition.

The performance of African identity was a complicated affair. Even hair and fashion became arenas of expression and debate. The "Afro" trend that blossomed during the mid- to late 1960s was inexorably linked to Africa; the term itself suggested a "nationalistic orientation toward African heritage." While some artists sported "natural" hairdos in the early '60s, it was only after the death of Malcolm X and the 1965 eruption of Watts that the Afro truly began to emerge as an emblem of pride, defiance, and glamour. For some, the coiffure promised to "reverse the brainwashing" of European aesthetic standards. As a political symbol, however, the style was hardly uncontested. "A lot of cats get their Natural thing up tight," Gaston Neal of Washington, DC's New School of Afro-American Thought observed in 1967, "and then come down the street with some ofay chick hanging on them."[71]

Personal names offered another index of African affinity. As in other parts of the black world, the campaign to recapture African cultural heritage in the United States included efforts to shed the appellations of "the oppressor." Cultural nationalist organizations like the Institute for Positive Education in Chicago, the East in New York City, and New Jersey's Committee for a Unified Newark urged black people to renounce European-derived names. Some younger African Americans abandoned their birth names altogether. When a member of a cultural nationalist cadre in Durham, North Carolina, delivered a written marriage proposal to another member in 1970, he headed the communiqué, "From Muga Karega Ajanaku (former Negro Clarence Henderson) to Oba Sima Ajanaku (former Negro Ida Jackson)." In a playful riff on the renaming trend, one contemporary writer concluded her letters with an elaborate signature: "Ronda Davis (English): Rahnduh Deyvihss (Africanese)."[72]

In the postwar era, groups like the Nation of Islam had reintroduced the concept of African Americans repudiating their European or "slave" names. "You don't even know your true family name, you wouldn't recognize your true language if you heard it," Malcolm X declared in his 1965 autobiography. After Malcolm's death, cultural nationalists like Maulana Karenga (nee Ron Everett) helped popularize the adoption of African names. "Have you ever seen a Chinese named Jones or a Japanese named Whitfield?" Karenga asked a howling audience of Watts teenagers in 1966. A generation of Pan African nationalists later embraced the reclamation of African names as a means of resisting European mind-conditioning and reorienting a people who had been "separated from our cultural forms."[73]

Like other campaigns for cultural renewal, the drive for African names occasionally depicted African-American practices as haphazard or unrefined. "All people have names they as a people have chosen to define themselves except the Africans-in-America," the Committee for Unified Newark asserted in its 1971 *Swahili Name Book*. Denial of African-American cultural legitimacy accompanied fantasies about the cultural purity or authenticity of continental Africans. Ironically, even as U.S. nationalists lamented the Anglo-Saxon names of black Americans, some African nationalists bemoaned the European and Biblical names borne by many of that continent's elites.[74]

The transformation of personal names was part of a larger conversion that also witnessed the shift to "black" and "Afro-American." For years, nationalists had rejected the label "Negro" as a degrading vestige of slavery. "As long as you call yourself a Negro," Malcolm X insisted, "nothing is yours." Civil rights veteran Bayard Rustin argued that the problems confronting black people would "not be solved by altering a name, or by dressing differently, or by wearing one's hair in a new way." Yet as philosopher Tsenay Serequeberhan later observed, the principle that "the self-appellation of a people is a central component of the process of its liberation" ultimately prevailed.[75]

On the eve of the 1970s, *Newsweek, Jet*, and other publications offered conflicting assessments of the extent of lingering black approval for the designation "Negro." Among intellectuals and younger African Americans, however, the term's status as an anachronism reserved for expressions of irony or ridicule was incontrovertible. Responding to pressure from readers, editors of *Negro Digest* tested the alias *Black World* in the May 1968 and May 1969 editions of the monthly. By spring 1970, when the new title was installed, a formal rechristening to mark the publication's growing emphasis on "the essential unity of African peoples" was long overdue.[76]

No less remarkable than the renaming trend was the depth of emotional identification with Swahili (formally "Kiswahili"). By the late 1960s, the language had become a prominent symbol of black awareness among younger African Americans. The national tongue of Nyerere's Tanzania, Swahili was spoken by millions of Eastern and Central Africans. Yet for many black Americans, the idiom's political significance outstripped its linguistic utility. Proponents of cultural revitalization saw Swahili—a lingua franca that crossed ethnic and national boundaries—as a vehicle for Pan African awareness. For some, the variety served as the exemplary African language and the quintessential expression of the search for cultural roots.[77]

By 1967, Swahili instruction had emerged as a popular curricular demand of African-American high school and college students. When a handful of urban public schools began offering classes in the East African tongue, however, a storm of protest arose. Critics ridiculed the courses, portraying them as irrelevant to the future prospects of "disadvantaged" youths. A contemptuous *New York Times* condemned "the manufacture of artificial linguistic and pseudo-nationalistic rallying points." Other detractors noted that the East African lingua franca had been used by Arab slave raiders and European colonialists, and that, ironically, the West African ancestors of African Americans had spoken varieties like Hausa and Yoruba—not Swahili. Some black intellectuals insisted that knowledge of French would enable communication with greater portions of the continent, or that familiarity with Russian would prove more relevant to the social forces of the future.[78]

Defenders of Swahili, on the other hand, argued that attacks on the variety reflected a larger campaign to stifle anything that "tends to arouse the consciousness of Afro-Americans who identify themselves with their former mother continent."[79] Neither repression nor ridicule stemmed the growing affinity for the language. Expressions of African kinship served the intellectual and psychological needs of a generation seeking new concepts of sovereignty. A broad segment of black America embraced African cultural reidentification as a formula for self-determination and as a potent politics in its own right. No one did more to promote this outlook, or to lay the groundwork for its popular practice, than Maulana Ron Karenga.

"Harvesting the People": Cultural Nationalism and the Myth of Authenticity

Karenga constructed the intellectual edifice of cultural nationalist education. The theorist rose to prominence in the wake of the death of Malcolm X and the 1965 Watts rebellion. A specialist in African languages, he had completed graduate work in political science and linguistics when he emerged as one of Los Angeles's major black nationalist figures. From texts like Jomo Kenyatta's *Facing Mount Kenya* and Sékou Touré's *Toward Full Reafricanization*, he acquired a view of culture as a holistic force and a formidable weapon against the subjugation of a people.[80]

Karenga formed the self-help group "US" (as opposed to "them") in late 1965, hoping to channel the political energy of the recent street uprising toward the goal of revolutionizing African-American culture. He had internalized Malcolm's belief that black people must recapture their heritage to escape the psychological burdens of the oppressed. Modeled after the tight, internal discipline of the Nation of Islam, US was designed to disseminate a critical body of ideas while winning converts to the cause of cultural regeneration. "The battle we are waging now is the battle for the minds of black people," Karenga proclaimed.[81]

US advocates strove to embody the total conversion that Karenga espoused. They studied Swahili, took African names, sported the bubas and talismans favored by their charismatic leader, and adhered to stern protocols and strictures. They emphasized political education, operating Los Angeles's School of Afroamerican Culture and other institutions designed to promulgate black nationalist ideals. US also exhibited many of the ills that afflicted other Black Power formations. Karenga, who translated his name as "master teacher," constructed a personality cult over which he presided as chief theoretician and supreme leader. US followers memorized his aphorisms and hailed his utterances with cries of "Speak, Maulana!" and "Tell the Truth!"[82]

US was intensely patriarchal. Its doctrines cast male supremacy and female submission as a return to African tradition. Women were confined to the role of inspiring male leaders through the performance of domestic tasks and the duties of "social development." The fact that such ideas surpassed the routine sexism of contemporary American life hardly impeded Karenga's growing popularity. A major presence at Black Power conferences between 1966 and 1968, the leader espoused "unity without uniformity," winning audiences with grassroots charm and an aura of sagely wisdom.[83]

Karenga's seminal contribution to black nationalist theory was "Kawaida." Ostensibly a product of painstakingly culled African traditions and analysis of African-American realities, Kawaida was a collection of quasi-religious principles that claimed to provide a pathway to a more rational and enriching way of life. According to historian Keith A. Mayes, the philosophy "integrated knowledge from Africa and Black American history, knowledge from Africa's past with the lived reality of Black America's present. The objective was to operationalize a new intellectual synthesis that could inform the black freedom struggle."[84] The centerpiece of Kawaida was the seven principles of the Nguzo Saba: umoja (unity), kujichagulia (self-determination), ujima (collective work and responsibility), ujamaa (cooperative economics), nia (purpose), kuumba (creativity), and imani (faith).

The doctrine of Kawaida appealed to many young African Americans who sought a roadmap to social change and personal enlightenment amid the fragmented landscape of black protest politics. Karenga provided a normative value system that appeared natural and essential, and that required only the convert's dedication to adopting a more deliberate and rigorous lifestyle. "To go back to tradition is the first step forward," proponents of the creed declared.[85] Yet Kawaida nationalism contained a labyrinth of fallacies. Among them were the beliefs that cultural battles must precede political and economic struggles; that the practice of "values" offers a viable defense against the material realities of structural racism; that black "unity" across lines of ideology, class, and gender is inherently liberating; and that a single leader, group, or ideology may possess the formula for black freedom.

US adherents saw themselves as an enlightened cadre whose duty was to re-educate the black masses. Ignoring black America's indigenous traditions of dignity and resistance, they adopted the astonishing position that African Americans actually lacked a genuine, coherent culture. "Bloods [black people] only have elements of a culture such as song and dance," US disciples asserted, "but it takes a composite of the Seven Criteria for Culture to make up a total culture."[86] Once this conclusion was reached, it was a simple matter to contrive a divine truth, a panacea for black America's putative vices and psychosocial ills. Reaching into the distant past, cultural nationalists synthesized a novel and eclectic Africa, a mystical ideal that they believed could reanimate latent characteristics.

This feat of reinvention produced Kwanzaa, Karenga's other major bequest to black America. The fledgling holiday demonstrated the perils of the attempt to glean from African antiquity some cultural essence applicable to modern African-American circumstances. Karenga developed the weeklong "first fruits"

celebration in 1966. The December 26–January 1 ritual, an idealized composite of traditional African harvest festivals, called for affirmation of the Nguzo
Saba, with each day of observance representing a different principle. Kwanzaa's
purpose was to provide an alternative to the Eurocentrism and wanton commercialism of Christmas and other Western holidays while reviving "lost"
practices that could restore a sense of black heritage and collectivity. In the
words of one early advocate, the holiday offered temporary refuge from "the
white man's ways."[87]

Like other cultural nationalist rituals, Kwanzaa was replete with contradictions. Many African Americans struggled to survive amid the all-too-real inse-
curity of industrial or service sector employment; most lacked the luxury or
desire to simulate a romantic return to agrarian life. Kwanzaa's creation by a
contemporary *African-American* theorist, moreover, seemed to undermine the
festival's symbolic recovery of an authentic African past. Confusion on this score
led to many misconceptions, including the belief that Kwanzaa had existed on
the African continent "centuries before Christ." US officials acknowledged that
while Kwanzaa borrowed from traditional practices, the holiday was a creative
adaptation designed "to fulfill our needs in America." Yet some Kwanzaa observers continued to imagine that their unknown African relatives retired to straw
mats at Christmastime, encircled by the harvest, to consecrate in quaint, pastoral
ceremonies "the enormous gifts of love and common experiences in the quiet
comfort of a rich and bountiful land."[88]

Such mythmaking was not the principal challenge faced by early organizers of Kwanzaa fetes, who struggled in the late 1960s simply to attract viable
audiences to the midwinter festivities. Kwanzaa was initially celebrated within
urban centers by grassroots organizers and avowed black nationalists. Growing
numbers of African-American schoolchildren were exposed to Kwanzaa events
in the early 1970s, especially in major cities. In general, however, the holiday was
observed in isolated ceremonies attended mainly by the converted.

Much of the success of Kwanzaa in subsequent years stemmed from the
efforts of independent black institutions, whose promotion of the holiday
helped sustain a vibrant counterpublic of Black Power practices.[89] Though establishments like Durham's Pan African Early Education Center continued to celebrate Christmas in the early 1970s, most black independent schools became
stalwart Kwanzaa advocates years before the festival was widely known among
African Americans. Uhuru Sasa and its parent organization, the East, introduced
Kwanzaa to Brooklyn in 1968. The East later partnered with the Committee
for a Unified Newark and Brooklyn's School of Common Sense to host joint
celebrations of the holiday. Larger collaborations occurred in Chicago, where
Shule Ya Watoto, Arusha Konakri Institute, the Institute of Positive Education,
the Communiversity, the Black Topographical Research Center, and the Center

for New Horizons cosponsored Kwanzaa observances devoted to black separatist themes and the reclamation of "a comfortable and real" way of life.[90]

Black nationalist schools and related establishments held Kwanzaa pageants
and concerts, commissioned Kwanzaa documentaries (including one that was
screened in a Trenton, New Jersey, maximum security prison), and circulated
books and other materials explaining the significance of the Nguzo Saba. In
1971, both the East and Atlanta's Pan African Work Center released Kwanzaa
pamphlets designed for parents and educators. One publication featured a recitation for young children: "We celebrate Kwanza because we are Afrikan people.
We all sit around and hold hands and meditate quietly. Our Afrikan brothers and
sisters do this, too."[91]

If grassroots Kwanzaa productions helped raise the holiday's profile, the waning of the festival's radical implications also expanded its popularity. Visions
of Kwanzaa as a repudiation of Christmas faded; by the early 1970s, Christian
ministers in Harlem openly touted the holiday's cultural benefits, while *Essence*
magazine wished its readers "Season's Greetings, Happy Kwanza and Merry
Christmas." The Kwanzaa events that began drawing large audiences in cities like
New York, Los Angeles, and Boston were hardly paragons of militancy. By the
late 1970s, celebration of the holiday in Washington, DC, transcended class and
ideology, drawing both "street activists and Brahmins of city hall."[92]

Some cultural nationalists accepted the decline of Kwanzaa's oppositional
character. In 1979, an official from Washington's Nationhouse Watoto School
acknowledged that the holiday necessarily encompassed a wide range of political
perspectives. Other ideologues vowed to re-establish Kwanzaa's "revolutionary"
significance as a rejection of white, Western ideals. As early as 1972, observers
complained that the festival was "becoming a fad." In 1975, a New York activist
called on his peers to "Afrikanize" the holiday by rescuing it from white cooptation. "Kwanza is jive only if we are jive," he declared.[93]

Jitu Weusi of Uhuru Sasa criticized black families who observed Kwanzaa
at home but continued to display a Christmas tree. Some nationalists sought
in vain to revive the element of daytime fasting once loosely associated with
the holiday. Other contemporary attempts to promote alternatives to holiday
commercialism—from the Black Panther's indictment of the "Pig's Xmas"
to Shule Ya Watoto's advocacy of a somber, cultural nationalist substitute for
Thanksgiving revelry—were no more successful in changing the behavior of the
black rank and file. In the end, models of black piety and asceticism held little
appeal as surrogates for popular rituals of consumption. By contrast, Kwanzaa
prospered in later years, propelled not by its contrarian dimensions, but by its
adaptability to the commercial imperatives of American culture.[94]

Over the course of the 1970s, it grew abundantly clear that Kwanzaa
offered no real alternative to social or economic relations under capitalism.

As political scientist Adolph Reed later observed, the holiday created "a mythology that paints Christmas black without really upsetting conventional practices." Kwanzaa provided another opportunity for corporations to market consumer goods to a niche audience. The festival, Mayes notes, "fit snugly into the new discourse on corporate and institutional multiculturalism." Many black professionals embraced Kwanzaa's emphasis on internal racial cohesion. The notion that all African Americans share a basic set of values helped ease the class anxieties of this relatively privileged stratum, even as it separated itself from the economic and political realities of the African-American majority.[95]

Early champions of Kwanzaa adapted to the shifting discourse. Karenga welcomed black elite observance of the festival and accepted the holiday's status as an affirmation of black camaraderie rather than an explicit rejection of bourgeois liberalism and Western capitalism. The Kwanzaa founder began characterizing the holiday as "a harvesting of the people" and as an opportunity to turn inward and renew bonds of racial solidarity.[96] Kwanzaa's assertions of fictive kinship offered a dose of psychological succor amid the liberation struggle's chaotic decline.

In the mid-1970s, a Harlem group coined the slogan, "The real 'Kwanza' is in Southern Africa!"—an attempt to use the holiday to bolster African-American support for assaults on European settler colonialism on the continent. Such efforts to trade abstraction for substantive political engagement proved all too rare. Many Kwanzaa celebrants remained content to perform superficial acts like eating "without European utensils" and uttering "harambee" or "Habari gani?"[97] In so doing, they promoted reductionist and ahistorical conceptions of Africa. Such narrow expressions of identity threatened to equate symbolism with struggle, obscuring the need for ongoing, principled confrontation with concrete political and economic conditions on the continent and throughout the diaspora.

The renaissance of African identity thus contained deep contradictions. Many younger activists were staunch anti-imperialists who equated Western finance capital with global white supremacy. Yet the new black nationalism also anchored transnational solidarity in the metaphysics of "African blood." Was blackness a timeless racial essence, or was it a "fellowship of the disinherited"—a product of historical exploitation within the world system? Shared belief in culture as resistance could not long forestall this critical debate.[98]

"To Lose Our Negro Minds": Black Nationalism's Cultural Turn

The African restoration movement viewed culture as a decisive sphere of struggle. Its central premise was that cultural revitalization was necessary to liberate

African Americans from the complex of the oppressed. "We must recapture our heritage and our identity if we are ever to liberate ourselves from the bonds of white supremacy," Malcolm X had proclaimed. "We must launch a cultural revolution to unbrainwash an entire people."[99]

A host of postcolonial thinkers, from Frantz Fanon to Ngugi wa Thiong'o, argued that cultural practices were central to the task of liberation. "A people who free themselves from foreign domination will not be culturally free unless, without underestimating the importance of positive contributions from the oppressor's culture and other cultures, they return to the upward paths of their own culture," Amilcar Cabral, leader of the anticolonial struggle in Guinea-Bissau and Cape Verde, famously observed. Gatherings like the 1966 First Festival of Negro Arts in Dakar affirmed culture as a critical element of postcoloniality. The launching of China's Great Proletarian Cultural Revolution provided another captivating (if deeply flawed) ideal of mass regeneration.[100]

Many emerging nations strove to consolidate their independence by eliminating the cultural and spiritual residue of the colonizer. The Tanzanian government urged resistance to the "imperialist cultural aggression" that flooded the country with debasing films, fashion, music, literature, and other "retrogressive importations." Guinean leader Sékou Touré blamed the vestiges of colonialism for distorting the tastes and aesthetics of his nation's young people and transforming them into "lovers of the tango or of the waltz." Efforts to "decolonize the African mind" and to "effect a renaissance of African civilization" inspired parallel black American struggles to escape the standards and values of the oppressor.[101]

Yet narrow conceptions of culture produced a number of errors. Few proponents of African-American cultural renewal displayed a nuanced understanding of the ways culture actually functions as a liberating force. They saw culture as static or pure rather than as a dynamic and multidimensional phenomenon. They imagined culture as a gift to be conferred rather than as an organic product of struggle and a means of popular participation in the creation of the new society. They envisioned culture as inherently liberatory rather than as an integral component of larger battles for the transformation of political and material realities.

Recognition of the limitations of culturalism led to the discrediting of cultural nationalism in the eyes of much of the black radical intelligentsia. By the late 1960s, many young activists regarded revolutionary nationalism as a potent alternative to narrow cultural politics. Revolutionary nationalists saw themselves as the offspring of Third World rebellions and as the true heirs of Malcolm X and North Carolina militant Robert F. Williams. They rejected cultural nationalism as an escapist ideology that glorified blackness while failing to seriously engage the question of imperialism or the social category of class. As the influence of radical internationalism increased, "cultural nationalist" became a term of derision among a growing segment of Black Power ideologues.

The divide between revolutionary and cultural nationalism was never as absolute as contemporary nomenclature implied. Both strains acknowledged the interrelatedness of culture and politics, venerated anticolonial struggles, and recognized the need to foster black consciousness. As scholars have noted, shades of emphasis rather than fundamental differences often separated black nationalist tendencies. Still, the conflict between revolutionary and cultural nationalism was both genuine and intense. Revolutionary nationalists viewed adherence to Marxism-Leninism and commitment to armed resistance and state transformation as antithetical to preoccupation with African costume, cultural heritage, and paraphernalia.[102]

The ideological rivalry affected all aspects of contemporary nationalist practice. One convert to revolutionary nationalism resigned from Washington, DC's New School of Afro-American Thought as early as 1967, concluding that the institution's cultural emphasis precluded direct forms of political confrontation, especially the strategy of "halting state power and bargaining from that position for a black nation-state." The following year, John Churchville of Philadelphia's Freedom Library Day School released a pamphlet in which he denounced cultural nationalists as "attitudenalists" who elevated "Afro-oriented" slogans and dress while avoiding political positions that might genuinely antagonize the ruling class.[103]

The most destructive manifestation of nationalism's internal conflict was the feud between Maulana Karenga's US organization and the Black Panther Party. Panther officials raised principled objections to the rival organization's brand of identity politics. "Culture itself will not liberate us," Huey Newton declared. "We're going to need some stronger stuff." As the Panthers grew more apprehensive about police infiltration and repression, however, members of the group couched their critiques in increasingly derisive language. Not content merely to mock the "mangled Swahili" of US adherents or to castigate them as rhetoricians and African fetishists, Panthers demonized Karenga's minions as "pork-chop nationalists" and as collaborators with reactionary politicians and police in the quest to "confuse the masses" and subvert black radicalism. In turn, cultural nationalists dismissed their ideological adversaries as self-abnegating "neo-leftists" and as dupes of white racists masquerading as radical allies. As the quarrel unfolded, paranoia and dogmatism enveloped both camps.[104]

The dispute degenerated into a fratricidal war whose most violent clash occurred in January 1969 when a Panther–US confrontation on the UCLA campus left two Panthers dead. The repercussions of the encounter lasted throughout the 1970s and beyond, fracturing the ranks of black radicalism and nationalism and intensifying the strife that plagued many independent black institutions.[105]

By the early 1970s, sectarianism, repression, and discord had imperiled national-ism's fragile status as the ascendant political tendency of the freedom struggle.

The drive for self-definition galvanized communities like East Palo Alto, whose activists pursued a pragmatic brand of nationalism that addressed everyday needs. Other visions of black autonomy and cultural identity proved esoteric and abstract. A wide array of organizers saw culture as a critical realm of struggle. Yet the elegant simplicity of "We Are an African People" concealed a host of competing impulses, from principled political engagement to outright fantasy. Only the re-emergence of modern Pan Africanism seemed capable of synthe-sizing contemporary theories of race and revolution and reinvigorating a frag-mented movement.

MAE MALLORY AND DAUGHTER. Activist Mae Mallory and daughter at
a New York City courthouse in the late 1950s. Mallory was the leader of the
"Harlem 9," a group of African-American mothers who boycotted the substandard,
segregated public schools to which their children were assigned. Such efforts were
important precursors to the mass black educational struggles of the 1960s. Burley
Versatile Photography. Courtesy of *New York Amsterdam News*.

RALPH FEATHERSTONE AND STANLEY WISE OF SNCC. Ralph Featherstone and Stanley Wise of the Student Nonviolent Coordinating Committee (SNCC), both future participants in Pan African nationalist schools, express support for the Palestinian struggle in 1967. The demise of SNCC and the radicalization of its staffers in the late 1960s contributed to the birth of a host of Pan African nationalist institutions. Featherstone and another activist were killed in a mysterious car blast in 1970. Wide World Photos. Courtesy of *New York Amsterdam News*.

NASHVILLE LIBERATION SCHOOL. A student instructor conducts a black history class in 1967 as Fred Brooks (seated at extreme left), a founder of the Nashville Liberation School, looks on. The school was forced to meet in a park after political pressure led to its eviction from its original quarters.

AMIRI AND AMINA BARAKA. Amiri and Amina Baraka (LeRoi Jones and Sylvia
Wilson) at a New Jersey courthouse in 1967. Amina took the lead in founding African
Free School, an innovative program that the couple developed to serve children from the
neighborhood surrounding their tenement theater in Newark, New Jersey. World Wide
Photos. Courtesy of *New York Amsterdam News*.

GERTRUDE WILKS. Gertrude Wilks near the school that she founded in East Palo Alto, California. Wilks, a former militant advocate of school desegregation, created Nairobi Day School and High School in the late 1960s to offer African-American residents of the San Francisco–area town an alternative to deteriorating public schools. Associated Press.

LESLIE CAMPBELL AT JHS 271 DEMONSTRATION. Junior High School 271 teacher Leslie Campbell (later "Jitu Weusi") addresses students outside the Brooklyn school during the community control struggles of 1968. Campbell, an outspoken leader in the experimental Ocean Hill–Brownsville district, founded Brooklyn's Uhuru Sasa Shule after being fired by the New York City Board of Education. Bettmann/Corbis, AP Images.

BLACK PANTHER LIBERATION SCHOOL, SAN FRANCISCO. A teacher leads students in political chants at a Black Panther Liberation School in San Francisco, California. Such schools were among the "survival programs" created by the Panthers in 1969 to meet the everyday needs of black residents of urban centers. Bettmann/Corbis.

HAKI MADHUBUTI. Poet and institution builder Haki Madhubuti (Don L. Lee) conducts a community workshop at a meeting of the Congress of African People. Along with Safisha Madhubuti (Carol Lee), Haki founded Chicago's New Concept Development Center, an independent school, in 1972 as the educational arm of the Institute of Positive Education, a cultural center. Courtesy of *New York Amsterdam News*.

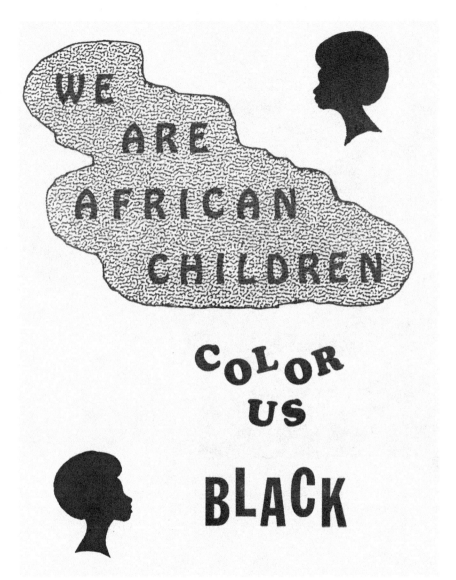

We Are African Children Coloring Book Cover. A coloring book created by a communications class at the Clifford McKissick Community School in Milwaukee. The secondary school was named after an unarmed young man who was shot and killed by police during the city's 1967 street uprising. Courtesy of Milwaukee County Historical Society.

KALAMU YA SALAAM KWANZAA CELEBRATION. Poet Kalamu Ya Salaam of Ahidiana Work/Study Center in New Orleans holds an ear of corn during a celebration of Kwanzaa, an African-themed African-American holiday. Ahidiana was both a Pan African nationalist collective and a small, independent primary school. Courtesy of *New Orleans Times-Picayune*.

5

The Maturation of Pan African Nationalism

To think of imperialism in terms of race is disastrous.
—C. L. R. James[1]

The years 1969–1972 offered a number of signs that the black nationalist resurgence was losing momentum. Ironically, this was a moment of unparalleled assertiveness and cultural expression. The sheer volume of intellectual production reinforced the sense that a long-term political realignment was underway. Yet neither the energy nor the inventiveness of militant nationalists could stem the crises that seized black America. Amid the nation's abandonment of its cities, the violence of counterinsurgency campaigns, and the dialectic of economic decline and drug crimes, a generation of organizers sought new directions.

Pan Africanism appeared to provide solutions. The Pan Africanist reawakening was hailed as a natural extension of the Black Power theme. But the advent of "Pan African nationalism" (or "Neo-Pan Africanism," as the movement was dubbed) produced no panaceas. Confronted with complex realities of power, many activists were forced to rethink their ideals. Some rejected the assumptions of "Racial Pan Africanism." They abandoned reductionist visions of the African world, seeking more rigorous frameworks and, in some cases, engaging feminist and proletarian struggles. Encounters with figures like West African revolutionary Amilcar Cabral inspired the transition to "Left Pan Africanism," an approach that attempted to root itself in the material circumstances of race and class.

"A Life Superior": Pan African Nationalism and the Rise of the Cadre Model

The crises of black liberation increased the appeal of Neo-Pan Africanism. Cultural nationalism's reputation had been damaged by the Panther–US conflict;

its status was further diminished by the emergence of "revolutionary national-ism" as the preferred self-designation of young militants. The Black Panthers had been virtually decimated by the state. Other radical formations fared no bet-ter. Police and counterintelligence crusades eliminated, captured, or drove into exile a small army of black political figures. What the power structure could not accomplish with repression it achieved through cooptation. Corporate America thoroughly commoditized "blackness." (Afro wigs could be purchased from Macy's in shades of black, brown, blonde, and "auburn gray.") President Nixon's equation of Black Power with "black capitalism" subjected the latter phrase to derision while signaling the former phrase's dwindling utility.[2]

The nationalist movement had reached a plateau. Cynicism swept through the ranks. Even condemnation of militant posturing began to seem for-mulaic. The quest for correct political models led to contests over which ideological tendencies could claim the banner of revolution. Amid these developments, the reassertion of Pan Africanist ideals by Stokely Carmichael (Kwame Ture) and other activists had an electrifying effect. By 1969, the com-monality of black struggles across the globe had resurfaced as a central tenet of African-American thought.[3]

Pan Africanism had arisen in the Western Hemisphere as a means of linking campaigns for freedom and dignity throughout the black world. After World War II, the movement's impetus had shifted from African-American and Caribbean luminaries to the African masses themselves, who seized the historical initia-tive by achieving formal independence and self-rule. To a large extent, modern Pan Africanism was a project of governments and heads of state whose primary agenda was the consolidation of formal power. Constrained by the politics of national formation, the Pan African movement had lost much of the radical meaning it had possessed as an insurgent social force.[4]

The contradictions of the postcolonial world hardly troubled most American exponents of Pan Africanism. Even as political crises swept across Africa, black America's popular conceptions of the continent remained sentimental, abstract, and rooted in domestic racial sensibilities. This reality only deepened enthusiasm for Pan Africanism, helping to ensure its status as a "consensus ideology" of the early 1970s. African-American theorists hailed the arrival of a genuine philosophy of the people—perhaps even the impetus for a revital-ized mass movement. "We Are an African People" provided the intellectual grounding for an array of institutions, publications, and organizations.[5]

"Pan African nationalism"—the simultaneous pursuit of black national-ist development and global black solidarity—emerged as the new precept of struggle. Hope for its fulfillment rested on the cadre model. Radical theorists held that disciplined, tight-knit circles of organizers working within individual communities constituted the vanguard of black liberation. These militants would disseminate the political concepts of Pan African nationalism. They would propel the struggle beyond sloganeering, building alternative institutions and delivering essential services to black urban neighborhoods. "It is the cadre or small unit of dedicated Nationalists [that] must be at the base of any conscious movement the total community will make," artist-activist Amiri Baraka declared in 1972. Such units, he maintained, should be established "in each black community across this land" and "wherever Afrikan peoples are in the world."[6]

An old organizing tool, the cadre model had reappeared in the 1960s as young militants searched for decisive methods of revolution. In 1966, members of the Student Nonviolent Coordinating Committee's (SNCC's) Atlanta Project had sought new configurations that would allow organizers to pursue self-discipline, ideological development, and "a life superior to the former way of life" without forming de facto colonies or becoming "exiles among our own people." The cadre, a Student Organization for Black Unity communiqué stressed in 1971, "is not a clique cut off from our people" but "an integral segment of the black community." Yet the nature of the Pan African nationalist cell, an entity designed to support a strenuous lifestyle of work and study, suggested that some degree of detachment from the masses was inevitable. Part of the rationale for such formations, Baraka acknowledged, was the willingness of their members to practice "a value system superior to the one that enslaves our community."[7]

A further paradox of the cadre lay in its aims. While proponents of Pan African nationalism hoped to demonstrate the ideology's practical relevance, they also regarded alternative institutions as mechanisms for socializing the black rank and file. Traditional issues like welfare rights, housing, job discrimination, and school reform were subordinated to the conceptual strategies of "national" development. Narrow preoccupation with the daily crises of oppression was seen as an error to be resolved through the political guidance of the cadre. "Without such a vanguard," the Pan African Students Organization in America asserted in 1970, "the popular masses, abandoned in oblivion, cannot be awakened to revolutionary consciousness; they are like an army without headquarters."[8]

If Pan African nationalism was hampered by such elitism, it was also crippled by political myths. In the early 1970s, most U.S. Pan Africanists remained mired in the provincialism of cultural nationalism. The influence of Kawaida, Maulana Karenga's "neo-traditionalist" doctrine, lent the Pan Africanist revival a mystical orientation. Its politics rehashed the racialism and anticommunism of Garvey while eschewing the progressive anti-imperialism of Du Bois. Only a closer encounter with the realities of revolution would engender a more critical approach.

"Masters of Our Own Space": Amiri Baraka and the Congress of African People

Amiri Baraka embodied the Pan African nationalist quest. Baraka was a Greenwich Village Beat poet known as LeRoi Jones when he was struck by revolutionary black consciousness. A Newark, New Jersey, native, he fled the "superfluities" of Howard University and the "sickness" of the Air Force before embarking on a life of letters whose early offerings included *Dutchman* (a land-mark play) and *Blues People* (a cultural history). A 1960 trip to Fidel Castro's Cuba shattered his illusion of artistic purity. In ensuing years, he demonstrated against Congolese Prime Minister Patrice Lumumba's assassination and worked with left-leaning black organizations, captivated by Malcolm X's rebuke of white supremacy. Awash with resentment and self-loathing after Malcolm's death, he renounced the bohemianism of Greenwich Village and, abandoning his white wife and two children, headed uptown in 1965 to help fashion the cultural edifice of black militancy.[9]

Baraka built the Black Arts Repertory Theatre/School (BARTS), the spring-board for the Black Arts Movement, in a Harlem brownstone. Toiling alongside a remarkable assemblage of cultural workers, including Harold Cruse, Larry Neal, and Sonia Sanchez, he helped establish the venture as a pioneering expression of the hunt for a "Black Aesthetic." BARTS hosted festivals, political gatherings, and cultural productions. It prefigured black studies programs and Black Power liberation schools, offering classes for children and adults in everything from "Afro-American Cultural Philosophy" to drumming, drawing, and literature. It attempted to embody the ideal of black self-determination. "No vague ghosts with pale tongues" would obstruct the attempt to transform Harlem young-sters into "warriors gifted with the powers of creation," a pamphlet pledged. But plagued by internal turmoil, the institution remained largely disconnected from the surrounding black community.[10]

Though BARTS collapsed after several months, the short-lived effort spawned cultural institutions across the country. Meanwhile, Baraka returned to Newark, determined to produce "art that would reach the people" and to formalize the "national" consciousness within black central cities. In Sylvia Wilson he found an able partner for both missions. Wilson (soon to become Amina Baraka) was herself a talented poet, dancer, and cultural worker. As Baraka's wife, she would devote her skills to the charismatic leader's political projects, even as she chafed under the patriarchy that cultural nationalism portrayed as African traditionalism.[11]

Throughout 1966 and 1967, nationalist development remained Amiri Baraka's primary concern. Despite its more than 60% black population, Newark was a grim industrial hub ruled by an Italian-American political machine and an ownership class of absentee landlords and merchants. Inspired by the nascent Black Power cry and the spirit of street revolts, Baraka resolved to transform the city into a center of black self-activity. Urban disorders had demonstrated the need for alternative infrastructure that could foster political awareness while addressing bread-and-butter needs. As the writer Robert L. Allen observed, "The rebellions put nationalist leaders on notice that, while more black people might be inclined toward nationalism, they were not in the least interested in idle dreams or obscure mysticism."[12]

Striving once more to forge an institution on the axes of revolutionary art and politics, Baraka created Spirit House, a theater and multipurpose center, in a drab tenement within Newark's Central Ward. He and Amina Baraka lived and worked in the rehabilitated building, producing plays and propaganda with the aid of a growing troupe of cultural workers. They used the residence as a base for grassroots organizing, attempting to influence educational struggles and other local issues. Then historical events interceded. Newark, a nexus of the police brutality, vanishing social services, dilapidated housing, and steep unemployment that had sparked conflagrations in other cities, finally erupted in summer 1967. The resulting violence caused more than two dozen deaths. Thousands of National Guardsmen and police invaded black neighborhoods. Amiri Baraka was savagely beaten and arrested during the uprising, and his tenement theater was ransacked. Yet the destruction fostered a sense of renewal. "For me, the rebellion was a cleansing fire," Baraka later said.[13]

As his political resolve deepened, the intellectual began conceptualizing Spirit House as the command post of a more purposeful mission. He embraced the teachings of Maulana Karenga, whose Kawaida philosophy and US organization exemplified the paramilitary discipline that many organizers associated with revolution. Baraka fashioned his Committee for a Unified Newark (CFUN), the umbrella organization for a host of grassroots projects, into a similarly regimented enterprise. Only highly trained, doctrinaire nationalists, he believed, could bring about the cultural regeneration of black neighborhoods. CFUN evolved into a coterie of more than 100 adherents whose zeal, asceticism, and African garb became paradigmatic elements of cultural nationalist practice.

CFUN represented the next phase of Baraka's campaign to develop a science of black urban revolution. He saw the crusade to reconfigure inner cities as a struggle to control existing social structures while forming radical, alternative institutions. Despite Newark's poverty and loss of industry and jobs, the leader continued to envision the city as a base for the implementation of Black Power. "We want our whole new Black selves as absolute masters of our own space," he proclaimed.[14]

CFUN's network of programs included cultural and educational centers, job training initiatives, theater and dance troupes, cooperatives, a community newspaper, and a small publishing house. The organization played a key role in the 1970 election of Kenneth Gibson, Newark's first black mayor. Rather than acting as "cultural pundits inveighing from on high," Baraka later insisted, CFUN workers became devoted servants of black Newark.[15]

But the organization also exhibited many weaknesses. CFUN failed to address the practical limitations of "community control," even as massive divestment ravaged urban centers. Its veneration of Kawaida doctrines precluded more rigorous analysis of structural racism. Its racial fundamentalism and patriarchy denied class distinctions and relegated women to subordinate roles. Its rigid social hierarchies mocked the idea of a creative, democratic movement based on widespread participation and grassroots leadership. Its preoccupation with the metaphysical wisdom of Karenga, its arcane ceremonies and rituals, its lack of self-criticism, its virtual deification of Baraka (who dropped "LeRoi Jones" for a designation meaning "blessed prince" while assuming the title "Imamu" or "spiritual leader"), and its obsession with moral and political re-education rendered its mission unintelligible to many working people.[16]

Similar shortcomings plagued the Congress of African People (CAP), the body that succeeded CFUN as the major expression of Baraka's leadership. An outgrowth of the national Black Power conferences of 1966–1968, CAP emerged from a 1970 summit that attracted more than 2,000 registrants, including a curious mélange of political luminaries. The purpose of the gathering was to establish a national black coalition, a united-front organization constructed upon the principle of "operational unity" and encompassing scores of nationalist-oriented affiliates in urban areas. Baraka and other CAP organizers hoped the new formation would spur the transition from "abstract ideological disagreements to a unity based on blacks working together on concrete programs."[17]

CAP conventions strove to create "an atmosphere of renewed seriousness" throughout the movement.[18] By promulgating abstract political concepts, however, the organization also demonstrated the pitfalls of black nationalist thought. CAP proclamations like "Land is changing hands!" sustained the fantasy that black empowerment was imminent or inevitable and largely a matter of stoking nationalist sentiment. The organization's militant pronouncements masked its collaboration with a rising class of African-American professionals and functionaries who answered to Democratic Party elites.[19]

The 1972 National Black Political Convention in Gary, Indiana, further highlighted the limitations of contemporary Pan Africanism and black nationalism. The summit, which drew more than 8,000 attendees to the task of setting "a black agenda," represented "the watershed experience" of the era of Pan African nationalist hegemony in African-American politics. The affair's ideological and organizational diversity seemed to validate the resounding cries of "Nation Time!" Gary advanced a comprehensive agenda for restructuring the social landscape. Its demand for redistributive economic policies reflected the influence of rank-and-file delegates and the momentum of countless grassroots struggles.

In the end, however, both the historic gathering at Gary and the National Black Assembly, the formation that it generated, represented less "a repudiation of existing American politics" than a confirmation of the political anemia of bourgeois nationalism. One of Gary's principal failings was its pursuit of all-black unity—the notion that achieving symbolic, intraracial accord is an inherently progressive political end. By embracing blackness as the ultimate social reality and dismissing ideological, class, and gender divisions, convention organizers elided conflicts that must serve as points of principled debate and struggle in any genuinely transformative movement.

Professions of black solidarity failed to disguise the patriarchal nature of the CAP and Gary summits. Women who appeared on daises at such events—figures like Dorothy Height, Queen Mother Moore, Betty Shabazz, and Coretta Scott King—played only symbolic roles in the proceedings. The male personalities, for their part, hailed largely from the ascendant, managerial class that benefited disproportionately from social spending and the expanding ranks of black elected officials. Their preoccupation with centralized, bureaucratic organizations and the rituals of electoral politics signaled a retreat from grassroots battles for democratic rights waged in neighborhoods, workplaces, and schools.[20]

"It Must Be Liberation That You Teach": African Free School and the Reclamation of Newark

The black political conventions of the early 1970s revealed the significance of independent schools as vehicles for Pan African nationalism. Organizers from the School of Common Sense and Uhuru Sasa Shule of Brooklyn; Malcolm X Liberation University of Durham (and later Greensboro) North Carolina; the Nairobi complex of East Palo Alto, California; and Washington, DC's Center for Black Education attended the founding CAP assembly in 1970. Creators of current or future Pan African nationalist academies played key roles during the conference, which called for the formation of a nationwide system of independent black education.[21]

As the major Pan African nationalist federation of the day, CAP strongly influenced the black independent school movement. Baraka, the guiding force and eventual chairman of CAP, was a leading proponent of Kawaida-style Pan

Africanism as the philosophical framework for parallel institutions. His own African Free School (AFS) provided a critical prototype.

Like many grassroots initiatives in Newark's Central Ward, AFS began at 33 Stirling Street, the site of Spirit House. In a dreary tenement that had been converted into a theater and arts workshop, Amiri and Amina Baraka began building a block association in 1967. A group of neighborhood children frequented the center, where they helped produce a newspaper and perform plays, some of which Amiri Baraka had written for the youngsters. Many of the children struggled to learn the scripts; it soon grew clear that they could not read. The Barakas had wanted to politicize the neighborhood and promote the Black Power concept. Now a more basic intervention was in order.

Amina Baraka and other young women from a Spirit House study circle began gathering children from surrounding buildings and bringing them to the center for academic tutoring. Many of the youngsters attended the old, battered Robert Treat Elementary School nearby, where the average student scored three years below national reading norms. Intrigued by the relationship between childhood education and nationalist consciousness, Amina Baraka developed a rendering of the alphabet that linked each letter to a word associated with the black freedom struggle. A "Community Free School" (soon renamed "African Free School") took shape as an after-school class within Spirit House. Though CFUN literature identified Amiri Baraka as the policymaker, Amina Baraka directed the venture and performed much of the intellectual and administrative work.[22]

AFS initially operated three days a week, serving elementary and junior high students and rapidly expanding to include a preschool and full-time offerings. Amiri Baraka further enlarged the enterprise, writing a grant proposal and struggling with the city's board of education and "reactionary forces in the community" before winning federal Title One funds in 1970 to create an offshoot AFS course in an experimental classroom at Robert Treat. There, under a red, black, and green flag, 30 youngsters, grades five through eight, many of whom officials had labeled "chronic slow learners," studied Swahili, hieroglyphics, and Zulu folklore along with more traditional subjects. Though opponents of black nationalism criticized the public school component of AFS, Amiri Baraka vigorously defended the curriculum. "Nobody thinks of teaching the Bantu philosophers to the white middle class," he noted.[23]

AFS reflected CFUN's short- and long-term visions of nationalist development. Amina Baraka's original aim was to help students acquire basic academic skills. AFS operators also strove to influence public education in Newark. The premise behind the semiautonomous AFS class at Robert Treat was that the public school system, moribund though it seemed, was likely to remain the primary mechanism for educating black children, at least for the foreseeable future. The Robert Treat extension enabled the incorporation of Pan African nationalist concepts and the construction of a model that could be replicated by other African-American schools.

The approach bespoke the larger strategy of infiltrating white-controlled institutions in black inner cities. CFUN hosted conferences and produced literature designed to challenge public school materials that treated slavery as the origin of black history. The goal was to critique the anachronistic perspectives of "Negro history" while transforming mainstream education.[24]

Ultimately, however, AFS was an expression of the search for permanent alternatives. Reducing black dependency on "enemy" structures, CFUN officials believed, required the provision of equivalent or superior services. "The most revolutionary Afrikans as far as the community will be concerned will be those who can deliver those goods and services," Amiri Baraka insisted. Though the leader acknowledged that AFS would never educate more than a fraction of the city's black children, he believed that the construction of educational prototypes could help demonstrate black nationalism's legitimacy. Amina Baraka continued to manage the expansion of the independent AFS operation, which acquired new furnishings and a handsome plant when it moved to a building on Clinton Avenue. There she pursued Pan African nationalism's central objective: the forging of a new people.[25]

Even the name of the CFUN school reflected this mission. The original "African Free School" had been founded in New York during the late eighteenth century as a means of educating the children of free and enslaved African Americans. Established by white philanthropists, the institution had become an instrument of black self-determination, producing an august procession of abolitionists, educators, and black nationalists, from Alexander Crummell to Henry Highland Garnet. Newark's AFS sought to generate an equally gifted leadership class, a body that could help "transform the values of our community from white and Negro values to black revolutionary values."[26]

The practical challenges of this crusade were daunting. AFS charged no tuition and relied on tens of thousands of dollars in grants from the federal government, foundations, and private donors. One of the more generously subsidized Pan African nationalist institutions of the day, the school received tax-exempt status in 1972. The tithes of CFUN workers and the volunteer labor of parents supplemented the operation, but the absence of a major endowment meant continued dependence on external benefactors.[27]

Whatever contradictions marred their rhetoric of black autonomy, AFS officials remained trenchant critics of public education. Amiri Baraka maintained that *all* public institutions—"even the rundown schools full of black children deep in the ghettos"—were strongholds of white supremacy. Without an effort to both control and circumvent such establishments, he argued, "we leave our children to be crippled for life by enemies as old and deadly as our residence in the West." The activist described the typical Newark teacher (a white, nonresi-dent of the city) as "a mind distortion specialist" who extracted "hunks of black matter" from the minds of African-American children, only to "replace that liv-ing tissue with cancerous growths."[28]

Newark's educational realities hardly invalidated such rhetoric. The deteriora-tion of the city's schools had accelerated during the 1960s as the African-American student population had climbed from 55% to close to 80%. Most black stu-dents attended congested, aging schools that had been abandoned by Newark's dwindling middle class. The high school dropout rate exceeded 30%; unofficial sources placed it closer to 50%. While 50 of its 75 schools were predominantly black, the district employed no African-American principals at the time of the 1967 uprising. A Governor's Commission on Civil Disorders reported in 1968 that thousands of children in the city "either cannot read, or are such poor read-ers that there is little hope for an escape from the ghetto."[29]

This was not news to black Newark, some portion of which had expressed its outrage in the streets the preceding summer. That was also the year that Spirit House organizers had joined the struggle for educational justice. Amiri Baraka had led an effort to oust the principal and assistant principal of Robert Treat while attempting to cultivate the nationalist sensibilities of local parents. ("Wouldn't it be better to have a black principal at an all-black school?" he asked.) As the scale of miseducation at Robert Treat and other schools was revealed, he, Amina Baraka, and other activists turned to open agitation. "We began to harass the school administration at Robert Treat to find out why the children couldn't read," he later recalled.[30]

Amiri Baraka's gadfly role deepened in 1970–1971 as the public school crisis took the form of violent, deeply divisive teacher strikes. Like New York's Ocean Hill–Brownsville conflict, the Newark affair pitted a largely white teacher's union against the board of education and black parents and activists. The battle involved a complex blend of race, ethnicity, class, and gender. A predominantly Jewish- and Italian-American union struggling to assert collective bargaining rights clashed with an African-American community striving to translate demo-graphic strength and the election of the city's first black mayor into genuine social gains.[31]

Over the course of the conflict, teachers endured mass arrests and jail while many African-American parents resisted the unionist agenda, fighting what they saw as a further threat to their children's education. Supporters of the teach-ers accused Baraka and other Newark militants of fueling racial antagonism for political ends while obscuring the class dimensions of a complicated issue. Meanwhile, Baraka continued to castigate not only the teacher's union but also black and Puerto Rican members of the school board and other figures who he believed had stymied the efforts of the black working class to seize control of

Newark. "The Neo-colonial negro [*sic*] has now conspired with the white boy to break the growing power of the black masses in this city over the educational system," he declared.[32]

Despite such assertions, black Newark's newfound influence *did* produce some changes, symbolic and otherwise, in the early 1970s. In the former category was the official rechristening of Robert Treat (originally named for a colonial-era governor, the school was now known as "Marcus Garvey") and an effort to authorize the flying of black liberation flags in African-American schools. As time passed, however, the failure of a rising class of black officials to effectively address urban decay and other social crises led to Baraka's disillusionment with electoral politics. Once hailed as a folk hero, Mayor Kenneth Gibson proved to be a prosaic bureaucrat who possessed neither the ability nor the inclination to oversee a transfer of power and resources to Newark's working class. Contemporary developments thus reinforced the appeal of alternative institutions.[33]

For its organizers, of course, AFS had remained a priority. It fell to Amina Baraka, who served as AFS principal, and to other mostly female teachers from the ranks of CFUN to educate the dozens of children—many of them sons and daughters of the organization's members—who attended the community school. The instructors showed signs of creativity. Students learned hieroglyphics in art class and fashioned bead necklaces or African skirts and dashikis in home economics. They performed political plays and studied *The Autobiography of Malcolm X*. They visited not only libraries, museums, and theaters but also welfare offices and housing projects. "We want them to understand the community," explained Mama Furaha, a veteran AFS teacher.[34]

In general, however, instruction proved highly regimented. Students chanted slogans and saluted a red, black, and green flag. Catechisms and rote methods were used from preschool through the upper-level classes. Amina Baraka trained scores of teachers in such practices, preparing them for service in AFS and other Pan African nationalist schools. The emphasis on discipline and collective response was said to complement the communitarian nature of black children. Instilling the "master teachings" of Kawaida and purging "the alien value system" were explicit aims. Education was defined as the inculcation of values. Pupils were graded on a seven-point system, with the highest rank defined as "the total African Free School student, with an African Personality."[35]

The preoccupation with values enhanced the status of female AFS teachers. Women were primary bearers of morality and social ethics in cultural nationalism's worldview. Since achieving nationhood was thought to require systematic transmission of such knowledge, women were seen as essential agents of national formation. "It must be survival and liberation that you teach, Sister," Amiri Baraka commanded. Of course, women's symbolic value rested on their willingness to accept male authority. Submission was celebrated as a sign of familial loyalty and devotion. By labeling female teachers "Mamas" and male instructors "Babas," AFS officials enforced both the bonds of fictive kinship and the principle of obedience.[36]

Ultimately, AFS was designed to produce the disciplined sons and daughters an embryonic nation requires. Children ages 4 to 14 were taught a uniform system of symbols based on a central premise: *Sifa Ote Mtu Weusi* (All Praises to the Black Man). The dictation of standards, the exaltation of conformity, the standardization of black life—all were regarded as indispensable to the task of building community amid what was frequently described as the "chaos" of the inner city. An exacting education was seen as a means of imposing order and "predictability." As Amiri Baraka noted, "Tradition in a degenerated situation becomes innovation."[37]

"An Incorruptible Generation": CAP Sites North and South

AFS influenced black independent schools across the country. Congress of African People units in more than a dozen cities developed similar systems, with circles of committed organizers creating and operating private schools. AFS also helped generate an educational renaissance within Newark. The 1967 insurrection that fueled Amiri Baraka's imagination produced other local enterprises designed to satisfy a generation's hunger for self-knowledge. The Chad School was among the ventures that emerged as part of the rebellion-inspired drive for experimentation and self-sufficiency. The establishment, which served youngsters up to age 15, was named after a Central African nation that had initiated a major campaign to develop its educational system. The Black Youth Organization, the coalition of high school and college students that founded the school, vowed to expand the institution through grade 12 before sending graduates to postsecondary ventures like Malcolm X Liberation University and the Center for Black Education.[38]

AFS inspired institutions in Chicago as well. Desegregation battles in the 1960s had failed to win educational justice for the city's black children, whose schools were ravaged by white flight, shrinking tax revenue, and systematic discrimination. As in other locales, increasingly assertive black parents and educators had clashed with an incipient teacher's union whose attempts to expand professional rights were seen as endangering efforts to improve inner-city education. As was the case elsewhere, the cumulative pressure of structural racism had combusted, igniting a 1966 uprising that spread both destruction and dreams of rebirth.

Those dreams included efforts to expand Chicago's traditions of black educational autonomy. Since the 1930s, the city had been home to one of the original branches of the Nation of Islam school system. In the 1960s, the Ruth B. Lott School, CAM Academy, and Communiversity furnished additional models of self-determination. By the early 1970s, New Concept Development Center and Shule Ya Watoto had emerged as leading sites within the latest cohort of independent institutions.

New Concept was the creation of a ring of educators and organizers led by Black Arts poet Haki Madhubuti. Madhubuti (née Don L. Lee) had grown up on the streets of East Side Detroit and West Side Chicago. After college, the army, and a series of odd jobs, he had found success as a poet, publishing popular volumes like *Think Black* and *Black Pride*. Madhubuti's didactic poems lamented what their creator saw as black people's psychological dependence on white majority culture. Madhubuti viewed the black artist as a "culture stabilizer" whose task was to uplift and enlighten African Americans, a people who had strayed from their true spiritual selves.[39] Black America's foes, Madhubuti maintained, had

> raped our minds with:
> T.V. & straight hair,
> *Reader's Digest* & bleaching creams,
> tarzan & jungle jim,
> used cars and used homes,
> reefers & napalm,
> european history & promises.[40]

The solution to such debasement was black awareness and institution building. While a poem might momentarily capture an audience, Madhubuti reasoned, an institution could offer direction for years to come. In 1967, the poet joined writers Carolyn Rodgers and Johari Amini in founding Third World Press, a small publishing house. However, it was the Institute for Positive Education (IPE), an establishment formed in 1970, that truly embodied Madhubuti's political visions.

IPE was conceived as a total resource for Chicago's South Side. A cultural center and political forum, it was designed to elevate the consciousness of children and adults and to serve as a vehicle for the "redefinition and reeducation of our people." In coming years, the storefront enterprise would issue pamphlets, develop food cooperatives, and offer tutoring services, youth programs, lecture series, and consumer advice. Madhubuti saw IPE as a means of correcting social deficiencies while offering concrete alternatives to the values of the white mainstream.

IPE served as the organizational framework for a cadre fashioned in the style of CFUN. The institution's cluster of young, marginally middle-class workers and volunteers included high school teacher and IPE cofounder Carol Hall (later Safisha Madhubuti, Haki's wife). The group followed a strict regimen of work, study, diet, and exercise. Separate men's and women's councils enforced stringent protocols and duties. The IPE structure even included a naming committee, a body that bestowed on the former Don L. Lee a designation meaning "justice" (*Haki*) and "precise, accurate, and dependable" (*Madhubuti*).[41]

Madhubuti and his associates continued to seek practical methods of purveying values, which they defined according to the neo-Africanist tenets of Kawaida. Carol Hall convinced Madhubuti that early childhood, especially the preschool years, was the critical moment for academic and social intervention. Conceding that his own generation's schooling had done little more than produce "white nationalists," Madhubuti concluded that only autonomous black education, starting as early as age 3, could reverse the pattern of cultural destruction.[42]

In late 1972, along with several comrades, Carol Hall and Madhubuti (then just 27 and 30, respectively) established New Concept Development Center, the educational arm of IPE. Located in the African-American neighborhood of South Shore, the venture began as a storefront Saturday school for children ages 12 and younger. Academic subjects included "History of the Black Man," "Geography of Black Nations," reading, mathematics, Swahili, and nutrition. IPE staffers served as teachers; Carol Hall doubled as principal and instructor. By 1974, Hall had become Safisha Madhubuti, and New Concept had expanded to a full-time day school. Its aims included the cultivation of basic skills, the inculcation of a "black value system," and the creation of what Haki Madhubuti described as "a secure, competent, work-oriented, incorruptible generation of black men and women."[43]

Chicago's Shule Ya Watoto ("School for Children") pursued a similar mission. However, rather than emerging from the efforts of a disciplined coterie of activist-intellectuals, it arose amid grassroots struggles for educational justice. Watoto's senior founder, Hannibal T. Afrik, was a central figure in the Chicago school insurgencies of the 1960s. Born Harold E. Charles in Greenville, South Carolina, Afrik studied biology as an undergraduate at Ohio's historically black Central State University before completing a master's degree at Chicago Teachers College in 1962. He later did additional graduate work and served as an assistant biochemist at the University of Chicago. Afrik's advanced education helped him secure a position as chair of the science department at Farragut High School on the city's West Side.

As he began teaching in 1963, mass struggles were engulfing the city's public schools. The 29-year-old joined the desegregation crusade. He marched with King in 1966 when the leader visited Chicago to confront northern racial oppression. He helped organize Operation Breadbasket, an economic initiative of King's Southern Christian Leadership Conference. Yet the nonviolent civil rights movement brought real democracy to neither the neighborhoods nor the classrooms of black Chicago. Educational struggles of the late 1960s grew increasingly militant, with African-American parents, students, and instructors seeking greater control over crowded schools with mushrooming black populations. Farragut was a locus of discontent, with an enrollment of 3,000 in a dilapidated building designed for half that number. While the school's student body was more than 90% black, its principal and four assistant principals were white, as was more than half its faculty.

Amid the 1968–1969 community control battles, Afrik launched a campaign to remold Farragut. He led a coalition of African-American parents and teachers in crafting a "black manifesto," a series of demands that included a black assistant principal, black studies, and the re-evaluation of disciplinary policies. The drive for more African-American staff reflected the belief that a black image of authority would serve the psychological and educational needs of Farragut students, most of whom hailed from the depressed, North Lawndale area. Afrik staged a series of protests at the school to underscore the manifesto's demands, organizing sit-ins, "sick-ins," and a marathon "teach-in" on black history before an overflow crowd of students. The Farragut movement helped fuel a larger rebellion of the city's black and Puerto Rican students and teachers, who mounted school boycotts and mobilized for community control.[44]

Afrik joined other black instructors in opposing Chicago Teachers Union strikes in 1969 and 1971. He assailed the union for failing to press for upgrades in black schools, and helped organize "liberation schools" to maintain the education of African-American students during the strikes. He also denounced local and federal desegregation edicts that he believed would strip experienced black teachers from African-American schools. The solution to educational inequality, he insisted, lay in community control and parity in school funding, not in "playing musical chairs with a few pupils based on tokenism and pseudo liberalism."[45]

Now cochair of Operation Breadbasket's teacher division, Afrik rejected "cultural deprivation" as an explanation for the educational plight of Chicago's black children. He dismissed efforts to attribute to "home environment" low African-American achievement on citywide academic tests. Evidence that the system itself had failed, he maintained, lay in the fact that black kindergarteners, initially on par with their white peers academically, fell progressively further behind as they matriculated through primary school.

Afrik sought alternative approaches to liberating the minds of African-American children. He designed a school governance plan featuring a parent–teacher–student council. He directed a black studies program that

produced African fashion shows and other cultural events. He organized education conferences with workshops like "Gifts of Africa" and "Myths of White
History."[46]

Meanwhile, he envisioned a more sustained exercise in "nation building."
He had called for "severing the umbilical cord" of black cultural dependency.
Working with three college students, all recent Farragut graduates, he now began
planning a new model of educational autonomy. As members of the school's
Black Student Alliance, Shebeta, Akidinimba, and Tiyi had been mentored
by Afrik, who abandoned his given name (Harold) for that of a third-century
North African military commander (Hannibal). The three young women took
African names as well. With Afrik's encouragement, they began exploring alter-
natives to public education. They traveled to Newark to observe African Free
School, visited Black Panther political education classes in Chicago, and toured
Pan African nationalist schools in Milwaukee and Washington, DC.

Later that year, Shebeta and other Black Student Alliance members designed
the curriculum for a free Saturday school stressing "African folkways." Afrik persuaded a Westside community organization to donate funds and two sparsely
furnished rooms in its storefront building. In February 1972, Shule Ya Watoto,
a program for Lawndale children ages 3 to 14, enrolled its first six students.
Watoto conveyed concepts of African "familyhood" while covering basic academic subjects. Students studied Swahili and discussed the social origins of
drug abuse. The volunteer staff of 10 instructors included Afrik and his Black
Student Alliance cofounders. During the first four-month term, 60 children
attended the school, with 30 youngsters enrolling in its summer program. By
that fall, organizers began looking toward full-time operation, recognizing that
Watoto students received "five days of garbage" during the regular school week.
As Afrik declared, "We have so many negative aspects to overcome."[47]

The quest for re-education was not just a northern affair. Pan African nationalist institutions emerged in the South as well. One such effort was Ahidiana
Work/Study Center of New Orleans. Like many of its counterparts, Ahidiana
sprang from a disciplined cadre designed to inspire a reorientation of black consciousness. However, the New Orleans venture developed a stronger ethic of
self-criticism and a deeper appreciation for indigenous black culture than that
which characterized many nationalist formations.

Much of the impetus for Ahidiana flowed from the art and activism of jazz
poet Kalamu Ya Salaam. Born Valery Ferdinand III, Salaam helped lead the 1969
student revolt at Southern University's New Orleans campus (SUNO). A native
of the city, Salaam had entered the army and served in Korea before returning
to Louisiana and enrolling at SUNO. In the spring of 1969, he emerged as a
major organizer of a strike at the predominantly black, working-class school.
Frustrated by inferior facilities and limited academic offerings, students at the

state institution demanded major changes, including a black studies department, a draft counseling office, and the upgrade of physical structures.

The symbolic climax of the conflict came that April when students repeatedly lowered the American flag at the college and replaced it with the banner of black liberation. On one occasion, Salaam himself mounted a ladder to hoist the black nationalist colors over the administration building. Ongoing disturbances brought skirmishes with police, and the National Guard was later summoned to end a student occupation of the campus. But Salaam saw the protests as highly organized and democratic, with strikers meeting on a daily basis for collective strategy sessions designed to maximize the input of all participants.[48]

Even before the SUNO rebellion, Salaam had begun to hone his political skills as a leader of the Free Southern Theater (FST), both an expression of and a forerunner to the Black Arts Movement. FST began as a cultural arm of the desegregation struggle. Founded by SNCC organizers in 1963 as a means of combating Jim Crow's grip on black life, FST was designed to help nurture a vocabulary of resistance and an ethic of creative self-expression among poor, African-American southerners. The touring company's integrated cast performed plays like *Waiting for Godot*, free of charge, in humble, sometimes makeshift settings in some of the rural South's most embattled locales. Its spirited productions were reviled by segregationists and cheered by black audiences. But the changing sensibilities of the freedom struggle soon exposed the contradictions in the troupe's integrationist orientation, Eurocentric repertoire, and condescending mandate to fill a "cultural void."[49]

FST underwent a radical transformation in the mid-1960s, becoming an all-black company and shifting its base of operations from Mississippi to the New Orleans district of Desire, an impoverished African-American neighborhood. Deeply engaged in the thrust for Black Arts, the ensemble of activists and actors—increasingly composed of native southerners rather than northern sympathizers—strove to develop a form of "black theater" relevant to the local community. Rejecting material authored by white playwrights, the troupe dedicated itself to celebrating an indigenous black, southern, working-class aesthetic. "Any theater which attempts to grow, to live by itself, justifying its own artistic ideals but failing to relate to the people around it, to the community, is grafted theater," Tom Dent, an FST administrator, declared in 1968. "We have all realized by now that not only can this not be done, but the black masses have no need of such benevolence."[50]

Salaam joined FST in 1968 amid the company's quest for black cultural affirmation. The pursuit of relevant material and the desire to furnish black people with "true images of themselves" inspired the creation of BLKARTSOUTH, the community-based writing and acting workshop that Salaam helped develop within FST. BLKARTSOUTH led to a democratization of artistic production in New Orleans. A collection of cultural workers whose diversity reflected the character of the city's native black population, the body gathered regularly to produce scripts and, more frequently, to create the kind of oral poetry that had recently been popularized by the Harlem group The Last Poets.

By 1969, BLKARTSOUTH had become a dynamic, local base for cultural and political activities, an enterprise roughly analogous to the Spirit House in Newark and the East in Brooklyn. The group staged performances of original poetry and one-act plays in public spaces—from bars to schools to churches to housing projects—in New Orleans and other southern cities. Often rendered in the vernacular, its compositions valorized black proletarian life while emphasizing political awareness and struggle. The aim was to stimulate black consciousness and combat self-destructive "Negro" mindsets.[51]

BLKARTSOUTH eventually separated from FST. Like its parent outfit, it played a major role in cultivating a radical black public sphere in the South. The company continued to create popular material that celebrated the everyday life and culture of African-American communities. As its members strove to define their relationship to the liberation struggle, however, they were forced to confront critical questions. Were they to anchor themselves in the daily realities of black life, resisting an "outsider" mentality? Or should they adopt a purely Pan African lifestyle, rejecting all vestiges of "the American way of death?"

These questions lingered throughout 1970 and 1971. Some members of the ensemble stressed the need to avoid distancing themselves from the larger community. Others emphasized regimens of self-development designed to purge internalized "white" pathologies. In the end, the search for higher consciousness prevailed. The objective, Salaam maintained, was to escape the psychological bonds of "this straightjacket society."[52]

A core group of BLKARTSOUTH members concluded that cultural nationalism and Pan Africanism were paramount social realities. Artistic performance was subordinate to the tangible work of nation building. In their lives and labors, progressive nationalists needed to prefigure the kind of society that could succeed the current order. "We can design right-on sets and scenery," Salaam noted, "but the question is, can we build a nation?"[53]

Embracing an ethic of self-sacrifice that required synchronizing one's personal life and political struggles, the cohort of 20 or so working- and middle-class intellectuals and artists reorganized as a study group, then a collective. Many of the participants were husband and wife; most had young children. The coterie gathered on weekends to exercise, study, and debate revolutionary theory. Its members bought and prepared food collectively and practiced communal child care, striving to eradicate individualism and model the transition to a communitarian society.[54]

Like many of their New Left counterparts, the collective's participants were drawn to the task of transforming themselves while building the archetype of a more harmonious civilization. Aline St. Julien came to the group amid a search for racial identity. Rejecting the privileged social status that her fair skin and creole background provided, she learned to embrace rather than deny her African heritage. She relished the opportunity to instill communitarian values in her children, discovering in the collective "a whole new cooperative way of living, caring and loving each other." For Tayari Kwa Salaam (formerly Cicely St. Julien), Kalamu Ya Salaam's spouse, what was most compelling was the chance to counteract black America's "mentality of self-hatred." She longed to help create an alternative cultural reality and style of living. She also wished to spare her children from the city's public schools.[55]

In late 1971, the collective organized Dokpwe Work/Study Center, a preschool. "We came to the conclusion that the education of our children was the key to making real and positive change in our people," one member later recalled. The institution's name, drawn from the West African work teams traditionally mobilized to perform communal tasks, reflected the collective's belief in a continual process of practice informing theory (and vice versa). While some Dokpwe workers envisioned the project as a base for political struggle, others proposed a narrower pedagogical focus. As the divide deepened, some collective members adopted the name "Ahidiana," meaning "promise" or "mutual agreement" in Swahili, as a reminder of their pledge to pursue communalism and Pan African transformation in every aspect of their lives.

In 1973, the group opened a second school, Ahidiana Work/Study Center, in the Lower Ninth Ward of New Orleans. The institution, which served preschool through third grade, was to be financed with tuition checks (fees had reached $75 a month by 1980) and the pledges of cadre members. Tayari Kwa Salaam served as head teacher and handled much of the curriculum development, fundraising, and administration. The school was small (for years enrollment hovered below 25) and largely working class. "We were not interested in operating a little 'private academy' populated mainly by the children of black professionals," Kalamu Ya Slaaam later recalled.[56]

Ahidiana (the organization) operated a bookstore and a small press, hosted lectures by figures like Amiri Baraka and Haki Madhubuti, sponsored Kwanzaa celebrations, and participated in political demonstrations. Like Ahidiana (the school), these "mass-based" operations were designed to cultivate the surrounding, working-class black community. Yet like other Pan African nationalist collectives, Ahidiana also offered a kind of cultural insulation, shielding its members from elements of social decay within inner cities. "If you don't believe change has gone down," Kalamu Ya Salaam wrote in 1972, "check how black people are dressing. Check how black people are living. Check what we dancing to. Check what we're smoking and shooting into our bodies."[57] Even at the height of Pan African nationalist activity, it was difficult to determine whether tight-knit cadres were bunkers against "white" cultural values or simply shelters from the most troubling symptoms of black demoralization.

"To Live Our Own Culture": Africanization Versus Transformation

The central theme of Pan African nationalist rebirth was "Africanization." The term originally had denoted the replacing of colonial administrations with African officials and emblems in the age of independence. Within the United States, Africanization (or "Re-Africanization") signified the cultivation or revival of essential black cultural traits.[58] Both versions of the concept masked conservative realities. Africanization on the continent had meant exchanging European bureaucrats for African elites without fundamental social transformation. Attempts to "Africanize" black America proved no more effective as a means of altering power relations.

For Pan African nationalist intellectuals, Africanization meant saturating black America with particular cultural symbols. Operators of independent black institutions circulated images and ideas designed to foster radical consciousness. Ruwa Chiri of Chicago's Arusha-Konakri Institute created and distributed a "Not Yet Uhuru" map that depicted Africa's neocolonial subjugation. The goal was to highlight the need for a permanent African and African-American revolution that sought total autonomy rather than nominal self-rule. Chiri oversaw a crusade to persuade nationalists to spell "Afrika" with a "K," a form he regarded as consistent with the dominant linguistic patterns of precolonial Africa. Adherence to the "K" spelling, he argued, constituted an act of intellectual "purification" that could help stimulate "the rebirth of the total Afrikan personality."[59]

Organizers of Pan African nationalist schools distributed an "Afrikan Date Book" rendered in Swahili and English. They offered an adult correspondence course in the East African language, an endeavor designed to restore "ancestral bonds" and contribute to the creation of "a new people." Even personal events furnished models of alternative practices. Held in a Chicago park, the African-styled wedding of the Institute of Positive Education's Haki and Safisha Madhubuti featured homemade garments, elaborate vows, and a procession that included invited guests and "bloods from the street." The ceremony was designed to demonstrate that "the best way to effectively fight an alien culture is to live our own."[60]

Africanization campaigns reinforced the idea that African descendants around the world share defining cultural attributes. Undergirding this principle was a collection of myths meant to sustain a counterhegemonic mystique of black-ness. Chief among them was the concept of Negritude. Originally promoted by Francophone African and Caribbean intellectuals and literary figures during the period between the world wars, Negritude encompassed an array of ideas. A the-ory of racial essentialism, it was also a counterracist creed. A sentimental fallacy, it also provided a stimulus for anticolonial movements. Historically, however, radical critics had dismissed Negritude as a misguided fantasy that reproduced imperialism's racist logic of European reason and African emotion.

Negritude's origins lay in various black cultural movements of the early twentieth century. The related concept of the African Personality, another prin-ciple redeployed by Neo-Pan Africanism, had an even older pedigree rooted in black nationalist theories of the nineteenth century. More recently, eminent African spokesmen like Kwame Nkrumah and Sékou Touré had promoted the ideal—defined by the former leader as "the cluster of humanist principles which underlie the traditional African society"—as a way to bolster pride in African heritage and identity.[61]

The tropes of Negritude and African Personality appealed to US Pan African nationalists because they offered a vocabulary of reaffirmation. They provided intellectual grounding for the vindicationist principles embedded in the con-cept of "blackness." They justified therapeutic responses to white supremacy's "depersonalization" of African Americans. They reinforced the belief that libera-tion requires a retrieval of lost values, a return to authenticity, and a metamor-phosis from Negro to "Afrikan."

Such schemas, however, were deeply flawed. Theories of universal African ontology attempted to reclaim a homogeneity that never existed. They repli-cated elements of the European thought they were designed to repudiate. They prescribed cultural and behavioral solutions for structural maladies. Failure to consider political economy compounded these errors. Few African-American theorists acknowledged that Leopold Senghor's lyrical defenses of Negritude had facilitated the reconquest of Senegal by French capital. Nor did they recog-nize how effectively Mobutu Sese Seko's policies of Africanization and cultural "authenticity" had abetted that leader's autocratic and corrupt rule of Zaire, the former Congo.[62]

The concept of "African Socialism" was equally misleading. Neo-Pan Africanism reinvigorated the theory of black people's natural collectivism. African Socialism held that pristine traditions of agrarian communalism pre-dated the continent's colonial subjugation and continued to orient Africa's scattered peoples toward the practice of cooperative economics. The doctrine found a concrete model in Julius Nyerere's Tanzania, the East African country whose "Ujamaa" system of agricultural collectivization, partial nationalization, and socialistic development provided an ideological beacon for progressive black intellectuals worldwide. However, African Socialism also reinforced the seductive belief that black people could escape capitalism's ills simply by restoring ancestral practices. "We are historically a communal people," members of Washington, DC's Center for Black Education insisted. "Independent Africa worked to satisfy the basic needs of all our people."[63]

Despite its romantic ideals, African Socialism mirrored the conservative logic of anticommunism. Many U.S. Pan Africanists denounced capitalism as a symptom of white immorality while dismissing scientific socialism as equally invalid. They echoed anticolonial pioneer George Padmore's characterization of world socialism (delivered in his 1955 treatise, *Pan-Africanism or Communism*) as merely another system of white domination. Socialism, they argued, was as steeped in white supremacy as was capitalism; its "prolet-aryan" outlook, the author of an Institute of Positive Education tract opined, was incapable of advancing black freedom. Dialectical materialism was incompatible with black communitarianism. Class analysis was irrelevant because all black people belonged to the "class of the dispossessed."[64]

Ultimately, African Socialism proved to be another delusion. The concept had been deployed by nations like Kenya, where governing elites had used its abstract tenets to justify or disguise policies of authoritarianism and neocolonial clientilism. Even staunch Pan Africanists like Nkrumah had come to recognize that visions of socialism must be rooted in the universal clash between laboring classes and their exploiters.[65] Ultimately, Pan African nationalism's romance with African Socialism reflected a crude repudiation of materialist struggle and a stubborn refusal to mesh theories of race and class.

"Submission Is Peace": Bourgeois Nationalism and Patriarchy

Neo Pan Africanism's utopian formulas revealed the movement's adherence to bourgeois thought. By and large, Pan African nationalist theories reflected the mindsets and interests of a relatively privileged middle class. Infatuation with vanguardism signaled a commitment to leadership by "experts" and a denial of "ordinary" people's capacity for self-emancipation. Many operators of independent black institutions viewed themselves and their political comrades as "a handful of genuine revolutionaries" (to borrow Nkrumah's formulation). They believed that the duty and wherewithal to conduct the struggle resided with those ideologues who possessed "neither the consciousness of the colonizer [nor] the consciousness of the colonized."[66]

Historian Rod Bush notes that "The very idea of a cadre of professional revolutionaries seems like an astonishing departure from reality, but the world of the 1970s was still part of the era of 1968, when revolution seemed to be on the agenda everywhere." Cadre formation also reflected the cessation of street rebellions, a signal to some that a period of vanguardism had succeeded the stage of mass spontaneous mobilization. It was only later that activists like Amiri Baraka embraced the ideal of collective leadership and the principle that radical intellectuals must harmonize their struggles with the perceptions and will of "the great masses" of working people.[67]

What author Robert L. Allen called "the vulgarization of the whole idea of black culture" further separated Pan African nationalism from the daily struggles of black urbanites. Attempts to substitute an imaginary African heritage for the lived experience of black America revealed a certain contempt for indigenous African-American folkways. This disdain was especially pronounced in the rhetoric of Haki Madhubuti, who lamented the ignorance and pathology of the American Negro—a "filthy invention" of the white oppressor. "We sick," Madhubuti wrote, "because we don't know *who we are*." Disregard for the cultural validity of the black working class fueled campaigns of moral and social uplift. The need to reclaim "captive minds" and to foster a more "admirable" way of life served as rationales for imposing paternalistic visions of social control. "Most people are not rational, or they are just rational," Baraka declared in 1969. "They function on a less than conscious level. The reason you have to teach people values, values, values is so they will do things that are in their best interest without trying to reason about it."[68]

The further Pan African nationalism strayed from objective African-American realities, the more its theories degenerated into crude orthodoxies. Attempts to recapture "our traditional greatness" by reviving feudalistic African practices hastened the descent into idealism. Topics as obscure as ancient African architecture were presented as germane to black liberation. Racial fundamentalism deepened the confusion. Baraka of Newark's African Free School celebrated African "biological roots." Ruwa Chiri of Chicago's Arusha-Konakri Institute exalted "our most ancient genes." Kalamu Ya Salaam (Ahidiana of New Orleans) stressed the need to "genetically remain an Afrikan people." Such formulations demonstrated the primacy of dogma over material reality and scientific analysis.[69]

Pan African nationalism's myths converged in the doctrine of male supremacy. Neo-Pan Africanists subjected women to astonishing levels of repression in the name of "national liberation." Karenga's reactionary teachings about black women's social "complementarity" (as opposed to equality) continued to define the movement. The use of what historians Barbara Ransby and Tracye Matthews call "a slightly modified language of biological determinism and essentialism" cloaked sexism in the mantle of cultural heritage. Black male domination was seen as an antidote to—rather than a symptom of—the values of the dominant order.[70]

Even the crassest expressions of patriarchy were couched in the language of reverence. The West African–derived coronation ceremony designed by Baraka for use in African-American beauty pageants exemplified Pan African nationalism's ritualistic exaltation of black women. Such adulation constituted what the feminist Frances Beale called "hypocritical homage," for African-American women were to be both adored and controlled.[71] Visions of women as objects of male power and manipulation shaped decrees about everything from clothing to human reproduction.

The righteous black woman was to shun abortions, which many African Americans associated with racist schemes of population control. In a 1972 missive to *Essence*, Jitu Weusi of Brooklyn's Uhuru Sasa Shule denounced "family planning" and government-sponsored birth control initiatives as conspiracies to thin the ranks of black resistance. Similarly, Haki Madhubuti condemned "western butchers" who performed abortions on black women. Beneath such critiques lay the historical reality of forced sterilization of women of color. Yet Pan African nationalism's assault on reproductive freedom also reflected retrograde ideas about African-American women's function as breeders of the black nation, a perspective rooted in long-standing beliefs about the link between "racial destiny" and reproduction.[72]

Of course, black women were not only to accept male control; they were also to provide inspiration. Pan African nationalists portrayed women's acquiescence and deference as motivating factors for black men, the putative agents of revolution. While "the brothers" engaged in forthright political action, "the sisters" would nurture "the seeds of liberation" by lightening black men's burdens. They would dutifully imbue children with black consciousness while laboring in the kitchen and bedroom to encourage masculine initiative.

Promoting patriarchy was hardly the exclusive domain of men. Gifted organizers like Amina Baraka were active collaborators in attempts to regiment women's personal habits, dress, and behavior; to condemn abortion as a threat to the black family; and to portray submissiveness as natural and proper. At times the endorsement of masculine control bordered on self-abnegation. "Submission is peace," Amina declared in a 1973 essay. If African-American women were to wash their men's feet in the evening, she maintained, "it would probably be a cultural attitude . . . it would probably be nothing wrong with that."[73]

Underlying such sentiments was the recognition that patriarchy offered security, as well as confinement. Scholars like Farah Jasmine Griffin have explored the attraction of some black women to the promise of patriarchal protection, an amenity that provided a measure of psychic and physical safety, as well as a historically denied "guarantee of purity," even as it imposed an obligation to obey.[74] Many Pan African nationalist women viewed "complementarity" as a genuinely liberating philosophy. For them, the reaffirmation of separate spheres heralded a return to dignity and order. Contributing to black liberation by inspiring and supporting male activists was seen as an essential task of "Afrikan womanhood."

Women's activities were to be confined to the arenas of education and "social development." Ironically, such gendered roles enabled organizers like Amina Baraka (Newark's African Free School), Safisha Madhubuti (Chicago's New Concept Development Center), and Tayari Kwa Salaam (Ahidiana of New Orleans) to assume leadership positions in independent schools, occupying top administrative posts and shaping curricula and pedagogy.[75] The flourishing of black feminist thought in the 1970s nevertheless deepened elements of dissent within hypermasculinist organizations. As the consciousness of Pan African nationalist women expanded to encompass class and gender analysis, even the most ideologically rigid cadres experienced internal challenges.

Resistance generally occurred underground. However faithfully they parroted party rhetoric, in practice, the women's assemblies of groups like the Committee for a Unified Newark and Ahidiana rejected the outright subservience demanded by orthodox Kawaida. Female cadres opposed extreme expressions of male supremacy, struggling to avoid relegation to "the decorative fringe" of political activities. Combining elements of submission and self-assertion, "the Malaika" ("angels") of CFUN embraced domestic duties like the maintenance of "Afrikan house décor" even as they claimed the right to set policy in African Free School. They insisted that black women were obliged to do "whatever is needed by the nation" and maintained that "all who can work" on behalf of the nationalist cause were entitled to do so.[76]

The political evolution of female activists unfolded mostly in private, in contrast to the abrupt, public shifts that marked the ideological epiphanies of some male leaders. In time, however, struggles for equality within Neo-Pan Africanist formations transcended what Margo Natalie Crawford describes as black women's "deft maneuvers" to subvert hypermasculinism.[77] As female activists came to see themselves as political comrades rather than mere consorts of men, they assumed more explicitly antisexist positions, demanding meaningful participation in all aspects of day-to-day organizing.

International influences aided their cause. Pan African nationalist women discovered in Third World models evidence that nation building meant marshaling *all* available human resources, irrespective of gender. Several African-American organizers attended the 1972 All Africa Women's Conference in Dar es Salaam, Tanzania, where they met revolutionaries from Southern Africa and the Middle East and discussed the role of women in national liberation. Women's conferences and retreats in the United States, including a key Newark summit in 1974, provided further opportunities for social analysis, political growth, and sisterhood. Female activists began forming their own support groups and seeking opportunities to engage in autonomous self-development.[78]

Some organizers adopted avowedly feminist perspectives. Amina Baraka had once defined her social value in terms of the doctrine of complementarity. An accomplished organizer and the founder of Newark's African Free School, she once described her primary role as the sustenance and encouragement of her husband, who she strove to inspire to create something "beautiful and beneficial to Afrikan people." After the leftward political turn of the Newark cadre in 1974, however, she and Amiri Baraka abandoned the philosophy of Kawaida and began critiquing male supremacy as a manifestation of bourgeois culture. She now saw complementarity as counterrevolutionary. As her feminism deepened, she recognized that Pan African nationalism had absorbed the repressive characteristics of capitalist patriarchy. No longer willing to accept masculinist dogma, she resolved to explore new visions of freedom.

Tayari Kwa Salaam of Ahidiana, the New Orleans organization, underwent a similar metamorphosis. Feminism taught her that black freedom required the dismantling of *all* forms of oppression, including male domination. As she participated in women's conferences and study groups in the mid- to late 1970s, awareness of black women as "triply oppressed based on race, sex and class" replaced her narrow cultural nationalist worldview. She began to define liberation not in terms of the "imposed reality" of idealized African culture, but rather, as the reversal of her own racist and sexist socialization under capitalism.

Ahidiana also evolved. Through strenuous self-criticism, the collective began formulating a genuinely antisexist ideology. By the late 1970s, its male members were expected to participate in the shared duties of child care and housework, and women were encouraged to take the lead in social and political initiatives. Yet struggles over gender equity continued. "Some of our men will not be willing, will not be able to give up their control over our lives, will be deeply fearful of the results, will believe that their manhood is weakened by the strengthening of our womanhood," Tayari Kwa Salaam concluded. "We sisters must be keenly aware of the threat we present to our men, [who were] born and reared in a male-dominated society."[79]

"A Mystical Unity": The Pitfalls of Infantile Pan Africanism

If Pan African nationalism was to evolve, its adherents would need to address its underlying weaknesses, especially its attempts to recast provincial black nationalism as a creed of global liberation. In his final days, Malcolm X had mobilized a cosmopolitan anti-imperialism, identifying "white world supremacy" as the enemy of all revolutionary people. In the early 1970s, however, many of his intellectual heirs continued to practice what some contemporaries called "infan-tile" or Racial Pan Africanism.[80]

Racial Pan Africanism reinforced the myth of uniform blackness. African-American theorists, political scientist Alex Willingham notes, "Started to speak of the African world as an organic community capable of systemic action." International black unity was seen as a natural phenomenon. Haki Madhubuti pictured "an African people moving toward oneness" worldwide, while Baraka envisaged an "African World Party." Illusions of homogeneity fostered dreams of a universal black ideology. During the 1970 Congress of African People, Baraka imagined the entire black world, "whether in Harlem or Johannesburg," conven-ing as "one people, one flag, one leadership, one identity."[81]

Neo-Pan Africanism thus consigned itself to the realm of metaphysics. The Pan African idea, writes sociologist Paul Gilroy, suggests "a mystical unity out-side the process of history or even a common culture or ethnicity which will assert itself regardless of determinate political and economic circumstances." Universalized blackness transcended the realities of time and place. Activists depicted transnational black harmony not as a fanciful abstraction but as a return to a coherent past. As Ruwa Chiri of Chicago's Arusha-Konakri Institute declared in a poem about the African and African-American bond, "We are stone BROTHERS reuniting after four hundred years."[82]

Such ahistoricism preserved a blissful ignorance. The Nigeria–Biafra cri-sis provides a good example. Seeing "tribalism" as an anachronism that mod-ern nationalism would supplant, many African Americans viewed Nigeria's 1967–1970 civil war as an intraracial feud instigated by white, neocolonial agents, rather than as a consequence of long-standing ethnic, cultural, and regional antagonisms. Theorists like Haki Madhubuti presented the conflict as a case of European manipulation of petty factions. The issue in Nigeria was straightforward, operators of Washington, DC's Center for Black Education insisted: "Africa for the Africans, or Africa for the Europeans."[83]

This binary logic led Neo-Pan Africanists to support authoritarian regimes. Black nationalism in the United States had a troubling record of backing reac-tionary political leaders—from "Papa Doc" Duvalier of Haiti to Mobutu of the Congo—whose rhetoric fostered the mystique of blackness. In the early 1970s, Idi Amin became the latest strongman to win the sympathy of some African-American intellectuals. Initially denounced as a neocolonial stooge, the Ugandan despot grew in the estimation of many Pan African nationalists as the Western press pilloried him as a tyrant and a buffoon. Some African-American ideologues reasoned that, considerable shortcomings notwithstanding, Amin was at least a nationalist who appeared to champion black self-determination.[84]

Ostensibly progressive leaders were afforded greater leeway. Many African-American activist-intellectuals venerated Pan African protagonists like

Sékou Touré of Guinea, Kenneth Kaunda of Zambia, and Forbes Burnham of the Caribbean country of Guyana, seeing such heads of state as symbols of uncompromising "black manhood" and national vigor. Racial ideology and patriarchy shielded these figures and their administrations from critical scrutiny.

This shortsightedness was especially acute in the treatment of Kwame Nkrumah. The Ghanaian patriarch was both a torchbearer of African liberation and, prior to his ouster in 1966, the chief executive of a state controlled by a corrupt ruling party and a parasitic petit bourgeoisie. Yet U.S. Pan African nationalists all but canonized the leader after his 1972 death. Bristling at accusations of demagoguery leveled at the late statesman in the mainstream media, activists like Jitu Weusi of Brooklyn's Uhuru Sasa Shule strove to counteract the defamation of an African hero. "You gave birth to black immortality," Chicago's Ruwa Chiri proclaimed in one tribute.[85]

According to these supporters, the very agents of "Negro mentality" and white deception that had toppled Nkrumah's government were now conspiring to assassinate his character. There was little acknowledgment of what radical Pan Africanist thinkers (notably the eminent Trinidadian Marxist C. L. R. James and Guyanese historian Walter Rodney) stated forthrightly—that for all his genius, Nkrumah had "fail[ed] to lead a successful social transformation" in Ghana, an error that enabled the maneuvers of the opportunistic class that helped orchestrate his downfall.[86]

Many Neo-Pan Africanists remained blind to the crimes of Amin and the flaws of Nkrumah. Such rulers personified patriarchal authority and the maintenance of highly centralized, hierarchical structures—characteristics that defined vanguardist black formations within the United States. Adulation of charismatic heads of state precluded consideration of the popular aspirations of those they governed. Pan African solidarity was defined as the unity of presiding elites, rather than as a democratic expression of class struggle from below.[87]

"Strangers in a Strange Land": Neo-Pan Africanism and the Quest for a Land Base

Contemporary Pan Africanism's tendency toward abstraction fueled a debate over whether the United States or Africa represented the critical "land base," or optimal site of African-American struggle. The revival of this "ancient riddle" of nationalist consciousness highlighted sharp philosophical conflicts.[88] On one end of the spectrum lay Kwame Ture (Stokely Carmichael), an exponent of the position that Africa (and especially Ghana) was the essential arena for nation building in concert with revolutionary elements of the black world. Similar outlooks motivated many of the radical, black American expatriates who in the

1960s and '70s settled in Tanzania, Ghana's successor as the primary site of politically inspired African-American emigration to Africa.

Organizations like Washington, DC's Center for Black Education declined to wholly reject struggle within the United States. The center's strategists deferred the question of whether African-American nationhood could flourish only on the Mother Continent or in scattered enclaves within America, as well. By 1970–1971, however, the institution began consciously prioritizing political work in East Africa. It initiated plans to shift 75% of its operations overseas, viewing activities within the United States as secondary to the struggle for "an independent African continent." This outlook matched the line of Kawaida adherents, who strove to strengthen black American identification with Africa until the United States came to be seen "only as a sad but real political circumstance."[89]

Some Neo-Pan Africanists sought a synthesis of priorities. While refusing to identify the United States as the permanent home of Africans Americans, Amiri Baraka acknowledged that "black people, circa 1970, ain't going anywhere." The physical territory African Americans currently occupied, he argued, must remain a principal social battlefront. Organizers of Chicago's Center for New Horizons, a Pan African nationalist preschool, concurred. "America is ours by virtue of vested interest," they proclaimed, "and Africa is our redeeming strength and physical land base."[90]

Offering a competing vision, the territorial nationalists of the Republic of New Africa argued that African Americans could "create Israel here" by claiming a portion of the Deep South as their sovereign domain. Meanwhile, left-leaning groups like the Revolutionary Action Movement and the Black Panthers continued to regard urban centers as the realm of revolutionary possibility. Some intellectuals noted that the drive to flee to distant spheres ignored the logistical obstacles of mass emigration and reflected an underlying political defeatism. The re-emergence of emigrationist rhetoric was a "symptom of withdrawal." Expatriation was tantamount to "jumping into the sea to avoid the rain."[91]

As the debate continued, the complications of African "solutions" began to emerge. The trend of African-American travel to "the Motherland" brought to the continent sojourners who arrived replete with sentimental notions of "blackness," only to confront sobering realities. "Africa is a continent riddled by external and internal subversion and division," Black Panther theorist Kathleen Cleaver reported in 1972. Visitors who expected an expanse of militancy discovered a sea of neocolonialism. Rather than "Mau Mau Power," the Center for Black Education's Charlie Cobb observed, "we find European power."[92]

Those who sought kinship and solidarity at times encountered misunderstanding, mistrust, or indifference. Guests who ventured beyond the orbit of the petit bourgeoisie learned that in many cases, the material conditions of the masses had not dramatically improved since the formal departure of colonialism. African-American activists resented the efforts of U.S. opinion makers to dismiss as misguided or naïve the idea of meaningful political and cultural exchange between Africans and black Americans. Yet no simple homecoming awaited Africa's dispossessed children as they fled the West. "Whether we realize it or not," Ahidiana's Kalamu Ya Salaam later said, acknowledging black America's distinctiveness, "we are a tribe."[93]

One Harlem encounter underscored the tensions of the Pan African reunion. In 1969, Kenya Economics Minister Tom Mboya offended the sensibilities of a troupe of black American nationalists, an act, *Jet* later noted, that saw the visitor "driven out of probably the most afro-minded community in the country." During a U.S. tour, the East African official stopped at a Harlem library and uttered what he presumed to be a truism: mass black emigration to Africa would constitute an act of surrender in the domestic freedom struggle. African Americans must not run from The Problem. Moments later, Mboya was booed and pelted with eggs. A local contingent of black nationalists had come to the talk prepared to censure the minister, who recently had opposed a proposal that Kenya offer automatic citizenship to African Americans. Amid the uproar (protesters cried, "Get with it, Mboya!" and "Africa is our home, too!"), the politician was escorted from the library auditorium by police. The ideal of mass flight to Africa had suffered another blow.[94]

As abstract visions of an African homeland clashed with intricate realities, a more concrete proposal surfaced. The notion that African Americans could best serve the cause of African redemption by sending skilled technicians overseas to participate in nation building became a defining tenet of Neo-Pan African thought. The premise, a classic theme of nineteenth- and early twentieth-century Pan Africanism, had been revitalized in the 1960s by the rise of independent African and Caribbean nations. The call of Nkrumah, Tanzania's Julius Nyerere, and other Third World leaders for African-American technical assistance further energized the concept.

As early as 1967–1968, SNCC activists had attempted to create an "Afro-American skills bank" to help Africa develop its resources and escape the clutches of neocolonialism. As the polemics of land base theory intensified, the idea of equipping the continent and diaspora with black American technicians emerged as a rare consensus position. Proponents of the strategy argued that African Americans represented "the world's largest pool of black teachers and candidates for skilled and technological posts in the budding economies." Rather than join corporate America, college graduates could put their skills to use "where they can do the most good."[95] Aiding the development of young nations offered an opportunity to exchange abstract notions of racial kinship for more substantial ties.

The New York City–based Pan African Skills Project (PASP) served as a clearinghouse for the provision of African-American specialists to the black world. Headed by former SNCC worker Irving Davis, the organization was established in 1970 as a means of recruiting African Americans to address skilled labor shortages in countries like Tanzania, Zambia, and Guyana. PASP officials insisted that African solidarity must transcend symbolism. African Americans, they suggested, were uniquely equipped to help free black nations from reliance on the technical expertise of "white, Anglo-Saxon countries." PASP, which had sent 300 African Americans to Tanzania and other sites by 1973, was regularly accused of "ripping off brothers and sisters" from the domestic movement. Yet by highlighting the indivisibility of African and African-American struggles, the project enriched the philosophical framework of Pan Africanism. "When you work in Africa," PASP representatives told black trainees, "you are working for yourself and for your people."[96]

"Return to the Source": The Maturation of Pan African Nationalism

Though hardly devoid of romanticism, the shift toward providing technical aid for the black world signaled a positive rejection of political abstraction. By 1972, the deficiencies of a Pan Africanist worldview rooted in racial mysticism were conspicuous. The ideological turn of the late 1960s had hardened the lines of theory. Infantile Pan Africanism had produced mechanistic formulas and true believers while failing to galvanize a mass base. The movement's dearth of coherent political strategies precluded engagement with popular forms of resistance at home and abroad. "If we can't help Mississippi," Atlanta's Institute of the Black World acknowledged, "we can't help Mali or Mozambique."[97]

Radical intellectuals searched for ways to reinvigorate the struggle. Some resumed the quest for objective analysis, quietly shedding fanciful doctrines. Without relinquishing the principle of vanguardism, they again sought modes of struggle informed by the everyday needs of the black populations they aspired to serve.

International developments spurred the reappraisal. One such event was the summer 1969 Festival of Pan-African Culture in Algiers, Algeria. Among the African Americans attending the affair were artists and intellectuals Ted Joans, Ed Bullins, and Michele Russell; political leaders Kwame Ture (Stokely Carmichael) and Eldridge and Kathleen Cleaver of the Black Panthers; and Pan African nationalist organizers Jimmy Garrett and Charlie Cobb of the Center for Black Education and Haki Madhubuti of the Institute of Positive Education.

Many of these figures arrived in Algiers eager to witness an affirmation of Pan African heritage. What ensued was a dismantling of cultural nationalist ideals.

At the time, Eldridge Cleaver and Ture were engaged in a public dispute over the role of white radicals in anti-imperialist struggle. Yet the very setting of Algiers, a sanctuary for revolutionary movements from around the world, seemed to transcend racial binaries, including the divide between North Africa and the Sub-Saharan portion of the continent. Algeria's capital city had been immortalized by *The Battle of Algiers*, the 1966 film about the Algerian revolution that had become an instant cult classic within New Left circles. Now African Americans themselves navigated the famous metropolis while conferring with insurgents from Palestine, Vietnam, and Southern Africa.

The festival reinforced leftist influences. Third World figures rose in multiple sessions to denounce Negritude as a reactionary myth. Sékou Touré of Guinea and other prominent intellectuals dismissed black cultural essentialism as an anachronism, a mystification of the material and political dimensions of liberation. Festivalgoers were urged to view culture not according to a vague "theory of melaninism," but as an arm of economic and social struggle. If the summit's predecessor, the 1966 First World Festival of Negro Arts in Dakar, Senegal, had showcased Negritude and its notions of racial ethos, the 1969 gathering represented a sharp turn toward scientific rationalism and anti-imperialism.[98] In Algiers, African Americans received a firm reminder that the racialism that shaped Neo-Pan Africanism at home had been repudiated by much of the revolutionary world.

Other international encounters further discredited elements of idealism in black American struggle. Two visits by West African revolutionary Amilcar Cabral proved especially significant. Cabral, leader of the liberation movement in Guinea-Bissau and Cape Verde, communed with African-American activists during trips to the United States in 1970 and 1972. Cabral had orchestrated the armed struggle that emancipated portions of Guinea-Bissau ("Portuguese Guinea"), an agricultural country of 800,000 people and a remaining outpost of European colonialism. The leader was well known among African-American activists; identification with guerilla campaigns in Southern Africa and the Portuguese colonies was a defining characteristic of contemporary black radicalism. Cabral was a brilliant philosopher-tactician, a heterodox Marxian thinker who generated strikingly original revolutionary theories. His U.S. appearances prodded Pan African nationalists toward greater lucidity.

During his initial visit, Cabral lectured at Syracuse University in Upstate New York, delivering remarks that were circulated widely among African-American theorists. The winter 1970 talk addressed the role of culture in national liberation. Cabral offered a portrait of the social dynamics of revolutionary struggle. An oppressed people's culture, he maintained, is inseparable from their history and economic and political circumstances. Failure to recognize culture as "an element of resistance" may cripple liberation movements. Yet culture reflects prevailing material conditions; it is neither an abstraction nor the possession of elites. In the process of self-liberation, oppressed people must "return to the upward paths of their own culture," rediscovering their native vitality and strengths. The movement's leaders must embody and defend the popular character of indigenous culture.

Invariably, however, the petit bourgeoisie from which the revolutionary leadership hails becomes estranged from mass culture. To avoid replicating the colonial order, revolutionary leaders must subordinate their economic and social privileges to the aspirations of the people. They must undergo a process of cultural reconversion, a change that occurs only as they fight alongside the popular masses. Male chauvinism and other retrograde traditions must be rejected. In the end, however, revolutionary leaders who immerse themselves in grassroots struggle will discover in their own elitism and colonial mentality the movement's greatest cultural impediment. In Cabral's words,

> The leaders realize, not without a certain astonishment, the richness of spirit, the capacity for reasoned discussion and clear exposition of ideas, the facility for understanding and assimilating concepts on the part of population groups who yesterday were forgotten, if not despised, and who were considered incompetent by the colonizer and even by some nationals.[99]

Cabral explored similar themes during his fall 1972 return to the United States His appearance at historically black Lincoln University in Pennsylvania drew a throng of activists; platform guests included Amiri Baraka, Haki Madhubuti, Ruwa Chiri, Nelson Johnson (of Student Organization for Black Unity), Gene Locke (of Lynn Eusan Institute, a school in Houston, Texas), and Malcolm X Liberation University's Owusu Sadaukai. Cabral warmly embraced an adolescent who presented him with a check for the Guinean and Cape Verdean movements on behalf of the Congress of African People. Then he issued his remarks, addressing the question of "Identity and Dignity in the Context of National Liberation."

The indigenous population under colonial domination, Cabral asserted, retains the weapon of culture, a means of resistance that persists even when political, economic, and military measures fail. However, having internalized the ruling culture, indigenous elites form a marginal class positioned between workers and the colonialists. In the course of national struggle, the revolutionary petit bourgeoisie must relearn its identity from "the native masses." Not simply a matter of reviving "tradition," this "return to the source" entails absolute identification with the revolutionary desires of the lower stratum. It means explicit rejection by the petit bourgeoisie of "the pretended supremacy of the culture of the dominant power." Black America's claim to an exclusively African identity, Cabral suggested, was "another proof, possibly a rather desperate one, of the need for a return to the source"—a reaffirmation of the cultural values of the African-American masses.[100]

A few days later a remarkable gathering of organizers enjoyed a more intimate exchange with Cabral. At the West African leader's behest, 30 black American organizations spanning a range of ideologies sent representatives to an informal meeting with the theorist. More than 120 activists responded to the call, squeezing into a small reception room in Harlem to converse with a man they considered one of Africa's preeminent freedom fighters.[101]

Cabral offered greetings on behalf of the people of Guinea-Bissau and Cape Verde, declaring that "All in this life concerning you also concerns us." He suggested that the relationship between insurgent Africans and African Americans must transcend fraternal affinity, becoming a genuine fellowship of struggle. He assured the gathering that he and his compatriots were aware of black America's circumstances. "We think that our fighting for Africa against colonialism and imperialism is a proof of understanding of your problem and also a contribution for the solution of your problems in this continent," he said. The inverse was also true; achievements in the African-American movement represented "real contributions to our own struggle." Revolutionary Africa, Cabral reported, was encouraged to learn that "each day more of the African people born in America become conscious of their responsibilities to the struggle in Africa." While black Americans should not relinquish their African heritage, he added, they must never abandon the struggle to transform the United States.

Cabral confronted the question of racialism, proclaiming, "We cannot answer racism with racism." Despite the terrorism of the colonialists, Africa's enemy was neither the Portuguese masses nor all white people. Only principled antiracism and anti-imperialism could defeat the true global adversary. "If a bandit comes in my house and I have a gun, I cannot shoot the shadow of this bandit, I have to shoot the bandit," Cabral said. Beneath the global fallacy of race lay the reality of imperialism—the material basis of oppression. It was necessary, the theorist cautioned, to avoid conflating the two.[102]

Cabral emphasized the need to wage struggle based on the concrete realities of one's society. He rejected the colonial analogy of black American oppression. Though the systems were related, subjection to racial caste was not equivalent to domination by a foreign power. In response to a question about the role of women, the African revolutionary affirmed the need for full gender equality in the struggle and in the new society. "We have (even myself) to combat ourselves on this question," he acknowledged.[103]

Finally, the theorist made a plea for painstaking, methodical organizing. "You see, my sister, you here in the United States, we understand you," he said, replying to a question. "You are for Pan Africanism and you want it today. Pan Africanism now!" Yet meeting the challenges of political, social, and economic transformation—on the African continent and elsewhere—demanded patient groundwork; it required commitment to "preparing the field" of possibility for tomorrow.

Cabral then left the gathering to attend to diplomatic duties, expressing regret that he could stay no longer, and inviting the assembled to "come to my country and see me and see our people."[104] Precisely four months later, at the age of 48, Cabral was assassinated by Portuguese agents operating within his own party. News of the revolutionary's death stunned African-American activists and intellectuals. The enthusiastic response of Pan African nationalists to Cabral's U.S. visits had reflected their immense respect for the leader's versatility and integrity as a revolutionary thinker.[105]

Though shaken by the assassination, black American theorists continued to digest the ideas of the man they had addressed as "Comrade Cabral." The late leader had broadened their conceptions of liberation, revealing that political links between Africa and African America trumped putative ties of blood. Cabral had rejected racial chauvinism, positing anticolonialism and anti-imperialism as causes that belong to all the world's exploited classes. However, the theorist's greatest contribution was his modeling of a deliberate, reflexive, revolutionary praxis. Cabral demonstrated that liberation requires sober confrontation of objective realities, not utopian or derivative formulas; that successful movements rally the oppressed around material needs, not obtuse doctrines; and that the duty of radical leaders is to foster critical consciousness, not blind conformity.

Some African-American activists embraced Cabral's insights. According to Maulana Karenga, the martyred rebel had "taught us through his service and sacrifice the profound possibilities inherent in man." He had "demonstrated that the decisive element in the struggle for national liberation is the people and their internal capacity to create progress, their flexibility and moral fiber—regardless of external forces." Ultimately, Cabral had shown that truly revolutionary culture enlarges and liberates consciousness. In so doing, Karenga concluded, "he took us all beyond ourselves."[106]

"Preparing the Field": The Transition to Left Pan Africanism

Many activist-intellectuals recognized that rebuilding the liberation movement required new approaches. This realization led to intensified combat with

Neo-Pan Africanism's regressive elements. Some proponents of the philosophy overcame their entrenched aversion to Marxist thought. International travel, exposure to veteran radicals and revolutionary texts, and growing identification with armed liberation struggles hastened the transition to a left-oriented Pan Africanism anchored in anticapitalism and anti-imperialism.

Though the shift to Left Pan Africanism was neither uniform nor universal, some activists began gleaning from the writings of Cabral and other figures the intellectual tools of a more scientific critique. Amiri Baraka's leftward turn accelerated as his disgust with "the sellout of black mayors and neocolonial leaders the world over" increased, and as he developed a new pantheon of revolutionary heroes that included Mao, Samora Machel of Mozambique, and leaders of South Africa's Pan African Congress. Under Baraka's influence, the political rhetoric of the Congress of African People evolved from Kawaida to "Revolutionary Kawaida" to "Nationalism, Pan-Africanism, and Socialism." Some of the organization's leaders began invoking the concept of dialectical materialism.[107]

The Student Organization for Black Unity (SOBU) also underwent a rapid transformation. Formed in 1969 by young activists, SOBU was closely linked to Malcolm X Liberation University and the Center for Black Education. An advocate of black independent schools, the organization sought to politicize African-American college students and prepare them for nation-building activities in Africa and the Caribbean. SOBU organizers initially viewed blackness as an all-encompassing reality. They saw class conflict within black communities as a divisive force that undermined the quest for political independence.

By 1971, however, SOBU leaders had revised their racial triumphalism. They groped for more rigorous analytical frameworks, striving to combat dogmatism. They combined race and class critiques. They strove to rescue Pan Africanism from the formulations of "bourgeois opportunists." They rejected sloganism and escapism, viewing engagement with African-American social and economic realities as an essential expression of radical internationalism. "It will be necessary to destroy colonialism, racism, imperialism and all the other obstacles we face from the bottom up," SOBU workers declared, "not merely chase them away from our window to prey upon other Africans elsewhere."[108]

SOBU exemplified the philosophical changes that reshaped many Pan African nationalist organizations. Awareness that "We cannot be free in Chicago if we remain oppressed in Conakry, or vice versa" replaced crude political analogies. The turn to materialist analysis, and ultimately to Marxism-Leninism, was hardly devoid of mechanistic thought. Yet two developments heralded continued intellectual growth. First, Pan African nationalists, recognizing the political complexity of Africa and the scope of neocolonial sabotage, shifted their focus from independent nations to liberation fronts engaged in armed campaigns against

Portuguese colonialism and white settler regimes. Second, some of these organizers rediscovered the lessons of SNCC. They strove to reunite with the struggles of black students and workers, conceding that, "A cadre can never be a substitute for working with the people," and reaffirming the need to relate to, intermingle with, and learn from nonideologues.[109] Few people embodied these revelations more fully than did Owusu Sadaukai of Malcolm X Liberation University.

6

The Black University
and the "Total Community"

> In an underdeveloped country an authentic national middle class
> ought to consider as its bounden duty to betray the calling fate has
> marked out for it, and to put itself to school with the people.
> —Frantz Fanon[1]

The ideal of the "Black University" provided a crucial theoretical framework for
the politics of institution building in the late 1960s and early 1970s. Though
it existed mainly as an abstraction, the concept took shape in several postsecondary, Pan African nationalist establishments. North Carolina's Malcolm X
Liberation University (MXLU) was one of several prototypes of an enterprise
of higher learning devoted to the pursuit of black consciousness. MXLU leader
Owusu Sadaukai (Howard Fuller) was also the main force behind the creation of
African Liberation Day, the period's most promising expression of transnational
black awareness. Large turnouts for the event in multiple cities convinced Pan
African nationalists that their movement was gaining a grassroots constituency.

Yet MXLU remained largely isolated from surrounding black communities,
first in Durham, then in Greensboro. Its strong orientation toward Africa and
the Caribbean precluded more sustained engagement with local black realities.
Meanwhile, decrying their own institutions' remoteness from everyday black
life, students at Howard University and other "Negro" colleges attempted to convert those campuses to the new mores of blackness. The failure of similar efforts
led founders of the Center for Black Education in Washington, DC, and Nairobi
College in East Palo Alto, California, to construct insurgent models of higher
education in poor and working-class African-American neighborhoods. These
initiatives reflected the hunt for a model of adult education capable of serving
the "total black community," a crusade that offered another critical test of Pan
African nationalism.

"The Arms of the Community":
MXLU and the Theory of Counterinstitutions

The odyssey of MXLU began with the political education of Howard Fuller. Born in Shreveport, Louisiana, in the early 1940s, Fuller moved to Milwaukee with his mother as a child. The two settled in a housing project in the city's Near Northside. A star basketball player in high school, Fuller attended Caroll College on academic and athletic scholarship, becoming one of the first black students to integrate the Wisconsin school. He later completed graduate studies in social work at Western Reserve University in Cleveland, where he joined the early 1960s crusades against segregation in northern public schools. Fuller worked for the Chicago Urban League before moving to Durham, North Carolina, in 1965 as a community organizer—first for Operation Breakthrough and then for the Foundation for Community Development, both antipoverty outfits.

In the African-American section of Durham, Fuller encountered dirt streets, "shotgun shacks," and a whole new dimension of poverty and marginalization. "You could tell when you were in a black community in North Carolina," he later recalled. "Hell, you could close your eyes, drive your car and just be going on this paved road, then when you hit them railroad tracks, and you got off on them dirt roads, then you knew you was in our place." The antipoverty worker helped mobilize residents to confront routine indignities. He mounted grass-roots campaigns to have homes repaired, rats eliminated, and streets repaved. He worked throughout the state to develop effective African-American leaders while encouraging the formation of "counterinstitutions" like cooperatives that could ensure black survival amid ongoing struggles for social justice. Through it all he stressed concrete, everyday issues, embracing the contemporary emphasis on empowering poor people to participate in the decision-making processes that affected their lives.[2]

Fuller recognized that simply petitioning local structures of power, from city councils to welfare boards, failed to address the underlying problem of white domination. He saw a need for black people to move toward controlling social services. Progress meant not joining the prosperous, white mainstream, but reworking the terms of separation to achieve black autonomy. The call for Black Power in 1966 struck Fuller as eminently correct. By 1967, he had emerged as one of North Carolina's most powerful and charismatic militants.

As Fuller strove to organize the black poor, a parallel struggle unfolded at Durham's Duke University. African-American students had begun pressuring the school to make curricular and institutional changes. Their efforts coincided with the university's attempts to escape its segregated past. While Duke integrated its undergraduate population in 1964, by 1969 its enrollment of 5,000 included only about 100 black undergraduates. Despite their modest numbers, African-American students successfully appealed for a ban on the use of segregated facilities by campus groups. In 1968, they organized as the Afro-American Society and issued a set of demands. They called for increased black enrollment and the appointment of a black faculty adviser, and pressured Duke to support a selective buying campaign in downtown Durham designed to fight housing discrimination. They also sought a "meaningful Afro-American studies program" built on the principle of black self-determination. Duke responded with mild concessions, hiring an African-American barber and forming a faculty committee that autumn to explore the prospect of black studies.

Meanwhile, Fuller and other activists escalated battles against the exploitation of African Americans, who represented 30,000 of Durham's 75,000 residents. Groups like the Foundation for Community Development, for which Fuller now worked, strove to empower the black poor, attempting to involve them in the administration of a local community action program. Campaigns for improved stop signs, playground equipment, and streetlights produced piecemeal victories. Residents pursued more substantive reforms like housing repairs and street repaving, meeting staunch resistance from landlords and municipal authorities. Outspoken public housing tenants received eviction notices and inflated utility bills. Grassroots organizers grew more aggressive, pushing for autonomy from the antipoverty agency. Over the course of two years, an observer later noted, "petitions changed to pickets; picketing evolved into mass marches; mass meetings gave way to protests at a mildly violent level."[3]

Fearless and magnetic, Fuller established deep roots in black communities within and beyond Durham. He led street demonstrations and supported the labor struggles of black nonacademic employees in area universities. He also worked with African-American college students. Drawn to the militancy of local groups, some of Duke's black undergraduates participated in a summer 1968 internship that enabled them to live and organize in Durham's poor neighborhoods. Students increasingly linked their own activism with community aspirations, raising "the critical question of the relevance of the entire educational process to the needs of the black community."[4]

This ideological awakening led the Afro-American Society to back the campaign of Duke's mostly black cafeteria workers for unionization and higher wages. Underpaid foodservice employees also struck at nearby North Carolina A&T and University of North Carolina, Chapel Hill, as black laborers, activists, and students strove to apply the freedom struggle's growing militancy to questions of economic justice. Duke students continued to agitate for a robust black studies program, rejecting compromises from the university that they felt violated the principle of black autonomy.

The struggle intensified in January 1969 when 15% of Duke's black freshmen flunked out of school. This statistic led many black students to conclude that African Americans required special training to overcome the alienation they often faced on predominantly white campuses. The following month, Mississippi organizer Fannie Lou Hamer, comedian Dick Gregory, and other prominent activists participated in a student-sponsored "Black Week" at Duke. Inspired by Hamer's personal testimony of courage, and angered by the intransigence of the university on the question of black studies and the rights of cafeteria workers, 75 black students seized the school's administration building that February, reiterating demands for curricular and other changes, including the formation of an Afro-American studies dormitory. They dubbed the site of their occupation "Malcolm X Liberation School," honoring Black Power's patron saint on the fourth anniversary of his death.

The takeover was among the first of its kind at a major southern university. Hours into the occupation, as police and state highway patrolmen in riot gear massed nearby, Howard Fuller climbed into the window of the barricaded building to advise the protesting students. The standoff ended in chaos hours later. As black protesters evacuated the building under threat of suspension and arrest, riot police lobbed tear gas canisters and clashed with throngs of white students sympathetic to the uprising.[5]

Though the crowd dispersed, the dream of a truly meaningful black education endured. Fuller and African-American student leaders continued to negotiate with university officials, but the distance between the two sides increased. A conservative institution, Duke was controlled by staunchly antiunion tobacco and textile industry businessmen and law-and-order proponents. The students, by contrast, had been radicalized by acts of solidarity with black campus workers and the larger African-American community. They now felt that a genuine experience of higher learning must equip them with the political tools necessary to advance black liberation. Declaring Duke a "brick wall of racism," they embraced Fuller's counterinstitution strategy, announcing that March that an initial contingent of 25 black undergraduates would withdraw from the school and construct a new, relevant black university—one that offered an alternative to "the assumptions, practices and priorities of white supremacy." That spring, the student protesters marched through downtown Durham to the city's largest African-American church, where they were "received into the arms of the black community."[6]

Fuller, who took a sabbatical from antipoverty work to devote himself to the proposed "Malcolm X Liberation University," vowed that the school would be no "publicity stunt." The 28-year-old activist recognized that by forgoing an elite education, the student radicals who had withdrawn from Duke were forfeiting prestige and status. On the other hand, planners of the forthcoming school viewed individual mobility within white society as morally bankrupt. They proposed an alternate rationale for higher learning: Durham's black populace would assist them in creating a practical institution, teaching them about the problems of poor and working-class African-American neighborhoods and helping them devise sound educational solutions. Eradicating barriers between black students and the community remained essential to their bid for black consciousness.[7]

"He Who Controls Minds": The Construction of MXLU

From the earliest stages of MXLU's development, this grassroots focus diverged from the school's broader political philosophies. Fuller embodied this duality. A community organizer who prioritized bread-and-butter issues, he was also an ideologue who shared Stokely Carmichael's visions of African nation-building. His ties to Carmichael and to the theorists of Washington, DC's Center for Black Education (an MXLU sister institution) reflected his commitment to Pan African principles. Fuller might stress community control of black inner cities one minute, and in the next breath, emphasize African battles against neocolonialism. It was never clear how MXLU would combine these ideals.

Plans for the institution continued. An abortive attempt to offer an 11-week course increased the determination of organizers to create a full-time university. Meetings were held throughout that spring and summer at the Washington home of the Center for Black Education's Jimmy Garrett and at a Bricks, North Carolina, retreat. A host of Pan African nationalists joined the effort, including former Student Nonviolent Coordinating Committee (SNCC) worker Cleveland Sellers and North Carolina A&T student Nelson Johnson (a founder that fall of the Student Organization for Black Unity). Carmichael, who remained in self-imposed exile in Guinea, West Africa, served on the MXLU advisory board, as did cultural figures like black writer John Oliver Killens. Most of the institution's visible leaders were men, though women like Duke student Bertie Howard and Cornell University's Faye Edwards played key organizing roles.[8]

MXLU's institutional vision evolved. A planning committee imagined a revolutionary school designed to advance "the whole Pan-African liberation struggle." The establishment would accept no white involvement; any consultation between MXLU and white technicians was to occur off campus. (This principle did not prevent organizers from securing the necessary educational charter from the State of North Carolina.) A two-year curriculum would "fulfill the needs of a nation" by training technicians to build self-governing black societies, either in the United States or in Africa. The first year of study would address "development of Pan Africanist perspective and decolonization of the mind." A history program would cover broad themes: from "independent African civilization" to slavery, colonialism, and neocolonialism. Core courses would include "Psychology of Racism" and "The Role of the Black Church in the Black Revolution." Swahili, "Revolution and the Third World," and "Speech Dynamics" would serve as electives. More mundane subjects, from journalism and drama to creative writing and business management, would also be offered.[9]

The second half of the curriculum would provide technical instruction, training engineers, architects, medics, teachers, and food scientists to perform services needed by black communities and nations. Faculty members (borrowed from "African revolutionary countries," as well as from institutions like Duke, Howard University, Rutgers, and Washington, DC's Federal City College) would include both PhDs and poor people with "specialized knowledge" of the realities of black survival. Students—grassroots activists, returning GIs, casualties of campus radicalism, and young people who simply wished to "get their minds together"—would converge on MXLU, their admission hinging on work ethic and "past political achievement." During their course of study, they would travel to Africa to witness the application of concepts they had explored in the classroom. "This is a nation-building school," Fuller explained, "a school for people who want to build an independent African nation someday and who want to be doing the right things right now."[10]

Fuller viewed MXLU as the culmination of a political journey. He once had counseled poor people to "work within the system" to fulfill the promise of full citizenship. He now saw his task as "liberating minds" by counteracting Western values. MXLU offered an opportunity to teach "the real history of our people." Fuller regarded education as a means of self-defense. He embraced historian Lerone Bennett's theory of formal learning as "a question of power, the power to name, to define and control minds."[11]

Fuller also saw independent establishments as a path to sovereignty. Black studies programs on white campuses, he believed, had bred only tokenism. "We can continue taking buildings and disrupting classes," Fuller wrote in 1970. "But in the final analysis institutions developed in the interest of white people can in no way deal with the nature of our oppression."[12]

As MXLU's fall 1969 opening approached, the challenges of political and financial autonomy loomed. The school's accreditation was to be granted by "the black community." Fuller would oversee the institution's daily functions, his official title, "HNIC," drawn from the colloquialism "Head Nigger in Charge." (As Fuller explained to one visitor, "We don't believe in fooling around with titles like 'chancellor.'") Yet it seemed unlikely that the venture could rely on black funding alone. A preliminary budget projected $380,000 in annual expenses. Tuition was $300; organizers refused to charge a fee that would preclude grassroots participation. The bulk of the school's operating funds would need to come from private donations.

Small contributions arrived from African-American workers and academics who expressed "unequivocal" support for MXLU. Fuller sought additional backing among black professionals and the rank and file, addressing a National Bar Association convention in Durham and a Fayetteville rally and MXLU benefit sponsored by the local poor people's organization. He and the school's other planners continued grappling with practical questions of self-reliance. They hoped to solicit donations from progressive foundations, black student unions, and African-American entertainers, resolving to pursue funding sources whose goals would not jeopardize those of the institution.[13]

In the end, the school relied heavily on contributions from religious groups. MXLU received grants from the Unitarians, the Interreligious Foundation for Community Organizations (IFCO), and the World Council of Churches (WCC). Spurred by urban rebellions, these and other progressive formations supported projects devoted to antiracism and black self-determination. The minority-controlled IFCO, a coalition of national church agencies committed to "total liberation of African people wherever we may be," subsidized MXLU as part of a campaign that also aided the American Indian Movement and revolutionary fronts in Southern Africa. Resolving to help the oppressed "determine for themselves the social system under which they want to live," the predominantly white WCC backed both the nascent Durham school and Cesar Chavez's farmworker movement. Unitarians aligned with the denomination's black caucus assisted MXLU through a fund reserved for the fight against white supremacy.[14]

The largest and most contested MXLU grant exposed the limits of mutual interest between liberal white congregants and self-proclaimed black revolutionaries. In 1969, the National Episcopal Church gave MXLU $45,000, a good portion of the total resources of the school, which had reduced its annual operating budget to a more realistic $80,000. Taken from a $9 million "urban crisis" fund approved at the church's general convention in 1967—a year of massive uprisings—the donation caused a minor insurrection of its own. Some parishioners balked at the idea of supporting a black separatist enterprise devoted to battling "racist, western imperialism." The grant threatened to provoke a schism, with some of the strongest resistance erupting within the North Carolina diocese.[15]

Fuller appeared at Durham's Church of the Good Shepherd that fall to describe the tenets of his fledgling operation. He denied that MXLU was violent, but he acknowledged that it rejected the philosophy of nonviolence. "We do not intend to let anybody spit on us or beat on us," he said. He assured the parishioners that MXLU was not a communist front, noting that both communism and socialism contain "a lot of racism," and insisting that the school accepted money from neither camp. "We're just as hard on them," he maintained. He bristled, however, when someone asked whether MXLU would instill hatred of white people. "You don't have to teach it," he replied. "Get serious."[16]

Fuller saw sponsorship by the "white-controlled" Episcopal Church as a temporary if necessary contradiction. Meanwhile other matters demanded attention. He and the school's other founders devoted themselves to acquiring a building, securing a disheveled warehouse alongside the southern railroad, a boundary that divided black Durham from the city's business district. Organizers and volunteers helped resurrect the plant, reclaiming it from rodents and overgrown vines and applying a coat of paint in the familiar hues of black liberation. The building contained only some battered equipment, metal folding chairs, a mimeograph machine, and an incongruous bunk bed—all donated or procured as part of a campaign of "liberating resources for the people." Students completed the renovation by telephoning the city and requesting that sanitation trucks be sent to aid the "community cleanup drive" in progress. According to one observer, MXLU's future home was "the brightest structure in an otherwise drab Negro slum."[17]

MXLU's dedication ceremony captured the pride and expectation that surrounded the institution. Late that October, a procession of militants, revelers, conga drummers, black personages, and curious spectators stretching more than half a mile in length departed Durham's Hillside Park—where a crowd of as many as 3,500 had enjoyed soul food, gospel music, and rhythm and blues—and trekked through the African-American community to the gritty corridor of black businesses where the new school had found a home. A chant arose from the head of the column: "Who shall survive America? Very few niggers and no crackers at all!" The marchers, many of them clad in African garb, arrived at Pettigrew and Ramsey Streets, where a platform rested before the building that would house MXLU. Once grimy with neglect, the two-story, six-room structure now gleamed.[18]

Men in dashikis patrolled the rooftops nearby. Betty Shabazz, widow of Malcolm X, took the lectern before an audience of 5,000 and vowed that neither treachery nor assassination would stall the revolution. "You have renewed some hope in me," she said. Courtland Cox of Washington, DC's Center for Black Education called for a vast network of radical, independent institutions (kindergartens, high schools, technical and agricultural schools) to govern "the consciousness of our people." As the crowd chastised several inebriated onlookers, Fuller approached the microphone and delivered a rhetorical masterstroke. "Whether we drunk, whether we high, whether we cripple, whether we short, tall, whether we young or old, we are black people, we are African people!" he declared. Stokely Carmichael underscored the point, having sent from Guinea remarks to be read during the ceremony. Carmichael hailed the emergence of MXLU as a seminal event in the history of black struggle. He reported that he had shared plans for the university with Guinean president Sékou Touré and ousted Ghanaian leader Kwame Nkrumah, and that both figures supported the project and its underlying concept—"that we are all an African people."[19]

"A New Peoplehood": The Early Life of MXLU

In MXLU's early months, its mandate to chart a course for the transformation of both higher education and black America almost seemed achievable. More than 50 students ages 15 to 40 registered, including those undergraduates who had withdrawn from Duke in the spring and several Durham residents who attended night classes at the nascent school. MXLU's first cohort included African Americans from the East Coast, the Midwest, and the South. Some had left or been expelled from predominantly white or black colleges and high schools for their political activities. Others were simply "brothers and sisters off the block" looking for an alternative path. Most were urbanites, though some hailed from rural areas and brought with them knowledge of basic farming or experience working in agricultural cooperatives.[20]

Admission to the school required no high school diploma; a screening committee simply verified that applicants harbored no ideas "hopelessly opposed to Pan Africanism." One enrollee, a woman who had spent a total of two years at Radcliffe College and American University, came to MXLU seeking tutelage in the science of nation building. "This is the beginning of my education," she said. Another student, a refugee of recent Duke protests, saw no option but to continue his education at the fledgling institution; after participating in the seizure of Duke's administration building the previous winter, he explained, he was neither physically nor psychologically capable of returning to the predominantly white school.

MXLU's faculty was eclectic. Local activists and scholars, graduate students, former SNCC staffers, and student radicals volunteered to teach at the institution. Most received only nominal compensation, despite an early projection of $10,000 salaries for full-time professors. Bunny Small, a leader of student struggles at Duke, joined the faculty, as did Philip N. Lee, a Pan Africanist and Harvard Law graduate who agreed to teach MXLU seminars on political economy and ideology. The science instructor was a Cornell University student who had participated in an armed takeover of that school's student center. A Vietnam veteran was placed in charge of physical education. A 19-year-old high school graduate was tapped to head the agricultural program.[21]

The institution defied simple ideological classification. Pan Africanism was an overarching creed; every aspect of the school reinforced the premise that African people throughout the world share enduring bonds. Yet whether MXLU's central thrust was revolutionary ("We are at war with the Europeans," an internal missive proclaimed) or more narrowly cultural ("Ujamaa—loving cooperation—is the natural spirit of black people," another document asserted) remained unclear. At times, leaders of the institution espoused a broad, multiracial Third Worldism. On other occasions, they seemed to embrace a chauvinistic nationalism that eschewed coalitions with nonblack people.

MXLU's gender outlooks were no more consistent. During a talk at Greensboro's Bennett College, Fuller accused the historically black women's institution of producing "proper Negro women" who were qualified only to perform domestic tasks and "marry a doctor or lawyer." What was truly needed, he argued, was "sisters with revolutionary minds." Yet MXLU itself reinforced gender orthodoxies. While the school arranged for local restaurants to provide its male students with two daily meals, its female students were expected to prepare all their own food.[22]

MXLU was unequivocal on the matter of Marxism. Operators of the institution rejected theories of intraracial class conflict as antithetical to black liberation. Marxism, they argued, was merely another extension of racist white Western civilization. Racial animosity was the true source of the Sino-Soviet split. Left-wing outlooks, they insisted, would only distract and distort black liberation.

MXLU's curricular strategies were also clear-cut. The institution adhered to a two-year structure, with the first year of instruction geared toward Pan African nationalist concepts and the second year devoted to intensive technical training and field work. Pupils studied everything from black political thought to topography. They participated in freewheeling discussions, watched political films, and read texts like Lerone Bennett's *Before the Mayflower* and Nkrumah's *Neocolonialism*. "The Portuguese in Kongo History," a typical seminar, examined a record of violent conquest dating back to the sixteenth century. The course demonstrated how European colonialist expansion had unleashed the forces of slavery and genocide, and explained how its bloody legacy had been whitewashed.[23]

Such themes fostered spirited exchanges. Critiques of Duke's institutional rigidity and dearth of meaningful student participation led MXLU to pursue more egalitarian approaches. Students presented papers in seminar-style classes. Cooperative work was stressed; one-upmanship and competitiveness were discouraged. To ensure an equitable distribution of power, the Political Committee, one of the institution's governing bodies, comprised an equal proportion of students, instructors, and neighborhood residents. Administrators strove to nurture dialogue and critical thought, and to ensure that no student was "allowed to feel comfortable waiting to be fed information."[24]

Overall, however, MXLU maintained an atmosphere of strict discipline. Daytime classes were in session from 6 AM to 6 PM. Academic rigor was combined with an intense regimen of physical conditioning and labor. Judo exercises and brisk jogs between campus and a nearby farm were mandatory. Students were responsible for the upkeep of the institution and were constantly reminded of the virtues of strenuous work. Violation of injunctions against liquor, drugs, "abusive language," and fraternization with white people was grounds for expulsion.[25]

This hardline approach was designed to disabuse newcomers to the school of romantic conceptions of revolutionary education. The aim was to correct the decadence and egoism engendered by the dominant culture—characteristics seen as inimical to "the long, hard task necessary to rid ourselves of our chains." If some students found the strictures intolerable, MXLU officials reasoned, others would adjust, developing the necessary work habits and outlook. "A whole new lifestyle is being developed among the young men and women at MXLU," an administrator declared. Kalamu Ya Salaam of Ahidiana, the New Orleans collective, later recognized the school as one of the most significant "manifestations of Pan-Afrikan thought" in the country. By summer 1970, MXLU had attracted another set of applicants for the upcoming academic year, including an auto mechanic, a secretary, a tailor, a nurse, a hotel manager, and a barber.[26]

"Underdeveloped Areas": MXLU, the Black Community, and the Boundaries of Nationhood

MXLU's ultimate purpose was to foster a "meaningful sense of 'peoplehood.'" The institution's leaders vowed that the school would never "strive to be a black Duke or UNC." Nor would it seek formal accreditation, a symbol, its operators believed, of acceptance of the status quo. Instead, MXLU would redefine "blackness," converting an emphasis on externalities like Afros and dashikis into a deep craving for liberation. It would serve as an example for "traditionally Negro colleges," inspiring them to become truly relevant, "black universities." And it would train technicians to meet "the basic needs of our people," creating capable purveyors of food, clothing, shelter, and medicine.[27]

MXLU organizers regarded this last task as their central mission. By its second year, the school had expanded its commitment to preparing skilled workers for the cause of black nationhood and self-sufficiency. It refashioned its academic unit as an "African Peoples' Ideological and Technical Institute"—an effort to transmit expertise that could be put to immediate use "for the benefit of African people." Laboratories and other facilities were upgraded to enable intense study in biomedics, agriculture, and civil and electrical engineering. Students were to spend at least 18 hours a week training in general skill areas. As one visitor observed, MXLU more resembled a trade school than it did a hotbed of militancy.[28]

The science and technology focus reflected a traditional black nationalist priority. "The wars of the future, whether they be physical or mental, will be fought along scientific lines," Marcus Garvey had once predicted, "and the race with the highest degree of scientific knowledge will ultimately triumph." MXLU companion projects like the Student Organization for Black Unity and the Pan African Skills Project shared the school's conviction that black college students' overemphasis on the liberal arts contributed to a shortage of technical expertise needed to modernize black communities and nations. Some African-American intellectuals argued that black colleges should shift from teacher education to the hard sciences as a contribution to global black development.[29]

Even as MXLU's devotion to the construction of "the African world" increased, the question of precisely where its graduates would practice their trades lingered. The institution remained strongly oriented toward Africa and the Caribbean as zones of future endeavor. Administrators planned to place alumni in countries like Tanzania or Guyana, where they would serve as long-time workers or permanent residents. They prioritized skills seen as relevant to rural life in such areas, from water purification to snakebite treatment, and they promoted the development of overseas "land bases" as the major task of Pan African nationalists. "We cannot savor the thought of victory until Africa is free and united and all African people are liberated from the shackles of white oppression and 'niggerisms,'" Fuller declared.[30]

MXLU theorists dismissed the notion that black self-determination could be achieved on American soil. African Americans had no hope of controlling the means of production or rivaling the power of American political and economic elites. By helping secure "Africa for the Africans," however, black people could aid in harnessing the continent's abundant minerals and resources, creating viable alternatives to a life of scarcity in American ghettos. This line of reasoning led almost inexorably to the deprecation of African-American social realities. Encouraged by Fuller to question the validity of American "Negro" culture, participants in one MXLU seminar concluded that "Anglo-Saxon" values had severely damaged black Americans. "We're operating at a very low spiritual level," one student maintained.[31]

In some ways, however, MXLU appeared to affirm the value of political work in African-American communities. At times, the institution's leaders seemed to suggest that the creation of truly sovereign African nations was a long-term goal that must be supplemented in the short term by efforts to empower local neighborhoods. Service to "the African Nation" did not have to mean overlooking African America; with some imagination, black communities in the United States could be seen as potential extensions of the African "liberated zones" that had been wrested from European colonial control. Viewed in this light, local neighborhoods offered crucial arenas for the dissemination of revolutionary concepts and techniques, and vital settings for the field work of MXLU students.

MXLU's evening classes, "The Law and Black People" and "Independent African Civilization," signaled the institution's desire to remain "rooted in the masses of our people." Between 20 and 30 Durham residents regularly attended the seminars. Administrators also launched a farming project designed to benefit the agriculture department while providing area residents with inexpensive produce. The school's most significant community-based initiative was its collaboration with two poor people's organizations to create the Betty Shabazz Early Education Center. The preschool served 30 three- to five-year-olds, delivering hot meals and positive cultural images based on the theme "We Are an African People."[32]

The fate of these projects, and the nature of MXLU's relationship to its surrounding neighborhood, was cast into doubt early in 1970 when operators of the school began to consider moving the institution to nearby Greensboro. Practical considerations prompted the discussion. MXLU had outgrown its Durham quarters as it continued to amass supplies and technical equipment. The institution and several blighted, adjacent structures had also been slated for removal under an urban renewal plan. Political concerns further inspired the move. Greensboro, a city of 150,000 people, about one-third of whom were African American, was a locus of black self-activity and the birthplace of the 1960 sit-in movement, an event that had inaugurated a new era of radicalism. The site promised to provide a highly politicized base.

Elements of estrangement from the Durham community spurred the relocation. MXLU had generated intense political opposition from members of the city's black and white establishments. Ironically, even the institution's efforts to support local causes had soured relations with neighbors. MXLU delegations had participated in several political demonstrations within and beyond Durham. However, expectations on the part of black, working-class residents that the institution would dispatch a complement of militants to reinforce every protest strained MXLU's capacities, intensifying police harassment of the school and leaving little time for internal development.[33]

MXLU made the Greensboro move in summer 1970, inhabiting a large church annex in the city and quartering its students in several nearby houses. After the transition, the school's community-based activities increased. While the Betty Shabazz Early Education Center continued operation in Durham,

MXLU helped establish or staff additional satellite projects in both Durham and Greensboro, including the Pan African Early Education Center; the Willie Grimes Community School (a secondary institution named after a North Carolina A&T student who had been killed during Greensboro's 1969 campus uprising); and the Young African Warriors, a group for adolescents. The farm program also expanded; MXLU students joined neighborhood youths and other volunteers in raising poultry and cultivating vegetables on 25 leased acres. The venture enabled community members to buy fresh eggs at discounted prices and yielded corn, okra, squash, tomatoes, cucumbers, and greens for consumption by MXLU students and distribution to a black cooperative supermarket.[34]

MXLU pupils and personnel developed a first aid manual for the local community, volunteered as health aides in the surrounding neighborhood, and supported a strike at a Greensboro manufacturing plant staffed by blind African-American workers. Even some of the school's international endeavors served local interests. In 1971, athletes representing several African nations converged on Durham for the USA–Pan Africa track-and-field meet. Driven by Cold War calculations, U.S. officials attempted to promote the competition as a symbol of ongoing racial progress in the South. Looking to foil the maneuver, MXLU activists distributed to members of the African delegation a self-published, illustrated booklet that highlighted the miserable poverty endured by many black North Carolinians.[35]

Despite such efforts, MXLU never became an integral part of the local black community. When operators of the school again began contemplating a new plant in late 1971, they were forced to acknowledge that misunderstanding and suspicion continued to separate the institution from much of black Greensboro. They had made plans to purchase the Palmer Memorial Institute, a historic but debt-ridden African-American prep school in nearby Sedalia, North Carolina. The sale would have furnished MXLU with additional space and valuable farmland, but the proposal died amid the furor raised by black and white residents who refused to see the landmark site in the hands of avowed revolutionaries.

In truth, MXLU theorists were too enamored with the masculine ideal of nationhood to relate fully to the mundane problems of most African-American communities. Self-determination was a prize to be won on rugged and remote frontiers, not in local campaigns for tenant and labor rights. Deploying a gendered discourse with roots in both European thought and Third World ideologies, Fuller cast national development as a process of conquest—both of the physical environment and of psychological deficiencies. Mining and constructing roads and dams—these were the kinds of virile acts that he hoped MXLU students would perform. "When we speak of a land base," he said in early 1971 after returning from a trip to Guyana's interior, "we are talking about jungles, dirt, snakes, etc. We are not talking about Brooklyn, Accra, Durham, Georgetown.

We are talking about the land areas ignored and underdeveloped by the oppressor, now lying dormant in Africa and in other places."[36]

"A Solidarity in Deeds": African Liberation Day and the Proletarianization of Pan Africanism

A month of revolutionary realism helped dispel romantic notions of nation building. Fuller had worked since 1970 to solidify bonds of transnational blackness. He attended the Seminar of Pan Africanist and Black Revolutionary Nationalists in Georgetown, Guyana; led a rally at the United Nations on behalf of Southern African anticolonial campaigns; visited West Africa to pave the way for future MXLU trips; and participated in efforts to develop a North American "day of solidarity" on behalf of armed struggles on the African continent. Fuller hoped to re-establish a central role for black America in "the liberation of our Motherland." Recognized as a pioneer in this crusade, he received a new name from his MXLU colleagues. He was now "Owusu Sadaukai," a designation translated as "one who clears the way for others."[37]

In August 1971, the MXLU chief visited Dar-es-Salaam, Tanzania, to attend a conference on black identity and solidarity. Sadaukai delivered a lecture about black education and made inquiries about MXLU's future involvement with rural development projects in the East African nation. While in Tanzania, he also met with agents of the Mozambique Liberation Front (FRELIMO) and was offered a rare opportunity to travel inside Mozambique with the movement's armed forces. Sadaukai accepted the invitation, eager to demonstrate revolutionary camaraderie. He planned to spend about two weeks in the embattled Southern African country. The trip actually spanned a grueling 31 days.

Trekking through the Mozambican countryside, swaths of which FRELIMO had emancipated from the Portuguese, Sadaukai experienced firsthand the rigors of revolutionary commitment. The unit with which he was embedded was bombed and strafed once, a harrowing incident that on this occasion took no lives. The bulk of the campaign involved endless hikes through punishing elephant grass. The expedition journeyed deep into the interior, covering 25 miles a day over narrow mountain trails and through swamps and streams. Men and women toted 70-pound loads and endured gnats and oppressive heat and cold, subsisting on a diet of corn, cassava, tea, and beans and rice. In the evenings, they sang FRELIMO songs and dreamed of new lives beyond the degradation of colonialism.

Sadaukai was awed by the fighters. He was struck by the sight of a woman in traditional African dress with an AK-47 slung over her shoulder. Women, he

discovered, were "total comrades" in the armed struggle. The tremendous sacrifices of the FRELIMO rebels contrasted with the posturing and extravagant
rhetoric that Sadaukai believed plagued the black American struggle. In the
African bush, he noted, there were "no speeches, no rallies, no newspaper articles, no press conferences"—just an exemplary ethic of revolutionary labor. At
one encampment he witnessed the organization of a makeshift school. "A freedom fighter, one day out of combat with the Portuguese, will put up a blackboard
on a tree and with his gun still strapped over his shoulder, begin to teach these
younger brothers and sisters—that's a revolutionary brother," he later recalled.[38]

Sadaukai returned to the United States imbued with "spirited resolve to struggle harder" and armed with political lessons that reshaped his consciousness.
Having witnessed the practice of gender equality, he began to recognize that
"there is no place for weak-kneed chauvinism" in the struggle. Having discovered
the pitfalls of racialism, he acknowledged that "The very essence of imperialist
domination was its capacity to use persons of all races to suppress the legitimate
aspirations of the popular masses." African revolutionaries were fighting neither for "blackness" nor for "traditional" culture. Their commitment to a global,
anti-imperialist vanguard convinced Sadaukai of the need for black American
activists to re-examine the nature of oppression and critically analyze the links
between race, class, and Western finance capitalism.[39]

As he absorbed these epiphanies, the MXLU leader contemplated other revelations. During meetings with Sadaukai, Samora Machel and other FRELIMO
leaders had stressed the significance of U.S. support for Portugal and other colonial settler regimes on the African continent. Southern Africa's liberation fronts
did not need African-American recruits to travel to their lands; what they needed
was intervention within the United States to counteract the superpower's international policies. True camaraderie with Africa, Sadaukai now realized, required
concrete deeds and material support, not mere "rap sessions." Practicing Pan
African solidarity meant fighting the agents of imperialism "at home."[40]

In early 1972, Sadaukai launched a national campaign that, as political scientist Cedric Johnson notes, established him as "a principal force in the movement to end Portuguese colonialism and white oligarchy in Southern Africa."
The MXLU helmsman summoned to Greensboro America's leading Pan African
nationalists to begin planning the largest African solidarity demonstration since
the days of Marcus Garvey. African Liberation Day (ALD) was designed to coincide with similar observances on the African continent and around the world.
The North American version of the event stemmed from a venerable tradition of
exposing the entanglement of U.S. capital and European colonialism.[41] Still, the
breadth of the ALD groundswell was extraordinary.

Virtually the entire corpus of progressive black artists, activists, intellectuals,
and politicians worked on ALD's behalf. Joining the effort were Angela Davis,

Stokely Carmichael, Georgia legislator Julian Bond, Roy Innis of CORE, Jesse Jackson of People United to Save Humanity, George Wiley of the National Welfare Rights Organization, Nelson Johnson of the Student Organization for Black Unity (SOBU), and Ohio activist Ron Daniels. Black Panthers Huey Newton, Bobby Seale, Elaine Brown, and Ericka Huggins participated. H. Rap Brown expressed solidarity from his Rikers Island jail cell. Michigan Congressmen John Conyers and Charles Diggs (chairman of the House Subcommittee on Africa) and California Congressman Ron Dellums played key roles, as did civil rights leaders Ralph Abernathy and Walter Fauntroy.

Pan African nationalists and independent school organizers composed the core ALD leadership. Sadaukai chaired the central ALD committee. Cleveland Sellers of MXLU and Dawolu Gene Locke of the Lynn Eusan Institute of Houston, Texas, served as national coordinators, as did Haki Madhubuti of Chicago's New Concept Development Center, Amiri Baraka of Newark's African Free School, and Florence Tate, a movement veteran with ties to various Pan African nationalist groups. Chicago's ALD chapter included members of the Communiversity, Shule Ya Watoto, and the Arusha-Konakri Institute. Atlanta's Pan African Work Center spearheaded that city's organizing committee. Brooklyn's Uhuru Sasa rallied black New York, Peoples College (an independent, leftist formation) mobilized Nashville, and Ahidiana galvanized New Orleans.[42] Scores of students, workers, church groups, and protest organizations helped promote the day of commemoration. Support for struggles against the remaining outposts of European colonial rule in Africa constituted the definitive consensus issue of the day.

The main impetus for ALD was the need to demonstrate opposition to Western involvement with Southern Africa's settler-colonialist regimes. As armed resistance to minority rule on the continent had intensified in the late 1960s and early '70s, African-American denunciation of the role of U.S. corporations and the Nixon administration in the region had increased. It was widely understood that Portugal, a small, economically "backward" country, was able to suppress liberation movements in its colonies only because it was buoyed by "a worldwide conspiracy of western imperialists and agents of neocolonialism." The United States and NATO remained prime sources of assistance to racist forces in South Africa, Angola, Namibia, Mozambique, Zimbabwe, and Guinea-Bissau.[43]

The ALD mobilization also provided an opportunity to expand political consciousness. Most African Americans remained unaware of the dynamics of African liberation movements and the nature of the colonial and neocolonial forces that the continent's freedom fighters were confronting. Organizers believed that mass demonstrations could help foster understanding of armed, anticolonial resistance in Africa as an international dimension of black America's quest for freedom. Such expressions of solidarity, they insisted, reflected revolutionary self-interest and recognition of the global character of black oppression.

Supporters hoped ALD would spur the transition "from the vagueness of a mystical 'cultural brotherhood' to what Guyanese Pan Africanist Eusi Kwayana defined as 'a solidarity in deeds and camaraderie.' "[44]

On May 27, 1972, solidarity propelled tens of thousands of black people into the streets. Rallies were held in U.S., Canadian, and Caribbean cities. The main ALD demonstration occurred in Washington, DC. As many as 30,000 people participated in that protest march, which wound from Malcolm X Park (formerly Meridian Hill Park) to the grounds of the Washington Monument, a site organizers had renamed "Lumumba Square" for the occasion. The procession through the city's diplomatic quarter featured speeches (before the Rhodesian information center and the South African and Portuguese embassies) denouncing the colonialist regimes. The route included a stop at the State Department, where speakers condemned U.S. government and corporate collaboration with colonial administrations.

At one point Queen Mother Moore addressed the crowd. "I have waited 54 years for this day!" the veteran organizer exclaimed. Dawolu Gene Locke recited an "African People's statement of indictment" against the United States. Haki Madhubuti read poetry. The Harambee Singers, a group associated with Atlanta's Pan African Work Center, sang a rendition of "Hands Off Nkrumah." Cleveland Sellers relayed Carmichael's message from overseas. ("Africa is ours," the expatriate wrote. "Her total liberation and unification under scientific socialism must be our only creed.") Finally, Sadaukai stood before the assemblage. "We are no longer buying the argument that Africans on the continent are different from us," he declared. "We understand that this racist, capitalist monster that we are struggling against is the same one that oppresses our people in Africa and all over the world." The MXLU chief led the crowd in chants of "We . . . are . . . an African people! We . . . are . . . an African people!"[45]

ALD '72 raised thousands of dollars for liberation fronts on the continent. It also marked a promising political moment. The mobilization effort belied the notion that African Americans "have their hands too full" with domestic concerns to think globally. When author Inez Smith Reid surveyed militant black American women in the early 1970s, many of them could not define "Pan Africanism" or feared that transnational black politics undermined efforts to "take care of business" at home. However, ALD revealed that a broad segment of African Americans embraced the radical, international dimensions of black consciousness. Transcending "Back-to-Africa" outlooks, participants affirmed the idea that racial capitalism and imperialism linked the fates of black populations around the world.[46]

ALD's success convinced many Pan African nationalists that they were witnessing the proletarianization of their movement. Mwalimu Shay, a teacher at Shule Ya Watoto in Chicago, reveled in the display of popular consciousness.

"We can no longer underestimate the mentality of the black masses," he declared. Independent black institutions mobilized throughout 1972 and 1973, promoting boycotts of corporations with investments in colonial Africa, linking the search for decent jobs and public services in the United States to the drive for self-determination on the continent, and extending anti-imperialist critiques to the war in Southeast Asia. In Oberlin, Ohio, members of Shule Ya Kujitambua circulated leaflets that asserted that until all of Africa had been liberated, "no black people anywhere can be completely free and respected." Washington, DC's Center for Black Education published a collection of original articles about colonialism in Southern Africa, believing that such knowledge could inspire African Americans to reject incremental social change in the United States.[47]

ALD illustrated the popular appeal of united-front politics, an approach that enabled a variety of organizations and political tendencies to cooperate for a common cause. What appeared to be the genesis of a new age of Pan African solidarity, however, was actually the prelude to a period of fragmentation. Beneath the aura of ecumenical harmony, ideological lines diverged.

The issue of Southern African "Bantustans" represented one area of philosophical difference. Some operators of right-leaning nationalist institutions saw the creation by white minority regimes of artificial black territories or "homelands" as opportunities to pursue "separate development," a strategy roughly analogous to the African-American bid for community control. In early 1972, Brooklyn's Uhuru Sasa Shule sponsored a lecture by a representative from "The Republic of Transkei," a South African Bantustan. The visitor's staunch anticommunism and vision of revolution as an inexorable clash between black and white antagonists matched the worldview of his African-American hosts.

Yet many of Uhuru Sasa's ALD allies denounced Bantustans as reservations and likened them to discredited "black capitalist" programs in the United States, seeing both schemes as attempts to confuse the popular masses while creating a reactionary native elite. "The oppressors who keep our people enmeshed in poverty, disease and 'Bantu' programs here are the same oppressors of our Ndugu na Dada [brothers and sisters] in Southern Africa," Sadaukai declared.[48] The issue at the heart of the disagreement—whether whiteness or imperialism itself was the inimitable enemy of the African revolution—had begun to undermine the renaissance of black American internationalism.

"Our People Are Ready": The Rebirth of Localism

ALD '72 was another revelation for Sadaukai. The display of popular anti-imperialism reinvigorated the intellectual's commitment to grassroots action. The demonstrations suggested that a potent political awareness was growing—

a consciousness not primarily derived from speeches, books, or international travel, but rather, from a sense that the oppression of African Americans was symptomatic of larger processes of domination. As Sadaukai declared, "Our people are ready to move again."[49]

ALD led Sadaukai to reassess the meaning of solidarity work. While the MXLU leader had once seen bolstering revolutionary Africa as the special duty of African Americans, he now envisioned a transatlantic relationship based on political mutuality. His analysis of political economy deepened. He honed explanations of how the transfer of manufacturing from the United States to South Africa exacerbated domestic unemployment while intensifying the exploitation of black labor overseas. He developed an understanding of Pan Africanism as a critique of the global system that forced black workers to toil for subsistence wages in North Carolina tobacco fields and South West African (Namibian) mines while depriving them of land in both Georgia and Mozambique. He came to view ALD and MXLU as instruments for cultivating concrete rather than romantic conceptions of transnational blackness.[50]

Amid these breakthroughs, MXLU rededicated itself to its surrounding community. Students and staff agitated for prison reform, restored a building for a new Greensboro community center, printed pamphlets for a community drive against police brutality, and opened another preschool designed to counteract children's susceptibility to mental "colonization." The institution's theorists continued to believe that "Every piece of ground won by African guerillas is another piece of our freedom restored." Sadaukai strengthened relations with African embassies and with heads of state like Tanzania's Julius Nyerere and Zambia's Kenneth Kaunda. Yet he insisted that the struggle against imperialism also meant waging local battles in areas like housing and public education.[51]

The revival of a domestic agenda prompted a reconceptualization of revolutionary leadership. African Americans again appeared capable of enlightened self-activity. Sadaukai rejected the idea that mass politics could be orchestrated from above by charismatic elites. Leaders bore a responsibility to participate in the daily struggles of working people, whether this meant joining picket lines or voting drives. "We [Pan African nationalists] talk of the masses but avoid any actions that involve the masses," Sadaukai charged in a 1972 pamphlet. "We then are left to theorize and criticize while the masses continue to suffer. We can no longer bury Pan Africanism in the halls of the intelligentsia."[52]

The search for clarity accelerated Sadaukai's transformation. The activist had once rejected Marxian analysis in favor of ill-defined traditions of communalism. His African sojourns, however, had convinced him of the perils of liberation without genuine social transformation. In the wake of ALD '72, he and other MXLU leaders embraced class struggle and scientific socialism. The idea that "the export of U.S. capital increases the misery of our people" became one of the institution's defining principles. Seminars on political economy were expanded. Renowned black Marxist C. L. R. James was booked as a guest lecturer. Sadaukai dropped "HNIC" and assumed the title "Mwalimu" ("teacher"), the honorific borne by the leftist Nyerere. MXLU students who rejected Marxism too hastily risked censure for exhibiting "European phobia" and "unsound" analysis.[53]

Even as it evolved, however, MXLU remained mired in crises. Attrition was a constant concern. By early 1972, fewer than 25 students remained, down from a high of about 60 in 1969–1970. Only five pupils returned for their third year, and the 13 full-time students who arrived in fall 1972 represented the smallest incoming class yet. Meanwhile, the corps of full-time faculty fell from 10 to 6 members. Rigid discipline was one reason for the turnover. Sadaukai continued to run an exacting organization. By 1972, student responsibilities included 35 hours of instruction per week along with a grueling physical workload. Yet MXLU granted no formal degrees and made no effort to send graduates to four-year institutions. Pupils who quit in exhaustion were accused of harboring bourgeois impulses. "They left Harvard but they also wanted Harvard in a sense," Sadaukai maintained.[54]

MXLU's Council of Elders hoped to attract students who were prepared to "do what needs to be done." Three-day entrance interviews no longer seemed sufficient as a means of barring "adverse interests." News reports about the federal government's underground war on black radicalism heightened MXLU concerns about internal subversion and lapses of discipline. The council briefly discussed hiring an investigator to screen applicants. (The idea was abandoned after someone pointed out that ideological purity was an unreasonable criterion for admission). Allies cautioned that the school's strictures would breed insularity and cut off potential avenues of support. But administrators continued to see student deviation from the line of the institution as a threat to be combatted with isolation and expulsion.[55]

External pressures compounded these problems. MXLU's reputation for extremism brought the school unwelcome scrutiny. Operators of the establishment were powerless to dispel allegations that Sadaukai was a bomb expert, and that they and their colleagues routinely conducted guerilla training exercises on nearby farmland. Civil rights leaders castigated the institution for misleading "our young people," and Greensboro authorities repeatedly interceded to block the sale or lease of facilities to the school.[56] Meanwhile police and city building inspectors harried the operation. MXLU leaders faced multiple arrests in connection with political activities. Sadaukai's involvement in strikes and demonstrations yielded a litany of charges, from "disorderly conduct" to "engaging in a riot." The activist received frequent traffic citations. It was later revealed that the FBI had surveilled the school since the establishment's inception in 1969, viewing its purpose as "the training of militant Negroes for Revolutionary Tactics."

The intelligence agency fed the news media information designed to discredit the institution and deter its sponsors.[57]

MXLU's biggest worry was money. By 1972, most major grants had ceased; expenses were met mostly with proceeds from Sadaukai's speaking engagements. MXLU continued to assume almost total financial responsibility for most of its students. Maintaining facilities and obtaining equipment and materials—from electron microscopes to a dairy cow—increased mounting costs. The school's notoriety diminished the prospect of continued support from past benefactors. (Even the Episcopalians, MXLU's erstwhile patrons, now dismissed the institution as a "dubious" experiment mounted by "frustrated, angry blacks.")[58] Proscriptions against white people within the walls of the school precluded the site visits required by other potential funders. Third World sources that might have offered support were put off by the institution's lack of accreditation.

So MXLU scrimped. Administrators imposed a hiring freeze. A security officer was asked to double as a janitor. Several rounds of cuts left Sadaukai's salary at $6,000—the ceiling of a pay scale that began at a meager $900. Operators of the institution discussed a plan to draft Betty Shabazz and actor Ossie Davis as fundraisers. Proposals to print "Right On!" greeting cards and to open cooperative laundromats were considered. Yet the school never stabilized financially. The institution was struggling to survive by fall 1972, the start of its fourth year. Its leaders wondered aloud whether "the masses" were truly prepared for an enterprise like MXLU.[59]

The Community as Campus: Relevance and the Black University

MXLU was a prominent model of the "Black University," one of the most evocative themes of the nationalist renaissance. The concept denoted a process of adult education that addressed the internal needs of African-American communities. The Black University ideal sprang from a convergence of forces, including the quest for black self-determination, critiques of the Cold War "multiversity," and attempts to fulfill the prophetic social role of education articulated by pioneers like Du Bois.

The drive for the Black University began with the 1960s rebellions of African-American students. The numbers of black college students were increasing, enlarged by social gains, civil rights initiatives, and the new recruiting efforts of postsecondary institutions. Black undergraduates had launched off-campus campaigns for social justice earlier in the decade. In the late 1960s, African Americans formed the vanguard of campus-based revolts. Students at historically black institutions helped initiate the escalation of campus unrest after the mid-1960s, with African-American pupils at predominantly white schools joining the militant surge by 1967–1968. Black agitation swept college campuses from coast to coast; African Americans participated in more than half of the 300 student protests that flared nationwide in the first six months of 1969. Black studies, new admissions policies, and more African-American instructors and staff were among their demands. Above all they sought social "relevance," repudiating "a hopelessly white educational apparatus which maims illiterate blacks and trains literate blacks to be enemies of their own people."[60]

Increasingly, black students defined their challenges to the white, Western hegemony of higher education—and to the traditional isolation of black students from poor, African-American neighborhoods—in terms of the struggle for the Black University. The search for a paradigm of postsecondary education that could empower the entire black community captured the imagination of an array of thinkers. Enthusiasm for the Black University crested between 1968 and 1970, as students and intellectuals discussed the theme in conferences and journals. The deliberations of these thinkers, one observer noted, marked one of the most fervent debates over African-American higher learning "since Du Bois defended his 'talented tenth' philosophy against Booker T. Washington's concept of craft education."[61]

Part of the allure of the Black University was its ambiguity. All proponents of the concept wished to use knowledge as an instrument of liberation. All affirmed the need to seek psychological independence from "the oppressor" and transcend Western ideals of scientific detachment and intellectual abstraction. Attempts to identify other unifying principles revealed a spectrum of beliefs. Was the task of the Black University to imbue African-American professionals with race pride or to engineer the "new man"—a personality totally committed to liberation? Would the institution instill "blackness" exclusively or take a more "cosmopolitan" approach? Would it serve as a skills bank for underdeveloped countries or form the nucleus of a new nation? Would it prepare its students to revolutionize the United States or to hasten its downfall?[62]

Could the Black University be built within the structure of higher education, as a supplemental presence on white campuses or as an effort to transform "predominantly Negro" colleges? Or was it necessary to conceive new models based on the idea that "the very sidewalks of the black community" could become a campus? Some believed an incipient Black University already existed. In the eyes of Black Arts poet Nikki Giovanni, Harlem's 500 churches and 300 bars represented 800 potential school buildings. "It would be a beautiful sight," she wrote in 1970, "to see a sign hanging from Small's Paradise Lounge, Afro-American History from 1664 to 1886, 8a.m. to 4p.m. daily. Professor Lerone Bennett Guest Lecturer This Week."[63]

A cadre of Philadelphia nationalists insisted that the Black University must nurture "an indigenous intelligentsia from the hardcore unemployed element of the black community." Other thinkers saw more traditional scholars as the Black University's personnel. Some felt the Black University should be based in the urban North. Others believed the institution, or at least its mother campus, should reside in the South, the historic birthplace of the black community. Many advocated an all-black establishment. Others reserved the right to determine the extent and nature of white participation.[64]

Pragmatists acknowledged that the Black University might require sponsorship by affluent white institutions. They insisted, however, that this did not have to mean abandoning the principle of black autonomy. Such aid, they maintained, could be considered a form of restitution by an empire to its former colony. In 1968, black economist Robert S. Browne proposed the creation of a $3 million Black University capital fund, a sum to be drawn from the endowments of northern, white schools. A more ambitious plan was advanced by former SNCC leader James Forman, whose 1969 "Black Manifesto" included a demand for the establishment of a $130 million Black University.[65]

The relationship of the Black University to black studies represented another area of debate. Some theorists considered the two concepts virtually synonymous. Others saw competing ideals. The early black studies revolt had seemed full of promise; its first major victory had seen the creation of an academic department at San Francisco State College in 1967, and the struggle had evolved into a genuine social movement after King's assassination the following year. To some, the emergence of "Afro-American" courses and programs constituted a nascent Black University. "It could very well be that the next chapter in our tense struggle will be a move from the scholar-oriented black studies program on white campuses to a community-oriented Black University," sociologist William Julius Wilson asserted in 1970.[66]

By then, however, some African-American progressives had begun to view the spread of black studies programs on predominantly white campuses with a degree of scorn. The proliferation of superficial programs detached from the aspirations of the black masses alienated those who hoped that black studies would complement grassroots organizing in African-American neighborhoods. Many black studies programs seemed geared toward "sterile dissection of the black experience" rather than "immersion" in blackness.[67] As uncertainty and suspicion engulfed black studies, theorists turned with new purpose to the Black University concept.

The notion of a Black University had arisen during the 1967 Black Power Conference in Newark. Participants had called for the formation of a central institution of higher learning with subsidiary black colleges in every major city. An education workshop at the 1968 Black Power Conference in Philadelphia had raised $1,500 toward the creation of such an establishment. The session included a proposal for the formation of "intelligence squads" designed to infiltrate "Negro" colleges and convert them into "true black institutions." Conferees also discussed the prospect of a wholly independent Black University, with Queen Mother Moore's sprawling Catskills, New York, property identified as a possible site for such an endeavor.[68]

Dialogue on the Black University continued during the 1968–1969 summits of the National Association of Afro-American Educators (NAAAE). The organization's founding meeting in 1968 had convinced some participants that realization of the Black University ideal was imminent. The concept had emerged as a major theme during the conference. Inspired by student insurgencies, attendees had discussed the development of an independent educational system able to serve the entire black community and had prioritized the pursuit of such ventures over the "short-range goal" of reforming existing institutions.

The tentative accord dissolved in 1969 at the NAAAE's Atlanta conference. Billed as a temporary Black University, the gathering was designed to showcase the creative potential of such an endeavor. Yet a series of internal disputes exposed the divide between so-called organizationalists (who wished to reform current educational systems), and institutionalists (who advocated the creation of parallel establishments in black communities). Questions arose about who would control new educational models. Critics charged that the organization's black professional elite remained far removed from the "mother wit" and "lifestyle" of the black grassroots—essential cultural elements of the Black University.[69]

A more auspicious effort to envision a socially relevant program of higher learning occurred in 1968 during the Toward a Black University (TABU) conference at Howard University, the black school in Washington, DC. Organized by Howard's student association, the event saw 2,000 educators, artists, activists, intellectuals, community residents, and students assemble to help define the structure and mechanics of the Black University. The summit came on the heels of a disavowal of the Black University concept by Howard's trustees. (Nothing in the school's charter would support such a model of "discrimination," the board had proclaimed.)[70] TABU reflected specific concerns about the isolation of the Washington school from "the larger masses of black people," as well as broader objections to the systematic acculturation of black students to "a society which debilitates black people."[71]

The scope of the gathering was impressive. Intellectuals and artists like Amiri Baraka, Harold Cruse, Ossie Davis, and Sonia Sanchez were among the guests. Panelists included scholar-activists Gerald McWhorter (Abdul Alkalimat) and Jimmy Garrett. A group of students presented a paper on "Black Liberation and Higher Learning in an Advanced Industrialist Neocolonialist Society." Stokely Carmichael stressed the need to counteract a white educational system that favored technological advancement over human development. Maulana Karenga predicted that the advent of the Black University would hasten the demise of the "Career Nigger" and foster a generation of students devoted to nation building.[72]

Despite its serious purpose, TABU exhibited many of the problems that bedeviled other explorations of the Black University idea. Though conference organizers resolved "to allow the widest possible representation from the black community" and arranged for some panels to occur off campus, few sessions seemed genuinely designed to facilitate grassroots participation. Halfway through Cruse's talk, a disgruntled audience member rose, denounced "phony" theorizing, and proclaimed that the true intellectuals of the black revolution were in the streets of the ghettos and not in universities. All in all, TABU was long on rhetoric and short on concrete plans. "I am here to find out how to establish a Black University," one University of Wisconsin student complained. "Instead I'm getting a lot of useless words."[73]

TABU's success lay not in the proposals that it generated, but in the consciousness that it helped precipitate. Five days of deliberation yielded far more than a set of resolutions. Nation of Islam ministers and restless high schoolers were among the conference participants. A student delegation arrived from Detroit's Wayne State University armed with a 30-page manifesto. Despite the diatribes, grandstanding, and interminable debates over whether the intelligentsia or proletariat would set the revolution in motion, an audacious spirit was spreading. New frontiers lay ahead.[74]

"Forced into Blackness": The Transformation of Howard University

Some proponents of the Black University believed the concept might find expression in one or more of the nation's anachronistically titled "predominantly Negro" colleges and universities. Founded in the years after the Civil War, the more than 100 southern-based institutions had played a crucial role in the development of black America, cultivating leaders and providing an essential means of social mobility. They had educated generations of students that white colleges had excluded, and they continued to serve as avenues to higher education for at least half the nation's black collegians. But traditions of dignity and social responsibility at black colleges mingled with patterns of provincialism. The attempts of the institutions to groom an African-American professional class often reflected elite notions of racial uplift and Victorian standards of respectability.[75]

In 1967, two prominent, white social scientists lambasted black colleges in a lengthy report, labeling them caricatures of white universities and "purveyors

of super-American, ultra-bourgeois prejudices and aspirations." Black nationalists were no gentler in their criticism of the schools' assimilationist tendencies and acquiescence to white paternal control. In 1965, Max Stanford of the
Revolutionary Action Movement described the institutions as "freak factories"
that imparted an ersatz whiteness and instilled an escapist desire to "succeed"
in racist America. "The so-called Negro Colleges," Amiri Baraka later declared,
"ought to be the first to be forced into blackness."[76]

By the mid-1960s, some African-American students had resolved to do just
that. Agitation at historically black colleges and universities (HBCUs) initially
addressed compulsory Reserve Officers' Training Corps (ROTC) exercises,
paltry facilities, and draconian social regulations and curfews. Galvanized by
the cry for Black Power, student dissent evolved into broader critiques of the
Vietnam War and white supremacy. During 1966 and 1967, a "storm of unrest"
swept black colleges. Demonstrations erupted on campuses in Houston, Baton
Rouge, Durham, Jackson, Memphis, Nashville, and other cities. Student radicals
complained of being conditioned by ROTC "to further the cause of American
imperialism throughout the nonwhite world." Many began to view "Negro"
college officials as arms of the white establishment, and to regard their campuses as "islands of whiteness" amid exploited black neighborhoods. Rejecting
expectations that they learn to "forget and scorn the ghetto," they demanded an
education geared toward liberation and the forging of "a perpetual reciprocal
relationship with the entire black community."[77]

A dramatic revolt unfolded at Howard University. Hailed as "the capstone of
Negro education," the school had long been recognized as one of the nation's
premiere black institutions. Though it had nurtured generations of civil rights
leaders, Howard also exemplified the tendencies of white mimicry that characterized many HBCUs. Much of its curriculum venerated Western civilization
while largely ignoring black history and culture. Its traditions fostered a climate of privilege, preserving a sanctuary for the brown bourgeoisie amid one of
Washington's poverty-stricken black neighborhoods.

When a handful of student organizers formed the Nonviolent Action Group
(NAG) in the early 1960s, they constituted "a tiny, activist island in Howard's
vast, bourgeois sea." NAG's members (including future Pan African nationalist
organizers Stokely Carmichael, Courtland Cox, and Cleveland Sellers) eventually went south to join the burgeoning civil rights revolution. The ferment of
struggle again penetrated Howard's docility in the mid-'60s. Against the backdrop of the antiracist campaign in Selma, Alabama, a contingent of Howard
students began protesting mandatory ROTC and the university's constraints
on academic freedom. Congressman Adam Clayton Powell, Jr.'s counsel to
Howard graduates, at the school's May 1966 commencement, to eschew narrow

integrationism and "seek audacious power" provided another prologue to the coming political renaissance.[78]

Howard's revolution began that fall with the selection of brown-skinned, Afro-crowned activist Robin Gregory as the campus's first "natural look" homecoming queen. Gregory had sought the title, which traditionally had gone to fair-skinned women with flowing hair, as a means of promoting a "black aesthetic" and demonstrating the political prowess of African-American women. Jubilation erupted during the ceremony in which she was revealed as the new queen. Students chanted "Umgawa, Black Power! Umgawa, Black Power!" as they marched out of the auditorium and into the city streets.[79]

The quest for "blackness" dismayed Howard patriarchs, who envisioned a different destiny for the university. Responding to the political and legal pressures of desegregation, Howard president James M. Nabrit in September 1966 announced his intention to transform the school into a 60% white institution, a plan opposed by the overwhelming majority of students on campus. Once a crusading civil rights lawyer, Nabrit was seen by many undergraduates as an autocrat who appeased the university's white benefactors while ignoring the need for a cultural overhaul of the institution. Nabrit had denounced early student protesters as Communist inspired; in turn, they derided him as a stooge of white power.[80]

The inevitable confrontation between the school's overseers and its pupils occurred the following spring when Lt. Gen. Lewis B. Hershey of the Selective Service ventured onto campus to deliver a talk about the military draft. A group of 35 students disrupted the proceedings, surging onto the stage brandishing posters of lynching victims and shouting "America is the black man's battleground!" as some onlookers cheered. The next day a fledgling "Black Power Committee," a coalition of student activists advised by radical Howard sociologist Nathan Hare, held a press conference in which they advocated "the overthrow of the Negro college with white innards" and indicted such institutions for having "swept potential theorists from the black community and converted them into sterile lackeys for an oppressive and morally decadent society."[81]

The rest of the spring unfolded in a crescendo of dissent. When Howard officials summoned four activists before a disciplinary board in connection with the Hershey incident, incensed students tried to force their way into the hearing room, and an effigy of Nabrit bearing around its neck a sign that read "60% white, 40% other" was hanged from a tree in the center of campus. Denied access to an auditorium by university authorities, heavyweight boxing champion Muhammad Ali, then in the throes of his struggle against the military draft, delivered an impromptu "black is best" speech from the steps of Frederick Douglass Hall, explaining to a crowd of 4,000 students precisely why "the black man is still catching hell." Thousands of undergraduates later boycotted classes to protest the punishment of the Hershey demonstrators. Conservative observers warned of "the shattering of Howard prestige" and the conversion of the institution into a training ground for Black Power. Appearing before a congressional subcommittee on civil disorders, Nabrit vowed to "deal with" the campus unrest—the product, he maintained, of an unruly fringe element.[82]

Howard officials cracked down, imposing new restrictions on student expression (only "orderly picketing" would be tolerated) and firing or expelling five professors and as many as 19 students in a summer purge of militants. These measures only fueled the resistance, mobilizing an array of campus forces against the display of repression. Student groups closed ranks, temporarily bridging ideological divides and forging a "shaky but growing solidarity." During the formal exercises marking the resumption of classes that fall, 125 students staged a walkout in opposition to the university "dictatorship."[83]

A cultural revolution was unfolding. The school's accountability to the community emerged as the movement's paramount question, surpassing matters of academic and personal liberty. Prior to the urban insurrections of 1967, some Howard students had planned to teach "black brothers" in the ghettos to fight the racist power structure without resorting to rioting. In the end, it was the street insurgents of Detroit and Newark who imparted the political lessons. Their rebellions "caused many students to realize the gap between the aggression of the black community and the complacency of the university campus," a student later noted. Howard organizers saw HBCUs as a critical means of closing that divide. While white campuses might pursue curricular reform, black schools were capable of "reorienting themselves" and adopting entirely new roles. Once inner-city uprisings had subsided, one student explained, "we are going to have to be prepared to rebuild a nation of people, either within the present governmental setup or in a completely new context."[84]

The autumn of 1967 brought more sporadic clashes between students and university officials. Howard became a political mecca, with agitators and theorists from across the country visiting the campus to cajole, exhort, and debate students between classes. Forced to grant concessions, administrators readmitted ousted pupils, abolished mandatory ROTC, and liberalized campus rules. The struggle languished until March 1968 when UJAMAA, a new student coalition, demanded that Howard make an explicit commitment to the welfare of the surrounding community. "It's not enough to talk of past glories when pressing problems of the black community are apparent just outside the gates of campus," student leader Adrienne Manns declared.[85] After university officials failed to respond to the challenge, a group of students disrupted the school's Charter Day ceremony, seizing the microphone and proclaiming the demise of the old Howard University.

In the ensuing days, a "New Howard" was born. Angered by the announcement that 39 of the Charter Day demonstrators would face disciplinary action, more than 200 students occupied the university's administration building, staging an overnight sit-in. The next day the number of strikers doubled. By day three, more than 2,000 students had joined the takeover, embracing the effort to vanquish forever the "Uncle Tom version of higher education." Using psychedelic lettering, fine arts majors fashioned a sign reading "Black University" and taped it to the face of the captured building.[86]

The coup generated extensive support. Expressions of solidarity arrived from scores of universities and Black Power groups. Students from HBCUs as far away as Ohio traveled to Washington to join the protest. Local restaurant owners sent turkey dinners, a welcome alternative to Howard's cafeteria fare. At night, students slept on the floors of the seized building. They did not vacate the site until the occupation's fifth day, having secured what amounted to a pledge of amnesty for all strikers. The takeover, which preceded the more widely remembered student protests at Columbia (1968) and Cornell University (1969), transformed its participants. Barricaded students donned African robes, played Malcolm X records, and cultivated Afros.[87]

The administration building became a seedbed of radicalism. Students declared that "The Vietnamese and the black people in this country are being oppressed by a common enemy" and urged their peers to "develop our own anti-draft and antiwar base" independent of white antiwar forces. Someone floated a proposal to form freedom schools in the community, with student instructors earning academic credit while teaching and politicizing area children. Anticipating a lengthy occupation, strikers discussed with operators of the New School of Afro-American Thought, a local Pan African nationalist outfit, plans to establish a parallel school—"The Black People's University"—for the continuation of their education. The protest even generated a kind of shadow government. Law school students organized a legal aid office. Medical students staffed the first aid station. English majors created press releases. There was a food service, a security detail, and a janitorial committee—evidence not just of a student strike, but also of a "liberated zone" in search of self-sufficiency.[88]

The tumult of '68 and the force of subsequent demonstrations helped bring about substantial changes. Howard officials continued to reject the Black University theme, seeing the concept as inimical to the goal of bringing the Negro "into the mainstream of American business activity." Yet Nabrit made concessions, acknowledging, "There is a spirit of revolt at work which will not be satisfied until a new order is established." Shortly before the Toward a Black University conference that fall, he asked faculty and staff to support the summit, expressing hope that it might "prove to be highly beneficial to Howard University and to our people." The surge of student activism generated reforms in the governance of the institution, the handling of student discipline, and the nature of academic content. The university launched an Afro-American studies department and began weaving black history and culture into its core curriculum.[89]

Nabrit's succession by 36-year-old James Cheek in 1969 offered further cause for optimism. The young theologian acknowledged the need for institutions of higher learning "that are recognized as being black" and that "are clearly identified with the black community." Under Cheek, Howard displayed a strong ethic of political leadership. In 1970, when six black men were shot in the back in Augusta, Georgia, and two African-American students were killed at Jackson State College, Cheek suspended normal course work to allow for discussion of the crises, and delivered a speech before 2,000 students in which he linked the slayings to "a long series of acts of lynching, slaughter, murder and tyranny exercised against men and women whose skins are black." Howard's engagement with surrounding neighborhoods increased. No longer was the school considered "separate and distinct from the total black community," a representative of Washington's Black United Front acknowledged in 1969. "There is now a united black community of which a black university becomes the educational apparatus for defining black values and black goals," the spokesman maintained.[90]

Ironically, just as some HBCUs began internalizing the mores of blackness, other crises engulfed the institutions. Black colleges found their legitimacy challenged by a new set of forces as the larger society focused on questions of integration in the 1960s and '70s. The *Brown v. Board of Education* ruling of 1954 and the Civil Rights Act of 1964 bolstered the logic and legal authority of desegregation, casting an ominous shadow over the future of the schools. Black colleges faced unprecedented pressure between the mid-'60s and the mid-'70s, as institutions associated with "racial isolation" were portrayed as obsolete and unconstitutional. Severely underfunded, forced to compete with wealthy white colleges for students and faculty, and facing elimination or "death by merger" under federal or state decrees, the schools were compelled to justify their existence, even as they struggled to survive.[91]

Some black radicals emerged as unlikely allies of HBCUs, defending the former targets of their disdain in the face of this latest attack. They reasoned that despite "neocolonialist" administrators and a historical pattern of reproducing a black buffer class, the institutions remained essential organs of black education and political culture. SOBU launched a "Save Black Schools" campaign to meet the threat of the wholesale integration or dissolution of the colleges, acknowledging their enduring utility as bases of black identity and mechanisms for pursuing "solutions to our oppression." The rise of political consciousness among black students, the organization asserted, had made HBCUs "a clear and present danger" to white power. The value of the institutions lay "not in what they have been but in what they can be."[92]

Yet many theorists denied that HBCUs were anything but bulwarks of the status quo. Schools like Howard had evolved, critics argued, but they had not genuinely become institutions of the people—resources upon which the entire community could draw. The outward transformation of black and predominantly white colleges had failed to meaningfully challenge the racist nature and bourgeois orientation of higher education. Student rebellions had been largely symbolic; they had not seriously disrupted the link between higher learning and global capitalism. Observers noted that student movements had been shaped by reformist rather than revolutionary ideals, that many protestors wanted a gateway to comfort and wealth, and that "the system" had absorbed much of the force of dissent. These critiques intensified in the 1970s as campus activism began to subside and self-interested careerism resurfaced as an explicit priority of student life. "The tragedy of building takeovers, confrontations and shouting sessions," SOBU leader Nelson Johnson wrote in 1972, "was that they gave the illusion of power but never processed the internal values and discipline to withstand and organize systematic opposition."[93]

By 1969, the year of MXLU's formation, some black militants (like many of their white, New Left counterparts) had determined that radical change was not possible within the apparatus of higher education. Though confrontations continued at some colleges, the early 1970s brought more evidence that the stage of seizing university buildings had passed, a reality that vindicated the view of campus revolts as precursors to action in other arenas. As one black studies advocate maintained, "The essential struggle will not be on the campus but in the community which is the focus for controlling the masses." Many organizers saw physical transition from the campus to the community—a path that SNCC workers had traveled in the early 1960s, and that Bobby Seale and Huey Newton had followed in 1966 when they left Oakland, California's Merritt College and established the Black Panther Party—as an essential political passage. They concluded that if the Black University were to escape the frivolities of college life and impart an education based on nationalist ideology, its "tentative beginnings" would have to occur within black neighborhoods.[94] This epiphany, so vital to the birth of MXLU, also produced the Center for Black Education and Nairobi College.

"In Service to Our People": The Emergence of the Center for Black Education

The Center for Black Education in Washington, DC, and Nairobi College in East Palo Alto, California, were forged by many of the pressures that drove the nascent MXLU from Duke's campus in 1969. Both ventures emerged from failed attempts to establish centers of black militancy within the structures of higher education. Both evolved into fully independent entities rooted in poor and working-class African-American neighborhoods. Necessity ushered both down the path to autonomy—survival on traditional campuses proved untenable. Yet withdrawal from mainstream education deepened the critiques upon which each institution stood.

While a host of activist-intellectuals helped organize the Center for Black Education, its principal founder was SNCC veteran Jimmy Garrett. Garrett spent his childhood in Dallas and East Texas, but he was reared from age 13 in South Central Los Angeles, and it was there that he first recognized education as a form of routinized hypocrisy. Public schools in the city's poor, black areas, Garrett discovered, were as degrading as were the decaying tenements and police brutality that also marked his adolescence. As he later recalled,

> One of the great contradictions of my life in the Los Angeles ghetto school was beginning the morning by saluting the flag of this country, then spending the remainder of the day being taught that I played no part in its development, that I was a slave—a parasite, a blight of blackness—that my only contribution to this society would be by turning white or venting rage.[95]

Garrett chose the latter path, joining a violent street gang in the 1950s. Sent down south during the summer, he participated in the sit-in movement and Freedom Rides of 1960 and 1961, and soon found himself "hooked" on the struggle. He joined SNCC in 1964, working briefly in the South before returning to Los Angeles as one of the group's fundraisers. He advocated extending the Freedom School prototype to the North, viewing the formations as tools for challenging unjust authority. Garrett saw such initiatives as signs of the northern movement's promise. "What started as tutorials are now autonomous organizations capable of being vehicles for effective change," he wrote in 1965.[96]

Though still a teenager, Garrett had experienced brutal repression at the hands of white racists, and had begun to articulate the criticisms of nonviolence and liberal reform that were reshaping the larger movement. The terror inflicted on the black population of Los Angeles during the "Watts Riot" of 1965 hastened his politicization. When the uprising began that summer, Garrett abandoned fundraising and moved into the streets. There he witnessed an organic black unity and spontaneity that broadened his awareness of the indigenous power of the African-American masses. "Burn, baby, burn!" struck him as a pure expression of defiance. He saw black businesses spared from the flames. He saw residents cooperate to expropriate the consumer goods that society had dangled before them as symbols of their exclusion.[97]

Garrett later dramatized the L.A. revolt in *We Own the Night*, a popular play. Performed at Black Panther rallies and in productions at Amiri Baraka's Spirit House in Newark, the piece depicted the clash between an older generation of "Negro" accommodationists and the young, street-savvy militants that Garrett viewed as the advance forces of black insurgency. The strikingly misogynistic play portrayed black "manhood" as the catalyst for liberation while depicting the emasculating black matriarch as its antithesis. (At the end of the script, the protagonist reclaims his thwarted masculinity and revolutionary prerogative by killing his domineering mother!) Yet the production also reflected its author's keen awareness of street rebellions as instruments of personal and collective transformation.[98]

Garrett sought to mobilize a radical ethic of blackness in 1966 when he enrolled as an undergraduate at San Francisco State College. Drawing on his experience as an organizer, he helped form the nation's first Black Student Union (BSU) and led the struggle that resulted in the creation of the original black studies department. Garrett and a corps of activists painstakingly built the radical movement at San Francisco State. They developed a critical blueprint for black studies while helping transform the petit bourgeois values of many students into a desire for "national liberation." They established a power base in San Francisco's African-American neighborhoods, sponsoring youth projects and boosting efforts to fight the draft and resist urban redevelopment. In so doing, they encouraged identification with the dispossessed and demonstrated that campus resources could be marshaled for the benefit of poor, black communities.

The struggle at San Francisco State featured a number of innovations. Garrett helped redesign the school's student-run Experimental College as a vehicle for black culture and history. He and other BSU leaders recruited figures like Amiri Baraka and Sonia Sanchez to serve as lecturers and instructors. They converted a tutorial program in the city's African-American slums into an instrument of black identity, wresting it from the control of white liberal students. They challenged the isolation and irrelevance of an educational system geared toward matriculation rather than social justice. And they helped promote the construction of black counterinstitutions as mechanisms of self-affirmation and self-learning.[99]

Garrett's quest to redefine black education and to infuse public establishments with nationalist ideals continued in fall 1968 when he accepted a position as humanities instructor and head of black studies at Federal City College (FCC), a new, experimental institution in downtown Washington. The urban land grant school (an establishment later absorbed by the University of the District of Columbia) was designed to serve a local population whose dearth of social opportunities had been highlighted by the unrest that followed King's assassination that spring. Created by an act of Congress, the small, tax-supported college featured an "open admissions" policy. Its tuition was just $25 a quarter, and its overwhelmingly black and working-class student body included Vietnam veterans, high school dropouts, and participants in a degree program for local prisoners. One black newspaper hailed FCC as a rare gesture of government largesse. Others saw the college as an attempt to placate a population that had demonstrated its capacity to destroy the nation's capital.[100]

Garrett, however, believed the school could become a base for black consciousness. He pushed for the hiring of activist instructors, including fellow SNCC veterans Courtland Cox, Jean Wiley, and Charlie Cobb. Assisted by a cadre of radical organizers, he began developing a "Black Education Program," a four-year curriculum that he envisioned as the nucleus of a degree-granting department. The course of study was designed to "decolonize the mind" and purge "white values" while developing technicians for the building of "a durable and productive African nation." Classes in math, science, history, and culture stressed practical skills and strategies for sustaining black communities and countries. The immersion program included instruction in self-defense, agronomy, and "development of land resources." It reflected a desire to "Africanize" students and stimulate "a lasting and meaningful black peoplehood."[101]

Controversy engulfed Garrett's proposal in fall 1968, just weeks into the college's inaugural year. Opponents of the Black Education Program, including key FCC faculty and administrators, denounced the prospectus as an attempt to inflame racial strife while trading academic principles for revolutionary dogma. Some suggested that the proposed curriculum had jeopardized the refunding of the fledgling college, an institution wholly reliant on congressional appropriations. Yet Garrett and his allies, including a few radical, white instructors, insisted that engagement with the ethics and practice of black liberation was essential to grassroots education in riot-torn Washington.

The dispute over black studies consumed much of the academic year. In time, however, the feud began to seem immaterial. FCC militants came to believe that they played an unwitting part in government efforts to contain black insurgency. Authorities, they concluded, had adopted a new approach to counterrevolution; rather than confront the radical wing of the liberation struggle, they would absorb it through offers of formal employment. Putting militants on the payroll would enable guardians of the status quo to maintain "an image of relevancy" in the eyes of the black poor. The scheme, Garrett suggested, represented "stage two of the antipoverty program—promise the niggers a prize and keep them fighting one another for it." The leader of the nation's first BSU thus joined those who rejected campus struggles as paradoxical campaigns pursued "under the economic and political auspices of white institutions they [are] attempting to challenge."[102]

Refusing to remain in hostile territory, Garrett and a coterie of radical FCC students and faculty withdrew from the school in the summer of 1969. "We reached a stage where we said that we've got to stop holding other people's coats while they fought," Garrett later recalled. "We couldn't tell students to seek other ways of educating themselves while we drew big salaries." Joined by other allies, including militant Howard professors and the circle of former SNCC staffers that had founded Washington's Drum & Spear Bookstore the year before, the activists reorganized the embryonic Black Education Program and "moved deeply into the black community," establishing the Center for Black Education in two adjoining, three-story brownstones in a depressed section of Northwest Washington. There they began pooling funds, gathering classroom supplies, and discussing "the preparation of a small group of black people to spend their lives in direct service to our people and our land."[103]

"Our Own Thing": The Birth of Nairobi College

Nairobi College followed a similar trajectory. The school emerged in fall 1969 in the aftermath of an intense struggle at the College of San Mateo, a San Francisco–area junior college. Nairobi College's founder, Bob Hoover, was an engineer of the 1960s East Palo Alto renaissance that also produced Nairobi Day School and High School. Born poor in segregated North Carolina, Hoover served in the Air Force and matriculated at Penn State before heading to Northern California to pursue graduate degrees at San Francisco State and Stanford University. He found work as a physical therapist and moved to East Palo Alto in the early 1960s amid an influx of African-American migrants.

An athlete who had competed in the Pan-American Games, Hoover aspired to become a baseball coach or athletic trainer. But encounters with housing discrimination and a growing desire to help refashion East Palo Alto as a black cultural stronghold led him to the arena of local struggle. By 1964, he was running a youth center in which members of the town's rival street gangs received counseling while hanging out and shooting pool. He helped form a coalition of black activists, joined SNCC, and attempted to apply the community organizing methods of theorist Saul Alinsky to East Palo Alto's quests for self-determination and educational justice. Both causes benefited in 1967 when Hoover and fellow SNCC worker Syrtiller Kabat became the first "militants" elected to the board of the community's elementary school district. Viewing self-reliance as an essential strategy for empowering black neighborhoods, the North Carolina native strove to create cooperatives and other indigenous institutions and supported grass-roots efforts to gain control of a local Upward Bound program and job-training center.[104]

Hoover carried the drive for black autonomy onto the nearby campus of the College of San Mateo (CSM), where he was hired in 1967 to direct an academic "readiness" program, an initiative designed to increase minority enrollment at the two-year school. Energetic and outspoken, Hoover helped expand the recruitment project, which admitted poorer students of color irrespective of high school education or grade point standing and enrolled them in special reading and counseling classes. He clashed with administrators, however, after alleging that the underfunding and marginalization of the 500-student program reflected entrenched patterns of racism. Hoover saw the readiness initiative as an opportunity to nurture black consciousness while boosting academic skills. CSM officials contended that he was using the project to foster black separatism. "I used to say the purpose of our program was to train leaders to build black communities," Hoover later recalled. "The college people always insisted that wasn't the college's job, but I said, 'Why not? You do it for white people all the time.'"[105]

The dispute took a fateful turn in 1968. Hoover and many CSM students of color (including Chicanos, Asians, Puerto Ricans, and Samoans) grew increasingly resentful of what they saw as coordinated efforts to subvert the readiness program and thwart an agenda of progressive change on campus. Then the college further slashed funding, dropping 200 of the program's enrollees and denying admission to others. During a demonstration that December, 150 irate students, most of them black, rampaged across campus, assaulting white students and faculty, scuffling with riot police, and doing $8,000 worth of damage to facilities. Administrators blamed Hoover for cultivating revolutionary ideas and assigned him to other duties. By summer 1969, he had resigned.[106]

Disgusted by what they viewed as a campaign of political repression at CSM, Hoover and several students who had been expelled from the college decided to take their destinies into their own hands. "Let's try to get our own thing going," the students said. "We want to build an institution that has meaning for us. We want to use our own sweat." Now in his late 30s, Hoover agreed to head the new endeavor. He was convinced that white institutions would never meet "the real needs of our communities," and that junior colleges in the area severely neglected students of color, making only token attempts to educate the oppressed. He concluded, moreover, that the moment of racial liberalization at predominantly white schools had passed. Though black student enrollment had surged nationwide, there was simply "not enough of us here in this country that we are going to take over a college or anything else." The time had arrived "to do our own thing."[107]

Hoover formed a multiracial committee of more than 25 Bay Area educators and activists, including militant Stanford BSU members, a radical Chicano organizer, and a few white allies. Within months the group had laid plans for

Nairobi College—a two-year school based in East Palo Alto but with satellite campuses scattered throughout the black, Latino, and Asian neighborhoods of the San Francisco Peninsula. Patterned after SNCC's philosophy of nurturing local activists, the establishment would offer "Third World" pupils academic preparation for four-year institutions while training them to provide progressive leadership for their native communities. Founders of the school envisioned "an alternative to an educational system which serves many people badly and people of color not at all."[108]

Initial contributions of almost $100,000, including donations from area residents and grants from private foundations, produced a modest but innovative venture. A small, private home in East Palo Alto served as the college's "main campus." (The primary and secondary schools of the Nairobi system lay nearby.) As the institution began limited operation that fall, more than 100 working-class, mostly black and Chicano students, some of them high school dropouts and many of them casualties of the CSM upheaval, enrolled in classes taught by volunteer instructors in area homes, churches, social service agencies, and even a local bank. The faculty consisted of about 40 volunteers, including community organizers and students and professors from nearby universities. An appeal for books yielded 20,000 donated texts from schools, individuals, and publishers. Lacking a formal library, administrators piled the volumes in two residential garages.[109]

Crude conditions hardly dampened spirits. Organizers imagined a campus fused with its surrounding community. They could afford no physical plant, apart from the dilapidated, white shingle structure that housed an administrative office. And they desired none. The vision of a constellation of campuses in places like San Francisco's Mission District and Chinatown never materialized. Yet the belief that "the community is the campus" inspired a true "college without walls"—a highly improvised but welcome alternative to the cultural isolation of the "ivory tower." At a time when the expansion of universities in urban centers threatened to displace many communities of color, Nairobi College's founders rejected the idea of leveling functional buildings to create a "fortress of hallowed learning."[110]

The college's admissions policy was equally democratic: anyone 16 or older could enroll. Classes were initially free. By 1971, a $500 tuition charge had been implemented, but federal financial aid was available, and fees were often waived. The idea was total access for those most estranged from formal learning, not only students of color who had experienced cultural alienation in area junior colleges, but also streetwise youngsters from communities like East Palo Alto who remained socially and physically isolated from higher education. "Our college will accept the hustlers and the rip artists from the streets who have found that conventional schools don't equip them for the real world," Hoover declared.[111]

Courses ranged from mathematics, English, electronics, and business to revolutionary art, black psychology, Chicano history, and Swahili. Instructors included Tello Nkhereanye, a leftist, Southern African scholar and associate of the revolutionary leader Amilcar Cabral; Frank Omowale Satterwhite, a community organizer and former student militant; Aaron Manganello, a Marxist activist and minister of education for the Brown Berets, a Latino nationalist group; Mary Hoover, a Stanford education specialist and pioneer in the effort to harness Black English to enhance academic proficiency; and Hoover himself. Students—many of them older, full-time workers who attended classes in the evening—performed three hours of mandatory service a week, volunteering in East Palo Alto health centers, schools, libraries, and welfare agencies. Organizers hoped to foster practical skills that could transform community aspirations into concrete social programs.

At its core, Nairobi College was an expression of the dream of East Palo Alto as a model black city. It aimed to furnish "our people and communities" with professional and technical expertise seen as vital for collective self-development. Created in the aftermath of urban insurrections and campus turmoil, the institution was conceived as "an alternative to tearing down." It was a response not only to social despair but also to the growing exodus from their native communities of black and brown college graduates, a trend that some feared would drain such enclaves of their potential for economic and political self-rule. East Palo Alto was gradually losing its skilled residents and civic leaders—traditional organizers of the crusade for self-determination—to expanding housing and employment opportunities in racially integrated environments. "If we are going to meet the needs of people of color," Hoover maintained, "we will have to educate leaders who want to work within the community—doctors, lawyers, engineers. We don't want all Stokely Carmichaels, but certainly we want some."[112]

"Struggle Toward Nation": The Parallel Development of CBE and Nairobi College

As Nairobi College was evolving on the West Coast, the Center for Black Education (CBE) was developing—in ways both similar and markedly different—on the East Coast. The parallel growth of the institutions demonstrated that a shared political language of Pan African Nationalism could produce diverse practices. Having seceded from Federal City College, CBE found itself compelled, during the fall of 1969, to define its mission as an independent venture. Its proprietors faced immediate pressure to disprove naysayers who dismissed the school as the work of impetuous radicals who would soon abandon their plans and return to the sanctuary of the academy. Affirming the principle that "the only people who can legitimize us are our own people," CBE organizers agreed to construct an establishment that could carry Pan African nationalism "past the cultural, mystical and faddish stage" while producing technicians devoted to worldwide black liberation.[113]

This mission attracted an assortment of intellectuals. Cultural critic Acklyn Lynch; former Howard student activists Marvin Holloway and Geri Stark; anti-imperialist organizer Clairmonte Moore; SNCC veterans Jean Wiley, Ralph Featherstone, Judy Richardson, Courtland Cox, and Ivanhoe Donaldson; and Kojo Nnamdi, the Guyanese-born journalist who went on to become a major radio personality, all joined the CBE cadre. Among the senior figures who supported the operation were longtime civil rights worker Hilda Howald M. Mason and C. L. R. James, the elder statesman of Left Pan Africanism, whose "fatherly influence" helped propel a generation of militants beyond racial fundamentalism. By late 1970, these theorists labored alongside more than 60 students, ages 16 and up, who studied everything from politics to civil engineering within CBE's spacious twin brownstones.[114]

Classes at the school reflected egalitarian ideals. Like Nairobi College, CBE embraced progressive pedagogy. Both institutions favored communal methods of instruction and strove to humanize the educational process. Students at Nairobi College participated in curriculum development. They were encouraged to transcend models of passive learning and to view instructors as equals rather than "keepers and dispensers of knowledge." Both CBE and Nairobi stressed practical skills. Students in both institutions served as health and teacher aides and legal counselors in black neighborhoods. CBE pupils who learned welding or carpentry practiced their trade while completing small contracting jobs in the community. The school's food science majors applied their expertise to problems of malnutrition in black Washington, DC, with a special focus on the dietary needs of pregnant mothers and welfare recipients.[115]

A more politically exclusive institution, CBE required students to endorse its Pan Africanist philosophy prior to enrollment. Unlike Nairobi, which rooted its curriculum in the humanities, the Washington, DC, school viewed science as a cornerstone of national development and offered technical training in biology, chemistry, engineering, and mathematics. Yet both institutions attempted to groom disciplined leaders to work in black neighborhoods.[116] CBE and Nairobi also strove to cultivate surrounding communities. The latter institution provided weekly tutoring and free books for inmates in a Northern California penitentiary. It offered East Palo Alto's ex-offenders transportation from prison upon release, $300 for clothes and necessities, enrollment in and employment with the college or job placement elsewhere, and temporary lodging in the homes of student and faculty volunteers.[117]

CBE hoped to build a Northwest Washington, DC, coffee house upon similar themes. More a cultural center than a café, the establishment was seen as a way to extend the school's reach beyond the classroom while providing an informal setting for political organizing, seminars on drug abuse, and screenings of films like *The Battle of Algiers*. Though the coffeehouse never materialized, CBE successfully launched other community-based ventures, including a free medical clinic housed in its building and featuring a volunteer staff of licensed doctors and nurses. The project, which received 200 patients a week, was designed to address health crises spawned by poverty and racism. (CBE's block alone contained 18 cases of tuberculosis.) The institution also operated a neighborhood preschool and a library. By meeting basic needs and enabling residents to participate in their own development—a reappropriation of the strategy of the poverty programs—CBE workers hoped to expose the inadequacy of existing social institutions while highlighting viable alternatives. "If we cannot relate to and work with our own people," the organizers acknowledged, "all the ideology in the world won't save us."[118]

Though promising, this approach was hampered by financial crises. While CBE anticipated a 1970 income of less than $30,000—a sum that included private donations, tuition fees ($100 for those students who were able to pay), and the tithes of instructors—its expenses that year topped $100,000. The school received occasional windfalls; a $60,000 grant from the Episcopal Church ultimately composed more than half its 1970 budget. Its staff concocted creative fundraising ideas including cocktail dinners with African ambassadors and cultural events in Washington's Malcolm X Park. But the establishment never achieved financial security. CBE operators refused to seek federal funding. They dismissed government grants as attempts to capture and bureaucratize the social institutions upon which poor people depended. "White people, in spite of liberal masochism, will not consciously finance the instruments of their own destruction," they declared. Until black communities were willing to devote time, money, and skills to their own internal development, "confusion and disorganization" would prevail.[119]

Nairobi College also struggled to sustain itself. A 1970 audit found the institution grossly understaffed and operating "hand to mouth." A review conducted the following year by an accrediting commission for junior colleges revealed that the school could barely meet its $200,000 operating budget and lacked an adequate system of accounting and record-keeping. Though the concept of a college without walls was "commendable," the commission asserted, effective teaching and learning over the long term required permanent facilities. Nairobi's willingness to seek public funding, however, provided some stability. Virtually all its students offset $500 tuition fees with federal grants and loans. Enrollment eventually reached 300 and the college hired a faculty of 10 full-timers. By 1972, the school's yearly budget stood at $320,000, though reliance on government support troubled some students and staff. "I tell the brothers and sisters here that they have to face reality," Nairobi's business manager declared. "If they are going to accept white money, then they have got to expect white accountability."[120]

Meanwhile, CBE faced growing repression. Washington officials shuttered the organization's health center in early 1971, citing building code violations and inadequate fireproofing. Leaders of the institution saw the move as an assault on black self-determination. (They were not mistaken: FBI agents had informed the city of the unlicensed operation.) The closure raised doubts about the viability of American cities as centers of Pan African nationalist development, while the FBI's overt surveillance of CBE signaled an official campaign of intimidation. Intelligence agents regarded the school as "a training ground for guerillas," despite copious evidence that the institution's activities were confined to political education and community service.[121]

In the end, CBE succumbed not only to external pressures but also to its own ideological rigidity. Though Nairobi College lacked CBE's rigor as a center of radical theory, the California school's pragmatism and adaptability produced a more sustainable operation. The question of multiracialism represented one area of divergence. Nairobi considered itself a "Third World college"—an institution that embodied the complexions and sensibilities of a nonwhite world struggling to consolidate its independence from the West. The school's governing board and staff included Chicanos, Native Americans, Asians, and a Filipino. Its founders had planned to open campuses in the Latino community of South San Francisco and on the nearby island of Alcatraz, the site of an abandoned federal penitentiary that had been occupied by a group of American Indians.

Nairobi College's Third Worldism also allowed for white participation. A handful of progressive white people served on the school's staff, including Jean Wirth, a CSM supervisor who had been fired during the institution's 1969 purge of radicals. An antiracist who rejected the anemia of liberal integrationism and the paternalism of "white missionary syndrome," Wirth had played a key role in the creation of Nairobi College. The school was open to white students as well; it had been dedicated to people of color as well as "others dissatisfied with the present educational system." Nairobi educators vowed to avoid "separating . . . race from race so that one may climb on the shaky foundation of the destruction of the other."[122]

Interracial alliances proved tenuous. Six white staffers left the college in late 1969. The following year most Chicano students departed to start their own institution—Vencerémos ("We shall overcome") College—in Redwood Park, a neighboring city. By 1973, almost all Nairobi College faculty and students were African American. But openness to multiracial organizing strengthened the school, providing channels of support that otherwise might not have existed. By contrast, CBE viewed racial coalitions as a "fallacy." Representatives of the Washington school and its twin institution, MXLU, who attended a fall 1970 conference at Nairobi College concluded that the organization's Third Worldism masked a dangerous faith in white benevolence. "Nairobi and others like it are not independent financially, diplomatically, tactically, physically or culturally," the educators reported.[123]

Career placement further separated Nairobi College and CBE. The former establishment ensured that students acquired skills that enhanced prospects for employment or transition to four-year schools. Administrators negotiated job programs for graduates with electronics companies and other San Francisco–area firms. Social mobility and professional development, they believed, could serve the cause of collective empowerment. A student who wished to "rebuild his community" by creating alternatives to urban renewal could intern in an architect's office before launching a career in planning or design. Ultimately, Nairobi College hoped to construct a corps of conscientious black and brown professionals.[124]

CBE took a different approach. The institution scorned the idea that a relevant black education would provide the training and credentials necessary to function within white society. "We are not charting a route to mainstream America," its officials proclaimed. The school granted no degrees. It counseled students to abandon expectations of a secure passage to the business world. For CBE, the purpose of education was to sustain "the culture of a nation" while honing skills that could satisfy "national" needs. No black self-development could occur, its operators believed, without control of land, goods and services, mechanisms of violence, and minds. "Revolution," they insisted, "is the process of struggle toward nation."[125]

CBE and Nairobi College's differences reflected the distinction between efforts to revive African-American neighborhoods and attempts to perform some of the rudimentary functions of an autonomous state. Nairobi College's efforts to develop East Palo Alto evoked the tradition of the nineteenth- and early twentieth-century black town movement, an attempt to cultivate an ethic of solidarity and cooperation that could provide shelter from a racist society. CBE's political strategies, on the other hand, recalled the logic of African-American emigrationism, the drive for territorial independence based on the conviction that black people needed to withdraw from America altogether and establish a power base in a foreign land.

Nairobi College's vision of nationhood meant exercising municipal authority. It meant controlling local policing and the maintenance of streets and parks, building a viable tax base and generating decent jobs, vanquishing drug dealers, and educating one's children according to the indigenous values of one's neighborhood. "We're trying to rescue people, to give them direction, to bring back skills and expertise to our community," Hoover said. "All the rhetoric about revolution, about change—it's no good if you don't know what you're after, and if a lot of talk is all you've got, you're not going anywhere."[126]

While Nairobi College strove to draw people and resources inward toward the community, CBE oriented its cadre outward toward Africa and the Caribbean. The latter institution's leaders came to see the quest for black American self-reliance as a prelude to African repatriation. They viewed the defeat of Western imperialism overseas as an alternative to—rather than a component of—the democratization of American political and economic institutions. Some CBE students began spending their summers working with agricultural cooperatives in Guyana. By late 1970, the school had finalized plans to shift most of its operations overseas, maintaining educational and agrarian projects in rural Tanzania. "Anything of permanent value must be set up in Africa," CBE organizers concluded.[127]

"In Quest of Self-Knowledge": The Black University at the Neighborhood Level

Though CBE, Nairobi College, and MXLU were visible prototypes, other models of the Black University appeared. Among them were Drum & Spear Bookstore, the New School of Afro-American Thought, and the New Thing Art and Architecture Center—autonomous, community-based ventures built on the conceptual foundations of black consciousness and designed to perform some of the functions of junior colleges, museums, art galleries, cultural centers, and meeting halls. Remarkably, Drum & Spear, the New School, and the New Thing occupied roughly the same section of Northwest Washington, DC, clustering near the 14th and U Street corridor that had formed the epicenter of unrest following King's 1968 assassination.

All three institutions sprang from the late 1960s milieu of "Black DC." With its large, African-American population subjected to ghetto conditions and denied formal political representation as a result of the city's status as a ward of Congress, Washington served as a critical locus for campaigns of black self-determination. The nation's capital became a hub of second-wave civil rights activity, especially after organizer Marion Barry arrived there in 1965 to establish a major SNCC project. The influx of movement veterans invigorated local black politics. Energized by the prospect of a new, urban movement, young activists embraced the issue of home rule and the quest to transform Washington into a truly black city.

Drum & Spear was a cornerstone of their crusade. Former SNCC workers founded the bookstore in a gutted, 14th Street storefront in June 1968, on the heels of the local uprising. The shop featured an impressive inventory of black literature; staples like *Wretched of the Earth* and *The Autobiography of Malcolm X* were perennial bestsellers. Drum & Spear also played a larger role as a source of empowerment "for a community in quest of self-knowledge," providing a forum for Pan Africanist organizing, poetry and book readings, children's programs, and other cultural events. Closely linked to CBE and to Howard University activists, the store became a major node of educational experimentation and creativity. Its press published black coloring books, maps of the African world, a C. L. R. James reprint (*A History of Pan-African Revolt*), and a high school social studies text featuring African parables.[128]

Even before the emergence of Drum & Spear, the New School of Afro-American Thought had served as a nexus of Washington's black artistic and political vanguard. The establishment's founders included jazz poet Gaston Neal, a colorful booster of Washington's Black Arts scene. Born in 1934, Neal spent his young adulthood drifting through drug addiction and crime. As a youngster growing up in Pittsburgh's slums, he dropped out of middle school after a teacher convinced him that he was incapable of academic success. Petty vandalism and other infractions landed him in reform school. He later served as a busboy, porter, and elevator attendant before joining the army, only to chafe under the regimentation and racism of the military. Neal came to view America's North Korean adversaries as his "black" comrades. Discharged after a psychiatric assessment and court-martial, he "bummed around" for a time, floating from city to city and experimenting with poetry and drugs before joining Washington's beatnik scene.[129]

Hooked on dope, Neal was arrested on a drug offense in 1960 and confined to St. Elizabeth's Psychiatric Hospital. He read voraciously and developed a staunchly black nationalist worldview. He continued to struggle with addiction after leaving St. Elizabeth's. Yet he also discovered "the beauty of my blackness" and managed to secure a position as a poverty worker in Washington's Cardozo section. Neal resolved to approach antipoverty efforts on his own terms. His political commitments lay not with the tan bourgeoisie of Howard, whose admissions officers had rebuffed him after his stint at St. Elizabeth's ("They thought I was a hoodlum," he later said), but with those on the city's social margins. He rejected integrationist civil rights groups, which he believed shunned "brothers like me—brothers from the street." The concept of civil rights without ownership of social resources struck him as a fantasy conceived by cunning rulers. Besides, he reasoned, "civil rights" had produced no concrete mechanisms of black nationhood. Searching for cultural alternatives, he and other neighborhood organizers formed the Cardozo Arts Committee. The group sponsored public exhibitions and, in 1966, hosted a popular "Three Days of Soul" music festival, a celebration of African and African-American heritage.[130]

Buoyed by the event's success, Neal and his fellow cultural workers began looking for a follow-up initiative. They hoped to de-emphasize antipoverty measures and shift local organizing toward a focus on self-help. Neal had come to reject the idea of reliance on government aid to rejuvenate African-American communities. Black America, he believed, needed a cultural revolution to achieve self-respect. Activist Don Freeman (later Baba Lumumba), a former Howard University student, urged Neal to imagine a permanent structure. "We need an institution," he said, "not a program." Freeman, who saw Howard as a "Negro" establishment that emulated "white values," shared Neal's view of HBCUs as aristocratic, superfluous enterprises. The pair of organizers hoped to apply the ideals of the Black Power and Black Arts movements to the build-your-own ethic of the Nation of Islam. They envisioned a formation that could help reverse the psychology of "self-hatred," the internalized logic of racism evident in many of the homeless denizens and street addicts of Washington.[131]

Determined to craft a "think-black" institution, Neal and Freeman launched a fundraising campaign with the assistance of local musicians and artists. They produced first an arts center and then a more comprehensive workshop, school, gallery, and performance venue, an establishment housed in a converted auto repair shop on 14th Street in the heart of the Cardozo ghetto. The New School was designed to serve "the man out here on the streets and the man from college," with a particular focus on helping the former population "rediscover" its cultural heritage. The institution's founders hoped to provide "a factory for black minds" and a nerve center for artists and intellectuals looking to fashion a revolutionary black aesthetic.[132]

The New School offered evening and weekend classes in African and African-American history and politics, as well as literature, painting, drumming, photography, jazz, dance, drama, poetry, Swahili, Arabic, data processing, first aid, and sewing. As many as 400 neighborhood residents attended the free courses, which were taught by volunteer instructors. The school hosted concerts designed to expose black Washington to jazz musicians like Sun Ra and Horace Silver. It featured poetry readings by Amiri Baraka and Sterling Brown, screened avant-garde films, exhibited the work of black painters, and provided a venue for cultural groups like Philadelphia's Yoruba Temple Dancers. In July 1968, amid the riot-fueled atmosphere of radical public discourse, Howard critic Acklyn Lynch delivered a series of lectures on Fanon to a packed New School audience. After returning to Washington in 1968, Stokely Carmichael used the school as his base of operations, as the headquarters of Washington's Black United Front, and, following King's assassination, as the site of the press conference in which he famously announced that white America had "declared war on us."[133]

The New School's main constituents were the rank-and-file citizens of Cardozo, some of whom received tutoring at the institution as they prepared to

take the high school equivalency exam. Sunday seminars on "Our Problem" provided counseling on topics ranging from diet and household budgets to interest
rates. The school became a theater of democratic engagement, a setting in which
neither dirty clothes nor addiction precluded participation. Neal and Freeman
recognized that most local African Americans remained alienated from nearby
Howard, its efforts to reorient itself toward "blackness" notwithstanding. The
New School demonstrated that poor and working-class audiences would attend
cultural events if they had a hand in planning the programs and access to a facility they considered their own.[134]

The institution, however, faced multiple crises. It received neither large grants
nor major outside funding. Proceeds from concerts and other events barely covered regular expenses. Administrators were always two months behind on the
$150 rent. Viewed as a nucleus of black militancy, the operation was routinely
"maligned and misunderstood" in the mainstream press and hounded by agents
of law enforcement. "Whenever civil disturbance breaks out here in the nation's
capital," *Muhammad Speaks* reported in 1969, "police, the National Guard, the
FBI and the Secret Service focus upon one block between V and W streets on
14th NW"—the one occupied by the New School.[135]

The organization was also plagued by internal strife. Ideological feuds among
its leaders led to the implementation of a rotating chairmanship as a means of
averting further power struggles. (One dispute between Neal and Freeman
resulted in an armed occupation of the school by supporters of the former
leader.) Yet Neal believed the institution would continue to rise from the ashes
of the 1968 rebellion. "White people are saying that, 'We want to control your
destiny because your destiny is wrapped up with me,'" he said in 1968, appropri-
ating a classic King refrain. "And we're saying, 'You're a goddamn lie! My destiny
ain't wrapped up with you, it's wrapped up with me and my own people, and we
are going to take it the way we see it.'"[136]

The other installment in Washington's network of independent black establishments was the New Thing. The "art and architecture center" was the brain-
child of Colin "Topper" Carew, former Howard student and SNCC staffer.
Recognizing that only a fraction of the city's cultural institutions were controlled
by African Americans, Carew launched the New Thing in a converted storefront
in the Adams Morgan neighborhood in 1967. The center offered adult and children's workshops in African dance, drumming, photography, filmmaking, music,
graphics, and fashion design, enrolling as many as 450 students, many of them
high school dropouts.

Like the New School, the institution embraced the quest for a black aesthetic.
It strove to expose poor people to art forms like jazz and blues while helping
them earn equivalency diplomas and reconstruct their neighborhoods. The New
Thing shared some of the characteristics of its more militant counterparts; in

1967, it nearly became the scene of a riot after street-corner youths gathered there to discuss rumors of the police murder of two black residents. But the New Thing's brand of nationalism was considerably milder than that of the New School, and its proprietor was more palatable to the white liberal establishment. The New Thing welcomed white board members and visitors, and received enough backing from private sources and from the poverty programs to expand to multiple buildings.[137]

"Study and Struggle!": The Black University's Left Turn

Though no city rivaled Washington as a base for the Black University, Chicago came close. The metropolis gave rise to several black nationalist ventures in adult education. A "Black Communiversity" appeared there in 1969 after a month-long series of cultural programs. Designed as an instrument of resistance and a means of forging "new life-styles," the temporary formation offered free, politically oriented classes for youngsters and adults.[138] The Black Peoples' Topographical Research Center constituted another local version of the Black University. Inspired by growing awareness of the social geography of oppression, the South Side establishment consisted of a windowless room ringed with maps depicting the distribution of the black population of Illinois. The images highlighted the cramped, concentrated nature of black "reservations" and their proximity to minimum-wage labor markets. Created by a collection of young, African-American researchers, the center demonstrated how black people had been "gerrymandered out of any real chance to establish economic, educational and political independence."[139]

Even Chicago's junior college system offered a prototype of black nationalist education. In 1969, a student-led cultural "revolution" at the overwhelmingly black Crane College, an ancient eyesore on the city's West Side, resulted in the school's overhaul and official rebirth as Malcolm X College. A major resource for high school dropouts and underemployed youths, the public institution offered training in conventional academic subjects while clothing itself in the symbols and ideals of the Black University. Charles G. Hurst, Jr., its young, African-American president, strove to relate learning to community problems, to ensure "relevance" to the task of liberation, and to generate a "new kind of human being." Hurst also promoted mainstream standards of professionalization, even as he embraced the notion of "a university of the street." Nationalists nevertheless praised the "blackening" of Crane and the effort to "Africanize" its students.[140]

Like most incarnations of the Black University, Chicago's independent black institutions embraced cultural reorientation as a central pedagogical aim. By 1973, however, new visions of mass education had arisen to challenge Neo-Pan Africanism's preoccupation with enculturation. The emergence of Lynn Eusan Institute in Houston and Peoples College of Nashville reflected the ideological shift to Left Pan Africanism. Created by Marxist-Leninists or emerging socialists, both formations promoted a race–class analysis that emphasized the structural and material foundations of power.

Peoples College was originally a network of theorists, a body that published analyses of current events and engaged in collective study. Under the leadership of radical Fisk University sociologist Abdul Alkalimat (Gerald McWorter), the collective developed a program of community education, offering a series of political classes in a Nashville student center. The five-week courses were designed to enable "workers, housewives [and] students" to examine problems of local African-American neighborhoods, as well as those of the black world. Fall 1973 classes included Pan-Africanism, the Third World, black history, and community analysis. Designed to foster a dialectical critique of power relations in Nashville and around the globe, the curriculum covered topics as varied as socialist development in Africa and the state of local health care.

Peoples College was part of an effort to nudge black intellectuals toward acts of "class defection" and enable African-American students and scholars to engage the black community on its own terms, rather than on the basis of the pathologizing visions of cultural elites. The task of the black intellectual, Alkalimat believed, was to affirm the indigenous strength of the black community and to help build a body of pertinent social knowledge. As part of that mission, Peoples College issued a black studies primer devoted to the science of revolution and bearing the slogan, "Study and struggle! Struggle and study!"[141]

The left model of the Black University found more concrete expression in Houston's Lynn Eusan Institute. Established in 1972, the training center for black organizers bore the name of a Pan African nationalist activist who had been brutally slain the year before. Eusan had become a conscientious "worker with the grassroots" while matriculating at the University of Houston during the late 1960s. The undergraduate had been an active member of Friends of SNCC and the Committee on Better Race Relations. As her political outlook shifted from integrationism to nationalism, she had helped form Africans in America for Black Liberation (AABL), a campus group. In 1968, Eusan became the University of Houston's first black homecoming queen, mounting a significant challenge to the social invisibility of nonwhite students. She later participated in the school's turbulent black studies struggle. After graduating in 1970, Eusan and other AABL members continued organizing in black Houston, now under the banner of Pan Africanism. The San Antonio native made plans to continue her political education at Malcolm X Liberation University. But in 1971, at age 23, she accepted a ride from a stranger in a thunderstorm and, during an apparent rape attempt, was stabbed to death.[142]

Eusan's AABL comrades founded Lynn Eusan Institute (LEI) as a means of combatting "the oppressive contradictions of black life" that the late activist had fought. They saw the institution as a vehicle for propagating Pan African ideology, promoting social change, and, ultimately, overthrowing "the system" that had "murdered Sis. Lynn." LEI staffers included Dawolu Gene Locke, former national coordinator for the 1971 World Solidarity Day for African Freedom Fighters, and community activists Imani Betty Milligan, Dwight Allen, and Sherra L. Locke. Over the years, as these and other Pan African nationalists organized around local and international issues, they discovered that such campaigns were hindered by a dearth of political skills. They learned that those who sought radical change required not only sincerity and commitment but also concrete techniques of resistance. They envisioned a school that could impart such expertise, arming community workers with practical organizing tools.[143]

In early 1973, LEI's first cohort of nine full-time students moved into the center's small dormitory, a facility supported by private grants. The pupils, including college students, a welfare mother, and a high school dropout, studied political, economic, and social theory, honing organizing tactics in workshops like "fundamentals of mobilizing." They agreed to become full-time organizers upon graduation, and to perform practical community work while enrolled at LEI. During the institution's first 10-month term, its trainees assisted a tenant group, a high school black studies club, and the city's welfare rights organization. One LEI student, a young woman from Los Angeles, was assigned to a community center that offered free health and welfare services. She helped residents navigate the bureaucracy of the federal food stamp program, a form of support in great demand as poor people struggled with the sharply rising cost of living.[144]

LEI represented a striking departure from most Neo-Pan African establishments. Its emphasis on grassroots, democratic tactics reflected the pragmatism and material needs of the people it endeavored to serve. By contrast, the Center for Black Education continued to embody the principle that the essential task of Pan African nationalists was to "take control of our minds" through strenuous resocialization. Preparation for the rigors of nation building, CBE theorists believed, required cadre members "to live a new style of subsistence." Efforts to combat sloth, "to stifle our psychological needs," and to transcend the old world of comfort and vice reflected a puritanism that obscured the realities of the poor and working class. Administrators dreamed of the day when students would willingly reside "three or four to a room" as an expression of revolutionary discipline. The irony, of course, was that poverty forced many families to live this way.[145]

The dream of expatriation deepened elements of idealism in CBE's politics. By 1971, the Washington school had fully embraced the notion of Africa as the locus of revolution, all but renouncing struggle within the United States. The organization explicitly rejected political escapism. Yet its vision of the continent as the authentic site of fieldwork; as a cornucopia of cultural, political, and economic resources; and as the "natural home" of black Americans conveyed a certain estrangement from quotidian African-American life.[146]

LEI staffers, on the other hand, acknowledged that people's workplaces and homes are critical sites of struggle. The Houston institution encouraged recognition of the interconnection of domestic and international oppression. As Imani Milligan noted, "The problems of exploited communities and classes of people here are linked with the problems of exploitation, poverty and wars of aggression by this country abroad." Transnational kinship was to be forged upon mutual circumstances and ideals. Blackness alone was not enough.[147]

To truly engage the "total black community," LEI activists argued, Pan African nationalists needed to address everyday concerns of working people while continuing to support liberation movements overseas. By emphasizing concrete economic issues and painstaking, grassroots work, LEI repudiated vanguardism and the quest for the "correct" political line. Trainees at the Houston center studied Marx, Lenin, Mao, Nkrumah, and Cabral, yet they were urged to test multiple approaches and perspectives, drawing on ideas they found sound and relevant while rejecting rigid "blueprints" for revolution. LEI courses were designed to accommodate the lives, schedules, and practical needs of workers, prisoners (some of whom enrolled in LEI correspondence classes), and poor people, and to acknowledge their capacity to build their own movements without the direction of political elites.[148]

The appearance of autonomous Black University models demonstrated the appeal of institution building and the range of practices and ideals encompassed by Neo-Pan Africanism. Founders of Malcolm X Liberation University, the Center for Black Education, and Nairobi College withdrew their educational programs from existing institutions and replanted them in black neighborhoods, while students at Howard attempted to transform their university from within. The New School of Afro-American Thought and other grassroots establishments embodied the concept of a campus fused with the cultural and intellectual life of its surrounding community. Lynn Eusan Institute endeavored to train political organizers while emphasizing class struggle and the material realities of the oppressed. By 1973, Pan African nationalists were rethinking not only the mechanics of organizing but also many of the movement's fundamental theories. The implications of this philosophical diversity would be revealed during African Liberation Day and the Sixth Pan-African Congress of 1974.

Owusu Sadaukai at Malcolm X Liberation University Registration
Desk. Owusu Sadaukai (Howard Fuller) at the registration desk of Malcolm X Liberation
University (MXLU), initially located in Durham, North Carolina. Sadaukai and other
activists founded MXLU in 1969 in the wake of a black student struggle at Duke University.
Courtesy of Durham Civil Rights Project, North Carolina Collection, Durham Public Library.

Owusu Sadaukai at Lectern. Malcolm X Liberation University founder Owusu
Sadaukai discusses the political situation in Rhodesia (now Zimbabwe) in 1972.
Sadaukai was a leading figure in contemporary efforts to strengthen ties between
liberation movements in black America, Africa, and the Caribbean. Courtesy of *New York
Amsterdam News*.

AFRICAN LIBERATION SUPPORT COMMITTEE LEADERS AT PRESS CONFERENCE.
African Liberation Support Committee (ALSC) leaders at a 1973 press conference.
Operators of Pan African nationalist schools played a central role in forming ALSC and
organizing African Liberation Day, an annual observance designed to raise awareness
of and funds for anticolonial struggles on the African continent. Harris Photo. Courtesy of
New York Amsterdam News.

JITU WEUSI RECEIVES CERTIFICATE. Jitu Weusi (left), founder of Brooklyn's Uhuru
Sasa Shule, is honored for his community service at the African Street Festival, an event
he helped establish. Courtesy of *New York Amsterdam News.*

A CLASS AT UHURU SASA. Students at Uhuru Sasa strike a pose of preparedness and determination. Behind them are world maps and a map of the African continent. Courtesy of Osei Chandler.

STUDENTS LINE UP OUTDOORS. Like the political organizations that produced them, many Pan African nationalist schools enforced rigid gender roles. Here, girls at Uhuru Sasa assume a position of deference and support while boys adopt a more assertive stance. Courtesy of Osei Chandler.

HANNIBAL AFRIK AND STUDENTS. Longtime educational activist Hannibal Afrik (Harold E. Charles) and the "Zulu level" (six- and seven-year-old) students of Shule Ya Watoto in Chicago. Courtesy of Juba Kalamka.

LYNN EUSAN AND GENE LOCKE. Lynn Eusan, a Pan African nationalist student activist at the University of Houston, is pictured with Dawolu Gene Locke. Eusan was murdered by an assailant in 1971. Locke went on to direct Houston's Lynn Eusan Institute, a training school for grassroots organizers. Courtesy of Special Collections, University of Houston Libraries.

CUBAN DELEGATE AT UHURU SASA. A Cuban delegate to the United Nations visits Uhuru Sasa in Brooklyn. Pan African nationalist schools were centers of internationalist thought and practice. Courtesy of *New York Amsterdam News*.

OAKLAND COMMUNITY SCHOOL CLASS. A class at Oakland Community School in 1976. Formed by Black Panthers in 1971, the school survived into the 1980s, providing a counterexample of radical adaptation as many Black Power–era independent schools folded or adopted conservative political outlooks. Courtesy of Department of Special Collections and University Archives, Stanford University Libraries.

7

The Black Institution Depression

> To educate the masses politically does not mean, cannot mean, making
> a political speech. What it means is that everything depends on them;
> that if we stagnate it is their responsibility, and that if we go forward it
> is due to them, too, that there is no such thing as demiurge, that there is
> no famous man who will take the responsibility for everything, but that
> the demiurge is the people themselves and the magic hands are finally
> only the hands of the people.
>
> —Frantz Fanon[1]

Many Pan African nationalists expected the cultural ferment of the late 1960s and early 1970s to subside. Few were prepared for the intensity of the counter-revolution. By the mid-1970s, their crusade to revolutionize black America had been stymied by the forces that beset the larger liberation struggle, reversing the progressive thrust of Black Power and signaling the demise of the age of mass movements. Independent schools foundered amid the waning vitality of popular struggle. Those that survived confronted a grim sociopolitical landscape. As an era of reaction supplanted a period of rebellion, contradictions in the thought and practice of black militants were exposed.

While the contemporary freedom struggle faced intense repression, internal political conflict proved almost as destructive. Operators of independent institutions were drawn into protracted feuds between right-leaning nationalists and black Marxists. The "two-line struggle," a fierce ideological conflict, drained the political promise of African Liberation Day. The Sixth Pan African Congress and the Angolan Civil War exacerbated the factionalism and disorientation of black internationalists. Pan African nationalism splintered into warring sects as much of its institutional apparatus dissolved. By the end of the 1970s, Afrocentrism, a more conservative elaboration of black nationalist and Pan Africanist ideals, had emerged to fill the void.

"The Soul of Feather": Political Violence
and the Clutches of Despair

The forces of counterinsurgency battered African-American political life and culture in the early to mid-1970s. While black militants faced heightened state surveillance and subversion during the 1960s, especially after the FBI's counterintelligence program began systematically targeting Black Power groups, it was not until the 1970s that the full extent of official treachery came to light. Black America learned that many of its dynamic political institutions, organizations, and leaders had been sabotaged by federal agents. Revelations about the FBI's illegal operations blended with news of the overseas assassination of figures like West African freedom fighter Amilcar Cabral, revealing the breadth of the contemporary counterassault.[2]

A number of independent schools came under attack. Federal agents continued to plot against the Center for Black Education, initiating local zoning and permit inspections designed to mire the Washington institution in legal troubles, halt its community activities (even the operation of a preschool serving poor families was considered suspect), and hasten its downfall. Efforts to destabilize the establishment included plans to reveal the "illicit relationships" that one of its staffers was purportedly conducting with several of its female cadres. Intelligence officials also conspired to undermine Baltimore's Soul School. Anonymous phone calls were used to fuel a dispute between the organization and its political rivals. The scheme exacerbated the fear and conflict that decimated the institution's enrollment. In the case of the Black and Proud Liberation School of Jackson, Mississippi, the attack involved covert targeting of the establishment's funding sources, as well as overt acts of police and FBI harassment.[3]

Court battles furnished another tool of repression. By the early 1970s, an assortment of Pan African nationalist leaders were embroiled in criminal proceedings. Cleveland Sellers of Malcolm X Liberation University, Willie Ricks of the Pan African Work Center, Gaston Neal of the New School of Afro-American Thought, Olugbala of the Soul School, and Sonny Carson of the School of Common Sense faced charges ranging from "conspiracy to riot" to weapons possession to murder. Other forms of intimidation, from predawn shotgun blasts through the windows of Newark's African Free School to repeated attempts to evict Brooklyn's Uhuru Sasa Shule, deepened the sense of many militants that powerful adversaries were mobilizing against them.[4]

The most unsettling symbols of real or reputed conspiracies of violence were the mysterious deaths of two Pan African nationalist organizers—Ruwa Chiri of Chicago's Arusha-Konakri Institute and Ralph Featherstone of Washington's Center for Black Education (CBE). Featherstone, 30, an administrator at CBE and the Drum & Spear Bookstore, was a beloved former Student Nonviolent Coordinating Committee (SNCC) staffer known for his pioneering work in southern freedom schools and African-American cooperatives. He had joined Washington's coterie of militants in the latter 1960s, becoming an admired proponent of Left Pan Africanism. Late one night in March 1970, he and young activist William "Che" Payne—both close associates of Black Power spokesman H. Rap Brown—were killed when the vehicle they were driving exploded near a Maryland town where Brown was to stand trial on conspiracy charges.[5]

The deaths shocked and enraged the freedom movement. Authorities concluded that Featherstone and Payne had knowingly transported a bomb that accidentally detonated, instantly dismembering them and mangling the car in which they were traveling. Few activists accepted this verdict. Featherstone's comrades denounced the FBI for completing its probe "almost before the wreckage of his borrowed automobile was cool," and for alleging that the slain organizer, who had been married only three weeks earlier, had been toying with explosives. Critics noted that heavy skid marks left by the doomed car moments before the blast had not been adequately explained.[6]

The liberation struggle saw Featherstone and Payne's deaths as further evidence of the ruthless design behind the call for "law and order." Militants blamed "the citizens and institutions of white nationalism" for the atrocity, concluding that government agents or their accomplices had planted the bomb in the hopes of eliminating Brown. Activists made vitriolic speeches, and some black, Washington-area high schoolers rallied under the slogan "Aggression is the order of the day!" Beneath the anger, the ranks of Pan African nationalism shuddered. The amiable brother they knew as "Feather," an interpreter of Marxist tracts, a survivor of white terrorism in southwest Mississippi, had perished on a bleak stretch of asphalt. News of the killings, Daphne Muse of Drum & Spear later recalled, "unhinged my soul like no death, no murder, no atrocity had before." Gaston Neal of the New School of Afro-American Thought was equally distraught. "Every law-and-order minute, black sons of Africa die," he wrote in a poem dedicated to Featherstone.[7]

More carnage lay ahead, including the grisly, February 1974 death of Ruwa Chiri, another passionate, 30-year-old ex-SNCC worker. The mutilated corpse of the Arusha-Konakri Institute director, *Afrika Must Unite* editor, and former instructor at Chicago's Communiversity and Milwaukee's Clifford McKissick Community School was discovered early one morning on the tracks near a Harlem, New York, subway station. Chiri had been struck by an oncoming train. Authorities could not determine whether the activist had walked or been carried deep into the subway tunnel and onto the tracks. They suggested, however, that Chiri, a Zimbabwean exile who had fought deportation from the United

States, and who apparently suffered from depression and paranoia, had committed suicide.

Chiri supporters rejected the idea. Yes, the outspoken organizer had waged a lengthy battle with U.S. officials who charged that he had been living in the country illegally. He had become edgy and peripatetic, and his belief that federal agents lurked behind every keyhole had troubled his friends. But Chiri's resolve had deepened, and his efforts to resist deportation and to seek asylum in progressive African countries had yielded encouraging results. These circumstances compounded the horror of his death. Dozens had mobilized to defend the Zimbabwean against the machinations of immigration officers, who monitored his speeches and statements, pressed him for information about political associates, and—in a move seemingly linked to his vigorous opposition to U.S. imperialism in Southern Africa—advised him that he was under constant surveillance. In the end, Chiri's supporters refused to rule out foul play in the activist's demise. "I know how this system works," one ally bitterly proclaimed.[8]

Chiri's body was flown to Zimbabwe for traditional Mashona burial rites while additional services were held in Chicago. But it was Ralph Featherstone's memorials that would haunt movement veterans for years to come. A Washington ceremony drew hundreds of mourners. The Harambee Singers performed an original song decrying political treachery. "Ralph Featherstone is going to Africa," one eulogist declared. "America is his murderer." Featherstone's ashes were later transported to Lagos, Nigeria, by an African-American delegation, where they were sanctified in a ceremony that blended Pan African sentiment and Yoruba chants. A procession of Nigerian youth, students, trade unionists, and artists paid their respects as the remains were interred. "The soul of Feather is now safe on African soil," an African-American observer reported, "and his spirit is entrusted to us in work and in deed."[9]

Such sentiments provided a measure of comfort, but there was no escaping the trauma that enveloped Pan African nationalism. Some cadres reaffirmed the principle of self-sacrifice. "We must recognize the vulnerability of our position," Center for Black Education workers declared. "We must tighten our ranks without succumbing to paranoia." Suspicion nevertheless eroded the optimism that had sustained the quest for a new peoplehood. It was a time of martyrs, of informers and agents provocateur, of intercepted letters and tapped phones. Jitu Weusi of Brooklyn's Uhuru Sasa Shule requested his FBI files in 1974 and discovered that agents had monitored his activities for years.

Fear of infiltration and sabotage drained energy that once had been devoted to the delivery of community services. Psychological strain left organizers frazzled and cagey. "After you've seen so many people killed . . . people are more cautious," Ahidiana's Kalamu Ya Salaam acknowledged in 1975. Despair threatened to overwhelm many dissidents. Malcolm X Liberation University's Cleveland

Sellers, a former SNCC member, almost grew accustomed to the chill that gripped him with each violent death of a comrade. "The trick is to control the emotion, deal with it and use it," he explained in 1973. "Otherwise it becomes an area of weakness."[10]

"How Shall We Organize?" Cultural Dissipation and the Exhaustion of Ideas

Assaults on independent black institutions came from many quarters, including the streets of the urban neighborhoods that their founders had conceptualized as Afro America's sovereign territory. As unemployment, economic decline, dwindling social spending, and the onslaught of drugs eviscerated many African-American communities, "lumpen" elements that a few years before had launched spontaneous attacks on the structures of racial oppression turned their destructive power on the very institutions that their rebellions had inspired. On separate occasions, burglars within Atlanta's African-American neighborhoods broke into the Learning House and the Martin Luther King, Jr. Community School and made off with prized equipment. Arsonists repeatedly struck Nairobi Elementary and High School of East Palo Alto, California, apparently in retaliation for the institution's leadership of a citizen's crusade against drug traffic, a cause championed by Nairobi founder Gertrude Wilks.[11]

Social attrition and the scourge of drug crimes mocked the populist ethic of black solidarity. At times, the decisive weapon of "neocolonial" subjugation appeared to be the heroin needle. Some black nationalist groups formed block patrols to defend urban neighborhoods against the proliferation of dope peddlers and street criminals; occasionally they embraced vigilantism as a means of combatting the drug menace, a move that further undermined the ideal of cohesive blackness. In the 1970s, Wilks attempted to rally East Palo Altans against local drug dealers, publicly rebuking hoodlums who demanded cash payments in return for the cessation of hostilities against the Nairobi campuses. "How long will our communities tolerate this kind of mess without saying a mumbling word?" the veteran organizer asked. By the early 1980s, crime in East Palo Alto had gotten so bad that Wilks and her staff began carrying classroom supplies home at night to thwart burglars.[12]

The response of many Pan African nationalists to these and other social crises was predictable; what was needed, they asserted, was a reorganization of values. The disarray of many black communities was rooted in the realities of economic and political retrenchment, postindustrial decay, and the oppressive policing of militarized urban centers. But most Neo-Pan Africanists—even some who displayed an affinity for Marxian language and analysis—continued to prescribe the cultural solutions of self-help, African consciousness, and revolutionary discipline. Such responses only deepened the atrophy of oppositional politics.

Signs of retreat and regression multiplied. The 1974 National Black Political Convention in Little Rock, Arkansas, lacked even the symbolic vitality and glamour of its 1972 predecessor. Hope for a truly independent national politics withered amid the accommodationism of the Congressional Black Caucus and the squabbling of the National Black Political Assembly. Scores of college-level black studies programs were dismantled. The conditions of black life under African-American mayors across the country underscored the limitations of local government as an agent of social change. Once imagined as "the fulcrum of black power," the urban core symbolized the neglect of people of color and the diminution of the public sector in the name of corporate profit. As monopoly capitalism entered a period of volatility and transition, large segments of the black poor and working class were relegated to welfare, joblessness, and prison.[13]

New forms of cultural dissipation accompanied the decline. The popularity of Blaxploitation films within African-American communities dismayed Pan African nationalists, who condemned the genre as a form of "mind genocide." Hollywood's black film boom promoted crude stereotypes, exalted mercenary values, portrayed women as sexual ornaments, and trivialized the task of "beating the system." However, many of the pictures also depicted gritty ghettos whose intense poverty neither civil rights nor Black Power had overcome, and whose criminal elements white racism and greed had spawned. Too disdainful to consider these aspects of social realism, many militants simply mirrored Hollywood's "brainwashing operations" with propaganda campaigns of their own.[14]

Pan African nationalists struggled to adapt to changing social and political circumstances. As historian Manning Marable has observed, "A full account of the decline of black nationalism would assume encyclopedic proportions." During the 1970s, he noted, black nationalism and Pan Africanism followed the familiar arc of American leftist politics: on the upswing, popular adoption of progressive political themes radicalizes discourse; on the downswing, accommodation, cooptation, sabotage, and isolation spawn internal discord and separate the movement from its popular base.[15] However, "internal" factors—including the rigidity and idealism of political elites—greatly accelerated the deterioration of the movement. In the denouement of popular struggle, the ideological purists of black consciousness lost their way, divorcing themselves from the pragmatism and lived experiences of "the masses."

As stagnation replaced an era of black progress, a clear vision of the role of radical intellectuals escaped many militants. Some retreated to the comfort of revolutionary illusions, unwilling or unable to face complex realities. Ideological confusion and wish fulfillment again eclipsed engagement with concrete conditions. Mysticism shrouded the task of confronting the existing system while striving to create the new society. Few activist-intellectuals were prepared to answer the challenge posed by astute black philosophers: "How shall we organize ourselves for the transformation from a period of mass movement to a time of grueling, protracted struggle?"[16]

Disdain for democratic ethics stimulated the backward tendencies of Pan African nationalism. The vanguardist impulse, the faith in exclusive corps of revolutionaries, the search for transcendent political formulas, and the narrow quest to "recapture" minds helped lay the groundwork for coming polemics. The politics of cultural reconversion had become a substitute for addressing existing circumstances.

Independent black institutions exhibited the exhaustion of ideas that characterized the broader liberation struggle. As social crises enveloped black America, the movement's theorists promoted the usual remedies. They pushed black unity and uplift. They advocated the construction of more community schools and cooperatives. They called for "ripping off the pusher" and seizing "psychological control of our lives." They urged regimens of self-development and moral reconstruction. Seldom did they commit themselves to developing new, relevant political directions and practices alongside the black rank and file. As one African-American activist-intellectual remarked in 1975, "We are also a class with a deep affection for our ideas."[17]

"We Are What We Believe": The Two-Line Struggle and the Quest for Clarity

Amid the mounting pessimism, Pan African nationalism experienced a momentary revival. African Liberation Day (ALD) events in summer 1972 and 1973, the simultaneous demonstrations in U.S., Canadian, and Caribbean sites on behalf of liberation movements on the continent, galvanized progressive black consciousness. The rallies helped energize popular internationalism and anticolonialism. They provided a model of grassroots action, a symbol of reciprocity between African-American activist-intellectuals and black working people, and a sign of the transition from abstract identity to concrete awareness.

By 1974, the drive for philosophical purity had eroded these gains. The loosely structured ALD coordinating committee originally had encompassed multiple political tendencies, most of which fell within the spectrum of nationalism and Pan Africanism. Pursuit of a permanent governing structure and firmer theoretical grounding led to the creation of the African Liberation Support

Committee (ALSC) in late 1972. Based primarily in the United States, ALSC comprised dozens of local chapters. Its central leadership consisted of heads of various Pan African nationalist institutions, including Dawolu Gene Locke (Lynn Eusan Institute of Houston), Amiri Baraka (Congress of African People and the African Free School of Newark), Abdul Alkalimat (Peoples College of Nashville), Haki Madhubuti (Institute of Positive Education in Chicago), and Owusu Sadaukai (Malcolm X Liberation University of Greensboro).

The emergence of ALSC reflected the larger shift to Left Pan Africanism. Influential ALD organizers wished to transcend "operational unity," narrow emphasis on racial affinity, and the simplistic rhetoric of "white man's hands off black man's lands." They sought a broader intellectual framework for challenging Western imperialism, exposing the role of multinational corporations in global exploitation, and casting black liberation as part of the international struggles of working people. They hoped to demonstrate the need for total reconstruction of American society, in part by highlighting links between imperialist domination in Angola, Mozambique, Guinea-Bissau, Zimbabwe, Namibia, and South Africa and the everyday problems of black people who faced political repression, police brutality, runaway plants, and vanishing social programs in the United States. As Locke declared, "We have a responsibility to the world to fight exploitation and oppression in its very stronghold."[18]

Meanwhile, the leftist turn within ALSC continued. Locke, Sadaukai, and Alkalimat had made decisive shifts toward Marxism-Leninism. Determined to merge radical black politics with "the process of world revolution," they promoted scientific solutions to racial capitalism and stressed the special historical role of the working class. They viewed ALSC as a forum for internal ideological struggle, seeing theory as a tool of conversion and revolutionary doctrine as a quest for "clarity."

Amiri Baraka underwent one of the most abrupt political metamorphoses. Between 1973 and 1975, historian Manning Marable observed, Baraka "moved rapidly from his position as high priest of cultural nationalism to [become] the avatar of Marxism-Leninism-Mao Tse Tung thought." The Congress of African People chairman's explanation for his volte-face amounted to a repudiation of most varieties of Neo-Pan Africanism. Baraka insisted that close study of revolutionary literature and growing recognition of political realities had occasioned the shift. He renounced his former "metaphysical" adherence to Kawaida, a philosophy that exalted social mores drawn from the feudal African past. He indicted "reactionary" black chauvinism; blanket condemnation of all white people, he now believed, constituted "charlatanism."[19]

Right-leaning Pan African nationalists mostly tolerated the initial drift toward socialism. Rhetorically, all tendencies recognized monopoly capitalism as a prime enemy of the black world. While cultural nationalists deployed anti-imperialist and anticapitalist language, they regarded annual ALD gatherings as vehicles for conveying familiar themes: the values of the Nguzo Saba, the mystique of the African Personality, and the mantra "We Are an African People." More rigorous socialist prescriptions, especially the notion of *intraracial* class struggle, required abandonment of the ideal of black world unity, a concession so-called Kawaida nationalists found unthinkable.

The leftist offensives that followed ALD '73 thus widened existing fissures within the movement. During a series of contentious retreats in the latter half of 1973 and early 1974, ALSC's neo-Marxists swapped ecumenical black solidarity for the pursuit of ideological consolidation. Sadaukai, Alkalimat, and their allies drafted an organizational mission statement consistent with their evolving vision. The document identified not just racism but also imperialism and capitalism as inexorable foes of black people. It acknowledged the existence of classes throughout the black world, declared that African-American workers must play the key role in ALSC organizing efforts, and expressed kinship with revolutionary movements across the globe.[20]

Kawaida nationalists balked. For them, the proliferation of "soviet" jargon and "workers take the lead" rhetoric indicated that a mutiny had occurred in the ranks of black liberation. The new ideological focus, Kalamu Ya Salaam of the New Orleans group Ahidiana believed, constituted "a rejection of Pan Afrikanism." Since the late 1960s, a broad swath of activists had understood Pan African nationalism as the critical tool for harnessing the political energy of the African-American masses. Now a handful of apostates had abandoned that apparent consensus, courting dubious white allies in pursuit of what ALD organizer Florence Tate called a "'workers of the world unite' utopia." This was an unforgivable affront—a manifest violation of the principle of black self-determination. As Jitu Weusi of Brooklyn's Uhuru Sasa Shule proclaimed, "If we make mistakes they shall be our mistakes and not errors emanating from the back room meetings of committees of CP [Communist Party] USA."[21]

Some neophyte Marxists attempted to explain their transformation. Their purpose was not to derail black struggle. On the contrary, they insisted, the hunt for a politics relevant to the material needs of African-American working people had pushed them beyond nationalism. They now recognized that black liberation required the destruction of capitalism. As Baraka wrote in an essay titled "Why I Changed My Ideology," "merely putting black faces in high places, without changing the fundamental nature of the system itself, simply served to make that system more flexible and more dangerous." Overall, however, leftists spent little time explicating their epiphanies. Instead, they escalated crusades for doctrinal supremacy. Believing that two lines of analysis had emerged in ALSC—a race theory and a class theory—and that building an ideologically sound movement meant exposing "incorrect" ideas, they sought a public resolution of internal differences. The "two-line struggle" had begun.[22]

The conflict intensified in 1974, reaching an apex that summer during the "Racism and Imperialism" conference in Washington, DC. Billed as a debate over the future direction of the movement, the gathering confirmed the dominance of ALSC's Marxist forces over their nationalist adversaries. Kwame Ture (Stokely Carmichael), of the All African Peoples Revolutionary Party, and Kwadwo Akpan, of the Pan African Congress—USA, defended the position that racism was the primary evil and that capitalism and imperialism were secondary. Their opponents, including Sadaukai, Alkalimat, and the latest proselyte—Amiri Baraka—promoted scientific socialism. Though the summit was titled "Which Way Forward," its excessive sloganeering hardly suggested progress. The theories of Cabral were invoked, but with none of the humanism or creativity that the late revolutionary had possessed. Less noticed amid the heated pronouncements was the evolution of Amina Baraka, who declared in one workshop that though their political roles required further refinement, women belonged alongside men in the forefront of struggle.[23]

"Racism and Imperialism" highlighted the movement's transition from a "united front" phase to a period of diatribes. Pan African nationalists and Marxist-Leninists retreated to their respective kingdoms and traded insults and accusations via black periodicals. Personal antagonism and ideological quarrels had already driven Haki Madhubuti and Jitu Weusi from Amiri Baraka's Congress of African People; it was not long before both intellectuals bolted ALSC as well. Other resignations followed. As the battle for position degenerated into campaigns of aspersion, bickering supplanted productive theorizing.

Right-leaning Pan African nationalists engaged their opponents in a flurry of articles. They charged that under the thrall of "foreign values and beliefs," and in a noxious "mood of clarification," born-again Marxists were attempting to fracture the movement. Members of the East, the parent body of Uhuru Sasa Shule, blamed "Moscow-minded negroes" for transforming ALD into a "hippie style freak out." Virtually overnight, it seemed, old allies had embraced "white philanthropists and European saviors." Haki Madhubuti castigated "turncoat nationalists" for letting the white Left infiltrate the Congress of African People and ALSC. Kalamu Ya Salaam shared Madhubuti's indignation. The assumption of the neo-Marxists, he maintained, was that "some white boy, or group of white boys" held the ultimate political solution.[24]

Black leftists struck back, accusing their opponents of clinging to racial superstition while ignoring socioeconomic realities. Baraka's rebuttals were especially scathing. He denounced Racial Pan Africanism as counterrevolutionary, disparaging Madhubuti and Weusi as paragons of "petit bourgeois individualism." He derided "primitive nationalists" as purveyors of "mysticism" and "bohemianism." He mocked "black capitalists in cheap dashikis" and cultural nationalists in "dime store prints" who "recite one word of Swahili, play drums, put down white people."[25]

By late 1974, the production of polemical essays had eclipsed grassroots organizing. Both sides of the dispute fueled the conflict. Right-leaning ideologues developed a bunker mentality, embedding themselves in the logic of race. They adopted increasingly superficial and anti-intellectual outlooks, unwilling to replace the fantasy of universal black kinship with more rigorous analytical frameworks. They envisioned "blackness" and "whiteness" as discrete and homogenous categories, hermetically sealed and locked in combat. This crude schema had little relevance to the material conditions of masses of black workers and peasants around the world.

As the right wing came under fire, it reverted to discourses of decline. Madhubuti bemoaned African-American emulation of white values and urged reclamation of "lost" characteristics. "Most of us are on the bare edge of insanity," he maintained, depicting black Americans as culturally debased and politically confused. Such postulations revealed the conservatism of Racial Pan Africanism. Having internalized the anticommunism of the larger society, Madhubuti and company refused to recognize democratic socialism as an expression of black America's organic aspirations. By dismissing black Marxists as flunkies, conspirators, and "integrationists" and portraying socialism and capitalism as equivalent white pathologies, "race-first" proponents spurned visions of social and economic reorganization that had long shaped African-American consciousness.[26]

Many of their leftist counterparts were equally myopic. Neo-Marxists wished to "unite with the working class" and address the concrete, everyday problems of the lower strata. Their rigid theories and mechanical conceptions of class struggle hardly served those ends. They reduced Marxism-Leninism's intellectual heritage to a collection of dictums and decrees. They pursued an inert economism, failing to adequately address the fact that the privileges and racism of many white workers severely constrained the politics of class unity. If this oversight constituted an "abuse of Marxism," as activist Gwendolyn Patton charged, so did the black Left's abandonment of the concept of "principled participation of all black progressives" in the anti-imperialist cause. As one veteran radical noted, "There is no understanding here of Leninist tactics of struggle, of the need to organize and unite the people, to form alliances and coalitions, however temporary and wavering, that will advance the black struggle."[27]

Several theorists criticized the neo-Marxist impulse to purge the liberation struggle of racial references. Maulana Karenga, originator of the Kawaida doctrine, made a surprisingly nuanced plea for more measured approaches. The black nationalist resurgence of the 1960s, he reminded his colleagues, had helped free African Americans from the psychology of dependence and transform them into agents of self-liberation. Despite its limitations, that nationalism had arisen "as a *collective response* to our oppression and exploitation" and "as a *social corrective* for the structured denial and deformation of our historical personality" by the combined processes of racism and capitalism. Black leftists might also have heeded the interventions of A. Sivanandan, the United Kingdom–based editor of *Race & Class*, who wrote that

> The hierarchical concept of society may help to explain the internal dynamics of particular societies but, as between the West (including Russia) and the Afro-Asian countries, the line of demarcation is the color line. That the color line is also the line of poverty makes the division that much more inexorable. The sickness of racism has overtaken the economics of colonialism. To allege in these circumstances (as the international socialists do) that the racial myth is a capitalist red herring is to obscure the psychological barrier between black and white which, in our time, has assumed pathological proportions. Capitalism is indeed the prime cause of racial prejudice as we know it today, but prejudice itself has set up categories which need to be defeated on their own ground.[28]

In a sense, both tendencies in the two-line struggle were trapped by their formulations. Despite their ideological differences, ALSC's rival factions shared a number of theoretical blunders. One of the most damaging was adherence to what one writer called "the tyranny of a purist ideology." Many of the dispute's combatants viewed compromise as defeat. Believing that their side possessed pristine knowledge, they regarded conflicting versions of reality as manifestations of treason or false consciousness. Their dogmatism and arrogance transformed a major vehicle of the contemporary freedom movement into a game of "competing utopias."[29]

Amid the polemics, the body of radical theories that had emerged in the late 1960s and early 1970s hardened into a cult of ideas. The call to "put theory in lead of practice" reflected a host of fallacies, including the notion that intense study would unlock the mysteries of revolution, that conflict was the path to clarity, and that ideology was the ultimate political weapon. For true believers in both camps, heterodoxy was anathema; failure to elaborate an "advanced" theoretical position was indefensible. "Our movement is underdeveloped because our theory is underdeveloped," Haki Madhubuti declared. Jitu Weusi was more blunt. "We are the sum total of what we believe," he proclaimed.[30]

Such outlooks led to a proliferation of "wordy forums" in which participants preached and proselytized, asserting their authority by demonstrating mastery of hallowed texts, whether drawn from the works of Chancellor Williams (author of *The Destruction of Black Civilization*) or Lenin. As Abdul Alkalimat of Nashville's Peoples College later recalled, "People began to worship books and spew forth quotations like Moses with the Ten Commandments."[31] Conceived as a dogged march toward philosophical certainty, the quest for black liberation became a clinical, joyless exercise. The task of refining a science of struggle had trumped the values of creativity and compassion. As political scientist Cedric Johnson has written,

> Equally important to the ALD mobilizations' strength and the popular anti-imperialism it entailed was the capacity of organizers to develop propaganda which appealed to black vernacular culture and its commonsensical notions of justice, fairness and equality; to convey the complexities of the emergent transnational politico-economic system through references to those institutions which organize black life in the United States; and to construct tangible, concrete opportunities for black citizens to contribute to the decolonization effort and act in solidarity with blacks across the diaspora. The Marxist-nationalist debate represented the negation of this political methodology and, as such, signaled the abandonment of an open-ended, popular radicalism by many black activists.[32]

A different path was possible. The contradictions of nationalism might have been addressed in the course of principled practice, and in a spirit of camaraderie rather than conquest. The domestic race/class question was but one iteration of a debate that was unfolding in the Caribbean, on the African continent, and throughout much of the Third World.[33] Its belligerent character in the United States reflected the rehashing of earlier Black Power disputes (and those of previous generations of black intellectuals), as well as the narcissism of black-consciousness elites whose brand of patriarchal, charismatic leadership had entered a period of obsolescence. The egotism, ad hominem attacks, and dearth of self-criticism that defined the two-line struggle were emblematic of a bankrupt model of spokesmanship.

Ultimately, the pursuit of "ideological clarity" only increased the toxicity of contemporary black politics. Some participants had expected the two-line struggle to usher in a new age of radicalism. Instead, the confrontations generated animosities that smoldered for decades. Militants found themselves battling opposing tendencies rather than fighting racism and imperialism. The rancor deepened the organizational trend toward centralization and suspicion. The toll on ALD was immediate; mass participation declined sharply amid competing rallies and widespread confusion. ALSC dissolved, only to reappear in weaker, dramatically different forms later in the decade.[34]

The fervor for parallel institutions also waned. Once widely regarded as a progressive and unifying strategy, the construction of separate black establishments was now seen as the domain of those Pan African nationalists who stressed racial identity. Amiri Baraka made plans to begin phasing out Newark's African Free School. Eventually, he and the enterprise parted ways. Other neo-Marxists retained their institutional bases, but their view of such ventures changed. In 1975, ALSC organizer Mark Smith shared his new outlook:

> Build "independent" institutions? Okay, but what about the 99% of black children who didn't go to your "independent" school, who continued to suffer the abuse of the public school system? None of this is to say that these efforts are *bad* things, but that they were, and are, wholly inadequate—they do not address themselves to the needs of the masses, the starting point for any revolutionary movement.[35]

The perspectives of ALSC veterans continued to diverge. In time, some organizers recognized the vulgarity of their dogmas. A few strove to rekindle grassroots efforts that had been abandoned amid the ideological clashes of the mid-1970s. They returned to local communities, joining day-to-day struggles against police repression, cutbacks in social programs, and economic exploitation. Many still envisioned—and expected—"revolution in our lifetime."[36] Yet the creative marriage of theory and practice that had sustained a larger vision and sense of destiny had been severed, and much of the movement's vitality was lost. What's more, the ideological skirmishes persisted. Just weeks after the chaos of ALD '74 came the debacle of the Sixth Pan African Congress (Six-PAC).

"All Diplomacy Is Bourgeois": The Sixth Pan African Congress

Preparations for Six-PAC, an event that took place in Tanzania, East Africa, in summer 1974, again raised hopes for a reinvigoration of Pan Africanism. This would be the first Pan African Congress on African soil. (The Fifth Pan African Congress of 1945 had been held in Manchester, England, and the early congresses of the interwar years had occurred in Western cities.) The summit was designed to address the development of the black world in the postindependence age. More than 1,000 delegates and observers from 50 countries were expected to participate in the attempt to redefine modern Pan Africanism.

To many African-American intellectuals, a Pan African congress seemed like the apotheosis of black solidarity. Here was an opportunity to elaborate a vision of liberation alongside representatives from throughout the black world. African-American theorists hoped to use the gathering to build unity, propel progressive initiatives (a proposal for a Pan African Academy of Science and Technology on the African continent sounded especially promising), and discuss the path to socialism. For them, Six-PAC symbolized the desire to move to the next level of struggle while reconciling competing visions of Pan Africanism.[37]

Operators of independent black institutions played a central role in the evolution of the congress. Originally proposed by Caribbean Black Power leader Roosevelt Brown, the summit took shape in a series of meetings in the United States and other parts of the black diaspora in the early 1970s. Members of CBE in Washington, DC, did much of the organizational work. Among them were Winston Wiltshire, Jimmy Garrett, Geri Stark, Edie Wilson, and Courtland Cox. Other key players included Sylvia Hill, founder of the Institute for African Education in St. Paul, Minnesota, and Beatrice Waiss of the Clifford McKissick Community School in Milwaukee. Hill and the CBE cadre formed the core of the Six-PAC steering committee. They took the lead in drafting its guiding documents and embarked on a frenetic schedule of travel on multiple continents to help bring the congress to life.[38]

The young volunteers worked closely with eminent Marxist and Pan Africanist C. L. R. James, Tanzanian president Julius Nyerere, and other prominent figures. The African-American organizers were an intrepid bunch—historian Lerone Bennett called them a "little band of dreamers." Yet they encountered significant difficulties from the start. Political rivalries complicated attempts to build support for Six-PAC among individuals and organizations in Europe, the Caribbean, and the United States. Ideological divisions among African-American intellectuals were intensifying. Conflict between activists who emphasized racial consciousness and those who stressed economic factors belied the spirit of unity that the congress symbolized.[39]

Forming the North American delegation to Six-PAC posed additional problems. Planners had to navigate the suspicion, jealousy, and egos of prominent activists. Figures like Baraka and Sadaukai had serious misgivings about the event's timing, purpose, and sponsors. As CBE's Jimmy Garrett later recalled, these and other detractors "felt the congress had arisen from a closed circle (which it had), was isolated (true), and had dubious purposes (which was not true)." Objections to the policies of the "Cox coterie" (Courtland Cox of CBE served as secretary general of the event) were openly expressed. The process of delegate selection was equally fraught. Leading intellectuals believed they were uniquely qualified to represent black America at the congress, a conviction at odds with the desire of organizers to ensure a democratic gathering.[40]

None of these issues proved as divisive as the Caribbean question. African-American planners had envisioned Six-PAC as a largely nongovernmental affair in which heads of state would simply take part. This, however, was not the vision of the event's host (TANU—the Tanzanian governing party), nor that of the states providing the bulk of the congress's sponsorship and resources. The latter parties included Caribbean governments that insisted, as a matter of protocol, that political opposition groups from their region were to be barred from the congress. In essence, this meant that Six-PAC would be a state affair rather than a true people's assembly. It also meant that African-American organizers who had declared that the conference would reject postcolonial regimes that "hide behind the slogan and paraphernalia of national independence while allowing finance capital to dominate and direct their economic and social life" were orchestrating a parlay that would welcome the Caribbean's neocolonial agents while repudiating embattled dissidents like Eusi Kwayana of Guyana and Geddes Granger of Trinidad.[41]

When this matter was raised by critics, Cox and company pleaded for understanding. In their estimation, *all* states were either imperialist or neocolonial. The choice, Garrett later recalled, was to "hold the meeting in one or the other [state] or not at all." Most African-American planners believed the congress had to take place, for better or worse. International organizers, they argued, lacked the luxury of making political distinctions between conference participants, especially given the need to marshal the power of state actors. "The truth is that those who advocate the most militant steps for African liberation and the building of a cooperative political-social order for our people don't even have the money to get together to talk," Cox declared in an open letter to Sadaukai. "We need the participation of Africans who have some of that capacity, but may not share our politics."[42]

This rationale failed to quell the growing outcry. Nor did it ease concerns that the congress was becoming a tool of the status quo rather than an instrument of political change. Privately, some African-American organizers hoped that Six-PAC might help generate solutions to ongoing struggles between black nation-states and opposition groups within their territories. Yet many North American activists regarded *any* association with the Caribbean's ruling elites as counterrevolutionary. Some detractors accused Six-PAC planners of capitulating to neocolonial interests. C. L. R. James immediately announced his intention to boycott the congress. Walter Rodney, the respected Guyanese theorist, maintained that Six-PAC planners had failed to recognize the class identity and reactionary nature of petit-bourgeois nationalist leaders. The congress, he asserted, would be "attended mainly by spokesmen of African and Caribbean states which in so many ways represent the negation of Pan-Africanism."[43]

After this inauspicious beginning, matters got worse. A fragmented and unwieldy North American delegation landed in Tanzania in June 1974 to participate in Six-PAC. The group of 200 delegates included professionals, activists, journalists, and several influential leaders of independent black institutions: Sadaukai, Gene Locke, Haki Madhubuti, Jimmy Garrett, Amiri Baraka, and Kalamu Ya Salaam, as well as Bob Hoover (of East Palo Alto's Nairobi College) and Barbara Huell (of Atlanta's Martin Luther King, Jr. Community School). Hoping to project a spirit of unity, Cox and Sylvia Hill had asked African-American delegates to submerge egos, cliques, stale rhetoric, and "petty gripes" for the duration of the summit. During the flight to Tanzania, however, existing ideological conflicts resurfaced. Queen Mother Moore of Harlem, the 76-year-old militant, sought to unify the factions long enough to formulate a North American position on political matters the congress was expected to address. The effort failed. As Garrett recalled, "The North American group arrived in Tanzania as individuals, small constituencies and personalities." Many of the delegates coalesced into a Pan African nationalist camp and a Marxist camp.[44] The two-line struggle had gone abroad.

The African Americans spent the early days of the congress trying to regroup. They were deeply divided and uncertain about their role within the scope of the proceedings. Unprepared to present a coherent platform to other attendees, they scrambled to organize themselves into committees and develop proposals. Their nightly caucuses only confirmed what was evident to other participants; they were a conglomeration of clashing agendas, interests, and ideologies without a unifying mission or an acknowledged chief. At one point a Tanzanian official asked a group of black Americans to identify their leader. "We are all leaders," someone said. "That can be very dangerous," the official replied.[45]

The North Americans were by far the largest and most diffuse group at the summit. Many delegations consisted of government bureaucrats authorized to represent well-defined state interests. The African Americans were at a distinct disadvantage. They were unaccustomed to the diplomatic conventions of an international forum, and their nongovernmental composition deprived them of the clout needed to influence congress maneuverings. "Few nation-states took us seriously," Madhubuti later remembered. Though most North American participants held delegate credentials, all but a few were effectively relegated to observer status, with no opportunity to directly address the conference's main sessions. The Americans were granted five "floor delegates," but it soon grew clear that many of the existing committees had already drafted their resolutions. Much of the meaningful work of Six-PAC was complete.

Several Americans argued in vain that their delegation ought to be accorded government status. When the North American floor delegates finally addressed the body, the stridency of their remarks ruptured the air of formality that characterized much of the nine-day congress. (In a fiery speech, Baraka asserted that the exclusion from the conference of Caribbean revolutionaries provided "screeching testimony" to the pervasiveness of neocolonial domination.) All in

all, the Americans appeared naïve, ineffective, and ill-prepared. They soon realized that their priorities—including demands for the formation of skills banks
and a Pan African Center of Science and Technology—would not receive genuine consideration. "We see this congress is not going to meet our needs," one
black American complained.[46]

Six-PAC speeches and resolutions further dismayed many of the African-
American delegates. The congress drew an aggressive line against "racial thinking" in all its permutations. In a prerecorded speech, Sékou Touré of Guinea
stressed that *all* philosophies of skin color were tools of imperialism. A representative of FRELIMO, the Mozambican liberation front, insisted that Six-PAC's
aim must be "a new order based on the power of the working masses," and not
the mere "Africanization of exploitation." He characterized Pan Africanism as "a
movement to liquidate exploitation, which has no color, colonialism, which has
no people, and imperialism, which has no country." Julius "Mwalimu" Nyerere of
Tanzania, a figure universally revered by the North Americans, also cast Six-PAC
as staunchly opposed to racialism, as did the congress's General Declaration,
which asserted that "Revolutionary Pan Africanism inscribes itself within the
context of the class struggle. Not to be conscious of this would be to expose ourselves to confusion which imperialism would not fail to exploit."[47]

Many of the Americans were aghast. What was being rejected, they felt,
was not just racism but *race itself* as a valid category of analysis. The political
intrigue behind some of the more rigid interpretations of class—including
the long-standing ideological war between Guinean and Senegalese leaders,
as well as efforts by several governments to distance themselves from the
opportunistic racial policies of Uganda's Idi Amin—were beyond the ken of
some of the African-American attendees. What *was* evident to them was that
the true nature of their plight in North America, as constituted by the historical conjuncture of race *and* class, would not be reflected in the great documents and pronouncements of the most significant Pan African event of the
modern era.

The class-first orthodoxies of Six-PAC perplexed many black American participants. Even Baraka, who called for socialist revolution during his floor speech,
was taken aback. He later lamented that "progressives" at the congress had
adopted a doctrinaire stance that "dismissed all reference to National Liberation
struggle" and neglected to mention the fact that much of the white working class
"has been bribed by imperialism." James Turner of Cornell University, a member of the North American delegation, lobbied for inclusion in the conference
resolutions of language recognizing the realities of the racial situation in the
United States. Ultimately, however, advocacy of class struggle overrode pleas for
racial consciousness. Once again, Madhubuti groused, "The Marxists were in
command."[48]

Six-PAC generated some positive results. The gathering affirmed the need for total emancipation of African people—both from lingering structures of formal colonialism and from neocolonial domination. It endorsed the provision of material support for liberation movements on the continent. It offered "critical lessons" for African-American attendees, including the "shortsightedness of the race *or* class debate," and the fact that African identity "requires more than skin pigment." Finally, the planning and execution of Six-PAC helped hone the organizing skills of a number of women—including Geri Stark of Washington's Center for Black Education and Sylvia Hill of Milwaukee's Institute for African Education—whose leadership challenged patriarchal models of internationalism and Neo-Pan Africanism.[49]

That said, the congress failed to revitalize Pan African nationalism within the United States. By denying that "blackness" retained any progressive political or intellectual value, Six-PAC intensified the disillusionment of many African-American activists. The North American delegates brought to Tanzania the accumulated fantasies of returning exiles. Naiveté inflated their expectations about what the congress would or could accomplish. They hoped to aid in the formation of a corps of technologists that might spur African development and "produce nation-builders." They pondered concepts of African-American dual citizenship and a "right of return" comparable to Israel's policy for Jews. They envisioned a permanent Pan African secretariat, the forging of an official political link to Africa, perhaps even a seat for black America in the Organization of African Unity.[50]

Racial Pan Africanists raised questions of land, kinship, and identity. Kalamu Ya Salaam of Ahidiana, only 26 at the time, hailed the "unification of Afrikan people everywhere." Nairobi College's Bob Hoover, then 42, imagined the harnessing of Africa's natural resources for the collective benefit of the black world. Meanwhile, the leftists pictured a revolutionary parlay devoted to indicting both imperialism and its neocolonial black functionaries. North Americans of all ideological tendencies anticipated explicit expressions of solidarity with African-American struggle.[51]

What black Americans actually received was a lesson in realpolitik. African governments feared that the proposed Pan African Academy of Science and Technology would become "a breeding ground for CIA-type infiltration." Though some conferees greeted the U.S. delegation in a spirit of camaraderie, their exchanges with the Americans reflected their own particular priorities. Nyerere's private audiences with North American delegates were not intended to convey abstract notions of unity, but to recruit specialists for ongoing Tanzanian projects. Representatives from FRELIMO, Mozambique's revolutionary organization, communed with African Americans on the basis of anti-imperialism rather than racial fellowship. Like the entire Six-PAC assemblage, they dismissed "the utopian idea of returning to promised lands."[52]

In the end, African-American idealism collided with affairs of state. The diplomatic obligations of African and Caribbean nations dashed black American hopes for a deeply ideological congress devoted to expressions of Pan African sentiment. "The very existence of African governments sometimes moves us to such rapture that we cannot be objective," Baraka acknowledged. Six-PAC was an accordingly sobering demonstration of the limitations of the nation-state as a progressive force. In a moment of candor, Nyerere all but conceded the point. "*All* governments are conservative," he declared during his chat with African Americans. The Cubans conveyed a similar message. "There's no radical diplomacy and bourgeois diplomacy," they told Geri Stark of the Center for Black Education. "All diplomacy is bourgeois." This was a jarring repudiation of the presumption that national sovereignty would redeem the oppressed.[53]

Whether the North American delegates fully absorbed the lessons of Six-PAC is unclear. Some activist-intellectuals gained insight into the realities of power, knowledge that proved valuable during future struggles. However, many U.S. participants recoiled from the bitter disappointment of the congress. They felt that their expressions of solidarity had not been properly reciprocated, that they had been cast as provincial and chauvinistic, and that the promise of "We Are an African People" had been betrayed. They might have seized the opportunity to examine their own contradictions as Westerners and middle-class intellectuals. Doing so would have meant confronting their interpretation of Pan Africanism as what Azinna Nwafor called "a unity imposed from above and not one emanating from the base in the real conditions of the impoverished masses."[54]

As it happened, the experience of Six-PAC accelerated the two-line struggle's degeneration into an open-ended war of attrition. The leftists believed that their crusade against "skin nationalism" had been vindicated. Many of them continued to seek "revolutionary clarity" in the intricacies of doctrine. Meanwhile, the right-leaning camp withdrew further into racial fundamentalism, concluding that "an Arab-Marxist world clique" was conspiring to strip Pan Africanism of color consciousness.[55] Bitter illusions proliferated on both sides amid the fracturing of the African liberation support movement in North America.

"A Tremendous Blunder": Angola and the Error of Arrogance

Signs that Six-PAC had not inspired universal self-reflection surfaced almost immediately. As the conference adjourned in late June 1974, several African Americans departed Tanzania on dubious political excursions. State tours of Somalia and Zanzibar were among the free junkets to East African sites accepted by members of the American delegation. These forays enabled African elites to recruit professionals and technicians from the West. They also allowed right-leaning Pan Africanists to indulge in the racial sentimentalism that Six-PAC had disavowed.

The most troubling expedition was to Idi Amin's Uganda. Amin, whose bloody reign cost hundreds of thousands of Ugandans their lives, sent his private jet to whisk a dozen black Americans to the beleaguered land. There, the Westerners toured a textile mill and other businesses, all of which were run by indigenous Africans, since Amin had expelled Asians from the country. How refreshing to see Africans in control, one black American noted, rather than serving as "window dressing for a Jew or an Asian." The North Americans enjoyed a state dinner with Amin, who announced that he would grant the visitors Ugandan citizenship, an offer that the guests heartily applauded. "Here we were after 400 years being reclaimed!" one traveler exulted. The Ugandan despot, a figure widely known as "the Butcher of Kampala," then played his accordion for the doting Americans. As a member of the East, the Brooklyn institution, later remarked, it was "a heavy experience."[56]

The Ugandan tour was also a perverse example of racial reductionism and the moral and political blindness that it can cause. It was the sort of venture that validated criticism of Pan Africanism as a conceit of the petit-bourgeois intelligentsia. Even amid the early planning stages of Six-PAC, some observers had predicted that such elements would dominate the congress. "It is not surprising that neither at Manchester nor in Dar es Salaam will the problem of the masses ever enter anybody's mind," Kenyan leftist Philip Ochieng wrote in 1971. "Nor does it matter if the same masses know anything about the movement. Pan Africanism was a movement of a self-interested class."[57]

A final misadventure framed the internationalist politics of the mid-1970s. The relationship of African-American activist-intellectuals to the Angolan Civil War highlighted the confusion of contemporary radicalism. The situation in the Southern African country was complex. After winning independence from Portugal in 1975, Angola plunged into a violent civil conflict driven by rival liberation fronts. The main antagonists were the MPLA (People's Movement for the Liberation of Angola) and UNITA (the National Union for the Total Independence of Angola). Cold War dynamics complicated matters, combining with ethnic and historical antipathies compounded by colonialism and a protracted independence struggle. Despite these dynamics, some black American theorists interpreted the crisis according to their own narrow political formulas.

Many African-American intellectuals, including large segments of the progressive and Pan African nationalist communities, had supported UNITA since the early '70s. Elements within both ideological currents of ALSC backed the Angolan organization, which was headed by the charismatic Jonas Savimbi.

UNITA devotees in the United States regarded the faction as "a supreme fighting force" in Southern Africa, a popular movement that had built a powerful infrastructure within the liberated zones. UNITA reportedly received funding from China, a fact that boosted its appeal among black American Maoists and other followers of the "Chinese line." By contrast, MPLA was said to be sponsored by the Soviet Union, a state many progressive African-American theorists disparaged as "social imperialist" (socialist in words, imperialist in deeds.)[58]

In truth, UNITA's high regard among black American activists stemmed largely from the group's efforts of self-promotion. Savimbi's movement waged an extensive propaganda campaign to win African-American support. Its representatives met with Black Power leaders and organizations in the United States, and arranged for African-American intellectuals and organizers like the ALSC's Florence Tate to visit the Angolan territories under its control. A key goal of this outreach was to discredit MPLA, UNITA's nemesis. The primary strategy for doing so was to paint the competing movement as inauthentically "black."[59]

UNITA spokesmen claimed that most MPLA officers were "mulatto"; that while UNITA fighters had African peasant wives, many of their MPLA counterparts had married Portuguese women; and that under MPLA rule, Angola would be controlled by white sympathizers and their mixed-race and "assimilado" allies, groups that the colonialists had favored over the African majority. This line of argument proved remarkably effective in the United States. Jitu Weusi saw the "white wives" issue as a major contradiction. His Brooklyn organization raised funds for UNITA and planned to distribute propaganda on its behalf. Madhubuti was another staunch admirer. "UNITA has been the most credible and African of all the liberation movements," he declared in 1974.[60]

Over the course of 1975, these and other figures discovered in horror that the CIA, South Africa's apartheid government, and other imperialist forces had quietly armed and funded UNITA to forestall genuine social transformation in Angola. African-American theorists, including many who considered themselves advanced revolutionary thinkers, had aided and abetted a tool of Western reaction. When Jimmy Garrett of the Center for Black Education visited Angola in 1976, hoping to better understand conditions there, he found compelling evidence of MPLA's status as the legitimate representative of the Angolan people's historical struggle for self-rule. UNITA, he learned, commanded little popular support within Angola; the organization had not been extensively involved in reconstruction efforts, and had committed major atrocities. He concluded that the UNITA publicity drive of recent years had constituted "one of the best public relations hoaxes ever run on the Afro-American nationalist/progressive community."[61]

The Angola revelations deepened the crisis of transnational black consciousness in the United States. Once touchstones of radical African-American awareness, Southern Africa's guerilla movements now appeared to be a labyrinth of foreign intrigue. "Our motherland is plunged into a sea of ideological struggle," Weusi lamented. Many activists believed they had been duped into supporting counterrevolutionaries. In reality, the UNITA fiasco reflected the shortcomings of contemporary radical thought. Neo-Marxists had been blinded by rigid allegiance to China, whose role in Angola reflected the exigencies of Sino-Soviet hostility rather than political ideology. Conservative Pan African nationalists, on the other hand, had been misled by simplistic theories of race. In both cases, a priori formulations had eclipsed careful analysis.[62]

As they strove to understand the lessons of Angola, progressives like Jimmy Garrett and Anthony Monteiro urged African-American radicals to expand their consciousness. Rather than simply focus on the elimination of white racist regimes in Africa and elsewhere, they argued, anti-imperialists needed to recommit themselves to visions and programs of total liberation. Meaningful postcoloniality required the construction of a new social order based on qualitative changes in relations of production and in the lives of the peasantry and working class.

Walter Rodney echoed the call for self-criticism. During a spring 1976 address at Howard University, the Caribbean intellectual condemned the arrogance of those who had transposed onto Angolan society the American idiosyncrasies of race. The error, he suggested, reflected an aversion to examining the actual shape of society and the true nature of power within any revolutionary situation. Hubris and dogma had generated much of the confusion that surrounded the Angola question. The challenge now was to recognize that a "tremendous blunder" had occurred, and to confront its root causes. "It is not unrevolutionary to make an error," Rodney said. "But it's certainly unrevolutionary not to accept that when it becomes clear that it is true."[63]

"What Happened to Liberation?": The Black Institution Depression

The Angola conflict exacerbated the factionalism that marked black solidarity work in the United States. The mid-1970s witnessed the advance of African sovereignty, the collapse of Portuguese colonialism, and the conquest of American imperialism in Vietnam. Plagued by internal turmoil, African-American internationalists drew little solace from these developments. Some activist-intellectuals displayed their confusion by shifting from wholesale support for UNITA to superficial readings of the Angolan civil war as a case of "black-on-black slaughter."[64]

Other African-American radicals developed more critical perspectives; in time, they realized that not even Tanzania, the embodiment of their love affair with the nation-state, had escaped the clutches of neocolonialism. As they transcended romanticism, they recognized that solidarity did not mean sameness. African and African-American political realities were not interchangeable. As Frantz Fanon had observed, "The Negroes of Chicago only resemble the Nigerians or the Tanganyikans insofar as they were all defined in relation to the whites."[65]

Such epiphanies inspired a reorientation toward local organizing. By 1973, the Center for Black Education had transitioned from training technical workers for Africa to sponsoring community forums and other practical initiatives in Washington. Houston's Lynn Eusan Institute also hosted a series of community discussions in black neighborhoods. Topics included "Inflation and the People," "Decent Health Care Is a Human Right," and "The Defeat of Portuguese Colonialism in Africa—Its Meaning to Blacks in the USA and to the World Fight for Human Dignity." Other cadres, like Jitu Weusi's East in Brooklyn, remained wedded to Racial Pan Africanism. They continued to regard Uganda's Idi Amin as a fearless nationalist, delighting in his harangues of Western powers and attributing to the mendacity of the white media accounts of his tyranny and mass murders.[66]

Members of the East also supported Forbes Burnham, the Pan Africanist, socialist, and increasingly repressive leader of the Caribbean country of Guyana. The dimensions of their error were revealed in 1980 when the Burnham regime orchestrated the assassination of Walter Rodney, a theorist known to African-American activists through his radical scholarship and extensive political work within the Caribbean, the United States, and Tanzania. Rodney's death, in a blast that mutilated the car in which he was seated, provided an eerie replay of the 1970 Ralph Featherstone slaying and raised troubling questions about the role of the CIA in Guyana.[67]

Sobering events overseas mirrored developments at home. Erupting two decades after *Brown v. Board of Education*, Boston's violent, mid-1970s busing skirmishes suggested not only a resurgence of white nationalist reaction but also the reinvigoration of integration as a dominant paradigm of black consciousness. Meanwhile, the death of Elijah Muhammad and the reorganization of his Nation of Islam signaled the dismantling of another model of black unity and cohesion—one that, notwithstanding its innumerable faults, had served as a crucial symbol of a "separate psychological world." In some respects, the 1976 publication of Alex Haley's *Roots* represented another setback. The book and accompanying television miniseries helped reframe the politics of African identity, subordinating questions of liberation to matters of genealogy and kinship.[68]

As the decade wore on, the search for alternatives to the decadence and corruption of American mainstream culture assumed increasingly escapist forms.
The ultimate symbol of African-American spiritual distress arose not in the
inner city but in a dense jungle paradise. In 1978, the bodies of more than 900
members of the People's Temple, a disproportionately black religious cult led
by white mystic Jim Jones, were discovered in a remote settlement deep within
the Guyanese rainforest. The suicide-murders at "Jonestown" (the deceased had
opted—or been forced—to drink a cyanide-laced cocktail) stunned black leaders. Jitu Weusi characterized the deaths as an act of genocide. In truth, People's
Temple was a warped expression of a larger hunt for communalism, autonomy,
and cultural rebirth, a quest that had also spawned a generation of independent
black institutions. Indeed, Weusi's East had for years maintained a secluded
farming cooperative just miles from Jonestown in the Guyanese interior.[69]

By the mid- to late 1970s, political demobilization had given way to despair.
The African-American renaissance of the 1960s and early '70s seemed to have
all but evaporated. No major renewal of mass activity was underway. Stagnation,
crime, unemployment, and repression had smothered the revolutionary initiative. Activists everywhere echoed the same question: "*Whatever happened to the
politics of black liberation?*" Social malaise hastened the collapse of independent
black establishments. Washington's New School of Afro-American Thought
folded in the early 1970s, dissolving amid ideological strife and the exhaustion
of its organizers. By the decade's end, several more Black Power formations had
succumbed to the "black institution depression."[70]

Sheer overwork spurred the decline. Independent institutions demanded
of their staff nothing less than missionary zeal. Oberlin's Shule Ya Kujitambua
required "a firm commitment to educating our youth for the good of the black
community, and dedication to the values of cooperation and self-reliance." In
practice, this meant performing classroom duties, learning rudimentary Swahili,
attending parent meetings, and contributing to the school's coffers. Chicago's
New Concept Development Center asked teachers to embody the Nguzo Saba
while meeting the "total needs" of students. Our School, a short-lived, New York
City venture, conveyed its expectations in a 1976 ad: "Wanted: Teachers.
Interviewing now for Sept. Full or part-time. Low pay. Long Hours. Hard
Work."[71]

Despite such rigors, most teachers in independent institutions were underpaid. The six full-time faculty members at Brooklyn's Uhuru Sasa made $8,500
each in 1975, the equivalent of about $36,000 in 2013 dollars. Instructors at the
impoverished Black and Proud School of Jackson, Mississippi, received stipends
of just $2,800 in 1977 (or the equivalent of less than $11,000 in 2013 dollars).
Meager pay led to the temporary resignation of Portia Coombs from the teaching staff of Atlanta's Martin Luther King, Jr. Community School. Though her

stint at the King School had provided "a glimpse of a beautiful future" and "a major highlight in my life as an African forced to live, for the time-being, in an alien land," financial realities had intervened.[72]

Parental expectations posed another challenge. Many of the parents who were drawn to independent schools hailed from the striving working class. They were young and relatively stable, possessed at least a rudimentary education, and were willing to make sacrifices, financial and otherwise, for the education of their children. Some appeared happy with the results: after enrolling in Pan African nationalist academies, children often seemed more focused, orderly, and race conscious. "Since my kids came here they are not uptight about fad dress," one Uhuru Sasa mother observed in 1974. "They are more inquiring, more responsible and less willing to run the street."[73]

For many families, the appeal of independent institutions lay in their role as alternatives to public schools. Yet parents expressed conventional concerns about individual development and the mastery of academic skills. Whatever their political commitments might have been, they saw private education as a way to prepare youngsters for gainful employment and full participation in society. "A child should have a black education to inform him about what his ancestors have contributed to this nation," a Pan African Early Education Center parent told school representatives in 1972. The value of independent institutions, another parent at the Durham, North Carolina, establishment asserted, lay in their capacity to teach students "about the many black people that have made our country what it is today." Excessive "emphasis on black alone," one parent at Boston's Highland Park Free School cautioned in 1973, would stifle academic achievement. "Our children must be taught to compete," another Highland Park mother insisted.[74]

Organizers had to consider such perspectives, even as they pursued larger political goals. "Our black children must not suffer because we refuse to step down from the dais of rhetoric," an instructor at Atlanta's King Community School declared. John Churchville of Philadelphia's Freedom Library Day School suggested that student academic progress could help mitigate parents' "ideological disparities." He acknowledged that if independent institutions imparted "slogans and handshakes and pledges, and no learning no building, no change of behavior and character at home—that parent is going to revert and say, 'that black stuff is a mess.' "[75]

Stretching budgets may have been even more difficult than managing parents. The recessionary economy compounded the financial woes of independent black establishments. Even the 200-student Uhuru Sasa Shule faltered. The primary and secondary school's 1975 income of $160,000 reflected a $3,000 deficit. The institution met its costs in 1976–1977, thanks largely to a benefit concert by jazz musicians Max Roach and Pharoah Sanders. Uhuru Sasa continued to provide scholarships for 20% of its pupils and allow parents to off-set tuition debts by working on campus. But tax debt and mounting expenses forced administrators to raise annual tuition fees from $450 to $500, an onerous burden for working-class families.[76]

All independent institutions felt the pressure of stagnant incomes and declining philanthropic donations and social spending. Operations like the Black and Proud Liberation School of Jackson, Mississippi, experienced the greatest hardship. By summer 1976, the 25-pupil, kindergarten through fifth-grade establishment had raised only $5,000 toward its $29,000 operating budget for the upcoming academic year. Meanwhile, drought decimated its cooperative farm, its clothing cooperative languished, and economic desperation seized its staff. In 1977, Spencer requested emergency grants from several foundations to help cover the personal utility bills and rent of his six teachers, most of whom were mothers and welfare recipients. The prospect of eviction from his own home forced Spencer to solicit funding on his family's behalf as well.

Black and Proud could not risk alienating its struggling families by raising its $38 monthly tuition. In 1976, Spencer turned to a local parents' association for donations of textbooks and other essential materials. A year later, Black and Proud still lacked crucial supplies, including typewriters, encyclopedias, and a deep freezer to preserve vegetables from its farm. Atlanta's King Community School also opted against a tuition hike. Half its families were on public assistance, and none could afford an increase in the $160 monthly fee. The school resorted to patching its budget with proceeds from raffles and poker parties.[77]

Some independent institutions joined forces to avoid destitution. In 1973, a coalition of Pan African nationalist organizations came to the aid of the impoverished Black Peoples' Topographical Research Center in Chicago. Other signs of solidarity appeared. After moving from Atlanta to Philadelphia in 1974, Vincent and Rosemarie Harding of the Institute of the Black World and the King Community School enrolled their children at John Churchville's storefront academy, seeing "any secondary differences that we might have with Freedom Library Day School only as sources of healthy, comradely discussion and debate."[78]

However, many independent schools continued to drift toward organizational chauvinism and rigidity. Dogmatism hastened the demise of Columbus, Ohio's Umoja Sasa Shule, which collapsed in 1973 after operating for just two years. The school had creatively blended internationalism and everyday concerns. Its July 1973 newsletter advertised an evening seminar in African history, called for a local boycott of Gulf Oil (a major investor in Southern Africa), and warned against department store finance plans. "Credit," an editor cautioned, "is the white man's game."[79] Yet ideological struggle against "rhetorical Pan Africanists" and emphasis on re-educating activists—"remolding one's life," as cofounder Lubengula put it—also defined the institution. "Certain attitudes can be tolerated in Amerika," Lubengula declared, "but they are totally inadmissible in a struggle to build Afrikan institutions."

Umoja Sasa's operators believed they had successfully sown "seeds of struggle" in their students, and remained optimistic about the fate of independent schools.[80] The 1973 dissolution of Greensboro, North Carolina's Malcolm X Liberation University (MXLU), however, dealt the black consciousness movement a staggering blow. MXLU's fiscal crisis had expanded after 1969. By February 1970, the institution operated on an $80,000 budget with only $12,000 in hand. Grants and individual contributions failed to cover monthly expenses of nearly $9,000. Director Owusu Sadaukai acknowledged in 1971 that he and his fellow organizers had underestimated the task of "building a truly black institution in the midst of a colonial existence."[81]

In early 1973, administrators reorganized, curtailing or suspending most projects and adopting austerity measures. The changes reduced expenses while allowing personnel "to better root themselves in the black community and see the practical usefulness of the skills" taught at MXLU. But the school continued to flounder. Its staff recognized that "revolutionary black institutions" throughout the United States were succumbing to the "massive co-optation efforts" of government and private agencies. Refusing to adopt a more accommodationist politics, and unable to resolve the philosophical conflict between focusing on Africa or black America, MXLU shut its doors that summer after four years of operation.

Overemphasis on Africa "as a major determinant in the future welfare of the masses of black working people in this country" had contributed to MXLU's downfall, Sadaukai acknowledged in a closing statement. The error had led to isolation from the black community and failure to build an effective local base. Sadaukai called for a revival of radical political resistance, urging those "resolved to end oppression" to combat all forms of racism and exploitation. In the end, he noted, MXLU was merely one vehicle of struggle. "It is necessary to change the vehicle from time to time," he said, "but that does not mean that the struggle will end."[82]

"To Neglect Our True Selves": The Rightward Drift of Pan African Nationalism

By the late 1970s, Philadelphia's Freedom Library Day School, Washington's Center for Black Education, Houston's Lynn Eusan Institute, Chicago's Arusha-Konakri Institute, and a host of other independent schools and storefront operations had folded. The campuses that survived faced political isolation and crushing debt. Autonomous black institutions had been touted as a means of reconstructing a people and practicing the values of self-determination. Some theorists had predicted that the establishments would serve "generations yet unborn."[83]

Now, amid the widespread reversal of political gains, the crusade for parallel institutions appeared to be another relic of Black Power exuberance. Long-standing critiques of independent schools resurfaced, including the claim that they were inherently elitist, that they failed to meet the needs of masses of black children trapped in decaying urban schools, and that they tended to foster "another group of people who have lost interest" in public education. Private ventures, critics argued, could never solve public crises. As Bill Strickland of the Institute of the Black World asserted, "All education of white people, by white people and for white people in this country [has been] subsidized by the state."[84]

Doubt and ennui enveloped many institutions. After the demise of his New School of Afro-American Thought in 1971, a depressed and exhausted Gaston Neal reverted to the heroin abuse of his bohemian days. In 1972, he checked into a Washington, DC, hospital, where he spent two months recovering. Battle fatigue also claimed Sadaukai, who suffered a near breakdown in 1976, three years after closing MXLU. The unraveling of both the school and the African Liberation Support Committee, and a grueling union job organizing Duke University hospital workers, finally depleted the activist-intellectual. He left North Carolina and returned to Milwaukee to recuperate.[85]

Meanwhile, in the mid-1970s, Churchville quit the Council of Independent Black Institutions (CIBI), the federation of Pan African nationalist schools he had helped establish. Conflict with political adversaries and other ideological and financial pressures had left him drained and disillusioned. "I just felt it was not worth it," he later remembered. In 1978, he shuttered Freedom Library and sent his four children—all of whom had attended the North Philadelphia storefront—to public school. "I was so turned off, burned out," he recalled.[86]

Jitu Weusi of Uhuru Sasa resisted the attrition. "Please don't lose touch with our struggle," he asked a fellow independent school organizer in 1974. Two years later, however, Weusi, CIBI's first chairman, resigned from the alliance, citing what he viewed as its impending obsolescence. Between 1972 and 1977, the organization had encompassed as many as 22 and as few as 8 institutions. Now its harried officials struggled to preserve the dream of a network of Pan African nationalist schools. "CIBI is at the crossroads," Weusi declared, insisting that the federation must regain its bearings or resign itself to irrelevance. The veteran educator himself stepped down as Uhuru Sasa headmaster in 1978.

CIBI leaders tried to halt the decay. "Some of you are tired, and we understand taking time for rest and recuperation," one of its administrators stated in a 1979 letter. "But the work is not finished, so we can't stop." Meanwhile, the ranks of the original institutions continued to thin. "Will another black school close?" a Brooklyn periodical asked in 1977 amid appeals for support from Oberlin, Ohio's Shule Ya Kujitambua. Even Chicago, once a breeding ground for Pan African nationalist schools, saw a decline in the establishments. By the early 1980s, only a handful of the city's Black Power–era campuses remained, serving a total student population of about 200.[87]

Eventually, the erosion slowed. Some of the autonomous institutions of the late 1960s and early 1970s survived into the 1980s and beyond. The approximately 100 "African-centered" sites operating across the United States in 1980 included several holdovers from this generation. Brooklyn's Uhuru Sasa Shule remained one of the nation's most active Pan African nationalist establishments until 1986, when it succumbed to financial strain. The school had opened in 1970 without heat or running water, and with a severe shortage of instructors and materials. It had grown into a viable pre-kindergarten through grade 12 facility with a faculty of 20 and an enrollment of more than 300, and had served as the cornerstone of a cultural center that featured a food co-op, a daycare center, a community news magazine, and an annual street carnival designed to convey "the flavor of our African heritage."[88]

Nairobi Day School of East Palo Alto, California, also operated through the mid-1980s, though always on a shoestring. Its debt-ridden high school closed during the 1976–1977 academic year, but its grade school endured for another decade, serving 50 students while striving to meet annual costs of $125,000 with private donations, corporate gifts, fundraisers, and tuition fees. Nairobi Day School continued to provide an alternative to a 90% black public school district in which sixth graders scored in the fourth percentile on standardized reading tests. The campus remained a symbol of pride and self-determination for many of the 20,000 residents of East Palo Alto, even as unemployment in the municipality climbed to 30% and a brisk narcotics trade overshadowed the aging institutions of black consciousness.[89]

There were other long-lived establishments. Ahidiana of New Orleans shut its doors in 1983 after 10 years, but Shule ya Watoto and New Concept Development Center of Chicago, Nidhamu Sasa of Philadelphia, and the Chad School of Newark endured. Meanwhile, new models appeared. Howard University students and former public school teachers founded Washington's 70-student Nationhouse Watoto in late 1974. Afrikan People's Action Movement, an organization devoted to the political philosophies of Ghana's late Kwame Nkrumah, created Trenton, New Jersey's Afrikan People's Action School, an establishment serving children ages 10 and younger, in 1976.[90]

Yet for many institutions, old and new, a retreat from radical ideals appeared to be part of the cost of survival. In the mid- to late 1970s, as the country moved to the right politically, a more conservative configuration of nationalism and Pan Africanism emerged as the dominant alternative to the integrationism and accommodationism of black elites. The anticapitalism, anti-imperialism, and Third Worldism that had intermingled with racialist and culturalist tendencies in the heyday of Black Power began to fade. The ideological currents that remained converged in the paradigm of Afrocentrism. Contemporary independent black institutions had arisen amid a search for radical alternatives, a quest animated by visions of a restructured society. Now the movement turned inward, embracing a conservative politics of identity.

This reorientation transformed the militant demand for collective self-determination into a feeble discourse of self-help. The former theme had complemented the fight for redistributive social policies; the latter motif reinforced the New Right's attacks on the welfare state. The critiques of political economy that had expanded the vision of Pan African nationalism dwindled as leftists abandoned the quest for parallel institutions. What lingered was an outlook that eschewed class struggle or dialectical thought, that promoted asceticism and self-discipline as solutions to black dependency, and that sought to rehabilitate rather than liberate the dispossessed.

In the 1970s and '80s, as progressives fought for full employment and the reconstruction of social democracy, many operators of what were now identified as "Afrocentric" schools characterized the black lower classes as "slaves to luxuries" who were "drunk on welfare" and lacked "initiative." Shule Ya Watoto's theorists called upon African Americans to become "totally independent of the white boy"—not by demanding living wages, dignified jobs, or the restoration of urban infrastructure, but by rejecting vices like cigarettes and alcohol. "The money you save from the elimination of useless self-indulgence could support a nation," they maintained. Operators of Pasadena, California's Omowale Ujamaa Community School held similar views. "Our children are taught to survive by living off the crumbs left on the government's table," one of the institution's officials argued in 1981. "We must teach them to move away from this 'give me, give me' welfare mentality."[91]

Such sentiments revealed an underlying contempt for the poor. Pan African nationalism had long vacillated between valorizing the African-American masses and demanding their reformation. Over the course of the 1970s, many of the philosophy's adherents embraced the latter position, indicting the alleged vices of the black rank and file. Shule Ya Watoto's Hannibal Afrik attributed black America's crises to its cultural failings, a category in which he included everything from Blaxploitation to black feminism. "We abandoned our cultural dress and appearance to adapt to the lifestyles of *Superfly* and the *Essence* woman," he complained in 1980. "It was not long before we began to imitate aliens and neglect our true selves."[92]

The reinvigoration of the culturalist worldview bolstered the premise that black Americans needed resocialization before the liberation movement could proceed. Only when cured of their purported backwardness could African Americans reassert the redemptive values of blackness. No longer primarily oriented toward anti-imperialism, many independent schools focused on pre-scribing "authentic" standards of behavior. Obsession with personal conduct led to the dictation of individual practices. In 1979, for example, Washington's Nationhouse Watoto denounced chemically treated hairdos as "European" and encouraged black women to observe traditional braiding techniques as an alternative to processed styles that bore "no relationship to us as an African people."[93]

Resisting the subversion of gender norms was another priority for conserva-tive Pan African nationalism. Like other traditionalists, the movement's adher-ents saw the ascent of women's and gay liberation and the flourishing of feminist theory as ominous developments. Black independent schools had long rein-forced essentialist and hierarchical notions of "manhood" and "womanhood." Amid a crescendo of perceived gender assaults—including the emergence of *Essence* magazine and the success of Ntozake Shange's *for colored girls who have considered suicide/when the rainbow is enuf,* a 1976 Broadway play that addressed the abuse of black women at the hands of black men—Afrocentric educators turned to rites-of-passage programs and black male caucuses as methods of reas-serting masculine authority.[94]

Patriarchal rituals and catechisms of self-help reinforced an ethic of social isolation. The radicalism of independent black institutions had resided in their status as sites of political engagement. The concept of schools as "liberated zones" suggested that the development of alternative educational models could help guide the reconstruction of society. Yet there was always the risk of psy-chic withdrawal, the possibility that rather than embody the new civilization, the establishments would simply become bulwarks against the existing one. During the 1970s and '80s, many surviving institutions accepted this diminished role. Rather than attempt to revive a radical public sphere, they endeavored to shield children and adults from the putative symptoms of social decay.

"Watoto School is one of the only safe zones where we can escape the enemy's attacks on our minds and those of our children," operators of the Washington enterprise declared in 1983. "It is also a base from which we can counterattack their lies with truth and their perversion with tradition, reason and purpose." Even pop singer Michael Jackson posed a moral threat. "Do you want your son to get a 'nose job,' have his eyes widened, use pancake makeup or bleaching cream, speak with a feminine voice, or escort white women?" a Watoto staff member asked. "Do you want your daughters to use Michael Jackson as the standard for a husband?"[95]

At times, the greatest cultural hazards appeared to emanate from black neighborhoods themselves. In a 1980 newsletter, Mama Lubaba Ahmed, headmistress of Brooklyn's Uhuru Sasa Shule, cited as evidence of African-American social and moral decline the proliferation of

> alcohol and drugs, unemployment, social service[s], food stamps, broken homes, poor nutrition, disrespect for elders, housing projects, Asian merchants, poor sanitation service, poor public education, broken glass in parks, writing on walls, homosexuality, [and] young black men filling up jails.[96]

The defensive posture of Pan African nationalist schools in the late 1970s and early '80s reflected the politics of late twentieth-century Afrocentrism, a modern variety of cultural nationalism. The academies embodied the revitalized quest to mold "the Afrikan personality." Their affirmations of "our Afrikanity" reflected the alleged imperatives of cultural rehabilitation and restoration. Their propagation of neo-traditional garb, language, and rituals—naming ceremonies, weddings, and Kwanzaa services—signaled a retreat to a mystical, ahistorical, homogenized Africa. Their preoccupation with Egyptology and the glories of dynastic Africa bolstered the search for a "high culture" of black antiquity. Their patronage of a burgeoning subfield of black chauvinist pseudo-science perpetuated biological theories of racial difference.[97]

By 1980, the year of the "Reagan revolution," black independent schools had helped engender an incipient Afrocentrism, an intellectual and cultural movement that gained momentum with the publication (also in 1980) of black studies scholar Molefi Kete Asante's *Afrocentricity*.[98] The schools' entrenched culturalism, patriarchy, heterosexism, and racial fundamentalism suggested that the quest for "nationhood" had come to mean little more than a cloistered, specialized lifestyle within the framework of monopoly capitalism. Largely detached from the social and economic realities of working and poor people in the United States and abroad, Afrocentric education sought a highly symbolic but politically anemic reaffirmation of blackness.

When leaders of the Council of Independent Black Institutions visited West Africa in 1981, they arranged an audience not with anti-imperialist activists, but rather, with an Ashanti king, the very symbol of traditional social hierarchy. Several of the federation's intellectuals had practiced a similar politics of black cultural transnationalism—an approach that emphasized bonds of identity while avoiding critical analysis of material conditions—during the Second World Black and African Festival of Arts and Culture (FESTAC) in Lagos, Nigeria, in 1977. They had relished FESTAC's message of racial solidarity, especially in the wake of the Marxian orthodoxies of the 1974 Sixth Pan African Congress. During FESTAC's closing ceremonies, members of the all-black U.S. delegation had marched around a modern stadium whose sleekness belied the hardship many ordinary Nigerians experienced under the nation's reigning military regime. As they processed, the African Americans had raised their fists and taken up a familiar chant: "We Are an African People!"[99]

Epilogue

Afrocentrism and the Neoliberal Ethos

The vast majority of the black institutions we need are yet to be born.
—Vincent Harding[1]

In many ways, independent black institutions embodied the promise of Black Power. They strove to meet the basic needs of exploited people while exposing the deficiencies of existing social structures. They helped concretize the principles of self-determination and self-definition. At their best, Pan African nationalist schools provided dynamic social alternatives and exemplified contemporary efforts to build "the new society within the shell of the old."

The concept of education for self-reliance and cultural regeneration outlived the mass activity of the 1960s and early '70s. The proliferation of black nationalist schools in the last quarter of the twentieth century signaled the survival of some Black Power ideas. It also demonstrated how social movements may be stripped of oppositional meaning. By the 1980s, many Afrocentric establishments practiced a brand of black nationalism that equated symbolism with struggle while eschewing systemic transformation. Some independent black institutions collaborated with conservative proponents of educational vouchers and charter schools, a sign of the symbiotic relationship between bourgeois identity politics and the corporate establishment. In organs like Northern California's Oakland Community School and Jackson, Mississippi's Black and Proud Liberation School, however, radical traditions were reborn.

"The Right Road": A Radical Redux?

The rightward drift of black alternative schools did not end the political development of individual activists. Many of the movement's participants regrouped after the mid-1970s, resisting assaults on black life in postindustrial urban

253

centers. Their activities belie accounts of an immediate "post–civil rights" era defined mainly by political accommodation and decline.[2] Veteran Pan African nationalists waged grassroots battles against a resurgent KKK, led antiapartheid and reparations movements, and supported the progressive efforts of African Liberation Day and the National Black Independent Political Party.

Activists like Jitu Weusi, founder of Brooklyn's Uhuru Sasa Shule, continued to convert liberation themes into concrete programs. In the late 1970s, he protested the police killing of a 15-year-old African-American boy, an incident that led to the birth of the Black United Front (BUF). As a leader of the organization's local and national formations, Weusi joined the often uneven and faltering attempts of nationalists and leftists to transcend political bickering, reunite race and class analysis, and revive engaged internationalism. BUF participants fought police brutality in the inner city while supporting Haitian boat people, the Sandanistas of Nicaragua, and the "New Jewel" revolution in Grenada. The organization eventually faded, and Weusi never overcame his inveterate hostility to feminism and gay liberation. Yet the seasoned organizer remained devoted to pressure tactics as a means of addressing the material realities of black Brooklyn.[3]

Kalamu Ya Salaam also strove to reinvigorate confrontation politics. The New Orleans–based cofounder of the Ahidiana school and collective protested the 1975 death sentence of Gary Tyler, a black teenager wrongfully convicted by an all-white jury for the murder of a white youth. He hosted KKK counterrallies and helped orchestrate demonstrations against police terrorism. He experimented with multiracial activism, joining white progressives in campaigns against South African apartheid and the construction of nuclear facilities near black neighborhoods. He honed a class critique. He rediscovered door-to-door organizing. In so doing, Salaam answered radical intellectuals like Manning Marable who challenged black nationalists to "make a decisive and uncompromising break from the black elite" and "come to terms with practical issues which touch the daily lives of blue collar and unemployed black America."[4]

Salaam's feminist awakening accelerated his metamorphosis. He once had upheld the standard Kawaida line on gender: "sisters" were "completers" whose vital tasks included "socializing children" and inspiring "the brothers." Day-to-day struggle, sustained theoretical work, and the influence of Tayari Kwa Salaam and other Ahidiana women spurred the New Orleans activist's evolution from hypermasculinism to antisexism. He now saw patriarchy as an element of capitalist hegemony. In a series of publications, he championed women's liberation as an essential component of human rights. While many Pan African nationalists denounced black feminists as race traitors, Salaam advocated a reconstruction of gender relations. "Instead of attacking black feminism," he declared in 1979, "we should be fanning the flames of struggle by heightening the anti-sexist critique of America and linking that critique with a critique of capitalism and racism."[5]

For a fleeting moment in the late 1970s, openness to reassessment and self-criticism seemed capable of transforming the black independent school movement. In summer 1977, 20 organizers of U.S. Pan African nationalist institutions visited China on a mission of political exploration and reflection. Brokered by the theorists of Ahidiana and the Friends of China Society, the trip was conceived as an intellectual exchange and an opportunity to observe the internal processes of "a revolutionary society." Participants included Kalamu Ya Salaam, Tayari Kwa Salaam, Haki Madhubuti, and Maulana Karenga, as well as activists from Philadelphia, New York, and other cities. The decision of the mostly orthodox Pan African nationalists to journey to the land of Mao surprised many observers. "Some in nationalist circles thought that we had sold out," Kalamu Ya Salaam later recalled. "Some in *Marxist* circles thought that we had crossed over."[6]

The trip held great potential as a catalyst for political re-evaluation. Though none of the delegation members were avowed leftists, they revered China as a traditional adversary of the West (despite the rapprochement of recent years), as a source of support for African anticolonial efforts (the nation's actual record on this score was decidedly mixed),[7] and as a revolutionary axis of the developing world. Many of the travelers had retreated from forthright Third Worldism in recent years. The three-week excursion helped restore international bonds and revive anticolonial sensibilities.

The African Americans toured Beijing, Shanghai, and other cities, visiting factories, communes, and schools; discussing foreign policy and socialist development with educators and Communist Party officials; and basking in the hospitality of their official hosts. Chinese schools emphasized productive labor and grooming successors for the revolution—principles that the black educators revered. The group met with black militant Robert F. Williams, the exiled North Carolina leader and armed self-defense advocate, who had lived for years in Cuba and China, and who was then visiting Beijing on a goodwill trip. This and other experiences helped puncture the isolationism of the African-American activists while reanimating radical solidarities. "When we argued the dual character of our oppression, i.e., racial and class," Karenga later recalled, "the Chinese did not deny the racial factor, only stressed that in the final analysis, class was determinative."[8]

In the end, however, the reunion with radical internationalism failed to mitigate the racial fundamentalism of Pan African nationalist education in the United States. The movement never abandoned its narrow ideological premises. Instead of prompting a reexamination of internal contradictions, the China tour reinforced the emphasis of the African-American delegates on "raising our children to be soldiers and warriors for our people" and convinced them that they were "on the right road to revolution."[9] By the early 1980s, internal transformation no

longer seemed desirable or necessary. Operators of many Pan African nationalist institutions continued to practice an inert politics of identity, unable to forge
an ethic of struggle relevant to the contemporary social crises of black America.

"Learning to Survive": Bourgeois Nationalism in the Age of Reagan

The post–civil rights era produced a new black middle class whose political
sensibilities represented major opportunities for Afrocentric schools. Many
upwardly mobile African Americans had absorbed the ideals of contemporary
black nationalism, even as they benefited from the social gains of the 1960s and
'70s. These professionals combined ambivalence toward integration with aversion to explicit separatism. They wished to expose their children to the popular
mores of black pride and awareness that they themselves had internalized during
the era of mass struggle.

Pan African nationalist educators recognized this population as an essential
constituency. Independent institutions of the Black Power era had largely served
working-class families. By the early 1980s, it was clear that a lingering aura of
militancy was preventing the establishments from enlarging their base and
avoiding obsolescence. A restyling was in order. Philadelphia's Nidhamu Sasa
reduced the use of Swahili in the classroom and implemented a battery of standardized tests. Brooklyn's Weusi Shule ("Black School") changed its name to the
Johnson Preparatory School. The Kubu Learning Center, another Philadelphia
operation, rechristened itself "The Lotus Academy." The Chad School of
Newark, New Jersey, adopted a "back to basics" academic approach and profes-
sionalized its staff, hiring more licensed instructors. Students at the establishment were encouraged to address one another as "brother" and "sister," but as a
visitor observed in 1982, few "obvious signs of black awareness" endured.[10]

Ahidiana also revamped its image. In the 1970s, the New Orleans school had
proclaimed its commitment to "raising warriors." By 1983, its brochures stressed
that upon graduation, its students "are able to excel and take their place at the
head of whatever public or private school they enter." Even Brooklyn's Uhuru Sasa
Shule mellowed. "Is our purpose to build a new nation or to survive within this
nation?" a 1980 parent handbook asked. "Could it be a combination of both: learn
to survive while developing skills that are essential for nation-building?"[11]

A milder profile helped some Afrocentric academies widen their clienteles.
Between the late '60s and the mid-'80s, enrollment at Newark's Chad School
leapt from 88 to 320 students. A 1986 survey circulated among parents at both
Chad and the Afrikan People's Action School in nearby Trenton, New Jersey,

yielded responses from a truck driver, an iron worker, and a secretary, as well as a physician, a realtor, an accountant, and other professionals. When asked why they had chosen a black independent school for their children, most respondents cited academic considerations like small classes, a personalized approach, and emphasis on basic skills, as well as factors like "cultural awareness" and "knowledge of black heritage."[12]

The moderate orientation of independent schools was not just an attempt to court a broader, more affluent constituency. The mainstream goals of Afrocentric education reflected contemporary black nationalism's basic political character. Divorced from its radical tendencies, the philosophy's entrepreneurial ethos prevailed. No longer preoccupied with training pupils to engender black America's "postcolonial" future or to render technical service to "the African world," the Council of Independent Black Institutions endeavored in 1986 simply to prepare "minority youth for the technologically sophisticated, capital intensive economy of the future."[13]

So long as the moral framework of the Nguzo Saba survived, such objectives were seen as compatible with the cultural imperatives of blackness. Some independent school operators viewed the movement's political adaptations as evidence of flexibility and growing sophistication. Indeed, politically moderate models of alternative education proved remarkably popular. By the late 1970s, a new breed of middle-class, African-American private school had emerged. These establishments shared some of the philosophical premises of their Pan African nationalist predecessors. They strove to transcend "dominant group culture," and they rejected the overtly accommodationist orientation of older black prep schools. Yet they were largely disconnected from the mass politics of Black Power and lacked both the rhetorical excesses and radical impulses of the movement.[14]

Such enterprises stressed "positive racial self-concept" and conventional academic success. Founded by black professionals rather than movement veterans, they promoted visions of a pluralistic society in which the cultivation of ethnic self-image and group identity could boost African-American achievement. These academies served a segment of the black middle class that rejected wholesale cultural assimilation yet desired for their children a comfortable and affirming passage to the mainstream.

Organizers of the part-time, kindergarten through grade 12 Patterson School in Harlem's elegant Sugar Hill section suggested that emphasis on "our rich African cultural and historical roots" could help prepare black children for individual achievement in the professions—a crucial metric, they believed, of racial progress. Chase Manhattan Bank (a longtime investor in apartheid South Africa) and other corporate sponsors of the school belonged to a business establishment eager to forge alliances with a growing, relatively prosperous black middle class; to frame "multiculturalism" as a corporate-friendly project; and to endorse the conciliatory political views that Patterson School founder Jamelle Patterson expressed in a 1976 parent newsletter: "As we have celebrated the 200th birthday of our nation—which highlighted the importance of heritage and encouraged the positive involvement of all our citizens—black parents and educators have turned anger and frustration into quiet and sober reassessment of the education of our youngsters."[15]

Such outlooks helped strengthen the rapprochement between capital and black identity politics. In the late 1970s and '80s, the 400-student Marcus Garvey Preschool and Elementary School of South-Central Los Angeles celebrated Kwanzaa, the great kings of Africa, and the Pan African ideal of worldwide black affinity. Urbane municipal and business elites now welcomed such themes as benign expressions of ethnic pride and as useful supplements to a cultural regimen of discipline and self-help. While earlier independent institutions had drawn the scrutiny of the FBI, the Marcus Garvey School was praised by the Los Angeles City Council for "tailoring educational techniques to meet the individual needs of each student."[16]

Bourgeois black nationalism equated private accumulation with group progress and hailed the elimination of barriers to individual African-American advancement. "Our children shouldn't have to work for others," a representative from Pasadena, California's Omowale Ujamaa Shule declared in 1981. "We want them to own their own businesses and to keep the money they make circulating inside the black community." Black youth were to undergo programs of cultural enrichment as part of their preparation to navigate the existing economic system. As operators of Nationhouse Watoto in Washington, DC, proclaimed, "The future of the world is one of cultural pluralism; a world where the prominent and powerful will be those who are uncompromising in projecting their culture, national identity and national agenda, and who speak with one voice."[17]

Despite its rhetoric of solidarity, bourgeois nationalism sought no basic transformation of social and economic relations, and generally distanced itself from the grassroots struggles of workers, women, and poor people. Its objective was psychological fortification, not mass mobilization or resistance. Indeed, its accommodationist logic served the interests of conservative forces that strove to harness the banal symbols of black unity and pride.

"An Unwavering Commitment": Independent Schools and Neoliberal Reform

The early 1980s witnessed a new convergence of Pan African nationalist educators and proponents of free market capitalism. Leaders of independent black institutions discovered that their long-standing critiques of public schools mirrored many of the themes of the educational reform movement promoted by the Reagan administration. In time, operators of some of the institutions forged a political kinship with neoliberal reformers intent on privatizing education.

Conservative opponents of public education found natural allies in black independent school proprietors. Since the community control battles of the late 1960s, organizers of the private institutions had condemned urban public education as a racist system that produced functional illiterates while subjecting students of color to "alien" curricula and values. Many Afrocentric educators continued to see inner-city public schools as sites of expropriation where the tax dollars of black and brown families were squandered on the salaries and benefits of incompetent instructors and administrators. Such perspectives complemented conservative visions of the public sector as a bloated and inept bureaucracy.[18]

For many free market advocates, the solution to chaotic and failing ghetto schools was the voucher system, a plan designed to furnish parents of schoolchildren with government-funded tuition certificates redeemable at public or private schools of their choice. Voucher experiments had long been linked to the Right; during the civil rights movement, southern state legislatures had used them to support "segregation academies," and President Nixon had made them a part of his efforts to mobilize opponents of busing. In the 1970s, some progressive activists had also touted voucher plans, seeing the programs as tools of democratic reform that could help black and Latino parents escape inferior, inner-city schools.[19]

After Reagan's 1980 election, conservatives increasingly viewed voucher proposals as a way to boost minority support for free market policies. Some parents of color accepted the central rationale for vouchers—the idea that they would enable innovative, private academies to compete for tuition funds that had been "monopolized" by ineffective public schools. Yet opponents of vouchers, including many parents and activists of color, charged that the programs would harm public education by further impoverishing underfunded urban districts. They saw such schemes as part of a larger assault on government services, organized labor, and the public sector itself.[20]

Vouchers were a major priority for a growing cohort of African-American conservatives, some of whom saw an opportunity to build alliances with Afrocentric schools. The Washington-based National Center for Neighborhood Enterprise (NCNE), a right-leaning black think tank, took the lead in promoting Reagan's "school choice" initiatives (including a "tuition tax credit" proposal) among proprietors of black private schools. Vouchers were a major component of the Republican strategy for wooing minority voters while fulfilling the neoliberal imperative of privatization. NCNE representatives framed voucher plans as an expression of the African-American self-help tradition and as a potential boon for cash-strapped Afrocentric schools. Building support for vouchers among Afrocentrists, conservatives recognized, would reinforce efforts to associate "choice" with black empowerment.[21]

In 1983, NCNE official Joan Davis Ratteray, a voucher advocate who believed public education had "outlived its usefulness," embarked on a cross-country trip in which she visited more than 40 minority-owned independent schools, most of them Afrocentric academies. Ratteray conducted a series of discussions with educators designed, in part, to bolster interest in voucher plans. The tour underscored the philosophical links between some black nationalists and traditional conservatives. Both parties resented state-mandated desegregation and centralized, highly regulated government bureaucracies. Both saw teachers unions as instruments of a complacent and profligate industry. Both viewed public schools as strongholds of liberal dogma and centers of mismanagement whose functions could be performed more effectively by private, specialized, neighborhood-based institutions.[22]

Many administrators and veterans of independent black institutions embraced the message of school choice. Anyim Palmer, founder of the powerful Marcus Garvey School in Los Angeles, praised vouchers as a way to increase the "competitiveness" of public education and ensure the autonomy of minority parents. John Churchville of Philadelphia's defunct Freedom Library Day School was more emphatic: the programs, he argued, would encourage reform and force urban school districts "up off their duff." Such views were hardly universal; some Pan African nationalists saw vouchers as right-wing schemes to erode the tax base of urban schools. NCNE's winter 1983 "Give a Child a Choice" conference, a gathering designed to build a minority constituency for voucher plans, nevertheless drew organizers from Omowale Ujamaa of Pasadena, California, and other black institutions, as well as representatives from American Indian "survival" schools and Chicano heritage academies.[23]

Because most contemporary voucher plans eventually stalled, the tuition credit system became an enduring source of neither funding nor controversy for black independent schools. In the 1990s, however, a more widespread reform left Afrocentric educators deeply divided. Early in the decade, "charter schools"— or independent academies authorized by individual states to operate as public schools—began proliferating in the United States. During the preceding quarter century, Pan African nationalist institutions had faced police and intelligence agents, state authorities, city inspectors, and the Internal Revenue Service. Few of these threats proved as destructive as the schism that ensued when several of the schools opted to convert to charters.

Aisha Shule of Detroit was among the first Afrocentric academies to gain access to public funds by successfully applying for a charter. Launched in the

1970s, the pre-kindergarten through grade eight enterprise had expanded to 90 students by 1995. After becoming a charter under Michigan guidelines the following year, the institution's enrollment more than doubled. The tax dollars that charter status provided enabled the establishment to purchase computers, increase teacher salaries, and offer more African-American students an alternative to overcrowded, underperforming schools. The Nsoroma Institute of Highland Park, Michigan, experienced a similar turnaround. Before receiving a charter in 1997, the school had operated hand-to-mouth, with many of its families struggling to afford its relatively modest, $2,730 annual tuition. Once granted a charter, Nsoroma became a far more viable institution. As an administrator at the establishment assured black independent school colleagues, "Our commitment to nationbuilding remains unwavering."[24]

Many Pan African nationalists were unconvinced. Like the older conflict over vouchers, the charter issue revived long-standing debates about the true meaning of black autonomy. Traditionalists like Hannibal Afrik of Chicago's Shule Ya Watoto saw the struggle to remain largely independent of government agencies and corporations as an essential principle of black nationality. "You cannot rely on aid and comfort from your enemy," he insisted in a 1997 position paper. Public funding would undermine the quest to "train Afrikan youth to become freedom fighters and nation-builders." Theorists from Trenton, New Jersey's Afrikan People's Action School agreed. Reliance on "outside assistance" as a primary funding source, they asserted, would breed dependency and encourage "intellectual isolation from the black masses and cultural arrogance to their needs and attitudes."[25]

The more influential voice in contemporary discussions of African Americans and school "restructuring" belonged to Howard Fuller. As Owusu Sadaukai, Fuller had presided over Greensboro, North Carolina's Malcolm X Liberation University. In the years after the school's 1973 demise, he had returned to Milwaukee and reverted to his birth name. In the late 1970s and '80s, Fuller held several academic, administrative, and municipal government posts. He also led a major campaign against police brutality and a struggle to resist a desegregation plan that threatened to strip Milwaukee's North Division High School of its distinctive black character. In 1987, he promoted a controversial proposal to create the city's first independent black school district. In the 1990s, he briefly served as superintendent of Milwaukee's public schools before emerging as one of the country's most visible proponents of educational vouchers.

Over the course of almost four decades, Fuller had undergone an extraordinary transformation from integrationist to black nationalist to Pan Africanist to Marxist-Leninist to advocate of free market educational reform. As he had entered his 50s, still grappling with the dilemmas of race and class, he had come to see "school choice" as a pragmatic way to win greater freedom and opportunity for African-American children. A charismatic spokesman with impressive activist credentials, Fuller was able to leverage black nationalist themes on behalf of a cause cherished by the Right. "We must heed Malcolm X's words and declare that our children must be educated 'by any means necessary,'" he declared in 2002.[26]

Despite the view of such ideological changes as inevitable adaptations, the rightward drift of some independent school organizers after the 1970s constituted a stunning reversal of the movement's liberatory impulses. At the heart of Black Power's struggle for parallel black institutions was the concept of prefigurative politics, the idea that alternative social and cultural models could help demonstrate the advantages of a fundamentally reordered society. The shift of movement veterans to accepting the profit motive as an agent of reform and the marketplace as the arbiter of social provisions signified more than acquiescence; it represented defeat.

In the final analysis, charter schools and voucher plans mainly benefited corporate interests and the forces of privatization. They could not answer questions of dignity, democracy, and citizenship inherent in struggles for decent education as a human right. As Uhuru Sasa's Jitu Weusi noted amid the charter school debates of the 1990s, the search for collective social solutions was incompatible with the private plunder of public funds. "Black schools have to realize the situation they're in and not play into the hands of those who are trying to do away with public education," Weusi cautioned in 1997, "because those are our children."[27]

"Vehicles of the Masses": Progressive Adaptation in the Post–Civil Rights Era

In some ways, the institutional thrust of Black Power did not fully materialize until the 1990s. While Pan African nationalist schools of the early 1970s had numbered in the dozens, by 1991, roughly 350 Afrocentric academies existed nationwide, and several major public school systems had adopted curricula and other programs inspired by the philosophy. Though such initiatives often proved controversial, black nationalist educational themes gained a measure of acceptance and even respectability as expressions of "multiculturalism" and "diversity."[28]

Yet neither public nor private Afrocentric institutions offered robust models of political opposition or social change. Operators of the schools continued to deploy some of the radical language of the 1960s and '70s. Some imagined their enterprises as instruments of "Revolutionary Pan Afrikan Nationalism," as alternatives to the decadence and materialism of mainstream America, and as critical sites of resistance. "African Centered Education Can Smash White Supremacy" one of the movement's partisans proclaimed in 1993.[29] However, few contemporary manifestations of nationalism or Pan Africanism were rooted in grassroots or international struggles. Fewer still were guided by social theories directly relevant to the lives of poor and working-class African Americans.

Afrocentric pedagogy reflected Black Power's emphasis on psychocultural conversion. As Sonia R. Jarvis notes, "Afrocentric curriculum advocates accept *Brown*'s premise that stigma is the greatest obstacle to black students' educational opportunities."[30] The principles and practices of anti-imperialism, anticapitalism, and Third Worldism were lost, or had grown so feeble that they lacked significance. No viable critique of political economy remained. Indeed, few of the lessons about class, gender, and power relations that Pan African nationalism had gleaned from the postcolonial world—and from the rank-and-file inhabitants of black America—appeared to be meaningfully represented in the curricula, programmatic life, or political imaginary of most modern Afrocentric schools. In their patriarchy, emphasis on racial personality, and static, essentialist conceptions of Africa, the institutions more closely recalled the Garveyite and Nation of Islam formations of the early to mid-twentieth century than they did the radical establishments of the 1960s and '70s.[31]

Of course, not all Black Power enterprises succumbed to provincialism in the postsegregation era. For a few independent schools, the aftermath of the age of mass protest brought both adversity and sustained, radical adaptation and growth. Northern California's Oakland Community School and the Black and Proud Liberation School of Jackson, Mississippi, continued to practice a resilient, progressive politics that creatively addressed the material realities of exploited black communities while embodying the humane, anticapitalist relations envisioned by their founders. Oakland Community School and Black and Proud refashioned some of Black Power's essential cultural elements, providing counterexamples of social relevance and vitality amid the political regression and alienation of the 1970s and early '80s.

The Oakland Community School began as the Intercommunal Youth Institute, an outgrowth of the Black Panther Party's liberation schools and "survival programs." By the time the institute appeared in 1971, the Panthers were reeling from internal crises of leadership and political direction combined with intense external pressures. The five-year-old party had been the target of a massive and brutal campaign of state repression; many of its most talented leaders were behind bars, exiled, or dead. The battered cadre that remained struggled to regroup while sustaining the organization's service projects, activities that strove to meet the basic needs of residents of black central cities. Fragmented and weakened, the party labored to shed the paramilitary image of its past.[32]

Oakland, the Panthers' birthplace, resurfaced as the center of the group's political and social efforts. It was there that a small group of Panthers, including parents and teachers who wished to shield their children from the "harshness and cruelty" of inner-city public schools, began planning a community institution for chronically undereducated, poor and working-class black youth. The nascent school occupied private homes and storefronts before the Panthers purchased its permanent quarters: a former church building with 25 classrooms, located in the heart of Oakland's black community.

The Intercommunal Youth Institute served not only children of party members but also scores of youngsters who had been labeled "troublemakers" and forced out of local public schools. Initially led by Brenda Bay, the institute grew from 40 to 100 students, ages 2 to 11. (Older children were later enrolled as well.) Ericka Huggins replaced Bay as director in early 1974. Huggins was a party veteran whose husband had been killed by members of the rival US organization in 1969. She herself had been jailed in connection with a Panther-related murder in New Haven, Connecticut, before being acquitted in 1971. A gifted theorist, Huggins viewed public schools as factories designed to instill capitalist values, stifle free development, and perpetuate the status quo; in their present form, she argued, they would "never meet the needs of black and oppressed people." Under her leadership, the institute, renamed the Oakland Community School (OCS) in 1975, forged a powerful alternative, building an enrollment of 160—most of it drawn from outside the party—while constructing a vibrant model of emancipatory education.[33]

The primary task of OCS was to equip alienated children with survival skills, including the capacity "to think in an analytical fashion in order to develop creative solutions to the problems we are faced with." Party leaders stressed that their aim was not to transmit a received doctrine; they took pains to distinguish OCS from earlier Black Panther liberation schools, many of which had delivered heavy doses of rhetoric. The Intercommunal Youth Institute had originally offered "Ideology of the Black Panther Party" as a core subject. By the time of its name change, OCS had abandoned the course, a sign that the school had positively resolved the tension between indoctrination and liberation that had once shaped Panther pedagogy. Barriers between students and teachers were minimized. Youngsters were encouraged to openly critique all areas of the school and to help devise daily menus and lesson plans. "We try to teach the children, in essence, how to think as opposed to what to think," Black Panther Party Chairman Elaine Brown explained.[34]

Pupils ages 14 and younger discussed Watergate and other current events. Eight- and nine-year-olds were exposed to political theory. ("What is a contradiction?" they were asked.) Students learned what might be described as a "people's math": "We have one pie to divide among eight comrades," one test stated. "What fraction of the pie does each comrade get?" Curricular offerings included martial arts, yoga, and meditation. Youngsters performed renditions of the score from the Blaxploitation film *Shaft*. They created their own plays. They read classics like *Animal Farm*. They studied Harriet Tubman and Julius Caesar, Ethiopia and the British Empire, China before and after 1949, France before and after 1789, the Amazon River and the Aegean Sea, the koala bear and the African elephant, the temperature at the poles and along the equator.[35]

Supported by federal and private funds, the school played a major role in the community. It provided students with three free, hot meals a day, as well as free medical services and family counseling. It served as a conduit to the George Jackson People's Free Health Clinic in nearby Berkeley, and it spawned awareness groups like the Oakland Community School Committee Against Infant Mortality. The Community Learning Center in which it was housed, also a Panther facility, offered a number of cultural and social services. Such activities seemed mundane when compared to the armed exploits that had shaped the party's image in the late 1960s. Some critics accused the organization of reformism and "working within the system."[36]

But by offering a viable counterinstitution amid the underdevelopment of the urban core, OCS taught in practical ways the principles of democratic participation and socialism. "The children cannot become full human beings without a collective experience," Huggins reminded OCS parents in a 1979 memo. While the school was overwhelmingly black, it conveyed communal values without resorting to racial dogma or essentialism. Its student body and faculty included Asians, Latinos, and a few white people, and it regarded itself as "a place where our differences are minimized and our similarities blossom." Long the last remaining Black Panther program, OCS dissolved in 1982, a victim of financial crises, hostile authorities, and the strange fusion of moribundity and chaos that marked the party's waning years. Yet the school had helped illuminate a future for which many staff, parents, students, and residents remained willing to fight.[37]

The commitment to democratic, grassroots activity that defined OCS also shaped the Black and Proud Liberation School. Black and Proud was an arm of the Jackson Human Rights Project (JHRP), an effort by radical activists to organize the poor, African-American residents of Georgetown, a depressed section of Jackson, Mississippi. Georgetown was an enclave of powerlessness and police violence in which none of the requisite provisions of dignity—from decent jobs and housing to humane schools and medical services—were in adequate supply. Howard Spencer, a former Tougaloo College student activist and a principal force behind JHRP, saw "individual and group loss of identity and pride" as a key factor in the community's marginalization. He helped launch the JHRP in 1968, hoping to address Georgetown's dearth of social services while "providing the people with a knowledge of their true history and heritage."[38]

JHRP created several survival programs, establishing a poor people's medical project and emergency welfare services. By 1969, Black and Proud had emerged as the organization's central initiative. Originally Georgetown Liberation School, the venture began as an alternative to unjust desegregation; after witnessing the ferocious response of some white Jacksonians to the prospect of racially mixed schools, some African-American parents vowed to spare their children the trauma of facing hostile teachers on remote campuses. But as JHRP absorbed the ideals of black self-determination and self-definition, Black and Proud embraced a more affirmative mission. Spencer, its director, hoped to equip dropouts, unwed mothers, and other poor youths with technical skills and "knowledge of self." In time, Black and Proud would provide a vehicle for transmitting "the academic and technical skills necessary to advance the world struggle against colonialism and imperialism."[39]

Initially an after-school and Saturday program for children ages 7 to 15, Black and Proud became a full-time operation with five staffers. From 13 youngsters gathered in a dilapidated house, it evolved into an enterprise that served 170 students in a modest, two-classroom facility sustained by grants from church groups and monthly tuition fees of $38. Courses covered English and math as well as history, geography, farming, sewing, first aid, leather craft, African dance, drumming, and French or Swahili. Kindergarteners learned how the ocean gets its color. Third graders studied Fannie Lou Hamer and Frederick Douglass.[40]

What truly distinguished Black and Proud were its functions as a parallel authority—an alternative model of governance and communal living. The institution distributed welfare rights information and provided free transportation to and from welfare offices. Its staffers formed block organizations and youth groups, and linked parents and other residents to JHRP's free medical services and clothing program. In 1975, the school opened a modest clothing factory and retail outlet, operations that had evolved from a sewing cooperative of welfare recipients and the unemployed. The businesses hired jobless locals while advancing JHRP's efforts to create a miniature planned economy in which the production and distribution of goods served the needs of destitute families rather than the imperatives of corporate profit.

The outlet sold inexpensive dashikis and maxi dresses. Much of the proceeds went to the school's cooperative farm, which provided fresh, organic vegetables to the children of Black and Proud and to community members, especially the elderly, pregnant, sick, and disabled. In turn, residents participated in the work teams that labored on the farm. Spencer viewed such programs as "vehicles of the masses" that could gradually "cut off dependence in respective areas of human need."[41]

Black and Proud was not without contradictions. Its commingling of cultural nationalist and Marxist-Leninist themes produced an awkward ideological marriage. At times, its valorization of poor people "doing for themselves and not having to depend on the system" echoed conservative discourses of "self-help." Yet Black and Proud's concept of self-reliance never denied the responsibility of the state to provide dignified employment or reasonable income for those who had been systematically undereducated and then abandoned by the economy. Indeed, the school's multiple services exposed the stinginess of the existing social wage and the chronic failures of capitalist society. At a time when standardization and "accountability" were supplanting participatory democracy and critical thinking as guiding values of educational reform, Black and Proud remained a center of dialectical analysis, internationalism, and rigorous engagement with social theory. Its Pan Africanist activities—study groups, rallies on behalf of Southern Africa, and Spencer's travel to Mozambique—complemented its local work on behalf of meaningful social change.[42]

Over the years, Black and Proud experienced fewer victories than defeats. Its staff members faced harassment by reactionary forces within Jackson (persecution by authorities forced the school to relocate twice in its first year and a half of operation) while enduring a vicious FBI campaign of misinformation and sabotage. By the late 1970s, the institution was too impoverished to repair or replace the rotting floors of its plant. The regressive economic policies of the early 1980s only exacerbated the school's financial plight.[43] Yet there were signs of success as well. Among them was Hattie, the precocious Black and Proud third grader who chronicled the school's 1977 graduation for a Jackson newspaper. As she noted:

> The graduation ceremonies were attended by approximately 35 parents with one family absent and one family with four generations present. The school colors are red, black, green and yellow. Red is for blood; black is for culture; green is for land and yellow is for the sun that gives energy. The Black and Proud school teaches pride, manners and respect for elders. Their waiting list consists of 21 students. The class motto is *A Luta Continua* (struggles continue).[44]

NOTES

Introduction

1. Otto Lindenmeyer, *Of Black America: Black History: Lost, Stolen, or Strayed* (New York: Avon Books, 1970), 229–237.
2. "Lost-Stolen-Strayed," *Los Angeles Sentinel*, June 27, 1968, B5; George Gent, "Television: Exit Darkies, Enter Blacks," *New York Times*, July 3, 1968, 71; Gent, "Show on Negroes Arouses Viewers," *New York Times*, July 4, 1968, 41; Ed Dowling, "How to Survive the Schoolmarms," *New Republic*, July 27, 1968, 21; Toni Cade, "The Children Who Get Cheated," in *Deprivation in America*, ed. Victor B. Ficker and Herbert S. Graves (Beverly Hills, CA: Glencose Press, 1971), 88; O. Musgrave Coombs, "Books Noted," *Negro Digest*, November 1968, 75; Lawrence Laurent, " 'Black America' Series Shatters Clichés," *Washington Post*, July 4, 1968, F7.
3. California Association for Afro-American Education and Nairobi College, "The Independent Black Institution," in *African Congress: A Documentary of the First Modern Pan-African Congress*, ed. Amiri Baraka (New York: William Morrow & Company, 1972), 285.
4. For a discussion of "black consciousness" in the context of Black Power, see Waldo E. Martin, *No Coward Soldiers: Black Cultural Politics in Postwar America* (Cambridge, MA: Harvard University Press, 2005), 36.
5. For a discussion of 1960s freedom schools, see John Dittmer, *Local People: The Struggle for Civil Rights in Mississippi* (Champaign: University of Illinois Press, 1994), 242–261; Clarence Taylor, *Knocking at Our Own Door: Milton A. Galamison and the Struggle to Integrate New York City Schools* (New York: Columbia University Press, 1997). For a discussion of Afrocentric education and ideology, see Diane Pollard and Cheryl Ajirotutu, eds., *African-Centered Schooling in Theory and Practice* (Westport, CT: Greenwood, 2000); Algernon Austin, *Achieving Blackness: Race, Black Nationalism and Afrocentrism in the Twentieth Century* (New York: New York University Press, 2006); Patricia Hill Collins, *From Black Power to Hip Hop: Racism, Nationalism, and Feminism* (Philadelphia: Temple University Press, 2006).
6. For a discussion of the nineteenth- and early twentieth-century origins of this idea, see Wilson Jeremiah Moses, *The Golden Age of Black Nationalism, 1850–1925* (New York: Oxford University Press, 1978). For rich and extensive discussions of independent educational institutions in the Black Power era, see Martha Biondi, *The Black Revolution on Campus* (Berkeley: University of California Press, 2012); Komozi Woodard, *A Nation Within A Nation: Amiri Baraka (LeRoi Jones) and Black Power Politics* (Chapel Hill: University of North Carolina Press, 1999); Richard D. Benson, II, *Fighting For Our Place in the Sun: Malcolm X and the Radicalization of the Black Student Movement, 1960–1973* (New York: Peter Lang, 2015); Kwasi Konadu, *A View From the East: Black Cultural Nationalism and Education in New York City* (Syracuse, NY: Syracuse University Press, 2009).
7. In the mid-1970s, for example, a coalition of Pan African nationalist institutions in Brooklyn, New York, enrolled about 650 mostly grade-school students, while New York City's Catholic

Archdiocese alone enrolled more than 12,000 black elementary school students. (Gladstone Modele Clarke, "New York Family Schools: Head Start for Black Children?" unpublished 1979 essay, KKP, INP.)

8. Frantz Fanon, *The Wretched of the Earth* (New York: Grove Press, 1963).

9. Institute of the Black World, ed., *Education and Black Struggle: Notes from the Colonized World* (Atlanta: Institute of the Black World, 1974), 31. See, for example, Ama Mazama and Garvey Musumunu, *African Americans and Homeschooling: Motivations, Opportunities and Challenges* (New York: Routledge, 2013). See also M. A. Farber, "'Africa Centered' School Plan is Rooted in 60's Struggles," *New York Times*, February 5, 1991, B1–B2.

10. Peniel E. Joseph, ed., *Neighborhood Rebels: Black Power at the Local Level* (New York: Palgrave Macmillan, 2010).

11. Vincent Harding "Fighting the 'Mainstream' Seen for 'Black Decade,'" *New York Times*, January 12, 1970, 63.

12. Alex Willingham, "Ideology and Politics: Their Status in Afro-American Social Theory," in *Race, Politics, and Culture: Critical Essays on the Radicalism of the 1960s*, ed. Adolph Reed, Jr. (Westport, CT: Greenwood Press, 1986), 24.

13. Amilcar Cabral, "Connecting the Struggles: An Informal Talk with Black Americans," in *Return to the Source: Selected Speeches by Amilcar Cabral*, ed. Africa Information Service (New York: Monthly Review Press, 1973), 90.

14. Nikhil Pal Singh, ed., *Climbin' Jacob's Ladder: The Black Freedom Movement Writings of Jack O'Dell* (Berkeley: University of California Press, 2010), 53; Robin D. G. Kelley, *Freedom Dreams: The Black Radical Imagination* (Boston: Beacon Press, 2002).

15. Here I have in mind a dissident politics of culture, not the pluralistic "cultural citizenship" associated with multiculturalism. For the latter, see Renato Rosaldo, "Cultural Citizenship and Educational Democracy," *Cultural Anthropology* 9 (1994): 402–411.

16. Thomas J. Sugrue, *Sweet Land of Liberty: The Forgotten Struggle for Civil Rights in the North* (New York: Random House, 2008), 449–492.

17. Milton A. Galamison, "Educational Values and Community Power," *Freedomways*, Winter 1968, 313.

18. Harry Morgan, *Historical Perspectives on the Education of Black Children* (Westport, CT: Praeger, 1995); James M. McPherson, *The Abolitionist Legacy: From Reconstruction to the NAACP* (Princeton, NJ: Princeton University Press, 1975), 196; James D. Anderson, *The Education of Blacks in the South, 1860-1935* (Chapel Hill: University of North Carolina Press, 1988), 104–105; Heather Andrea Williams, *Self-Taught: African-American Education in Slavery and Freedom* (Chapel Hill: University of North Carolina, 2005); Steven Hahn, "To Build a New Jerusalem," in *Teach Freedom: Education for Liberation in the African-American Tradition*, ed. Charles M. Payne and Carol Sills Strickland (New York: Teachers College, 2008), 16–17; Vanessa Siddle Walker, *Their Highest Potential: An African American School Community in the Segregated South* (Chapel Hill: University of North Carolina Press, 1996); David S. Cecelski, *Along Freedom Road: Hyde County, North Carolina, and the Fate of Black Schools in the South* (Chapel Hill: University of North Carolina Press, 1994); C. Eric Lincoln, *The Black Muslims in America* (Boston: Beacon Press, 1961), 119–122.

19. Vincent P. Franklin, *The Education of Black Philadelphia: The Social and Educational History of a Minority Community, 1900-1950* (Philadelphia: University of Pennsylvania Press, 1979); Jack Dougherty, *More Than One Struggle: The Evolution of Black School Reform in Milwaukee* (Chapel Hill: University of North Carolina Press, 2004); Matthew J. Countryman, *Up South: Civil Rights and Black Power in Philadelphia* (Philadelphia: University of Pennsylvania Press, 2006); Dionne Danns, *Something Better for Our Children: Black Organizing in Chicago Public Schools, 1963-1971* (New York: Routledge, 2003); Adina Back, "'Exposing the Whole Segregation Myth': The Harlem Nine and New York City's School Desegregation Battles," in *Freedom North: Black Freedom Struggles Outside the South, 1940-1980*, ed. Jeanne Theoharis and Komozi Woodard (New York: Palgrave Macmillan, 2003), 65–91; Jeanne Theoharis, "Alabama on Avalon: Rethinking the Watts Uprising and the Character of Black Protest in Los Angeles," in *The Black Power Movement: Rethinking the Civil Rights—Black Power Era*, ed. Peniel E. Joseph (New York: Routledge, 2006), 27–54; Jim Haskins, *Diary of a Harlem Schoolteacher* (New York: Grove Press, 1970); Ernest W. Chambers, "We Have Marched,

We Have Cried, We Have Prayed," *Ebony*, April 1968, 29–38; Inner City Parents Council, "Detroit Schools—A Blueprint for Change," *Liberator*, September 1967, 8; "Thought Stimulator #423: Schools as Prisons," Box 23, PWP, SCR; Preston Wilcox, "The Kids Will Decide—and More Power to Them," *Ebony*, August 1970, 136; Jerald E. Podair, *The Strike That Changed New York: Blacks, Whites, and the Ocean Hill-Brownsville Crisis* (New Haven, CT: Yale University Press, 2002), 134; "Proposal for McKissick Community School," 1970, CSP, ACC.

20. Podair, *The Strike That Changed New York*; Daniel H. Perlstein, *Justice, Justice: School Politics and the Eclipse of Liberalism* (New York: Peter Lang, 2004); William Ayers and Michael Klonsky, "Navigating a Restless Sea: The Continuing Struggle to Achieve a Decent Education for African American Youngsters in Chicago," *Journal of Negro History* 63 (1994): 13.
21. Sheryl McCarthy, "Black Parents Consider the Alternatives," *Village Voice*, August 29, 1977, 53; Thomas A. Johnson, "Black-Run Private Schools Lure Growing Numbers in New York," *New York Times*, April 5, 1980, 1, 23; William Overend, "Emergence of the Black Private School," *Los Angeles Times*, June 26, 1980, G1, G12–G15; Diana T. Slaughter and Deborah J. Johnson, *Visible Now: Blacks in Private Schools* (Westport, CT: Greenwood Press, 1988); Black Child Development Institute, *Black Children Just Keep on Growing: Alternative Curriculum Models for Young Black Children* (Washington, DC: Black Child Development Institute, 1977); Allen Graubard, *Free the Children: Radical Reform and the Free School Movement* (New York: Pantheon Books, 1972); Ronald & Beatrice Gross, eds., *Radical School Reform* (New York: Simon & Schuster, 1969); Kenneth W. Haskins, "A Black Perspective on Community Control," *Inequality in Education*, November 1973, 27.
22. Ponchitta Pierce, "Street Academies: New Way to Reach Ghetto Dropout," *Ebony*, August 1967, 158–162; Larry Cuban, *How Teachers Taught: Constancy and Change in American Classrooms, 1890-1990* (New York: Teachers College Press, 1993), 175–176; V. Lawson Bush, "Independent Black Institutions in America: A Rejection of Schooling, an Opportunity for Education," *Urban Education* 32 (1997): 98–116.
23. Julie L. Davis, *Survival Schools: The American Indian Movement and Community Education in the Twin Cities* (Minneapolis: University of Minnesota Press, 2013); Guadalup San Miguel, *Chicana/o Struggles for Education: Activism in the Community* (Houston: University of Houston, 2013); Johanna Fernandez, *When the World Was Their Stage: A History of the Young Lords Party, 1968-1974* (Princeton, NJ: Princeton University Press, forthcoming); Mark Lai, *Becoming Chinese American: A History of Communities and Institutions* (Lanham, MD: Rowman & Littlefield, 2004), 282–284; Daniel J. Elazar, "The National-Cultural Movement in Hebrew Education in the Mississippi Valley," in *Hebrew in America: Perspectives and Prospects*, ed. Alan L. Mintz (Detroit: Wayne State University Press, 1993), 129–154.
24. "Black Education," *Black News*, December 10, 1970, 8; June 7, 1972, Kasisi Jitu Weusi to Dear Brothers and Sisters, Box 18, PWP, SCR.
25. "Council of Independent Black Institutions: Summary from 1st Work Meeting," 1972 pamphlet, JAL, UMI.
26. Peniel E. Joseph, *Waiting 'Til the Midnight Hour: A Narrative History of Black Power in America* (New York: Henry Holt, 2006), 260; Clayborne Carson, *In Struggle: SNCC and the Black Awakening of the 1960s* (Cambridge, MA: Harvard University Press, 1981), 265, 299, 306; Hasan Kwame Jeffries, *Bloody Lowndes: Civil Rights and Black Power in Alabama's Black Belt* (New York: New York University Press, 2009), 213; Fanon Che Wilkins, "The Making of Black Internationalists: SNCC and Africa Before the Launching of Black Power, 1960-1965," *Journal of African American History* 92 (2007): 469; Fanon Che Wilkins, "'In the Belly of the Beast': Black Power, Anti-Imperialism, and the African Liberation Solidarity Movement, 1968-1975" (PhD diss., New York University, 2001). Also see James Forman, *The Making of Black Revolutionaries* (New York: Macmillan, 1972); Cleveland Sellers, *The River of No Return: The Autobiography of a Black Militant and the Life and Death of SNCC* (New York: William Morrow, 1973); Faith S. Holsaert et al., eds., *Hands on the Freedom Plow: Personal Accounts by Women in SNCC* (Champaign: University of Illinois Press, 2010).
27. See Max Elbaum, *Revolution in the Air: Sixties Radicals Turn to Lenin, Mao and Che* (New York: Verso, 2002); Roderick Bush, *The End of White World Supremacy: Black Internationalism and the Problem of the Color Line* (Philadelphia: Temple University, 2009);

Brenda Gayle Plummer, *In Search of Power: African Americans in the Era of Decolonization, 1956-1974* (New York: Cambridge University Press, 2013); Nikhil Pal Singh, *Black Is a Country: Race and the Unfinished Struggle for Democracy* (Cambridge, MA: Harvard University Press, 2004).

28. Africa Information Service, "Mozambique: The Struggle Continues," *Black Scholar*, October 1973, 44–51.

29. See Malcolm X, "Statement of the Organization of Afro-American Unity," in *Let Nobody Turn Us Around: An African American Anthology*, ed. Manning Marable and Leith Mullings (Lanham, MD: Rowman & Littlefield, 2009), 417. For further discussion of the quest to remake African-American identity, see Clare Corbould, *Becoming African Americans: Black Public Life in Harlem, 1919-1939* (Cambridge, MA: Harvard University Press, 2009); Austin, *Achieving Blackness*.

30. Council of Independent Black Institutions, "Planning a New Institution: A Conference Call," KLC, INP; "The Al-Karim School," 1972 pamphlet, Box 1, IIE, CUK; Lula Strickland-Abuwi, "Cush Campus School: 20 Years of Curriculum of Inclusion," *New York Amsterdam News*, November 23, 1991, 9; "New School for Blacks Opens Fall Registration," *New York Amsterdam News*, September 28, 1968, 27; "Carson Quits Core," *New York Amsterdam News*, October 12, 1968, 26; Elombe Brath, "A Salute to Abubadika Sonny Carson: A Freedom Fighter Against All Odds," *Everybody's*, January–February 2003, 20.

31. Paulo Freire, *Pedagogy of the Oppressed* (New York: Herder & Herder, 1970); Julius K. Nyerere, *Freedom and Socialism/Uhuru na Ujamaa* (London: Oxford University Press, 1968), 267–290.

32. Diane Nash, "Black Woman Views Genocidal War in Vietnam," *Black Liberator*, May 1969, 2; Michelle Wallace, "Erased, Debased, and Encased: The Dynamics of African Educational Colonization in America," *College English*, April 1970, 671–681; "Cuba Under Castro," *SNCC Newsletter*, May 1967, Box 3, SCLS, SUS; "Education in Mozambique," *African World*, June 16, 1973; James Turner, "Universal Education and Nation-Building in Africa," *Journal of Black Studies*, September 1971, 3–27; Africa Information Service, "Mozambique: The Struggle Continues," 44–52.

33. "Tanzanian Education System," *African World*, September 16, 1972, 14; "Tanzania Secondary School Seeks: Education for Self-Reliance," *African World*, February 5, 1972, 11; Owusu Sadaukai, "Inside Liberated Mozambique," *African World*, February 5, 1972, 8.

34. Sellers, *The River of No Return*, 167; H. Rap Brown (Jamil Abdullah al-Amin), *Die Nigger Die! A Political Biography* (Chicago: Lawrence Hill Books, 2002), 39; Stokely Carmichael, "Toward Black Liberation," *Massachusetts Review*, Autumn 1966, 649.

35. F. Nunes, "The Anti-Poverty Hoax," *Freedomways*, Winter 1970, 24; Harold Cruse, *The Crisis of the Negro Intellectual* (New York: William Morrow, 1967), 93; Ralph H. Metcalf, Jr., "Chicago Model Cities and Neocolonization," *Black Scholar*, April 1970, 23–30; Leila O. Evans, "Neo-Colonialism and Development of the Black Ghetto: Model Cities," *Black Lines*, Fall 1970. For an account of how urbanites constructed "alternative models" of revitalized city centers in the 1960s and '70s, see Mandi Isaacs Jackson, *Model City Blues: Urban Space and Organized Resistance in New Haven* (Philadelphia: Temple, 2008).

36. Sugrue, *Sweet Land of Liberty*, 334; Singh, *Black Is a Country*, 192; Manuel Castells, *The City and the Grassroots: A Cross-Cultural Theory of Urban Social Movements* (Berkeley: University of California Press, 1983), 49–53; J. H. O'Dell, "The July Rebellions and the 'Military State,'" *Freedomways*, Fall 1967, 295; Kenn M. Freeman, "The Colonized of North America," *Soulbook*, Winter 1965–1966, 308; "Proposal for McKissick Community School," Box 11, Folder 9, CSP, ACC.

37. Derrick Morrison, "By Any Means Necessary," *Militant*, February 4, 1972, 9.

38. For other valuable discussions of contemporary black institution building, see Alondra Nelson, *Body and Soul: The Black Panther Party and the Fight Against Medical Discrimination* (Minneapolis: University of Minnesota, 2011); Derrick E. White, *The Challenge of Blackness: The Institute of the Black World and Political Activism in the 1970s* (Gainesville: University Press of Florida, 2012); James Smethurst, *The Black Arts Movement: Literary Nationalism in the 1960s and 1970s* (Chapel Hill: University of North Carolina Press, 2005). For more on the politics of Black Power and independent education, see Maisha T. Fisher, *Black Literate Lives:*

Historical and Contemporary Perspectives (New York: Routledge, 2008); Austin, *Achieving Blackness*; Dougherty, *More Than One Struggle*; Devin Fergus, *Liberalism, Black Power and the Making of American Politics, 1965–1980* (Athens: University of Georgia Press, 2009); Elizabeth Todd-Bredland, "To Reshape and Redefine Our World: African American Political Organizing for Education in Chicago, 1968-1988" (PhD diss., University of Chicago, 2010); Alphonso Pinkney, *Red Black and Green: Black Nationalism in the United States* (Cambridge: Cambridge University Press, 1979).

39. Bayard Rustin, "From Protest to Politics: The Future of the Civil Rights Movement," *Commentary*, February 1965, 25, quoted in Cynthia Griggs Fleming, *Soon We Will Not Cry: The Liberation of Ruby Doris Smith Robinson* (Lanham, MD: Rowman & Littlefield, 1996), 177.

40. See Heather Ann Thompson, *Whose Detroit? Politics, Labor, and Race in a Modern American City* (Ithaca, NY: Cornell University Press, 2001), on the League of Revolutionary Black Workers, and, in general, Judson L. Jeffries, ed., *On the Ground: The Black Panther Party in Communities Across America* (Jackson: University Press of Mississippi, 2010), on the Panther Survival Programs. *Rhythm Magazine* quoted in "Around Our Way—By Big Black," *Black News*, September 26, 1970, 10.

41. The African-American theorist who appears to have contemplated this question most extensively is Jack O'Dell, the radical *Freedomways* editor. See Singh, ed., *Climbin' Jacob's Ladder*.

42. Vladimir Ilyich Lenin, "Dual Power," in *Collected Works*, vol. 24 (London: Lawrence & Wishart, 1977), 38; Leon Trotsky, *History of the Russian Revolution* (Chicago: Haymarket Books, 2014 [1932]), 149–155; Nicos Ar Poulantzas, *State, Power, Socialism* (New York: Verso, 2000), 257–261; Singh, *Black Is a Country*, 205.

43. Steven Hahn, *A Nation Under Our Feet: Black Political Struggles in the Rural South from Slavery to the Great Migration* (Cambridge, MA: Belknap Press, 2003); Colin Grant, *Negro with a Hat: The Rise and Fall of Marcus Garvey and His Dream of Mother Africa* (New York: Oxford University Press, 2008); Grace and James Boggs, "The City Is the Black Man's Land," *Monthly Review*, April 1966, 39; Jack O'Dell, "On the Transition from Civil Rights to Civil Equality," in *Climbin' Jacob's Ladder*, 237; "African Congress Opens," *New York Amsterdam News*, September 5, 1970, 38.

44. See, for example, James Boggs, "Books Notes: Handbook of Revolutionary Warfare," *Negro Digest*, November 1969, 83.

45. For narratives of black nationalism as political and cultural disruption, see Diane Ravitch, *The Troubled Crusade: American Education, 1945-1980* (New York: Basic Books, 1983); David L. Kirp, *Just Schools: The Idea of Racial Equality in American Education* (Berkeley: University of California Press, 1982). For discussion of black nationalist, radical, and liberatory traditions in black educational thought, see Sandra Richards and Sidney J. Lemelle, "Pedagogy, Politics and Power: Antinomies of the Black Radical Tradition," in *Black Protest Thought and Education*, ed. William H. Watkins (New York: Peter Lang, 2005), 7; Noel S. Anderson and Haroon Kharem, eds., *Education as Freedom: African American Educational Thought and Activism* (Lanham, MD: Lexington Books, 1964).

46. For declension narratives of Black Power, see Carson, *In Struggle*; Charles M. Payne, *I've Got the Light of Freedom: The Organizing Tradition and the Mississippi Freedom Struggle* (Berkeley: University of California Press, 1995); David Garrow, *Bearing the Cross: Martin Luther King, Jr., and the Southern Christian Leadership Conference* (New York: HarperCollins, 1986). For alternative accounts, see Singh, *Black Is a Country*; Joseph, *Waiting 'Til the Midnight Hour*; Joseph, ed., *The Black Power Movement*, Robert O. Self, *American Babylon: Race and the Struggle for Postwar Oakland* (Princeton, NJ: Princeton University Press, 2003); Scot Brown, *Fighting for Us: Maulana Karenga, the US Organization and Black Cultural Nationalism* (New York: New York University Press, 2003); Countryman, *Up South*; Patrick Jones, *The Selma of the North: Civil Rights Insurgency in Milwaukee* (Cambridge, MA: Harvard University Press, 2009); Jeffries, *Bloody Lowndes*; Woodard, *A Nation Within a Nation*; Smethurst, *The Black Arts Movement*; Biondi, *The Black Revolution on Campus*.

47. William H. Chafe, *Civilities and Civil Rights Civilities and Civil Rights: Greensboro, North Carolina, and the Black Struggle for Freedom* (New York: Oxford University Press, 1980); Countryman, *Up South*; Yohuru Williams, *Black Politics/White Power: Civil Rights, Black*

Power, and the Black Panthers in New Haven (St. James, NY: Brandywine Press, 2000); Christina Greene, *Our Separate Ways: Women and the Black Freedom Movement in Durham, North Carolina* (Chapel Hill: University of North Carolina Press, 2005).

48. For examples of the declension narrative applied to African-American liberation pedagogy and education, see Daniel Perlstein, "Minds Stayed on Freedom: Politics, Pedagogy, and the African American Freedom Struggle," *American Educational Research Journal* 39 (2002): 249–277; Taylor, *Knocking at Our Own Door*; David B. Tyack, *The One Best System: A History of American Urban Education* (Cambridge, MA: Harvard University Press, 1974). For an alternative perspective, see Fannie Theresa Rushing, "Minds Still Stayed on Freedom? Reflections on Politics, Consensus, and Pedagogy in the African American Freedom Struggle," in *Teach Freedom*, 95–99.

49. Stokely Carmichael, "Pan-Africanism—Land and Power," *Black Scholar*, November 1969, 40.

50. Clayborne Carson, "African-American Leadership and Mass Mobilization," *Black Scholar*, Fall 2001, 4; Joe Walker, "The Blacks Are in Motion All Over This Land," *Muhammad Speaks*, September 27, 1968, 14. See also Daniel H. Watts, "Black Is Not Enough," *Liberator*, August 1968, 3.

51. See, for example, Todd Gitlin, *The Twilight of Common Dreams: Why America is Wracked by Culture Wars* (New York: Metropolitan Books, 1995).

52. See, for example, Robert C. Smith, *We Have No Leaders: African-Americans in the Post-Civil Rights Era* (Albany: State University of New York Press, 1996).

53. See James H. Meriwether, *Proudly We Can Be Africans: Black Americans and Africa, 1935-1961* (Chapel Hill: University of North Carolina Press, 2002); Kevin K. Gaines, *American Africans in Ghana: Black Expatriates and the Civil Rights Era* (Chapel Hill: University of North Carolina Press, 2006).

54. Dan Berger, ed., *The Hidden 1970s: Histories of Radicalism* (New Brunswick, NJ: Rutgers University Press, 2010); Aaron Brenner, Robert Brenner, and Cal Winslow, eds., *Rebel Rank and File: Labor Militancy and Revolt from Below During the Long 1970s* (London: Verso, 2010); White, *The Challenge of Blackness*; Stephen Tuck, " 'We Are Taking Up Where the Movement of the 1960s Left Off': The Proliferation and Power of African American Protest During the 1970s," *Journal of Contemporary History* 43 (2008): 641; Jacquelyn Dowd Hall, "The Long Civil Rights Movement and the Political Uses of the Past," *Journal of American History* 91 (2005): 1254.

55. Quoted in Sidney J. Lemelle, "The Politics of Cultural Existence: Pan-Africanism, Historical Materialism and Afrocentricity," *Race & Class* 35 (1993): 196; E. Frances White, " 'Africa on My Mind': Gender, Counter Discourse and African-American Nationalism," *Journal of Women's History* 2 (1990): 73–97.

56. See, for example, Eddie S. Glaude, ed., *Is It Nation Time? Contemporary Essays on Black Power and Black Nationalism* (Chicago: University of Chicago Press, 2002); Reed, ed., *Race, Politics, and Culture*; Sidney Lemelle and Robin D. G. Kelley, *Imagine Home: Class, Culture and Nationalism in the African Diaspora* (London: Verso, 1994); Michael O. West, William G. Martin, and Fanon Che Wilkins, eds., *From Toussaint to Tupac: The Black International Since the Age of Revolution* (Chapel Hill: University of North Carolina Press, 2009); Cedric Johnson, *From Revolutionaries to Race Leaders: Black Power and the Making of American Politics* (Minneapolis: University of Minnesota Press, 2007); Dean E. Robinson, *Black Nationalism in American Politics and Thought* (Cambridge: Cambridge University Press, 2001).

57. Greene, *Our Separate Ways*, 165.

58. See, for example, Fergus, *Liberalism, Black Power and the Making of American Politics, 1965-1980*; Noliwe Rooks, *White Money/Black Power: The Surprising History of African American Studies and the Crisis of Race in Higher Education* (Boston: Beacon Press, 2006); Johnson, *From Revolutionaries to Race Leaders*.

59. Baraka, ed., *African Congress*, 117. Ironically, marketers and commercial interests promoted a similar redefinition of revolution. See Adolph L. Reed, Jr., "Black Particularity Reconsidered," in *Is It Nation Time?*, 39.

60. James Jefferson Doughty, "A Historical Analysis of Black Education Focusing on the Contemporary Independent Black School Movement" (PhD diss., Ohio State University, 1973), 252–256.

61. For international outlooks on Black Power, see Nico Slate, ed. *Black Power Beyond Borders: The Global Dimensions of the Black Power Movement* (New York: Palgrave Macmillan, 2012); West et al., *From Toussaint to Tupac*; Robeson Taj Frazier, *The East Is Black: Cold War China in the Black Radical Imagination* (Durham, NC: Duke University Press, 2015); Bush, *The End of White World Supremacy*; Plummer, *In Search of Power*.

Chapter 1

1. George Jackson, *Soledad Brother* (New York: Bantam Books, 1970), 12. For related discussions of community control, black educational thought, and black self-determination, see Daniel H. Perlstein, *Justice, Justice: School Politics and the Eclipse of Liberalism* (New York: Peter Lang, 2004); Dionne Danns, *Something Better for Our Children: Black Organizing in Chicago Public Schools, 1963–1971*; Matthew Countryman, *Up South: Civil Rights and Black Power in Philadelphia* (Philadelphia: University of Pennsylvania Press, 2006); Jack Dougherty, *More Than One Struggle: The Evolution of Black School Reform in Milwaukee* (Chapel Hill: University of North Carolina Press, 2005); Bill Dahlk, *Against the Wind: African Americans and the Schools in Milwaukee, 1963–2000* (Milwaukee: Marquette University Press, 2010); Craig Steven Wilder, *A Covenant with Color: Race and Social Power in Brooklyn* (New York: Columbia University Press, 2000).
2. "Operation Shut-Down," pamphlet, January 21, 1965, Box 15, Folder "Boycott 1965," ASP, CUL; Harlem Youth Opportunities Unlimited, *Youth in the Ghetto* (New York: HARYOU, 1964), 188. For early references to "educational genocide," see Robert L. Levey, "Hint Defiance of Collins During Dr. King's Visit," *Boston Globe*, April 21, 1965, 7, and Ray Rogers, "Watts Group Charges School Discrimination," *Los Angeles Times*, June 8, 1967, 11.
3. Hope R. Stevens, "Economic Structure of the Harlem Community," *Freedomways*, Summer 1963, 343–354; Editors, "Harlem—A Community in Transition," *Freedomways*, Summer 1963, 262; "Junior High School 139: A School So Bad Even Teachers Picket," *New York Amsterdam News*, December 21, 1963, 3; Sylvester Leaks, "Talking About Harlem," *Freedomways*, Summer 1963, 263.
4. Sara Slack, "We'd Rather Go to Jail," *New York Amsterdam News*, December 13, 1958, 24; Jennifer de Forest, "The 1958 Harlem School Boycott: Parental Activism and the Struggle for Educational Equity in New York City," *Urban Review* 40 (2008): 21–41; Adina Back, "Up South in New York: The 1950s School Desegregation Struggles" (PhD diss., New York University, 1997).
5. Clarence Taylor, *Knocking at Our Own Door: Milton A. Galamison and the Struggle to Integrate New York City Schools* (Lanham, MD: Lexington Books, 2001); Editors, "Harlem—A Community in Transition," 262.
6. *Views* [Harlem Parents Committee newsletter], February 1965, Box 15, Folder "Boycott 1965," ASP, CUL; "An Analysis of the Board of Education Open Enrollment Policy," Box 14, Folder 99, MGP, SCR.
7. Fred Powledge, "Leaders of Protest Foresee a New Era of Militancy Here," *New York Times*, February 4, 1964, 1; Annie Stein, "Strategies for Failure," *Harvard Educational Review* 41 (1971): 158–204; Harlem Parents Committee, "The Education of Minority Group Children in the New York City Public Schools," pamphlet, 1965, Box 1, Folder 28, JWJ, SCR; *Views*, August 1965, Box 13, Folder 27, EJB, SCR; "A Slice of IS 201 History, April,1966: Parents Council District #4," Box 24, Folder 1, PWP, SCR; Fred M. Hechinger, "I.S. 201 Teaches Lessons on Race," *New York Times*, September 25, 1966, 166; "Battle to Control Black Schools," *Ebony*, May 1969, 48; Herbert Kohl, "Integrate with Whom?" *Interplay*, June–July 1968, 27; Thomas K. Minter, "Intermediate School 201, Manhattan: Center of Controversy," pamphlet, Box 53, Folder 17, UFT, RFW; Jason Epstein, "The Politics of School Decentralization," *New York Review of Books*, June 6, 1968, 26–32; "A Summary of the Controversy at I.S. 201," *IRCD Bulletin*, Winter 1966–1967, 1–2; Diane Ravitch, *The Great School Wars: A History of the New York City Public Schools* (New York: Basic Books, 1988).

8. *Views*, April and May 1966, Box 15, Folder "Views/HPC," and February 12, 1965, Joseph Patterson and Calvin Oba letter to Parents, Box 15, Folder "Boycott 1965," and "Action Training Clearing House Notes on Decentralization," and "Community Control of Schools—'We Couldn't Do Worse," Box 1, Folder 6, ASP, CUL.
9. *Views*, July 1966, Box 13, Folder 25, EJB, SCR; *Views*, November 1967, Box 52, Folder 17, UFT, RFW.
10. Laurence T. Sorkin, "Anarchists and Royalists in the Promised Land: I.S. 201 and Single School Autonomy," unpublished paper, 1967, LGL, YLS; Gene Currivan, "Board Sets Talks in School Dispute," *New York Times*, September 11, 1966, 79; Marlene Nadle, "Ghetto Fight: Quality, Segregated Education," *Village Voice*, September 29, 1966, 11; Andrew Kopkind, "Down the Down Staircase: Parents, Teachers, and Public Authorities," *New Republic*, October 22, 1966, 12; Preston R. Wilcox, "Issues and Answers: Black Male Principal," *Renewal*, October–November 1966.
11. Dorothy S. Jones, "The Issues at I.S. 201: A View from the Parent's Committee," *Integrated Education*, October–November, 1966, 23; "Events and Issues Surrounding Intermediate School 201," 1966, Box 21, Folder 33, JHC, SCR.
12. Preston Wilcox, "The Kids Will Decide—And More Power to Them," *Ebony*, August 1970, 134; George Todd, "Say 'School Chaos Harder on Blacks,'" *New York Amsterdam News*, September 16, 1967, 25; "A Proposal for a Neighborhood Education Committee," 1966, Box 10, Folder 9, PWP, SCR; Merelice Kundratis, "Roxbury Unit Seeks School Control," *Christian Science Monitor*, July 25, 1968, 13.
13. Quoted in James C. Harvey, *Black Civil Rights During the Johnson Administration* (Jackson: University Press of Mississippi, 1973), 202; see, for example, Diane Ravitch, *The Troubled Crusade: American Education 1945-1980* (New York: Basic Books, 1983), 162, 174.
14. Will Lissner, "Harlem Proposes a Special Panel to Operate I.S. 201," *New York Times*, October 3, 1966, 1, 37; untitled essay, 1966, Box 1, Folder 6, ASP, CUL; "Conflicting Images of the Community's Role in the School," unpublished essay, Box 11, Folder 19, PWP, SCR; quoted in Jeremy Larner, "I.S. 201: Disaster in the Schools," *Dissent*, January–February 1967, 33.
15. Robert Self, *American Babylon: Race and the Struggle for Postwar Oakland* (Princeton, NJ: Princeton University Press, 2003), 11.
16. Thomas J. Sugrue, *Sweet Land of Liberty: The Forgotten Struggle for Civil Rights in the North* (New York: Random House, 2008): 170–171.
17. Danns, *Something Better for Our Children*, 13, 22–23; Michael W. Homel, *Down from Equality: Black Chicagoans and the Public Schools, 1920-41* (Champaign: University of Illinois Press, 1994), x; Jean Anyon, *Ghetto Schooling: A Political Economy of Urban Educational Reform* (New York: Teachers College Press, 1997), 50–63; Jeanne M. Theoharis, "'Exposing the Whole Desegregation Myth': The Harlem Nine and New York City's School Desegregation Battles," in *Freedom North: Black Freedom Struggles Outside the South, 1940-1980*, ed. Theoharis and Komozi Woodard (New York: Palgrave Macmillan, 2003), 67, 69; Sugrue, *Sweet Land of Liberty*, 174–179; David M. Douglas, *Jim Crow Moves North: The Battle Over Northern School Segregation, 1865-1954* (New York: Cambridge University Press, 2005), 7, 10, 192; Gregory S. Jacobs, *Getting Around Brown: Desegregation, Development and the Columbus Public Schools* (Columbus: Ohio State University Press, 1998), 7–10; Vincent P. Franklin, *The Education of Black Philadelphia: The Social and Educational History of a Minority Community, 1900-1950* (Philadelphia: University of Pennsylvania Press, 1979), 48–49, 71–73, 150, 188–197.
18. Sara Lawrence Lightfoot, "Families as Educators: The Forgotten People of Brown," in *Shades of Brown: New Perspectives on School Desegregation*, ed. Derrick A. Bell, Jr. (New York: Teachers College Press, 1980), 3.
19. Barbara Ransby, *Ella Baker and the Black Freedom Movement: A Radical Democratic Vision* (Chapel Hill: University of North Carolina Press, 2005), 151–155; Martha Biondi, *To Stand and Fight: The Struggle for Civil Rights in Postwar New York City* (Cambridge, MA: Harvard University Press, 2003), 241–248; Jack Dougherty, *More Than One Struggle: The Evolution of Black School Reform in Milwaukee* (Chapel Hill: University of North Carolina Press, 2003), 37–45; Robert L. Carter, "A Reassessment of Brown," in *Shades of Brown*, 22; David B. Tyack, "Growing Up Black: Perspectives on the History of Education in Northern Ghettos," *History*

of Education Quarterly 9 (1969): 291; Alton Hornsby, *Black Power in Dixie: A Political History of African Americans in Atlanta* (Gainesville: University Press of Florida, 2009), 226–230; Paula S. Fass, *Outside In: Minorities and the Transformation of American Education* (New York: Oxford University Press, 1989), 7; Manning Marable, *Race, Reform & Rebellion: The Second Reconstruction and Beyond in Black America* (Jackson: University Press of Mississippi, 2007), 53.

20. Richard Kluger, *Simple Justice: The History of Brown v. Board of Education and Black America's Struggle for Equality* (New York: Knopf, 1976), 510; Jacobs, *Getting Around Brown*, 17; Howell S. Baum, *Brown in Baltimore: School Desegregation and the Limits of Liberalism* (Ithaca, NY: Cornell University Press, 2011), 76.

21. Ravitch, *Troubled Crusade*, 175–177; Sugrue, *Sweet Land of Liberty*, 181–189, 451–466.

22. Anyon, *Ghetto Schooling*, 71–81; Franklin, *The Education of Black Philadelphia*, 200; David B. Tyack, *The One Best System: A History of American Urban Education* (Cambridge, MA: Harvard University Press, 1974), 284; Thomas J. Sugrue, *The Origins of the Urban Crisis: Race and Inequality in Postwar Detroit* (Princeton, NJ: Princeton University Press, 1996); Self, *American Babylon*, 211.

23. Ronald P. Formisano, *Boston Against Busing: Race, Class and Ethnicity in the 1960s and 1970s* (Chapel Hill: University of North Carolina Press, 1991), 12; Douglas, *Jim Crow Moves North*, 266–68; Jacobs, *Getting Around Brown*, 10–16; Biondi, *To Stand and Fight*, 248.

24. Leonard Buder, "Picketing Quiet at School Board," *New York Times*, July 16, 1963, 13.

25. Fred Powledge, "Leaders of Protest Foresee a New Era of Militancy Here," *New York Times*, February 4, 1964, 1, 20; Danns, *Something Better for Our Children*, 33–42; Taylor, *Knocking at Our Own Door*, 121, 129.

26. Christopher Jencks, "Private Schools for Black Children," in *Restructuring American Education: Innovation and Alternatives*, ed. Ray C. Rist (New Brunswick, NJ: Transaction Publishers, 1972), 172.

27. See, for example, Countryman, *Up South*, 156.

28. Manuel Castells, *The City and the Grassroots: A Cross-Cultural Theory of Urban Social Movements* (Berkeley: University of California Press, 1983), 67; Mel King, *Chain of Change: Struggles for Black Community Development* (Cambridge, MA: South End Press, 1981), xxvi, 129, 153.

29. Marilyn Gittell, *Local Control in Education: Three Demonstration School Districts in New York City* (New York: Praeger Publishers, 1972), 24.

30. Steven V. Roberts, "Brownsville Sinks in Decay and Fear," *New York Times*, March 7, 1968, 45. See also Sylvester Leaks, "Is Community Control of Schools New Lever for Black Liberation?" *Muhammad Speaks*, September 8, 1968, 15; Milton A. Galamison, "Bedford-Stuyvesant—Land of Superlatives," *Freedomways*, Summer 1963, 420.

31. May 9, 1967, Oliver Leeds, Bob Carson, Maurice Fredericks, Mary Phifer Letter, Box 52, Folder 17, UFT, RFW; "Chronology: The People's Board of Education, New York City," *Views*, 1967, 3, Box 15, Folder "Views/HPC," ASP, CUL.

32. New York Civil Liberties Union, "The Burden of Blame: A Report on the Ocean Hill-Brownsville School Controversy," *Urban Education*, April 1964, 9; L. Alexander Harper, "School Daze in Ocean Hill-Brownsville: The Death of Classroom Colonialism," *Church in Metropolis*, Winter 1968, 26.

33. Fred Ferretti, "Who's to Blame in the School Strike," *New York Magazine*, November 18, 1968, 23; Preston Wilcox, "'Troublemakers at the Board of Education: Fact or Fantasy," *Equity and Excellence in Education*, June 1967, 47–53; Jerald E. Podair, *The Strike That Changed New York: Blacks, Whites and the Ocean Hill-Brownsville Crisis* (New Haven, CT: Yale University Press, 2002), 71–74; "Report to Governing Board Ocean Hill School District from Personnel Committee, Mrs. Clara Marshall, Chairman," n.d., Box 1, Folder 6, ASP, CUL; Leonard Buder, "Ghetto Residents Seeking New Role," *New York Times*, January 11, 1967, 27, 33; Maurice J. Goldbloom, "The New York School Crisis," *Commentary*, January 1969, 43–48; "Chronology of the Events in the City's School Crisis," *New York Times*, November 4, 1968, 54.

34. William W. Sales, Jr. and Rod Bush, "The Political Awakening of Blacks and Latinos in New York City: Competition or Cooperation?" *Social Justice* 27 (2000): 35.

35. Merelice Kundratis, "Roxbury Unit Seeks School Control," *Christian Science Monitor*, July 25, 1968, 13; "An Open Letter to Teachers," *Foresight*, February 1969, 5; "Community Control Across the Nation," *Community* [Queens College Institute for Community Studies], February 1969, 1–2; Fred M. Hechinger, "Negroes' Priority Demand," *New York Times*, October 13, 1968, 1; Joe Walker, "Harlem Struggles for Voice in the Control of Black Schools," *Muhammad Speaks*, October 4, 1968, 36.

36. See, for example, James Goodrich, "Black Confab Hears Political Action Call," *Los Angeles Sentinel*, June 1, 1967, A1; C. Gerald Fraser, "Survival Is a Topic at Black Power Conference," *New York Times*, August 30, 1968, 24; "Black Survival," *Black Panther*, October 5, 1968, 4. Also see Civil Rights Congress, ed. *We Charge Genocide: The Historic Petition to the United Nations for Relief from a Crime of the United States Government Against the Negro People* (New York: International Publishers, 1970), and William L. Patterson, "'We (Still) Charge Genocide,'" *Muhammad Speaks*, June 26, 1970, 23; "Let Freedom Ring!" flyer, n.d., Box 15, Folder "Boycott 1965," ASP, CUL.

37. Transcript of Jim Leeson Interview with Preston Wilcox, Brooklyn, May 1968, CRD, MSR.

38. February 17, 1972, unnamed letter, Box 24, Folder 9, UFT, RFW.

39. See, for example, Dahlk, *Against the Wind*, 41.

40. Derrick A. Bell, Jr., "School Desegregation: Seeking New Victories Among the Ashes," *Freedomways*, Winter 1977, 35–38; US Commission on Civil Rights, *Racial Isolation in the Public Schools* (Washington, DC: Government Printing Office, 1967), 199; Carl Bernstein, "Norfolk: Learning to Live with Busing," *Washington Post*, November 29, 1971, 1; Dionne Danns, "Racial Ideology and the Sanctity of the Neighborhood School in Chicago," *Urban Review* 40 (2008): 64–75; Alex Poinsett, "Ghetto Schools: An Educational Wasteland," *Ebony*, August 1967, 54.

41. Shirley Chisholm, "The Black as a Colonized Man," *Afro-American Studies* 1 (1970): 8. "What kind of a hypocrite am I to tell black children to do their thing in school and college so that they can take their rightful place in society?" Ocean Hill–Brownsville school administrator Rhody McCoy fumed in 1970. "Where is that place?" ("Does Integration Still Matter to Blacks?" *Time*, March 9, 1970, 14.)

42. Derrick A. Bell, Jr., "Integration—Is It a No-Win Educational Policy for Blacks?" in *Federal Pre-School and Early Childhood Programs From a Black Perspective*, ed. Evelyn K. Moore (Washington, DC: National Policy Conference on Education for Blacks, 1972), 7.

43. William E. Nelson, Jr., "School Desegregation and the Black Community," *Theory Into Practice* 17 (1978): 122–130. For a discussion of desegregation and the loss of black cultural traditions, see David S. Cecelski, *Along Freedom Road: Hyde Country, North Carolina and the Fate of Black Schools in the South* (Chapel Hill: University of North Carolina Press, 1994), and Vanessa Siddle Walker, *Their Highest Potential: An African American School Community in the Segregated South* (Chapel Hill: University of North Carolina Press, 1996). For a discussion of black education and social and cultural capital, see Marion Orr, *Black Social Capital: The Politics of School Reform in Baltimore, 1986-1998* (Lawrence: University Press of Kansas, 1999); "Genocide by Desegregation/White Control," pamphlet, Institute of Afrikan Research, Harlem, 1982, Box 24, Folder 9, PWP, SCR; David K. Shipler, "Busing in New York: Ambivalence, Not Outrage," *New York Times*, March 20, 1972, 39; Daniel Zwerdling, "White Militance in Michigan—Block Those Buses," *New Republic*, October 23, 1971, 14. See also Milton A. Galamison, "Educational Values and Community Power," *Freedomways*, Fall 1968, 311–318.

44. Lesley Oelsner, "Goal of Integration in Schools Elusive," *New York Times*, November 20, 1977, 64.

45. Floyd McKissick, "A Communication: Is Integration Necessary?" *New Republic*, December 3, 1966, 34; "African-American Teachers Association Demands Self-Control, Self-Determination, and Self-Defense for Schools in the Black Community," flyer, September 1967, Box 24, Folder 8, UFT, RFW.

46. "Jist Funin'," cartoon, *Community Advocate* (Ocean Hill-Brownsville), n.d., Box 53, Folder 2, UFT, RFW.

47. Mel King, "Thoughts on Busing: 1972, not 1954," manuscript, March 1972, Box 25, Folder 10, PWP, SCR; Philip Green, "Decentralization, Community Control, and Revolution," *Massachusetts Review* 11 (1970): 437; Shipler, "Busing in New York," 39.

48. As a measure of African-American ambivalence toward the most contentious desegregation method—busing—during the height of Black Power, consider the 1972 antibusing resolution passed by the National Black Political Convention in Gary, Indiana. After the resolution sparked an outcry from some of the gathering's 7,000 attendees, delegates rushed to pass a qualifying resolution that opposed busing where it destroyed high-quality education in black communities and supported it where it "serves the end of equal education for black people." (See "Hatcher Reviews Parley of Blacks," *New York Times*, March 16, 1972, 34; "Inside the Black Convention," *New York Amsterdam News*, March 18, 1972, 1.)

49. Jean Carey Bond, "The New York School Crisis: Integration for What?" *Freedomways*, Spring 1964, 201.

50. Quoted in Marable, *Race, Reform & Rebellion*, 97.

51. Preston Wilcox, "The Controversy over IS 201," *Urban Review* 1 (1966): 13.

52. Larner, "IS 201: Disaster in the Schools," 29; Lillian S. Calhoun, "New York: Schools and Power—Whose?" *Integrated Education*, January–February 1969, 33. This stance was somewhat distinct from that of the NAACP, which offered tepid support for community control while maintaining its traditional stance against the nationalist position. "We do not believe that community control and desegregation are inherently incompatible or in conflict unless they are made to be by the advocates, white or black, of racial separatism," the organization's national office proclaimed. See Alan Altshuler, *Community Control: The Black Demand for Participation in Large American Cities* (New York: Bobbs-Merrill, 1970), 60–61.

53. "Battle to Control Black Schools," 44.

54. One academic wrote, "Negroes who have become discouraged with the slow pace of progress toward desegregation in the schools are increasingly receptive to the separatist argument of militant black nationalists." Daniel U. Levine, "Confused Reform Rhetoric in the Big Cities," *Integrated Education*, September–October 1968, 30. The origins of nationalist revolt were actually more homegrown. For example, the first demonstration staged by Harlem's incipient Black Panther cadre in September 1966 targeted a local school that many of the young picketers once had attended. (See Thomas A. Johnson, "Black Panthers Picket a School," *New York Times*, September 13, 1966, 38).

55. Examples of media bias abound. On the occasion of a triumphant, largely black and Puerto Rican march from city hall to the Board of Education headquarters in Brooklyn, an event hailed by the *Black Panther* newspaper as "one of the largest demonstrations of strength in the history of black struggle in New York City," the *New York Times*, ever faithful to the cause of portraying northern black protest as disruptive and illegitimate, snubbed the demonstration as a temporary nuisance for rush-hour commuters. ("20,000 in N.Y. March for Black Control," *Black Panther*, October 26, 1968, 15; Maurice Carroll, "School Protest Blocks Traffic on Brooklyn Bridge," *New York Times*, October 4, 1972, 38.) For examples of UFT rhetoric, see "The Black and the Jew: A Falling Out of Allies," *Time*, January 31, 1969, 55–59; and "Who Should Run the Schools," *Newsweek*, October 28, 1968, 84.

56. "They Must Kill Ocean Hill/Brownsville . . . ," Rhody McCoy press release, n.d. (c. 1968), Box 1, Folder 6, ASP, CUL; "The Talk of the Town: Notes and Comment," *New Yorker*, October 26, 1968.

57. "Black Solidarity Day," 1970 flyer, Box 24, Folder 9, and "Let's Take Our Schools!" flyer, n.d. (c. 1968), Box 55, Folder 16, UFT, RFW; Thomas A. Johnson, "Protesters Carry Cause from School to School," *New York Times*, December 11, 1968, 36; "Black Mother Speaks On: Mis-Education of the American Child," *Muhammad Speaks*, October 11, 1968, 34; Grace Lee Boggs, "Education: The Great Obsession," *Monthly Review*, September 1970, 29.

58. Herbert Hill, "Letter to the Editor," *Issues in Industrial Society* 1 (1970): 69; Charles Isaacs, "Colonial Politics in the Schools: A Case Study," unpublished manuscript, Box 1, Folder 6, ASP, CUL; "On the Line: Who Will Control New York City Schools," *Guardian*, October 26, 1968, 11.

59. Agee Ward, "Ocean Hill: Education, Community, Power and the Media," *Center Forum*, November 13, 1968, 1–10; "Ocean Hill Target for Black Militants," *New York Amsterdam News*, March 22, 1969. For early examples of internal colony analysis, see Jack O'Dell, "Colonialism and the Negro American Experience," *Freedomways*, Fall 1966, 296–308; and O'Dell, "A Special Variety of Colonialism," *Freedomways*, Winter 1967, 8; Larner, "I.S. 201: Disaster in the Schools," 33, 39.

60. Calhoun, "New York: Schools and Power—Whose?" 25; *Soul* [Newsletter of Brooklyn Black Caucus], July 4, 1968, Box 55, Folder 17, and "Position Paper—The Parent-Community Council, from JHS 271," May 15, 1968, Box 55, Folder 16, UFT, RFW.

61. Miriam Wasserman, "The I.S. 201 Story," *Urban Review*, June 1969, 4; Preston Wilcox, "Changing Conceptions of Community," *Educational Leadership* 21 (1972) [original emphasis].

Chapter 2

1. Gunnar Myrdal, *An American Dilemma*, vol. 2 (New York: McGraw-Hill, 1964 [1944]), 879. For related discussions of the curricular implications of black "relevance," see chapter nine of Daniel H. Perlstein, *Justice, Justice: School Politics and the Eclipse of Liberalism* (New York: Peter Lang, 2004); chapter three of Maisha T. Fisher, *Black Literate Lives: Historical and Contemporary Perspectives* (New York: Routledge, 2008); and Donna Murch, *Living for the City: Migration, Education, and the Rise of the Black Panther Party in Oakland, California* (Chapel Hill: University of North Carolina Press, 2010).

2. J. Anthony Lukas, "Schools Turn to Negro Role in U.S.," *New York Times*, July 8, 1968, 1, 26. (Sputnik and Cold War anxieties had prompted the first "textbook revolution.")

3. "Reflections on Black Studies," version of July 1970 lecture, Box 27, Folder 59, and "Black Studies: Toward an Intellectual Framework," transcript of September 23, 1969, lecture, Box 27, Folder 19, SCD, SCR.

4. Lerone Bennett, Jr., "Confrontation on the Campus," *Ebony*, May 1968, 28; Kenneth Gross, "Pupils' Target Praises Them," *New York Post*, May 14, 1968, 28; "Demands of Black & Puerto Rican High School Students," flyer, May 14, 1969, Box 5, Folder 8, ASP, CUL; "NYC's School Picture: It's 'in' to Be Out!" *New York Amsterdam News*, December 7, 1968, 1; George Todd, "Ocean Hill Showdown as JHS 271 Is Padlocked," *New York Amsterdam News*, December 7, 1968, 1; George Todd, "10 Policemen Hurt in Model Schools Area," *New York Amsterdam News*, October 5, 1968, 23; Margie Stamberg, "NY Schools Erupt," *Guardian*, December 7, 1968, 6; "Program of the High School Coalition," flyer, n.d., Box 52, Folder 26, and "To the Real Black Men of Boys High School," flyer, April 10, 1968, Box 55, Folder 16, UFT, RFW; Sara Slack, "Push for Shake-Up of Boys High Staff," *New York Amsterdam News* [Brooklyn Edition], May 11, 1968, 1; Michael Stern, "Teen-Agers Protesting Too," *New York Times*, January 9, 1969, 79; John Herbers, "High School Unrest Rises, Alarming U.S. Educators," *New York Times*, May 9, 1969, 1; "New Explosion of Black Youths Sweeping High Schools," *Muhammad Speaks*, October 25, 1968, 10; Ruth B. Stein, "Black Protests Spur Teaching of Negro History," *Jet*, February 15, 1968, 16–22; see also Countryman, *Up South*, 228.

5. "Do You Want Your Child Taught This?" flyer, n.d., Box 55, Folder 22, "The Following Material Was Distributed in J.H.S. 271, Ocean Hill-Brownsville," transcript of Ralph Poynter letter, Box 52, Folder 19, and "Baird Visits Africa," *Ocean Hill-Brownsville Community Advocate*, August 1969, Box 55, Folder 13, UFT, RFW.

6. C. Gerald Fraser, "Workshop Is Held in Brooklyn to Teach Parents How to Teach," *New York Times*, September 7, 1967, 18.

7. Charles V. Harrison, "Black History and the Schools," *Ebony*, December 1968, 113; "Schools Are Fast Putting Blacks Back into History," *Chicago Daily Defender*, February 7, 1970, 28; Rose Marie Levey, *Black Studies in Schools: A Review of Current Policies and Programs* (Washington, DC: National School Public Relations Association, 1970), 11.

8. Raymond H. Giles, *Black Studies Programs in Public Schools* (New York: Praeger, 1974), 44; Florence Mouckley, "Black History Instruction Varies Across U.S.," *Christian Science Monitor*, January 4, 1974, 5; Harrison, "Black History and the Schools," 113; Ernest Kaiser, "The Negro Heritage Library and Its Critics," *Freedomways*, Winter 1967, 64; "Book Trade Journal Comments on Hearings" [Excerpt from September 19, 1966, *Publisher's Weekly* Editorial],

Interracial Books for Children, Winter 1967, Box 8, Folder 2, ASP, CUL; James Garrett, "Black Power & Black Education," *Washington Free Press*, April 16–30, 1969, 9.

9. Ragni Lantz, "Adam Powell Probes Bias in Textbooks," *Jet*, September 8, 1966, 16; Paul Delaneys, "Use of 'Multi-Ethnic Textbooks' Grows," *New York Times*, June 7, 1971, 1; Letitia W. Brown, "Section F: Why and How the Negro in History," *Journal of Negro Education* 38 (1969): 447; "The Best Way to Study Black History" (Promotion for CES Negro History Transparencies), Box 140, Folder 4, UFT, RFW; Yosef ben-Jochannan, *Cultural Genocide in the Black and African Studies Curriculum* (New York: Alkebu-lan Book Association, 1972), 1.

10. "The East Harlem Coalition for Community Control Makes the Following Resolutions," 1968 flyer, Box 52, Folder 18, UFT, RFW; New York City Board of Education Press Release, April 13–14, 1966, Box 8, Folder 2, ASP, CUL.

11. Margaret Burroughs, "Integration of Learning Materials . . . Now!" *Negro Digest*, March 1966, 31–32; "Statement of Roy Wilkins, NAACP Executive Director," press release, September 21, 1970, Box 46, Folder 6, EGP, SCR.

12. Sara Slack, "Angered People Vow to Keep Teachers Out of School," *New York Amsterdam News*, October 5, 1968, 35; James A. Banks, "Teaching Black Studies for Social Change," *Journal of Afro-American Issues* 1 (1971): 141–163.

13. "The Advisory Board of Nairobi Schools Presents Afro-American History Week Celebration," February 14, 1970, Box 27, Folder 43, SCD, SCR. Nationalists were among the most outspoken critics of public school curricula. See, for example, "Objects to Textbook; Keeps Daughter from Class," *Jet*, October 13, 1966, 13.

14. Maude White Katz, "End Racism in Education: A Concerned Parent Speaks," *Freedomways*, Winter 1968, 347.

15. Henry Hampton and Steve Fayer with Sarah Flynn, *Voices of Freedom: An Oral History of the Civil Rights Movement from the 1950s Through the 1980s* (New York: Bantam Books, 1990), 502; *Black News*, April 10, 1970; "Negro History Week Now; Black Liberation Week Next," *New York Amsterdam News*, February 14, 1970, 16; "Seek Black Unity, Says McKissick," *Chicago Daily Defender*, June 25, 1968, 5.

16. Margie Stamberg, "NY Schools Open, but Parents Angry," *Guardian*, November 30, 1968, 6; Hugh Wyatt, "Harlem Fears Johnny Won't Learn to Read," *Daily News*, November 18, 1969, 5; "NY School Crisis Deadlocked," *Guardian*, November 2, 1968, 6.

17. "Chronology of the UFT-Community Confrontation, 1967-1968," in *Schools Against Children: The Case for Community Control*, ed. Annette T. Rubinstein (New York: Monthly Review Press, 1970), 267; "The 'So-Called' Disruptive Child," August 1967 flyer, Box 24, Folder 8, UFT, RFW; Teacher's Freedom Party of UFT, "Anatomy of a Cop-Out: Harlem vs. Shanker," *Liberator*, January 1968, 16.

18. Charles S. Isaacs, "A J.H.S. 271 Teacher Tells It Like He Sees It," *New York Times Magazine*, November 24, 1968, 52; Herman Ferguson, "A Black Survival Curriculum," *Guardian*, March 9, 1968, 16; "Education-Self Learning, Dr. Nathan Hare, Chairman, Third International Conference on Black Power," 1968 pamphlet, Box 21, PWP, SCR. The need to challenge law-and-order practices in schools grew more evident by 1970, as African-American parents began to mobilize against the stigma of "hyperactivity" that led some primary schools to "drug black children into quiet submission" with Ritalin and other behavioral medications. (See Robert Maynard, "Omaha Pupils Given 'Behavior' Drugs," *Washington Post*, June 29, 1970, 1.)

19. November 28, 1969, Preston Wilcox to M. Lee Montgomery, Box 24, Folder 7, PWP, SCR; Preston R. Wilcox, "The Community-Centered School," in *The Schoolhouse in the City*, ed. Alvin Toffler (New York: Frederick A. Praeger, 1968), 102; James E. Campbell, "Struggle: The Highest Form of Education," *Freedomways*, Winter 1968, 407.

20. Preston Wilcox, "Education for Black Liberation," *New Generation*, Winter 1969, 18, 20; Garrett, "Black Power & Black Education," 9; Joyce A. Ladner, "Labeling Black Children: Social-Psychological Implications," *Journal of Afro-American Issues* 3 (1975): 50.

21. Charles V. Hamilton, "An Advocate of Black Power Defines It," *New York Times Magazine*, April 14, 1968, 82; Charles V. Hamilton, "Race and Education: A Search for Legitimacy," *Harvard Educational Review* 38 (1968): 683.

22. Wilcox, "The Community-Centered School," 105–106; Kenneth W. Haskins, "A Black Perspective on Community Control," *Inequality in Education*, November 1973, 28–29; *I.S. 201 Complex Community Information Manual, 1968-69* (New York: Intermediate School 201

Complex, 1968), GRD, SCR; Preston Wilcox, "One View and a Proposal," *Urban Review*, July 1966, 14; David Bresnick, Seymour Lachman, and Murray Polner, *Black, White, Green, Red: The Politics of Education in Ethnic America* (New York: Longman, 1978), 4; Charles H. Moore and Ray E. Johnston, "School Decentralization, Community Control and the Politics of Public Education," *Urban Affairs Quarterly* 6 (1971): 423.

23. See in general Bresnick et al, eds., *Black, White, Green, Red*; Keith E. Baird, "Semantics and Afro-American Liberation," *Social Casework*, May 1970, 266–267.

24. For the literature of cultural deprivation, see Frank Riesman Frank, *The Culturally Deprived Child* (New York: Harper and Row Publishers, 1962); Benjamin Samuel Bloom et al., *Compensatory Education for Cultural Deprivation* (New York: Holt, Rinehart and Winston, 1965); Lester Donald Crow et al., *Educating the Culturally Disadvantaged Child: Principles and Programs* (New York: David McKay Co., 1966).

25. Kenneth B. Clark, "Clash of Cultures in the Classroom," in *Learning Together: A Book on Integrated Education*, ed. Meyer Weinberg (Chicago: Integrated Education Association, 1964), 22; see also Dougherty, *More Than One Struggle*, 65. One very powerful narrative of pathology is Daniel Patrick Moynihan, *The Negro Family: The Case for National Action* (Washington, DC: Office of Policy Planning and Research, U.S. Department of Labor, 1965).

26. "Parents Boycott Busses, Hold Freedom Schools," *The Movement*, February 1966, 1; Ravitch, *The Great School Wars*, 299.

27. James S. Coleman, *Equality of Educational Opportunity* (Washington, DC: U.S. Government Printing Office, 1966); Inner City Parents Council, "Detroit Schools—A Blueprint for Change," *Liberator*, September 1967, 9; "Approaches to Black Education," Transcript of Chester Davis lecture at Institute of the Black World, Atlanta, June 3, 1970, 2, Box 44, Folder 22, IBW, SCR.

28. Nathan Glazer and Daniel Patrick Moynihan, *Beyond the Melting Pot: The Negroes, Puerto Ricans, Jews, Italians and Irish of New York* (Cambridge, MA: Harvard University Press, 1963), 53. For examples of this vindicating style of scholarship, see Andrew Billingsley, *Black Families in White America* (Upper Saddle River, NJ: Prentice-Hall, 1968), and Joyce A. Ladner, *Tomorrow's Tomorrow: The Black Woman* (Garden City, NY: Doubleday, 1971).

29. "Day Care and the Black Community: Myths and Realities," Transcript of April 27, 1971, lecture, p. 6, Box 34, Folder 8, PWP, SCR. See also Toni Cade, "The Children Who Get Cheated," *Redbook*, January 1970.

30. Garrett, "Black Power & Black Education," 9; Alton D. Rison, "How to Teach Black Children," *African-American Teachers Forum* (undated clipping), Box 24, Folder 8, UFT, RFW; Nathan Hare, "Bourgeois Teachers in Black Schools," *Liberator*, March 1967, 6.

31. Charles V. Hamilton, "Education in the Black Community: An Examination of the Realities," *Freedomways*, Fall 1968, 320.

32. "Our Children Need 'Teachers with Soul'" [Advertisement], *New York Amsterdam News*, April 4, 1970, 32; "Proposal for the Recruitment and Training of Teachers for Disadvantaged Areas," ATA Pamphlet, n.d., Box 24, Folder 8, UFT, RFW; Ralph Poynter, "Liberation Forum: Community Control of Education," *Guardian*, May 25, 1968, 11.

33. "Negro Teachers' Association Conference," *Integrated Education*, August–September 1967, 37; March 13, 1967, Milton A. Galamison to Kenneth Clark, Box 14, Folder 100, MGP, SCR; "Resolutions; Negro Teachers' Association's Conference, Saturday, May 28, 1967," pamphlet, Box 24, Folder 8, UFT, RFW; Hare, "Bourgeois Teachers in Black Schools," 4–6; M. Lee Montgomery, "Educating Black Children," in *What Black Educators Are Saying*, ed. Nathan Wright, Jr. (New York: Hawthorne Books, 1970), 50; Leslie J. Campbell, "The Black Teacher and Black Power," *African-American Teachers Forum*, May–August 1967, 2.

34. Ronald Evans, "On the Education of Our Children," *Freedomways*, Winter 1969, 77; "Declaration of Black Teachers," *Foresight*, February 1969, 4; Richard Parrish, "How the System Twists Attitudes: The Miseducation of Black Teachers," *Washington, D.C. Teacher*, April 1970.

35. "Interracial competition" quote is from Roy Wilkins (see "Black Leaders Speak Out on Black Education," *Today's Education*, October 1969, 3); Marie Syrkin, "Don't Flunk the Middle-Class Teacher," *New York Times Magazine*, December 15, 1968, 70, 75. For a

discussion of conceptions of racial values in black liberation movements, see Jerald E. Podair, " 'White' Values, 'Black' Values: The Ocean Hill-Brownsville Controversy and New York City Culture, 1965-1975," *Radical History Review* 59 (1994): 41–42.

36. "First Regional Conference on Black Power: Statement and Resolution by Workshop on Education," in *Black Power and Black Education*, ed. National Association for African American Education (Harlem, NY: National Association for African American Education, 1970), 11; J. Caroll Williams, "Chicago Viewpoint: Black Education," *Black Liberator*, August 1969, 6.

37. "What Is to Be Done?" 1969 pamphlet, Muhammad Ahmad, Black Power Movement Part 3—Revolutionary Action Movement, Series 2 (Microfilm); "Battle to Control Black Schools," *Ebony*, May 1969, 45.

38. Robert C. Smith, "Black Power and the Transformation from Protest to Politics," *Political Science Quarterly* 96 (1981): 431–443. Also see James Aronson, "The New Politics of Black Power," *Monthly Review*, October 1967, 11–21, and Albert B. Cleage, Jr., " 'We Have Become a Black Nation,' " *Negro Digest*, January 1969, 30–38.

39. "Resolutions: Negro Teachers' Association's Conference, Saturday, May 28, 1967," Box 24, Folder 8, and "Black Solidarity Day," flyer, and Albert Vann to Albert Shanker, n.d., and Negro Teachers Association Press Release, n.d., Box 24, Folders 8 and 9, UFT, RFW; "Separatism for Negro Educators," *Education Summary*, October 1, 1968, 5–6; George Todd, "Rump Teachers Group Threat at Conference," *New York Amsterdam News*, June 3, 1967, 21, 30; Will Lissner, "Rustin Warns on School Separatists," *New York Times*, April 7, 1968, 60; *African-American Teachers Forum*, November–December 1967, 1; "The Chicago African-American Teachers Association," *CATA Newsletter*, Fall 1968, 4; "The Chicago African-American Teachers Association" and "Farmer to Address Dinner for Retiring Teachers," *CATA Newsletter*, Spring 1969, 1, 4, VGH, CGW.

40. Gerald Grant, "1300 Teachers Debate Textbook Negro Image," *Washington Post*, December 10, 1966, A4; Nan Robertson, "Teacher Opposes the Term 'Negro,' " *New York Times*, December 10, 1966, 27; *Liberator*, January 1967, 22; "A Study Unit to Aid in the Teaching of Afro-American Life and Culture," Miller District Demonstration Project Workshop, Materials Committee, Racism in Education Conference, Series 3, RPP, SCR; "What Do You Do with An Ugly Fact? Can We Teach the Truth?" 1966 James E. Campbell pamphlet, Box 6, RBP, SCR.

41. "Racism in Education," *Changing Education*, Winter 1967, 6–7; "Curriculum Changes Planned Quietly in Ocean Hill," *New York Times*, September 18, 1968, 32; "A Brief History of the AFT Black Caucus, 1967-1974," pamphlet, Series 3, RPP, SCR; Richard Parrish, "The New York City Teachers Strikes," *Labor Today*, May 1969; John Henrik Clarke, "Black Power and Black History," *Negro Digest*, February 1969, 17.

42. "Black Control of Schools: Selected Viewpoints," pamphlet, 1968, Box 4, PWP, SCR.

43. Nan Robertson, "Four-Day Poverty Parley Described as 'Emotional Catharsis,' " *New York Times*, January 22, 1968, 20; see also, Michael Lipinsky, ed., *Synopsis of Upward Bound Winter Conference: New Orleans, Louisiana, January 16-10, 1968* (Washington, DC: Office of Economic Opportunity, 1968). ERIC, ED 021931.

44. July 31, 1968, Albert Vann letter, Box 22, PWP, SCR.

45. "Preston Wilcox 1ˢᵗ Chairman of Association of Afro-American Educators," *Hometown News*, July 16, 1968; Campbell, "Struggle: The Highest Form of Education," 408; *Report of the Meeting of the National Organization Planning Committee of the National Association of Afro-American Educators* (Chicago: NAAAE, 1968), 1, 25.

46. Leon R. Forrest, "Blacks Meet in Atlanta to 'Make Education Relevant,' " *Muhammad Speaks*, September 5, 1969, 4; Charles V. Hamilton, "An Advocate of Black Power Defines It," *New York Times Magazine*, April 14, 1968, 80; John Rhodes, "5,000 Black Educators Convene in Atlanta; Coin Term 'BACON,' " *Philadelphia Tribune*, August 30, 1969, 6; Francis Ward, "Black Meeting Mired in Factional Dispute," *Los Angeles Times*, September 1, 1969, B12; Preston Wilcox, "A Letter to Black Educators in Higher Education," *Annals of the American Academy of Political and Social Science* 404 (1972): 110; June 17, 1968, Preston Wilcox to Rev. Lucius Walker and July 2, 1968, Wilcox to Muriel Hamilton, Box 31, Folder 33, IFCO, SCR.

47. Hugh J. Scott, "The National Alliance of Black Educators," *Crisis*, June–July 1978, 203; Clarke, "Black Power and Black History," 19; Preston Wilcox, "A Black Educator's View of Us All,"

Black Liberator, July 1969, 8; David B. Kent, ed., *Proceedings of the First National Association of Afro-American Educators Conference* (Chicago: NAAAE, 1968), 22–23; NAAAE Milwaukee Regional Conference Steering Committee memorandum, 1968, Box 31, SAV, WHI.

48. Charles Thomas, "Black Parley OKs Drive for Own Party," *Philadelphia Inquirer,* September 2, 1968, 1, 8; Betty Washington, "Educators Agree They Must Overhaul Nation's Schools," *Daily Defender,* June 12, 1968, 8.

49. "What Happened to Community Control of Our Schools," *New York Amsterdam News,* December 11, 1971, A7.

50. "The Decentralization Bill Is a Recentralization Bill" and "Decentralization or Community Control," flyers, c. 1969, Box 52, Folder 7, UFT, RFW; "Cowardly Racists Dissolve Black Schools," *Muhammad Speaks,* January 16, 1969, 6.

51. Fred M. Hechinger, "When Schools Join the Power Struggle," *New York Times,* December 8, 1968, 237; Rhody A. McCoy, "Educational Issues Swamped by Politics," *New York Amsterdam News,* December 11, 1971, A7; Charles Wilson, "School Problem Show We're in Deep Trouble," *New York Amsterdam News,* December 11, 1971, A7; Lesly Jones, "I.S. 201 Complex No More, But—," *New York Amsterdam News,* July 3, 1971, B6.

52. Les Ledbetter, "Youths' Lunches Get Latin Flavor," *New York Times,* July 16, 1972, 52; "Uses Black Awareness," *New York Amsterdam News,* February 5, 1972, B5; Diane Divoky, "New York's Mini-Schools," *Saturday Review,* December 18, 1971, 60; Babette Edwards, "Trouble in I.S. 201," *Integrated Education,* July–August 1971, 23–25; Charlayne Hunter, "Division and Unrest on Rise in Harlem School Complex," *New York Times,* March 23, 1971, 39; "Community School," undated memo on black professional role in community school, Box 13, Folder 25, EJB, SCR; Martin Arnold, "2 on I.S. 201 Board Resign in Protest," *New York Times,* March 9, 1971, 44.

53. R. Sakolsky, "The Myth of Government-Sponsored Revolution: A Case Study of Institutional Safety-Valves," *Education and Urban Society* 5 (1973): 21–44; "Report to Governing Board Ocean Hill School District from Personnel Committee, Mrs. Clara Marshall, Chairman," n.d., Box 1, Folder 6, ASP, CUL; Robert Wright Interview with Jose Stevens, Transcript, p. 24, CRD, MSR; Michael B. Katz, "The Present Moment in Educational Reform," *Harvard Educational Review* 41 (1971): 351; Ivor Kraft, "There Is No Panacea," *Nation,* January 20, 1969, 73.

54. Diane Ravitch, "Community Control Revisited," *Commentary,* February 1972, 69; Edward B. Fiske, "Community-Run Schools Leave Hopes Unfulfilled," *New York Times,* June 24, 1980, A1. See also David S. Seeley, "Decentralization's Disastrous Decade," *New York Daily News,* June 3, 1980, 34.

55. James A. Geschwender, "Negro Education: The False Faith," *Phylon,* Fall 1968, 371; C. Eric Lincoln, "The Relevance of Education for Black Americans," *Journal of Negro Education* 38 (1969), 222; Doxey Wilkerson, "Inequalities in Education and Powerlessness," 1974 pamphlet, Box 17, Folder 8, DWP, SCR; *Ebony* study cited in Otter M. Scruggs, "The Education of the Afro-American: An Historic View," in *Education and the Black Experience,* ed. Kenneth Hall and Alfred Young (Palo Alto, CA: R&E Research Association, 1989), 9.

56. Charles E. Wilson, "Beyond Reform: The New York City School System," *Freedomways,* Spring 1971, 141. For findings on gains made in the demonstration districts in terms of parent involvement and democratization of the schools, see "Findings on Demonstration Schools," *New York Amsterdam News,* December 18, 1971, and David McClintick and Art Sears, Jr., "Educational Hot Spot; Decentralized District in a New York Ghetto Claims Gains in Schools," *Wall Street Journal,* April 10, 1969, 1, 28.

57. See *Kweli* (Published by IS 201 Educational Complex), December 1970, GRD, SCR; "Assemblyman Al Vann: Exclusive Interview," *Black News,* October 1978, 12; "Invisible Windows," Arthur A. Schomburg School Yearbook, 1966–1969, GRD, SCR.

58. "Master Teacher Ferguson Rips White Frame-Up," *Muhammad Speaks,* August 20, 1968, 22; "Community Education Center Rally a Black Power Forum," *Long Island Press,* September 5, 1968; "SUBJECT: An Independent Black School or a Dependent Nigger School," August 1969 proposal, Box 5, PWP, SCR.

59. Roy Innis and Victor Solomon, "A Proposal for an Independent Board of Education for Harlem" (New York-Harlem CORE, March 1, 1967), in *Proposals for Black Studies Programs*

for Various Types of Educational Institutions (East Palo Alto, CA: Black Liberation Publishers, 1969); Leonard Buder, "Separate Schools for Harlem Urged by 2 Civil Rights Chiefs," *New York Times*, November 22, 1967, 54; Thomas A. Johnson, "CORE Urges City to Let Harlem Run Own Schools," *New York Times*, March 4, 1969, 28; Basil A. Paterson, "Independent School System Called for in Harlem," *New York Amsterdam News*, October 19, 1968, 1, 43; "Meeting of Document Committee Meeting 11/16/67," Box 9, Folder 14, ASP, CUL; Dorothy S. Jones, "Tentative, Preliminary Plans for an Independent Community Educational System for Central Harlem, New York," February 9, 1970, Box 48, Folder 1, EGP, SCR.

60. "Basic Aims and Objectives of the Organization of Afro-American Unity," in *Let Nobody Turn Us Around*, ed. Manning Marable and Leith Mullings (Lanham, MD: Rowman & Littlefield, 2009), 438–439; Steven R. Weisman, "Black Teachers Discuss Control," *New York Times*, April 23, 1972, 36; Derrick Morrison, "NYC Black Teachers Hold Convention," *The Militant*, May 12, 1972, 14; Albert Vann, "View of the Black Teachers' Conference," *New York Amsterdam News*, May 20, 1972, A5; "Black Teachers Hold 3-Day Meeting Here," *New York Amsterdam News*, April 22, 1972, C1.

61. Albert Vann, "Look to the East," *African-American Teachers Forum*, January–February 1972; Albert Vann, "The State of Education for Black People—1973," *New York Amsterdam News*, September 1, 1973, A5; Donald Freeman, Rollie Kimbrough, and Brother Zolili, "The Meaning of Education," *Journal of Negro Education* 3 (1968): 433–434; "Resolutions of Workshop on Education, African People's Conference, Cleveland, Ohio, December 25, 1970," Black Movement Part 3—Revolutionary Action Movement, Series 7 (Microfilm).

62. "Assemblyman Al Vann: Exclusive Interview," 10.

63. Uhuru Hotep, "Dedicated to Excellence: An Oral History of the Council of Independent Black Institutions, 1970-2000" (PhD diss., Duquesne University, 2001), 36–38; Kasisi Jitu Weusi, *A Message from a Black Teacher* (New York: East Publications, 1973), 4, 19; Transcript of Les Campbell Interview, November 3, 1988, Eyes on the Prize Interviews II, HHC, WUF; "On the Shoulders of Our Freedom Fighters: Baba Jitu Weusi," accessed January 5, 2008, http://www.assatashakur.org/forum/shoulders-our-freedom-fighters/17691-baba-jitu-weusi-print.html.

64. Steven Mufson, "A Dream Deferred: Ocean Hill-Brownsville Remembers," *Village Voice*, June 6, 1989, 29; Carlos E. Russell, *Perspectives on Power: A Black Community Looks at Itself* (unpublished manuscript), 589, Box 6, RBP, SCR; Hotep, "Dedicated to Excellence," 40–42; Podair, "'White' Values, 'Black' Values," 46; Leslie J. Campbell, "The Black Teacher and Black Power," *Forum*, May–August 1967, 2.

65. Akyeame Kwame, "Baba Jitu Weusi," Assata Shakur Forums, accessed January 5, 2008, http://www.assatashakur.org/forum/shoulders-our-freedom-fighters/17691-baba-jitu-weusi.html; Sara Slack, "The Inside Story of the Malcolm X IS 201 Memorial," *New York Amsterdam News*, March 2, 1968, 1, 40.

66. Slack, "The Inside Story of the Malcolm X IS 201 Memorial," 40; Leonard Buder, "Teacher Is Shifted for Taking Pupils to Anti-White Rally at I.S. 201," *New York Times*, February 27, 1968, 32; Daniel H. Watts, "The Program," *Liberator*, March 1968, 3; Transcript of Les Campbell Interview, November 3, 1988, Eyes on the Prize Interviews II, HHC, WUF; Weusi, *A Message from a Black Teacher*, 7–8; "Teacher Who Took Pupils to Malcolm Event Loses License," *Chicago Daily Defender*, March 30, 1968, 31; Leonard Buder, "Negroes Protest at School Inquiry," *New York Times*, March 6, 1968, 54L; Les Campbell, "Letter to the Editor: 'An Open Letter to My Young and Old Brothers and Sisters at Junior High School No. 35,'" *Forum*, January–April, 1968, 4.

67. Charles S. Isaacs, "A J.H.S. Teacher Tells It Like He Sees It," *New York Times*, November 24, 1968, SM70; Emanuel Perlmutter, "Course on Rebellion Listed at J.H.S. 271," *New York Times*, October 8, 1968, 1; "What Black Power Teaches," *Education News* (undated clipping, c. 1968), Box 24, Folder 8, and "Mr. Papaleo Lesson Plan," n.d., Box 55, Folder 22, UFT, RFW.

68. Martin Mayer, "The Full and Sometimes Very Surprising Story of Ocean Hill, the Teachers' Union and the Teacher Strikes of 1968," *New York Times Magazine*, February 2, 1969, 63; Henry Hampton and Steve Fayer, eds., *Voices of Freedom: An Oral History of the Civil Rights Movement from the 1950s Through the 1980s* (New York: Bantam Books, 1990), 492–502.

69. Mufson, "A Dream Deferred," 30; Russell, *Perspectives on Power*, 630; Thomas R. Brooks, "Tragedy at Ocean Hill," *Dissent*, January–February 1969, 33.

70. Nancy Hicks, "Nine Are Indicted for Obstruction in School Dispute," *New York Times*, December 20, 1968, 1; "9 to Fight Coercion Charges," *New York Amsterdam News*, December 28, 1968, 29; Leslie R. Campbell, "The Devil Can Never Educate Us," *Forum*, November 1968, 1, 3.

71. Isaacs, "A J.H.S. Teacher Tells It Like He Sees It," SM70; "The Mason-Dixon Line Moves to New York," *I.F. Stone's Weekly*, November 4, 1968, 2; Hampton and Fayer, *Voices of Freedom*, 506–507.

72. "Back Campbell in Bias Dispute," *New York Amsterdam News*, January 25, 1969, 23; Mufson, "A Dream Deferred," 30.

73. "The Black and the Jew: A Falling Out of Allies," *Time*, January 31, 1969, 55–59. For a discussion of prewar northern black resentment of Jews, see St. Clair Drake and Horace R. Cayton, *Black Metropolis: A Study of Negro Life in a Northern City* (Chicago: University of Chicago, 1993 [1945]), 432n.

74. Transcript of Les Campbell Interview, November 3, 1988, Eyes on the Prize Interviews II, HHC, WUF; Arnold H. Lubasch, "Racism Aired at Rally Backing Community Control of Schools," *New York Times*, February 17, 1969, 68; Les Campbell, "In Search of the New World," *Black News*, December 19, 1969, 4; Leonard Buder, "5 Black Teachers Reported Ousted," *New York Times*, June 19, 1969, 10.

75. "Brooklynites Spearhead Tribute for Nkrumah," *New York Amsterdam News*, May 13, 1972, C1; Hampton and Fayer, *Voices of Freedom*, 402–403.

76. "The New Breed of Black Youth," *Black News*, December 10, 1970, 2–4, and January 14, 1971, 2; "Black Power in N.Y.C.H.S.," flyer, n.d., Box 55, Folder 21, UFT, RFW; Big Black, "Around Our Way," *Black News*, September 26, 1970, 10; Emanuel Perlmutter, "Student Violence Shuts 2 City Highs," *New York Times*, April 24, 1969, 1, 35; Steven V. Roberts, "White Principal at Boys High Who Became Symbol Asks Shift," *New York Times*, May 29, 1968, 28; James P. Sterba, "School Protest Leader Defines Action," *New York Times*, December 3, 1968, 41; M. A. Farber, "Boys High Students Rampage and Set Two Fires; Scheduled Strike by Pupils Is Called Ineffective," *New York Times*, May 6, 1969, 31; "George Washington High Disrupted," *New York Times*, May 7, 1969, 33; Transcript of Les Campbell Interview, November 3, 1988, Eyes on the Prize Interviews II, HHC, WUF; "Say Students Already Have Power Board Would Give Them," *New York Amsterdam News*, November 8, 1969, 1, 47; Peter Kihss, "8 Arrested, Student Leaders Call Off Revolt in City," *New York Times*, December 6, 1968, 41.

77. C. Gerald Fraser, "Youths Protest at School Board," *New York Times*, August 27, 1969, 25; Transcript of Les Campbell Interview, November 3, 1988, Eyes on the Prize Interviews II, HHC, WUF; "The New Breed of Black Youth," 2–4; "Brother Les Campbell Is Dead," flyer, n.d., Box 55, Folder 22, UFT, RFW.

78. Mufson, "A Dream Deferred," 30; Hotep, "Dedicated to Excellence," 43; "The East: A Model of Nationhood," *Imani*, August–September 1971, 30–31; Jitu K. Weusi, "The East Legacy," *Journal of Community Advocacy and Activism* 1 (1996): 17; Les Campbell, "Ocean Hill-Brownsville Revisited: 1969," *Black News*, October 1969, 1–3; Black, "Around Our Way," 10.

79. Black, "Around Our Way," 10; "The East: A Model of Nationhood," 30–31; Weusi, "The East Legacy," 17; Ronald Walters, *Pan Africanism in the African Diaspora: An Analysis of Modern Afrocentric Political Movements* (Detroit, MI: Wayne State University Press, 1993), 303–305.

80. "Uhuru Sasa Shule," Parent Newsletter, 1971, KKP, INP; "Uhuru Sasa School," 1970 pamphlet, Box 48, Folder 1, EGP, SCR; "The Uhuru (Freedom) Sasa (Now) School," 1970 pamphlet, Box 24, Folder 9, UFT, RFW; "The East: A Model of Nationhood," 34, 56; Kierna Mayo, "Independents' Day," *City Limits Magazine*, January 1997; Hotep, "Dedicated to Excellence," 44, 46; "To Open Black School," *New York Amsterdam News*, February 7, 1970, 28; "The East Mental Ministry Report," 1972 pamphlet, Box 18, PWP, SCR; Joseph Lelyveld, "City High Schools Affected," *New York Times*, February 9, 1970, 1.

81. See Julius K. Nyerere, *Freedom and Socialism/Uhuru na Ujamaa: A Selection from Writings and Speeches, 1965-1967* (London: Oxford University Press, 1968); "Outline for a New African Educational Institution: The Uhuru Sasa School Program," 1972 pamphlet, JAL, UMI.

82. "Community School Pays Tribute to First Graduates," *New York Amsterdam News*, January 7, 1978, B1; "The East: A Model of Nationhood," 33–36; "The East Mental Ministry Report," 1972 pamphlet, Box 18, PWP, SCR.

Chapter 3

1. Staughton Lynd, "The New Radicals and 'Participatory Democracy,'" *Dissent*, July 1965, 328. For a sampling of the extensive literature on the radicalization of the black freedom struggle in the 1960s, see Hasan Kwame Jeffries, *Bloody Lowndes: Civil Rights and Black Power in Alabama's Black Belt* (New York: New York University Press, 2009); Yohuru Williams, *Black Politics/ White Power: Civil Rights, Black Power, and the Black Panthers in New Haven* (St. James, NY: Brandywine Press, 2000); Matthew J. Countryman, *Up South: Civil Rights and Black Power in Philadelphia* (Philadelphia: University of Pennsylvania Press, 2006); Christina Greene, *Our Separate Ways: Women and the Black Freedom Movement in Durham, North Carolina* (Chapel Hill: University of North Carolina Press, 2005); William H. Chafe, *Civilities and Civil Rights: Greensboro, North Carolina, and the Black Struggle for Freedom* (New York: Oxford University Press, 1980); Todd J. Moye, *Let the People Decide: Black Freedom and White Resistance Movements in Sunflower County, Mississippi, 1945–1986* (Chapel Hill: University of North Carolina Press, 2004); Richard D. Benson, II, *Fighting for Our Place in the Sun: Malcolm X and the Radicalization of the Black Student Movement, 1960–1973* (New York: Peter Lang, 2015); Donna Murch, *Living for the City: Migration, Education, and the Rise of the Black Panther Party in Oakland, California* (Chapel Hill: University of North Carolina Press, 2010); Robert O. Self, *American Babylon: Race and the Struggle for Postwar Oakland* (Princeton, NJ: Princeton University Press, 2003).

2. Charles M. Payne, "Introduction," in *Teach Freedom: Education for Liberation in the African-American Tradition*, ed. Charles M. Payne and Carol Sills Strickland (New York: Teachers College Press, 2008), 9–10; Sandra Richards and Sidney J. Lemelle, "Pedagogy, Politics and Power: Antinomies of the Black Radical Tradition," in *Black Protest Thought and Education*, ed. William H. Watkins (New York: Peter Lang, 2005), 6.

3. For more on the uplift tradition in African-American politics, see Kevin Kelly Gaines, *Uplifting the Race: Black Leadership, Politics, and Culture Since the Turn of the Century* (Chapel Hill: University of North Carolina Press, 1996).

4. William L. Van DeBurg, ed., *Modern Black Nationalism: From Marcus Garvey to Louis Farrakhan* (New York: New York University, 1997), 11; Richards and Lemelle, "Pedagogy, Politics and Power," 11–12; Judith Stein, *The World of Marcus Garvey: Race and Class in Modern Society* (Baton Rouge: Louisiana State University Press, 1986), 30; Cary D. Wintz, *African-American Political Thought, 1890-1930: Washington, Du Bois, Garvey and Randolph* (New York: M. E. Sharpe, 1996), 11.

5. Barbara Bair, "Pan-Africanism as Process: Adelaide Casely Hayford, Garveyism, and the Cultural Roots of Nationalism," in *Imagine Home: Class, Culture and Nationalism in the African Diaspora*, ed. Sidney J. Lemelle and Robin D. G. Kelley (New York: Verso, 1994), 130–132; Tony Martin, *Race First: The Ideological and Organizational Struggles of Marcus Garvey and the Universal Negro Improvement Association* (Dover, MA: Majority Press, 1976), 36–37; Barbara Bair, "Garveyism and Contested Political Terrain in 1920s Virginia," in *Afro-Virginian History and Culture*, ed. John Saillant (New York: Taylor & Francis, 1999), 230.

6. "Great Excursion to Liberty University," *Negro World*, September 25, 1926, 3, 6; "Liberty University to Help Furnish the New Education for the Negro," *Negro World*, September 4, 1926, 3.

7. Bair, "Garveyism and Contested Political Terrain in 1920s Virginia," 230; Robert A. Hill and Barbara Bair, eds., *Marcus Garvey: Life and Lessons* (Los Angeles: University of California Press, 1987), 264–265.

8. Hill and Bair, *Marcus Garvey*, 264; Tony Martin, ed., *Message to the People: The Course of African Philosophy* (Dover, MA: Majority Press, 1986), xix, xxi. For an analysis of the "civilizationist" tendencies of early black nationalism, see Wilson Jeremiah Moses, *The Golden Age of Black Nationalism: 1850-1925* (Camden, CT: Archon Book, 1978).

9. Hakim M. Rashid and Zakiyyah Muhammad, "The Sister Clara Muhammad Schools: Pioneers in the Development of Islamic Education in America," *Journal of Negro Education* 61 (1992): 179; Elijah Muhammad, *Message to the Blackman in America* (Chicago: Muhammad Mosque of Islam No. 2, 1965), 39–41; Clemmont E. Vontress, "Threat, Blessing, or Both? The Black Muslim Schools," *Phi Delta Kappan*, October 1965, 86; Barbara J. Whiteside, "A Study of the Structure, Norms and Folkways of the Educational Institutions of the Nation of Islam in the United States from 1932 to 1975," (EdD diss., Wayne State University, 1987); Bayyinah Sharief Jeffries, "'A Nation Can Rise No Higher Than Its Women': The Critical Role of Black Muslim Women in the Development and Purveyance of Black Consciousness, 1945-1975" (PhD diss., Michigan State University, 2009), 195; Mattias Gardell, *In the Name of Elijah Muhammad: Louis Farrakhan and The Nation of Islam* (Durham, NC: Duke University Press, 1996), 61; Karl Evanzz, *The Messenger: The Rise and Fall of Elijah Muhammad* (New York: Random House, 1999), 99–100.

10. "Senator Asks Black Muslim School Probe," *Chicago Daily Tribune*, May 13, 1962, 10; "Educator, Legislator View Muslim School," *Chicago Daily Tribune*, May 22, 1962, 1; "Behind the Muslim Curtain," *New York Amsterdam News*, June 9, 1962, 15.

11. Charlayne Hunter, "Muslim Center Blends Business, School and Mosque," *New York Times*, August 25, 1970, 38; Elijah Muhammad, *Salaam*, July 1960, 7; Alvin Adams, "Fight Looms over Charge School Teaches Race Hatred," *Jet*, July 12, 1962, 18; "Educator, Legislator View Muslim School," *Chicago Daily Tribune*, May 22, 1962, 1.

12. Clifton E. Marsh, *The Lost-Found Nation of Islam in America* (Lanham, MD: Scarecrow Press, 2000), 43–44; Edward E. Curtis, *Black Muslim Religion in the Nation of Islam, 1960-1975* (Chapel Hill: University of North Carolina Press, 2006), 156–157; Joe Walker, "Opening of the University of Islam No. 7," *Muhammad Speaks*, January 2, 1970, 8; Hunter, "Muslim Center Blends Business, School and Mosque," 38; Vontress, "Threat, Blessing, or Both?," 88, 90; "The Muslim Way," *Newsweek*, September 25, 1972, 106, 109–110.

13. See, for example, Daryl Michael Scott, *Contempt and Pity: Social Policy and the Image of the Damaged Black Psyche* (Chapel Hill: University of North Carolina Press, 1997).

14. Sister Agnita X, "The Fruits of Muhammad's Amazing Education Program," *Muhammad Speaks*, June 14, 1968; Vontress, "Threat, Blessing, or Both?," 86; Walker, "Opening of the University of Islam No. 7," 8; Zakiyyah Muhammad, "Faith and Courage to Educate Our Own: Reflections on Islamic Schools in the African American Community," in *Black Education: A Transformative Research and Action Agenda for the New Century*, ed. Joyce Elaine King (Mahwah, NJ: American Educational Research Association, 2005), 272–273; Gardell, *In the Name of Elijah Muhammad*, 61; Brother Theodore 4X Marshall, "Black Children Need Black Teachers," *Muhammad Speaks*, August 1, 1969; "Politicians, Teachers to Aid Muslim Schools," *New York Amsterdam News*, August 16, 1969, 28; "Muslim Call for Separate School System for Blacks," *Jet*, October 9, 1969, 7.

15. Ula Taylor, "Elijah Muhammad's Nation of Islam: Separatism, Regendering, and a Secular Approach to Black Power After Malcolm X (1965-1975)," in *Freedom North: Black Freedom Struggles Outside the South, 1940-1980*, ed. Jeanne Theoharis and Komozi Woodard (New York: Palgrave Macmillan, 2003), 189; Brother Lovett X and Sister Remel X, "To the Editor," *Pittsburgh Courier*, November 23, 1957, B7; "The Original Black Capitalists," *Time*, March 7, 1969, 29; "U. of Islam Students Tour Printing Plant," *Muhammad Speaks*, June 19, 1970, 15.

16. William Sturkey, "'I Want to Become a Part of History': Freedom Summer, Freedom Schools, and the *Freedom News*," *Journal of African-American History* 95 (2010): 349–354; Daniel Perlstein, "Teaching Freedom: SNCC and the Creation of the Mississippi Freedom Schools," *History of Education Quarterly* 30 (1990): 308; Carleton Mabee, "Freedom Schools, North and South," *The Reporter*, September 10, 1964, 30–32; Charles L. Sanders, "Playing Hooky for Freedom," *Ebony*, April 1964, 153–162.

17. Dorothy Cotton, "CEP: Challenge to the 'New Education,'" *Freedomways*, Winter 1969, 66; Septima Clark, "Literacy and Liberation," *Freedomways*, Winter 1964, 122 (emphasis is mine); David P. Levine, "Citizenship Schools" (PhD diss., University of Wisconsin-Madison, 1999); David P. Levine, "The Birth of the Citizenship Schools: Entwining the Struggles for Literacy and Freedom," *History of Education Quarterly* 44 (2004): 388–414.

18. Joe Street, "Reconstructing Education from the Bottom Up: SNCC's 1964 Mississippi Summer Project and African American Culture," *Journal of American Studies* 38 (2004): 274; Charles Cobb, "Prospectus for a Summer Freedom School Curriculum," *Radical Teacher*, Fall 1991, 36; Charles M. Payne, *I've Got the Light of Freedom: The Organizing Tradition and the Mississippi Freedom Struggle* (Berkeley: University of California Press, 1995), 302–303; Perlstein, "Teaching Freedom," 297–324; George W. Chilcoat and Jerry A. Ligon, "'We Talk Here. This Is a School for Talking.' Participatory Democracy from the Classroom out into the Community: How Discussion Was Used in the Mississippi Freedom Schools," *Curriculum Inquiry* 28 (1998): 167–168; George W. Chilcoat and Jerry A. Ligon, "'Helping to Make Democracy a Living Reality': The Curriculum Conference of the Mississippi Freedom Schools," *Journal of Curriculum and Supervision* 15 (1999): 48; Jon Hale, "'The Student as a Force for Social Change': The Mississippi Freedom Schools and Student Engagement," *Journal of African-American History* 96 (2011): 331.

19. John Dittmer, *Local People: The Struggle for Civil Rights in Mississippi* (Chicago: University of Illinois Press, 2004), 259; Payne, *I've Got the Light of Freedom*, 302–303; Elizabeth Sutherland, ed., *Letters from Mississippi* (New York: McGraw-Hill, 1965), 96; Sturkey, "'I Want to Become a Part of History,'" 356.

20. Henry Hampton and Steve Fayer, eds., *Voices of Freedom: An Oral History of the Civil Rights Movement from the 1950s Through the 1980s* (New York: Bantam Books, 1990), 181; Howard Zinn, "Schools in Context: The Mississippi Idea" (reprint of *Nation* article), Box 72, Folder 14, AMP, SCR; Clayborne Carson, ed., *The Student Voice, 1960-1965: Periodical of the Student Nonviolent Coordinating Committee* (Westport, CT: Meckler, 1990), 180–181.

21. Charlie Cobb, "Prospectus for a Summer Freedom School Program," December 1963, Box 9, Folder 2, EJB, SCR; Daniel Perlstein, "Teaching Freedom: SNCC and the Creation of the Mississippi Freedom Schools," *History of Education Quarterly* 30 (1990): 297–324; Jimmy Garrett, "Freedom Schools," *Radical Teacher*, Fall 1991, 42–43.

22. Chilcoat and Ligon, "'Helping to Make Democracy a Living Reality,'" 46; Dittmer, *Local People*, 259.

23. Christopher Jencks and Milton Kotler, "A Government of the Black, by the Black, and for the Black," *Ramparts*, July 1966, 53–54, and Jencks and Kotler, "A Strategy of Para-Government for Negro Mississippi: The Prospects of Direct Federal Relations" (report prepared for Presbyterian Church, October 1964), Box 6, NLC, HIA; Eric Burner, *And Gently He Shall Lead Them: Robert Parris Moses and Civil Rights in Mississippi* (New York: New York University, 1994), 216; Dittmer, *Local People*, 326; Rod Bush, *We Are Not What We Seem: Black Nationalism and Class Struggle in the American Century* (New York: New York University Press, 1999), 166.

24. Sharon Harley, "'Chronicle of a Death Foretold': Gloria Richardson, the Cambridge Movement, and the Radical Black Activist Tradition," in *Sisters in the Struggle: African-American Women in the Civil Rights-Black Power Movement*, ed. Bettye Collier-Thomas and Vincent P. Franklin (New York: New York University Press, 2001), 176; James Forman, *The Making of Black Revolutionaries* (Seattle: University of Washington Press, 2000 [1972]), 360, 448; Ibram Rogers, "Remembering the Black Campus Movement: An Oral History Interview with James P. Garrett," *Journal of Pan African Studies* 2 (2009): 33; Cleveland Sellers, *The River of No Return: The Autobiography of a Black Militant and the Life and Death of SNCC* (New York: William Morrow, 1990), 167.

25. Cynthia Griggs Fleming, *Soon We Will Not Cry: The Liberation of Ruby Doris Smith Robinson* (Lanham, MD: Rowman & Littlefield, 1996); Clayborne Carson, *In Struggle: SNCC and the Black Awakening of the 1960s* (Cambridge, MA: Harvard University Press, 1981), 129; Charlie Cobb, "Revolution: From Stokely Carmichael to Kwame Ture," *Black Scholar* 27 (1997): 36; Sellers, *The River of No Return*, 167.

26. John Lewis, *Walking with the Wind: A Memoir of the Movement* (Orlando, FL: Harcourt Brace, 1998), 365; Forman, *The Making of Black Revolutionaries*, 445; Charles Cobb, "Atlanta to Zimbabwe," *Southern Exposure*, Spring 1981, 85–88; Fanon Che Wilkins, "The Making of Black Internationalists: SNCC and Africa Before the Launching of Black Power, 1960-1965," *Journal of African American History* 92 (2007): 468–491; Wesley C. Hogan, *Many Minds, One Heart: SNCC's Dream for a New America* (Chapel Hill: University of North Carolina Press,

2001), 219; Seth M. Markle, "'We Are Not Tourists': The Black Power Movement and the Making of 'Socialist' Tanzania, 1960-1974," (PhD diss., New York University, 2011).

27. Transcript of October 21, 1988, Interview with Cleveland Sellers, HHC, WUF; Lewis, *Walking with the Wind*, 297; Kwame Ture and Ekwueme Michael Thelwell, *Ready for Revolution: The Life and Struggles of Stokely Carmichael* (New York: Scribner, 2003), 440.

28. Howard Zinn, "Schools in Context: The Mississippi Idea" (reprint of *Nation* article), Box 72, Folder 14, AMP, SCR.

29. "Negroes in American History: A Freedom Primer," Box 1, Folder 14, and Frank Cieciorka to Cleveland Sellers, n.d. (c. September 1965), Box 1, Folder 7, RYP, SCR.

30. Fannie Theresa Rushing, "Minds Still Stayed on Freedom?" in *Teach Freedom*, 98; "Residential Freedom School Report," Judy Richardson, August 1965, Box 1, Folder 12, RYP, SCR.

31. Payne, *I've Got the Light of Freedom*, 328–330, 343; Dittmer, *Local People*, 369.

32. Donald W. Robinson, "Head Starts in Mississippi," *Phi Delta Kappan*, October 1965, 91–95; "Shriver Drops CDGM," *New Republic*, October 15, 1966, 7; Joan Bowman, "Mississippi Counterattacks the War on Poverty," *The Movement*, October 1965, 7; Polly Greenburg, "CDGM . . . An Experiment in Preschool for the Poor—by the Poor," *Young Children*, May 1967, 310.

33. "Accusations and Answers," Child Development Group of Mississippi, Box 159-2, Folder 18, CRV, MSR; Pat Watters, "CDGM: Who Really Won?" *New South*, Spring 1967, 49–63; Faith S. Holsaert et al., *Hands on the Freedom Plow: Personal Accounts by Women in SNCC* (Champaign: University of Illinois Press, 2010), 551; Jean Smith, "I Learned to Feel Black," in *The Black Power Revolt*, ed. Floyd Barbour (Boston: Extending Horizons Books, 1968), 216.

34. May 15, 1966, "Dear Sirs" letter, SNCC Atlanta Project, Box 1, Folder 12, VCP, WHI; "Freedom Schools: The Reason Why" and minutes of April 25, 1966, Freedom School Meeting, Atlanta, 1966, Box 9, Folder 2, EJB, SCR.

35. "Nashville Instruction in Black History: Whites Call It Teaching 'Reason for Black Hate,'" *Muhammad Speaks*, September 1, 1967, 20, 22; "Nashville Black Consciousness Advocates Charge City Is Conspiring to Crush Them," *Muhammad Speaks*, December 1, 1967, 18; "Liberation School: Correction Sent to Eastland," *Chicago Daily Defender*, August 10, 1967, 10; "I Will Tell Them What Is Going On," *Baltimore Afro-American*, August 12, 1967, 1–2; "'Hate-White' School Hit in Riot Probe," *San Francisco Chronicle*, August 4, 1967, 1, 11.

36. "Repression vs. Liberation in Nashville," *The Movement*, September 1967, 8; "Nashville Movement Attacked," *The Southern Patriot*, October 1967; "School Kids Act Out Slave Revolt," *Chicago Daily Defender*, August 17, 1967, 5. See also Carson, *In Struggle*, 258–260, and Audio Cassette of Fred Brooks Interview, CRD, MSR.

37. "OAAU Liberation School," pamphlet, Box 6, JCP, ACC; Muhammad Ahmad (Max Stanford), "Malcolm X: Human Rights and Self-Determination," 9–13 March 1990; William W. Sales, Jr., *From Civil Rights to Black Liberation: Malcolm X and the Organization of Afro-America Unity* (Boston: South End Press, 1994), 121; Max Stanford, "What Road for Black Power," December 1967, Black Power Movement Part 3 (Microfilm).

38. Angela Davis, *Angela Davis: An Autobiography* (New York: International Publishers, 1988 [1974]), 183; H. Rap Brown to Vincent Harding, n.d. (c. 1969), Box 36, Folder 13, VHP, EUM.

39. "Liberation Means Freedom," *Black Panther*, July 5, 1969, 3–4; Ryan J. Kirkby, "'The Revolution Will Not Be Televised': Community Activism and the Black Panther Party, 1966-1971," *Canadian Review of American Studies* 41 (2011): 36; Paul Alkebulan, *Survival Pending Revolution: The History of the Black Panther Party* (Tuscaloosa: University of Alabama Press, 2007); JoNina M. Abron, "'Serving the People': The Survival Programs of the Black Panther Party," in *The Black Panther Party Reconsidered*, ed. Charles E. Jones (Baltimore, MD: Black Classic Press, 1998), 177–192; Craig Peck, "'Educate to Liberate': The Black Panther Party and Political Education" (PhD diss., Stanford University 2001), 196–203; David McClintick, "The Black Panthers: Negro Militants Use Free Food, Medical Aid to Promote Revolution," *Wall Street Journal*, August 29, 1969, 1, 12; Earl Caldwell, "Black Panthers Serving Youngsters a Diet of Food and Politics," *New York Times*, June 15, 1969, 57; Eldridge Cleaver, "On Meeting the Needs of the People," *Ramparts*, September 1969, 34.

40. "Black Panther Party Platform," in *Black Protest: History, Documents and Analysis, 1619 to the Present*, ed. Joanne Grant (New York: Fawcett Premier, 1968), 519; "Liberation School," *Black Panther*, August 16, 1969, 14; Emory Douglas, "On Revolutionary Culture," *Black Panther*, September 13, 1969, 6.
41. "Black Panther Party Liberation Schools (Summer)," memorandum, Box 1, Folder 7, BPFBI, SCR; "Liberation Means Freedom," *Black Panther*, July 5, 1969, 3–4; "Letters to Chairman Bobby from Seattle Liberation School," *Black Panther*, September 13, 1969, 8; Charlayne Hunter, "Panthers Indoctrinate the Young," *New York Times*, August 18, 1969, 31.
42. Hunter, "Panthers Indoctrinate the Young," 31; "Liberation School from a Mother's Point of View," *Black Panther*, July 12, 1969, 3; "The Liberation School," *Black Panther*, August 2, 1969, 14; "The Youth Make the Revolution," *Black Panther*, August 2, 1969, 12; "San Francisco Liberation School," *Black Panther*, November 15, 1969, 17; "Liberation Means Freedom," *Black Panther*, July 5, 1969, 3–4.
43. Mike Evans, "Community Schools," *Black Panther*, February 5, 1970, 7; Assata Shakur, *Assata: An Autobiography* (Chicago: Lawrence Hill, 1987), 220.
44. Joy Ann Williamson, "Community Control with a Black Nationalist Twist: The Black Panther Party's Educational Programs," in *Black Protest Thought and Education*, ed. William H. Watkins (New York: Peter Lang, 2005), 138, 142; "San Francisco Liberation School," *Black Panther*, November 15, 1969, 17.
45. Earl Caldwell, "Black Panthers Serving Youngsters a Diet of Food and Politics," *New York Times*, June 15, 1969, 57; "Black Panther Party Liberation Schools (Summer)," memorandum, Box 1, Folder 7, BPFBI, SCR; "Liberation Means Freedom," 3–4; "Liberation Schools," in *The Black Panthers Speak*, ed. Philip S. Foner (Cambridge, MA: Da Capo Press, 1995), 171.
46. Williamson, "Community Control with a Black Nationalist Twist," 145; Bush, *We Are Not What We Seem*, 221; "Richmond Fascists Attempt to Stop Liberation School," *Black Panther*, August 2, 1969, 14.
47. "Liberation Means Freedom," 3–4; quoted in Peck, " 'Educate to Liberate': The Black Panther Party and Political Education," 195, 198–199.
48. Julius Lester, *Revolutionary Notes* (New York: Grove Press, 1969), 105; Carmichael (Kwame Ture) quoted in Van DeBurg, ed., *Modern Black Nationalism*, 15.
49. John Elliott Churchville, *Driven! Remembrance, Reflection & Revelation* (West Conshohocken, PA: Infinity Publishing, 2011), 4–6.
50. Alvin F. Poussaint and Joyce Ladner (untitled clipping, *National Observer*, August 12, 1968), Box 79, Folder 11, JKP, EUM; Churchville, *Driven!*, 8.
51. Harland Randolph, "The Northern Student Movement" (reprint from *The Educational Record*, Fall 1964), Box 10, Folder 8, EJB, SCR; "The Northern Student Movement," and Peter Countryman, "With Our Minds Stayed on Freedom," reprint, 1963, Box 117, Folder 2, JKP, EUM.
52. Karen Joyce Cook, "Freedom Libraries in the 1964 Mississippi Freedom Summer Project: A History" (PhD diss., University of Alabama, 2008); "Northern Student Movement Freedom Library Report," Box 7, Folder 18, NSM, SCR; Bill Strickland to John O. Killens, August 4, 1964, Box 117, Folder 2, JKP, EUM.
53. Al Hasbrouk, "Director Explains Freedom Library's Employment Policy," *Temple University News*, December 17, 1964; James Smart, "A Library Grows in the Riot Rubble," *Philadelphia Bulletin*, September 6, 1964, 4; Countryman, *Up South*, 185–186; Bill Strickland to John O. Killens, August 4, 1964, Box 117, Folder 2, JKP, EUM; John Churchville, "Freedom Library Day School," in *Curriculum Approaches from a Black Perspective*, ed. Black Child Development Institute (Washington, DC: Black Child Development Institute, 1973), 49.
54. "NSM Freedom Library: A General Statement," n.d., and "Northern Student Movement Freedom Library Report," Box 7, Folder 18, NSM, SCR; "Omowale Ujamaa Celebrates 10th Year," *Los Angeles Sentinel*, December 3, 1981, A11, C13; "Founder Keeps Project Going Despite Shortage of 'Sponsors,' " *Philadelphia Tribune*, September 3, 1966, 6; Joan D. Ratteray, "An Interview with John Churchville," July 1982 transcript, National Center for Neighborhood Enterprise, Box 6, IIE, CUK; John Churchville, "On Correct Black Education," *Black News*, January 25, 1970, 1–3; Bill Strickland, "Community Organization in the Ghetto, A Critique" (rough draft of statement), n.d., Box 117, Folder 2, JKP, EUM.

55. "Prospectus for NSM Project in Philadelphia," n.d., and August 5, 1964, William Strickland to Sylvester Leaks, Box 7, Folders 17 and 18, NSM, SCR; also see Carson, *In Struggle*, 195.
56. Bill Strickland, "Community Organization in the Ghetto, A Critique" (rough draft of statement), n.d., Box 117, Folder 2, JKP, EUM; Kenneth B. Clark, *Prejudice and Your Child* (New York: Beacon Press, 1955), 63; Michael Harrington, *The Other America: Poverty in the United States* (New York: Touchstone, 1997 [1962]), 64; Smart, "A Library Grows in the Riot Rubble," 4.
57. "Memorandum from National Office to Staff Re: The Philadelphia Youth Group's Trip to New York," n.d. (c. 1966) and John E. Churchville, "Pre-School and After-School Program of the NSM Freedom Library" (draft of program overview), n.d., Box 7, Folder 18, NSM, SCR.
58. Churchville, "Freedom Library Day School," 47–50; "15 Neighborhood Groups Confer On Phila. School Problems," *Philadelphia Tribune*, October 26, 1965, 2.
59. Countryman, *Up South*, 3, 190–201; Black Unity Movement Flyer, February 1966, and February 9, 1966, Mattie L. Humphrey to the Editor of the *Philadelphia Tribune*, Box 7, Folder 17, NSM, SCR; Paul Washington, *"Other Sheep I Have": The Autobiography of Father Paul M. Washington* (Philadelphia: Temple University Press, 1994), 46.
60. "Conviction of 373 Students Get Review," *Baltimore Afro-American*, March 3, 1963, 2; James Forman, *The Making of Black Revolutionaries* (New York: Macmillan, 1972), 467; " 'Testimony Proved Frame-Up' Says SNCC's Foreman,' " *Baltimore Afro-American*, September 3, 1966, 15; Countryman, *Up South*, 216; "Bar Ridge Group From Mon. Meet," *Philadelphia Tribune*, June 22, 1965, 4.
61. Churchville, *Driven!*, 10–11; Staughton Lynd, "The Freedom Schools: Concept and Organization," *Freedomways*, Spring 1965, 307.
62. Albert Vann, "We Must Educate Ourselves or Perish," *Forum*, January–February, 1972.
63. John E. Churchville, "Pre-School and After-School Program of the NSM Freedom Library" (draft of program overview), n.d., Box 7, Folder 18, NSM, SCR; Charlie Cobb, "What We Have Discovered," *Freedomways*, Spring 1965, 342; John E. Churchville, "On Correct Black Education, Part II: The Function, Basis, and Extent of Correct Black Education," *Maji-Maji*, January 1969, 9; John Churchville, "On Correct Black Education," *Black News*, January 25, 1970, 3; Austin D. Scott, "Negroes of North Set Up Campaign on Slum Housing," *Washington Post*, July 17, 1966, A7.
64. "The NSM Freedom Library, 2064 Ridge Avenue, Philadelphia," pamphlet, and "Northern Student Movement Freedom Library Report," Box 7, Folder 18, NSM, SCR; Black Child Development Institute, *Curriculum Approaches from a Black Perspective* (Washington, DC: Black Child Development Institute, 1973), 55.
65. John E. Churchville, "Jesus, Salvation, and YOU," 1967 pamphlet, Box 44, Folder 11, VHP, EUM; Churchville, *Driven!*, 19; "Teachers Don't Always Have the Right Answers," *Los Angeles Times*, October 9, 1968, C2; " 'Black Value System' Is Urged on Nuns," *New York Times*, August 20, 1972, 58.
66. See Freire, *Pedagogy of the Oppressed* (New York: Continuum, 1970); "NSM Freedom Library: A General Statement," n.d., Box 7, Folder 18, NSM, SCR.
67. Kasisi Jitu Weusi, "A View from the East: 'A Homecoming,' " *Black News*, March 1976, 3, 4; Vincent Harding, "On the Education of Children (and Parents) for a Time of Protracted Struggle," Box 35, Folder 31, JHC, SCR and CIBI, INP.
68. "Children Begin in This School at 2 ½-Year-Old," *Philadelphia Tribune*, September 3, 1966, 6.
69. "Prospectus for N.S.M. Project in Philadelphia," and "Honoring Tanzania" (Supplement to the Unity Bulletin), March 19, 1966, Box 7, Folder 18, NSM, SCR; John Wise, *It's a New Day*, Columbus, OH: Council of Independent Black Institutions, 1973.

Chapter 4

1. Amilcar Cabral, *Return to the Source: Selected Speeches by Amilcar Cabral* (New York: Monthly Review Press, 1974), 43. For another examination of East Palo Alto and independent black institutions,a see chapter seven of Martha Biondi, *The Black Revolution on Campus* (Berkeley: University of California Press, 2012). For an early discussion of culture and Black Power,

see William L. Van DeBurg, *New Day in Babylon: The Black Power Movement and American Culture, 1965–1975* (Chicago: University of Chicago Press, 1992). For a different interpretation that stresses the political significance of cultural work, see Scot Brown, *Fighting for Us: Maulana Karenga, the US Organization and Black Cultural Nationalism* (New York: New York University Press, 2002).

2. Phyllis Barusch and Harriet Nathan, "The East Palo Alto Municipal Advisory Council: A Black Community's Experiment in Local Self-Government," *Public Affairs Report*, October 1972, 185–191; Myron Meyers, "African Name of Nairobi Proposed for East Palo Alto," *Palo Alto Times*, April 2, 1968, 1–2; "E. Palo Altans Nix Name Change to Nairobi by 3 to 1 Margin," *Palo Alto Times*, November 6, 1968, 3; Earl Caldwell, "'Nairobi' Fight in California Pits Youth Against Oldsters," *Miami News*, January 8, 1969, 8A.

3. Caldwell, "'Nairobi' Fight in California Pits Youth Against Oldsters," 8A; Daryl E. Lembke, "East Palo Alto to Vote on Becoming Nairobi," *Los Angeles Times*, November 3, 1968, B26; "East Palo Alto Wants Freedom," *Black Panther*, September 25, 1968, 11.

4. "Congo Altering City Names: Leopoldville to Be Kinshasa," *New York Times*, May 8, 1966, 16; Meyer Avers, "African Names," *New York Times*, July 12, 1966, 16; "Action Stimulator No. #75: 'New Town' Movement: Black Style," flyer, September 10, 1971, Box 14, PWP, SCR.

5. Quoted in James H. Meriwether, *Proudly We Can Be Africans: Black Americans and Africa, 1935-1961* (Chapel Hill: University of North Carolina Press, 2002), 149.

6. Gerald Horne, *Mau Mau in Harlem? The U.S. and the Liberation of Kenya* (New York: Palgrave Macmillan, 2009), 238.

7. Romic Chemical Corporation, *A History of East Palo Alto* (East Palo Alto, CA: Romic Chemical Corporation, 1993), 1–2, 10–11, 16–17; Mark Stein, "East Palo Alto: Minority Cityhood: A Casebook," *Los Angeles Times*, January 21, 1987, B1; Veronique de Turenne, "East Palo Alto Looks to Its Past for a New Name," *Los Angeles Times*, November 8, 1998.

8. Albert M. Camarillo, "Blacks, Latinos, and the New Racial Frontier in American Cities of Color: California's Emerging Minority-Majority Cities," in *African American Urban History Since World War II*, ed. Kenneth L. Kusmer and Joe W. Trotter (Chicago: University of Chicago Press, 2009), 44–45; Barusch and Nathan, "The East Palo Alto Municipal Advisory Council," 185–188; Stephen Robitaille, "E. Palo Alto Coming of Age—Painfully City's History a Saga of Unfulfilled Promise," *San Jose Mercury News*, February 12, 1989, 1A.

9. Philip Hager, "E. Palo Alto Unites to Halt Rising Crime Rate," *Los Angeles Times*, May 24, 1970, B7; "Shaped by a Dream: A Town Called Boley," *Life*, November 29, 1968, 72–74; "Boley, Oklahoma: An All-Black Town Struggles for Survival," *Black Enterprise*, September 1970, 22–25; June Jordan, "Mississippi 'Black Home': A Sweet and Bitter Bluesong," *New York Times*, October 11, 1970, 249–251; Arthur L. Tolson, "Black Towns of Oklahoma," *Black Scholar*, April 1970, 22; Richard Hall, "A Stir of Hope in Mound Bayou," *Life*, March 28, 1969, 66–81; Joseph Huttie, Jr., "'New Federalism' and the Death of a Dream in Mound Bayou, Mississippi," *New South*, Fall 1973, 20–29.

10. Lembke, "East Palo Alto to Vote on Becoming Nairobi," 11; Stein, "Minority Cityhood," B1; Allan B. Jacobs, *Observing and Interpreting East Palo Alto, Working Paper No. 375, August 1982* (Berkeley: University of California Berkeley, 1982), 8; Barusch and Nathan, "The East Palo Alto Municipal Advisory Council," 185–188; "Black City Fights Crime," *New Pittsburgh Courier*, December 19, 1971, 6; "Nairobi Schools Offer Help to Health Center," *Palo Alto Times*, October 7, 1970; July 10, 1969, Executive Planning Committee, National Conference of Health Consumers to Leslie Dunbar, Box 2S437, Field Foundation Archives, Center for American History, University of Texas Austin; "East Palo Alto Opens War on Pushers, Burglars," *Sun Reporter*, September 18, 1971, 8; Philip Hager, "E. Palo Alto Unites to Halt Rising Crime Rate," *Los Angeles Times*, May 24, 1970, B7.

11. Jeanette Bradley, "East Palo Alto Name Changing . . . Gradually," *Palo Alto Times*, August 18, 1969, 35; Bill Lane, "People—Places 'n' Situwayshuns," *Los Angeles Sentinel*, April 17, 1975, B6.

12. Caldwell, "'Nairobi' Fight in California Pits Youth Against Oldsters," 8A; Transcript of Leigh Torrance and Danielle Moore Interview with Robert "Bob" Hoover, July 7, 2004, East Palo Alto, SOH, INP.

13. "The Nairobi Day School," 1970 KPFA Interview with Gertrude Wilks, PTL, MEC; Gertrude Dyer Wilks, *Gathering Together: Born to Be a Leader* (LaVergne, TN: Xlibris Corporation, 2010), 49–58.

14. Transcript of "Circle in the Dirt" Interview with Gertrude Wilks, n.d., Box 6, Folder 2, CMP, SUS; Transcript of Robert Martin Interview with Gertrude Wilks, July 28, 1969, East Palo Alto, CRD, MSR.

15. Aleta Watson, "Nairobi School Celebrates Its 14th Birthday," *San Jose Mercury News*, October 22, 1989, 1B, 3B; Transcript of John Rickford Interview with Gertrude Wilks, July 14, 2004, East Palo Alto, SOH, INP.

16. Robert Lowe, "Ravenswood High School and the Struggle for Racial Justice in the Sequoia Union High School District" (PhD diss., Stanford University, 1989), 9, 77, 87; Keith Hearn, "Program to Aid Deprived Students at an Early Stage," *Palo Alto Times*, January 19, 1966, 3; *National Policy Conference on Education for Blacks; Proceedings, March 29-April 1, 1972* (Washington, DC: U.S. House of Representatives, 1972), 136.

17. Transcript of Robert Martin Interview with Gertrude Wilks, July 28, 1969, East Palo Alto, CRD, MSR; East Palo Alto Day School, *Day School, E.P.A.* (East Palo Alto, CA: MEE Bookstore, 1970), 12; Gertrude Wilks, "Recipe for Building a School," 1971 pamphlet, GWC, INP.

18. East Palo Alto Day School, *Day School, E.P.A.*, 11, 27; "Ravenswood Moms to Demonstrate," *Palo Alto Times*, September 5, 1966, 1; "Ravenswood High Faces Student Walkout Threat," *Palo Alto Times*, September 22, 1966, 1; "Parents Form New Ravenswood Group," *Palo Alto Times*, March 28, 1968, 5.

19. Lowe, "Ravenswood High School and the Struggle for Racial Justice," 89; Sandra Blakeslee, "School for Blacks Offers Money-Back Guarantee," *New York Times*, June 4, 1975, 35.

20. "Negro Betterment Requires Competition, Organizer Says," *Palo Alto Times*, April 10, 1967, 2; "School Officials Decry Ravenswood Pullouts," *Palo Alto Times*, December 14, 1966, 1.

21. Sylvia Berry Williams, *Hassling* (Boston: Little, Brown, 1970), 110; Wilks, *Gathering Together*, 61; "And How Shall Our Children Be Educated?" *The Crisis*, August–September 1966, 398.

22. Charlotte K. Beyers, "Education by Degrees; Recipe for a Community School," *Essence*, October 1980, 42; Gertrude Wilks, "Recipe for Building a School," 1971 pamphlet, GWC, INP; East Palo Alto Day School, *Day School, E.P.A.*, 15.

23. Gertrude Wilks, "Recipe for Building a School," 1971 pamphlet, GWC, INP; East Palo Alto Day School, *Day School, E.P.A.*, 15; Ronald D. Goben, "A School Outside of School," *Southern Education Report*, October 1967, 32; Bill Shilstone, "Black Motivation, Quality Education—That's Nairobi School, Mrs. Wilks Says," *Palo Alto Times*, June 20, 1970, 1, 3.

24. Roger Rapoport, "Peninsula Busing Battle Takes a Strange Turn," *San Francisco Chronicle*, March 24, 1978, 2; "Nairobi High, 1970," yearbook (Microfilm), BL, UCB; "The Nairobi Day School," 1970 KPFA Interview with Gertrude Wilks, PTL, MEC.

25. "Palo Alto Residents Seek Negro Neighbors," *Los Angeles Times*, April 28, 1968, H6; Louis L. Knowles and Kenneth Prewitt, eds., *Racism in America* (Englewood Cliffs, NJ: Prentice-Hall, 1969).

26. "Too Militant to Teach," *Sun Reporter*, October 25, 1969, 12; "Palo Alto Wants Black Teachers for Multicultural Project," 1968 pamphlet, Box 26, PWP, SCR; Jeanette Bradley, "Private High School for Blacks Now Open," *Palo Alto Times*, April 16, 1969; *Equal Educational Opportunity Hearings Before the Select Committee of the U.S. Senate, 92nd Congress, First Session, Part 9A—San Francisco and Berkeley, CA* (Washington, DC: U.S. Government Printing Office, 1971), 4301–4302.

27. "What Can I Do?" 1969 flyer, Box 38, NLC, HIA; Transcript of "Circle in the Dirt" Interview with Gertrude Wilks, n.d., Box 6, Folder 2, CMP, SUS.

28. "The Nairobi Day School," 1970 KPFA Interview with Gertrude Wilks, PTL, MEC; Bradley, "Private High School for Blacks"; Williams, *Hassling*, 16, 116–117, 173, 188, 191.

29. Austin Scott, "New Negro Spirit Based on Organization, Pride," *San Jose Mercury News*, September 26, 1967, 17.

30. Transcript of Leigh Torrance and Danielle Moore Interview with Robert "Bob" Hoover, July 7, 2004, East Palo Alto, SOH, INP.

31. Lowe, "Ravenswood High School and the Struggle for Racial Justice."

32. Daryl Lembke, "1,000 Join in School Switch," *Los Angeles Times*, August 24, 1971, 2, 20; Shilstone, "Black Motivation, Quality Education"; Warren C. Hayman, "Community Control of the Educational System," in *Black Is . . . A Publication from a Conference on the Emerging Trends in the Education of Black Students*, ed. Lanny Berry and Barbara Shaw (Larkspur, CA: Tamalpais Union High School District, 1972), 66.

33. Transcript of John Rickford Interview with Gertrude Wilks, July 14, 2004, East Palo Alto, SOH, INP; Jack Slater, "Learning Is an All-Black Thing," *Ebony*, September 1971, 91.

34. Bradley, "Private High School for Blacks"; Michele Fuetsch, "Her Concern: Black People; Her Goal: Social Change," *Palo Alto Times*, January 26, 1970, 11.

35. Nairobi Day School, *The Nairobi Day School, E.P.A.*; Slater, "Learning Is an All-Black Thing," 90.

36. Frank Koch, *The New Corporate Philanthropy: How Society & Business Can Profit* (New York: Plenum Press, 1979), 143–145; "The Nairobi Day School," 1970 KPFA Interview with Gertrude Wilks, PTL, MEC; Barbara Mouton, "Nairobi Day and High Schools, Inc.," in *Education by, for and About African Americans: A Profile of Several Black Community Schools*, ed. Deborah Daniels (Lincoln, NE: Student Commission on Undergraduate Education and the Education of Teachers, 1973), 44–45; Blakeslee, "School for Blacks," 35; Robert Strand, "Blacks Make Own School in Calif. Area," *Chicago Daily Defender*, March 20–March 26, 1971, 5.

37. Charlotte K. Beyers, "Mothers Organize School to Help Blacks 'Stand Tall,'" *Christian Science Monitor*, December 10, 1973, B4; Blakeslee, "Schools for Blacks," 35; Mouton, "Nairobi Day and High Schools, Inc.," 46; Evelyn Wallace and Pat Hendrix, "MEE Day Care Center," in *Curriculum Approaches from a Black Perspective*, ed. Black Child Development Institute (Washington, DC: Black Child Development Institute, 1973), 67; "Nairobi School Benefits From Show," *Palo Alto Times*, April 3, 1973; "Ministers Give $400 to Nairobi," *Palo Alto Times*, April 13, 1971.

38. "Nairobi High, 1970," yearbook (Microfilm), BL, UCB; Shilstone, "Black Motivation, Quality Education," 1, 3.

39. "Plan School System to Meet Blacks' Needs," *Jet*, February 5, 1970, 26; Barusch and Nathan, "The East Palo Alto Municipal Advisory Council," 190; Terry Hansen, "Nairobi School Founder Completely Optimistic," *Palo Alto Times*, October 7, 1969; Aleta Watson, "Nairobi School Celebrates Its 14th Birthday," *San Jose Mercury News*, October 22, 1980, 1B.

40. "The Nairobi Day School," 1970 KPFA Interview with Gertrude Wilks, PTL, MEC.

41. Mary Hoover, "You in Debt for Life," *Journal of African/Black Writing* 1 (1989): 90–91; Nairobi Day School 1972 Yearbook, GWC, INP; Fuetsch, "Her Concern: Black People," 11.

42. Bill Shilstone, "Nairobi Conducting Niggerology Course," *Palo Alto Times*, February 12, 1971, 16; "Private School for Blacks Only Charts Course," *New York Times*, July 7, 1970, 3.

43. "Nairobi Day School Dedicated; Opens First Full Academic Year," *Palo Alto Times*, September 15, 1969; "Murray Nairobi Teacher," *San Jose Mercury News*, September 13, 1969; Goben, "A School Outside of School," 32; Scott, "New Negro Spirit," 17.

44. Mary Eleanor Rhodes Hoover, "The Nairobi Day School: An African-American Independent School, 1966-1984," *Journal of Negro Education* 61 (1992): 203; Scott, "New Negro Spirit," 17.

45. "'Educational Revival' Planned," *Palo Alto Times*, May 18, 1972.

46. "The Nairobi School System, East Palo Alto, California," Transcript of 1969 Gertrude Wilks Lecture, Box 31, Folder 30, IFCO, SCR.

47. East Palo Alto Day School, *Day School, E.P.A.*, 30, 43.

48. *Equal Educational Opportunity Hearings Before the Select Committee of the U.S. Senate, 92nd Congress*, 4321.

49. Beyers, "Education by Degrees," 49, 53; Wallace Stegner, "East Palo Alto," *Saturday Review*, August 1, 1970, 54; Joseph Horton, "Interracial Partnership for Community Betterment," *Sepia*, June 1973, 72–80; Don Davies et al., *Patterns of Citizen Participation in Education Decisionmaking*, vol. 2 (Boston: Institute for Responsive Education, 1979), 17–22; "'Hate Courses' Not Taught," *Palo Alto Times*, November 28, 1968.

50. "Nairobi High, 1970," yearbook (Microfilm), BL, UCB.

51. Gertrude Wilks, "Recipe for Building a School," 1971 pamphlet, GWC, INP.

52. *Equal Educational Opportunity Hearings Before the Select Committee of the U.S. Senate, 92nd Congress,* 4321; "The Nairobi School System, East Palo Alto, California," Transcript of Gertrude Wilks Lecture, October 20, 1969, Wright Institute, Berkeley, CA, Box 31, Folder 30, IFCO, SCR.

53. Transcript of Robert Martin Interview with Gertrude Wilks, July 28, 1969, East Palo Alto, CRD, MSR.

54. Ibid.; Ana Simones film on GWC, INP.

55. Gertrude Wilks, "Recipe for Building a School," 1971 pamphlet, GWC, INP.

56. Hoover, "The Nairobi Day School," 203.

57. Nairobi Day School's administrators regularly used mainstream standardized exams despite their misgivings about "socioeconomic" biases embedded in some such tests. The point was that mastery of even culturally foreign academic tasks was essential. As Wilks declared, "When we get through with a fellow he can pass your test, his test, anybody's test." (Mary Hoover, "The Politics of Education: Illiteracy and Test Bias," *National Black Law Journal* 10 [1987]: 72.)

58. Mary Rhodes Hoover, "Characteristics of Black Schools at Grade Level: A Description," *Reading Teacher,* April 1978, 761; Mary Rhodes Hoover, "Community Attitudes Toward Black English," *Language in Society* 7 (1978): 65–87; Mary Hoover, "The Nairobi Day School," 205; Mary R. Hoover, Robert L. Politzer, and Shirley Lewis, "A Semiforeign Language Approach to Teaching Reading to Bidialectal Children," in *Applied Sociolinguistics and Reading,* ed. Robert E. Shafer (Newark, DE: International Reading Association, 1979), 68; Mary Hoover, "Models of Early Black Educational Excellence and Black Women," in *Working Papers: The Black Woman, Challenges and Prospects for the Future,* ed. The Ohio State University Department of Black Studies Community Extension Center (Columbus, OH: Amen-Ra Publishing, 1991), 149–150; "Calif. Parents Open Nairobi Day School," *The Black Child Advocate,* June 1971, 7.

59. Barbara Mouton, "Nairobi Day and High Schools, Inc.," in *Education by, for and About African Americans,* 45; December 17, 1973, Henry P. Organ to Ray Santiago, Box 31, Folder 30, IFCO, SCR; *Equal Educational Opportunity Hearings Before the Select Committee of the U.S. Senate,* 4313, 4316, 4323.

60. Robert Hoover, "Meeting Community Needs," in *The Minority Student on the Campus: Expectations and Possibilities,* ed. Robert A. Altman and Patricia O. Snyder (Boulder, CO: Western Interstate Commission for Higher Education, 1970), 193–194.

61. Mary Hoover, "Models of Early Black Educational Excellence and Black Women," in *Working Papers: The Black Woman,* 152, 157, 162.

62. "Nairobi High, 1970," yearbook (Microfilm), BL, UCB.

63. Ibid.

64. "The Advisory Board of Nairobi Schools Presents Afro-American History Week Celebration," February 1970 program, Box 27, Folder 43, SCD, SCR; East Palo Alto Day School, *Day School, E.P.A.,* 29.

65. John Stanton, "Mostly Whites Hear Stokely," *Palo Alto Times,* February 24, 1968; East Palo Alto Day School, *Day School, E.P.A.,* 68–69.

66. Bernard Magubane, *The Ties That Bind: African-American Consciousness of Africa* (Trenton, NJ: Africa World Press, 1989), 100, 129; Elliott P. Skinner, *Afro-Americans and Africa: The Continuing Dialectic* (New York: Urban Center of Columbia University, 1973), 15; Martin Kilson, "African Americans and Africa: A Critical Nexus," *Dissent,* Summer 1992, 361–69; Robert G. Weisbrod, *Ebony Kinship: Africa, Africans and the Afro-American* (Westport, CT: Greenwood Press, 1973), 185; Meriwether, *Proudly We Can Be Africans,* 6, 91, 121; James T. Campbell, *Middle Passages: African American Journeys to Africa, 1787-2005* (New York: Penguin, 2006).

67. Weisbrod, *Ebony Kinship,* 185–186; Skinner, *Afro-Americans and Africa,* 384; Johnnetta B. Cole, "Africanisms in the Americas: A Brief History of the Concept," *Anthropology and Humanism Quarterly* 10 (1985): 123; Harold R. Isaacs, *The New World of Negro Americans* (New York: Viking Press, 1964), 140; Ronald W. Walters, *Pan Africanism in the African Diaspora: An Analysis of Modern Afrocentric Political Movements* (Detroit, MI: Wayne State University Press, 1993), 113; Penny M. Von Eschen, *Race Against Empire: Black Americans and Anticolonialism, 1937-1957* (Ithaca, NY: Cornell University Press, 1997); Thomas

Borstelmann, *The Cold War and the Color Line: American Race Relations in the Global Arena* (Cambridge, MA: Harvard University Press, 2001).

68. Kevin K. Gaines, *American Africans in Ghana: Black Expatriates and the Civil Rights Era* (Chapel Hill: University of North Carolina Press, 2006); E. U. Essien-Udom, "The Relationship of Afro-Americans to African Nationalism," *Freedomways*, Fall 1962, 405; Magubane, *The Ties That Bind*, xxix; John Henrik Clarke, "The New Afro-American Nationalism," *Freedomways*, Fall 1961, 285; Richard B. Moore, "Africa Conscious Harlem," *Freedomways*, Summer 1963, 314–334; Meriwether, *Proudly We Can Be Africans*, 121; Brenda Gayle Plummer, *In Search of Power: African Americans in the Era of Decolonization, 1956-1974* (New York: Cambridge University Press, 2013), 5; Komozi Woodard, *A Nation Within a Nation: Amiri Baraka (LeRoi Jones) & Black Power Politics* (Chapel Hill: University of North Carolina Press, 1999), 161; Walters, *Pan-Africanism*, 55–61, 379.

69. William W. Sales, Jr., *From Civil Rights to Black Liberation: Malcolm X and the Organization of Afro-American Unity* (Boston: South End Press, 1994); Manning Marable, *Malcolm X: A Life of Reinvention* (New York: Penguin, 2011), 373; George Breitman, ed., *Malcolm X Speaks* (New York: Grove Press, 1966), 125.

70. Magubane, *The Ties That Bind*, 203; Walters, *Pan-Africanism*, 364–367; Meriwether, *Proudly We Can Be Africans*, 243; Skinner, *Afro-Americans and Africa*, 26–28; Earl Caldwell, "African Influence Thriving in Harlem," *New York Times*, March 12, 1968, 45, 49; Adelaide Cromwell Hill, "What Is Africa to Us?" in *The Black Power Revolt*, ed. Floyd Barbour (Boston: Extending Horizons Books, 1968), 134–135; C. Gerald Fraser, "Widow of Marcus Garvey, 'Black Moses,' Revisits Harlem," *New York Times*, August 17, 1968, 29.

71. Phyl Garland, "Is the Afro on Its Way Out?" *Ebony*, February 1973, 128; David Llorens, "Natural Hair: New Symbol of Race Pride," *Ebony*, December 1967, 142–143.

72. Takawira S. Mafukidze, "The Origin and Significance of African Personal Names," *Black World*, July 1970, 4–6; Committee for a Unified Newark, *Swahili Name Book* (Newark, NJ: Jihad Productions, 1971); The East, "African Names . . . Why? Which to Choose: What It Means: Where?" pamphlet, n.d., Brooklyn, Box 52, Folder 2, VHP, EUM; Haki R. Madhubuti, "Editorial," *Black Books Bulletin*, Spring 1974, 3; "More Afro-South American Taking Back Original Names," *Muhammad Speaks*, March 7, 1969, 14; Muga Karega Ajanaku (Clarence Henderson) to Oba Sima Ajanaku (Ida Jackson), n.d., Box 11, Folder 10, CSP, ACC; August 14, 1969, Ronda Davis to Preston Wilcox, Box 10, Folder 23, PWP, SCR.

73. Malcolm X and Alex Haley, *The Autobiography of Malcolm X* (New York: Grove Press, 1965), 161; Thomas A. Johnson, "Black Nationalist Leader Stirs Watts Teen-Agers," *New York Times*, May 27, 1966, 30; *Reclaim Your African Name* (New York: Pan African Students Organization, 1972); Ben L. Martin, "From Negro to Black to African American: The Power of Names and Naming," *Political Science Quarterly* 106 (1991): 93–94; The East, "African Names . . . Why? Which to Choose: What It Means: Where?" pamphlet, n.d., Brooklyn, Box 52, Folder 2, VHP, EUM.

74. Committee for a Unified Newark, *Swahili Name Book*, 7; "Honoring One's Origin," *Christian Science Monitor*, August 5, 1968, B10; Kiteme Katumi, "What Is Our Name in Africa?" *Negro History Bulletin*, April 1972, 81–83.

75. Richard B. Moore, *The Name Negro: Its Origins and Evil Roots* (Baltimore, MD: Black Classics Press, 1992), 11; Rosalyn Terborg-Penn, "Naming Ourselves: Politics and Meaning of Self-Designation," in *The Columbia Guide to African American History since 1939*, ed. Robert L. Harris, Jr. and Terborg-Penn (New York: Columbia University Press, 2006); Malcolm X, quoted in *Malcolm X: The Man and His Times*, ed. John Henrik Clarke (New York: Collier Books, 1969), 323; Bayard Rustin, "What's in a Name," *New York Amsterdam News*, January 23, 1971, 14; Tsenay Serequeberhan, *Our Heritage: The Past in the Present of African-American and African Existence* (Lanham, MD: Roman & Littlefield, 2000), 22.

76. February 26, 1971, Afroamerican Institute press release, Box 46, Folder 5, EGP, SCR; Ben L. Martin, "From Negro to Black to African American: The Power of Names and Naming," *Political Science Quarterly* 106 (1991): 93–94; Lerone Bennett, Jr., "What's in a Name?" *Ebony*, November 1967, 46–54; "Interview with Hoyt Fuller," *Black Collegian*, April–May 1971, 25–26; "Black Books Bulletin Interview Hoyt W. Fuller," *Black Books Bulletin*, Fall 1971, 18–19.

77. Alex Poinsett, "Inawapasa Watu Weusi Kusema Kiswahili," *Ebony*, December 1968, 163–168; Adhama Oluwa Kijeme, "Swahili and Black Americans," *Negro Digest*, July 1969, 5–8; Beverly Coleman, "Relevancy in Teaching and Learning Swahili," *Black World*, October 1970, 12–17; Beverly E. Coleman, "A History of Swahili," *Black Scholar*, February 1971, 13–25; Donald Bogle, "Black and Proud Behind Bars," *Ebony*, August 1969, 64–72; "Swahili at Rahway State Prison," *Black New Ark*, May 1972, 3.

78. Leonard Buder, "Bronx High School Plans to Teach Swahili," *New York Times*, November 18, 1967, 39; "Swahili in the Schools," *New York Times*, November 18, 1967, 36; John Chamberlain, "Teach Swahili to US Negroes? That Is Ridiculous," *Milwaukee Sentinel*, November 26, 1967, 16; Imim Konubi, "Why Swahili?" *African-American Teachers Forum*, September 1969, 8; "Teaching Swahili," *Chicago Daily Defender*, December 22, 1971, 15.

79. "Teaching Swahili," *New York Amsterdam News*, November 25, 1967, 14; "In Defence of Teaching Swahili in the United States Public Schools," *Pan-African Journal*, Winter 1968, 3–4; "Need for Third World Language Stressed," *Muhammad Speaks*, April 24, 1970, 19.

80. "Afro-American Assn. Forms L.A. Branch," *Los Angeles Sentinel*, August 15, 1963, A3; Johnson, "Black Nationalist Leader Stirs Watts Teen-Agers," 30; "Militant Negro Leader," *New York Times*, September 2, 1968; Brown, *Fighting for US*, 10–13; Keith A. Mayes, *Kwanzaa: Black Power and The Making of the African-American Holiday Tradition* (New York: Routledge, 2009), 59–60.

81. Woodard, *A Nation Within a Nation*, 71–72; Ron Karenga "Critique . . . and Response: Ron Karenga and Black Cultural Nationalism," *Negro Digest*, January 1968, 5.

82. Elaine Brown, *A Taste of Power: A Black Woman's Story* (New York: Anchor Books, 1992), 117; Scot Brown, "The US Organization, Black Power Vanguard Politics, and the United Front Ideal: Los Angeles and Beyond," *Black Scholar* 31 (2001): 21–27.

83. Brown, *Fighting for Us*, 35, 56; Maulana Ron Karenga, "Nation Time in Atlanta," *Liberator*, October 1970, 4; Woodard, *A Nation Within a Nation*, 105; Brown, "The US Organization," 23–24.

84. Mayes, *Kwanza*, 74.

85. LeRoi Jones, *Kawaida Studies: The New Nationalism* (Chicago: Third World Press, 1972), 10–13; Clyde Halisi, ed., *The Quotable Karenga* (Los Angeles: US Organization, 1967), 12.

86. Temple of Kawaida, *Kitabu: Beginning Concepts in Kawaida* (Los Angeles: US Organization, 1971), 5–6.

87. Brown, *Fighting for US*, 69; Mayes, *Kwanzaa*, 82; Florence E. Hill, "Readers Write: 'Dreams of Kwanza' Praised," *New York Amsterdam News*, February 5, 1972, A4.

88. "'Swanza Celebration' on WABC-TV," *New York Amsterdam News*, December 23, 1973, D13; Temple of Kawaida, *Kitabu*, 14; Lee Cook, "Dreams of Kwanza," *New York Amsterdam News*, December 25, 1971, 4–5.

89. Mayes, *Kwanzaa*, xxiii.

90. *Pan African Early Education Center Monthly Newsletter*, January 1971, and "1973 Kwanza 1973," flyer, Box 18, PWP, SCR; Barbara Campbell, "Harlem Pupils Get Early Start on Kwanza," *New York Times*, December 20, 1972, 47; "Children Participate in Traditional African Xmas," *New York Amsterdam News*, December 30, 1972, D1; Judith Cummings, "City Blacks Begin Fete of Kwanza," *New York Times*, December 27, 1973, 41; Joann Stevens, "Kwanzaa Holiday Helps Preserve African Cultural Festival," *Washington Post*, December 20, 1979, DC3; Adeyemi Bandele, "Ten Years of Struggle," *Black News*, December 1978, 3; "Kwanza 1972 Events Schedule," *New York Amsterdam News*, December 23, 1972, A9; Studio Museum in Harlem, *Kwanza* (New York: Studio Museum in Harlem, 1972).

91. "Jihad Productions Kwanza Festival Proposal," 1973, Box 25, Folder 49, IFCO, SCR; December 27, 1973, Preston Wilcox to Ndugu John Wise, Box 14, PWP, SCR; *Kwanzaa: An African-American Holiday That Is Progressive & Uplifting* (Chicago: Third World Press, 1972); John "Watusi" Branch, *A Story of Kwanza: Black/Afrikan Holy Days* (New York: East Distribution and Publications, n.d.); Pan African Work Center, *Kwanza: In the Beginning: A Storybook for African Children* (Atlanta: Pan African Work Center, 1971); *The First Book of Kwanzaa* (New York: East Publications, 1971).

92. Robert J. McCartney, "More People Dream of a Black Christmas as Kwanzaa Spreads," *Wall Street Journal*, December, 25, 1971, 1; H. Carl McCall, "Why Bother with Christmas?" *New York Amsterdam News*, December 22, 1973, A5; *Essence*, December 1973; Joann Stevens, "Kwanzaa Holiday Helps Preserve African Cultural Festival," *Washington Post*, December 20, 1979, DC3.

93. Stevens, "Kwanzaa Holiday Helps Preserve African Cultural Festival," DC3; *Kwanzaa: An African-American Holiday*, 9; Basir Mchawi, "Which Way Kwanza," *Black News*, December 1975.

94. McCartney, "More People Dream of a Black Christmas," 1; Basir Mchawi, "Kwanza: By Any Means Necessary!" *Black News*, December 1974, 4; Brenda Presley, "Pigs Xmas Sham Ending," *Black Panther*, December 21, 1968, 4; "Shule Ya Watoto: Position Paper: What Does Thanksgiving Mean to Afrikan People in America?" November 1976 flyer, CIBI, INP. For more on the evolution of Kwanzaa, see Elizabeth Pleck, "Kwanzaa: The Making of a Black Nationalist Tradition, 1966-1990," *Journal of American Ethnic History* 20 (2001): 4–28, and Anna Day Wilde, "Mainstreaming Kwanzaa," *The Public Interest*, Spring 1995, 68–79.

95. Adolph Reed, Jr., *Class Notes: Posing as Politics and Other Thoughts on the American Scene* (New York: New Press, 2000), 8; Mayes, *Kwanzaa*, xxi; see in general Pleck, "Kwanzaa."

96. Maulana Karenga, *The African American Holiday of Kwanzaa: A Celebration of Family, Community & Culture* (Los Angeles: University of Sankore Press, 1988), 17.

97. "Naturally '75 Has a Real Kwanza Theme This Year: Women's Liberation," *New York Amsterdam News*, December 13, 1975, D7; *The First Book of Kwanzaa*.

98. Dean E. Robinson, *Black Nationalism in American Politics and Thought* (New York: Cambridge University Press, 2001), 1, 5; Robin D. G. Kelley, *Freedom Dreams: The Black Radical Imagination* (Boston: Beacon Press, 2002), 21; Singh, *Black Is a Country*, 189.

99. David Gross, "Culture, Politics and 'Lifestyle' in the 1960s," in *Race Politics and Culture: Critical Essays on the Radicalism of the 1960s*, ed. Adolph Reed, Jr. (Westport, CT: Greenwood Press, 1986), 103; Larry Neal, "New Space/The Growth of Black Consciousness in the Sixties," in *The Black Seventies*, ed. Floyd B. Barbour (Boston: Porter Sargent, 1970), 12; Woodard, *A Nation Within a Nation*, 43; "Editorial: 1970—Ain't It Funky Now!" *Soulbook*, Fall–Winter 1970, 2; John Runcie, "The Black Culture Movement and the Black Community," *Journal of American Studies* 10 (1976): 192–195; Larry Neal, "The Black Arts Movement," in *The Black Aesthetic*, ed. Addison Gayle Jr. (New York: Doubleday, 1971), 272; quoted in Brown, *Fighting for Us*, 23.

100. Horace Campbell, "Pan Africanism and African Liberation," in *Imagine Home: Class, Culture and Nationalism in the African Diaspora*, ed. Sidney Lemelle and Robin D. G. Kelley (London: Verso, 1994), 305; Amilcar Cabral, *Unity and Struggle: Speeches and Writings* (New York: Monthly Review Press, 1979), 143; Plummer, *In Search of Power*, 7; James Baldwin, "Black Colloquium in Paris," in *Black Homeland/Black Diaspora*, 99; Roderick D. Bush, *The End of White World Supremacy: Black Internationalism and the Problem of the Color Line* (Philadelphia: Temple University Press, 2009), 192; St. Clair Drake, "Diaspora Studies and Pan-Africanism," in *Global Dimensions of the African Diaspora*, 2nd ed., ed. Joseph E. Harris (Washington, DC: Howard University Press, 1993), 478; Maulana Ron Karenga, "Nation Time in Atlanta," *Liberator*, October 1970, 4; Robert Allen, "China Since the Great Cultural Revolution," *Black Scholar*, November 1973, 49.

101. "Tanzanians Call for Black African Cultural Revolution," *Muhammad Speaks*, November 3, 1967, 8; Sekou Toure, "The African Elite in the Anti-Colonial Struggle," *Black Scholar*, January 1972, 6–9; Chinweizu, *Decolonising the African Mind* (London: Pero Press, 1987), 5–6; "America Is the Blackman's Battle Ground!" Black Power Movement Part 3—Revolutionary Action Movement (Microfilm), Series 2.

102. Singh, *Black Is a Country*, 196–197; James Edward Smethurst, *The Black Arts Movement: Literary Nationalism in the 1960s and 1970s* (Chapel Hill: University of North Carolina Press, 2005), 16, 18; Brown, "The US Organization," 12, 22; Woodard, *A Nation Within a Nation*, 9; Francis Njubi Nesbitt, *Race for Sanctions: African Americans against Apartheid, 1946-1994* (Bloomington: Indiana University Press, 2004), 43–44; Robin D. G. Kelley, "Stormy Weather: Reconstructing Black (Inter)Nationalism in the Cold War Era," in *Is It Nation Time?*, ed. Eddie S. Glaude (Chicago: University of Chicago Press, 2002), 73–76;

Reed, ed., *Race, Politics, and Culture*; Sidney Lemelle and Robin D. G. Kelley, *Imagine Home*; Cleaver, "Culture and Revolution," 34; S. E. Anderson, "Revolutionary Black Nationalism and the Pan-African Idea," in *The Black Seventies*, 99–128; S. E. Anderson, "The Fragmented Movement," 8; Earl Ofari, "Cultural Nationalism and Black Revolution," *Guardian*, November 23, 1968, 24; John Runcie, "The Black Culture Movement and the Black Community," *Journal of American Studies* 10 (1976): 208; Drake, "Diaspora Studies," 455.

103. John Lewis, "Kimani Says He's Political Prisoner," *Afro-American*, October 7, 1967, 14; John Churchville, "On Correct Black Education," September 1968 pamphlet, Box 4, PWP, SCR.

104. Philip S. Foner, ed., *The Black Panthers Speak* (New York: J. B. Lippincott, 1970), 50; "An Interview with Huey P. Newton," in *Black Nationalism in America*, ed. John H. Bracey Jr., August Meier, and Elliott Rudwick (Indianapolis: Bobbs-Merrill Company, 1970), 534; Brown, *Fighting for Us*, ix; Woodard, *A Nation Within a Nation*, 117–118; Brown, *A Taste of Power*, 143; Runcie, "The Black Culture Movement," 207; Imamu Amiri Baraka, *Raise, Race, Rays, Raze: Essays Since 1965* (New York: Random House, 1971), 130–131; Cleaver, "Culture and Revolution," 34–36.

105. Woodard, *A Nation Within a Nation*, 118–119; Brown, "The US Organization," 28; Smethhurst, *The Black Arts Movement*, 17–18; Brown, *Fighting for Us*, x.

Chapter 5

1. C. L. R. James, *The Black Jacobins: Toussaint L'Ouverture and the San Domingo Revolution* (New York: Vintage, 1963), 283. For more on the cadre model of Black Power organizing and the institutional and organizational life of the Congress of African People, see Komozi Woodard, *A Nation Within a Nation: Amiri Baraka (LeRoi Jones) and Black Power Politics* (Chapel Hill: University of North Carolina Press, 1999), and Michael Simanga, *Amiri Baraka and the Congress of African People* (New York: Palgrave Macmillan, 2015).

2. Manning Marable, *Race, Reform & Rebellion: The Second Reconstruction and Beyond in Black America, 1945-2006* (Jackson: University Press of Mississippi, 2007), 112–130; "Instant Niggers," *Liberator*, July 1970, 3; "Black Thing Coopted," *Black Panther*, October 25, 1969, 5.

3. See, in general, Ronald W. Walters, *Pan Africanism in the African Diaspora: An Analysis of Modern Afrocentric Political Movements* (Detroit, MI: Wayne State University Press, 1997), and Manning Marable, *African & Caribbean Politics: From Kwame Nkrumah to Maurice Bishop* (London: Verso, 1987).

4. Walters, *Pan Africanism in the African Diaspora*; Marable, *African & Caribbean Politics*.

5. Alex Willingham, "Afro-American Pan-Africanist Ideology in the 1960s," in *Pan Africanism: New Directions in Strategy*, ed. W. Ofuatey-Kodjoe (Lanham, MD: University Press of America, 1986), 95–122; Nathan Hare, "Wherever We Are," *Black Scholar*, March 1971, 34; Marable, *Race, Reform & Rebellion*.

6. LeRoi Jones, *Kawaida Studies: The New Nationalism* (Chicago: Third World Press, 1972), 44.

7. Handwritten notes attached to "African Project Suggestions," pamphlet, Box 1, Folder 14, VCP, WHI; "Developing Effective Cadres," *SOBU Newsletter*, April 17, 1971, 4; Amiri Baraka, "Strategy and Tactics of a Pan African Nationalist Party," *Black News*, September 10, 1971, 4.

8. "The Student Organization for Black Unity: A Look Backward and Forward," July 1970, Box 11, Folder 1, and "Ideological Manifesto of the Pan-African Students Organization in the Americas, Inc.," PASO National Executive Council, August 1970, Box 11, Folder 7, CSP, ACC.

9. Amiri Baraka, "Confessions of a Former Anti-Semite," *Village Voice*, December 17–23, 1980, 1, 19–20; Cedric Johnson, *Revolutionaries to Race Leaders: Black Power and the Making of African American Politics* (Minneapolis: University of Minnesota Press, 2007), 52; Jerry Watts, *Amiri Baraka: The Politics and Art of a Black Intellectual* (New York: New York University Press, 2001), 16.

10. Flyers and materials on Black Arts Repertory Theater and School, 1965-1966, Box 26, Folders 22–23, JOP, ARC; Werner Sollors, *Amiri Baraka/LeRoi Jones: The Quest for a "Populist Modernism"* (New York: Columbia University Press, 1978), 6; Amiri Baraka, *The Autobiography of LeRoi Jones* (Chicago: Lawrence Hill Books, 1997), 224.

11. Baraka, *The Autobiography*, 204, 231, 241, 269; Sollors, *Amiri Baraka/LeRoi Jones*, 6.

12. Robert L. Allen, *Black Awakening in Capitalist America* (New York: Doubleday, 1969), 126.

13. Woodard, *A Nation Within a Nation*, 70–71, 84–86; Alex Poinsett, "Newark a Year Later," *Ebony*, November 1971, 125–132; Baraka, "Confessions of a Former Anti-Semite," 1; Baraka, *The Autobiography*, 241, 266.

14. Baraka, *The Autobiography*, 253; "CFUN's Goal: Political Empowerment for New Ark's Blacks," *IFCO News*, September–October, 1972, 1–2; Imamu Amiri Baraka, "Black (Art) Drama Is the Same as Black Life," *Ebony*, February 1971, 74–82; "Ameer (LeRoi Jones) Baraka," *Ebony*, August 1969, 75–83; Woodard, *A Nation Within a Nation*, 88–89, 115; LeRoi Jones, *Kawaida Studies: The New Nationalism* (Chicago: Third World Press, 1972), 21.

15. Baraka, *The Autobiography*, 392.

16. See, in general, Woodard, *A Nation Within a Nation*.

17. Alex Poinsett, "It's Nation Time!" *Ebony*, December 1970, 98–106.

18. Ibid.; July 24, 1970, Hayward Henry, Jr. letter to multiple recipients, Box 32, Folder 17, VHP, EUM.

19. Oba Simba T'shaka, "Make the Past Serve the Present: Strategies for Black Liberation," *Black Scholar*, January–February 1983, 21–37; "History of the Congress of African People," *Unity & Struggle*, June 1976, 5; Tony Thomas, "Can a Black Party Be Built by Supporting Democrats," *Militant*, May 31, 1974, 20.

20. April 7, 1972, Bill Strickland Memo to Alex Poinsett, Box 35, Folder 2, VHP, EUM; "New Politics for Black People: A Statement of Principles, Goals, Guidelines, Definitions and Direction of the National Black Political Assembly," *Black World*, October 1975, 61–65; "Gary—Beyond the Unity," *African World*, May 27, 1972, 6; Ronald Walters, "The New Black Political Culture," *Black World*, October 1972, 14; Bill Strickland, "The Gary Convention and the Crisis of American Politics," *Black World*, October 1972, 18–26; Tony Thomas, "Issue Facing Congress of African People: Black Party or Support to Democrats," *Militant*, September 8, 1972, 24; Vincent Harding, "'A Long Hard Winter to Endure': Reflections on the Meaning of the 1970's," *Black Collegian*, December–January 1980, 90; Ronald Walters, "The New Black Political Culture," *Black World*, October 1972, 14; William Strickland, "Whatever Happened to the Politics of Black Liberation?" *Black Scholar*, October 1975, 25.

21. Amiri Baraka, ed., *African Congress: A Documentary of the First Modern Pan-African Congress* (New York: Morrow, 1972), 470–473.

22. African Free School Proposal, 1973, Box 22, Folder 6, IFCO, SCR; Komozi Woodward January 4, 1986, Interview with Amiri Baraka, Black Power Movement Series, Part 1—Amiri Baraka (Microfilm); Crispin Campbell, "Tutoring Program Spurs New School," *Times-News*, October 17, 1974, 10; Fox Butterfield, "Experimental Class in Newark School is Indoctrinated in Black Subjects," *New York Times*, April 10, 1971, 42; "Jersey Public School Teaches Class in African Culture," *Chicago Daily Defender*, January 23, 1971, 18; Woodard, *A Nation Within a Nation*, 88; Afrikan Free School, *Education Text* (Newark, NJ: Jihad Publishing Co., 1974), 1–3; "African Free School," *Black New Ark*, September 1972, 4.

23. "CFUN's Goal: Political Empowerment for New Ark's Blacks," *IFCO News*, September–October, 1972, 1–2; Butterfield, "Experimental Class in Newark School," 42; "Attacking a School," *New York Amsterdam News*, June 26, 1971, D2; Ronald Burns, "Jersey Public School Teaches Class in African Culture," *Chicago Daily Defender*, January 23, 1971, 18.

24. African Free School Proposal, 1973, Box 22, Folder 6, IFCO, SCR.

25. Jones, *Kawaida Studies*, 51–52; "Interview: Imamu Amiri Baraka," *Black Collegian*, March–April 1973, 33; Baraka, *The Autobiography*, 299; Imamu Amiri Baraka, "Strategy and Tactics of a Pan African Nationalist Party," 1972 pamphlet, Black Power Movement Part 1—Amiri Baraka (Microfilm).

26. Amiri Baraka, "Raise! Education for Liberation!" *Black New Ark*, November 1972.

27. "Grant for African Free School," *New York Amsterdam News*, July 24, 1971, D2; "CFUN Awarded $7,500 to Support Black Education," *Black New Ark*, October 1972; "AFS to Open New Classroom Building," *Black New Ark* October 1972; "African Free School in Newark," *New York Amsterdam News*, July 24, 1971, D3; "Baraka Raps On 'Like It Is,'" *New York Amsterdam News*, December 14, 1974, D20.

28. Amiri Baraka, "The Need for a Cultural Base to Civil Rites and Bpower Mooments," in *Raise, Race, Rays, Raze: Essays Since 1965* (New York: Random House, 1971), 45; Baraka, "Raise! Education for Liberation!"; Imamu Amiri Baraka, "White Suburban Teachers Union vs. Black New Ark," *Black News*, July 17, 1971, 20.

29. "Report for Action," 1968, Governor's Select Commission on Civil Disorder, State of New Jersey, New Jersey State Library.

30. Baraka, *The Autobiography*, 247.

31. Fox Butterfield, "Newark School Strike Splits Blacks," *New York Times*, February 14, 1971, 45; "The Newark School System: A Study in Urban Decay," *Imani*, August–September 1971, 7–10; Steve Golin, *The Newark Teacher Strikes: Hope's on the Line* (New Brunswick, NJ: Rutgers University Press, 2002), 112.

32. Joe Walker, "Ocean Hill-Brownsville Veteran Tells Why He Supports Newark Teacher Strike," *Muhammad Speaks*, March 5, 1971, 24; Baraka, "Raise! Education for Liberation!"

33. Joseph F. Sullivan, "Hanging of Blacks' Flag in Jersey Schools Argued," *New York Times*, January 15, 1972, 25; Derrick Morrison, "Black Nationalist Flag Stirs Newark Debate," *Militant*, January 14, 1972, 19; "Educators Support Liberation Flag-Flying," *New York Amsterdam, News*, January 8, 1972, A1, A11; T'shaka, "Make the Past Serve the Present," 24; Amiri Baraka, "Black Liberation Today," *Unity & Struggle*, May 1976, 12.

34. Butterfield, "Experimental Class in Newark School," 42; African Free School Proposal, 1973, Box 22, Folder 6, IFCO, SCR; "Ameer (LeRoi Jones) Baraka," 83; Burns, "Jersey Public School Teaches Class in African Culture," 18.

35. "The Newark School System: A Study in Urban Decay," 11; "African Free School Sets Pre-School for Newark Young," *New York Amsterdam News*, March 25, 1972, B9; Jones, *Kawaida Studies*, 26; Crispin Campbell, "Tutoring Program Spurs New School," *Times-News*, October 17, 1974, 10.

36. Jones, *Kawaida Studies*, 27; "The Newark School System," 11.

37. Imamu Amiri Baraka, "Strategy and Tactics of a Pan African Nationalist Party," 1972 pamphlet, Black Power Movement Part 1—Amiri Baraka (Microfilm); Jones, *Kawaida Studies*, 26; Burns, "Jersey Public School Teaches Class in African Culture," 18.

38. "Chad-A Pan Africanist School," *Black New Ark*, September 1972, 4; Simba Risasi, "New-Ark School—A Community Institution," *Black New Ark*, September 1972, 4; "The Chad School: Heart of Africa," 1975 Proposal, Box 25, Folder 6, IFCO, SCR; "Chad School: Student Perseverance Builds Strong, Natural Program," *SOBU Newsletter*, December 19, 1970, 12.

39. Haki R. Madhubuti, *YellowBlack: The First Twenty-One Years of a Poet's Life* (Chicago: Third World Press, 2006), xv, xvi; Don L. Lee, *Think Black* (Detroit, MI: Broadside Press, 1969), 6; "Interview: The World of Don L. Lee," *Black Collegian*, February–March 1971, 26–27.

40. Don L. Lee, *Black Pride* (Detroit, MI: Broadside Press, 1970), 24.

41. *Kwanza—The First Fruits: An African Holiday* (Chicago: Institute of Positive Education, 1972); D. H. Malhem, *Heroism in the New Black Poetry: Introductions & Interviews* (Lexington: University Press of Kentucky, 1990), 87; Haki R. Madhubuti, *From Plan to Planet: The Need for African Minds and Institutions* (Chicago: Third World Press, 1973), 9; Janice Cobb, "A Closeup of Genius," *Sun Reporter*, June 2, 1973, 12; Regina Jennings, *Malcolm X and the Poetics of Haki Madhubuti* (Jefferson, NC: McFarland, 2006), 168–169; Carole D. Lee, "Profile of an Independent Black Institution: African-Centered Education at Work," in *Teach Freedom: Education for Liberation in the African-American Tradition*, ed. Charles M. Payne and Carol Sills Strickland (New York: Teachers College Press, 2008), 210–212; Elizabeth Todd-Breland, "To Reshape and Redefine Our World: African American Political Organizing for Education in Chicago, 1968-1988" (PhD diss., University of Chicago, 2010), 76–78, 85–86.

42. Gary Rivlin, "Eyes on the Prize," *Chicago Reader*, May 23, 1997, 26; "Interview: The World of Don L. Lee," 33.

43. "New Concept School to Open Here Saturday," *Chicago Daily Defender*, September 28, 1972, 11; Lisa Michele Stulberg, "Teach a New Day: African American Alternative Institution-Building and the Politics of Race and Schooling Since Brown" (PhD diss., University of California Berkeley, 2001), 156–159; Madhubuti, *From Plan to Planet*, 13.

44. Hannibal T. Afrik resumé, HAC, INP; John F. Lyons, *Teachers and Reform: Chicago Public Education, 1929-1970* (Urbana: University of Illinois Press, 2008), 171–194; "Farragut Teachers Issue Demands," *Chicago Daily Defender*, September 4, 1968, 3; "Farragut Students Backing Black Profs," *Chicago Daily Defender*, September 7, 1968, 1; "Support Grows for 'Manifesto' at Farragut," *Chicago Daily Defender*, September 18, 1968, 4, 5; "Farragut's Black Teachers Win Demands," *Chicago Daily Defender*, September 28, 1968, 1; Donald Mosby, "Black Students Plan Big Walkout Today," *Chicago Daily Defender*, October 14, 1968, 3, 4; Faith C. Christmas, "700 Teachers Join Second School Boycott," *Chicago Daily Defender*, October 22, 1968, 3; Clark Kissinger, "Chicago Schools Disrupted," *Guardian*, October 19, 1968, 9; "Farragut Walkout Today," *Chicago Daily Defender*, June 23, 1969, 3; "Black Teachers Support Chicago Student Boycott," *Muhammad Speaks*, November 1, 1968, 2; Faith C. Christmas, "Farragut Teachers Stage All-Day Teach-In, Threaten More Action," *Chicago Daily Defender*, December 21, 1968, 1–2; Faith C. Christmas, "Community Control Trial: A New Focus for Farragut," *Chicago Daily Defender*, May 26, 1970, 2; Faith C. Christmas, "A New Focus for Farragut," *Chicago Daily Defender*, May 29, 1970, 2; Faith C. Christmas, "Students Strike Called Today; Honor Malcolm X," *Chicago Daily Defender*, May 19, 1970, 1.

45. Faith C. Christmas, "900 Black Teachers Vow Not to Strike," *Chicago Daily Defender*, January 10, 1970, 1, 4; Faith C. Christmas, "Black Teachers Start 'Liberation Schools,' " *Chicago Daily Defender*, January 13, 1971, 3, 23; Faith C. Christmas, "Teachers Fear Ouster Plot," *Chicago Daily Defender*, October 22, 1969, 3, 28; "2 Educators Rap Busing Edict," *Chicago Daily Defender*, April 21, 1971, 3; Marion B. Campfield, "Educators Withhold Comment," *Chicago Daily Defender*, November 23, 1971, 3, 23.

46. "Set Breadbasket Teachers Panel," *Chicago Daily Defender*, July 30, 1969, 4, 24; Toni Anthony, "Black Educators Agree: Home Life Not 'Cause' in Scoring," *Chicago Daily Defender*, February 3, 1970, 6; Harold E. Charles, "From Our Readers; Impressed," *Chicago Daily Defender*, December 16, 1970, 19; "W. Siders Back School Plan," *Chicago Daily Defender*, June 12, 1969, 4; "Hold Black Liberation Month at Farragut High School," *Chicago Daily Defender*, March 1, 1972, 16; "Feast Honors Marcus Garvey," *Chicago Defender*, August 25, 1973, 6; Toni Anthony, "Black Teachers Map Liberation Plans," *Chicago Daily Defender*, January 19, 1971, 7; "Teachers Meet to Learn Ghetto's Needs," *Chicago Daily Defender*, January 30, 1969, 4.

47. Mwalimu Hannibal Tirus Afrik, "On the Operational Philosophy of the Shule Ya Watoto: An Analysis; Education for National Liberation," September 1980 pamphlet, HAC, INP; Shule Ya Watoto Kwanza Term Fact Sheet and Letter, 1972, Box 24, Folder 10, Box 22, Folder 6, IFCO, SCR; Faith C. Christmas, "W. Side Unit Fills Gap," *Chicago Daily Defender*, April 22, 1972, 4; Faith C. Christmas, "A Is for Awareness, B Is for Blackness," *Chicago Daily Defender*, April 29, 1972, 5.

48. "Flag Lowering Incident at Southern U.," *Chicago Daily Defender*, April 10, 1969, 8; "Black Students at Southern University Scuffle with Cops," *Chicago Daily Defender*, April 10, 1969, 5; "New Orleans Struggles with School Turmoil," *Christian Science Monitor*, April 12, 1969, 6; "Fly 'Black Flag' at Southern," *Chicago Defender*, April 16, 1969, 8; "Governor Pledges Action to New Orleans Black Students," *Christian Science Monitor*, April 23, 1969, 4; "Black Students Yield After La. Guard Called," *Washington Post*, May 6, 1969, A10; "Guard Stands by at Negro Campus," *New York Times*, May 6, 1969, 32; "Crisis in New Orleans Fades, Guard Called Off," *Los Angeles Times*, May 6, 1969, A26; Jerry W. Ward, "Perspectives," *Black World*, January 1974, 83–85; Catherine Michna, " 'We Are Black Mind Jockeys': Tom Dent, The Free Southern Theater, and the Search for a Second-line Literary Aesthetic in New Orleans," *Journal of Ethnic American Literature* 1 (2011): 47n; Jeffrey A. Turner, *Sitting In and Speaking Out: Student Movements in the American South, 1960-1970* (Athens: University of Georgia Press, 2010), 198.

49. Doris Derby, Gilbert Moses, and John O'Neal, "The Need for a Southern Freedom Theatre," *Freedomways*, Winter 1964, 109–112; Elizabeth Sutherland, "Theatre of the Meaningful," *The Nation*, October 19, 1964, 254–255; Thomas C. Dent, "The Free Southern Theater," *Negro Digest*, April 1967, 44, 95–98; Larry Neal, "Conquest of the South," *The Drama Review* 14 (1970): 169–172; Floyd Gaffney, "The Free Southern Theater: What Price Freedom?" *Black World*, April 1971, 11–14; "Enriching the Paper Trail: An Interview with Tom Dent," *African*

American Review 27 (1993): 333–338, 343; Michna, "'We Are Black Mind Jockeys,'" *Journal of Ethnic American Literature* 1 (2011): 36–37, 42; G. Lenoir-Kingham, "The Free Southern Theater," *World Theatre*, September 1965, 50–51.

50. Tom Dent, "Black Theater in the South: Report and Reflections," *Freedomways*, Summer 1974, 247–54; Thomas C. Dent, Richard Schechner, and Gilbert Moses, eds., *The Free Southern Theater by the Free Southern Theater: A Documentary of the South's Radical Black Theater* (Indianapolis: Bobbs-Merrill, 1969), 232.

51. Martha M. Jones, "An Interview with Gil Moses," *Black Creation*, Winter 1972, 20; "Echoes from the Gumbo," pamphlet, Box 46, Folder 26, FST, ARC, Amistad Research Center; Michna, "'We Are Black Mind Jockeys,'" 53; Geneviève Fabre, "The Free Southern Theatre, 1963-1979," *Black American Literature Forum* 17 (1983): 56–57; Tom Dent, "Black Theater in the South: Report and Reflections," *Freedomways*, Summer 1974, 248–250; Kalamu Ya Salaam, "News from BLKARTSOUTH," *Black Theatre* 4 (1970): 4; Val Ferdinand, "New Orleans," *Negro Digest*, April 1970, 29–31; Jerry Ward, "Southern Black Aesthetics: The Case of 'Nkombo' Magazine," *Mississippi Quarterly* 44 (1991): 145–147.

52. "Food for Thought," *Nkombo*, December 1969, Box 88, Folder 6, and "From the Kitchen," *Nkombo*, August 1972, Box 88, Folder 7, FST, ARC, Amistad Research Center; Kalamu Ya Salaam, "Blk Art South—New Orleans," *Black World*, April 1972, 41; Hoyt Fuller, "The New Nkombo," *Black World*, November 1971, 72; "Enriching the Paper Trail: An Interview with Tom Dent," 327; Val Ferdinand, "BLKARTSOUTH/Get on Up!" in *New Black Voices: An Anthology of Contemporary Afro-American Literature*, ed. Abraham Chapman (New York: Mentor, 1972), 470; Kalamu Ya Salaam, *Art for Life*, accessed July 29, 2012, http://www.nathanielturner.com/artforlifetable.htm.

53. Charles H. Rowell, "Hofu Ni Kwenu," *Black World*, September 1974, 87–91; Kalamu Ya Salaam, "Blk Art South—New Orleans," *Black World*, April 1972, 43.

54. Mtumishi St. Julien, *Upon the Shoulders of Elephants We Reach the Sky: A Parent's Farewell to a Collegian* (New Orleans: Runagate Press, 1995), 2–4, 61, Index; Tayari Kwa Salaam, "So-Journeying: Creating Sacred Space in Education" (PhD diss., Louisiana State University, 1993), 3, 98–99, 116; "Schools Without Funding: The Economic Plight of the Independent Black School Movement Today!" 1983 pamphlet, HAC, INP.

55. Val Ferdinand, *The Blues Merchant: Songs (Poems) for Blkfolk* (New Orleans: Nkombo Publications, 1969); Aline St. Julien, *Colored Creole: Color Conflict and Confusion in New Orleans* (New Orleans: Ahidiana, 1977), 10; Kwa Salaam, "So-Journeying," 2.

56. Salaam, "Blk Art South—New Orleans," 43; Kalamu Ya Salaam, *Pamoja Tutashinda/ Together We Will Win* (New Orleans: Ahidiana, 1974); Kwa Salaam, "So-Journeying," 2–4; St. Julien, *Upon the Shoulders of Elephants We Reach the Sky*, 3–4; Wekesa Madzimoyo, "Afrikan-Americans Educate Their Own," *Southern Exposure*, Fall 1980, 45; Kalamu Ya Salaam Resumé, Box 2, Folder "SPAC Na Delegates," 6PAC, MSR; Kalamu Ya Salaam, *Art for Life*, accessed July 29, 2012, http://www.nathanielturner.com/artforlifetable.htm.

57. Kalamu Ya Salaam Delegate Questionnaire Application, Box 2, Folder "SPAC Na Delegates," 6PAC, MSR; Kalamu Ya Salaam, "Food for Thought," *Nkombo*, June 1974, Box 88, Folder 7, FST, ARC.

58. Robin D. G. Kelley, "Stormy Weather: Reconstructing Black (Inter)Nationalism in the Cold War Era," in *Is It Nation Time?* ed. Eddie S. Glaude (Chicago: University of Chicago Press, 2002), 76–77.

59. Marable, *African & Caribbean Politics*, 112; "Remapping Africa: A Black Perspective," *SOBU Newsletter*, May 15, 1971, 9; Ruwa Chiri, "Why We Use 'K,'" *Afrika Must Unite*, 1973, 6.

60. *Afrikan Date Book in Swahili* (Chicago: Institute of Positive Education, 1972); February 5 and March 1 and 14, 1972, Malcolm X Liberation University Swahili Department to Swahili Student and "Floating Swahili Program" materials, Box 30, Folder 40, IFCO, SCR; "MXLU Initiates Project: Floating Swahili," *African World*, September 30, 1972, 17; Njoki McElroy, "Alternative to a Traditional Wedding," *Essence*, April 1974, 59; Haki and Safisha Madhubuti, "Facing the Coming Nation: The Union of Haki R. Madhubuti (Don L. Lee) and Safisha N. Laini (Carol Easton)," *Black Collegian*, September–October 1974, 32.

61. Marable, *African & Caribbean Politics*, 45–46; Adekunle Ajala, *Pan-Africanism: Evolution, Progress and Prospects* (New York: St. Martin's Press, 1973), 106; Stephen Howe,

Afrocentrism: Mythical Pasts and Imagined Homes (London: Verso, 1998), 24–25. Quoted in Anthony Bogues, *Black Heretics, Black Prophets: Radical Political Intellectuals* (New York: Routledge, 2003), 108.

62. Marable, *African & Caribbean Politics*, 1, 46.
63. See, for example, Jim Cleaver, "Karenga, Black Panthers Speak Out," *Los Angeles Sentinel*, March 6, 1969, D2; Maulana Ron Karenga, "Nation Time in Atlanta," *Liberator*, October 1970, 6; Imamu Amiri Baraka, *Raise, Race, Rays, Raze: Essays Since 1965* (New York: Random House, 1971), 138; LeRoi Jones, *Kawaida Studies: The New Nationalism* (Chicago: Third World Press, 1972), 13–14; Temple of Kawaida, *Kitabu: Beginning Concepts in Kawaida* (Los Angeles: US Organization, 1971), 10; Stokely Carmichael, "Pan-Africanism—Land and Power," in *Modern Black Nationalism: From Marcus Garvey to Louis Farrakhan*, ed. William L. Van Deburg (New York: New York University Press, 1996), 207–208; John Lewis, "Black Voices," *Baltimore Afro-American*, August 9, 1969, 5.
64. Marable, *African & Caribbean Politics*, 46–47; Sidney J. Lemelle, "The Politics of Cultural Existence: Pan-Africanism, Historical Materialism and Afrocentricity," *Race & Class* 35 (1993): 100; Baraka, *African Congress*, 61–62; Jones, *Kawaida Studies*, 15; Carlos Moore, *Were Marx and Engels White Racists? The Prolet-Aryan Outlook of Marx and Engels* (Chicago: Institute of Positive Education, 1972); Clyde Halisi, ed., *The Quotable Karenga* (Los Angeles: US Organization, 1967), 5.
65. Adolph L. Reed, "Marxism and Nationalism in Afroamerica," *Social Theory and Practice* 1 (1971): 16–17; Marable, *African & Caribbean Politics*, 79, 81, 87; Jock McCulloch, *In the Twilight of Revolution: The Political Theory of Amilcar Cabral* (London: Routledge, 1983), 61–62; Bogues, *Black Heretics, Black Prophets*, 102; Kwame Nkrumah, *Class Struggle in Africa* (London: Panaf Books, 1970).
66. Kwame Nkrumah, *Handbook of Revolutionary Warfare: A Guide to the Armed Phase of the African Revolution* (London: Panaf Books, 1968), 49; Imamu Amiri Baraka, "The Concept of a Black United Front," *Black News*, February 1974, 8.
67. Roderick D. Bush, *The End of White World Supremacy: Black Internationalism and the Problem of the Color Line* (Philadelphia: Temple University Press, 2009), 165; Charlie Reilly, ed., *Conversations with Amiri Baraka* (Jackson: University Press of Mississippi, 1994), 110.
68. Allen, *Black Awakening in Capitalist America*, 168; Don L. Lee, *We Walk the Way of the New World* (Detroit, MI: Broadside Press, 1970), 11; Don L. Lee, *Book of Life* (Detroit, MI: Broadside Press, 1973), 29; "Ameer (LeRoi Jones) Baraka," 81–82.
69. Najib Peregrino-Brimah, *Architecture for the Afrikan* (Chicago: Institute of Positive Education, 1972); Majenzi Kuumba, "A Neo-Traditional African Architecture," *Black New Ark*, August 1972, 7; "Ideological Statement of the Congress of African Peoples," *African Congress*, 108; Ruwa Chiri, "The Pan-Afrikan Anthem," *Afrika Must Unite*, March–April 1972, 30; Kalamu Ya Salaam, *Pamoja Tutashinda/Together We Will Win* (New Orleans: Ahidiana, 1974).
70. Jones, *Kawaida Studies*, 25; Barbara Ransby and Tracye Matthews, "Black Popular Culture and the Transcendence of Patriarchal Illusions," *Race and Class* 35 (1993): 59.
71. Imamu Ameer Baraka, "The Coronation of the Black Queen," *Black Scholar*, June 1970, 46–48; Frances Beale, "Double Jeopardy: To Be Black and Female," in *The Black Woman: An Anthology*, ed. Toni Cade (New York: Signet, 1970), 91.
72. Howard Fuller, "[untitled]," in *African Congress*, 61; Jitu Weusi, "An Open Letter," *Black News*, October 1972, 12–14; Jitu Weusi, "Scribe Views *ESSENCE's* Descent into Dregs or Evil," *Muhammad Speaks*, September 22, 1972, 13, 14, 25; Haki R. Madhubuti, "Abortion," *Black Scholar*, March 1977, 48; Mary G. Rolison, *Grassroots Garveyism: The Universal Negro Improvement Association in the Rural South, 1920-1927* (Chapel Hill: University of North Carolina Press, 2007), 138.
73. Imamu Amiri Baraka, "Black Woman," *Black World*, July 1970, 11; "The Malaikas of CFUN," *Unity & Struggle*, February–March 1974, 11; "Black Women's Role in Society Morehouse Told," *Atlanta Daily World*, May 14, 1972, 2; Bibi Amina Baraka, "The Work of a Society," *Black New Ark*, October, 1972, 6; "Bibi Amina Baraka," *Black Collegian*, May–June 1973, 45.

74. Farah Jasmine Griffin, "'Ironies of the Saint': Malcolm X, Black Women, and the Price of Protection," in *Sisters in the Struggle: African American Women in the Civil Rights—Black Power Movement*, ed. Bettye Collier-Thomas and V. P. Franklin (New York: New York University Press, 2001), 216.

75. Kwa Salaam, "So-Journeying," 4, 98; Jones, *Kawaida Studies*, 28; Tayari Kwa Salaam, "The Malaika of CFUN," *Black Collegian*, May–June 1973, 43.

76. Michael Simanga, "The Congress of African People (1970-1980): History and Memory of an Ideological Journey" (PhD diss., Union Institute & University, 2008), 68; Baraka, "Confessions of a Former Anti-Semite," 20; Tayari Kwa Salaam, *Working Together We Can Make a Change: Towards Sisterhoods of Struggle* (New Orleans: Nkombo, 1981), 4; Kwa Salaam, "The Malaika of CFUN," 43–44; Muminans of CFUN, "Mwanamke Mwananchi (the Nationalist Woman)," 1971 pamphlet, Black Power Movement Part 1 (Microfilm).

77. Margo Natalie Crawford, "Must Revolution Be a Family Affair? Revisiting *The Black Woman*," in *Want to Start a Revolution: Radical Women in the Black Freedom Struggle*, ed. Dayo F. Gore, Jeanne Theoharis, and Komozi Woodard (New York: New York University Press, 2009), 188.

78. "Women in Africa Discuss Roles," *African World*, September 16, 1972, 4; Alberta Hill, "All-African Women's Conference, Dar es Salaam, Tanzania, July 24–31, 1972," *Black News*, November 1, 1972, 22–25; "The *Black Scholar* Interviews: Queen Mother Moore," *Black Scholar*, March–April 1973, 47–55; "Report from Tanzania," *Afrika Must Unite*, 1973, 14; "Mwanamke Weusi (Black Woman)," *Black News*, February 1974, 27; Amiri Baraka, "Black Women's United Front and National Black Assembly Meetings Analyzed," *Unity and Struggle*, February 1976, 12; Kwa Salaam, "So-Journeying," 112–114; "The Relationship Between the Sexes," pamphlet, n.d., Black Power Movement Part 1, Reel 4 (Microfilm).

79. "Bibi Amina Baraka," *Black Collegian*, May–June 1973, 45; Amiri Baraka, *The Autobiography of LeRoi Jones* (Chicago: Lawrence Hill Books, 1997), xv–xxiv; Kalamu Ya Salaam, *Our Women Keep Our Skies from Falling: Six Essays in Support of the Struggle to Smash Sexism/Develop Women* (New Orleans: Nkombo, 1980), 5–7; Kwa Salaam, *Working Together*, 3, 5–6, 14.

80. Bush, *The End of White World Supremacy*, 46.

81. Willingham, "Afro-American Pan-Africanist Ideology in the 1960s," 120; "Interview: The World of Don L. Lee," *Black Collegian*, February–March 1971, 33; Imamu Amiri Baraka, "Introduction," in *African Congress*, x.

82. Paul Gilroy, *"There Ain't No Black in the Union Jack": The Cultural Politics of Race and Nation* (Chicago: University of Chicago Press, 1991), 158; Ruwa Chiri, *An Acknowledgement of My Afro-American Brother* (Chicago: Free Black Press, 1968), 9.

83. Don L. Lee, *Don't Cry, Scream* (Detroit, MI: Broadside Press, 1970), 43; *The Pan African*, January 16, 1970, Box 54, Folder 4, JOP, ARC.

84. "Sadaukai: Cap Speech, Pt. II: We Need a Political Party," *African World*, October 14, 1972, 11; "Is Amin a Nationalist?" *Afrika Must Unite*, 1973, 4, 8, 19; "Press Conference by Hon. Wanume Kiebedi, Minister of Foreign Affairs of the Republic of Uganda," *Black News*, October 1972, 9.

85. W. C. Anas M. Luqman, "Malcolm X 'Black Manhood' Award," 1970 pamphlet, Box 154–32, Folder 73, KNP, MSR; "'Black Manhood' Prize to Guinea's President," *Chicago Daily Defender*, June 26, 1971, 2; "Resent the Scant Notice Given Nkrumah Death," *New York Amsterdam News*, May 6, 1972, C1; "Kwame Nkrumah: Dedicated Freedom Fighter," *Message African*, July–August 1972, 10, Box 47, Folder 2, FST, ARC; Jones, *Kawaida Studies*, 17; Dabu Gizenga, "On the Death of Osagyefo Dr. Kwame Nkrumah," *Afrika Must Unite*, June 1972; Dorothy Bannister, "Final Tribute to Kwame Nkrumah," *Black News*, July 1972, 2–3; Ruwa Chiri, "Osagyefo," *Afrika Must Unite*, March–April 1972, 26.

86. "The Black Scholar Interviews: Walter Rodney," *Black Scholar*, November 1974, 40; Marable, *African & Caribbean Politics*, 93.

87. See also J. K. Obatala, "Black Americans in Africa: A Critical View," *Pan African Notes*, Summer 1973, 54.

88. Daniel H. Watts, "The Carmichael/Cleaver Debate," *Liberator*, September 1969, 5.

89. Stokely Carmichael, "Pan-Africanism the Highest Stage of Black Power," *Rhythm*, Fall 1970, 37; "Center for Black Education: One Year Later," *Third World*, n.d. (c. 1970), Box 4,

UUA, AHT; Temple of Kawaida, *Kitabu: Beginning Concepts in Kawaida* (Los Angeles: US Organization, 1971), 8.

90. Imamu Amiri Baraka, "Coordinator's Statement," in *African Congress*, 117; see Appendix, Lathan Johnson, "The Role of Education in Western Culture History: Tanzania as a Model of Education for Self-Reliance" (PhD diss., Brandeis University, 1979).

91. Imari Abubakari Obadele I, "Yes—An Independent Black Nation in Our Time, in This Place!" in *African Congress*, 157; Harold W. Cruse, "The Little Rock National Black Political Convention," *Black World*, November 1974, 21; S. E. Anderson, "Revolutionary Black Nationalism and the Pan-African Idea," in *The Black Seventies*, ed. Floyd B. Barbour (Boston: Porter Sargent, 1970), 108; Nathan Hare, "Wherever We Are," *Black Scholar*, March 1971, 34.

92. Kathleen Cleaver, "Interview: Return to Babylon," *Black Collegian*, March–April 1972, 39; Charlie Cobb, "Africa Notebook: Views on Returning 'Home,' " *Black World*, May 1972, 29.

93. Kalamu Ya Salaam, "The Realities of Living and Working in Afrika," *Black Collegian*, September–October 1974, 28.

94. Era Bell Thompson, "Are Black Americans Welcome in Africa," *Ebony*, January 1969, 50; "Harlemites Boo African Who Tells Them to Stay in U.S.," *New York Amsterdam News*, March 29, 1969, 3; Joe Walker, "Why Harlem Hurled Eggs at Tom Mboya," *Muhammad Speaks*, April 4, 1969, 18, 30; Joseph Walker, "Part II: Why Harlem Threw Eggs at Kenya's Tom Mboya," *Muhammad Speaks*, April 11, 1969; Bayard Rustin, "Tom Mboya's Message in Harlem," *New York Amsterdam News*, April 19, 1969, 14; Selwyn R. Cudjoe, "Taking Whitey's Word," *Liberator*, May 1969; Immanuel Wallerstein, "Taking Whitey's Word: Replies," *Liberator*, July 1969, 9; Songha Wayandney Songha, "Mr. Mboya in Harlem," *Liberator*, July 1969, 10–11; Michael Knashie Searles, "It Ain't Necessarily So," *Liberator*, July 1969, 10–11; "Slain African's Legacy to Black Americans: 'Back to Africa' Views Chart Future of Blacks and Africans," *Jet*, July 24, 1969, 50–56.

95. James Forman, "The Concept of International Black Power," *Pan-African Journal*, Spring–Summer 1968, 93; Charles P. Howard, "Black Africa Recruiting Teachers from White Britain; Why Not Afro-Americans?" *Muhammad Speaks*, February 23, 1968, 2; Milton Coleman, "Nation Building in Africa," *SOBU Newsletter*, May 29, 1971, 1.

96. "Pan African Skills Project," proposal, November 1972, Box 36, Folder 4, VHP, EUM; "Become One of the PAS 4000," flyer, n.d., Box 46, Folder 12, FST, ARC, Amistad Research Center; Brother Ollis Douglas to unknown, n.d. (c. 1971), Box 128, Folder 23, DGC, MSR; "Pan-Africanism at Work: The Pan African Skills Project," *IFCO News*, January–February 1973, 2.

97. Institute of the Black World, *Black Analysis for the Seventies, 1971-1972*, vol. I (Atlanta: Institute of the Black World, 1973), 39.

98. "Cleaver and Seale Accept Algiers Bid," *New York Times*, July 14, 1969, 7; "Cleaver Arrives for Algiers Fete," *New York Times*, July 16, 1969, 9; Eric Pace, "African Nations Open 12-Day Cultural Festival with Parade Through Algiers," *New York Times*, July 22, 1969, 9; Eric Pace, "Carmichael Tells of Meeting Cleaver in Algiers," *New York Times*, July 25, 1969, 16; Conrad Clark, "Pan-African Cultural Festival Draws Blacks," *New York Amsterdam News*, July 26, 1969, 31; Eric Page, "Africans at Algiers Festival Denounce Concept of 'Negritude' as Outmoded," *New York Times*, July 28, 1969, 4; "Al Fatah, at Festival in Algiers, Seeks Black Africans' Support," *New York Times*, August 2, 1969, 3; "Ed Bullins Attends First Pan-African Festival," *New York Amsterdam News*, August 30, 1969, 21; Richard W. Fox, "Black Panthers in Africa," *Commonweal*, October 3, 1969, 6–7; Hoyt W. Fuller, "Algiers Journal," *Negro Digest*, October 1969, 73–87; Nathan Hare, "Algiers 1969: A Report on the Pan-African Cultural Festival," *Black Scholar*, November 1969, 2–10; Michele Russell, "Algerian Journey," *Freedomways*, Fall 1969, 355–364; Hare, "Wherever We Are," *Black Scholar*, 34.

99. Amilcar Cabral, "National Liberation and Culture," in *Return to the Source: Selected Speeches by Amilcar Cabral*, ed. Africa Information Service (New York: Monthly Review Press, 1973), 39–56.

100. "Identity and Dignity in Struggle, Part One," *African World*, October 28, 1972, 8, 14; "Identity and Dignity in Struggle, Part Two," *African World*, November 11, 1972, 9, 13; Amilcar Cabral, "Identity and Dignity in the Context of the National Liberation," *Pan-African Journal*, Autumn 1973, 369–378.

101. S. O. Claxton, "Warrior Battles for Freedom," *CORE*, Winter 1972, 48–50.

102. Amilcar Cabral, "Connecting the Struggles: An Informal Talk with Black Americans," in *Return to the Source*, 72–78, 83–85.
103. Ibid., 86.
104. Ibid., 85–92.
105. Forence Tate, "Freedom Fighters Close Ranks After Cabral Slain," *Afro-American*, February 3, 1973, 1, 2; Owusu Sadaukai, "A Tribute to Amilcar Cabral," *Black Collegian*, March–April 1973, 6.
106. Ron Karenga, "A Strategy for Struggle," *Black Scholar*, November 1973, 8–21; Maulana Ron Karenga, "A Tribute to Cabral's Triumph," *African World*, July 14, 1973, 11.
107. Kalamu Ya Salaam, *Art for Life*, accessed July 29, 2012, http://www.nathanielturner.com/artforlifetable.htm; Baraka, "Confessions of a Former Anti-Semite," 23; Simanga, "The Congress of African People," 69; "Nationalists Gather for 2nd Congress of African People," *African World*, September 30, 1972, 10; "CAP Summation," *Unity & Struggle*, October 2, 1975, 5; Reilly, *Conversations with Amiri Baraka*, 138, 205; Baraka, *The Autobiography*, 417.
108. "Developmental Background: The Student Organization for Black Unity," pamphlet, Black Power Movement Part 1, Reel 4 (Microfilm); "Student Organization for Black Unity: Proposal," December 20, 1969, Box 11, Folder 1, CSP, ACC; "SOBU Programs," *Muhammad Speaks*, November 6, 1970, 6; "Understanding Pan-Africanism," *SOBU Newsletter*, October 17, 1970, 4.
109. "The Student Organization for Black Unity: A Look Backward and Forward," July 1970, and "Student Organization for Black Unity: Ideological Paper," Box 11, Folder 1, CSP, ACC; "We Are an African People," *African World*, September 16, 1972, 19; Eldridge Cleaver, "Culture and Revolution: Their Synthesis in Africa," *Black Scholar*, October 1971, 33–39; "Developing Effective Cadres," *SOBU Newsletter*, April 17, 1971, 4.

Chapter 6

1. Frantz Fanon, *The Wretched of the Earth* (New York: Grove Press, 1963), 150. For other narrative histories of the "Black University" theme, see chapter five, Martha Biondi, *The Black Revolution on Campus* (Berkeley: University of California Press, 2012), and Richard D. Benson, II, *Fighting for Our Place in the Sun: Malcolm X and the Radicalization of the Black Student Movement, 1960–1973* (New York: Peter Lang, 2015).
2. "Background Information on the Malcolm X Liberation University," March 1969, Box 12, Folder 8, and "Suggested Solutions to Problem Areas," April 1969, Box 12, Folder 3, and Howard University Résumé, CSP, ACC; Interview with Howard Fuller, December 14, 1996, Southern Oral History Program Collection, Documenting the American South, accessed October 13, 2013, http://docsouth.unc.edu/sohp/O-0034/menu.html; Jack White, "Black University Survives in N.C.," *Race Relations Reporter*, July 6, 1971, 5–6; Report of Greensboro Local Committee, June 1972, Box 11, Folder 81, TFP, LRW; Elizabeth Tornquest, "Tear Gas Blurs the Image as Duke Opts for 'Law and Order,'" *New South*, Spring 1969, 28.
3. Report of Greensboro Local Committee, June 1972, Box 11, Folder 81, TFP, LRW; Tornquest, "Tear Gas Blurs the Image as Duke Opts for 'Law and Order,'" 21–29; Chuck Hopkins, "Malcolm X Liberation University," *Negro Digest*, March 1970, 39–42; Brent H. Belvin, "Malcolm X Liberation University: An Experiment in Independent Black Education" (master's thesis, North Carolina State University, 2004), 41–44; "Proposal for Malcolm X Liberation University," June 5, 1969, and "What You Can Do for MXLU," March 1969, CSP, ACC.
4. Proposal for Malcolm X Liberation University, Box 12, Folder 3, and "Proposal for Malcolm X Liberation University," June 5, 1969, CSP, ACC.
5. Report of Greensboro Local Committee, June 1972, Box 11, Folder 81, TFP, LRW; "Background Information on the Malcolm X Liberation University," March 1969, Box 12, Folder 8, and Proposal for Malcolm X Liberation University, Box 12, Folder 3, CSP, ACC; Hopkins, "Malcolm X Liberation University," 40; Tornquest, "Tear Gas Blurs the Image as Duke Opts for 'Law and Order,'" 21–29; Hopkins, 40; "Gas Routs Protesters After Sit-In at Duke," *Washington Post*, February 14, 1969, A1, A16.
6. Untitled March 11, 1970, document, Box 50, Folder 20, EGP, SCR; "Background Information on the Malcolm X Liberation University," March 1969, Box 12, Folder 8, and "Malcolm X

Liberation University Fact Sheet," Box 12, Folder 3, and "What You Can Do for MXLU," pamphlet, CSP, ACC; Tornquest, "Tear Gas Blurs the Image as Duke Opts for 'Law and Order,'" 27.

7. "Background Information on the Malcolm X Liberation University," March 1969, Box 12, Folder 8, and "Malcolm X Liberation University Fact Sheet," Box 12, Folder 3, and "What You Can Do for MXLU," pamphlet, CSP, ACC; "Fires Set, Nation's High Schools, Colleges Hit by Student Unrest," *Jet*, March 27, 1969, 46; Tornquest, "Tear Gas Blurs the Image as Duke Opts for 'Law and Order,'" 27–28.

8. Stokely Carmichael, "We Are All Africans," *Black Scholar*, May 1970, 15; August 20, 1969, John O. Killens to Howard L. Fuller, Box 117, Folder 13, JKP, EUM; "Malcolm X Liberation University Fact Sheet," Box 12, Folder 3, and September 29, 1969, Howard L. Fuller to Committee Member, CSP, ACC; Christina Greene, *Our Separate Ways: Women and the Black Freedom Movement in Durham, NC* (Chapel Hill: University of North Carolina Press, 2005), 82–88.

9. James T. Wooten, "Malcolm X University to Open In Durham as Militants' School," *New York Times*, October 28, 1969, 44; "Proposal for Malcolm X Liberation University," June 1969, Box 12, Folder 3, and "MXLU Bulletin, 1970-1971," Box 12, Folder 8, and "Malcolm X Liberation University Fact Sheet," Box 12, Folder 3, CSP, ACC.

10. "Position Paper for Malcolm X Liberation University," Box 4, PWP, SCR; "Background Information on the Malcolm X Liberation University," March 1969, Box 12, Folder 8, and "Foundation for Community Development Memorandum on MXLU," April 3, 1969, and "Malcolm X Liberation University Fact Sheet," Box 12, Folder 3, CSP, ACC; Wooten, "Malcolm X University to Open in Durham," 44.

11. Report of Greensboro Local Committee, June 1972, Box 11, Folder 81, TFP, LRW; Lucius Walker Jr., "Malcolm X Liberation University Closes to Engage a Larger Task," *IFCO News*, 1973, 6; Lerone Bennett, *The Negro Mood* (Chicago: Johnson Publishing, 1964).

12. Untitled March 11, 1970, document, Box 50, Folder 20, EGP, SCR.

13. "New Malcolm X School," *Chicago Daily Defender*, November 4, 1969, 13; "Malcolm X University Policies, Procedures Outlined," *Durham Morning Herald*, October 28, 1969, B1; "Lawyers Stress Role of Black Attorney in Meet," *New Journal and Guide*, August 23, 1969, A15; "Parade Held in Support of University," *Fayetville Observer*, November 30, 1969, B1; December 12, 1969, Mary Jane Barthwell, S. E. Anderson, and Howard Fuller to "Brothers and Sisters," and December 29, 1969, Howard L. Fuller to Ewart Guinier, Box 50, Folder 20, EGP, SCR; "Malcolm X Liberation University Fact Sheet," and "Progress Report on Malcolm X Liberation University," July 1969, and "Proposal for Malcolm X Liberation University," June 1969, Box 12, Folder 3, CSP, ACC; "Malcolm X Classes Set Oct. 27," *Shelby Daily Star*, October 10, 1969, A9.

14. Thomas Patrick, "Church Body Aids Drive Against Bias," *Washington Post*, September 10, 1971, A23; "Press Statement," *IFCO News*, July–August 1971; "Interreligious Foundation Grants Total Half Million," *New York Amsterdam News*, May 15, 1971, 31; "Foundation Gives 100G to U.S., Afro Movements," *New York Amsterdam News*, July 1, 1972, D8; George Dugan, "Black Action Unit Takes Aim At Bias," *New York Times*, March 19, 1972, 24; "White Cleric to Head Black Drive," *Chicago Defender*, October 7, 1971, 14.

15. "Church to Aid Negro School," *New York Times*, October 14, 1969, 35; "Progress Report on Malcolm X Liberation University," pamphlet, February 20, 1970, and "Foundation for Community Development Memorandum on MXLU," April 3, 1969, and "Episcopal Body Urges Grant Process Review," newspaper clipping, November 1, 1969, CSP, ACC.

16. Jim Lewis, "'No, We Do Not Teach Violence,' Fuller Says of Malcolm X Univ.," *Raleigh News & Observer*, November 3, 1969.

17. "Malcolm X School Rescinds Funds Appeal," *Baltimore Afro-American*, July 22, 1972, 17; "Malcolm X University institutes Alternative Educational System," *Afro-American*, January 3, 1970, 12; "Malcolm X College Fighting for Its Life," *Milwaukee Journal*, February 5, 1970, 8; Bradley Martin, "Malcolm X University: Alternative to the System," *Charlotte Observer*, December 1, 1969, 8C; Franklin Delano Williams biography, accessed October 27, 2013, http://www.crmvet.org/vet/fdw.htm; White, "Black University Survives in N.C.," 5; Rosemary Yardley, "Malcolm X University: Black Separation Symbol," *Greensboro Daily News*, November 30, 1969, B1, B12.

18. Milton Coleman, "Fuller Emphasizes Need for Continuing Struggle," *Milwaukee Courier,* November 2, 1969, 1, 9.

19. "'Liberation' University Opens," *Milwaukee Courier,* November 2, 1969, 1, 9; David Newton, "Idea of Independent Black Africa Gets Boost," *Durham Morning Herald,* October 26, 1969, 6A; Hazel Reid, "Dedication Held for Malcolm X U.," *Baltimore Afro-American,* November 8, 1969, 20; Coleman, "Fuller Emphasizes Need for Continuing Struggle," 9; "African Clad Group Marches to School," unidentified news clipping, Box 9, Folder 65, TFP, LRW; "'Liberation' University Opens," *Milwaukee Courier,* November 2, 1969, 1, 9; Carmichael, "We Are All Africans," 15–19.

20. "Memorandum on MXLU"; National Association for African American Education, *The Perspectives Gained: Findings of a Five-Day Black University* (Harlem, NY: National Association for African American Education, 1970), 68.

21. "Proposal for Malcolm X Liberation University," June 1969, Box 12, Folder 3, and "Background Information on the Malcolm X Liberation University," March 1969, Box 12, Folder 8, CSP, ACC; "Proposal for Malcolm X Liberation University," Box 30, Folder 39, IFCO, SCR.

22. Report of Greensboro Local Committee, June 1972, Box 11, Folder 81, TFP, LRW; Proposal for Malcolm X Liberation University, and "Progress Report on Malcolm X Liberation University," November 1969, Box 12, Folder 3, CSP, ACC.

23. Donald Stone, "MXLU Speaks," *Rhythm,* Winter 1970, 17; "Position Paper for Malcolm X Liberation University," Box 4, PWP, SCR; "Malcolm X Liberation University Community Seminars," brochure, n.d., and "The Portuguese in Kongo History," lesson plan, n.d., Box 30, Folder 38, IFCO, SCR; MXLU 1970-71 Bulletin, Box 12, Folder 8, CSP, ACC.

24. Martin, "Malcolm X University: Alternative to the System," 8C; MXLU brochure, Box 30, Folder 38, IFCO, SCR; "Student Organization for Black Unity Pan African Work Program," brochure, and "What You Can Do for MXLU," 1969 pamphlet, and "Background Information on the Malcolm X Liberation University," March 1969, Box 12, Folder 8, and April 10, 1969, Howard L. Fuller to Faculty, Box 12, Folder 3, and "Proposal for Malcolm X Liberation University," June 1969, Box 12, Folder 3, and "Internal Organization and Organizing," Box 12, Folder 4, CSP, ACC.

25. Report of Greensboro Local Committee, June 1972, Box 11, Folder 81, TFP, LRW; "Malcolm X Liberation University," *Black Collegian,* November–December 1972, 53; "DRAFT—For Internal Purposes Only," 1971 manuscript, and "Internal Organization and Organizing," Box 12, Folder 4, CSP, ACC.

26. MXLU Financial Report of Cummins Engine Foundation Grant, 1972, Box 30, Folder 39, IFCO, SCR; Kalamu Ya Salaam, "Tell No Lies, Claim No Easy Victories," *Black World,* October 1974, 21; "Internal Organization and Organizing," Box 12, Folder 4, and Minutes of the Council of Elders Meeting, May 1, 1970, CSP, ACC.

27. Malcolm X Liberation University Community Seminars, n.d., Box 30, Folder 38, IFCO, SCR; "Position Paper for Malcolm X Liberation University," Box 4, PWP, SCR; Stone, "MXLU Speaks," 15; "Background Information on the Malcolm X Liberation University," March 1969, Box 12, Folder 8, CSP, ACC.

28. "Student Organization for Black Unity Pan African Work Program," brochure, CSP, ACC; Progress Report, June 30, 1972, to December 1, 1972, Box 30, Folder 39, and "IFCO Project Evaluation and Recommendation," October 1970, Box 45, Folder 38, IFCO, SCR.

29. Adam C. Powell, "My Black Position Paper," in *The Black Power Revolt,* ed. Floyd Barbour (Boston: Extending Horizons Books, 1968), 260; Acklyn R. Lynch, *Blueprint for Change* (Chicago: Institute of Positive Education, 1972), 3–4.

30. "Student Organization for Black Unity Pan African Work Program," brochure, "DRAFT—For Internal Purposes Only," 1971 manuscript, Box 12, Folder 4, and Peter Leo, "At Malcolm X—Dawn to Dusk Education," newspaper clipping, Box 12, Folder 9, and Howard Fuller, "Mwalimu's Message," *Msaidizi,* August 1971, CSP, ACC.

31. "Understanding the African Struggle," *African Warrior,* December 4, 1970, 3, 11; "'Building Things,' but Not Here," newspaper clipping, Box 12, Folder 9, CSP, ACC.

32. Stone, "MXLU Speaks," 17; Martin, "Malcolm X University: Alternative to the System," 8C; "Progress Report on Malcolm X Liberation University," November 1969, Box 12, Folder

3, and Minutes from Council of Elders Meeting, September 25–26, 1970, and "Student Organization for Black Unity Pan African Work Program," brochure, CSP, ACC.

33. Minutes from Council of Elders Meeting, September 25–26, 1970, CSP, ACC; "Proposal for Malcolm X Liberation University," Box 30, Folder 39, IFCO, SCR; White, "Black University Survives in N.C.," 5–6; "Malcolm X Moves to Greensboro," *Greensboro Record*, August 20, 1970, D1, D5; "Malcolm X Univ. to Greensboro Site," *New Journal and Guide*, September 5, 1970, 1–2; Jim Grant, "Malcolm X Liberation University in Third Year," *Philadelphia Tribune*, January 1, 1972, 7; "Malcolm X Liberation University," 13–14.

34. White, "Black University Survives in N.C.," 6; "Malcolm X Liberation University," 14; "African Teachers Trained at MXLU," *African Warrior*, December 4, 1970, 4; "Malcolm X Liberation University Proposal Summary," Box 30, Folder 38, and "Malcolm X Liberation University African Peoples' Ideological and Technical Institute," Progress Report, June 30, 1972, to December 1, 1972, Box 30, Folder 39, IFCO, SCR; Jim Grant, "Malcolm X Liberation University in Third Year," *Philadelphia Tribune*, January 1, 1972, 7; "Minutes of the Council of Elders Meeting," May 1, 1970, and "Summer Work at Malcolm X," *Msaidizi*, August 1971, and Minutes from Council of Elders Meeting, September 25–26, 1970, CSP, ACC.

35. "Malcolm X Liberation University Proposal Summary," Box 30, Folder 38, IFCO, SCR; "Blind Workers Continuing Strike," *African Warrior*, December 4, 1970, 2; "Welcome from Malcolm X Liberation University," pamphlet, CSP, ACC.

36. October 22, 1971, Howard Fuller to Bishop Charles Golden, Box 30, Folder 37, IFCO, SCR; Report of Greensboro Local Committee, June 1972, Box 11, Folder 81, TFP, LRW; "Civil Engineers for African World," *African Warrior*, February 5, 1971, 1; "DRAFT—For Internal Purposes Only," 1971 manuscript, Box 12, Folder 4, and Jesse Poindexter, "Fuller: Mellowed by New Approach," newspaper clipping, Box 12, Folder 9, CSP, ACC.

37. Charles Wartts Jr., "African Liberation Support Group to Spearhead Year Round Drive," *Muhammad Speaks*, October 28, 1972, 5; Minutes from Council of Elders Meeting, September 25–26, 1970, and "Progress Report on Malcolm X Liberation University," 1970 pamphlet, Box 12, Folder 3, CSP, ACC; "World-Wide African Solidarity Day—May 25," *SOBU Newsletter*, May 15, 1971, 1; Report of Greensboro Local Committee, June 1972, Box 11, Folder 81, TFP, LRW.

38. "50 Black Clergymen to Meet in Tanzania," *New York Amsterdam News*, August 7, 1971, D10; Peter Leo, "Controversial School Comes of Age," newspaper clipping, Box 12, Folder 9, CSP, ACC; "Malcolm X Liberation University Mwalimu Mkuu Owusu Sadaukai," *Black Collegian*, March–April 1973, 50; Tom Bamberger, "The Education of Howard Fuller," *Milwaukee Magazine*, July 1988, 58; Owusu Sadaukai, "Inside Liberated Mozambique," *African World*, January 8, 1972, 8, 9.

39. Sarah Means, "Fighting for School Choice: One Man's Struggle from Africa to Milwaukee," *Washington Times*, July 5, 2000, A15; Sadaukai, "Inside Liberated Mozambique," 8–9.

40. Means, "Fighting for School Choice," A15; "Owusu's Speech," transcript, c. 1973, CSP, ACC;

41. Cedric Johnson, *Revolutionaries to Race Leaders: Black Power and the Making of African American Politics* (Minneapolis: University of Minnesota, 2007), 138–140; Signe Waller, *Love and Revolution: A Political Memoir: People's History of the Greensboro Massacre, Its Setting and Aftermath* (Lanham, MD: Rowman & Littlefield), 55; SNCC Research Department, "The Source of the South African Economy: A Study of the Chase Manhattan Bank in South Africa," 1966 pamphlet, Box 1, Folder 14, VCP, WHI; C. E. Wilson, "American Investment in Portuguese Africa: A Problem of Democratic Socialism," *Freedomways*, Summer 1967, 214–225; Daniel Schechter, "Polaroid Apartheid: Pull Tab, Wait 60 Seconds," *Ramparts*, February 1971, 46–50; William J. Pomeroy, "The Resistance Movement Against Apartheid in South Africa," *Freedomways*, Summer 1971, 243; Charles C. Diggs Jr., "My Visit to South Africa," *Africa Report*, November 1971, 16–17.

42. "The African Liberator," 1972 pamphlet, and "Africa for the Africans at Home and Abroad," pamphlet, n.d., Box 7, Folder 2, PWP, SCR; "African Liberation Day," *African World*, May 9, 1972, 8; "Afrikan Solidarity Demonstration," *Afrika Must Unite*, March–April 1972, 12; "African Liberation Day Set," *African World*, April 1, 1972, 3; "Origin of May 27 Protest Action on Africa," *Militant*, May 12, 1972, 14.

43. "The African Liberator," 1972 pamphlet, African Liberation Day Coordinating Committee, Box 7, Folder 2, PWP, SCR; "Pulling Together the African World," *SOBU Newsletter*, May 15, 1971, 3; "Black Organizations Protest Rhodesian Goods Shipment," *Los Angeles Sentinel*, April 27, 1972, A15; Institute of the Black World, *Black Analysis for the Seventies, 1971-1972*, vol. I (Atlanta: Institute of the Black World, 1973), 13.

44. "Amiri Baraka (Leroi Jones at the East)," *Black News*, March 28, 1972, 13; "Owusu's Speech," c. 1972 transcript, CSP, ACC.

45. Richard E. Prince, "12,000 Blacks March to Support Africa," *Washington Post*, May 28, 1972, A1; Tom Stokes, "Blacks Protest South Africa," *Chicago Daily Defender*, May 30, 1972, 4; "ALD International Success," *African World*, June 10, 1972, 1, 8; "African Liberation Day Speeches," *African World*, June 10, 1972, 10; Lonnie Kashif, "African Liberation Day," *Muhammad Speaks*, June 16, 1972, 13–14, 19; Larry Brown, "15,000 Join in Solidarity Call," *Baltimore Afro-American*, June 3, 1972, 1, 9; "ALD International Success," *African World*, June 10, 1972, 1, 8; "ALD March Orderly and Enthusiastic," *African World*, June 10, 1972, 9; John Hawkins, "Film: African Liberation," *Militant*, September 29, 1972, 20.

46. "America's Black Silent Majority," *Atlas*, June 1970, 27; Inez Smith Reid, *"Together" Black Women* (New York: Third Press, 1975), 253–254; Johnson, *Revolutionaries to Race Leaders*, 138–140.

47. Mwalimu Shay and Hannibal Tirus Afrik, "Vision on Afrikan Liberation Day," *Elimu Ya Kujitegemea* [Shule Ya Watoto newsletter], c. 1972, Box 18, PWP, SCR; "Africa for the Africans at Home and Abroad," 1973 flyer, Box 4, Subseries 4, COC, OCA; The Center for Black Education, *African Liberation: An Analytical Report on Southern Africa* (Washington, DC: Drum & Spear Press, 1973), 2.

48. "A South African Revolutionary," *Black News*, January 1972, 2–4; "Afrikan Solidarity Demonstration," *Afrika Must Unite*, March–April 1972, 12. Also see "Africa for the Africans at Home and Abroad," pamphlet, Box 7, Folder 2, PWP, SCR; "Understand the Struggle," *African World* [Special Section], May 27, 1972, 7.

49. John Hawkins, "Owusu Sadaukai on African Liberation and the '72 Elections," *Militant*, July 21, 1972, 10; Bruce Oudes, "The African Liberation Day March," *Africa Report*, June 1972, 12–13; "Our People Have Begun to Move," *African World*, June 24, 1972, 10.

50. "ALD Committee Continues to Work," *African World*, August 19, 1972, 14; "Cabral and PAIGC Honored," *African World*, October 28, 1972, 1, 9; February 16, 1973, Owusu Sadaukai and Florence Tate to Preston Wilcox, Box 7, Folder 2, PWP, SCR; Mwalimu Owusu Sadaukai, *The Condition of Black People in the 1970s* (Chicago: Institute of Positive Education, 1972), 1; Carole A. Parks, "Africa Is at War," *Black World*, May 1973, 79.

51. "MXLU Opens 4th Year," *African World*, October 14, 1972, 6; MXLU Financial Report of Cummins Engine Foundation Grant, 1972, Box 30, Folder 39, and MXLU Brochure, Box 30, Folder 38, and "Proposal for Malcolm X Liberation University," Box 30, Folder 39, IFCO, SCR; "Sadaukai Confers with African Presidents," *African World*, August 19, 1972, 14; "Malcolm X Liberation University," 53; "African Liberation Struggles: Angola, Guinea-Bissau, Mozambique," pamphlet, Box 7, Folder 2, PWP, SCR.

52. Florence Tate, "200 Students Meet to Plan Future of Black Community," *Natchez News Leader*, November 19, 1972, 7A; Wartts Jr., "African Liberation Support Group to Spearhead Year Round Drive," 23–24; Sadaukai, *The Condition of Black People in the 1970s*, 5, 9.

53. Malcolm X Liberation University African Peoples' Ideological and Technical Institute, Quarterly Report for IFCO, November 1, 1970, to January 31, 1971, Box 30, Folder 37, IFCO, SCR; "DRAFT—For Internal Purposes Only," 1971 manuscript, Box 12, Folder 4, and Minutes of the Council of Elders Meeting, May 1, 1970, CSP, ACC.

54. "Malcolm X Liberation University African Peoples' Ideological and Technical Institute," Progress Report, June 30, 1972, to December 1, 1972, Box 30, Folder 39, and Quarterly Report for IFCO November 1, 1970, to January 31, 1971, Box 30, Folder 37, and MXLU Brochure, Box 30, Folder 38, IFCO, SCR; Jesse Poindexter, "Fuller: Mellowed by New Approach," newspaper clipping, Box 12, Folder 9, CSP, ACC; Jim Grant, "Malcolm X Liberation University in Third Year," *Philadelphia Tribune*, January 1, 1972, 7; " 'No, We Do Not Teach Violence,' Fuller Says of Malcolm X Univ.," Box 9, Folder 66, TFP, LRW; "Malcolm X Lib. Univ. Support Committee Minutes, Dec. 2, 1972," Box 48, Folder 2, EGP, SCR; "Malcolm X Liberation University," 14.

55. "DRAFT—For Internal Purposes Only," 1971 manuscript, Box 12, Folder 4, and Minutes from Council of Elders Meeting, September 25–26, 1970, CSP, ACC.
56. "Malcolm X Liberation University Proposal Summary," Box 30, Folder 38, IFCO, SCR; Report of Greensboro Local Committee, June 1972, Box 11, Folder 81, TFP, LRW; Ed Martin, "Young Urges Black Power In Perspective," *Durham Morning Herald*, October 31, 1969, B1; "Malcolm X Liberation University," 14; "Malcolm X Lib. Univ. Support Committee Minutes, Dec. 2, 1972," Box 48, Folder 2, EGP, SCR.
57. Wooten, "Malcolm X University to Open in Durham," 44; MXLU Financial Report of Cummins Engine Foundation Grant, 1972, Box 30, Folder 39, IFCO, SCR; Report of Greensboro Local Committee, June 1972, Box 11, Folder 81, TFP, LRW; "Black Activist to Figure in Operations at School," *Greensboro Record*, August 20, 1970, D5; FBI Files on Black Extremist Organizations, microform, reels 4–5; Jesse Poindexter, "Fuller: Mellowed by New Approach," newspaper clipping, Box 12, Folder 9, CSP, ACC.
58. "$45,000 Grant to Malcolm X University Defended," *New Journal and Guide*, February 7, 1970, 11; "Malcolm X College Fighting for Its Life," *Milwaukee Journal*, February 5, 1970, 8; Report of Greensboro Local Committee, June 1972, Box 11, Folder 81, TFP, LRW.
59. "Malcolm X Lib. Univ. Support Committee Minutes, Dec. 2, 1972," Box 48, Folder 2, EGP, SCR; Malcolm X Liberation University materials, Box 12, Folder 14, DJB, RLC; "IFCO Project Evaluation and Recommendation," October 1970, Box 45, Folder 38, and Malcolm X Liberation University African Peoples' Ideological and Technical Institute, Quarterly Report for IFCO, November 1, 1970, to January 31, 1971, Box 30, Folder 37, IFCO, SCR; Minutes from Council of Elders Meeting, September 25–26, 1970, CSP, ACC; "MXLU Opens 4th Year," *African World*, October 14, 1972, 6.
60. "Black Pride," *Time*, October 6, 1967; Robert S. Browne, "The Challenge of Black Student Organizations," *Freedomways*, Fall 1968, 325–326; "Black Mood on Campus," *Newsweek*, February 10, 1969, 53; James Cass, "Can the University Survive the Black Challenge," *Saturday Review*, June 21, 1969, 700; "Student Strikes: 1968-1969," *Black Scholar*, January–February 1970, 66; Lerone Bennett Jr., "Confrontation on the Campus," *Ebony*, May 1968, 29.
61. Keith Lowe, "Towards a Black University," *Liberator*, September 1968, 5.
62. Gerald McWhorter, "The Nature and Needs of the Black University," *Negro Digest*, March 1968, 9; Vincent Harding, "Some Implications of the Black University," *Negro Digest*, March 1968, 37; Ronald Davis, "Response to Vincent Harding," *Negro Digest*, March 1970, 15; John O. Killens, "The Artist and the Black University," *Black Scholar*, November 1969, 64; Stokely Carmichael, "Pan-Africanism—Land and Power," *Black Scholar*, November 1969, 43.
63. Stephen E. Henderson, "The Black University: Toward Its Realization," *Negro Digest*, March 1968, 80; "The Black University: A Movement or an Institution," 1969 pamphlet, Box 22, PWP, SCR; Nikki Giovanni, "I Fell Off the Roof One Day (A View of the Black University)," in *The Black Woman*, ed. Toni Cade (New York: Signet, 1970), 135.
64. McWhorter, "The Nature and Needs of the Black University," 10; "National Black Institute," 1968, Black Power Movement Part 3—Revolutionary Action Movement, Series 3 (Microfilm); Davis, "Response to Vincent Harding," 14; quoted in McWhorter, "The Nature and Needs of the Black University," 8.
65. "Financing the Black University," November 1968 transcript, Box 22, Folder 9, RSB, SCR; James Forman, "Black Manifesto," in *Black Protest: History, Documents, and Analyses: 1619 to the Present*, ed. Joanne Grant (Greenwich, CT: Fawcett, 1968), 547.
66. Stephen Henderson, "Toward a Black University," *Ebony*, September 1970, 109; William J. Wilson, "'New Creation or Familiar Death': A Rejoinder to Vincent Harding," *Negro Digest*, March 1970, 58.
67. "Critique of a Colonizing Program," pamphlet, c. 1972, and Nelson N. Johnson, "Black Studies and Revolution," *SOBU Newsletter*, clipping, n.d., CSP, ACC; I. K. Sundiata, "Black Studies: A Cop-Out?" *Liberator*, April 1969, 10; Richard A. Long, "The Black Studies Boondoggle," *Liberator*, September 1970, 6–9; Davis, "Response to Vincent Harding," 17.
68. "Militants Snuff Out Moderates at Conference on Black power," *Call and Post*, July 29, 1967, 1A, 16A; "Education, Self-Learning and Report of Workshop on Education and Control of Schools in Black Community," 1968 pamphlet, Box 7, Folder 5, and "Control of Schools Within the Black Community," 1968 pamphlet, Box 24, Folder 1, PWP, SCR.

69. September 22, 1969, Hoyt W. Fuller to Preston Wilcox, Box 10, Folder 23, PWP, SCR; "National Association for African American Education," brochure, Box 34, Folder 16, VHP, EUM; "Black Educators' Conference Slated," *Los Angeles Sentinel*, June 5, 1969, A9; Betty Washington, "Black Educators Seek to Alter College Entry," *Chicago Daily Defender*, June 10, 1968, 3, 20; Association of Afro-American Educators, 1968 manuscript, Box 8, Folder 10, PWP, SCR; Leon R. Forrest, "Blacks Meet in Atlanta To: 'Make Education Relevant,'" *Muhammad Speaks*, September 5, 1969, 4.

70. "Howard University: A Policy Statement on the Black University," October 22, 1968, Box 159-4, Folder 16, SAV, WHI.

71. "Towards a Black University-November 13–17, 1968," *Hilltop*, November 8, 1968; "Faculty Engages in Tokenism," *Hilltop*, November 8, 1968, 8.

72. Thomas A. Johnson, "Howard Students Discuss Reforms," *New York Times*, November 15, 1968, 34; Thomas A. Johnson, "Negro Students Seek Relevance," *New York Times*, November 18, 1968, 25; "Howard University: A Policy Statement on the Black University," October 22, 1968, Box 159-4, Folder 16, SAV, WHI; "Towards a Black University-November 13–17, 1968," *Hilltop*, November 8, 1968; "The Conference Is a Learning Experience," *Hilltop*, November 8, 1968, 8; Lonnie Kashif, "New Confrontations Likely: Howard University Campus," *Muhammad Speaks*, November 8, 1968, 27; "Carmichael to Keynote Conference," *Hilltop*, November 8, 1968, 8; "Maulana Ron Karenga Will Address Conference Saturday," *Hilltop*, November 8, 1968, 9; "2MJQ to Participate in Sunday's Seminar," *Hilltop*, November 8, 1968, 10; Lonnie Kashif, "Toward a Black University Conference," *Muhammad Speaks*, November 29, 1968, 30; "Afro-Americans Move Towards a Black University," *Muhammad Speaks*, November 29, 1968, 30, 37; "'Towards a Black University' Conference Schedule," November 1968, Box 159-4, Folder 16, SAV, WHI.

73. "Dr. James M. Nabrit Endorses Proposed 'Towards a Black University Conference,'" *Muhammad Speaks*, November 15, 1968, 8; "Notes on Towards a Black University Conference, Submitted by Lois P. Johnson, November 18, 1968," Box 159-4, Folder 16, SAV, WHI.

74. "Notes from Keynote Addresses at the Towards a Black University Conference, November 13–17, 1968," Box 159-4, Folder 16, SAV, WHI; "Dr. James M. Nabrit Endorses Proposed 'Towards a Black University Conference,'" 8; George B. Davis, "The Howard University Conference," *Negro Digest*, March 1969, 47; "Notes on Towards a Black University Conference, Submitted by Lois P. Johnson, November 18, 1968," Box 159-4, Folder 16, SAV, WHI.

75. See, for example, critiques of historically black colleges and universities in E. Franklin Frazier, *Black Bourgeoisie: The Rise of a New Middle Class* (New York: The Free Press, 1957). Also see Nathan Hare, "Black Students and Negro Colleges: The Legacy of Paternalism," *Saturday Review*, July 20, 1968, 44–45, 57–58; Walter R. Allen and Joseph O. Jewell, "A Backward Glance Forward: Past, Present, and Future Perspectives on Historically Black Colleges and Universities," *Review of Higher Education* 25 (2002): 241–261; Cally L. Waite and Margaret Smith Crocco, "Fighting Injustice Through Education," *History of Education* 33 (2004): 573–583; Earl J. McGrath, *The Predominantly Negro Colleges and Universities in Transition* (New York: Columbia University Press, 1965); Fred M. Hechinger, "On the Ailing Negro College," *New York Times*, March 19, 1967, E9; M. A. Farber, "Negro Higher Education: Between 2 Worlds," *New York Times*, October 11, 1971, 26; Thomas H. Wirth, "'Predominantly Negro' Colleges: Gray Schools for Black Students," pamphlet, n.d., Box 48, Folder 16, VHP, EUM; Emory, "Black Body/White Mind," 1967 pamphlet, Box 1, Folder 14, RYP, SCR.

76. Christopher Jencks and David Riesman, "The American Negro College," *Harvard Educational Review* 37 (1967): 317–352; Max Stanford, "Revolutionary Nationalism and the Afroamerican Student," *Liberator*, January 1965, 13; LeRoi Jones, *Raise, Race, Rays, Raze: Essays Since 1965* (New York: Random House, 1971), 46.

77. Vincent Harding, "When Stokely Met the Presidents: Black Power and Negro Education," *Motive*, January 1967, 4–9; "Black Power Revolt at Texas Southern," *The Movement*, May 1967, 1; "Black Campuses Explode," *Southern Patriot*, May 1967; Ernest Stephens, "The Black University in America Today: A Student Viewpoint," *Freedomways*, Spring 1967, 134; "Black Students Vow Active Roles, Freedom Objectives," *Muhammad Speaks*, April 14, 1967, 4; "Rebellion of the Black Intellectuals," *Muhammad Speaks*, April 21, 1967, 4, 6, 27; Henry Leifermann, "See 'Black Consciousness' Sweeping Campuses," *Afro-American*,

December 9, 1967, 1; "Summary Analysis of Three Civil Disturbances Involving Negro College Students: The Cases of Nashville, Tennessee; Jackson, Mississippi; and Houston, Texas, Spring 1967," transcript of 1967 study, Center for Community Studies, Nashville, TN, Box 22, Folder 6, AOW, WHI; "A Proposal for the Formation of the National Association of Black Students," pamphlet, Box 34, Folder 15, VHP, EUM; Chester Higgins, ed., "Student Unrest, Tuskegee Institute: A Chronology," 1968 pamphlet, Box 164, USSA, WHI.

78. Charlie Cobb, "Revolution: From Stokely Carmichael to Kwame Ture," *Black Scholar*, Fall 1997, 34; Alphonso Pinkney, *Red, Black and Green: Black Nationalism in the United States* (Cambridge: Cambridge University Press, 1976); James L. Hicks, "Adam Powell Calls for a 'Black Renaissance,'" *New York Amsterdam News*, June 4, 1966, 1, 28; Adam Clayton Powell, "Call to the Barricades: Seek Audacious Power," *Negro Digest*, August 1966, 4–9.

79. Henry Hampton and Steve Fayer, eds., *Voices of Freedom: An Oral History of the Civil Rights Movement from the 1950s through the 1980s* (New York: Bantam, 1990), 433–435.

80. Transcript of January 1971 Allen Coleman Interview with John Warren, CRD, MSR; Leon Dash and Don Robinson, "Activism Emerges on Howard Campus: Hershey Talk Disrupted," *Washington Post*, March 23, 1967, D1, D2; Alex Poinsett, "The Metamorphosis of Howard University," *Ebony*, December 1971, 114.

81. Robert A. Malson, "The Black Power Rebellion at Howard University: Profile of a Crisis," *Negro Digest*, December 1967, 22; Dash and Robinson, "Activism Emerges on Howard Campus," D1, D2; Nathan Hare, "Final Reflections on a 'Negro' College," *Negro Digest*, March 1968, 45; Don Robinson, "College 'Black Power' Group Formed," *Washington Post*, March 23, 1967, D2; Ben A. Franklin, "Black Power at Howard," *New York Times*, September 24, 1967, E9; "A News Release for a Press Conference Announcing the Formation of the Black Power Committee, Cramton Auditorium, Howard University, March 22, 1967," Black Power Movement Part 3 (Microfilm).

82. Lowe, "Towards a Black University," 6; Leon Dash, "Black Consciousness Grips the Negro University," *Washington Post*, April 21, 1967, B1; Hare, "Final Reflections on a 'Negro' College," 45; "'Black Power' Threatens a Leading Negro College," *U.S. News & World Report*, July 31, 1967, 38–39; *Riots, Civil and Criminal Disorders: Hearings Before the Permanent Subcommittee on Investigations of the Committee on Government Operations, United States Senate* (Washington, DC: Government Printing Office, 1967), 4766–4769.

83. Malson, "The Black Power Rebellion at Howard University," 24; Michael Miles, "Colonialism on the Black Campus," *New Republic*, August 5, 1967, 15; Franklin, "Black Power at Howard," E9.

84. Dash, "Black Consciousness Grips the Negro University," B1; Anthony Gittens, "Black Student Movements," pamphlet, n.d. (c. 1968), SAV, WHI; Malson, "The Black Power Rebellion at Howard University," 24, 29.

85. Transcript of January 1971 Allen Coleman Interview with John Warren, CRD, MSR; Susan L. Jacoby, "In Search of a Black Identity," *Saturday Review*, April 20, 1968, 382.

86. Ralph Matthews, "Black Power at Howard U," *Baltimore Afro-American*, March 26, 1968, 16; Hampton and Fayer, eds., *Voices of Freedom*, 440–441; "New Howard University," *The Movement*, May 1968, 14–15; Chuck Porter, "Students Paralyze Historic School in Wash., D.C.," *Los Angeles Sentinel*, March 28, 1968, 8A; Gim Okoh, "Students End Howard Siege," *Baltimore Afro-American*, March 26, 1968, 1, 16.

87. Lonnie 2X, "Finds 'Peace' at Howard Uneasy; Sees Student Rebellion Ready to Erupt Again," *Muhammad Speaks*, April 12, 1968, 7; Hampton and Fayer, eds., *Voices of Freedom*, 444; Muhammad Ahmad, "On the Black Student Movement—1960-1970," *Black Scholar*, May–June 1978, 9; Porter, "Students Paralyze Historic School in Wash., D.C.," 8A.

88. Matthews, "Black Power at Howard U," 16; "Brothers and Sisters" flyer, November 1968, Box 159-4, Folder 13, Howard U.—Campus Unrest, 1968, SAV, WHI; "Howard University Closed by Student Protests; 'Stay-ins' Given Legal Assistance," *Baltimore Afro-American*, March 30, 1968, 1; Poinsett, "The Metamorphosis of Howard University," 116; Okoh, "Students End Howard Siege," 1, 16; "New Howard University," 14–15.

89. "Statement by Dr. James Edward Cheek, President of Howard University," press release, July 8, 1969, Box 159-4, Folder 13, Howard U.—Campus Unrest, 1968, SAV, WHI; Lonnie Kashif,

"Howard President Wins Respect," *Muhammad Speaks*, June 5, 1970, 5; Sanford J. Ungar and Vincent Paka, "Howard Strike Increases Attendance," *Washington Post*, May 19, 1970, C1; C. Gerald Fraser, "Howard Students Refuse to Relinquish Buildings," *New York Times*, May 9, 1969, 29.

90. Poinsett, "The Metamorphosis of Howard University," 114; "Howard University: A Policy Statement on the Black University," October 22, 1968, and October 28, 1968, Names M. Nabrit to Deans, Faculties, and Administrative Officers, memorandum, Box 159-4, Folder 16, SAV, WHI; Malson, "The Black Power Rebellion at Howard University," 30; Charles Alverson, "Howard University's 'Relevance' Throes," *Wall Street Journal*, June 17, 1968, 16; Poinsett, "The Metamorphosis of Howard University," 110–116; Transcript of January 1971 Allen Coleman Interview with John Warren, CRD, MSR; Fraser, "Howard Students Refuse to Relinquish Buildings," 29.

91. Benjamin E. Mays, "The Role and Future of the Negro College," *Crisis*, August–September 1965, 419–422; "Integration: Negro Colleges' Latest Challenge," *Ebony*, March 1966, 36–46; Fred M. Hechinger, "The Negro Colleges: Victims of Progress," *New York Times*, October 6, 1969, 46; Robert J. Levey, "Black Colleges Starved of Funds," *Boston Globe*, December 28, 1969, A43; "Are Negro Colleges Necessary?" *Sepia*, August 21, 1970, 16–21; Fred M. Hechinger, "'Should I Throw in the Towel?'" *New York Times*, June 20, 1971, E9.

92. April 15, 1970, Student Organization for Black Unity Press Release, Box 10, Folder 84, JCP, ACC; "Students Organize to Save 'Integrity' of Black Colleges," *Afro-American*, May 2, 1970, 7; Jim Grant and Milton Coleman, "Day of Solidarity to Save Black Schools," *African World*, November 13, 1971, 2; Nelson N. Johnson, "The Black Community and Black Schools," *African World*, October 14, 1972, 8; February 27, 1973, Nelson N. Johnson to "Black Student Leader," Box 42, Folder 4, GWP, WHI; "SOBU: Neo-Colonialist Administrators, Guardsmen Close Voorhees Again," pamphlet, Box 117, Folder 113, JKP, EUM; "National Black College Conference Maps Out 'Survival Strategy,'" *African World*, April 28, 1973, 1; December 26, 1969, Nelson N. Johnson to "Brother Ricks," and "The Student Organization for Black Unity: A Look Backward and Forward," 1970 pamphlet, and "We Are An African People," pamphlet, Box 11, Folder 1, CSP, ACC; Brenda Reese, "The Save Black Schools Movement," *Black Collegian*, March–April 1974, 21–24.

93. Davis, "Response to Vincent Harding," 60; Judith Cummings, "Return to Howard: The Turbulent 60's Seem Long Ago," *New York Times*, November 16, 1975, 14; Nelson N. Johnson, "Students in the Struggle," *SOBU Newsletter*, May 1, 1971, 4; Nelson N. Johnson, "What Happened to the 'Revolution?'" *African World*, October 28, 1972, 6. Also see Tim Thomas, "The Student Movement at Southern University," *Freedomways*, Winter 1973, 14.

94. James Turner, "Black Studies and a Black Philosophy of Education," *Black Lines*, Winter 1970, 8; Johnson, "Students in the Struggle," 4; Abdul Alkalimat, "1970s: What Must be Done by Black Students," *Black Lines*, Summer 1971, 35–36; Vincent Harding, "Toward the Black University," *Ebony*, August 1970, 157.

95. Jimmy Garrett, "The Negro Revolt in LA—From the Inside," *The Movement*, September 1965, 6.

96. Ibram Rogers, "Remembering the Black Campus Movement: An Oral History Interview with James P. Garrett," *Journal of Pan African Studies* 2 (2009): 33; Jimmy Garrett, "We Need Freedom Schools in the North," *The Movement*, May 1965, 1.

97. Garrett, "The Negro Revolt in LA—From the Inside," 6.

98. Jimmy Garrett, "And We Own the Night: A Play of Blackness," *Drama Review*, Summer 1968, 62–69.

99. Daniel Perlstein, "Minds Stayed on Freedom: Politics and Pedagogy in the African-American Freedom Struggle," *American Educational Research Journal* 39 (2002): 11–12; Fabio Rojas, *From Black Power to Black Studies* (Baltimore: Johns Hopkins University, 2007), 51–54; Ibram Rogers, "Celebrating 40 Years of Activism," *Diverse Issues in Higher Education* 10 (2006): 18–22; Rogers, "Remembering the Black Campus Movement: An Oral History Interview with James P. Garrett," 31–38; James P. Garrett, "The Student Strike at SFSU: 20th Anniversary Reunion; The Historical Development of the SFSU Strike," *Journal of African/Black Writing* 1 (1989): 82–89; Transcript of Robert Martin July 10, 1969, Interview with Octavious Tracy, CRD, MSR; John H. Bunzel, "Black Studies at San Francisco State," *Public Interest* 13 (1968): 22–38.

100. "City College's Paperback Library Features Negro-Oriented Books," *Washington Post*, July 24, 1968; "Federal City College—History of Struggle," *African World*, May 1975, 5; "Profile: Federal City College: The Concrete Campus in Washington, D.C.," *Black Collegian*, May–June 1972, 12–13, 46; "A Federal College," *Chicago Daily Defender*, May 1, 1968, 15; Lonnie Kashif, "D.C. City College Begins Community Involvement Test," *Muhammad Speaks*, October 25, 1968, 15.

101. "Interview with Jimmy Garrett, Center for Black Education," *Third World*, no. 6, Box 4, Folders 8–9, UUA, AHT; Peter Milius, "Racial Split Hits New College," *Washington Post*, November 13, 1968, A1; Thomas A. Johnson, "New Capital Negro College Debates 'Black' Studies," *New York Times*, November 17, 1968, 76; Herbert H. Denton, "Program Splits City College," *Washington Post*, March 6, 1969, A1; "Aims and Objectives of the Black Education Program—A Position Paper," pamphlet, n.d., Box 4, PWP, SCR; "Black Studies Program/ Federal City College/1968," in *Black Students*, ed. Harry Edwards (New York: Free Press, 1970), 206–215; "Black Studies Purpose: To 'Africanize' Students," *Washington Post*, March 13, 1969, B7.

102. Thomas A. Johnson, "New Capital Negro College Debates 'Black' Studies," *New York Times*, November 17, 1968, 76; "Curriculum Programs for Students of the Pan-African Community," 1970 pamphlet, and February 4, 1970, Jim McQueen to "Dear Brother or Sister" and attached proposal and materials, Box 4, Folders 8–9, UUA, AHT.

103. Lawrence Feinberg, "Revolt Climbs Social Ladder," *Washington Post*, March 8, 1970, 1; "Interview with Jimmy Garrett, Center for Black Education," *Third World*, no. 6, and February 4, 1970, Jim McQueen to "Dear Brother or Sister" and attached proposal and materials, Box 4, Folders 8–9, UUA, AHT; "Center for Black Education" in *The Perspectives Gained: Findings of a Five-Day Black University*, ed. National Association of Afro-American Educators (New York: National Association of Afro-American Educators , 1970); Jimmy Garrett, ed., *The Struggle for Black Education, 1968-1971* (Washington, DC: Drum & Spear Press, 1972), i, 1.

104. Valerie Miner Johnson, "Nairobi College," *Mademoiselle*, August 1970, 290–291; Transcript of July 7, 2004, Leigh Torrance and Danielle Moore Interview with Robert Hoover, SOH, INP; " 'Stanford Students Spur 'Betterment,' " *Pittsburgh Courier*, March 21, 1964, 13; Daryl Lembke, "Negro Plans All-Black College in E. Palo Alto," *Los Angeles Times*, July 10, 1969, 18; *Riots, Civil and Criminal Disorders, Parts 19-20: Hearings Before the Senate Committee on Government Operations, Permanent Sub Committee on Investigations* (Washington, DC: U.S. Government Printing Office, 1969), 4048–4049.

105. "Office of Economic Opportunity Community Action Program Proposal," 1970, and Transcript of Egerton Interview with Bob Hoover, JEP, VUA; "College in Bay Area for Blacks," *Sacramento Observer*, August 21, 1969, 29; " 'To Blacks, a High School Diploma Is a Worthless Piece of Paper' . . . Hoover," *Sun Reporter*, July 5, 1969, 2; John Egerton, "Success Comes to Nairobi College," *Change*, May 1972, 25; Lembke, "Negro Plans All-Black College," 18.

106. "Educator Resigns Calif. College Job," *Afro-American*, July 5, 1969, 22; " 'To Blacks, a High School Diploma Is a Worthless Piece of Paper' . . . Hoover," 2; Johnson, "Nairobi College," 290.

107. Mary Hoover, "Nairobi College," in Deborah E. Daniels, *Education By, For and About African Americans* (Lincoln, NE: Student Commission on Undergraduate Education and the Education of Teachers, 1973), 61; Orde Coombs, "Nairobi College: A Unique Experiment," *Education Digest*, October 1973, 39; Robert Hoover, "Meeting Community Needs," in *The Minority Student on the Campus: Expectations and Possibilities*, ed. Robert O. Altman and Patricia A. Snyder (Boulder, CO: Western Interstate Commission for Higher Education, 1970), 190; "Office of Economic Opportunity Community Action Program Proposal," 1970, and Transcript of Egerton Interview with Bob Hoover, JEP, VUA; "College in Bay Area for Blacks," *Sacramento Observer*, August 21, 1969, 29.

108. "A Proposal Requesting Financial Support of Nairobi College, East Palo Alto, California," and "Nairobi College Progress Report," August 1969, and "IFCO Grant Proposal Record: Nairobi College," 1970, Box 31, Folder 30, IFCO, SCR; "Nairobi College Looking for Students," *Sun Reporter*, September 13, 1969, 7; "College in Bay Area for Blacks," 29; "Nairobi College Operating on a Shoestring and a Faith," *Los Angeles Times*, May 23, 1971, B26; "Nairobi School System: Concern and Control," *Sacramento Observer*, April 22, 1971,

E27; Robert Strand, "Blacks Make Own School in Calif. Area," *Chicago Daily Defender*, March 20–March 26, 1971, 5; "Office of Economic Opportunity Community Action Program Proposal," 1970, and Transcript of Egerton Interview with Bob Hoover, JEP, VUA.

109. "Nairobi College Sign-up Starts; 100 in Classes," *Palo Alto Times*, October 2, 1969; "Donations of Books Asked to Aid New Library at Nairobi College," *Palo Alto Times*, November 6, 1969, 4; "Nairobi College Progress Report #2," October 1969, TSP, WHI.

110. "Nairobi College Looking for Students," 7; "IFCO Grant Proposal Record: Nairobi College," 1970, Box 31, Folder 30, IFCO, SCR; Reed L. Buffington et al. June 8, 1971, memo to Accrediting Commission for Junior Colleges, n.d., JEP, VUA; "New Black University Concept," *Muhammad Speaks*, September 12, 1969, 37.

111. "A Proposal Requesting Financial Support of Nairobi College, East Palo Alto, California," 1970, Box 31, Folder 30, IFCO, SCR; Reed L. Buffington et al. June 8, 1971, memo to Accrediting Commission for Junior Colleges, n.d., JEP, VUA; Lembke, "Negro Plans All-Black College," 18.

112. "Nairobi College Progress Report #2," October 1969, TSP, WHI; "Nairobi College Sign-up Starts; 100 in Classes"; "Nairobi College Progress Report #3," 1970, and "Nairobi College Progress Report," August 1969, Box 31, Folder 30, IFCO, SCR; Johnson, "Nairobi College," 290; H. Bruce Franklin, "Burning Illusions: The Napalm Campaign," in *Against the Vietnam War: Writings by Activists*, ed. Mary Susannah Robbins (Lanham, MD: Rowman & Littlefield, 1999), 74; "Office of Economic Opportunity Community Action Program Proposal," 1970, and Transcript of Egerton Interview with Bob Hoover, JEP, VUA; Valerie Jane Miner, "Nairobi College: Education for Relevance," December 1969 (ED 038131).

113. Garrett, ed., *The Struggle for Black Education*, 2, 11; "Curriculum Programs for Students of the Pan-African Community," 1970 pamphlet, Box 4, Folders 8–9, UUA, AHT; "The Center for Black Education: Nation-Building in Action," *SOBU Newsletter*, January 9, 1971, 9.

114. February 4, 1970, Jim McQueen to "Dear Brother or Sister" and attached proposal and materials, and "Interview with Jimmy Garrett, Center for Black Education," *Third World*, no. 6, Box 4, Folders 8–9, UUA, AHT; "The Center for Black Education: Nation-Building in Action," 9; Snigdha Prakash, "Kojo Nnamdi," *Washington Post*, July 1, 1990, L9; Paul Buhle, "Political Styles of C.L.R. James," in *C.L.R. James*, ed. Buhle (London: Allison and Busby, 1986), 28; John Lewis, "Black Voices," *Baltimore Afro-American*, August 9, 1969, 5.

115. "A Proposal Requesting Financial Support of Nairobi College," 1970, and "Nairobi College," report, n.d., and May 15, 1970, Lester Kleckley to Lucius Walker, Box 31, Folder 30, IFCO, SCR; "Nairobi College Looking for Students," 7; " 'To Blacks, a High School Diploma Is a Worthless Piece of Paper' . . . Hoover," 2; "Nairobi College," Pamphlet, TSP, WHI; Reed L. Buffington et al. June 8, 1971, memo to Accrediting Commission for Junior Colleges, n.d., JEP, VUA; "Durham, NC; Washington, DC," *Negro Digest*, March 1970, 38; Lewis, "Black Voices," 5; "Draft: Black Studies—Food Science Core," proposal, n.d., Box 4, PWP, SCR.

116. Center for Black Education pamphlet, and Black Teachers Conference packet, February 1970, Box 4, Folders 8–9, UUA, AHT; "Aims and Objectives of the Black Education Program—A Position Paper," pamphlet, n.d., Box 4, PWP, SCR; "Office of Economic Opportunity Community Action Program Proposal," 1970, and Transcript of Egerton Interview with Bob Hoover, JEP, VUA.

117. "Nairobi Community Re-entry Program," June 1972, Box 2S435, FFA, DBC.

118. "Proposal for Coffee House," n.d., Box 3, Folder 13, FLH, ARC; The Fund for Education and Community Development April 1971 newsletter, Box 48, Folder 5, FST, ARC; February 4, 1970, Jim McQueen to "Dear Brother or Sister" and attached proposal and materials, Box 4, Folders 8–9, UUA, AHT; Garrett, ed., *The Struggle for Black Education*, 24–25.

119. "Episcopal Cleric Backs Grants to Black Separatist Groups," *Washington Post*, March 7, 1970, C9; Staff of the Center for Black Education, "Schools Must Educate for Political Action," *New York Amsterdam News*, December 25, 1971, A7; February 4, 1970, Jim McQueen to "Dear Brother or Sister" and attached proposal and materials, and "Fund Raising Proposal," Box 4, Folders 8–9, UUA, AHT.

120. "IFCO Grant Proposal Record: Nairobi College," 1970, Box 31, Folder 30, IFCO, SCR; "Office of Economic Opportunity Community Action Program Proposal," 1970, Transcript

of Egerton Interview with Bob Hoover, and Reed L. Buffington et al. June 8, 1971, memo to Accrediting Commission for Junior Colleges, n.d., JEP, VUA; Orde Coombs, "The Necessity of Excellence: Nairobi College," *Change*, April 1973, 43–44.

121. The Fund for Education and Community Development April 1971 newsletter, Box 48, Folder 5, FST, ARC; Robert M. Smith, "IRS Team Collects Data on Extremists for Tax Use," *New York Times*, January 13, 1972, 1; February 4, 1970, Jim McQueen to "Dear Brother or Sister" and attached proposal and materials, Box 4, Folders 8–9, UUA, AHT.

122. Hoover, "Meeting Community Needs," 195; "Nairobi College Progress Report #2," October 1969, TSP, WHI; "Office of Economic Opportunity Community Action Program Proposal," 1970, and Transcript of Egerton Interview with Bob Hoover, JEP, VUA; John Egerton, "Readiness Instead of Remedies," *Southern Education Report*, November 1968, 22–23; "Nairobi Seeks Accreditation," *San Jose Mercury*, July 20, 1969.

123. Jeannette Bradley, "Nairobi Planning 2nd Campus," *Palo Alto Times*, December 18, 1969, 1; David Johnston, "2 Minority Colleges Near Split," *San Jose Mercury*, June 2, 1971; Reed L. Buffington et al. June 8, 1971, memo to Accrediting Commission for Junior Colleges, n.d., JEP, VUA; Nairobi College Official Recruits 17 Chicanos," *Palo Alto Times*, January 6, 1970; Egerton, "Success Comes To Nairobi College," 26; Coombs, "Nairobi College: A Unique Experiment," 40–41; "With the Rape and Penetration of the African Continent . . ." untitled pamphlet, n.d., Box 4, Folders 8–9, UUA, AHT; Minutes from Council of Elders Meeting, September 25–26 1970, CSP, ACC.

124. "Office of Economic Opportunity Community Action Program Proposal," 1970, and Transcript of Egerton Interview with Bob Hoover, JEP, VUA; "Nairobi College Progress Report #2," 1969, TSP, WHI; "Nairobi College Progress Report #3," 1970, and "A Proposal Requesting Financial Support of Nairobi College, East Palo Alto, California," 1970, Box 31, Folder 30, IFCO, SCR; Hoover, "Nairobi College," 81.

125. "With the Rape and Penetration of the African Continent . . .," untitled pamphlet, n.d., and February 4, 1970, Jim McQueen to "Dear Brother or Sister" and attached proposal and materials, and Center for Black Education Pamphlet, Box 4, Folders 8–9, UUA, AHT; Lewis, "Black Voices," 5; "Aims and Objectives of the Black Education Program—A Position Paper," pamphlet, n.d., Box 4, v.

126. Lembke, "Nairobi College Operating on a Shoestring and a Faith," 26.

127. "The Birth of a Pan-African School System," *Imani*, August–September 1971, 44; "Minutes From Council of Elders Meeting, September 25, 1970," pamphlet, CSP, ACC; "Center for Black Education: One Year Later," *Third World*, n.d., Box 4, UUA, AHT.

128. Faith Berry, "Washington, Like It Is," *Nation*, May 6, 1968, 589; Dilip Hiro, "Black Is Beautiful," *New Society*, September 12, 1968, 363; Greg Thomas, "Proud Flesh Inter/ Views: Acklyn Lynch," *Proudflesh* 6 (2007); Adrienne Manns, "Ghetto Book Shop Finds Untapped Literary Mart," *Washington Post*, August 27, 1968, B1; "Speaks on Black Center," *New York Amsterdam News*, October 17, 1970, 30; April 29, 1969, Charles Cobb to Sterling Brown, Box 13, SBP, MSR; The Fund for Education and Community Development April 1971 newsletter, Box 48, Folder 5, FST, ARC.

129. John Lewis, " 'Hey Man, It Will be a Gas,' " *Baltimore Afro-American*, October 14, 1967, 18; E. Fannie Granton, "New School of Afro-American Thought," *Negro Digest*, June 1967, 12–13; Transcript of James Mosby July 1, 1968, Interview with Gaston Neal, CRD, MSR.

130. Transcript of James Mosby July 1, 1968, Interview with Gaston Neal, CRD, MSR; Mary Stratford, "Soul Brothers Youth Center Could Be the Answer," *Baltimore Afro-American*, September 2, 1967, 5; Floyd Barbour, ed., *The Black Power Revolt* (Boston: Extending Horizons Books, 1968), 252; Granton, "New School of Afro-American Thought," 13; James O. Gibson, "Black Arts," *Washington Post*, January 26, 1969, G2; "3-Day African Festival of Music Stated Here," *Washington Post*, March 6, 1966, B4.

131. Leon Dash, "New Cardozo Area School Explores Afro-American Life and Culture," *Washington Post*, March 2, 1967, B1; Hiro, "Black Is Beautiful," 363; George Davis, "400 Attend Afro-American School Program," *Washington Post*, June 2, 1968, D5; Transcript of James Mosby July 1, 1968, Interview with Gaston Neal, CRD, MSR; Lorenz "Abeeku" Wheatley, "Under the Radar: The New School of Afro-American Thought," *DC Digital Museum*, accessed January 23, 2014, http://www.wdchumanities.org/dcdm/items/

show/1523; Jacqueline Trescott, "The Poet with An Active Voice; Gaston Neal Linked Arts and Politics," *Washington Post*, October 22, 1999, C1.

132. "'Think Black' Members Shun Newsmen," *Los Angeles Sentinel*, January 25, 1968, 7A; Granton, "New School of Afro-American Thought," 13; Transcript of James Mosby July 1, 1968, Interview with Gaston Neal, CRD, MSR.

133. Davis, "400 Attend Afro-American School Program," D5; "H. Rap Brown to Get 'Man of Year' Award," *Baltimore Afro-American*, October 14, 1967, 18; Granton, "New School of Afro-American Thought," 14; Jesse W. Lewis Jr., "Afro-American Arts Workshop Opens," *Washington Post*, October 27, 1966, C1; Louise D. Stone, "Sun Ra's Outerspace Music Makes a Hit Here," *Washington Post*, May 30, 1967, C10; Thomas, "Proud Flesh Inter/Views: Acklyn Lynch"; "Black Power Backers Take Pot Shots at Established Groups," *Baltimore Afro-American*, August 12, 1967, 14; Gibson, "Black Arts," G2; Rebecca Burns, *Burial for a King: Martin Luther King Jr.'s Funeral and the Week that Transformed Atlanta and Rocked the Nation* (New York: Scribner, 2011), 52–53.

134. Dash, "New Cardozo Area School Explores Afro-American Life and Culture," B1; Leroy F. Aarons, "Negro Arts, History School Will Open Today in Cardozo," *Washington Post*, October 15, 1966, B5; Lorenz "Abeeku" Wheatley, "Under the Radar: The New School of Afro-American Thought," *DC Digital Museum*, accessed January 23, 2014, http://www.wdchumanities.org/dcdm/items/show/1523.

135. Lewis, "'Hey Man, It Will Be a Gas,'" 14; Gibson, "Black Arts," G2; Johnstone Muthiora, "Black Identity: An African View," *GW: The George Washington University Magazine*, September 1968, 16; "Seeks to Provide Community With 'Orientation in Black,'" *Muhammad Speaks*, November 15, 1969, 26.

136. "Director Charges Armed Takeover of New School," *Washington Afro-American*, September 17, 1968, 1–2; "Black Culture Shop Opens Here Today," B9; Transcript of James Mosby July 1, 1968, Interview with Gaston Neal, CRD, MSR.

137. Hiro, "Black Is Beautiful," 363; Gibson, "Black Arts," G2; Faith Berry, "Washington, Like It Is," *Nation*, May 6, 1968, 590; Monroe Anderson, "The Young Black Man," *Ebony*, August 1972, 133; Angela Terrell, "'What's That New Thing up the Street?'—It's a Black Cultural Center," *Washington Post*, August 13, 1972, M1; Ike Ridley, "BSU: 'A Thief is a Thief, No Matter How He Does His Stealing,'" *Baltimore Afro-American*, May 10, 1969, 5; "The New Thing Heritage Dancers," *Baltimore Afro-American*, June 21, 1969, A1; Transcript of 1967 John H. Britton Interview with Lonnie King, CRD, MSR; "'Arts' Keep Students in Schools," *Baltimore Afro-American*, February 17, 1973, A4B; Paul W. Valentine, "'New Thing' Plans Culture for Poor," *Washington Post*, July 7, 1967, B1; New Thing Newsletter, n.d., Box 54, Folder 3, JOP, ARC.

138. "The Communiversity," *Negro Digest*, March 1970, 25–27; "Sociologist Speaks on 'Black Forum' Series," *Chicago Daily Defender*, February 24, 1970, 5.

139. "New Black Research Center to Conduct Census," *Muhammad Speaks*, September 13, 1968, 29, 32; "Center Tour Is Planned," *Chicago Daily Defender*, March 18, 1969, 5; Ethel L. Payne, "Militants Apprehensive About Detention Camps," *Chicago Daily Defender*, June 2, 1969, 3–4; "Black Awareness Featured at Auburn YMCA Day Camp," *Chicago Defender*, July 8, 1972, 25; "Confederation of Nationalist and Pan-Afrikan Organizations," 1972 pamphlet, Box 24, Folder 2, PWP, SCR; Lloyd Hogan, "Research Center Shows how Blacks are Isolated," *Chicago Daily Defender*, November 27, 1968, 4.

140. Chesly Manly, "Dr. Hurst's 'Revolution' at Malcolm X," *Chicago Tribune*, January 4, 1970, A1; Charles G. Hurst, "Malcolm X: A Community College with a New Perspective," *Negro Digest*, March 1970, 32; Alex Poinsett, "Dr. Charles G. Hurst: The Mastermind of Malcolm X College," *Ebony*, March 1970, 29–38; Charles G. Hurst Jr., "Malcolm X College: An Open Door," *Essence*, September 1971, 40–41, 74; "Profile: Malcolm X Community College," 11; Preston Wilcox June 5, 1969, To Whom It May Concern, Box 8, Folder 7, PWP, SCR; Charles G. Hurst, "The Black University," in *Black Is . . .: A Publication from a Conference on the Emerging Trends in the Education of Black Students*, ed. Lanny Berry and Barbara Shaw (Larkspur, CA: Tamalpais Union High School District, 1972), 126.

141. "Power: Key to Southern U.," *African World*, March 3, 1973, 8–9, 14; Abdul Alkalimat, "1970s: What Must Be Done by Black Students," *Black Lines*, Summer 1971, 35–41; "Peoples College Announces Basic College," 1973 brochure, Box 48, Folder 2, EGP, SCR; Gerald

A. McWorter, "Deck the Ivy Racist Halls: The Case of Black Studies," in *Black Studies in the University: A Symposium*, ed. Armstead L. Robinson, Craig C. Foster, and Donald H. Ogilvie (New Haven, CT: Yale University Press, 1969), 55–74; Peoples College, *Introduction to Afro-American Studies* (Chicago: Peoples College, 1975), vi.

142. Rick Campbell, "Queen Lynn: From Glory to Tragedy" *Houston Chronicle*, December 22, 2008, accessed November 14, 2013, http://blog.chron.com/40yearsafter/2008/12/queen-lynn-from-glory-to-tragedy/; Dawolu Gene Locke, "Pan-African Worker Slain," *African World*, October 2, 1971, 5; "Hold Texas Longshoreman in Stabbing Death of Black Homecoming Queen," *Jet*, September 30, 1971, 23.

143. Locke, "Pan-African Worker Slain," 5; "Lynn Eusan Institute Opens in Houston," *African World*, September 16, 1972, 13; "Lynn Eusan Institute: Instrument for Struggle," *IFCO News*, November–December 1973; "Training Organizers," *African World*, December 23, 1972, 12; "Lynn Eusan Program," *African World*, February 17, 1973, 4.

144. January 5, 1973, Dawolu Gene Locke to Martha Fritts and attached materials, Box 30, Folder 32, IFCO, SCR; "Training Organizers," *African World*, December 23, 1972, 12; "Lynn Eusan Institute: Instrument for Struggle"; "Lynn Eusan Institute Marks 1st Anniversary," *African World*, October 1973, 14; "LEI Student Spearheads Community Assistance Program," *The Call to Struggle*, August 1973, Box 30, Folder 32, IFCO, SCR.

145. Staff of the Center for Black Education, "Schools Must Educate for Political Action," A7; "The Center for Black Education: Nation-Building in Action," *SOBU Newsletter*, January 9, 1971, 9; "Living Our Commitment," *The Pan African*, October 16, 1970, Box 159–2, Folder 12, SAV, WHI.

146. Staff of the Center for Black Education, "Schools Must Educate for Political Action," A7; February 4, 1970, Jim McQueen to "Dear Brother or Sister" and attached proposal and materials, and "With the Rape and Penetration of the African Continent . . ." untitled pamphlet, n.d., Box 4, Folders 8–9, UUA, AHT; Garrett, ed., *The Struggle for Black Education*, 17; "The Center for Black Education: Nation-Building in Action," 9; CBE, "Center for Black Education," *Negro Digest*, March 1970, 44.

147. "Lynn Eusan Institute: Instrument for Struggle."

148. January 5, 1973, Dawolu Gene Locke to Martha Fritts and attached materials, Box 30, Folder 32, IFCO, SCR; "Lynn Eusan Institute—Organizer Training Program," 1974 pamphlet, GCRR, UMC.

Chapter 7

1. Frantz Fanon, *Wretched of the Earth* (New York: Grove Press, 1965), 197.

2. Manning Marable, *Race, Reform & Rebellion* (Boston: South End Press, 1991), 110–111; Ward Churchill and Jim Vander Wall, *The Cointelpro Papers: Documents from the FBI's Secret Wars Against Dissent* (Boston: South End Press, 1990); Derrick Morrison, "Watergate & the Black Struggle," *Militant*, June 29, 1973, 14; Chokwe Lumumba, "The African Prisoner of War Movement and the International African Prisoner Solidarity Day," *Black Collegian*, March–April 1973, 20–21, 49–51; Baxter Smith, "FBI Memos Reveal Repression Schemes," *Black Scholar*, April 1974, 43–48.

3. "COINTELPRO: Black Nationalist Hate Groups" (Microfilm; see 1969-1970 surveillance notes); Howard Spencer, "White Repression and Black Response in Mississippi," *Liberator*, April 1969, 11. Also see Robert M. Smith, "I.R.S. Team Collects Data on Extremists for Tax Use," *New York Times*, January 13, 1972, 1.

4. "Cleveland Sellers Jailed," *African World*, March 3, 1973, 4; John H. Britton, "Black Militants Face Showdown," *Jet*, January 16, 1969, 19; Robert F. Levey, "Gaston Neal Gets 90 Days in Gun Case," *Washington Post*, November 15, 1968, C1; "2 Militants Indicted in Plot," *Afro-American*, August 24, 1968, 31, 32; "Soul School Official Is Convicted," *Afro-American*, November 16, 1968, 23, 32; Elizabeth M. Oliver, "Claims Cops Planted Dope on Client," *Baltimore Afro-American*, January 25, 1969, 1; "Sonny Carson, Others Indicted for Murder," *New York Amsterdam News*, July 21, 1973, C1; "Sonny Carson Frame-Up!" *Black New Ark*, August 1973, 2; "Violence in Newark over Kawaida Court Decision," *New York Amsterdam News*, August 11, 1973, C3; "Community School Window Shot Out!" *Black New Ark*,

September 1973, 5; Charles Bail-Lou, "City Trying to Evict Uhuru Sasa School," *New York Amsterdam News*, October 11, 1986, 11.

5. Homer Bigart, "Friend of Rap Brown Dies with 2d Man in Auto Blast," *New York Times*, March 11, 1970, 1; "Step Up Hunt for Bombers," *Chicago Daily Defender*, March 14, 1970, 1, 4.

6. Floyd McKissick, "From a Black Point of View: 16 Years Too Late," *New York Amsterdam News*, March 28, 1970, 7; Ike Ridley, "Feather Was Bridegroom of Three Weeks," *Afro-American*, March 17, 1970, 1–2; Paul Good, "The American Dream of Cleveland Sellers," *New South*, Spring 1973, 18.

7. "The Official Statement on the Political Assassination of Ralph Featherstone and William 'Che' Payne," March 1970, Box 50, Folder 15, VHP, EUM; "Bomb Victim Wed Only Three Weeks," *New York Amsterdam News*, March 21, 1970, 1, 42; Center for Black Education, *The Struggle for Black Education, 1968-1971* (Washington, DC: Drum & Spear Press, 1972), 21; "Liberation Cycle," *Washington Post*, October 12, 1970, B4.

8. Ellis Cose, "African's Death Raises Questions," *Chicago Sun-Times*, February 15, 1974, 54; "For the Martyrs Have Imperishable Causes," *Community Action & Human Development Tearsheet*, January–February 1975, Box 47, Folder 17, FST, ARC; "Repression Continues to Plague Black Movement in U.S.," *African World*, September 16, 1972, 1, 19; "Ruwa Chiri Still Fights Deportation," *African World*, November 25, 1972, 8; K. T. K., "Letters & Notes," *Afrika Must Unite*, 1973, 2; "Help 'Save Ruwa,'" flyer (c. 1973), Box 23, Folder 24, UNIA, EUM; "U.S. Government Continues to Harass Ruwa Chiri," *African World*, April 13, 1973, 5; "Bira Ruwa Chiri, Memorial Rites for Pan-African Brother Maruwa Saunyama Chiri," February 1974 Memorial Service Program, Box 13, PWP, SCR.

9. "In Memory of Ruwa Chiri," *African World*, March 1974, 3; "Featherstone Wish Granted, Buried in Nigeria," *Muhammad Speaks*, May 1, 1970, 21; "Step Up Hunt for Bombers," *Chicago Daily Defender*, March 14, 1970, 1, 4; Okanlawan Subair, "Nigerian Admirer of Featherstone Urges Blacks to Build Life in U.S.," *Muhammad Speaks*, June 19, 1970, 19; Adrienne Manns, "Mourners Told He Had Love for All Mankind," *Afro-American*, March 17, 1970, 1–2; "Willie Ricks Wounded," *African World*, May 9, 1972, 3; "African Warrior Returns Home," *Rhythm*, Fall 1970, 32, 33.

10. "The Struggle Goes On," *Third World*, n.d., Box 48, Folder 16, IFCO, SCR; "Interview With Jitu Weusi on COINTELPRO Tactics," *Black News*, February 1979, 20–22; Janice C. Simpson, "Building a Base," *Wall Street Journal*, October 21, 1975, 1; Good, "The American Dream of Cleveland Sellers," 18.

11. "Burglars Hit Businesses of Atlantans," *Atlanta Daily World*, December 31, 1974, 3; "Burned Schools! Who'll Be Next?" April 29, 1975, newspaper clipping, EPA, PAH; "No 'Protection' Money from School Operator," *San Jose Mercury*, October 7, 1971; "Nairobi Educational Community Burns," *Sun Reporter*, March 8, 1975, 4; *Nairobi Schools '72*, (Nairobi Day School 1972 Yearbook), GWC, INP.

12. Les Matthews, "Black Crime Wave Chokes Harlemites," *New York Amsterdam News*, April 17, 1971, 1, 43; "What Is Nationhood—Talk or Substance?" *Black News*, October 1972, 37; Daniel H. Watts, "Two Cities," *Liberator*, May 1970, 3; Clayton Riley, "Drugs Are Real," *Liberator*, September 1970, 10–11; Baba Lumumba, "The Movement and the Drug Problem," *Soulbook*, Spring 1975; Rose L. H. Finkenstaedt, "Neocolonialism at Home: Narcotics in the Ghetto," *Liberator*, February 1963, 12–14; "Blackman's Development Center," pamphlets, Box 159–2, Folder 1, CRV, MSR; "On the Struggle Against Dope," *Black News*, June 1971, 26–29; Transcript of "Circle in the Dirt" Interview With Gertrude Wilks, n.d., Box 6, Folder 2, CMP, SUS.

13. Manning Marable, "Black Nationalism in the 1970s: Through the Prism of Race and Class," *Socialist Review*, March–June 1980, 57–107; Edward Greer, "The 'Liberation' of Gary, Indiana," *Trans-Action*, January 1971, 30–39, 63; Lenwood G. Davis and Winston Van Horne, "The City Renewed: White Dream—Black Nightmare?" *Black Scholar*, November 1975, 3; William W. Sales Jr., "New York City: Prototype of the Urban Crisis," *Black Scholar*, November 1975, 21–22; Robert Staples, "To Be Young, Black and Oppressed," *Black Scholar*, December 1975, 2–3; Robert S. Browne, "The U.S. Economy and Unemployment Prospects for Blacks," *Black Collegian*, March–April 1976, 66.

14. "'Super Fly' Star Tom O'Neal Denies Film Promotes Drug Use," *Afro-American*, September 23, 1972, 10; Francis Ward, *"Super Fly" A Political and Cultural Condemnation by the Kuumba*

Workshop (Chicago: Institute of Positive Education, 1972); Jim Williams, "Death to the Pusher," *Black News*, October 1972, 2–4.

15. Marable, "Black Nationalism in the 1970s," 79, 82.

16. Vincent Harding, "The Black Wedge in America: Struggle, Crisis and Hope, 1955-1975," *Black Scholar*, December 1975, 41.

17. Kalamu Ya Salaam, "Change Is Our Only Salvation," *Black Collegian*, March–April 1976, 13; "It's Hard Work Time," *Black News*, May 1972, 18; Kasisi Jitu Weusi, "The Control of Black Culture," *Black News*, January 31, 1975, 3–4; "New Orleans Position Paper," Ahidiana (c. 1974), Box 7, 6PAC, MSR; Bill Strickland, "Black Intellectuals and the American Social Scene," *Black World*, November 1975, 8.

18. "ALD Success Reveals Growth in Black Political Understanding," *African World*, June 16, 1973, 1, 3; "ALD Committee Continues to Work," *African World*, August 19, 1972, 14; Charles Wartts Jr., "African Liberation Support Group to Spearhead Year Round Drive," *Muhammad Speaks*, October 28, 1972, 5; February 16, 1973, Owusu Sadaukai and Florence Tate to Preston Wilcox, Box 7, Folder 2, PWP, SCR; "ALD Demonstrations Widespread: List of ALD State Coordinators," *African World*, April 28, 1973, 3; Owusu Sadaukai, "Our Responsibilities in the African Revolution," *Pan African Notes*, Summer 1973, 35–36; "African Liberation Support Committee: Statement of Principles," n.d., Reel 4, Black Power Movement Part 1 (Microfilm); "Pan-African Notes," *Black World*, August 1974, 66.

19. "Locke Elected National Head of ALSC," 1973 pamphlet, GCRR, UMC; Manning Marable, "Black Nationalism in the 1970s: Through the Prism of Race and Class," *Socialist Review*, March–June 1980, 86; Amiri Baraka, "'Why I Changed My Ideology': Black Nationalism and Socialist Revolution," *Black World,* July 1975, 30–42; Joseph F. Sullivan, "Baraka Abandons 'Racism' as Ineffective and Shifts to 'Scientific Socialism' of Marx," *New York Times*, December 27, 1974, 35.

20. "Afrikan Liberation Day: Its Meaning and Significance," *Black Collegian*, May–June 1973, 38–42.

21. Don L. Lee, "African Liberation Day," *Ebony*, July 1973, 38–46; Kalamu Ya Salaam, "Tell No Lies, Claim No Easy Victories," *Black World*, October 1974, 22; Florence Tate, "Which Way ALD?" *Afrika Must Unite* clipping, n.d., Box 10, Folder 5, CSP, ACC; Kasisi Jitu Weusi, "Around Our Way," *Black News*, August 4, 1973, 14.

22. "What We Mean by Class," *African World*, March 17, 1973, 15; Amiri Baraka, "'Why I Changed My Ideology,'" 32; "Toward the Ideological Unity of the African Liberation Support Committee: A Response to the Criticisms of the A.L.S.C. Statement of Principles Adopted at Frogmore, South Carolina, June-July 1973," and Dawolu Gene Locke "A Few Remarks in Response to Criticisms of ALSC," August 1974 pamphlet, Black Power Movement Part 1, Reel 4 (Microfilm).

23. "Background to the Conference," *African World*, July 1974, 3; "Summary, Debate, Plans Mark ALSC Conference," *African World*, March 1974, 1–2, 15; Abdul Alkalimat, *A Scientific Approach to Black Liberation* (Nashville: Peoples College, 1974), 1–23; Phil Hutchins, "Report on the ALSC National Conference," *Black Scholar*, July–August 1974, 48–53; "African Liberation Support Committee: Statement of Principles," n.d., Reel 4, Black Power Movement Part 1 (Microfilm); "Workshop on Women in the Struggle," *African World*, July 1974, 5.

24. "Haki Madhubuti and Jitu Weusi: Two Resignations," *Unity & Struggle*, October 1974, 8; Haki R. Madhubuti, "The Latest Purge: The Attack on Black Nationalism and Pan-Afrikanism by the New Left, the Sons and Daughters of the Old Left," *Black Scholar*, September 1974, 43; Kasisi Jitu Weusi, "Around Our Way," *Black News*, October 30, 1974, 15; Basir Mchawi, "Afrikan Liberation Day: Which Way Now???" *Black News*, June 1974, 3; Mwanza, "A.L.S.C. Resignation," *Black News*, June 1974, 18; Haki R. Madhubuti, "Enemy: From the White Left, White Right and In-Between," *Black World*, October 1974, 42; Kalamu Ya Salaam, "A Response to Haki Madhubuti," *Black Scholar*, January–February 1975, 40, 42.

25. "Comments of Chairman on Resignations of Haki Madhubuti and Jitu Weusi," May 1974 pamphlet, Black Power Movement Part 1 (Microfilm). Also see "Haki Madhubuti and Jitu Weusi: Two Resignations," *Unity & Struggle*, October, November, and December issues, 1974.

26. Madhubuti, "The Latest Purge," 43; Mwanza, "A.L.S.C. Resignation," 18; Haki Madhubuti, "From the Beginning: The Decision Is to Fight," *Black World*, March 1976, 26–31, 92–97.

27. Mark Smith, "A Response to Haki Madhubuti," *Black Scholar*, January–February 1975, 51; Gwendolyn M. Patton, "Open Letter to Marxists," *Black Scholar*, April 1975, 50; "The Potential of A.L.S.C.," *African World*, June 30, 1973, 6; Ernest Kaiser, "Book Reviews: Revealing the Dialectics of Black Liberation," *Freedomways*, Spring 1975, 120–121.

28. Maulana Ron Karenga, "Which Road: Nationalism, Pan-Africanism, Socialism," *Black Scholar*, October 1974, 21; A. Sivanandan, "Revolt of the Natives," *Liberator*, January–February 1971, 8.

29. Ladun Anise, "The Tyranny of a Purist Ideology," *Black World*, May 1975, 18–27; Lerone Bennett, *Unity in the Black Community* (Chicago: Institute of Positive Education, 1972), 5.

30. Madhubuti, "Enemy," 42; Kasisi Jitu Weusi, "Around Our Way," *Black News*, August 4, 1973, 15.

31. Amiri Baraka, "The Congress of Afrikan People: A Position Paper," *Black Scholar*, January–February 1975, 9; "Black Liberation and the United Front Against Imperialism," Transcript of 1977 Abdul Alkalimat speech, Box 50, Folder 8, FST, ARC.

32. Cedric Johnson, "From Popular Anti-Imperialism to Sectarianism: The African Liberation Support Committee and Black Power Radicals," *New Political Science* 25 (2003): 507.

33. For an overview of similar debates in the Caribbean, see Bukka Rennie, "The Conflicting Tendencies in the Caribbean Revolution," *Pan African Journal*, Summer 1975, 153–174.

34. Edward O. Erhagbe, "The African-American Contribution to the Liberation Struggle in Southern Africa: The Case of the African Liberation Support Committee, 1972-1979," *Journal of Pan African Studies* 4 (2011): 38.

35. Hutchins, "Report on the ALSC National Conference," 48; "Baraka Abandons 'Racism' as Ineffective and Shifts to 'Scientific Socialism' of Marx," *New York Times*, December 27, 1974, 35; Smith, "A Response to Haki Madhubuti," 51.

36. "Black Liberation and the United Front Against Imperialism," Transcript of 1977 Abdul Alkalimat speech, Box 50, Folder 8, FST, ARC; Kalamu Ya Salaam, "South View: We Can See Clearly Now," *Black News*, July 1975, 23; December 12, 1973, Kasisi Jitu Weusi to Imamu Amiri Baraka, KKP, INP.

37. Lawrence A. Still, "Jamaica, Guyana Promise Next Pan African Meet," *Afro-American*, July 20, 1974, 16; Benjamin F. Scott, "The Technology of Liberation: Proposal for a Pan-African Academy of Science," *Black World*, July 1972, 29–39; December 5, 1971, Winston Wiltshire memorandum to Secretariat Steering Committee Members, Box 36, Folder 3, VHP, EUM.

38. Minutes from Sixth Pan African Congress North Atlantic Delegation Midwest Working Meeting, November 23–24, 1973, Box 2, Folder SPAC NA Dist. LV, 6PAC, MSR; Transcript of William Minter interview with Sylvia Hill, September 23, 2003, Washington, D.C., "No Easy Victories" Interview Transcripts, accessed April 16, 2014, http://www.noeasyvictories. org/interviews/int11_hill.php; Transcript of Charles Cobb interview with Geri Augusto, January 26, 2005, Providence, Rhode Island, "No Easy Victories" Interview Transcripts, accessed April 16, 2014, http://www.noeasyvictories.org/interviews/int10_augusto.php; James Garrett, "The Six Pan African Congress: A Historical Sketch," *Black World*, March 1975, 4–20.

39. Lerone Bennett Jr., "Pan-Africanism at the Crossroads," *Ebony*, September 1974, 151; April 10, 1974, Sylvia Hill to Courtland Cox, Box 7, 6PAC, MSR.

40. Imamu Amiri Baraka, "Some Questions About the Sixth Pan-African Congress," *Black Scholar*, October 1974, 43; Garrett, "The Six Pan African Congress: A Historical Sketch," 7–13, 16; William Minter interview with Sylvia Hill, September 23, 2003, Washington, D.C., "No Easy Victories" Interview Transcripts, accessed April 16, 2014, http://www.noeasyvictories.org/ interviews/int11_hill.php.

41. Fanon Che Wilkins, "Line of Steel: The Organization of the Sixth Pan African Congress and the Struggle for International Blak Power, 1969-1974," in *The Hidden 1970s: Histories of Radicalism*, ed. Dan Berger (New Brunswick, NJ: Rutgers University Press, 2010), 97; "Radicals Criticize Governments," *New York Amsterdam News*, January 19, 1974, A10; Garrett, "The Six Pan African Congress: A Historical Sketch," 14, 17.

42. October 16, 1973, Owusu Sadaukai to Courtland Cox, and October 18, 1973, Courtland Cox to Owusu Sadaukai, Box 4, Folder SPAC Owusu/Courtland, and April 12, 1974, C.L.R. James to Forbes L. Burnham, Box 7, 6PAC, MSR.

43. Mamadou Lumumba, "To the Bothers and Sisters of the Pan-African World," *Soulbook*, Spring 1975, 82–85; Garrett, "The Six Pan African Congress: A Historical Sketch," 20; Walter Rodney, "Towards the Sixth Pan-African Congress: Aspects of the International Class Struggle in Africa, the Caribbean and America," in *Pan Africanism: The Struggle Against Imperialism and Neo-Colonialism* (Toronto, Canada: Afro-Carib Publications, 1975), 29.

44. Cynthia Jo Rich, "Americans Differ at African Congress," *Race Relations Reporter*, July 15, 1974, 2; David Lawrence Horne, "The Pan-African Congress: A Positive Assessment," *Black Scholar*, July–August 1974, 10; February 13, 1974, Courtland Cox to James Turner, Box 2, and April 10, 1974, Sylvia Hill to Courtland Cox, Box 7, 6PAC, MSR; Garrett, "The Six Pan African Congress: A Historical Sketch," 20.

45. Kalamu Ya Salaam, "6 P.A.C.," *Black News*, August 1974, 6; Alma Robinson, "A Meeting with Nyerere," *New Directions*, Summer 1974, 8.

46. Robinson, "A Meeting with Nyerere," 9; Haki R. Madhubuti, "Sixth Pan-Afrikan Congress: What Is Being Done to Save the Black Race," *Black Books Bulletin*, Fall 1974, 48; Imamu Baraka, "Revolutionary Culture and Future of Pan-African Culture," in *Pan Africanism: The Struggle Against Imperialism and Neo-Colonialism*, 124; Rich, "Americans Differ at African Congress," 3–5.

47. "Sixth Pan-African Congress," *Africa Research Bulletin*, June 1–30, 1974, 3261; Julius Nyerere, "President Nyerere's Speech to the Pan African Congress," and "From President Ahmed Sekou Toure to the Sixth Pan African Congress," and "General Declaration of the Sixth Pan-African Congress," in *Pan Africanism: The Struggle Against Imperialism and Neo-Colonialism*, 64, 77–80, 135.

48. Madhubuti, "Sixth Pan-Afrikan Congress: What Is Being Done to Save the Black Race," 48; Baraka, "Some Questions About the Sixth Pan-African Congress," 46; Bennett, "Pan-Africanism at the Crossroads," 158–160; Madhubuti, "Sixth Pan-Afrikan Congress," 49.

49. La Tasha Levy, "Remembering Sixth-PAC: Interviews with Sylvia Hill and Judy Claude, Organizers of the Sixth Pan-African Congress," *Black Scholar* 37 (2008): 39–47; Horne, "The Pan-African Congress: A Positive Assessment," 2–11.

50. J. Fletcher Robinson, "On Science and Technology: Self-Development in the Black World," *Black World*, March 1974, 29; Robinson, "A Meeting with Nyerere," 9; Bennett, "Pan-Africanism at the Crossroads," 158.

51. Kalamu Ya Salaam, Gene L. Locke, and Robert S. Hoover 6-PAC Delegate/Observer Applications, Box 2, Folder SPAC NA Delegates, 6PAC, MSR; Rich, "Americans Differ at African Congress," 3.

52. Robinson, "A Meeting with Nyerere," 8, 17; Sixth Pan-African Congress," 3261; "Pan-African Congress Seeks End to Racial Movements," *Jet*, August 1, 1974, 47–48; "General Declaration of the Sixth Pan-African Congress," 133.

53. Imamu Baraka, "Revolutionary Culture and Future of Pan-African Culture," in *Pan Africanism: The Struggle Against Imperialism and Neo-Colonialism*, 123; Transcript of William Minter interview with Sylvia Hill, September 23, 2003, Washington, D.C., "No Easy Victories" Interview Transcripts, accessed April 16, 2014, http://www.noeasyvictories.org/interviews/intl1_hill.php; Transcript of Charles Cobb interview with Geri Augusto, January 26, 2005, Providence, Rhode Island, "No Easy Victories" Interview Transcripts, accessed April 16, 2014, http://www.noeasyvictories.org/interviews/intl0_augusto.php. See also Julian Ellison, "The 1974 Sixth Pan-African Congress and Economic Needs of African Peoples," *Pan African Journal*, Summer 1974, 173–178.

54. Azinna Nwafor, "Liberation and Pan Africanism," *Monthly Review*, May 1973, 13.

55. Baraka, "Some Questions About the Sixth Pan-African Congress," 45; Horne, "The Pan-African Congress: A Positive Assessment," 10; Madhubuti, "Sixth Pan-Afrikan Congress," 50.

56. Kalamu Ya Salaam, "Zanzibar," *Black News*, August 1974, 35; Adeyemi Al Muqaddim, "Ugandan Experience," *Black News*, August 1974, 32–33.

57. Philip Ochieng, "Why the Pan-African Congress Is Foreign," *Black Star*, 1971, 61.

58. "Struggle in Portugal and Africa," *Southern Africa*, July–August 1974, 17; "The Angolan Struggle: Remarks by an MPLA Leader," *Black Scholar*, June 1976, 50–58; Hoyt W. Fuller, "The Angola Crisis and Afro-Americans," *Black World*, March 1976, 24–25, 72–73; Kasisi Jitu Weusi, "A View from the East: Angola—Afrika's Viet Nam?" *Black News*, December 1975, 4;

"The ALSC and CAP Abandon Pan-Afrikan Nationalism for the 'Chinese Line,'" May 1976 Patrice Lumumba Coalition position paper, Box 10, Folder 20, CSP, ACC; Jimmy Garrett, "The Lessons of Angola: An Eyewitness Report," *Black Scholar*, June 1976, 6; Herbert Boyd, "Angola: A Background," *Black World*, March 1976, 18.

59. "The Beginning of UNITA's Path to Socialist Reconstruction in Angola—An Eyewitness View," Florence Tate report, n.d., Box 46, Folder 18, FST, ARC; Transcript of review of *The Angolan Revolution: Exile Politics and Guerilla Warfare, 1962-1976, Volume II*, n.d., Box 7, Folder "Radio Interview," PNP, WHI.

60. Transcript of Charles Cobb interview with Geri Augusto, January 26, 2005, Providence, Rhode Island, "No Easy Victories" Interview Transcripts, accessed April 16, 2014, http://www.noeasyvictories.org/interviews/int10_augusto.php; Fuller, "The Angola Crisis and Afro-Americans," 25; Baraka, "Some Questions About the Sixth Pan-African Congress," 44; "National Union for the Total Independence of Angola," *Unity & Struggle*, June 1, 1976, 8; Weusi, "A View from the East: Angola—Afrika's Viet Nam?" 5; Kasisi Jitu Weusi, "Around Our Way," *Black News*, June 1974, 11; Kasisi Jitu Weusi, "Around Our Way," *Black News*, May 1974, 14; Haki R. Madhubuti, "Part II on 6th PAC," *Black News*, December 1974, 6.

61. Anthony Monteiro, "Angola's Second War of Liberation," *Freedomways*, Winter 1976, 47–59; Boyd, "Angola: A Background," 16–23; Garrett, "The Lessons of Angola," 2–7.

62. "Angola," *Black News*, January 1976, 8; undated and untitled position paper, Box 10, Folder 5, and "The ALSC and CAP Abandon Pan-Afrikan Nationalism for the 'Chinese Line,'" May 1976 Patrice Lumumba Coalition position paper, Box 10, Folder 20, CSP, ACC; Boyd, "Angola: A Background," 16–23.

63. Garrett, "The Lessons of Angola," 2–15; Monteiro, "Angola's Second War of Liberation," 47–59; "The Lessons of Angola," Transcript of April 22, 1976, Walter Rodney speech at Howard University, Washington, DC, Box 7, Folder "Liberation Struggles—Marxism in Africa," PNP, WHI.

64. "Angola," *Black News*, January 1976, 8.

65. Anise, "The Tyranny of a Purist Ideology," 21; Horace Campbell, "Socialism in Tanzania: A Case Study," *Black Scholar*, May 1975, 41–51; Fanon, *Wretched of the Earth*, 97.

66. K. A. Mtumishi, "From Washington: Dark City," *Black News*, June 2, 1973, 25; "Staff Evaluation Form on Quarterly Progress Reports," Lynn Eusan Institute, 1974, GCRR, UMC; Kasisi Jitu Weusi, "Around Our Way," *Black News*, July 1974, 13; Mustafa Ouma, "The Great Afrikan Debate," *Black News*, May 31, 1975, 3.

67. "Message to Carter," *Black News*, May 1977, 14–16; Kalamu Ya Salaam, "How and Why Rodney Was Downpressed," *Black Collegian*, October–November 1980, 107–111; July 25, 1980, Patricia Daly to IBW Members and Associates, PWP, SCR.

68. See "Busing: A Symposium," *Ramparts*, December 1974–January 1975, 38–46; Nathan Hare, "Can Blacks Ever Unite?" *Ebony*, September 1976, 98; Ronald-Bryant McFarland, "A Critique of the TV Presentation of Roots I," *Freedomways*, Winter 1979, 87–94. For a discussion of capitalist appropriation of sentimental motifs of Africa, see Grant Farred, "Feasting on Foreman: The Problematics of Postcolonial Identification," *Camera Obscura* 13 (1996): 52–76.

69. Jitu Weusi, "The Jonestown Massacre—An Act of Genocide," *Black News*, December 1978, 14–15, 34; John Hamill, "B'klyn Group Stunned by Guyana Neighbors," *Daily News*, November 24, 1978, 8.

70. Alex Poinsett, "Progress Report: 1975: Another Year of Erosion," *Ebony*, January 1976, 118–122; "Some Protesters Have 'Burned Out,' Others Say They're Regrouping," *New York Times*, September 30, 1977, 29; William Strickland, "Whatever Happened to the Politics of Black Liberation?" *Black Scholar*, October 1975, 20–26; "Doing More with Less," IBW Monthly Report, January–February 1974, Box 48, Folder 15, FST, ARC.

71. "Shule Ya Kujitambua: Summer 1973 Brochure" and "Mtoto Information Form," Shule Ya Kujitambua, Box 4, Subseries 4, COC, OCA; "Education Workshop Report," Congress of African People Eastern Regional Conference, Newark, New Jersey, September 1971, Box 35, Folder 20, JHC, SCR; "Action Stimulator No. 199: Mwalimu-Mwanafunzi Relationship," 1973 flyer, Box 23, PWP, SCR; Wilhemina E. Lockert Anthony, "Nairobi College: A Case Study: Faculty Recruitment and Turnover" (PhD diss., Claremont College, 1974), 22; *New York Amsterdam News*, July 10, 1976, B8.

72. May 1, 1975, Leslie R. Campbell to Robert Browne, and "Toward a Better Brooklyn and a Fair World," flyer, Box 8, Folder 15, and "Fact Sheet: The Black and Proud Elementary School," Box 11, Folder 1, TCF, SCR; August 29, 1977, Howard Spencer to Mr. and Mrs. Ferry, CWF, RLC; October 4, 1970, Portia A. Coombs to Barbara Huell, Box 23, Folder 10, VHP, EUM.

73. Ovid Abrams, "Uhuru Sasa: A School Devoted to Freedom and Education," *Black News*, January 28, 1974, 7.

74. Pan-African Early Education Center Newsletter, March 1972, Box 18, PWP, SCR.

75. October 4, 1970, Portia A. Coombs to Barbara Huell, Box 23, Folder 10, VHP, EUM; Council of Independent Black Institutions, "Summary from First Work Meeting, June 30-July 3, Frogmore, SC," 1972 pamphlet, JAL, UMI; John Churchville, "Freedom Library Day School," in *Curriculum Approaches from a Black Perspective*, ed. Black Child Development Institute (Washington, DC: Black Child Development Institute, 1973), 58.

76. May 1, 1975, Leslie R. Campbell to Robert Browne, and "Toward a Better Brooklyn and a Fair World," flyer, Box 8, Folder 15, and "Fact Sheet: The Black and Proud Elementary School," Box 11, Folder 1, TCF, SCR; "Uhuru Sasa School: Income and Expenses, Sept. 1976-June 1977," 1977 report, KKP, INP.

77. "Fact Sheet: The Black and Proud Elementary School," Box 11, Folder 1, TCF, SCR; August 29, 1977, Howard Spencer to Mr. and Mrs. Ferry, May 16, 1975, Bernard Parks to Carol Bernstein Ferry, CWF, RLC.

78. "Confederation of Nationalist and Pan-Afrikan Organizations," 1972 pamphlet, Box 24, Folder 2, PWP, SCR; "On the Education of Children (and Parents) for a Time of Protracted Struggle: A Personal/Organizational Note from Philadelphia," 1974 memorandum, Box 35, Folder 31, JHC, SCR.

79. July 1973 Umoja Sasa Newsletter, Box 18, PWP, SCR.

80. Margaret Bowers, "The Independent Black Educational Institution: An Exploration and Identification of Selected Factors that Relate to Their Survival" (EdD diss., Atlanta University, 1984), 180–183.

81. "Progress Report on Malcolm X Liberation University," June 1969 and February 20, 1970, and "Minutes of the Council of Elders Meeting," May 1 and September 25, 1970, and "Mwalimu's Message," *Msaidizi*, August 1971, CSP, ACC.

82. "Progress Report on Malcolm X Liberation University," June 1969 and February 20, 1970, and "Minutes of the Council of Elders Meeting," May 1 and September 25, 1970, and "Mwalimu's Message," *Msaidizi*, August 1971, CSP, ACC; December 20, 1972, Owusu Sadaukai to Members of Political Committee and Joint Command, Box 30, Folder 38, IFCO, SCR; "Malcolm X Liberation U. Begins Reorganization," *African World*, February 8, 1973, 11; January 12, 1973, Owusu Sadaukai to "Brothers and Sisters," Box 10, Folder 72, and June 27, 1973, Owusu Sadaukai Press Release, Box 10, Folder 73, TFP, LRW; "Malcolm X University Closes After 4 Years," *Afro-American*, July 14, 1973, 21; "Malcolm X Liberation Univ. Closed," *African World*, July 14, 1973, 1, 3; "Black Separatist University Closes," *Raleigh News and Observer*, June 28, 1973, 49; Diane King, "School's Days Were Stormy," *Greensboro Record*, June 27, 1973, D1–D2.

83. John Oliver Killens, "Wanted: Some Black Long Distance Runners," *Black Scholar*, November 1973, 2; Ronald Walters, "Critical Issues on Black Studies," *Pan African Journal*, Summer 1970, 535; Hoyt W. Fuller, "Another Fork in the Road," *Black World*, October 1974, 50; Peoples College, *Introduction to Afro-American Studies: A Peoples College Primer* (Chicago: Twenty-First Century Books, 1986), 240–241; S. E. Anderson, "Pitfalls of Black Intellectuals," *Black Scholar*, November 1973, 30.

84. "Black Education Conference, 1970," Notes from March 1970 planning meeting, Box 56, FHR, NEU; "Black Studies and the Struggle for Black Education," transcript of May 1, 1970, conference panel, Box 37, Folder 23, JHC, SCR.

85. Randolph P. Smith, "Poet and Former Addict Battles Heroin Epidemic," *Baltimore Afro-American*, October 4, 1980, 8; Jacqueline Trescott, "The Changing Face of D.C. Activism," *Washington Post*, August 6, 1988, A10; Tom Bamberger, "The Education of Howard Fuller," *Milwaukee Magazine*, July 1988, 59.

86. "An Interview with John Churchville," 1983 transcript, Box 6, IIE, CUK.

87. October 29, 1974, Kasisi Jitu Weusi to Patricia Fields, NFC, INP; Kasisi Jitu Weusi, "A View from the East: CIBI—A Critical Evaluation," *Black News*, June–July 1977, 8–10; "CIBI

Presents: Successful Teaching of Our Children," 1979 conference program, VFC, RJB; "Will Another Black School Close?" *Black News*, April–May 1977, 26–27; "Schools Without Funding: The Economic Plight of the Independent Black School Movement Today!" 1983 pamphlet, HAC, INP.

88. "Building a Pan African Preschool," *Black Child Journal*, September 1980, 38–40; Charles Baillou, "City Trying to Evict Uhuru Sasa School?" *New York Amsterdam News*, October 11, 1986, 11; "Direction, Identity, Purpose: Uhuru Sasa Shule: The Parent Handbook," 1980 pamphlet, KKP, INP; Adeyemi Bandele, "Ten Years of Struggle," *Black News*, December 1978, 3; "A Testimony to Jitu from Penda," *Black News*, December 1978, 36; "Community School Pays Tribute to First Graduates," *New York Amsterdam News*, January 7, 1978, B1; E. Curtis Alexander, "Uhuru Sasa 78: The Continuation of a Legacy of Struggle," *Black News*, November 1978, 12–17; June 7, 1978, Aminisha Weusi to "Dear Friend," NFC, INP.

89. Sharon Noguchi, "Nairobi School on Shoestring but Stepping," *Palo Alto Times*, October 12, 1978, 27; Roger Rapoport, "Peninsula Busing Battle Takes a Strange Turn," *San Francisco Chronicle*, March 24, 1978, 2; "Successful Minority Schools: The Responsibility Must Be Shared by All Involved," *Philadelphia Tribune*, June 10, 1978, 14; Noguchi, "Ravenswood Recreation District Affairs in Shambles," *Palo Alto Times*, October 12, 1978, 10; William Trombley, "Multidistrict Integration Plan Opens Schism," *Los Angeles Times*, September 29, 1977, B3, B35–36; Scott Herhold, "Prop. 13 Success Spells Hard Times for E. Palo Alto," *San Jose Mercury*, June 16, 1978; "Nairobi Day School: 'Our Children Can Learn,'" 1980 flyer, VFC, RJB.

90. APAS brochures and "Statement of Purpose of the Afrikan People's Action Movement," pamphlet, n.d., CIBI, INP; Afrikan People's Action School 1986 brochure, Box 1, and "Watoto School," pamphlet, n.d., and Nationhouse Watoto newsletter, Box 2, Folder 57, IIE, CUK.

91. Haki R. Madhubuthi, "Ten Reasons Why Black People Should Not Take White People as Mates, Lovers, Friends, Associates, Partners, or Comrades," *Black Books Bulletin*, Winter 1975, 30–32; Don L. Lee, "To Build the Nationalist-Pan Afrikanist Organization We Must Understand Why Many Black Organizations Failed in the Past," *Black News*, February 1974, 31; John E. Churchville, "May We Rest in Peace," *Black News*, December 1974, 9; "Malcolm X Memorial Committee Position Paper," *Black News*, May 1977, 16–17; Phyllis Bailey, "Children Taught to Be Future Leaders," *Los Angeles Sentinel*, November 19, 1981, A11. For related discussions of the retreat from radicalism, see Marable, "Black Nationalism in the 1970s," 75–79; S. E. Anderson, "Black Students: Racial Consciousness and the Class Struggle, 1960-1976," *Black Scholar*, January–February 1977, 35–43; Adolph L. Reed, "Back Particularity Reconsidered," *Telos*, Spring 1979, 71–93; Oba Simba T'Shaka, "Make the Past Serve the Present: Strategies for Black Liberation," *Black Scholar*, January–February 1983, 22–29.

92. Madhubuti, "From the Beginning: The Decision Is to Fight," 30; Hannibal Afrik, "On the Operational Philosophy of the Shule Ya Watoto," 1980 pamphlet, HAC, INP.

93. Ahidiana, "A Food Guide for Afrikan People," 1973 pamphlet, VGH, CGW; Johari M. Kunjufu, *Commonsense Approach to Eating: The Need to Become a Vegetarian* (Chicago: Institute of Positive Education, 1975); Aama Nahuja, "It's All About Food," *The Black Parent*, January 1976, NBP, WHI; *Nation Times*, December 1979, and Nzinga Latimer, "African Hairstyles," *Nation Times*, Nationhouse Watoto newsletter, December 1979, CIBI, INP.

94. "The Council of Independent Black Institutions," pamphlet, n.d., HAC, INP; Segun Shasaka, "A Journey of a Thousand Miles Begins with One Step," *New York Amsterdam News*, June 25, 1977, B3; Sis. Malika Iman and Sis. Aminisha Weusi, "Two Views: For Colored Girls," *Black News*, October 1976, 7–8; Mchawi, "Are Black Women Oppressed More Than Black Men," *Black News*, March 3, 1975, 7–8.

95. Yusef Waleiyaya, "On the Correct Black Educator," *Black News*, December 7, 1973, 21; Jitu Weusi, "Wherever America Is Heading New York Will Get There First," *New York Amsterdam News*, August 20, 1977, A3; Niani Kilkenny, "Should Television Be the Primary Educator of Our Youth?" 1979 pamphlet, KLC, INP; Hannibal Afrik, "On the Operational Philosophy of the Shule Ya Watoto," 1980 pamphlet, HAC, INP; *The Watoto Message*, March 1983, Shule Ya Watoto newsletter, and *The Message*, April 1984, Nationhouse newsletter, CIBI, INP.

96. "Direction, Identity, Purpose: Uhuru Sasa Shule: The Parent Handbook," 1980 pamphlet, KKP, INP.

97. Herb Boyd and Don Rojas, "The Contemporary Black Nationalist Roots of Afrocentricity," *New York Amsterdam News*, April 4, 1992, 6; "Direction, Identity, Purpose: Uhuru Sasa Shule: The Parent Handbook," 1980 pamphlet, KKP, INP; "The Council of Independent Black Institutions," pamphlet, n.d., HAC, INP; Agyei Akoto, "Nationhouse: A Direction," *Nation Times*, December 1982, Box 2, Folder 57, IIE, CUK; "CIBI Ritual Standardization," 1978 report, KLC, INP; Minutes of "Central Committee Meeting," April 1978, KKP, INP; Therese Mitchell, "African Festival to Herald New Year Here," *Times-Picayune*, December 26, 1976, 38; "The East Presents Kwanza," and "A Story of Kwanza," and "The Perfect Gift for Kwanza," and "Kwanza Is our African Holiday," flyers, n.d., Box 8, Folder 15, TCF, SCR; "Culture ... Culture ... Culture," *Black News*, December 1978, 4–5; E. Curtis Alexander, "Africa Mother of World Civilization: A Legacy of Black Antiquity, B.C.E.," *Black News*, October 1978, 18; Yosef ben-Jochannan, *Africa: Mother of Western Civilization* (New York: Alkebu-lan Publications, 1971); Chancellor Williams, *The Destruction of Black Civilization* (Chicago: Third World Press, 1974); Frances Cress Welsing, *The Cress Theory of Color Confrontation and Racism (White Supremacy)* (Washington, D.C.: C-R Publishers, 1974); Bobby Wright, "The Psychopathic Racial Personality," *Black Books Bulletin*, Fall 1974, 25–31; Chauncey Bailey, "Special Report: Mixed Emotions on the 'State of the Race,'" *Sun Reporter*, November 2, 1978, 4.
98. Molefi Kete Asante, *Afrocentricity: The Theory of Social Change* (Buffalo, NY: Amulefi, 1980).
99. "NS/CIBI in Afrika '81," *Fundisha!-Teach!*, 1981, HAC, INP; Hoyt W. Fuller, "FESTAC '77: A Footnote," *First World*, March–April 1977, 26–27; "A Report on Festac '77," *Black News*, June–July 1977, 19; "FESTAC '77: The Official Statement of the USA/FESTAC Committee," *Black Books Bulletin*, Summer 1977, 50–53; "FESTAC '77: A Festive Pan-Afrikan Success," *Black Collegian*, May–June 1977, 32, 64.

Epilogue

1. Vincent Harding, "IBW and the Vocation of the Black Scholar," in *Education and Black Struggle: Notes from the Colonized World*, ed. Institute of the Black World (Cambridge, MA: Harvard Educational Review, 1974), 26. For a discussion of Afrocentrism that stresses its considerable elements of political vibrancy and resilience, see Scot Brown, *Fighting for Us: Maulana Karenga, the US Organization and Black Cultural Nationalism* (New York: New York University Press, 2003).
2. See, for example, Robert Charles Smith, *We Have No Leaders: African Americans in the Post-Civil Rights Era* (Albany: State University Press of New York, 1996). Obviously I agree with Smith's larger emphasis on the decline of radical impulses in the postsegregation age.
3. Jitu Weusi, "The Re-Emergence of B'klyn Grassroots Politics," *New York Amsterdam News*, December 31, 1977, B1; Jitu Weusi, "A Brief History of Our Efforts to Establish a National Black United Front," Black Power Movement Part 1, Reel 7 (Microfilm); Andrew Marx, "Forward Together! Backward Never! An Interview with the National Black United Front," *Southern Africa*, July–August 1981, 3–5, 31; "NBUF Action Plan Targets Budget Cuts, Racism, War," *Guardian*, July 16, 1981; "The East and Jitu Weusi Under Attack," 1978 flyer, Box 17, PWP, SCR; "Interview with Rev. Herbert Daughtry Chairman of New York Metropolitan Area Black United Front," *Black News*, August–September 1979, 4–6; Jitu Weusi, "Statement of Chief of Operations, Black United Front, Brooklyn, New York, USA, to 11th Assembly of People's Democratic Party of Guinea," *Black News*, December 1978, 16–17.
4. Kalamu Ya Salaam, "Save Gary Tyler's Life," *Black News*, March 1977, 20–21; Kalamu Ya Salaam/Ahidiana, "Nuclear Power and the Black Liberation Struggle," *Black Scholar*, July–August 1978, 26–35; "New Orleans Demand: Destroy Racist Statue," *New York Amsterdam News*, December 9, 1976, 6; Scott Williams, "Slayings of Blacks Spark Protest in New Orleans," *Hartford Courant*, June 19, 1981, A5; Kalamu Ya Salaam, "In the Face of Oppression: A Case Study of New Orleans," *Black Scholar*, January–February 1981, 65–67; Manning Marable, "Beyond Coalition: Toward a New Strategy for Black Nationalist Politics," *First World*, September 1980, 18.
5. Kalamu Ya Salaam, *Hofu Ni Kwenu: My Fear Is For You* (New Orleans: Ahidiana, 1973); Kalamu Ya Salaam, *Our Women Keep Our Skies from Falling: Six Essays in Support of the*

Struggle to Smash Sexism/Develop Women (New Orleans: Nkombo, 1980); Kalamu Ya Salaam, "Revolutionary Struggle/Revolutionary Love," *Black Scholar*, May–June 1979, 22.

6. Kalamu Ya Salaam, "The Great Wall Does Not Divide Us," *Black Collegian*, January–February 1978, 48, 50, 80; "Black Alternative Educators Tour the People's Republic of China," *Black Scholar*, September 1977, 55; Basir Mchawi, "Black News Visits China," *Black News*, September 1977, 3, 7; "Five from Area School Invited to China on Educational Tour," *Philadelphia Tribune*, May 14, 1977, 2; Kalamu Ya Salaam/Ahidiana, "Nuclear Power and the Black Liberation Struggle," 27.

7. See the final chapters of Robeson Taj Frazier, *The East Is Black: Cold War China in the Black Radical Imagination* (Durham, NC: Duke University Press, 2015).

8. Basir Mchawi, "Black Educators Back from 'Eye-Opener' Tour of China," *New York Amsterdam News*, August 27, 1977, A2; Basir Mchawi, "China's Medical and Educational Institutions Contrast with Ours," *New York Amsterdam News*, September 3, 1977, B2; Kalamu Ya Salaam, "Why Do We Lie About Telling the Truth," in *Afro Asia: Revolutionary Political and Cultural Connections Between African Americans and Asian Americans*, ed. Fred Ho and Bill V. Mullen (Durham, NC: Duke University Press, 2008), 206–210; M. Ron Karenga, "Chinese Theory and Practice on the Nationalities Question," *In These Times*, September 14–20, 1977, 16.

9. Kalamu Ya Salaam, "Independent Black Educators Tour China," *Fundisha!-Teach!* n.d. (c. 1977); M. Ron Karenga, "Inside China: A Report on a New Reality," *Black News*, September 1977, 6.

10. Transcript of July 11, 1983, Joan D. Ratteray Interview with Renee Fluellen of Nidhamu Sasa Shule, Philadelphia, Box 6, IIE, CUK; Kierno Mayo, "Independents' Day," *City Limits*, January 1997, 21–22; Valeria M. Russ, "Learning to Win out of Deep Roots in Black Experience; Independent Phila. Academies Evolve into a Force for Community Building," *Philadelphia Daily News*, March 10, 1986, 14; Margaret King and Alfred L. Karlson, *A Non-Racist Framework for the Analysis of Educational Programs for Black Children* (Palo Alto, CA: R&E Research Associates, 1982), 86–87, 100–101.

11. "Ahidiana Work/Study Center: A Black Independent and Affirmative Institution of Vital Education," brochure, n.d., HAC, INP; "Direction, Identity, Purpose: Uhuru Sasa Shule: The Parent Handbook," 1980, KKP, INP.

12. W. Leon Moore to Dear Friends of Chad, n.d., and Transcripts of Institute for Independent Education Questionnaires, completed by parents of Chad School and Afrikan People's Action School, 1986, Box 1, Folder 26, IIE, CUK.

13. Paul Hill Jr., "Liberation Education," August 6, 1986 (ED 287926).

14. Deborrah Wilkinson, "New Hopes Come with New Home," *Philadelphia Tribune*, August 28, 1984; Transcript of July 22, 1983, Joan D. Ratteray Interview with Elaine Gills of W.E.B. Du Bois Institute, Los Angeles, Box 6, IIE, CUK; Sheryl McCarthy, "Black Parents Consider the Alternatives," *Village Voice*, August 29, 1977, 53; Thomas A. Johnson, "Black-Run Private Schools Lure Growing Numbers in New York," *New York Times*, April 5, 1980, 1, 23; William Overend, "Emergence of the Black Private School," *Los Angeles Times*, June 26, 1980, G1, G12–15; Laura Washington, "Decade of Growth: Chicago's Black Private Schools: Separate But More Than Equal," *Chicago Reporter*, January 1982, 1–2; Edmund Newton, "An Alternative to Public Education," *Black Enterprise*, September 1984, 61–65; Patrice Gaines-Carter, "Choices Difficult for Many Parents," *Washington Post*, February 14, 1985, 1, 8; Carolyn Hughes Crowley, "Pride, Heritage and Values," *Washington Post*, November 20, 1988, ER1, ER19–22.

15. J. Zamgba Browne, "Patterson Promotes Heritage While Students Learn," *New York Amsterdam News*, March 6, 1976, C11; Charlayne Hunter, "After-School School for Black Youngsters in Search of Heritage," *New York Times*, April 17, 1976, 34; Celia Knight, "The Patterson School in Harlem," *Africa Woman*, July–August 1977, 40–41; Rachelle Station, "The Patterson School Aiding Black Youngsters," *New York Amsterdam News*, September 23, 1978, C5; August 1976 Jamelle R. Patterson to Friends of the Patterson School, Box 9, Folder 1, TCF, SCR.

16. "Marcus Garvey School Elementary and Junior High," October 1990 Newsletter, Box 2, IIE, CUK; Legrand H. Clegg II, "Marcus Garvey School: New Hope for Black Children,"

Sepia, November 1980, 50–53; Pamela Douglas, "The Marcus Garvey School: A Successful Alternative," *National Leader*, December 23, 1982, 11.

17. Phyllis Bailey, "Children Taught to Be Future Leaders," *Los Angeles Sentinel*, November 19, 1981, A11; NationHouse Positive Action Center, Inc. brochure, Box 2, Folder 37, IIE, CUK.

18. Carol D. Lee, "Profile of an Independent Black Institution: African-Centered Education at Work," *Journal of Negro Education* 62 (1992): 175; "The Instructors," *Nation Times*, December 1982, Box 2, Folder 57, IIE, CUK; "Informational Brochure, Garvey Youth Service Corporation, Governing Body of the Shule Ya Watoto," pamphlet, n.d., CIBI, INP; Peter Harris and Hannibal Afrik, "On Redefining Educational Leadership," *Fundisha!-Teach!* [Council of Independent Black Institutions Newsletter, Vol. 8] (c. 1985), KKP, INP; 1983 Hannibal Afrik Memo to CIBI Central Committee ("Notes on [February 1983] *Reader's Digest* Article"), and Mwalimu Hannibal Afrik, "Black Parents Must Control Their Schools," flyer, n.d., and Hannibal Tirus Afrik, "'Neither One of Us Wants to Be the First to Say Good-Bye': An Analysis of the Agony of Black Parents' Dependency Upon the Public School System," 1976 pamphlet, HAC, INP; Harold E. Charles, "Most Important Black Issue," *Chicago Defender*, June 28, 1986, 14; Harold E. Charles, "Educational Self-Determination," *Chicago Defender*, August 2, 1986, 14; Harold E. Charles, "Seeds for Nation Harvest," *Chicago Defender*, August 5, 1986, 10; Hannibal Tirus Afrik, "The Role of Political Ideology in Teaching," 1975 pamphlet, KLC, INP; Transcript of July 12, 1983, Joan Ratteray Interview with John Churchville of Freedom Library Day School, Philadelphia, Box 6, IIE, CUK; Kofi Lomotey to "Dear New Member," n.d., Council of Independent Black Institutions Members Handbook, March 1985 Edition, CIBI, INP.

19. Theodore R. Sizer, "The Case for a Free Market," *Saturday Review*, January 11, 1969, 34–42, 93; Maurice R. Berube, "The Trouble with Vouchers," *Commonweal*, January 1971, 414–417; "The Case for Vouchers," *Black Scholar*, May–June 1973, 8–13; Albert Vann, "Black People in America: The State of Education for Black People—1973," *New York Amsterdam News*, September 1, 1973, 5; Felton E. Lewis, "Avoiding Elitism; And Promoting Democracy," *Amsterdam News*, October 22, 1975, A5; "Statement by E. Babette Edwards to the New York State Board of Regents at the Regents Legislative Conference, September 10, 1975," transcript, Box 13, Folder 26, EJB, SCR; Gertrude S. Goldberg, "Class Action, Community Organization and School Reform, Part II," *Freedomways*, Winter 1978, 28–35; Babette Edwards, "Future Directions in Obtaining Effective Education," *New York Amsterdam News*, January 19, 1980, 11.

20. A California Committee of Teachers, "The Voucher—Plot Against Free Public Schools," *Black Liberation Journal*, Summer 1979, 48–50.

21. Walter E Williams, "A Minority View," *Atlanta Daily World*, June 14, 1984, 4; Clarence Page, "Freedom of Choice for Poor Folks," *Chicago Tribune*, August 23, 1987, C3; "Editorial: The Tax Tuition Credit Plan," *Alternative Schooling News*, Fall 1982, 1–3; Keith B. Richburg, "Voucher Plan for Education Pushed Here," *Washington Post*, November 27, 1985, B7; John Chodes, "Public Education—Dump It," *New York Times*, December 19, 1988, A17; December 23, 1985, Robert L. Woodson to Hannibal Afrik, and Afram News Reprint on educational tuition tax credits, 1982, HAC, INP.

22. Karen Farkas, "Inner-City Public Schools Branded a Failure," *Plain Dealer*, March 7, 1987, 2B; Joan Davis Ratteray, "One System Is Not Enough: A Free Market Alternative for the Education of Minorities," *Lincoln Review*, Spring 1984, 27; Joan Davis Ratteray, "Independent Neighborhood Schools: A Framework for the Education of African Americans," *Journal of Negro Education* 61 (1992): 138–147.

23. Transcript of July 22, 1983, Joan D. Ratteray Interview with Anyim Palmer of Marcus Garvey Elementary school, Los Angeles, Box 2, and Transcript of July 12, 1983, Joan Ratteray Interview with John Churchville of Freedom Library Day School, Philadelphia, Box 6, IIE, CUK; "National Center for Neighborhood Enterprise, Neighborhood-Based Independent Schools: Give a Child a Choice Panelists and Participants," 1983 roster, Box 13, PWP, SCR; Susan Walton, "Local Independent Schools Offer Minorities 'Educational Option,'" *Education Week*, November 16, 1983, 1, 16; "Inner-City Schools Are Failing, Conference Speakers Say; Some Believe Choice and Competition Are Keys to Reform," *Cato Policy Report*, January–February 1990, 7.

24. Hugh Pearson, "An Urban Push for Self-Reliance," *Wall Street Journal*, February 7, 1996, A14; March 14, 1997, Malik Yakini memorandum to Mwalimu Shujaa, National Executive Officer, CIBI, KLC, INP.

25. Hannibal Tirus Afrik, "Towards National Liberation: On the Possibility and Desirability of Education for Self-Reliance: 'To Charter or Not to Charter? Clarity or Confusion?'" 1997 position paper, and November 18, 1996, Afrikan People's Action School Board to Members of CIBI Ndundu and Executive Committee, KLC, INP.

26. Kevin Merida, "Howard Fuller: '60s Activist Still Active," *Milwaukee Journal*, March 21, 1982, 5–9; Tom Bamberger, "The Education of Howard Fuller," *Milwaukee Magazine*, July 1988, 60–62; Paul Taylor, "Milwaukee's Controversial Private School Choice Plan Off to Shaky Start," *Washington Post*, May 25, 1991, A3; Alan J. Borsuk, "A Difference, 'But Not Enough': Dedicated to Fighting for Change, He Leaves in Frustration," *Milwaukee Journal Sentinel*, April 19, 1995, 1A; Howard Fuller, "Creating Educational Options for Low Income Parents," *Vital Speeches of the Day*, September 15, 2000, 721–725; Howard Fuller, "Educational Choice: A Core Freedom," *Journal of Negro Education*, Winter 2002, 3.

27. Mayo, "Independents' Day," 23.

28. T. Toch and B. Wagner, "Fighting a Racist Legacy," *U.S. News & World Report*, December 9, 1991, 74; Mark Walsh, "Black Private Academies Are Held Up as Filling Void," *Education Week*, March 13, 1991, 1, 28.

29. Kofi Lomotey, "Creating an Afrocentric Institution: A Working Paper," Council of Independent Black Institutions pamphlet (c. 1987), Box 4, IIE, CUK; Conrad W. Worrill, "African Centered Education Can Smash White Supremacy," *Philadelphia Tribune*, October 8, 1993, 7A.

30. Sonia R. Jarvis, "Brown and the Afrocentric Curriculum," *Yale Law Journal* 101 (1992): 1286–1287.

31. See, for example, M. A. Farber, "'Africa Centered' School Plan Is Rooted in 60's Struggles," *New York Times*, February 5, 1991, B1–B2; Joseph Berger, "'Africa-Centered' Proposal Outlined for a Trial School," *New York Times*, January 22, 1991, B3; Samuel Weiss, "Ethnic Plan for a School Seen Fading," *New York Times*, July 5, 1991, B1; Dwight Ott, "New Direction in Camden: A Man and His School Plan," *Philadelphia Inquirer*, September 3, 1988, 1B; Linda Stewart, "Schools Start by Giving Pupils Sense of Identity," *Detroit Free Press*, September 16, 1990; Gary Putka, "Curricula of Color," *Wall Street Journal*, July 1991, A2; Lynne Duke, "African-Centered Curricula: Reclaiming History or Rewriting It?" *Washington Post*, November 27, 1992, 1; Agyei Akoto, "Notes on an Afrikan-Centered Pedagogy," in *Nationbuilding: Theory and Practice in African-Centered Education*, ed. Mwalimu Shujaa (Trenton, NJ: Africa World Press, 1994), 319–337. For critiques of Afrocentrism, see Patricia Hill Collins, *From Black Power to Hip Hop; Racism, Nationalism and Feminism* (Philadelphia: Temple University Press, 2006), 75–82; E. Frances White, "Africa on My Mind; Gender, Counter Discourse and African-American Nationalism," *Journal of Women's History* 2 (1990): 73–97; Manning Marable, "Beyond Racial Identity Politics: Towards a Liberation Theory for Multicultural Democracy," *Race and Class* 35 (1993): 116–121; Sidney J. Lemelle, "The Politics of Cultural Existence: Pan-Africanism, Historical Materialism and Afrocentricity," *Race & Class* 35 (1993): 93–112; James P. Garrett, "Black/Africana/Pan African Studies: From Radical to Reaction to Reform?—Its Role and Relevance in the Era of Global Capitalism in the New Millennium," *Journal of Pan-African Studies* 1 (1998): 167–169.

32. Andrew Ross, "Can the Black Panthers Survive?" *New York Amsterdam News*, November 30, 1974, B10; Stanley O. Williford, "The Black Panthers Today," *Race Relations Reporter*, July 1974, 30–34.

33. Bob Lucas, "East Oakland Ghetto Blooms with Growth of Black Panther School," *Jet*, February 5, 1976, 20–24; "Dedication/Celebration to Mark Opening of Youth Institute and Son of Man Temple," *Black Panther*, October 20, 1973, 5; JoNina M. Abron, "Reflections of a Former Oakland Public School Parent," *Black Scholar*, Summer 1997, 15; "Bobby Seale Dedicates New Youth Institute and Son of Man Temple to Community," *Black Panther*, October 27, 1973, 3; "'The World Is Their Classroom,'" *Black Panther*, November 3, 1973, 4; "Youth Institute Succeeding Where Public Schools Failed," *Black Panther*, February 2, 1974, 7; "Blacks, Poor Win Voice on School Board," May 12, 1976 *Montclarion* reprint, Box 16,

Folder 11, HPN, SUS; "Busing: A Symposium," *Ramparts*, December 1974–January 1975, 42–43; " 'Mighty Panthers' Drill Team Highlights O.C.S. 'December Festival,' " *Black Panther*, December 27, 1975, 4; Jim Hoffman, "Reading, Writing and Fighting in the Oakland Ghetto," *Black Panther*, June 30, 1975, 23.

34. "Youth Institute Opens," *Black Panther*, September 15, 1973, 4; "Letters to Chairman Bobby and Ericka from the Youth Institute (Unedited)—March 1971," *Black Panther*, March 27, 1971; " '. . . Our Hope Is Placed on You' " *Black Panther*, March 27, 1971; Lucas, "East Oakland Ghetto Blooms with Growth of Black Panther School," 22.

35. "Youth Institute: Group 4: Language Arts with Novelty," *Black Panther*, April 13, 1974, 4; Williford, "The Black Panthers Today," 30–34; "Youth Institute: Group 7: Method Is Very Important," *Black Panther*, May 4, 1974, 4; "Bobby Seale Dedicates New Youth Institute and Son of Man Temple to Community," *Black Panther*, October 27, 1973, 3; "Youth Institute's Environmental Studies Project an Educational Experience," *Black Panther*, January 5, 1975, 5; Oakland Community School Instructor Handbook, Box 17, Folder 1, HPN, SUS.

36. Ross, "Can the Black Panthers Survive?" B10.

37. 1978-1979 Ericka Huggins Memoranda and Weekly School Reports to Huey P. Newton, Box 16, Folder 4, and "Oakland Community School," flyer, n.d., and "*Oakland Community Learning Center News*," November 1979 newsletter, Box 16, Folder 2, and "Black Babies Are Dying!" flyer, n.d., Box 16, Folder 13, and "George Jackson People's Free Medical Research Health Clinic: Child Health Care Program," brochure, n.d., Box 17, Folder 7, HPN, SUS; Craig Peck, " 'Educate to Liberate,' The Black Panther Party and Political Education" (PhD. diss., Stanford University, 2001), 212–229.

38. April 15, 1970, John O'Neal letter to Herb Callendar and attached materials, Box 22, Folders 6–7, JOP, ARC.

39. Ibid.; "Proposal for Funding the Jackson Human Rights Project," 1970 proposal, Box 22, Folders 6–7, JOP, ARC; December 6, 1975, Howard Spencer to Resist, Box 4, Folder 2, and January 12, 1976, Howard Spencer to Resist, Box 2, Folder 1, RES, WTC; Dylan Watson, "Frank Figgers," *Jackson Free Press*, October 31, 2012; "Black and Proud Liberation School, Basic Application Data," Box 11, Folder 1, and "Black and Proud Elementary School Fact Sheet," brochure, n.d., TCF, SCR.

40. "Proposal for Funding the Jackson Human Rights Project," 1970 proposal, Box 22, Folders 6–7, JOP, ARC; December 6, 1975, Howard Spencer to Resist, Box 4, Folder 2, and January 12, 1976, Howard Spencer to Resist, Box 2, Folder 1, RES, WTC.>>; Hattie L. Hayes, "Black and Proud Graduations," *Jackson Advocate*, June 7–June 13, 1979.

41. January 12, 1976, Howard Spencer to Resist, and February 23, 1977, and April 20, 1977, Howard Spencer to "Dear Friends in Resist," and "From 'Black and Proud Newsletter,' February 1977," Box 2, Folder 1, and February 4, 1976, Howard Spencer to "Friends in the Struggle," Box 4, Folder 2, and June 24, 1980, and July 15, 1980, Howard Spencer to Resist, Box 5, Folder 1, and January 26, 1981, Howard Spencer to Resist, Box 5, Folder 2, and March 21, 1982, Howard Spencer to Resist, Box 10, Folder 2, RES, WTC; April 15, 1970, John O'Neal letter to Herb Callendar and attached materials, Box 22, Folders 6–7, JOP, ARC.

42. August 29, 1977, Howard Jackson to "Mr. and Mrs. Ferry," CWF, RLC; July 11, 1979, Howard Spencer Letter to "Bob," Box 11, Folder 1, TCF, SCR.

43. August 29, 1977, Howard Jackson to "Mr. and Mrs. Ferry," CWF, RLC; July 11, 1979, Howard Spencer Letter to "Bob," Box 11, Folder 1, TCF, SCR; Howard Spencer, "White Repression and Black Response in Mississippi," *Liberator*, April 1969, 11; John M. Credson, "Black Pastor Got F.B.I. Threat in '69," *New York Times*, March 17, 1975, 1, 19.

44. Hayes, "Black and Proud Graduations."

ARCHIVAL SOURCES

6PAC, MSR	Sixth Pan African Congress Papers, Moorland-Spingarn Research Center, Howard University, Washington, DC
AMP, SCR	August Meier Papers, Schomburg Center for Research in Black Culture, The New York Public Library, New York, NY
AOW, WHI	Arthur Ocean Waskow Papers, Wisconsin Historical Society, Madison, WI
ASP, CUL	Annie Stein Papers, Rare Book and Manuscript Library, Columbia University, New York, NY
BL, UCB	Bancroft Library, University of California Berkeley, Berkeley, CA
BPFBI, SCR	Black Panther Party FBI File, Schomburg Center for Research in Black Culture, The New York Public Library, New York, NY
CIBI, INP	Council of Independent Black Institutions Records, In Private Hands, Trenton, NJ
CMP, SUS	Cherrie Moraga Papers, Stanford University Special Collections, Stanford, CA
COC, OCA	City of Oberlin Collection, Oberlin College Archives, Oberlin, OH
CRD, MSR	Civil Rights Documentation Project, Moorland-Spingarn Research Center, Howard University, Washington, DC
CRV, MSR	Civil Rights Vertical File, Moorland-Spingarn Research Center, Howard University, Washington, DC
CSP, ACC	Cleveland L. Sellers Jr. Papers, Avery Research Center, College of Charleston, Charleston, SC
CWF, RLC	Carol B. Ferry and W. H. Ferry Papers, Ruth Lilly Special Collections and Archives, Indiana University-Purdue University, Indianapolis, IN
DGC, MSR	Dabu Gizenga Collection, Moorland-Spingarn Research Center, Howard University, Washington, DC
DJB, RLC	DJB Foundation Records, Ruth Lilly Special Collections and Archives, Indiana University-Purdue University, Indianapolis, IN
DWP, SCR	Doxey Wilkerson Papers, Schomburg Center for Research in Black Culture, The New York Public Library, New York, NY
EGP, SCR	Ewart Guinier Papers, Schomburg Center for Research in Black Culture, The New York Public Library, New York, NY
EJB, SCR	Ella Baker Papers, Schomburg Center for Research in Black Culture, The New York Public Library, New York, NY
EPA, PAH	East Palo Alto Clipping File, Palo Alto Historical Society, Palo Alto, CA
FFA, DBC	Field Foundation Archives, Dolph Briscoe Center for American History, University of Texas, Austin, TX
FHR, NEU	Freedom House Records, Archives and Special Collections, Northeastern University, Boston, MA
FLH, ARC	Fannie Lou Hamer Papers, Amistad Research Center, New Orleans, LA

FST, ARC   Free Southern Theater Records, Amistad Research Center, New Orleans, LA

GCRR, UMC   Records of the General Commission on Religion and Race, General Commission on Archives and History, The United Methodist Church, Madison, NJ

GRD, SCR   General Research Division, Schomburg Center for Research in Black Culture, The New York Public Library, New York, NY

GWC, INP   Gertrude Wilks Collection, In Private Hands, East Palo Alto, CA

GWP, WHI   George Wiley Papers, Wisconsin Historical Society, Madison, WI

HAC, INP   Hannibal Afrik Collection, In Private Hands, Port Gibson, MI

HHC, WUF   Henry Hampton Collection, Film and Media Archive, Washington University Libraries, St. Louis, MO

HPN, SUS   Huey P. Newton Foundation Collection, Stanford University Special Collections, Stanford, CA

IBW, SCR   Institute of the Black World Records, Schomburg Center for Research in Black Culture, The New York Public Library, New York, NY

IFCO, SCR   Interreligious Foundation for Community Organizations Collection, Schomburg Center for Research in Black Culture, The New York Public Library, New York, NY

IIE, CUK   Institute for Independent Education Records, Carl A. Kroch Library Division of Rare and Manuscript Collections, Cornell University, Ithaca, NY

JAL, UMI   Joseph A. Labadie Collection, University of Michigan Special Collections, Hatcher Graduate Library, Ann Arbor, MI

JCP, ACC   James Campbell Papers, Avery Research Center, College of Charleston, Charleston, SC

JEP, VUA   John Egerton Papers, Jean and Alexander Heard Library, Vanderbilt University Archives, Nashville, TN

JHC, SCR   John Henrik Clarke Papers, Schomburg Center for Research in Black Culture, The New York Public Library, New York, NY

JKP, EUM   John O. Killens Papers, Manuscript, Archive and Rare Book Library, Emory University, Atlanta, GA

JOP, ARC   John O'Neal Papers, Amistad Research Center, New Orleans, LA

JPB, DCR   James P. Breeden Papers, Rauner Special Collections Library, Dartmouth College, Hanover, NH

JRC, INP   John R. Rickford Collection, In Private Hands, Palo Alto, CA

JWJ, SCR   James Weldon Johnson Community Center Papers, Schomburg Center for Research in Black Culture, The New York Public Library, New York, NY

KKP, INP   Kwasi Konadu Collection, In Private Hands, Brooklyn, NY

KLC, INP   Kofi Lomotey Collection, In Private Hands, Brooklyn, NY

KNP, MSR   Kwame Nkrumah Papers, Moorland-Spingarn Research Center, Howard University, Washington, DC

LGL, YLS   Lillian Goldman Library, Yale Law School, New Haven, CT

MGP, SCR   Milton Galamison Papers, Schomburg Center for Research in Black Culture, The New York Public Library, New York, NY

NBP, WHI   National Black Parents Organization Papers, Wisconsin Historical Society, Madison, WI

NFC, INP   Natelege Fields Collection, In Private Hands, Brooklyn, NY

NLC, HIA   New Left Collection, Hoover Institution Archives, Stanford University, Stanford, CA

NSM, SCR   Northern Student Movement Papers, Schomburg Center for Research in Black Culture, The New York Public Library, New York, NY

PNP, WHI   Prexy Nesbitt Papers, Wisconsin Historical Society, Madison, WI

PTL, MEC   Pacifica Tape Library, Charles Evans Inniss Memorial Library, Medgar Evers College, Brooklyn, NY

PWP, SCR   Preston Wilcox Papers, Schomburg Center for Research in Black Culture, The New York Public Library, New York, NY

RBP, SCR	Robert Beecher Papers, Schomburg Center for Research in Black Culture, The New York Public Library, New York, NY
RES, WTC	Resist Collection, Watkinson Library and College Archives, Trinity College, Hartford, CT
RPP, SCR	Richard Parrish Papers, Schomburg Center for Research in Black Culture, The New York Public Library, New York, NY
RSB, SCR	Robert S. Browne Papers, Schomburg Center for Research in Black Culture, The New York Public Library, New York, NY
RYP, SCR	Roberta Yancy Papers, Schomburg Center for Research in Black Culture, The New York Public Library, New York, NY
SAV, WHI	Social Action Vertical File, Wisconsin Historical Society, Madison, WI
SBP, MSR	Sterling Brown Papers, Moorland-Spingarn Research Center, Howard University, Washington, DC
SCD, SCR	St. Clair Drake Papers, Schomburg Center for Research in Black Culture, The New York Public Library, New York, NY
SCLS, SUS	Stokely Carmichael—Lorna D. Smith Papers, Stanford University Special Collections, Stanford, CA
SOH, INP	Stanford Oral History Project, John Rickford, In Private Hands, Palo Alto, CA
TCF, SCR	Twenty-First Century Foundation Papers, Schomburg Center for Research in Black Culture, The New York Public Library, New York, NY
TFP, LRW	Thomas A. Fraser Papers, Louis Round Wilson Special Collections Library, University of North Carolina, Chapel Hill, NC
TSP, WHI	Tom W. Shick Papers, Wisconsin Historical Society, Madison, WI
UFT, RFW	United Federation of Teachers Records, Robert F. Wagner Labor Archives, New York University, New York, NY
UNIA, EUM	Universal Negro Improvement Association Records, Manuscript, Archive and Rare Book Library, Emory University, Atlanta, GA
USSA, WHI	United States Student Association Records, Wisconsin Historical Society, Madison, WI
UUA, AHT	Unitarian Universalist Association Black Affairs Council Records, Andover-Harvard Theological Library Manuscripts and Archives, Harvard Divinity School, Cambridge, MA
VCP, WHI	SNCC Vine City Project Records, Wisconsin Historical Society, Madison, WI
VFC, RJB	Vertical File Collection, Ralph J. Bunche Center for African American Studies, UCLA, Los Angeles, CA
VGH, CGW	Vivian G. Harsh Research Collection of Afro-American History and Literature, Carter G. Woodson Library, Chicago Public Library, Chicago, IL
VHP, EUM	Vincent Harding Papers, Manuscript, Archive and Rare Book Library, Emory University, Atlanta, GA

BIBLIOGRAPHY

Abron, JoNina M. "'Serving the People': The Survival Programs of the Black Panther Party." In *The Black Panther Party Reconsidered*, edited by Charles E. Jones, 177–192. Baltimore: Black Classics, 1998.

Africa Information Service, ed. *Return to the Source: Selected Speeches by Amilcar Cabral.* New York: Monthly Review, 1973.

Alkebulan, Paul. *Survival Pending Revolution: The History of the Black Panther Party.* Tuscaloosa: University of Alabama Press, 2007.

Allen, Robert L. *Black Awakening in Capitalist America.* New York: Doubleday, 1969.

Altshuler, Alan. *Community Control: The Black Demand for Participation in Large American Cities.* New York: Bobbs-Merrill, 1970.

Anderson, James D. *The Education of Blacks in the South, 1860-1935.* Chapel Hill: University of North Carolina Press, 1988.

Anderson, Noel S., and Haroon Kharem, eds. *Education as Freedom: African American Educational Thought and Activism.* Lanham, MD: Lexington Books, 1964.

Anyon, Jean. *Ghetto Schooling: A Political Economy of Urban Educational Reform.* New York: Teachers College Press, 1997.

Austin, Algernon. *Achieving Blackness: Race, Black Nationalism and Afrocentrism in the Twentieth Century.* New York: New York University Press, 2006.

Ayers, William, and Michael Klonsky. "Navigating a Restless Sea: The Continuing Struggle to Achieve a Decent Education for African American Youngsters in Chicago." *Journal of Negro History* 63 (1994): 5–18.

Back, Adina. "'Exposing the Whole Segregation Myth': The Harlem Nine and New York City's School Desegregation Battles." In *Freedom North: Black Freedom Struggles Outside the South, 1940-1980*, edited by Jeanne Theoharis and Komozi Woodard, 65–91. New York: Palgrave Macmillan, 2003.

———. "Up South in New York: The 1950s School Desegregation Struggles." PhD diss., New York University Press, 1997.

Bair, Barbara. "Garveyism and Contested Political Terrain in 1920s Virginia." In *Afro-Virginian History and Culture*, edited by John Saillant, 227–249. New York: Taylor & Francis, 1999.

Bamberger, Tom. "The Education of Howard Fuller." *Milwaukee Magazine*, July 1988, 39–62.

Baraka, Amiri, ed. *African Congress: A Documentary of the First Modern Pan-African Congress.* New York: William Morrow & Company, 1972.

———. *The Autobiography of LeRoi Jones.* Chicago: Lawrence Hill Books, 1997.

Baum, Howell S. *Brown in Baltimore: School Desegregation and the Limits of Liberalism.* Ithaca, NY: Cornell University Press, 2011.

Bell, Derrick A. *Shades of Brown: New Perspectives on School Desegregation.* New York: Teachers College Press, 1980.

Belvin, Brent H. "Malcolm X Liberation University: An Experiment in Independent Black Education." Master's thesis, North Carolina State University, 2004.

ben-Jochannan, Yosef. *Cultural Genocide in the Black and African Studies Curriculum.* New York: Alkebu-lan Book Association, 1972.

Benson, Richard D, II. *Fighting For Our Place in the Sun: Malcolm X and the Radicalization of the Black Student Movement, 1960–1973.* New York: Peter Lang, 2015.

Berger, Dan, ed. *The Hidden 1970s: Histories of Radicalism.* New Brunswick, NJ: Rutgers University Press, 2010.

Biondi, Martha. *The Black Revolution on Campus.* Berkeley: University of California Press, 2012.

———. *To Stand and Fight: The Struggle for Civil Rights in Postwar New York City.* Cambridge, MA: Harvard University Press, 2003.

Black Child Development Institute, ed. *Black Children Just Keep on Growing: Alternative Curriculum Models for Young Black Children.* Washington, DC: Black Child Development Institute, 1977.

———. *Curriculum Approaches from a Black Perspective.* Washington, DC: Black Child Development Institute, 1973.

Bloom, Joshua and Waldo E. Martin. *Black Against Empire: The History and Politics of the Black Panther Party.* Berkeley: University of California Press, 2013.

Boggs, Grace Lee. "Education: the Great Obsession." *Monthly Review,* September 1970, 18–39.

Boggs, James, and Grace Lee. "The City Is the Black Man's Land." *Monthly Review,* April 1966, 35–46.

Bogues, Anthony. *Black Heretics, Black Prophets: Radical Political Intellectuals.* New York: Routledge, 2003.

Bowers, Margaret. "The Independent Black Educational Institution: An Exploration and Identification of Selected Factors that Relate to Their Survival." PhD diss., Atlanta University, 1984.

Bradley, Stefan. *Harlem vs. Columbia University: Black Student Power in the Late 1960s.* Champaign: University of Illinois Press, 2009.

Breitman, George, ed. *Malcolm X Speaks.* New York: Grove Press, 1966.

Brenner, Aaron, Robert Brenner, and Cal Winslow, eds. *Rebel Rank and File: Labor Militancy and Revolt from Below During the Long 1970s.* London: Verso, 2010.

Bresnick, David, Seymour Lachman, and Murray Polner. *Black, White, Green, Red: The Politics of Education in Ethnic America.* New York: Longman, 1978.

Brown, Elaine. *A Taste of Power: A Black Woman's Story.* New York: Anchor Books, 1992.

Brown, H. Rap (Jamil Abdullah al-Amin). *Die Nigger Die! A Political Biography.* Chicago: Lawrence Hill Books, 2002.

Brown, Scot. *Fighting for Us: Maulana Karenga, the US Organization and Black Cultural Nationalism.* New York: New York University Press, 2003.

Burner, Eric. *And Gently He Shall Lead Them: Robert Parris Moses and Civil Rights in Mississippi.* New York: New York University Press, 1994.

Bush, Roderick. *The End of White World Supremacy: Black Internationalism and the Problem of the Color Line.* Philadelphia: Temple University Press, 2009.

———. *We Are Not What We Seem: Black Nationalism and Class Struggle in the American Century.* New York: New York University Press, 1999.

Bush, V. Lawson. "Independent Black Institutions in America: A Rejection of Schooling, an Opportunity for Education." *Urban Education* 32 (1997): 98–116.

Cabral, Amilcar. *Unity and Struggle: Speeches and Writings.* New York: Monthly Review, 1979.

Campbell, James T. *Middle Passages: African American Journeys to Africa, 1787-2005.* New York: Penguin, 2006.

Carson, Clayborne. *In Struggle: SNCC and the Black Awakening of the 1960s.* Cambridge, MA: Harvard University Press, 1981.

———, ed. *The Student Voice, 1960-1965: Periodical of the Student Nonviolent Coordinating Committee.* Westport, CT: Meckler, 1990.

Castells, Manuel. *The City and the Grassroots: A Cross-Cultural Theory of Urban Social Movements.* Berkeley: University of California Press, 1983.

Cecelski, David S. *Along Freedom Road: Hyde County, North Carolina, and the Fate of Black Schools in the South.* Chapel Hill: University of North Carolina Press, 1994.

Chafe, William H. *Civilities and Civil Rights Civilities and Civil Rights: Greensboro, North Carolina, and the Black Struggle for Freedom*. New York: Oxford University Press, 1980.

Chilcoat, George W., and Jerry A. Ligon. "'Helping to Make Democracy a Living Reality': The Curriculum Conference of the Mississippi Freedom Schools." *Journal of Curriculum and Supervision* 15 (1999): 43–68.

———. "'We Talk Here. This Is a School for Talking.' Participatory Democracy from the Classroom out into the Community: How Discussion Was Used in the Mississippi Freedom Schools." *Curriculum Inquiry* 28 (1998): 165–193.

Chinweizu. *Decolonising the African Mind*. London: Pero Press, 1987.

Churchill, Ward, and Jim Vander Wall. *The Cointelpro Papers: Documents from the FBI's Secret Wars Against Dissent*. Boston: South End, 1990.

Churchville, John Elliott. *Driven! Remembrance, Reflection & Revelation*. West Conshohocken, PA: Infinity Publishing, 2011.

Clarke, John Henrik. *Malcolm X: The Man and His Times*. New York: Collier Books, 1969.

Cobb, Charlie. "Prospectus for a Summer Freedom School Curriculum." *Radical Teacher*, Fall 1991, 36.

———. "Revolution: From Stokely Carmichael to Kwame Ture." *Black Scholar* 27 (1997): 32–38.

Collins, Lisa Gail and Margo Natalie Crawford, eds. *New Thoughts on the Black Arts Movement*. New Brunswick: Rutgers University Press, 2006.

Collins, Patricia Hill. *From Black Power to Hip Hop: Racism, Nationalism, and Feminism*. Philadelphia: Temple University Press, 2006.

Conyers, James L, Jr., ed. *Engines of the Black Power Movement: Essays on the Influence of Civil Rights Actions, Arts, and Islam*. Jefferson, NC: McFarland & Co., 2007.

Corbould, Clare. *Becoming African Americans: Black Public Life in Harlem, 1919-1939*. Cambridge, MA: Harvard University Press, 2009.

Countryman, Matthew J. *Up South: Civil Rights and Black Power in Philadelphia*. Philadelphia: University of Pennsylvania Press, 2006.

Cruse, Harold. *The Crisis of the Negro Intellectual*. New York: William Morrow, 1967.

Cuban, Larry. *How Teachers Taught: Constancy and Change in American Classrooms, 1890-1990*. New York: Teachers College Press, 1993.

Curtis, Edward E. *Black Muslim Religion in the Nation of Islam, 1960-1975*. Chapel Hill: University of North Carolina Press, 2006.

Dahlk, Bill. *Against the Wind: African Americans and the Schools in Milwaukee, 1963–2002*. Milwaukee: Marquette University Press, 2010.

Daniels, Deborah, ed. *Education by, for and About African Americans: A Profile of Several Black Community Schools*. Lincoln, NE: Student Commission on Undergraduate Education and the Education of Teachers, 1973.

Danns, Dionne. *Something Better for Our Children: Black Organizing in Chicago Public Schools, 1963-1971*. New York: Routledge, 2003.

Davis, Julie L. *Survival Schools: The American Indian Movement and Community Education in the Twin Cities*. Minneapolis: University of Minnesota Press, 2013.

Dawson, Michael C. *Black Visions: The Roots of Contemporary African-American Political Ideologies*. Chicago: University of Chicago Press, 2001.

de Forest, Jennifer. "The 1958 Harlem School Boycott: Parental Activism and the Struggle for Educational Equity in New York City." *Urban Review* 40 (2008): 21–41.

Dittmer, John. *Local People: The Struggle for Civil Rights in Mississippi*. Champaign: University of Illinois Press, 1994.

Dougherty, Jack. *More Than One Struggle: The Evolution of Black School Reform in Milwaukee*. Chapel Hill: University of North Carolina Press, 2004.

Douglas, David M. *Jim Crow Moves North: The Battle over Northern School Segregation, 1865-1954*. New York: Cambridge University Press, 2005.

Drake, St. Clair. "Diaspora Studies and Pan-Africanism." In *Global Dimensions of the African Diaspora*, 2nd ed., edited by Joseph E. Harris, 301–402. Washington, DC: Howard University Press, 1993.

Elbaum, Max. *Revolution in the Air: Sixties Radicals Turn to Lenin, Mao and Che*. New York: Verso, 2002.

Erhagbe, Edward O. "The African-American Contribution to the Liberation Struggle in Southern Africa: The Case of the African Liberation Support Committee, 1972-1979." *Journal of Pan African Studies* 4 (2011): 26–56.

Evanzz, Karl. *The Messenger: The Rise and Fall of Elijah Muhammad*. New York: Random House, 1999.

Fanon, Frantz. *The Wretched of the Earth*. New York: Grove Press, 1963.

Fass, Paula S. *Outside In: Minorities and the Transformation of American Education*. New York: Oxford University Press, 1989.

Fergus, Devin. *Liberalism, Black Power and the Making of American Politics, 1965-1980*. Athens: University of Georgia Press, 2009.

Fernandez, Johanna. *When the World Was Their Stage: A History of the Young Lords Party, 1968-1974*. Princeton, NJ: Princeton University Press, Forthcoming.

Fisher, Maisha T. *Black Literate Lives: Historical and Contemporary Perspectives*. New York: Routledge, 2008.

Fleming, Cynthia Griggs. *Soon We Will Not Cry: The Liberation of Ruby Doris Smith Robinson*. Lanham, MD: Rowman & Littlefield, 1996.

Forman, James. *The Making of Black Revolutionaries*. New York: Macmillan, 1972.

Formisano, Ronald P. *Boston Against Busing: Race, Class and Ethnicity in the 1960s and 1970s*. Chapel Hill: University of North Carolina Press, 1991.

Franklin, Vincent P. *The Education of Black Philadelphia: The Social and Educational History of a Minority Community, 1900-1950*. Philadelphia: University of Pennsylvania Press, 1979.

Frazier, Robeson Taj. *The East Is Black: Cold War China in the Black Radical Imagination*. Durham: Duke University Press, 2015.

Freire, Paulo. *Pedagogy of the Oppressed*. New York: Herder & Herder, 1970.

Fuller, Howard. "Educational Choice: A Core Freedom." *Journal of Negro Education* 71 (2002): 1–4.

Gaines, Kevin K. *American Africans in Ghana: Black Expatriates and the Civil Rights Era* Chapel Hill: University of North Carolina Press, 2006.

———. *Uplifting the Race: Black Leadership, Politics, and Culture Since the Turn of the Century*. Chapel Hill: University of North Carolina Press, 1996.

Gardell, Mattias. *In the Name of Elijah Muhammad: Louis Farrakhan and the Nation of Islam*. Durham: Duke University Press, 1996.

Garrett, James P. "Black/Africana/Pan African Studies: From Radical to Reaction to Reform?—Its Role and Relevance in the Era of Global Capitalism in the New Millennium." *Journal of Pan-African Studies* 1 (1998).

Garrow, David. *Bearing the Cross: Martin Luther King, Jr., and the Southern Christian Leadership Conference*. New York: HarperCollins, 1986.

Giles, Raymond H. *Black Studies Programs in Public Schools*. New York: Praeger, 1974.

Gilroy, Paul. *"There Ain't No Black in the Union Jack": The Cultural Politics of Race and Nation*. Chicago: University of Chicago Press, 1991.

Gittell, Marilyn. *Local Control in Education: Three Demonstration School Districts in New York City*. New York: Praeger, 1972.

Glaude, Eddie S., ed. *Is It Nation Time? Contemporary Essays on Black Power and Black Nationalism*. Chicago: University of Chicago Press, 2002.

Goldberg, David and Trevor Griffey, eds. Black Power at Work: *Community Control, Affirmative Action and the Construction Industry*. New York: Columbia University Press, 2010.

Golin, Steve. *The Newark Teacher Strikes: Hope's on the Line*. New Brunswick, NJ: Rutgers University Press, 2002.

Grady-Willis, Winston A. *Challenging U.S. Apartheid: Atlanta and Black Struggles for Human Rights, 1960-1977*. Durham, NC: Duke University Press, 2006.

Grant, Colin. *Negro with a Hat: The Rise and Fall of Marcus Garvey and His Dream of Mother Africa*. New York: Oxford University Press, 2008.

Grant, Joanne, ed. *Black Protest: History, Documents and Analysis, 1619 to the Present*. New York: Fawcett Premier, 1968.

Graubard, Allen. *Free the Children: Radical Reform and the Free School Movement*. New York: Pantheon Books, 1972.

Greene, Christina. *Our Separate Ways: Women and the Black Freedom Movement in Durham, North Carolina*. Chapel Hill: University of North Carolina Press, 2005.

Griffin, Farah Jasmine. "'Ironies of the Saint': Malcolm X, Black Women, and the Price of Protection." In *Sisters in the Struggle: African American Women in the Civil Rights—Black Power Movement*, edited by Bettye Collier-Thomas and V. P. Franklin, 214–229. New York: New York University, 2001.

Hahn, Steven. *A Nation Under Our Feet: Black Political Struggles in the Rural South from Slavery to the Great Migration*. Cambridge, MA: Belknap Press, 2003.

Hale, Jon. "'The Student as a Force for Social Change': The Mississippi Freedom Schools and Student Engagement." *Journal of African-American History* 96 (2011): 325–348.

Hall, Jacquelyn Dowd. "The Long Civil Rights Movement and the Political Uses of the Past." *Journal of American History* 91 (2005): 1233–1263.

Hampton, Henry, and Steve Fayer with Sarah Flynn. *Voices of Freedom: An Oral History of the Civil Rights Movement from the 1950s Through the 1980s*. New York: Bantam Books, 1990.

Harding, Vincent. "'A Long Hard Winter to Endure': Reflections on the Meaning of the 1970's." *Black Collegian*, December 1979–January 1980.

Hill, Laura Warren and Julia Rabig, eds. *The Business of Black Power: Community Development, Capitalism, and Corporate Responsibility in Postwar America*. Rochester, NY: University of Rochester Press, 2012.

Hill, Robert A., and Barbara Bair, eds. *Marcus Garvey: Life and Lessons*. Los Angeles: University of California Press, 1987.

Hogan, Wesley C. *Many Minds, One Heart: SNCC's Dream for a New America*. Chapel Hill: University of North Carolina Press, 2001.

Holsaert, Faith S. et al., eds. *Hands on the Freedom Plow: Personal Accounts by Women in SNCC*. Champaign: University of Illinois Press, 2010.

Homel, Michael W. *Down from Equality: Black Chicagoans and the Public Schools, 1920-41*. Champaign: University of Illinois Press, 1994.

Horne, Gerald. *Mau Mau in Harlem? The U.S. and the Liberation of Kenya*. New York: Palgrave Macmillan, 2009.

Hornsby, Alton. *Black Power in Dixie: A Political History of African Americans in Atlanta*. Gainesville: University Press of Florida, 2009.

Hotep, Uhuru. "Dedicated to Excellence: An Oral History of the Council of Independent Black Institutions, 1970-2000." PhD diss., Duquesne University, 2001.

Howe, Stephen. *Afrocentrism: Mythical Pasts and Imagined Homes*. London: Verso, 1998.

Huggins, Ericka and Angela D. LeBlanc-Ernest. "Revolutionary Women, Revolutionary Education: The Black Panther Party's Oakland Community School. In *Want to Start a Revolution? Radical Women in the Black Freedom Struggle*, edited by Jeanne Theoharis and Komozi Woodard, 161–184. New York: New York University Press, 2009.

Institute of the Black World, ed. *Education and Black Struggle: Notes from the Colonized World*. Atlanta: Institute of the Black World, 1974.

Jackson, Mandi Isaacs. *Model City Blues: Urban Space and Organized Resistance in New Haven*. Philadelphia: Temple University Press, 2008.

Jacobs, Gregory S. *Getting Around Brown: Desegregation, Development and the Columbus Public Schools*. Columbus: Ohio State University Press, 1998.

James, C. L. R. *The Black Jacobins: Toussaint L'Ouverture and the San Domingo Revolution.* New York: Vintage, 1963.

Jefferson, James Doughty. "A Historical Analysis of Black Education Focusing on the Contemporary Independent Black School Movement." PhD diss., Ohio State University, 1973.

Jeffries, Bayyinah Sharief. "'A Nation Can Rise No Higher Than Its Women': The Critical Role of Black Muslim Women in the Development and Purveyance of Black Consciousness, 1945–1975." PhD diss., Michigan State University, 2009.

Jeffries, Hasan Kwame. *Bloody Lowndes: Civil Rights and Black Power in Alabama's Black Belt*. New York: New York University Press, 2009.

Jeffries, Judson L., ed. *Black Power in the Belly of the Beast. Champaign: University of Illinois Press*, 2006.

———, ed. *On the Ground: The Black Panther Party in Communities Across America*, Jackson: University Press of Mississippi, 2010.

Jennings, Regina. *Malcolm X and the Poetics of Haki Madhubuti*. Jefferson, NC: McFarland, 2006.

Johnson, Cedric. "From Popular Anti-Imperialism to Sectarianism: The African Liberation Support Committee and Black Power Radicals." *New Political Science* 25 (2003): 477–507.

———. *From Revolutionaries to Race Leaders: Black Power and the Making of American Politics.* Minneapolis: University of Minnesota Press, 2007.

Jones, Patrick. *The Selma of the North: Civil Rights Insurgency in Milwaukee.* Cambridge, MA: Harvard University Press, 2009.

Joseph, Peniel E., ed. *Neighborhood Rebels: Black Power at the Local Level.* New York: Palgrave Macmillan, 2010.

———, ed. *The Black Power Movement: Rethinking the Civil Rights—Black Power Era.* New York: Routledge, 2006.

———. *Waiting 'Til the Midnight Hour: A Narrative History of Black Power in America.* New York: Henry Holt, 2006.

Karenga, Maulana. *The African American Holiday of Kwanzaa: A Celebration of Family, Community & Culture.* Los Angeles: University of Sankore, 1988.

Kelley, Robin D. G. *Freedom Dreams: The Black Radical Imagination.* Boston: Beacon Press, 2002.

Kilson, Martin. "African Americans and Africa: A Critical Nexus." *Dissent,* Summer 1992, 361–369.

King, Joyce Elaine, ed. *Black Education: A Transformative Research and Action Agenda for the New Century.* Mahwah, NJ: American Educational Research Association, 2005.

King, Mel. *Chain of Change: Struggles for Black Community Development.* Cambridge, MA: South End Press, 1981.

Kirp, David L. *Just Schools: The Idea of Racial Equality in American Education.* Berkeley: University of California Press, 1982.

Kluger, Richard. *Simple Justice: The History of Brown v. Board of Education and Black America's Struggle for Equality.* New York: Knopf, 1976.

Konadu, Kwasi. *A View from the East: Black Cultural Nationalism and Education in New York City.* Syracuse, NY: Syracuse University Press, 2009.

Kusmer, Kenneth L., and Joe W. Trotter, eds. *African American Urban History Since World War II.* Chicago: University of Chicago Press, 2009.

Lai, Mark. *Becoming Chinese American: A History of Communities and Institutions.* Lanham, MD: Rowman & Littlefield, 2004.

Lazerow, Jama and Yohuru Williams, eds. *In Search of the Black Panther Party: New Perspectives on a Revolutionary Movement.* Durham, NC: Duke University Press, 2006.

Lee, Carol D. "Profile of an Independent Black Institution: African-Centered Education at Work." *Journal of Negro Education* 62 (1992): 160–177.

Lemelle, Sidney, and Robin D. G. Kelley, eds. *Imagining Home: Class, Culture and Nationalism in the African Diaspora.* London: Verso, 1994.

———. "The Politics of Cultural Existence: Pan-Africanism, Historical Materialism and Afrocentricity." *Race & Class* 35 (1993): 93–112.

Lenin, Vladimir Ilyich. "Dual Power." In *Collected Works,* vol. 24. London: Lawrence & Wishart, 1977.

Lester, Julius. *Revolutionary Notes.* New York: Grove Press, 1969.

Levine, David P. "The Birth of the Citizenship Schools: Entwining the Struggles for Literacy and Freedom." *History of Education Quarterly* 44 (2004): 388–414.

Levy, La Tasha. "Remembering Sixth-PAC: Interviews with Sylvia Hill and Judy Claude, Organizers of the Sixth Pan-African Congress." *Black Scholar* 37 (2008): 39–47.

Lewis, John. *Walking with the Wind: A Memoir of the Movement.* Orlando, FL: Harcourt Brace, 1998.

Lincoln, C. Eric. *The Black Muslims in America.* Boston: Beacon Press, 1961.

Lindenmeyer, Otto. *Of Black America: Black History: Lost, Stolen, or Strayed.* New York: Avon Books, 1970.

Lomotey, Kofi, ed. *Going to School: The African-American Experience.* Albany: State University of New York Press, 1990.

———. "Independent Black Institutions: African-Centered Education Models." *Journal of Negro Education* 61 (1992): 455–462.

Lowe, Robert. "Ravenswood High School and the Struggle for Racial Justice in the Sequoia Union High School District." PhD diss., Stanford University, 1989.

Lyons, John F. *Teachers and Reform: Chicago Public Education, 1929-1970.* Urbana: University of Illinois Press, 2008.

Madhubuti, Haki R. *From Plan to Planet: The Need for African Minds and Institutions.* Chicago: Third World Press, 1973.

———. *YellowBlack: The First Twenty-One Years of a Poet's Life.* Chicago: Third World Press, 2006.

Magubane, Bernard. *The Ties That Bind: African-American Consciousness of Africa.* Trenton, NJ: Africa World Press, 1989.

Malhem, D. H. *Heroism in the New Black Poetry: Introductions & Interviews.* Lexington: University of Kentucky Press, 1990.

Marable, Manning. *African & Caribbean Politics: From Kwame Nkrumah to Maurice Bishop.* London: Verso, 1987.

———. "Black Nationalism in the 1970s: Through the Prism of Race and Class." *Socialist Review* 10 (1980): 57–108.

———, and Leith Mullings, eds. *Let Nobody Turn Us Around: An African American Anthology.* Lanham, MD: Rowman & Littlefield, 2009.

———. *Race, Reform & Rebellion: The Second Reconstruction and Beyond in Black America.* Jackson: University of Mississippi Press, 2007.

——— and Elizabeth Kai Hinton, eds. *The New Black History: Revisiting the Second Reconstruction.* New York: Palgrave Macmillan, 2011.

Markle, Seth M. "'We Are Not Tourists': The Black Power Movement and the Making of 'Socialist' Tanzania, 1960–1974." PhD diss., New York University, 2011.

Marsh, Clifton E. *The Lost-Found Nation of Islam in America.* Lanham, MD: Scarecrow Press, 2000.

Martin, Ben L. "From Negro to Black to African American: The Power of Names and Naming." *Political Science Quarterly* 106 (1991): 83–107.

Martin, Tony, ed. *Message to the People: The Course of African Philosophy.* Dover, MA: Majority Press, 1986.

———. *Race First: The Ideological and Organizational Struggles of Marcus Garvey and the Universal Negro Improvement Association.* Dover, MA: Majority Press, 1976.

Martin, Waldo E. *No Coward Soldiers: Black Cultural Politics in Postwar America* Cambridge, MA: Harvard University Press, 2005.

Mayes, Keith A. *Kwanzaa: Black Power and the Making of the African-American Holiday Tradition.* New York: Routledge, 2009.

Mazama, Ama, and Garvey Musumunu. *African Americans and Homeschooling: Motivations, Opportunities and Challenges.* New York: Routledge, 2013.

McCulloch, Jock. *In the Twilight of Revolution: The Political Theory of Amilcar Cabral.* London: Routledge, 1983.

Meriwether, James H. *Proudly We Can Be Africans: Black Americans and Africa, 1935-1961.* Chapel Hill: University of North Carolina Press, 2002.

Michna, Catherine. "'We Are Black Mind Jockeys': Tom Dent, the Free Southern Theater, and the Search for a Second-line Literary Aesthetic in New Orleans." *Journal of Ethnic American Literature* 1 (2011): 31–68.

Minter, William et al., eds., *No Easy Victories: African Liberation and American Activists Over a Half-Century, 1950–2000.* Trenton, NJ: Africa World Press, 2007.

Moore, Evelyn K., ed. *Federal Pre-School and Early Childhood Programs from a Black Perspective.* Washington, DC: National Policy Conference on Education for Blacks, 1972.

Moore, Richard B. *The Name Negro: Its Origins and Evil Roots.* Baltimore: Black Classics, 1992.

Morgan, Harry. *Historical Perspectives on the Education of Black Children.* Westport, CT: Praeger, 1995.

Moses, Wilson Jeremiah. *Afrotopia: The Roots of African American Popular History.* Cambridge: University of Cambridge, 1998.

———. *The Golden Age of Black Nationalism, 1850-1925.* New York: Oxford University Press, 1978.

Moye, Todd J. *Let the People Decide: Black Freedom and White Resistance Movements in Sunflower County, Mississippi, 1945–1986.* Chapel Hill: University of North Carolina Press, 2004.

Muhammad, Elijah. *Message to the Blackman in America.* Chicago: Muhammad Mosque of Islam No. 2, 1965.

Muñoz, Carlos, Jr. *Youth, Identity, Power: The Chicano Movement.* New York: Verso, 1989.

Murch, Donna. *Living for the City: Migration, Education, and the Rise of the Black Panther Party in Oakland, California.* Chapel Hill: University of North Carolina Press, 2010.

Nelson, Alondra. *Body and Soul: The Black Panther Party and the Fight Against Medical Discrimination.* Minneapolis: University of Minnesota Press, 2011.

Nesbitt, Francis Njubi. *Race for Sanctions: African Americans Against Apartheid, 1946-1994.* Bloomington: Indiana University, 2004.

Nyerere, Julius K. *Freedom and Socialism/Uhuru na Ujamaa.* London: Oxford University Press, 1968.

Ogbar, Jeffrey O. G. *Black Power: Radical Politics and African American Identity.* Baltimore: Johns Hopkins University Press, 2004.

Orr, Marion. *Black Social Capital: The Politics of School Reform in Baltimore, 1986-1998.* Lawrence: University of Kansas Press, 1999.

Payne, Charles M. *I've Got the Light of Freedom: The Organizing Tradition and the Mississippi Freedom Struggle.* Berkeley: University of California Press, 1995.

———, and Carol Sills Strickland, eds. *Teach Freedom: Education for Liberation in the African-American Tradition.* New York: Teachers College Press, 2008.

Peck, Craig. "'Educate to Liberate': The Black Panther Party and Political Education." PhD diss., Stanford University Press, 2001.

Perlstein, Daniel H. *Justice, Justice: School Politics and the Eclipse of Liberalism.* New York: Peter Lang, 2004.

———. "Minds Stayed on Freedom: Politics, Pedagogy, and the African American Freedom Struggle." *American Educational Research Journal* 39 (2002): 249–277.

———. "Teaching Freedom: SNCC and the Creation of the Mississippi Freedom Schools." *History of Education Quarterly* 30 (1990): 297–324.

Pinkney, Alphonso. *Red Black and Green: Black Nationalism in the United States.* Cambridge: Cambridge University Press, 1979.

Pleck, Elizabeth. "Kwanzaa: The Making of a Black Nationalist Tradition, 1966-1990." *Journal of American Ethnic History* 20 (2001): 3–28.

Plummer, Brenda Gayle. *In Search of Power: African Americans in the Era of Decolonization, 1956-1974.* New York: Cambridge University Press, 2013.

Podair, Jerald E. *The Strike That Changed New York: Blacks, Whites, and the Ocean Hill-Brownsville Crisis.* New Haven, CT: Yale University Press, 2002.

Pollard, Diane, and Cheryl Ajirotutu, eds. *African-Centered Schooling in Theory and Practice.* Westport, CT: Greenwood, 2000.

Pritchett, Wendell E. *Brownsville, Brooklyn: Blacks, Jews and the Changing Face of the Ghetto.* Chicago: University of Chicago Press, 2002.

Purnell, Brian. *Fighting Jim Crow in the County of Kings: The Congress of Racial Equality in Brooklyn.* Lexington: University Press of Kentucky, 2013.

Ransby, Barbara. *Ella Baker and the Black Freedom Movement: A Radical Democratic Vision.* Chapel Hill: University of North Carolina Press, 2005.

Rashid, Hakim M., and Zakiyyah Muhammad. "The Sister Clara Muhammad Schools: Pioneers in the Development of Islamic Education in America." *Journal of Negro Education* 61 (1992): 178–185.

Ravitch, Diane. *The Great School Wars: A History of the New York City Public Schools.* New York: Basic Books, 1988.

———. *The Troubled Crusade: American Education, 1945-1980.* New York: Basic Books, 1983.

Reed, Adolph. *Class Notes: Posing as Politics and Other Thoughts on the American Scene.* New York: New Press, 2000.

———, ed. *Race, Politics, and Culture: Critical Essays on the Radicalism of the 1960s.* Westport, CT: Greenwood, 1986.

———. *Stirrings in the Jug: Black Politics in the Post-Segregation Era.* Minneapolis: University of Minnesota Press, 1999.

Reilly, Charlie, ed. *Conversations with Amiri Baraka.* Jackson: University of Mississippi Press, 1994.

Rist, Ray, ed. *Restructuring American Education: Innovation and Alternatives.* New Brunswick, NJ: Transaction Publishers, 1972.

Robinson, Dean E. *Black Nationalism in American Politics and Thought.* Cambridge: Cambridge University Press, 2001.

Rogers, Ibram. *The Black Campus Movement: Black Students and the Racial Reconstitution of Higher Education, 1965–1972.* New York: Palgrave Macmillan, 2012.

———. "Celebrating 40 Years of Activism." *Diverse Issues in Higher Education* 10 (2006).

———. "Remembering the Black Campus Movement: An Oral History Interview with James P. Garrett." *Journal of Pan African Studies* 2 (2009): 30–41.

Rojas, Fabio. *From Black Power to Black Studies.* Baltimore: Johns Hopkins University Press, 2007.

Rolison, Mary G. *Grassroots Garveyism: The Universal Negro Improvement Association in the Rural South, 1920-1927.* Chapel Hill: University of North Carolina Press, 2007.

Rooks, Noliwe. *White Money/Black Power: The Surprising History of African American Studies and the Crisis of Race in Higher Education.* Boston: Beacon Press, 2006.

Rushing, Fannie Theresa. "Minds Still Stayed on Freedom? Reflections on Politics, Consensus, and Pedagogy in the African American Freedom Struggle." In *Teach Freedom: Education for Liberation in the African-American Tradition,* edited by Charles M. Payne and Carol Sills Strickland, 95–99. New York: Teachers College Press, 2008.

Salaam, Kalamu Ya. "Why Do We Lie About Telling the Truth." In *Afro Asia: Revolutionary Political and Cultural Connections Between African Americans and Asian Americans,* edited by Fred Ho and Bill V. Mullen, 198–216. Durham, NC: Duke University Press, 2008.

Salaam, Tayari Kwa. "So-Journeying: Creating Sacred Space in Education." PhD diss., Louisiana State University Press, 1993.

———. *Working Together We Can Make a Change: Towards Sisterhoods of Struggle.* New Orleans: Nkombo, 1981.

Sales, William W. *From Civil Rights to Black Liberation: Malcolm X and the Organization of Afro-America Unity.* Boston: South End Press, 1994.

———, and Rod Bush, "The Political Awakening of Blacks and Latinos in New York City: Competition or Cooperation?" *Social Justice* 27 (2000): 19–42.

San Miguel, Guadalup. *Chicana/o Struggles for Education: Activism in the Community.* Houston: University of Houston Press, 2013.

Scott, Daryl Michael. *Contempt and Pity: Social Policy and the Image of the Damaged Black Psyche.* Chapel Hill: University of North Carolina Press, 1997.

Self, Robert O. *American Babylon: Race and the Struggle for Postwar Oakland.* Princeton, NJ: Princeton University Press, 2003.

Sellers, Cleveland. *The River of No Return: The Autobiography of a Black Militant and the Life and Death of SNCC.* New York: William Morrow, 1973.

Serequeberhan, Tsenay. *Our Heritage: The Past in the Present of African-American and African Existence.* Lanham, MD: Roman & Littlefield, 2000.

Shakur, Assata. *Assata: An Autobiography.* Chicago: Lawrence Hill, 1987.

Shujaa, Mwalimu. *Nationbuilding: Theory and Practice in African-Centered Education.* Trenton, NJ: Africa World Press, 1994.

———, ed. *Too Much Schooling, Too Little Education: A Paradox of Black Life in White Societies.* Trenton: Africa World Press, 1994.

Simanga, Michael. *Amiri Baraka and the Congress of African People: History and Memory.* New York: Palgrave Macmillan, 2015.

Singh, Nikhil Pal. *Black Is a Country: Race and the Unfinished Struggle for Democracy.* Cambridge, MA: Harvard, 2004.

———, ed. *Climbin' Jacob's Ladder: The Black Freedom Movement Writings of Jack O'Dell.* Berkeley: University of California Press, 2010.

Skinner, Elliott P. *Afro-Americans and Africa: The Continuing Dialectic.* New York: Urban Center of Columbia University, 1973.

Slate, Nico, ed. *Black Power Beyond Borders: The Global Dimensions of the Black Power Movement.* New York: Palgrave Macmillan, 2012.

Slaughter, Diana T., and Deborah J. Johnson. *Visible Now: Blacks in Private Schools.* Westport, CT: Greenwood, 1988.

Smethurst, James. *The Black Arts Movement: Literary Nationalism in the 1960s and 1970s.* Chapel Hill: University of North Carolina Press, 2005.

Smith, Robert C. *We Have No Leaders: African Americans in the Post-Civil Rights Era.* Albany: State University of New York Press, 1996.

Sollors, Werner. *Amiri Baraka/LeRoi Jones: The Quest for a "Populist Modernism."* New York: Columbia University Press, 1978.

St. Julien, Mtumishi. *Upon the Shoulders of Elephants We Reach the Sky: A Parent's Farewell to a Collegian.* New Orleans: Runagate Press, 1995.

Stein, Judith. *The World of Marcus Garvey: Race and Class in Modern Society.* Baton Rouge: Louisiana State University Press, 1986.

Street, Joe. "Reconstructing Education from the Bottom Up: SNCC's 1964 Mississippi Summer Project and African American Culture." *Journal of American Studies* 38 (2004): 273–296.

Stulberg, Lisa Michele. "Teach a New Day: African American Alternative Institution-Building and the Politics of Race and Schooling Since Brown." PhD diss., University of California Berkeley, 2001.

Sturkey, William. " 'I Want to Become a Part of History': Freedom Summer, Freedom Schools, and the *Freedom News.*" *Journal of African-American History* 95 (2010): 349–354.

Sugrue, Thomas J. *The Origins of the Urban Crisis: Race and Inequality in Postwar Detroit.* Princeton, NJ: Princeton University Press, 1996.

———. *Sweet Land of Liberty: The Forgotten Struggle for Civil Rights in the North.* New York: Random House, 2008.

Taylor, Clarence. *Knocking at Our Own Door: Milton A. Galamison and the Struggle to Integrate New York City Schools.* New York: Columbia University Press, 1997.

Terborg-Penn, Rosalyn. "Naming Ourselves: Politics and Meaning of Self-Designation." In *The Columbia Guide to African American History Since 1939*, edited by Robert L. Harris, Jr. and Terborg-Penn, 91–100. New York: Columbia University Press, 2006.

Theoharis, Jeanne. "Alabama on Avalon: Rethinking the Watts Uprising and the Character of Black Protest in Los Angeles." In *The Black Power Movement: Rethinking the Civil Rights—Black Power Era*, edited by Peniel E. Joseph, 27–54. New York: Routledge, 2006.

———. " 'Exposing the Whole Desegregation Myth': The Harlem Nine and New York City's School Desegregation Battles." In *Freedom North: Black Freedom Struggles Outside the South, 1940-1980*, edited by Theoharis and Komozi Woodard, 65–92. New York: Palgrave Macmillan, 2003.

———, and Komozi Woodard. *Freedom North: Black Freedom Struggles Outside the South, 1940-1980.* New York: Palgrave Macmillan, 2003.

Thompson, Heather Ann. *Whose Detroit? Politics, Labor, and Race in a Modern American City.* Ithaca, NY: Cornell University Press, 2001.

Todd-Bredland, Elizabeth. "To Reshape and Redefine Our World: African American Political Organizing for Education in Chicago, 1968-1988." PhD diss., University of Chicago, 2010.

Tuck, Stephen. " 'We Are Taking Up Where the Movement of the 1960s Left Off': The Proliferation and Power of African American Protest During the 1970s." *Journal of Contemporary History* 43 (2008): 637–654.

Ture, Kwame, and Ekwueme Michael Thelwell. *Ready for Revolution: The Life and Struggles of Stokely Carmichael.* New York: Scribner, 2003.

———. *Stokeley Speaks: From Black Power to Pan-Africanism.* Chicago: Chicago Review, 2007.

Turner, Jeffrey A. *Sitting In and Speaking Out: Student Movements in the American South, 1960-1970.* Athens: University of Georgia Press, 2010.

Tyack, David B. "Growing Up Black: Perspectives on the History of Education in Northern Ghettos." *History of Education Quarterly* 9 (1969): 287–297.

———. *The One Best System: A History of American Urban Education.* Cambridge, MA: Harvard University Press, 1974.

Tyner, James. *The Geography of Malcolm X: Black Radicalism and the Remaking of American Space.* New York: Routledge, 2006.

Van DeBurg, William L., ed. *Modern Black Nationalism: From Marcus Garvey to Louis Farrakhan.* New York: New York University Press, 1997.

———. *New Day in Babylon: The Black Power Movement and American Culture, 1965–1975.* Chicago: University of Chicago Press, 1992.

Von Eschen, Penny M. *Race Against Empire: Black Americans and Anticolonialism, 1937-1957.* Ithaca, NY: Cornell University Press, 1997.

Walker, Vanessa Siddle. *Their Highest Potential: An African American School Community in the Segregated South.* Chapel Hill: University of North Carolina Press, 1996.

Waller, Signe. *Love and Revolution: A Political Memoir: People's History of the Greensboro Massacre, Its Setting and Aftermath*. Lanham, MD: Rowman & Littlefield, 2002.

Walters, Ronald. *Pan Africanism in the African Diaspora: An Analysis of Modern Afrocentric Political Movements*. Detroit, MI: Wayne State University Press, 1993.

Washington, Paul. *"Other Sheep I Have": The Autobiography of Father Paul M. Washington*. Philadelphia: Temple University Press, 1994.

Watkins, William H, ed. *Black Protest Thought and Education*. New York: Peter Lang, 2005.

Watts, Jerry. *Amiri Baraka: The Politics and Art of a Black Intellectual*. New York: New York University Press, 2001.

Weisbrod, Robert G. *Ebony Kinship: Africa, Africans and the Afro-American*. Westport, CT: Greenwood Press, 1973.

West, Michael O., William G. Martin, and Fanon Che Wilkins, eds. *From Toussaint to Tupac: The Black International since the Age of Revolution*. Chapel Hill: University of North Carolina Press, 2009.

White, Derrick E. *The Challenge of Blackness: The Institute of the Black World and Political Activism in the 1970s*. Gainesville: University Press of Florida, 2012.

White, E. Frances. "'Africa on My Mind': Gender, Counter Discourse and African-American Nationalism." *Journal of Women's History* 2 (1990): 73–97.

Whiteside, Barbara J. "A Study of the Structure, Norms and Folkways of the Educational Institutions of the Nation of Islam in the United States from 1932 to 1975." PhD diss., Wayne State University, 1987.

Wilcox, Preston. "The Kids Will Decide—And More Power to Them." *Ebony*, August 1970, 134–137.

Wilde, Anna Day. "Mainstreaming Kwanzaa." *The Public Interest*, Spring 1995, 68–79.

Wilder, Craig Steven. *A Covenant with Color: Race and Social Power in Brooklyn*. New York: Columbia University Press, 2000.

Wilkins, Fanon Che. "'In the Belly of the Beast': Black Power, Anti-Imperialism, and the African Liberation Solidarity Movement, 1968-1975." PhD diss., New York University, 2001.

———. "Line of Steel: The Organization of the Sixth Pan African Congress and the Struggle for International Black Power, 1969-1974." In *The Hidden 1970s: Histories of Radicalism*, edited by Dan Berger, 97–114. New Brunswick, NJ: Rutgers University Press, 2010.

———. "The Making of Black Internationalists: SNCC and Africa Before the Launching of Black Power, 1960-1965." *Journal of African American History* 92 (2007): 467–488.

Wilks, Gertrude Dyer. *Gathering Together: Born to Be a Leader*. LaVergne, TN: Xlibris, 2010.

Williams, Heather Andrea. *Self-Taught: African-American Education in Slavery and Freedom*. Chapel Hill: University of North Carolina Press, 2005.

Williams, Rhonda Y. *Concrete Demands: The Search for Black Power in the 20th Century*. New York: Routledge, 2015.

Williams, Yohuru. *Black Politics/White Power: Civil Rights, Black Power, and the Black Panthers in New Haven*. St. James, NY: Brandywine Press, 2000.

Williamson, Joy Ann. *Black Power on Campus: The University of Illinois, 1965–1975*. Urbana: University of Illinois Press, 2003.

———. "Community Control with a Black Nationalist Twist: The Black Panther Party's Educational Programs." In *Black Protest Thought and Education*, edited by William H. Watkins, 137–158. New York: Peter Lang, 2005.

———. *Radicalizing the Ebony Tower: Black Colleges and the Black Freedom Struggle in Mississippi*. New York: Teachers College Press, 2008.

Willingham, Alex. "Afro-American Pan-Africanist Ideology in the 1960s." In *Pan Africanism: New Directions in Strategy*, edited by W. Ofuatey-Kodjoe, 95–122. Lanham, MD: University Press of America, 1986.

Wintz, Cary D. *African-American Political Thought, 1890-1930: Washington, Du Bois, Garvey and Randolph*. New York: M. E. Sharpe, 1996.

Woodard, Komozi. *A Nation Within a Nation: Amiri Baraka (LeRoi Jones) and Black Power Politics*. Chapel Hill: University of North Carolina Press, 1999.

Wright, Nathan, ed. *What Black Educators Are Saying*. New York: Hawthorne Books, 1970.

X, Malcolm, and Alex Haley. *The Autobiography of Malcolm X*. New York: Grove Press, 1965.

INDEX

Abdur-Razzaq, Abdullah, 11
Abdur-Razzaq, Ohra, 11
Abernathy, Ralph, 184
abortion, 154
African-American Student Association
  (ASA), 69–71
African Free School (AFS; Newark, NJ): the
  Barakas' departure from, 232; the Barakas'
  leadership of, 3, 138–39, 141–42, 155–56;
  Committee for a Unified Newark and,
  138–39, 141; establishment of, 138;
  expansion of, 139; funding for, 138–39;
  Pan African curriculum at, 138, 141–42;
  as a prototype, 139, 142, 146; racial
  fundamentalism and, 153; violent threats
  against, 220; women teachers at, 141–42
African Liberation Day (ALD): African
  Liberation Support Committee
  (ALSC) and, 225–26; decline of, 231;
  establishment (1972) of, 21, 168, 182–85;
  Sadaukai's role in establishing, 168, 182–85,
  187; "two-line struggle" ideological
  divisions and, 219, 226–28, 231–32; united
  front politics behind, 186; US policy as
  a focus on, 184–85; Washington DC
  celebration (1972) of, 185
African Liberation Support Committee
  (ALSC): African Liberation Day
  celebrations and, 225–26; Angolan civil
  war and, 239–40; decline of, 231, 247; Left
  Pan Africanism and, 226–28; Racism and
  Imperialism Conference (1974) and, 228;
  "two-line struggle" ideological conflict in,
  227–30, 232
African Personality concept, 141, 151, 227, 251
Africans in America for Black Liberation
  (AABL), 216–17
African Socialism, 151–52
Africa's Gift to America (Rogers), 77

Afrik, Hannibal T. (Harold E. Charles), 144–46,
  249, 261
Afrikan People's Action School (Trenton, NJ),
  248, 256–57, 261
Afro-American Teachers Association
  (ATA): African-American Student
  Association and, 69, 71; black studies
  curricula advocated by, 57; "disruptive
  child" rule and, 51; founding of,
  65; independent black schools and,
  63; Leslie Campbell discipline cases
  (1968-1969) and, 66, 68; militant
  political confrontation emphasized by,
  57; Nation of Islam schools and, 62–63;
  on orientations for white teachers
  in black neighborhoods, 55; school
  community control movement and, 42,
  57, 63, 65
Afrocentricity (Asante), 251
Afrocentrism: conservative nature of, 21, 219,
  249–51, 253, 256–58; criticism of black
  lower classes and, 249; patriarchy and,
  250–51; pedagogy at schools devoted to,
  262–63; positive racial self-concept and,
  257; school vouchers and, 259–60
Afro hairstyle, 120
Ahidiana Work/Study Center (New
  Orleans): academics emphasized at, 256;
  African Liberation Day and, 184; closing
  of, 248; community initiatives of, 149;
  feminism and, 156; funding of, 149;
  Kawaida doctrine and, 155; opening of,
  146, 149
Ahmed, Mama Lubaba, 251
Aisha Shule (Detroit), 260–61
Akpan, Kwadwo, 228
Algeria, 19, 162
Ali, Muhammad, 51, 195–96
Alinsky, Saul, 203

Blackwell, Unita, 80
Black World magazine, 122
Black Youth Organization (Newark, NJ), 142
Blaxploitation films, 224, 249, 265
BLKARTSOUTH (community art workshop in New Orleans), 147–49
Blues People (LeRoi Jones), 134
Boggs, Grace Lee, 15, 43
Boggs, James, 15
Boley (Oklahoma), 103
Bond, Julian, 184
Booker T. University (Harlem), 75
Boston (Massachusetts): black studies protests in, 47; busing desegregation controversy in, 32, 242; freedom schools in, 78–79; Kwanzaa celebrations in, 126; school community control movement in, 29
Boys High (Brooklyn), 69
Brooklyn (New York City). *See also* Bedford-Stuyvesant; Ocean Hill-Brownsville: Congress of Racial Equality (CORE) breakaway chapter in, 11, 36; school boycotts (1960s) in, 36; school community control movements in, 8, 28–29, 35–38, 40, 42–46, 65; school desegregation in, 26, 39–40
Brooks, Fred, 10, 87
Brown, Elaine, 184, 264
Brown, H. Rap, 50, 184, 221
Brown, John, 48
Brown, Roosevelt, 233
Brown, Sterling, 213
Brown Berets, 206
Browne, Robert S., 191
Brownsville (New York City). *See* Ocean Hill-Brownsville (New York City)
Brown v. Board of Education (1954), 25, 27, 31, 113, 198, 263
Bullins, Ed, 161
Burnham, Forbes, 158, 242
Burroughs, Margaret, 49
Bush, Rod, 152–53

Cabral, Amilcar: assassination of, 165, 220; critiques of Racial Pan Africanism by, 164–65; on grassroots nature of revolutionary struggle, 163; Guinea-Bisseau liberation movement and, 162, 164; on national liberation as an act of culture, 100; Pan-Africanism and, 19, 131, 164–65, 218, 228; on the role of culture in national liberation, 162–64; United States visit (1970) of, 162–63; United States visit (1972) of, 163–65; on the "upward paths of one's own culture," 128
Cade, Toni, 2
CAM Academy (Chicago), 143

Campbell, James E., 51, 57, 88
Campbell, Leslie. *See also* Weusi, Jitu: biographical background of, 64; black-Jewish relations and, 67–68; black studies curricula and, 66; on fostering skills and leadership in inner city schools, 55; at Junior High School 35 (Brooklyn), 64–66; at Junior High School 271 (Brooklyn), 66–68; King assassination protests (1968) and, 66–67; on Nkrumrah, 68–69; on school desegregation strategies, 40
Campbell, Robert, 64
Camus, Albert, 83
Cape Verde, 128, 162, 164
Cardozo Arts Community (Washington DC), 212
Carew, Colin "Topper," 214
Carmichael, Stokely. *See also* Ture, Kwame: African Liberation Day (1972) and, 184–85; Black Power movement and, 34, 83, 109, 113; on the "dictatorship of definition," 92; East Palo Alto visits (1967 and 1968) by, 109–10, 113, 119; Malcolm X Liberation University (North Carolina) and, 172, 175–76; Nashville protests (1967) and, 87; New School for Afro-American Thought and, 213; Nonviolent Action Group (NAG; Howard University) and, 194; on organization efforts in Northern inner cities, 12; Pan Africanism and, 119, 132, 172; on self-identifying as "African," vi; Student Nonviolent Coordinating Committee's Northern urban initiatives and, 12; on "taking control of the education of our children," 110; Toward a Black University Conference (1968) and, 192–93
Carson, Clayborne, 83
Carson, Sonny, 11, 36, 49, 67, 220
Carver, George Washington, 49, 80
Center for Black Education (CBE, Washington DC): Africa as locus of revolution for, 218; African Socialism and, 152; Biafra War and, 157; career and mainstream America de-emphasized at, 210; closing of, 246; community organizing emphasis at, 207; curriculum at, 207; Drum & Spear Bookstore and, 212; East Africa operations of, 159; establishment of, 20, 199–200, 203, 206; faculty at, 207; Federal Bureau of Investigation surveillance of, 209, 220; funding for, 208; on importance of solidarity against government opponents, 222; insurgent models of higher education and, 168; local community-based ventures of, 208, 242; Malcolm X Liberation University (North Carolina) and, 172;